The Supreme Court Compendium
Data, Decisions, and Developments
Third Edition

Lee Epstein
Washington University in St. Louis

Jeffrey A. Segal
State University of New York at Stony Brook

Harold J. Spaeth
Michigan State University

Thomas G. Walker
Emory University

CQ PRESS

A Division of Congressional Quarterly Inc.
Washington, D.C.

In memory of my grandfather, Martin Buxbaum

L.E.

For Michelle and Paul

J.A.S.

*For my coauthors, who made the compilation of this book
a thoroughly enjoyable endeavor*

H.J.S.

For Victoria Nowak and Ann Walker

T.G.W.

CQ Press
1255 22nd Street, N.W., Suite 400
Washington, D.C. 20037

202-729-1900; toll-free: 1-866-4CQ-PRESS (1-866-427-7737)

www.cqpress.com

Printed and bound in the United States of America

06 05 04 03 02   5 4 3 2 1

♾ The paper used in this publication meets the minimum requirements of the American National Standard for Information Sciences—Permanence of Paper for Printed Library Materials, ANSI Z39.48-1992.

Library of Congress Cataloging-in-Publication Data

The Supreme Court Compendium : data, decisions, and developments / Lee Epstein
. . . [et al.].—3rd ed.
    p. cm.
Includes bibliographical references and index.
ISBN 1-56802-592-0 (cloth : alk. paper)
    1. United States. Supreme Court—Outlines, syllabi, etc. 2. Constitutional law—United States—Outlines, syllabi, etc. 3. Judicial review—United States—Outlines, syllabi, etc. I. Epstein, Lee, 1958–

KF8742 .S914 2003
347.73'26—dc21

2002041345

Contents

5 The Justices: Post-Confirmation Activities and Departures from the Court

6 The Justices: Voting Behavior and Opinions

Preface to the Third Edition

As professors who teach courses and conduct research on courts and law, we became increasingly frustrated with the absence of a comprehensive collection of information on the U.S. Supreme Court. It seemed that each time we needed even the simplest datum, whether it be a Senate vote on a particular nominee or the number of cases argued during a given term, we had to consult three or four different books and articles to find the desired information. This sense of frustration led to the compilation of the first edition of *The Supreme Court Compendium: Data, Decisions, and Developments*.

Our goal for this third edition is the same as it was for the first two: to provide a comprehensive collection of data and relevant information on the U.S. Supreme Court. We have attempted to cover as many bases as possible, from characteristics of the Court and its members, to the environment in which it operates, to the public's views on its decisions and perceptions about the Court itself, and much more. We have sought to provide readers with some insight into how we collected the data and why we consider them important. We urge readers to use both the general introduction and the introductions included with each chapter as guides to the information presented in the tables and figures that follow. Readers should also pay particular attention to table notes, where we identify data sources and, when relevant, caution readers about potential irregularities in data interpretation.

Of course, there are differences between this edition and the previous editions—three of which deserve mention. First, in addition to updating virtually every table, we have retained the backdating included in the second edition. This was made possible largely through the efforts of Harold J. Spaeth, who has expanded his United States Supreme Court Judicial Database to include the Vinson Court (1946–1952 terms). Such data will be of particular use to researchers who wish to conduct longitudinal analyses of the Court and its members: They now have highly reliable data for a fifty-five-year period. Second, we have strengthened what we think was the most distinctive feature of the first two editions—the emphasis on the Supreme Court of the United States. Accomplishing this goal led us to both add and delete tables. New tables in this edition include a guide to oral arguments in the Court, a list of Court decisions reported on the front page of the *New York Times*, tables identifying the ideological mean and median justices in various areas of the law, the American Bar Association's ratings of Supreme Court nominees, and tables relating to public opinion about the Court in the wake of *Bush v. Gore* (2000). Most of the tables we deleted from the first and second editions concerned the lower federal courts and state courts of last resort. We felt that the information contained in these tables—caseload data, for example—detracted from our overall focus on the Court. Updated information on lower federal tribunals and state supreme courts is readily available from other sources, including the *Statistical Abstract of the United States* and *State Court Caseload Statistics*. For this edition, we continued to pare down data on tribunals other than the Supreme Court. For example, we eliminated information on the selection of state court justices because it, too, is readily available elsewhere. Third, with the goal of making tables derived from the U.S. Supreme Court Judicial Database easy to replicate, we have provided, for each table, the unit of analysis and decision type we used to produce it.

One final note about this edition: Putting it together required us to work with a great deal of data. Although we took pains to check and recheck all of the tables, it is possible that we committed errors of omission and commission. Naturally, we take full responsibility for both. We ask readers who find errors in the text or the tables to please contact us so that we may remedy them for subsequent editions. Email can be directed to Lee Epstein at epstein@artsci.wustl.edu.

****

Many people assisted us in producing this and earlier editions of *The Supreme Court Compendium*. The folks at CQ Press were, as always, terrific. We initially pitched the project to Brenda Carter, who provided a great deal of encouragement. Our editor for the first edition, Jeanne Ferris, could not have been more helpful or patient. She read the entire text and considered all the tables with an eye toward clarity and readability. This edition continues to reap the benefits of Jeanne's keen interest. Kerry V. Kern, our copy editor for this edition, performed her job with great skill. We are truly grateful for her assistance. We also appreciate the important contributions of Christopher Anzalone, Christopher Karlsten, Daphne Levitas, Paul Pressau, and Liza Sanchez. And, we wish to thank our indexer, Julia Petrakis.

We have terrific colleagues in the law and courts field—many of whom took the time to offer suggestions and even data. We are especially indebted to Judy Baer of Texas A&M, Gregory Caldeira of Ohio State University, Micheal Giles of Emory University, Leslie Goldstein of the University of Delaware, Valerie Hoekstra of Arizona State University, Jack Knight of Washington University, Andrew D. Martin of Washington University, Jan Palmer of Ohio University, and James Stimson of the University of North Carolina.

Students at our respective institutions performed various essential tasks throughout this undertaking. Since this edition builds on the first two, we want again to acknowledge research assistance provided by Scott Comparato, Paul Fabrizio, Marjorie George, Robert Howard, Tim Johnson, Madhavi McCall, Robert Oritz, Melissa Schwartzberg, and James Spriggs.

Ellen Baik, Scott Graves, Chris Hasselmann, Mark Hendershot, Chad King, Eddie Sindaco, and Jeff Staton cheerfully gathered data and helped to assemble the final version of this edition. In addition, we are grateful to Andrew Koshner, Andrew Martin, Kevin Quinn, Rorie Spill, and Christina Wolbrecht, who have allowed us to use some of their data.

Although a four-person collaboration was a great deal of fun, it was our home institutions that bore the costs of extended phone calls and faxes, as well as photocopying and mailing expenses. We also thank the Law and Social Science Program of the National Science Foundation for its continued support of Spaeth's U.S. Supreme Court Judicial Database, without which this volume would be considerably less comprehensive.

L.E.
St. Louis

J.A.S.
Stony Brook

H.J.S.
East Lansing

T.G.W.
Atlanta

Introduction

Before the first edition of *The Supreme Court Compendium* was published in 1994, there was no comprehensive collection of data on the U.S. Supreme Court. This was unfortunate, not only because of the importance of the Court in the American government but also because the absence of reliable data makes it hard to understand the Court, the justices, and case decisions. This volume is our effort to rectify this deficiency.

We hope that readers will find useful the data and information presented in the following pages. Before continuing, though, we urge them to read this introduction and the introductions opening each chapter so that they might better understand the choices we made in compiling this work. Here, we provide information on data sources, the scope of the data, data presentation, and the overall organization of the volume. In the introductions preceding each chapter, we provide more specific details on the tables they contain.

Data Sources and Scope of the Data

Our sources of information vary widely, depending on what dimension of the Court we are examining. The primary source is the reports of the Court's decisions. The official record is the *United States Reports*.[1] Three privately printed sources are also employed: *The Lawyers' Edition*,[2] *The Supreme Court Reporter*,[3] and *United States Law Week*.[4] In Tables 2-9 and 2-10 we provide additional information about these various systems. Two major legal electronic information retrieval systems, LEXIS and WESTLAW, also contain the Court's decisions. We used these sources when gathering data requiring specific search delimiters. Other sources of electronically transmitted information are various Web sites (see Table 1-8). The Legal Information Institute site, for example, contains recent decisions of the Court.[5]

We also obtained information from archived databases. The expanded version of Harold J. Spaeth's computer-dependent United States Supreme Court Judicial Database[6] provides a wealth of data beginning with the Vinson Court through to the present. Among the many attributes of Court decisions coded by Spaeth are the names of the courts making the original decision, the identities of the parties to a case, the policy context of a case, and the votes of each justice. It and accompanying documentation are freely available at the Web site for Michigan State University's Program for Law and Judicial Politics: www.polisci.msu.edu/pljp/. Along with the Gallup Poll, the Harris Survey, and unpublished press releases issued by the *New York Times*, we use data gathered by the National Opinion Research Center (and archived as the General Social Survey) as sources for information on public opinion. Because survey responses are extremely sensitive to question wording, we eschew one-time "snapshots" of public opinion on questions relevant to the judiciary and focus instead on trends over time.

We compiled additional data from government reports. *Historical Statistics of the United States, Colonial Times to 1970,*[7] and the *Statistical Abstract of the United States*[8] (published annually since 1878) are "the standard summar[ies] of statistics on the social, political, and economic organization of the United States."[9] For our purposes, they are particularly useful sources of court caseload statistics. Another very helpful source is *The Constitution of the United States of America: Analysis and Interpretation.*[10] Among other things, it lists all Court decisions overruled by subsequent decisions and all cases in which the Court held unconstitutional acts of federal, state, and local governments. We also rely on reports issued by various government actors and agencies. Examples include the *Register of the U.S. Department of Justice and the Federal Courts,*[11] which provides information on individuals who have served as attorneys and solicitors general; the Administrative Office of the United States Courts,[12] which issues annual reports on court caseloads; and the *Annual Report of the Attorney General of the United States,*[13] which contains various data on the processing of Court litigation. Such data are increasingly available via the Internet. When we obtained information from a Web site, we list the URL.

Finally, we scoured historical accounts and secondary material to fill in blanks and verify other sources. This was particularly the case in collecting information about the lives of the justices. While there has been a great deal written about the most famous of the justices, little is known about many of the others. Much of the data on the justices come from well-established biographical sources, including Leon Friedman and Fred Israel's *The Justices of the United States Supreme Court,*[14] The Judicial Conference of the United States' *Judges of the United States,*[15] *The National Cyclopaedia of American Biography,*[16] and *The Dictionary of American Biography.*[17] *The First One Hundred Justices*[18] by Albert P. Blaustein and Roy M. Mersky was especially helpful. Similarly, a great deal of information was gleaned from John Schmidhauser's classic study of the backgrounds of the justices.[19] Data from this important work are archived at the Inter-University Consortium for Political and Social Research.[20] Even with the wealth of information contained in these sources, significant gaps remained. We filled these holes by consulting scores of biographies on the justices, newspaper accounts, and studies of the various historical periods. At the end of this process, we were still plagued with missing information and instances where contradictory claims in the biographical literature could not be resolved to our complete satisfaction. Unfortunately, such difficulties are inevitable when dealing with incomplete historical records. Notes to the tables alert readers to these and other problems.

The scope of our information also varies considerably. Whenever possible we tried to present data dating back to the Court's inception in February 1790. Unfortunately, this was more the exception than the rule, as such longitudinal data have seldom been compiled and, when they have, are often riddled with inconsistency. We were especially handicapped in our ability to offer information on voting behavior prior to the Vinson Court era, as our most reliable source, Spaeth's U.S. Supreme Court Judicial Database, does not antedate 1946.

For data other than voting behavior, though, we were often able to locate information going back to the early 1900s and occasionally even the 1800s. We do want to alert readers to the fact that, while we sought to verify historical data against other sources, we did not attempt to research the primary data sources. In some instances, therefore, we cannot vouch for accuracy. Once again, table notes alert readers to these potential problems.

Presentation of the Data

Several major concerns guided our presentation of the data. First, we sought to be as comprehensive as possible. Accordingly, we provide data well fitted to tabular presentation as well as data that are not. Examples of the latter are a chronology of events in the Court's history (Table 1-1) and catalogs of landmark decisions (Tables 2-12 and 2-13). To organize and communicate the data in usable fashion, we exercised our judgment of how best to present them, as most of the data have either not been compiled at all or have not appeared in any systematic fashion. Where possible, we have conformed to customary and conventional categorization, such as chronological, alphabetical, or topical. But for the vast majority of the data, conventions simply do not exist. Hence, we proceeded on the bases of clarity and understanding.

Second, for those tables derived from the U.S. Supreme Court Judicial Database, we wanted to provide sufficient information for readers to understand, evaluate, build on, or reproduce them. Accordingly, for each table we provide two crucial pieces of information—what Spaeth labels "analu" and "dec_type." "Analu" is the unit of analysis under study, and Spaeth offers the following options:

- analu = 0: case citation. Sometimes the Court decides several cases under one opinion. Using this as the unit of analysis will identify only the lead case.

- analu = 1: docket number. In those instances when the Court decided several cases under one opinion, this unit of analysis will bring up all cases, not just the lead case. This can be useful when differences exist between or among cases consolidated under one citation, such as the court in which the case originated, the court whose decision the Supreme Court reviewed, the parties to the case, and so on.

- analu = 2: multiple-issue case. This is the identification of cases that contain multiple issues, such as a case that raised questions about federal taxation and self-incrimination.

- analu = 3: multiple legal-provisions case. This is the identification of cases that contain multiple legal provisions, such as a case in which the Court dealt with the Fourteenth Amendment Equal Protection Clause and the Civil Rights Act of 1964.

- analu = 4: split-vote case. This is the identification of cases that contain a split vote. This phrase refers to those cases with a common citation, docket number, legal provision, and issue in which one or more of the justices voted with the majority on one issue or aspect of the case and dissented on another.
- analu = 5: case with multiple issues and multiple legal provisions.

"Dec_type" refers to the types of decisions the Court renders. Again, Spaeth offers a number of options:

- dec_type = 1: cases in which the Court hears oral argument and which it decides by a signed opinion. These are the Court's so-called formally decided full-opinion cases.
- dec_type = 2: cases decided with an opinion but without oral argument—that is, per curiam.
- dec_type = 3: memorandum cases. These are summary decisions that deal with petitions for certiorari and appeals, requests of individuals and organizations to participate as amicus curiae, and various other motions, orders, and writs. These are segregated from other types of decisions by their location in the back of the various volumes of the *United States Reports*, beginning at page 801 or 901 or later.
- dec_type = 4: decrees. This infrequent type of decision usually arises under the Court's original jurisdiction and involves state boundary disputes. The justices will typically appoint a special master to take testimony and render a report, the bulk of which generally becomes the Court's decision. The presence of the label "decree" distinguishes this type of decision from the others.
- dec_type = 5: cases decided by an equally divided vote. When a justice fails to participate in a case or when the Court has a vacancy, the participating justices may cast a tie vote. In such cases the Reports merely state that "the judgment is affirmed by an equally divided vote" and give the name of any nonparticipating justice(s). Their effect is to uphold the decision of the court whose ruling the Supreme Court reviewed.
- dec_type = 6: a variant of the formally decided cases (dec_type = 1). It differs from type 1 only in that no individual justice's name appears as author of the Court's opinion. Instead, these unsigned orally argued cases are labeled as decided per curiam. The difference between this type and type 2 is that the former includes oral argument, whereas the latter does not. In both types the opinion of the Court is unsigned—that is, per curiam.
- dec_type = 7: judgments of the Court. This decision type is also a variant of the formally decided cases (dec_type = 1). It differs from type 1 in that less than a majority of the participating justices agree with the opinion produced by the justice assigned to write the Court's opinion.

Readers can learn more about "analu" and "dec_type," including which options to select for particular research projects, from at least two sources—Spaeth's documentation and Sara C. Benesh's "Becoming an Intelligent User of the Spaeth Databases," both of which are available on the Internet at www.polisci.msu.edu/pljp/. We wish to note here that users need not select only one "analu" and one "dec_type." Indeed, among the most common combinations appearing in our tables is one in which the unit of analysis equals case citation (analu = 0) and docket number (analu = 1), and the type of decision equals formally decided full-opinion cases, orally argued per curiams, and judgments of the Court (dec_type = 1, 6, or 7).

At the same time, while providing readers with sufficient information to replicate the tables, we sought to minimize the technical character of the data. This is not an easy task since the Court and its activities are complex matters typically characterized by a somewhat arcane vocabulary (notwithstanding the inroads made on legalese by the plain English movement of recent years). Although we eliminated technical terms to the extent possible, they are by no means absent. For this reason (and several others noted above), it is especially important that readers review the notes following the tables. Legal definitions typically lack even imprecise meaning. What rights, for example, are objectively within—or outside—"the very essence of a scheme of ordered liberty"?[21] What principles of justice are "so rooted in the traditions and conscience of our people as to be ranked as fundamental"?[22] Is a declaration of unconstitutionality or the overruling of a precedent beyond dispute? Moreover, many legal definitions create distinctions between things that arguably have no meaningful differences. A jurisdictional dissent, for example, includes dissents from the Court's refusal to decide a case, from the Court's affirmation of a lower court's decision without oral argument, and from the Court's assertion of jurisdiction over a case. None addresses the merits of the controversy. Should they be distinguished from one another or simply lumped together? Does it really matter? In short, we had to formulate our own operationally meaningful definitions, as the notes to the tables point out.

In addition, technical terms do not necessarily have conventional meanings. Jurisdictional dissents provide a good example, as do concurring opinions. Is a concurring opinion that fully agrees with the contents of the majority opinion to be treated the same as one that agrees only with the result reached by the majority? We do not think so; hence, we separate them into "regular" and "special" concurrences. In our view, the justices who join the former type are full-fledged members of the majority opinion coalition, while those joining the latter are not. And if enough justices specially concur, no opinion of the Court will result—only a judgment. In such a case, the decision provides little guidance either to the litigants or to others similarly situated. Consider also the basic question of how to count cases. Should each citation be treated separately, or should one count the number of docketed cases under a given citation? Further, should one limit analysis only to "formally" decided cases—that is, to those cases that have been orally argued? And if so, should orally argued cases with the prevailing opinion signed by a justice be included alone, or in tandem with those decided per curiam (in which no individual justice authors the prevailing opinion)? Because no convention dictates the answers to these and other matters, the explanatory notes following the tables (including the unit of analysis and decision type we invoked when working with Spaeth's database) are particularly important.

Finally, apart from convention, certain matters are sufficiently unusual that they must be treated in an ad hoc fashion. Although we sometimes report anomalies in separate tables (see Table 4-17, for example), such peculiarities will often affect the contents of related tables. This too points to the need to pay close attention to the notes that accompany the tables.

The fact that the Court operates in a technical fashion need not cloud comprehension and understanding. We have defined terms in a nontechnical fashion, and the tables themselves do not require advanced interpretive skills. The book is based on simple numerical data, not the results of complicated statistical analyses. It should be useful to the methodologically skilled and unskilled alike.

The Organization of the Book

Chapter organization progresses logically. We begin in Chapters 1 through 3 with an institutional overview of the Court's history, the constitutional and congressional provisions that govern the Court and its jurisdiction, the Court's caseload, and landmark decisions. We also identify various chronological and topical trends apparent in the Court's decisions and opinions.

Chapters 4, 5, and 6 shift the focus from cases to the individual justices. We identify family backgrounds, childhood environments, marital status, educational and employment histories, and political experiences; dates and circumstances of nomination and confirmation are supplied as well, as are dates of court service. The circumstances surrounding retirements, resignations, and deaths are reviewed. The justices' scholarly credentials are identified and quotations from classic opinions excerpted. The justices' voting behavior is viewed ideologically, and trends in voting agreement are presented. We also identify the justices' opinion-writing proclivities, and those who agreed between themselves.

Chapter 7 considers the political and legal environments in which the Court operates. In the first part of the chapter, we identify congressional legislation most frequently the subject of Court litigation, amendments ratified to alter Court decisions, and key congressional members whose legislative activities affect the judicial system (for example, the chairs of the House and Senate Judiciary Committees). We map the organization of the Justice Department and list the names and dates of service of persons heading these agencies. We also chart the success of the United States as a party before the Supreme Court and note the rates of success of various administrative agencies. Finally, we enumerate the frequency with which states participate in Court litigation and the rates of success they achieve in so doing. In the second part of Chapter 7 we focus on other courts within the judicial system: federal district courts, circuit courts of appeal, specialized federal courts, and state courts. At the federal court level, we specify, among other things, the extent to which the Supreme Court has reversed and affirmed lower court decisions. For the state courts, we detail Supreme Court review of state court decisions.

Chapter 8 summarizes the public's views of the Court, both overall and by subgroup. Questions reviewed include "How knowledgeable is the public about the Court?" and "To what extent does the public support the Court's resolution of specific controversial issues?"

Chapter 9 addresses the impact of the Court on certain public policy questions. Abortion, capital punishment, school desegregation, voter registration, and reapportionment are examples of issues covered.

In compiling the data contained in the pages that follow, detailed and voluminous though they be, we have made no attempt to resolve the questions and controversies that presently surround the Court. Questions such as "Are the justices overworked, too old, too unrepresentative?" "Is the Court rendering too many liberal decisions, or too many conservative ones?" "Is the Court addressing pertinent issues of broad public concern?" "Does the solicitor general exercise too much influence over the justices?" are not answered here. The data we supply are simply that: information about the Court and its environment. We have compiled and reported these data as accurately and as objectively as possible. They do not cover the totality of the activity that occurs within the confines of the justices' "Marble Palace." For example, we know little of what has transpired within the justices' secret conferences where they choose cases to be heard and decided and cast initial votes on the merits of the cases.[23] Our data, rather, are an appropriate starting point for analysis. But by no means are they the last word on the subjects to which they pertain.

Notes

1. *United States Reports* (Washington, D.C.: Government Printing Office).
2. *The Lawyers' Edition* (Rochester, N.Y.: Lawyers Co-operative Publishing Co.).
3. *The Supreme Court Reporter* (Minneapolis, Minn.: West Publishing Co.).
4. *United States Law Week* (Washington, D.C.: Bureau of National Affairs).
5. Accessed at www.law.cornell.edu/supct/. See Table 1-8 for other law-related sites.
6. Available at www.polisci.msu.edu/pljp. For information on the database (along with instructions on how to use it), see Spaeth's documentation and Sara C. Benesh, "Becoming an Intelligent User of the Spaeth Databases," presented at the 2002 annual meeting of the Southwestern Political Science Association. Both sources are available at the Web site listed above.

7. U.S. Bureau of the Census, *Historical Statistics of the United States, Colonial Times to 1970* (Washington, D.C.: Government Printing Office, 1975).

8. U.S. Bureau of the Census, *Statistical Abstract of the United States* (Washington, D.C.: Government Printing Office).

9. Ibid., v.

10. U.S. Library of Congress, Congressional Research Service, *The Constitution of the United States of America: Analysis and Interpretation: Annotations of Cases Decided by the Supreme Court of the United States* (Washington, D.C.: Government Printing Office).

11. U.S. Department of Justice, *Register of the U.S. Department of Justice and the Federal Courts* (Washington, D.C.: Government Printing Office).

12. Administrative Office of the United States Courts, *Annual Report of the Director of the Administrative Office of the United States Courts* (Washington, D.C.: Government Printing Office).

13. U.S. Department of Justice, *Annual Report of the Attorney General of the United States* (Washington, D.C.: Government Printing Office).

14. Leon Friedman and Fred L. Israel, eds., *The Justices of the United States Supreme Court: Their Lives and Major Opinions* (New York: R.R. Bowker, 1969–1978).

15. *Judges of the United States*, 2d ed. (Washington, D.C.: Judicial Conference of the United States, 1983).

16. *The National Cyclopaedia of American Biography* (New York: James T. White).

17. *The Dictionary of American Biography* (New York: Charles Scribner's Sons).

18. Albert P. Blaustein and Roy M. Mersky, *The First One Hundred Justices* (Hamden, Conn.: Shoe String Press, 1978).

19. John Schmidhauser, "The Justices of the Supreme Court: A Collective Portrait," *Midwest Journal of Political Science* 3 (February 1959): 1–57.

20. Ann Arbor, Mich., Inter-University Consortium for Political and Social Research, published as study #7240.

21. *Palko v. Connecticut,* 302 U.S. 319 (1937), at 325.

22. *Snyder v. Massachusetts,* 291 U.S. 95 (1934), at 105.

23. The exception is the Vinson Court (1946–1953). Jan Palmer's dataset draws on the private docket books of most of the justices who sat on that Court. See *The Vinson Court Era: The Supreme Court's Conference Votes* (New York: AMS Press, 1990). Having gained access to these docket books, Palmer systematically presents all the votes—preliminary and final—cast by each of the justices in every case in which the Vinson Court justices voted. The expanded version of the Supreme Court Database houses Palmer's data, as well as information of the Warren Court. See also H.W. Perry Jr., *Deciding to Decide: Agenda Setting in the United States Supreme Court* (Cambridge, Mass.: Harvard University Press, 1991); and Gregory A. Caldeira, John R. Wright, and Christopher J. Zorn, "Sophisticated Voting and Gate-keeping in the Supreme Court," *Journal of Law, Economics, and Organization* 15 (1999): 549.

1

The Supreme Court:
An Institutional Perspective

The material in this chapter provides an overview of the Supreme Court as an institution from a largely historical perspective. Tables 1-1, 1-2, and 1-3 offer a chronology of the Court's history with a look at its decisions and its personnel changes and at various unusual and noteworthy events.

While we have attempted to be reasonably detailed in compiling the contents of these tables, readers will note that more recent events appear with greater frequency than events of earlier years. For example, we provide at least one entry for each of the past fifteen years; by contrast, an entry appears for only half of the fourteen years between the Constitutional Convention and the ascension of John Marshall to the chief justiceship in 1801. To be sure, this may reflect a recency bias. More likely, however, it demonstrates the greater importance of the modern Court as a national policy maker (see Table 1-4).

Tables 1-5, 1-6, and 1-7 outline and specify the major legislation enacted by Congress to implement its constitutional powers concerning the federal judiciary in general and the Supreme Court in particular. As Table 1-5 indicates, this legislation typically addresses the number of justices and the scope of the Court's jurisdiction. Tables 1-6 and 1-7 contain the pertinent provisions of the United States Code that detail the organization of the Court and the types of cases it may hear and decide. The writ of certiorari (see Table 1-7) is the primary method by which those who have lost a case in a lower court bring their case to the Supreme Court's attention. Unlike the traditional writ of appeal, the justices can choose to grant or deny a petitioner's writ of certiorari.

Once the Court decides a case it has agreed to hear, it typically issues an opinion. The primary way of disseminating these opinions and other of the Court's decisions is through published reports. More so than most American courts, state or federal, the reports of the U.S. Supreme Court contain a relatively comprehensive record of the Court's decisions. Prior to the twentieth century, however, records are less than complete. During the 1790s, for example, fewer than half of the Court's decisions were published, and many of those were compiled from the notes of the attorneys who argued the cases.[1] Incompleteness continued to afflict the Court's reports until well after the Civil War. Numerous cases that are absent from the official *United States Reports* can be found in the privately published *Lawyers' Edition* of the Court's reports.[2] For at least the last half-century, though, the official reports do not materially differ from the privately printed ones. What differences do exist are largely limited to unofficial matters such as notes, summaries, and indices. (See Table 2-9 for a summary of the reporting systems available today.)

While virtually all law libraries contain at least one reporter dedicated to the Supreme Court, readers may be interested in obtaining copies of Court opinions (especially more recent ones) via various Web sites on the Internet. Table 1-8 provides a list of such sites, along with others that relate to law and the courts and various law lists. Because of the explosion of these Web sites and law lists in recent years, the table offers only those we think represent the best of the current Internet selection. Readers can use one of the many search engines also listed in Table 1-6 to locate others.

The remaining tables furnish information on a range of institutional features of the Court. Tables 1-9 through 1-12 provide a fairly complete set of data on the Court's budget, salary, and pension provisions. The data show that the Court comprises but a tiny fraction of the federal government's expenditures. The Court's rules, calendar, and processing of cases (from the initial filing to the publication of its decisions) are the subjects of Tables 1-13 and 1-14 and Figure 1-1. Finally, Tables 1-15 through 1-17 consider the Court's officers and employees. Table 1-15 details those sections of the United States Code pertaining to the Court's officers and employees, Table 1-16 identifies the number of full-time positions, and Table 1-17 provides the names and dates of service of the Court's administrative officials.

Notes

1. Susan W. Brenner, *Precedent Inflation* (New Brunswick, N.J.: Transaction, 1992), 84, 94–95.
2. For example, *Thatcher v. Kaucher,* 24 L. Ed. 511 (1877), *Keough v. Orient Fire Insurance Co.,* 24 L. Ed. 650 (1878).

Table 1-1   Chronology of Important Events in the Supreme Court's
History, 1787–1995

1787   The Constitutional Convention meets.

1789   The Constitution is ratified.
President George Washington signs the Judiciary Act of 1789, which establishes a federal court structure.

1790   The Supreme Court holds its first session in New York City.
The Court issues its first formal rule, creating the Office of the Clerk of the Court.
The first member of the Supreme Court bar, Elias Bordinot, is sworn in.

1791   The Bill of Rights becomes part of the Constitution.
The Court moves from New York City to Philadelphia.

1793   The Court announces its first major decision, *Chisholm v. Georgia*, which authorizes citizens of one state to sue another state in the Supreme Court. Ironically, the Eleventh Amendment, ratified in 1795, nullifies this decision.
The Court refuses Secretary of State Thomas Jefferson's request to answer questions concerning the appropriate role America should play in the ongoing English-French war. In so doing, it sets an important precedent regarding advisory opinions: issuing them would violate the separation of powers principle.

1795   The first chief justice, John Jay, resigns to become governor of New York. Washington nominates John Rutledge of South Carolina as Jay's successor, but for the first time the Senate refuses to confirm a Supreme Court nominee. In January of 1796, William Cushing, the senior associate, is nominated. He declines because of age. Washington then offers the post to Oliver Ellsworth, whom the Senate confirms the next day.
The Eleventh Amendment, prohibiting a nonresident from suing a state in federal court, is ratified.

1796   John Marshall makes his only appearance as an attorney before the Supreme Court when he argues the case of *Ware v. Hylton*. In stark contrast to the nationalist position he espoused as chief justice, Marshall here alleges the supremacy of state laws that conflict with federal treaties. He loses the case.

1801   Marshall is appointed chief justice by lame-duck president John Adams shortly before Jefferson takes office.
The Court moves to Washington, D.C., and holds sessions in a room in the Capitol building.
Congress passes the Circuit Court Act of 1801, which eliminates circuit court duty for the justices, reduces the number of justices from six to five, and increases the number of circuits from three to six.
Chief Justice Marshall begins the practice of issuing opinions of the Court, rather than having the justices deliver individual opinions in each case.

1802   Congress repeals the Circuit Court Act of 1801; the number of justices is returned to six.

1803   *Marbury v. Madison*, which enunciates the doctrine of judicial review, is decided.

1804   For the only time in history, the House of Representatives votes to impeach a Supreme Court justice, Samuel Chase. However, one year later the Senate fails to muster the two-thirds vote required to convict Chase on charges of partisan political behavior.

(Table continues)

Table 1-1   *(Continued)*

The Twelfth Amendment, governing the election of the president and vice-president, is ratified.

1805   Justice William Johnson delivers the Court's first opinion labeled as a dissent, in *Huidekoper's Lessee v. Douglass.*

1807   Congress creates a seventh circuit and, accordingly, increases the Court's membership to seven.

1810   The Court declares a state law unconstitutional for the first time in *Fletcher v. Peck.*

1811   On his fourth attempt to fill the vacancy created by the death of the last of the Court's original members, William Cushing, President James Madison nominates, and the Senate confirms, Joseph Story, at thirty two years old the youngest person ever to sit on the Court.

1813   The U.S. Attorney General files the Court's first *amicus curiae* brief (*Beatty's Administrator v. Burnes's Administrators*).

1816   The Court rules in *Martin v. Hunter's Lessee* that it, rather than the state courts, has final authority to determine the meaning of constitutional provisions and acts of Congress.

Henry Wheaton becomes the first Court reporter formally appointed by the Court. His two predecessors, Alexander J. Dallas and William Cranch, held the position on an unofficial basis.

Congress authorizes the official publication of Supreme Court decisions.

1819   The doctrine of implied powers is formulated in *McCulloch v. Maryland.*

In *Dartmouth College v. Woodward*, the Court broadly construes the contract clause to prevent states from abridging corporate charters as well as public grants.

1823   The longest period in the Court's history without a change of personnel (twelve years) ends with the death of Justice Henry Livingston.

Henry Clay files the first nongovernmental *amicus curiae* brief in a Supreme Court case (*Green v. Biddle*).

1824   The Court decides *Gibbons v. Ogden* in an opinion by Chief Justice Marshall that broadly defines the scope of Congress's power to regulate interstate commerce.

1832   An attempt by Georgia to subject Cherokee Indians to its authority, notwithstanding a Court decision to the contrary *(Worcester v. Georgia)*, ends when President Andrew Jackson reverses his pro-state position and supports expanded federal judicial power.

1833   *Barron v. Baltimore*, Chief Justice Marshall's last major constitutional opinion, holds that the Bill of Rights applies only to the federal government, not to the states.

1835   Chief Justice Marshall dies.

James M. Wayne of Georgia, the only incumbent member of the House of Representatives to be appointed to the Court, takes his seat.

1836   Because of Senate opposition to the nomination of Roger Taney as Marshall's successor, the Supreme Court, for the only term in its history, is without a chief justice.

Taney is finally confirmed by the Senate, notwithstanding the opposition of two giants of American constitutional law, Daniel Webster and Henry Clay.

1837   Three major decisions, *Charles River Bridge v. Warren Bridge, New York v. Miln,* and *Briscoe v. Bank of Kentucky,* portend an increase in the rights of

Table 1-1   *(Continued)*

the states vis-à-vis the national government by limiting the scope of the contract clause and upholding state regulations affecting interstate commerce.

Congress divides the United States into nine circuits and increases the Court's membership to nine.

1841   In *United States v. Libellants and Claimants of the Schooner Amistad,* Justice Story delivers the opinion of the Court that the African peoples aboard the ship *Amistad* be declared free.

Former president John Quincy Adams appears before the Court as an advocate in the *Amistad* case. Thirty-two years had passed since his last appearance.

1842   *Prigg v. Pennsylvania* holds that the federal government, not the states, has authority over fugitive slaves.

1844   The longest vacancy in Supreme Court history begins with the death of Justice Henry Baldwin. Because of partisan conflict between President John Tyler—the first nonelected president—and the Senate, Tyler is unsuccessful in filling the vacancy before he leaves office in 1845. Incoming president James Polk faces similar difficulties in naming a replacement for Baldwin. His first choice declines and his second choice is rejected by the Senate. Finally, twenty-seven months after Baldwin's death, the Senate confirms Robert Grier for the post.

1849   The Court places time limits on oral arguments: two hours per side.

1851   Benjamin Curtis, the only Whig to sit on the Court, takes his seat.

1857   The *Dred Scott* decision rules that slaves are property with which Congress may not interfere, and that neither they nor any of their descendants are citizens under the Constitution.

1861   Jeremiah Black, nominated by lame-duck president James Buchanan, is rejected by the closest vote in history, 25 to 26.

1863   The Emancipation Proclamation declares southern slaves free.

For the first time, a president clearly identified with one political party nominates a formally affiliated member of another political party to the Supreme Court when Abraham Lincoln selects Stephen J. Field.

Congress abolishes the Circuit Court of California, created in 1855, and replaces it with a tenth circuit. It also increases the size of the Court to ten. This gives Lincoln the opportunity to make his fourth appointment.

1864   Chief Justice Taney dies and is succeeded by Salmon P. Chase.

1865   General Robert E. Lee surrenders at Appomattox, ending the Civil War. Five days later John Wilkes Booth assassinates President Lincoln.

The Thirteenth Amendment, abolishing slavery, is ratified.

John S. Rock, the first black to become a member of the Supreme Court bar, is sworn in.

1866   Congress reduces the size of the Court from ten to seven to thwart President Andrew Johnson.

In *Ex parte Milligan,* the Supreme Court rules that military tribunals have no jurisdiction over civilians where civil courts are open and operating.

The number of circuit courts is reduced to nine.

1867   Congress establishes the Office of the Marshal of the Supreme Court, which manages the Court's chamber.

1868   The Fourteenth Amendment, prohibiting the states from depriving persons of due process or denying them equal protection of the laws, is ratified.

(Table continues)

Table 1-1   *(Continued)*

President Andrew Johnson is impeached.

After the Court hears arguments in *Ex parte McCardle,* Congress removes the Court's authority to hear appeals emanating under the 1867 Habeas Corpus Act. The justices then redocket the case, but decline to decide it. Their action indicates that Congress possesses the authority to remove the Court's appellate jurisdiction as it deems necessary.

1869   Congress increases the size of the Supreme Court to nine, where it has remained ever since.

1870   The last of the Civil War amendments, the Fifteenth, is ratified, prohibiting the states or the United States from denying anyone the right to vote because of race.

By a 4–3 vote, the Court rules in *Hepburn v. Griswold* that Congress has no power to authorize paper money as legal payment of debts, the method used to finance the Civil War. President Ulysses S. Grant fills the Court's two vacancies with individuals sympathetic to the use of paper money, and, fifteen months after the initial decision, the Court reverses itself and rules that the Legal Tender Acts were a proper exercise of congressional power.

Congress creates the Department of Justice and the post of solicitor general. Elias C. Boudinot becomes the first Native American to appear before the Court.

1873   By a 5–4 vote, the Court holds in the *Slaughterhouse Cases* that nothing in the Fourteenth Amendment expands the scope of individual rights against state action.

With only Chief Justice Chase dissenting, the Court rules in *Bradwell v. Illinois* that a state violates no constitutional provision in denying a woman a license to practice law because of her sex.

Chief Justice Chase dies.

1874   After two unsuccessful attempts to fill the chief justiceship—the most in history—Grant nominates Morrison Waite, a little-known Ohio attorney without judicial experience who had never argued a case before the Court.

1875   Court Reporter John W. Wallace retires. Because of a change in policy, he is the last to see his name on the cover of the reports of the Court. The official reports of the Court now are known as *United States Reports.*

1877   Five members of the Court serve on the electoral commission that resolves the disputed election of 1876. The justices split 3 to 2 along party lines, thereby making the Republican nominee, Rutherford B. Hayes, president.

In *Munn v. Illinois,* the Court reaffirms its 1873 decision in the *Granger Cases,* which asserted that the Fourteenth Amendment does not prevent states from regulating the use of private property.

1879   Belva Ann Lockwood becomes the first woman member of the Supreme Court bar.

1880   For the first time since the Civil War, President Hayes nominates a person from a Confederate state, William B. Woods, to sit on the Court. Woods, however, was not a native of the South, having migrated to Georgia after Appomattox.

1881   Stanley Mathews, the only person besides John Jay ever to be nominated to the same seat by two different presidents, is confirmed by the closest vote in history, 24 to 23.

Table 1-1   *(Continued)*

1882   Justice Horace Gray is the first Supreme Court justice to hire law school graduates as clerks.

1883   In the *Civil Rights Cases*, the Court narrowly defines what constitutes state action under the due process and equal protection clauses of the Fourteenth Amendment and, as a result, declares the Civil Rights Act of 1875 unconstitutional. Not until after World War II would the Court with any regularity support civil rights claims.

1886   In *Santa Clara County v. Southern Pacific R. Co.*, the Court claims that corporations are not citizens and thus not entitled to the protections afforded by the Fourteenth Amendment. They are nevertheless "persons" who cannot be deprived of liberty or property without due process of law. This decision heralds the Court's integration of the doctrines of laissez-faire economics into the Constitution.
Congress authorizes each justice to hire a stenographic clerk.

1887   The Interstate Commerce Act is passed, creating the first regulatory commission in U.S. history. Supreme Court decisions, however, sap the strength from its provisions, making the commission impotent to regulate the railroads, which are the focus of the Act.

1888   L.Q.C. Lamar of Mississippi is appointed to the Court. He is the first Democrat to be seated in a quarter century.
Chief Justice Waite dies. He is replaced by Melville Fuller, a Chicago railroad attorney.

1890   Congress enacts the Sherman Antitrust Act. Because of lax enforcement and hostile Court decisions, the law does little to curb the growth of concentrated economic power.

1891   Congress establishes federal appellate courts, allowing district court judges to sit in place of Supreme Court justices, virtually eliminating circuit-riding duty.

1894   Edward D. White, the first incumbent senator to be selected for the Court in forty-eight years, is nominated and confirmed on the same day. It will be another forty-three years before a subsequent incumbent senator, Hugo Black, is chosen.

1895   In *United States v. E. C. Knight Co.*, the Court rules that the Sherman Antitrust Act, which is based on Congress's power to regulate interstate commerce, does not apply to manufacturing because manufacturing is not commerce.
Overruling a 100-year-old precedent, the Court declares the income tax unconstitutional in *Pollock v. Farmers' Loan & Trust Co.*, occasioning the adoption of the Sixteenth Amendment eighteen years later.
A unanimous Court in *In re Debs* approves the use of federal judicial power to stop strikes through the use of the labor injunction.

1896   The Court formulates the separate but equal doctrine in *Plessy v. Ferguson*, thereby legitimizing the segregated society created by Jim Crow laws.

1897   In *Allgeyer v. Louisiana*, the Court holds that the Fourteenth Amendment protects the freedom of contract, including the right of individuals to sell their labor without governmental regulation of hours, wages, or working conditions.

1898   In *Smyth v. Ames*, the Court further extends its probusiness judicial activism, holding that if states set the rates railroads may charge, those rates must provide a fair return on investment, and that the federal courts will determine what is and is not fair.

(Table continues)

Table 1-1   *(Continued)*

1899   Former attorney general Augustus H. Garland collapses and dies while presenting oral arguments.

1902   Theodore Roosevelt appoints Massachusetts Supreme Court chief justice and legal scholar Oliver Wendell Holmes to the U.S. Supreme Court.

1905   *Lochner v. New York* is decided, precluding a state from restricting bakers to a ten-hour day and a sixty-hour week on the basis of freedom of contract.

1908   In *Adair v. United States,* freedom of contract also invalidates the act of Congress outlawing yellow-dog contracts, which employers utilize to fire employees if they join a labor union.

Although the Sherman Act does not particularly restrain labor activity, the Court construes it to ban secondary boycotts by labor unions in *Loewe v. Lawlor.*

As a result of the advocacy of Louis D. Brandeis, who would join the Supreme Court eight years later, the Court, in *Muller v. Oregon,* accepts limitations on freedom of contract in the case of women. Accordingly, a state may restrict women laundry workers to a ten-hour day.

1909   William Howard Taft takes the oath of office as president. During his tenure, six justices are seated, more than under any other single-term president. Only Washington's ten successful nominees and Franklin Roosevelt's nine exceed this number.

The first of Taft's nominees, Horace H. Lurton, at 65, is the oldest member to be seated as an associate justice in history. Harlan Fiske Stone and Charles Evans Hughes were 68 years, 8 months, and 67 years, 10 months, respectively, when promoted to the chief justiceship.

1910   Chief Justice Fuller dies. Taft is the first president to cross party lines, as an associate justice, Edward D. White, is promoted to the chief justiceship.

1911   In *Standard Oil Co. v. United States,* the Court states that the Sherman Act only outlaws unreasonable restraints of trade even though it contains no such qualification. The federal courts determine for themselves what is and is not reasonable.

Congress completely relieves justices of circuit-riding duty.

1913   The Sixteenth (income tax) and Seventeenth (popular election of senators) amendments are ratified.

1914   World War I begins.

The Clayton Antitrust Act, which supplements and strengthens the Sherman Act, is passed.

1916   President Woodrow Wilson nominates the first Jew, Louis Brandeis, to the Supreme Court. Over the opposition of former president—and soon-to-be chief justice—Taft and various bar and business leaders, Brandeis is confirmed after four months of acrimonious hearings. Although his opponents describe him as a trouble-making radical, anti-Semitism fuels much of the opposition.

1917   The United States declares war on Germany.

1918   By a 5–4 vote in *Hammer v. Dagenhart,* the Court declares unconstitutional Congress's effort to outlaw child labor.

The armistice ending World War I is signed.

1919   The "noble experiment," Prohibition, spearheaded by the Women's Christian Temperance Union and the Anti-Saloon League, is written into the Constitution as the Eighteenth Amendment.

1920   Women earn the right to vote with the ratification of the Nineteenth Amendment.

Table 1-1   *(Continued)*

1921   Chief Justice White dies. President Warren Harding chooses former president Taft as his successor.

1922   Congress's second effort to ban child labor, based this time on the power to tax rather than the interstate commerce clause, is struck down as a result of the Court's decision in *Bailey v. Drexel Furniture Co.*
Congress allows Court law clerks to be hired at government expense.

1923   The Court rules in *Adkins v. Children's Hospital* that a federal minimum wage law for women violates freedom of contract.

1925   In the course of upholding the conviction of a left-wing radical for distributing a pamphlet urging the overthrow of the government, the Court, in *Gitlow v. New York*, notes that freedoms of speech and of the press are among the fundamental rights and liberties that the Fourteenth Amendment protects from state abridgment.
Congress enacts the Judiciary Act of 1925, reducing significantly the proportion of cases the Court must hear.
The Court develops the Rule of Four: at least four justices must agree before the Court will hear a case under its discretionary jurisdiction.

1928   The Court reduces oral argument from two hours to one hour per side.

1929   The stock market crashes; the Great Depression begins.
The Tenth Circuit Court of Appeals is created.

1930   President Herbert Hoover replaces Chief Justice Taft, who resigns, with Charles Evans Hughes, who had left the Supreme Court in 1916 to accept the Republican nomination for president.
John J. Parker is rejected by a vote of 39 to 41. Not since 1894 has a nominee failed to gain confirmation, and not until 1968 will another one do so.

1931   In *Stromberg v. California*, the Court strikes down a California law prohibiting the display of a red flag as a symbol of opposition to government as a violation of First Amendment rights. Two weeks later, in *Near v. Minnesota*, the Court rules that a state law prohibiting publication of a scandal sheet violates the First Amendment's guarantee of freedom of the press.

1932   The Norris-LaGuardia Act forbids the federal courts to issue injunctions in labor disputes to prevent strikes, boycotts, or picketing.
Two months shy of his ninety-first birthday, Oliver Wendell Holmes resigns, the only nonagenarian ever to sit on the Supreme Court.

1933   Franklin D. Roosevelt takes office. The New Deal begins. Major regulatory legislation is enacted, including the Agricultural Adjustment Act and the National Industrial Recovery Act. Congress creates the Civilian Conservation Corps to provide outdoor work for unemployed males between the ages of eighteen and twenty-five, and establishes the Tennessee Valley Authority to construct dams and power plants in especially depressed parts of Appalachia.
The Twentieth Amendment, which ends the practice of congressional lame-duck sessions, is ratified.
The Twenty-first Amendment, repealing Prohibition is ratified.

1934   Major federal regulatory commissions are created, including the Securities and Exchange Commission, the Federal Communications Commission, and the Federal Housing Administration.
In *Nebbia v. New York*, the Court rules that the Fourteenth Amendment does not prevent a state from fixing the maximum and minimum prices of milk.

(Table continues)

Table 1-1 *(Continued)*

1935   Congress enacts the National Labor Relations Act, which gives labor the legal right to bargain collectively, and the Social Security Act, which provides unemployment compensation, old-age pension benefits, aid to blind and disabled persons, and aid to families with dependent children.

The Court declares unconstitutional the National Industrial Recovery Act and the Railroad Retirement Act, which established a comprehensive pension system for railroad workers.

May 27 goes down in history as Black Monday when the Court deals the Roosevelt administration three losses on a single day (*Schechter Poultry Corporation v. United States, Humphrey's Executor v. United States,* and *Louisville Joint Stock Land Bank v. Radford*).

Oliver Wendell Holmes dies. He leaves his estate to the United States, which uses the money to fund a study of the Court's history.

The Court meets in its new (and current) building, "the Marble Palace," in Washington, D.C. *Douglas v. Willcuts* is the first case argued in the new building.

1936   The Court continues to strike down major portions of the New Deal in *United States v. Butler* and *Carter v. Carter Coal Co.,* invalidating the Agricultural Adjustment Act and the Bituminous Coal Conservation Act, respectively.

The Court declares in *Morehead v. New York* and *ex rel. Tipaldo* that all state minimum wage laws, including those that apply to women and children, violate due process.

1937   The Court unanimously rules in *DeJonge v. Oregon* that the due process clause of the Fourteenth Amendment makes binding on the states the First Amendment's guarantee of freedom of assembly.

Following his landslide reelection in 1936, President Roosevelt submits to Congress a so-called Court-packing plan that will allow him to appoint additional justices to the Supreme Court for the unexpressed purpose of preventing further invalidation of New Deal legislation. But Justice Owen Roberts's switch in vote, immortalized as "the switch in time that saved nine," produces a pro–New Deal majority and makes Roosevelt's Court-packing scheme a moot issue.

West Coast Hotel Co. v. Parrish overrules the 1923 decision, *Adkins v. Children's Hospital,* and the 1936 decision, *Morehead v. New York ex rel. Tipaldo,* and upholds the state of Washington's minimum wage law. As the justices earlier read freedom of contract into the Constitution, they now read it out.

In *National Labor Relations Board v. Jones & Laughlin Steel Corp.,* the Court finally accepts that manufacturing is a part of commerce that Congress has power to regulate. As a result, the National Labor Relations Act is ruled to be constitutional.

Steward Machine Co. v. Davis upholds the unemployment compensation provisions of the Social Security Act. *Helvering v. Davis* upholds its old-age pension benefits.

Justice Willis Van Devanter retires. Roosevelt has his first opportunity to fill a seat on the Court and thereby increase judicial support for the New Deal. His selection, Senator Hugo Black, is confirmed five days after nomination.

1938   Justice George Sutherland becomes the second anti–New Deal member to resign. By the middle of 1941, Roosevelt has filled seven Court vacancies.

Table 1-1   *(Continued)*

The Fair Labor Standards Act prohibits child labor and establishes a nationwide minimum wage and maximum hour law. The Court upholds its constitutionality three years later in *United States v. Darby.*

1939 Felix Frankfurter, the last foreign-born justice, becomes an associate justice. World War II begins with the Nazi invasion of Poland.

1940 In an opinion by Justice Frankfurter in *Minersville School District v. Gobitis*, the Court holds that children attending public school may be compelled to salute the flag, notwithstanding their religious objections.

With President Roosevelt's elevation of Frank Murphy, his appointees now comprise a majority of the Court.

1941 Chief Justice Hughes resigns. For the second time in history, a president crosses party lines to select a chief justice when Roosevelt nominates Harlan Fiske Stone.

James F. Byrnes, the last justice to sit without having attended law school, is appointed. He neither attended college nor graduated from high school.

Japan attacks Pearl Harbor.

The last of the anti–New Deal justices, James McReynolds, leaves the Court.

1942 In *Wickard v. Filburn*, the justices unanimously assert that Congress's power to regulate interstate commerce gives it control over activities that are neither commercial nor interstate.

1943 The Court overrules its compulsory flag salute decision of 1940 in *West Virginia State Board of Education v. Barnette.*

1944 In *Korematsu v. United States*, the Court asserts that unsubstantiated "military necessity" permits citizens to be summarily imprisoned solely because of their race.

Justice William Douglas selects the first woman, Lucille Loman, to serve as a law clerk.

1945 President Roosevelt dies; Harry Truman succeeds him. World War II ends and the Cold War begins.

President Truman crosses party lines to nominate Republican incumbent senator Harold H. Burton to the Supreme Court.

1946 Chief Justice Stone dies. Fred Vinson succeeds to the chief justiceship.

1947 In *Everson v. Board of Education*, the First Amendment's religious establishment clause is made binding on the states.

1948 In *Shelley v. Kraemer*, the Court rules that state courts may not constitutionally enforce racially restrictive housing covenants.

Justice Frankfurter selects the first black, William T. Coleman, to serve as a law clerk.

1949 In *Wolf v. Colorado*, the Fourth Amendment's ban on unreasonable searches and seizures is held to apply to the states.

1950–
1952 A series of decisions upholds federal and state legislation curbing alleged subversive activity.

1951 The Twenty-second Amendment, limiting presidential terms, is ratified.

1952 In *Burstyn v. Wilson*, the Court rules that motion pictures are a significant medium of expression protected by the First Amendment.

The Court curbs presidential power in *Youngstown Sheet and Tube Co. v. Sawyer* by ruling unconstitutional President Truman's seizure of the steel mills to avoid a strike that would disrupt U.S. military actions in Korea.

(Table continues)

Table 1-1   *(Continued)*

1953	Chief Justice Vinson dies. California governor Earl Warren becomes chief justice.
	The Court meets in special session to decide the fate of Ethel and Julius Rosenberg. Its decision to lift the stay of their death sentences leads to their execution.
1954	The separate but equal doctrine of *Plessy v. Ferguson* is overruled in *Brown v. Board of Education,* paving the way for school desegregation.
	Three members of the Everett family are sworn in as members of the Supreme Court bar. This is believed to be the first time that three members of the same family were sworn in on the same day.
1955	The Court begins taping oral arguments.
	The Court announces that it will no longer hear oral arguments on Fridays, reserving that day for conference.
1956	The American Bar Association's Standing Committee on the Federal Judiciary begins screening and rating Court candidates.
1957	In *Yates v. United States,* the Court makes the conviction of alleged subversives more difficult by requiring prosecutors to show that the accused took some action to overthrow the U.S. government by force.
	The Court declares obscenity to be without constitutional protection in *Roth v. United States* and *Alberts v. California.*
1961–	
1969	The Warren Court begins to expand the rights of persons accused of crime by using various provisions in the Fourth to Eighth amendments to restrict state and local law enforcement activities.
1961	The Court holds in *Mapp v. Ohio* that the judicially created constitutionally based exclusionary rule prohibits the use of illegally seized evidence in state, as well as federal, trials.
	The Twenty-third Amendment is ratified, allowing the District of Columbia to participate in presidential elections.
	Ending an 1873 rule, the Supreme Court begins its sessions at 10:00 A.M. rather than noon.
1962	The Court rules in *Baker v. Carr* that redistricting malapportioned legislative bodies is a judicial, not a political, question. Within the next twenty-seven months, the Court formulates a "one person, one vote" rule and applies it to the House of Representatives and both houses of the states' legislatures. These decisions break the historical rural domination of legislative politics and shift power to cities and their suburbs.
	In *Engle v. Vitale,* the Court rules that officially sanctioned prayer in the public schools violates the Constitution's establishment of religion clause.
1963	The Court rules in *Gideon v. Wainwright* that the Sixth Amendment requires that all persons accused of serious crimes be provided an attorney.
	President John F. Kennedy is assassinated.
1964	The Twenty-fourth Amendment, prohibiting poll and other voting taxes, is ratified.
	In *New York Times v. Sullivan,* the Court determines that the First Amendment prevents public officials from collecting damages for libelous media statements unless they prove the statement was made "with knowledge that it was false or with reckless disregard of whether it was false or not."
	The Court holds in *Malloy v. Hogan* that the Fifth Amendment's protection against self-incrimination applies to state criminal defendants.

Table 1-1   *(Continued)*

The Court unanimously upholds the constitutionality of the Civil Rights Act of 1964 and its ban on discrimination in places of public accommodations in *Heart of Atlanta Motel v. United States.*

1965   In *Pointer v. Texas,* the Court makes defendants' Sixth Amendment right to confront and crossexamine their accusers binding on the state, as well as the federal, governments.

The Court rules in *Griswold v. Connecticut* that "penumbras" in the First, Third, Fourth, Fifth, Ninth, and Fourteenth amendments guarantee a right to personal privacy, which prohibits a state from criminalizing the use of contraceptives.

Abe Fortas, the fifth Jewish justice, takes his seat.

1966   In *South Carolina v. Katzenbach,* the Court upholds the constitutionality of the Voting Rights Act of 1965. As a result, for the first time since Reconstruction southern blacks are able to vote with relative ease.

In *Miranda v. Arizona,* the Court decides that suspects must be read their rights before police questioning. The collapse of law enforcement is widely forecast, and efforts to impeach Chief Justice Warren gain additional force.

1967   The Twenty-fifth Amendment, governing the order of succession in cases of presidential incompetence, is ratified.

A unanimous Court in *Loving v. Virginia* rules that criminalizing interracial marriage violates due process as well as equal protection.

In *Washington v. Texas,* the Court rules that defendants in state courts have as much right to obtain favorable witnesses as does the prosecution.

Thurgood Marshall, the first black nominated to the Supreme Court, takes his seat.

1968   The Court holds in *Duncan v. Louisiana* that the due process clause of the Fourteenth Amendment requires states to provide a trial by jury to persons accused of serious crimes.

A unanimous Court in *Green v. County School Board* terminates the "with all deliberate speed" formula for desegregating southern schools under the mandate of *Brown v. Board of Education* and orders desegregation "now."

The Court rules in *United States v. O'Brien* that the First Amendment does not protect draft card burning.

President Lyndon Johnson nominates Abe Fortas to succeed Earl Warren as chief justice and Homer Thornberry to occupy Fortas's seat as associate justice. Opposition from Republicans and conservative Democrats forces the lame-duck Johnson to withdraw Fortas's nomination, which also precludes action on Thornberry.

Richard Nixon defeats Hubert Humphrey in the presidential election.

1969   The Court rules in *Tinker v. Des Moines School District* that the First Amendment protects symbolic speech and applies to children as well as adults. Hence, students may wear armbands to protest the Vietnam War.

Under investigation for his dealings with a convicted felon, Justice Fortas resigns. He is the only justice to resign under threat of impeachment.

The Court rules in *Benton v. Maryland* that the due process clause prohibits the states from denying individuals protection from double jeopardy.

President Nixon nominates Warren Burger to succeed Chief Justice Warren, who has announced his intention to resign at the end of the Court's term.

(Table continues)

Table 1-1   *(Continued)*

1969–
1970   President Nixon's initial efforts to fill the Fortas vacancy are unsuccessful. The Senate rejects his first two nominees, Clement Haynsworth and Harrold Carswell. Not since 1894 have two successive nominees been rejected. The Senate, however, does confirm his third choice, Harry Blackmun, by a vote of 94 to 0.

1970   In *In re Winship* the Court determines that juvenile defendants are entitled to the same evidentiary standard as adults: beyond a reasonable doubt.

The Court in *Oregon v. Mitchell* rules that Congress has power to lower the voting age to eighteen only for federal, not state and local, elections. As a consequence, the Twenty-sixth Amendment is proposed and ratified one year later.

The Court reduces its dockets from three (original, appellate, miscellaneous) to two (original and all others).

The Court reduces the time allotted to oral arguments from one hour per side to one-half hour per side.

1971   The Court holds that cross-district busing, racial quotas, and redrawn school district boundaries are permissible means of ending southern school segregation in *Swann v. Charlotte-Mecklenburg County Board of Education.*

With each justice writing an opinion in *New York Times Co. v. United States,* the Court denies the government's request for an injunction prohibiting the publication of the "Pentagon Papers," classified documents pertaining to American involvement in Vietnam.

In *Reed v. Reed,* the Court for the first time voids a law because it discriminates against women.

At the cost of $8,600, the Court switches from a simple straight bench to a shallow "U"-shaped bench.

1972   White House aides break into Democratic headquarters in the Watergate office building in Washington, D.C.

In *Argersinger v. Hamlin,* the Court rules that the right to counsel applies to all cases in which a jail sentence is possible.

With each justice again writing an opinion, the Court voids all death penalty statutes in the United States in *Furman v. Georgia.*

1973   *Roe v. Wade* is decided. The due process clause entitles women to an abortion "without undue governmental interference."

The Court decides in *San Antonio Independent School District v. Rodriguez* that because the Constitution nowhere mentions education, it is not a fundamental right insofar as the equal protection clause is concerned. Hence, states are free to finance their schools by local property taxes even though the dollars available vary widely from district to district.

1974   By an 8–0 vote, the Court in *United States v. Nixon* requires President Nixon to comply with a subpoena of certain White House tapes dealing with the Watergate affair. Seventeen days later Nixon resigns.

The Court rules in *Milliken v. Bradley* that a multidistrict remedy for school desegregation may involve only districts that have themselves discriminated. Hence, suburban Detroit districts cannot constitutionally be required to participate in the desegregation of the Detroit schools.

The Supreme Court Historical Society is founded.

Table 1-1   *(Continued)*

New guidelines for dress and decorum for attorneys appearing before the Court are enacted. Policy changes include a switch from formal attire to conservative business dress.

1975   The justices unanimously agree in *O'Connor v. Donaldson* that the guarantee of liberty in the due process clause prevents involuntary confinement in mental hospitals of persons dangerous to no one and capable of surviving in the outside world.

Justice Douglas resigns after thirty-six years on the Court, longer than any justice in history.

The Court limits oral arguments to Mondays, Tuesdays, and Wednesdays.

1976   In *Gregg v. Georgia*, the Court determines that carefully crafted statutes authorizing the death penalty for first degree murder do not necessarily violate the Eighth Amendment.

1977   In a series of three decisions, the Court rules that neither the Constitution nor the Social Security Act requires states to pay for nontherapeutic abortions. Furthermore, public hospitals may, as a matter of policy, refuse to perform abortions. Such actions do not constitute unreasonable governmental interference with a woman's right to an abortion.

1978   The Supreme Court decides the *Bakke* case, the first major decision involving affirmative action. Numerical quotas are illegal, but goals are not. Furthermore, race may not be the sole criterion for such programs, but may be one of several.

1980   Ronald Reagan is elected president.

1981   Sandra Day O'Connor becomes the first woman to sit on the Supreme Court. In anticipation of her arrival, the justices change the traditional title of "Mr. Justice" to simply "Justice."

1982   In *Globe Newspaper Co. v. Superior Court*, the Court rules that a state may ban media coverage of the testimony of child molestation victims in criminal trials only on a case-by-case basis.

Michael A. Chatoff becomes the first deaf lawyer to appear before the Court, with the help of a computerized video display screen. This was also the first time such equipment was allowed in the Court.

1983   The one-house legislative veto is ruled unconstitutional in *Immigration and Naturalization Service v. Chadha*.

Michigan v. Long, posing a major threat to the autonomy of state courts, is decided. The Court overturns its traditional presumption that state court decisions containing a mixture of state and federal issues rest "on an adequate and independent state ground." Since *Long*, if the basis for the state court's decision is unclear, the Court assumes it to be based on federal grounds.

1984   The Court rules in *Lynch v. Donnelly* that the inclusion of a nativity scene in a city's secular Christmas display does not violate the Constitution's establishment clause.

1985   The Court determines in *New Hampshire Supreme Court v. Piper* that, although the privileges and immunities clause of Article IV of the Constitution allows states to discriminate against nonresidents for "substantial" reasons, New Hampshire's denial of a license to a Vermont lawyer does not qualify as such.

In *Wallace v. Jaffree*, the Court holds that a legislatively mandated moment of silence for meditation or voluntary prayer in the public schools violates the establishment clause.

(Table continues)

Table 1-1   *(Continued)*

1986   The Court in *Bowers v. Hardwick* holds that the Constitution confers no right on consenting adult homosexuals to engage in oral or anal sex.

The Court decides in *Wygant v. Jackson Board of Education* that affirmative action plans need not be "victim specific," but that racial preferences in hiring and promotion are constitutionally preferable to layoffs.

President Reagan promotes Justice William Rehnquist to replace Chief Justice Burger. Antonin Scalia takes Rehnquist's seat.

1987   The Court unanimously rules in *St. Francis College v. Al-Khazraji* that members of white ethnic groups are also protected from employment, housing, and other forms of discrimination.

The Court decides in *Edwards v. Aguillard* that a Louisiana law requiring schools that teach evolution to teach creation science too violates the establishment of religion clause.

President Reagan's first two attempts to fill the seat vacated by Lewis Powell fail when the Senate rejects Robert Bork by a 42–58 vote and Douglas Ginsberg withdraws because of allegations of marijuana use while a professor at Harvard Law School. In January 1988, the Democratically controlled Senate approves Reagan's third choice, Anthony Kennedy, by a 97–0 vote.

1988   Congress enacts legislation virtually eliminating the Court's nondiscretionary appellate jurisdiction.

1989   The Court rules in *Perry v. Lynaugh* and *Stanford v. Kentucky* that mentally retarded persons and those as young as sixteen may constitutionally be sentenced to death.

The Supreme Court announces that it will make its decisions available to the public electronically moments after they are handed down.

1990   In *Cruzan v. Missouri Department of Health*, the Court decides that, for persons making their wishes clearly known, the Constitution recognizes a right to die.

Justice William Brennan resigns after more than thirty-three years, the seventh longest tenure. President George Bush nominates, and the Senate confirms, David Souter to replace him.

1991   Thurgood Marshall, the first black justice, resigns. He is replaced by Clarence Thomas, the second black justice, after acrimonious hearings involving alleged sexual harassment.

For the first time a father and son argues on the same day. Robert G. Pugh represented Gov. Roy Roemer of Louisiana in *Chisolm v. Roemer* and *United States v. Roemer*, while his the son, Robert G. Pugh Jr., represented the governor in the case of *Clark v. Roemer*.

1992   In *Planned Parenthood of Southeastern Pennsylvania v. Casey*, the Court reaffirms the constitutional right to obtain an abortion.

In a unanimous ruling in *R.A.V. v. City of St. Paul*, the Court strikes down a "hate speech" ordinance as a violation of the First Amendment.

The Twenty-seventh Amendment, which provides that congressional pay raises shall not take effect until an intervening election has occurred, is ratified. The amendment was first proposed to the states in 1789.

1993   Justice Byron White announces his retirement from the Court. Accordingly, after eleven successive Republican appointments, President William J. Clinton is the first Democrat since Lyndon B. Johnson to appoint a Supreme Court justice. He nominates Ruth Bader Ginsburg, whom the Senate confirms by a 96–3 vote.

Table 1-1   *(Continued)*

1994   President Clinton nominates and the Senate, by a vote of 87-to-9, confirms, Stephen G. Breyer as the 108th Supreme Court justice. He replaces Harry A. Blackmun.

1995   In the affirmative action case of *Adarand Constructors, Inc. v. Pena*, the Supreme Court holds by a 5–4 vote that all racial classifications imposed by government must be narrowly tailored and closely related to a compelling governmental purpose.

In *U.S. Term Limits v. Thornton*, the justices by a 5–4 vote rule that states may not set a limit on the number of terms members of Congress can serve. Prior to this decision, nearly half the states had enacted term limits of one sort or another.

For the first time in Court history, Jeffrey P. Minear, assistant to the solicitor general of the United States, argues two cases in succession: *Kansas v. Colorado* and *Nebraska v. Wyoming*.

1996   In the longest time elapsed between arguments on the same case, Stanley Geller argues for *Agostini v. Felton*. The case first appeared on the docket in 1984 as *Aguilar v. Felton*.

The Court issues only seventy-five signed opinions—fewer than other term since 1953.

1997   John G. Roberts argues four cases in the October 1997 term. While this is unique for modern attorneys not on the staff of the solicitor general, history would probably show that others have equaled this record. Walter Jones, Francis Scott Key, Thomas Swann, and William Wirt are likely candidates to have equaled or surpassed Mr. Roberts's record.

In *Clinton v. Jones*, the Court decides that there is no constitutional provision to protect an incumbent president from civil litigation while in office.

1998   In *Clinton v. City of New York*, the Court strikes down the line-item veto for tax and spending measures.

The Court decides on four sexual harassment cases, finding that employers are liable for the acts of a supervisor, school districts are not liable for teachers who harass students if the school administration was unaware of the problem, and that harassment laws apply to those who engage in same-sex harassment.

1999   In *Chicago v. Morales*, the Court decides that cities cannot arbitrarily prevent loitering by those suspected of being in gangs.

2000   In *Boy Scouts of America v. Dale*, the Court holds that a private organization can restrict membership on the basis of sexual orientation.

In *California Democratic Party v. Jones*, the Court strikes down California's "blanket" primary, saying it violates a political party's First Amendment right of association.

Following the 2000 presidential election, the Supreme Court makes a series of decisions regarding the counting of votes in the state of Florida, culminating in a 7–2 decision on December 12 declaring the Florida recount unconstitutional and a 5–4 decision ordering Florida to desist from further recounting of ballots, thereby assuring George W. Bush's electoral victory.

2001   In *Alexander v. Sandoval*, the Court rules 5–4 that individuals do not have a private right of action to file a lawsuit to enforce disparate impact discrimination pursuant to Title VI of the Civil Rights Act of 1964.

(Table continues)

Table 1-1   *(Continued)*

On September 11, the United States experiences its worst terrorist attack, with hijacked airplanes destroying the World Trade Center towers and part of the Pentagon. Congress responds by enacting the Anti-Terrorist Act; the president issues orders allowing suspected terrorists who are not U.S. citizens to be tried by military tribunals.

For the first time since it moved into its present building in 1935, the Supreme Court convenes in another courtroom, after spores of anthrax are found in a building that handles mail for the Court.

Note: This list reflects the judgment of the authors.

Sources: Joan Biskupic and Elder Witt, *Guide to the U.S. Supreme Court,* 3d ed. (Washington, D.C.: Congressional Quarterly, 1997); Kermit L. Hall, ed., *The Oxford Companion to the Supreme Court* (New York: Oxford University Press, 1992); Robert Shnayerson, *The Illustrated History of the Supreme Court of the United States* (New York: Abrams, 1986); Mary Ann Harrell and Burnett Anderson, *Equal Justice Under Law* (Washington, D.C.: Supreme Court Historical Society, 1988); *United States Reports,* various years.

Table 1-2   Chronology of Important Events in the Supreme Court's History Pertaining to Women, 1787–2002

1873   With only Chief Justice Salmon P. Chase dissenting, the Court rules in *Bradwell v. Illinois* that a state violates no constitutional provision in denying a woman a license to practice law because of her sex.

1875   In *Minor v. Happersett* the Court finds that the state of Missouri did not violate the Fourteenth Amendment in denying women the right to vote.

1879   Belva Ann Lockwood becomes the first woman member of the Supreme Court bar.

1908   In *Muller v. Oregon,* the Court accepts limitations of freedom of contract in the case of women. Accordingly, a state may restrict women laundry workers to a ten-hour day.

1920   The Nineteenth Amendment is ratified, prohibiting state and federal governments from denying the right to vote on the basis of sex.

1923   The Court rules in *Adkins v. Children's Hospital* that a federal minimum wage law for women violates freedom of contract.

1936   The Court declares in *Morehead v. New York ex rel. Tipaldo* that all state minimum wage laws, including those that apply to women and children, violate due process.

1937   *West Coast Hotel Co. v. Parrish* overrules the 1923 decision, *Adkins v. Children's Hospital,* and the 1936 decision *Morehead v. New York ex rel. Tipaldo,* and upholds the state of Washington's minimum wage law.

1944   Justice William Douglas selects the first woman, Lucille Loman, to serve as a law clerk.

1948   In *Goesaert v. Cleary,* the Court upholds a Michigan law that prohibits women from becoming bartenders unless they are a member of the immediate family of the bar owner.

1961   In the case of *Hoyt v. Florida,* the Court finds that a system that repeatedly produces all-male juries does not deny equal protection to female defendants.

1965   The Court rules in *Griswold v. Connecticut* that "penumbras" in the First, Third, Fourth, Fifth, Ninth, and Fourteenth amendments guarantee a right to personal privacy, which prohibits a state from criminalizing the use of contraceptives.

1967   The Court finds in *Loving v. Virginia* that states cannot pass statutes banning marriages of mixed race.

1971   In *Reed v. Reed,* the Court for the first time voids a law because it discriminates against women.

1973   *Roe v. Wade* is decided. The due process clause entitles women to an abortion "without undue governmental interference."
        In *Doe v. Bolton,* the Court finds that a hospital committee on abortion as well as the need for the acquiescence of copractitioners are violations of a patient's right to an abortion.
        In *Frontiero v. Richardson,* the Court finds that spouses of enlisted military women are eligible for benefits, as are the spouses of enlisted military men.

1974   The Court finds in *Bigelow v. Virginia* that a Virginia statute making the promotion or advertisement of abortions a misdemeanor violates free speech.

1976   In *Planned Parenthood of Central Missouri v. Danforth,* the Court finds that a state cannot legislate the viability of a fetus in terms of weeks. The case also yields other ramifications in terms of abortion regarding spousal consent and minors, with the Court finding that neither can be enforced.

(Table continues)

Table 1-2   *(Continued)*

In *Craig v. Borden*, the Court adopts a heightened scrutiny standard for evaluating sex discrimination claims.

1977   In a series of three decisions, the Court rules that neither the Constitution nor the Social Security Act requires states to pay for nontherapeutic abortions. Furthermore, public hospitals may, as a matter of policy, refuse to perform abortions. Such actions do not constitute unreasonable governmental interference with a woman's right to an abortion.

In *Carey v. Population Services International*, the Court holds that a New York law banning the sale of contraceptives to minors and banning the display of contraceptives is unconstitutional.

In *Maher v. Roe*, the Court holds that a state that participates in the Medicaid program is not required to pay for nontherapeutic abortions, even though the state has made it a policy to pay for childbirth expenses. The justices make similar rulings in *Beal v. Doe* and *Poelker v. Doe*.

1979   The Court found in *Orr v. Orr* that women could also be ordered to pay alimony.

1980   The Court finds in *Harris v. McRae* that the Hyde Amendment, which severely limits the use of Medicaid monies for abortions, is not in violation of the Equal Protection Clause.

1981   Sandra Day O'Connor becomes the first woman to sit on the Supreme Court. In anticipation of her arrival, the justices change the traditional title of "Mr. Justice" to simply "Justice."

The Court holds in *Rostker v. Goldberg* that Congress may constitutionally restrict the military draft to males.

The Court finds in *Michael M. v. Superior Court* that statutory rape laws aimed specifically at males are constitutional.

1982   In *Mississippi University for Women v. Hogan*, Justice O'Connor finds that the Mississippi University of Women's policy concerning the exclusion of males to compensate for discrimination against women violates the Equal Protection Clause of the Fourteenth Amendment.

1983   In *Bolger v. Youngs Drugs Prods. Corp*, the Court finds that a law prohibiting the mailing of advertisements for contraceptives is unconstitutional.

In *Akron v. Akron Center for Reproductive Health, Inc.*, the Court finds that waiting periods and requirements that abortions after the first trimester be performed in hospitals are unconstitutional.

1984   The Court rules in *Roberts v. U.S Jaycees* that a state may constitutionally prohibit large, nonselective, private organizations from restricting membership on the basis of sex.

1986   In *Thornburgh v. American College of Obstetricians & Gynecologists*, the Court rules that attempts by a state to intimidate women into continuing pregnancies by giving her printed materials to that effect or informing her of a father's financial obligations are a violation of a woman's right to choose an abortion.

In *Meritor Savings Bank v. Vinson*, the Court finds that a "hostile environment" is a form of sex discrimination that is actionable under Title VII.

1987   In *Johnson v. Transportation Agency*, a male plaintiff, Johnson, argued that he was discriminated against when a promotion he was competing for was given to a woman. The Court finds that moderate, flexible, case-by-case plans to improve the representation of minorities and women in the agency's workforce do not violate Title VII.

Table 1-2 *(Continued)*

In *Rotary International v. Rotary Club of Duarte,* the Court finds that California's Unruh Act, which requires equal access to "business establishments," is constitutional.

1989 In *Webster v. Reproductive Health Services,* the Court upholds a statute passed by the state of Missouri concerning fetus viability, the definition of when life begins, as well as barring the use of federal money for abortions. The Court concludes that the Missouri statute did not contradict *Roe v. Wade* or other Court rulings on abortion.

1990 In *Hodgson v. Minnesota,* the Court finds that two-parent parental notification in cases where a minor is seeking an abortion is harmful to a woman's right to obtain an abortion.

1991 In *Rust v. Sullivan,* the Court upholds the "gag rule," denying federal funds to any facility that gives information about abortion.

1992 In *Planned Parenthood of Southeastern Pennsylvania v. Casey,* the Court reaffirms the constitutional right to obtain an abortion.

1993 Ruth Bader Ginsburg becomes the second woman to sit on the Supreme Court.

1996 With only one justice dissenting, the Court holds in *United States v. Virginia* that state military institutions of higher learning violate the Equal Protection Clause when they impose a males-only admissions policy.

1997 In *Clinton v. Jones,* the Court decides that there is no constitutional provision to protect an incumbent president from civil litigation while in office.

1998 The Court decides four sexual harassment cases, finding that: employers are liable for the acts of a supervisor; school districts are not liable for teachers who harass students, if the school administration was unaware of the problem; and that harassment laws apply to those who engage in same-sex harassment.

1999 In *Davis v. Monroe County School Board,* the Court finds that schools can be fined for failing to stop harassment among students.

2000 A Nebraska statute banning "partial-birth" abortions is struck down by the Court in *Stenberg v. Carhart.*

2001 Pamela Talkin becomes the first woman appointed as marshal of the Supreme Court.

Note: This list reflects the judgment of the authors, with guidance from Judith A. Baer and Leslie Goldstein.

Sources: Joan Biskupic and Elder Witt, *Guide to the U.S. Supreme Court,* 3d ed. (Washington, D.C.: Congressional Quarterly, 1997); Kermit L. Hall, ed., *The Oxford Companion to the Supreme Court* (New York: Oxford University Press, 1992); Robert Shnayerson, *The Illustrated History of the Supreme Court of the United States* (New York: Abrams, 1986); Mary Ann Harrell and Burnett Anderson, *Equal Justice Under Law* (Washington, D.C.: Supreme Court Historical Society, 1988); *United States Reports,* various years.

Table 1-3   Chronology of Important Events in the Supreme Court's History Pertaining to Minorities, 1787–2002

1841   In *United States v. Libellant and Claimants of the Schooner Amistad,* Justice Joseph Story delivers the opinion of the Court that the African people aboard the ship *Amistad* be declared free.

1857   The *Dred Scott* decision rules that slaves are property with which Congress may not interfere, and that neither slaves nor any of their descendants are citizens under the Constitution.

1858   The Court finds the fugitive slave law constitutional in *Ableman v. Booth.*

1865   The Thirteenth Amendment to the Constitution is ratified.

   John S. Rock is sworn in as the first black member of the Supreme Court bar.

1868   The Fourteenth Amendment is ratified.

1870   The Fifteenth Amendment is ratified.

1870   Elias C. Boudinot becomes the first Native American to appear before the Supreme Court.

1879   In *Strauder v. West Virginia,* the Court finds unconstitutional a West Virginia statute prohibiting blacks from sitting on juries.

1883   In the *Civil Rights Cases,* the Court narrowly defines what constitutes state action under the due process and equal protection clauses of the Fourteenth Amendment and, as a result, declares the Civil Rights Act of 1875 unconstitutional. Not until after World War II would the Court support civil rights claims with any regularity.

1896   The Court formulates the separate but equal doctrine in *Plessy v. Ferguson,* thereby legitimizing the segregated society created by Jim Crow laws.

1915   In *Guinn & Beal v. United States,* the Court finds that Grandfather Clauses, as well as suffrage and literacy tests in the Oklahoma constitution, violate the U.S. Constitution.

1917   In *Buchanan v. Warley,* the Court finds that cities may not forbid blacks from purchasing homes in neighborhoods that are primarily white. Nor may a white homeowner be banned from selling property to a black person.

1935   The Court finds in *Norris v. Alabama* that blacks cannot be prohibited from serving on juries or grand juries.

1938   In keeping with the separate but equal doctrine, the Court finds that the state of Missouri must provide a law school for black students in *Missouri ex rel. Gaines v. Canada.*

1944   In *Korematsu v. United States,* the Court asserts that unsubstantiated "military necessity" permits citizens to be summarily imprisoned solely because of their race.

   In *Smith v. Allwright,* the Court finds that people cannot be prohibited from voting in primaries due to their race.

1946   In *Morgan v. Virginia,* the Court strikes down provisions of the Virginia codes that require separation of white and black passengers on inter- and intrastate motor carriers. This decision is not based on the discriminatory aspects of the Virginia code, but rather on the fact that such provisions burden interstate commerce.

1948   In *Shelley v. Kraemer,* the Court rules that state courts may not constitutionally enforce racially restrictive housing covenants.

   Justice Felix Frankfurter selects the first black, William T. Coleman, to serve as a law clerk.

Table 1-3 *(Continued)*

1950 In *Sweatt v. Painter*, the Court finds that a black student must be admitted to the whites-only University of Texas Law School because the law school established for black students is not equal to the school for whites.

In *McLaurin v. Oklahoma State Regents*, the Court finds that if a black student is admitted to a white school, he or she must be treated the same as other students. Therefore, special seating requirements for the black student and state-ordered segregation within the school are not allowed.

1953 The Court again finds voting restrictions based on race or color unconstitutional in *Terry v. Adams*.

1954 The separate but equal doctrine of *Plessy v. Ferguson* is overruled in *Brown v. Board of Education*, paving the way for school desegregation.

In *Bolling v. Sharpe*, a case involving segregated schools in the District of Columbia, the Court finds that the federal government must comply with desegregation.

1960 In *Gomillion v. Lightfoot*, the Court strikes down a statue passed by the Alabama legislature that redrew the Tuskegee city boundaries in a blatant attempt to remove black residents from the city voting registration rolls.

1964 In *Heart of Atlanta Motel v. United States*, the Court unanimously upholds the constitutionality of the Civil Rights Act of 1964 and its ban on discrimination in places of public accommodations.

1966 In *South Carolina v. Katzenbach*, the Court upholds the constitutionality of the Voting Rights Act of 1965. As a result, for the first time since Reconstruction southern blacks are able to vote with relative ease.

The Court finds in *Evans v. Newton* that a park is operated in a municipal manner and therefore access to the park cannot be limited on the basis of race.

1967 A unanimous Court in *Loving v. Virginia* rules that criminalizing interracial marriage violates due process as well as equal protection.

Thurgood Marshall, the first black nominated to the Supreme Court, takes his seat.

1968 A unanimous Court in *Green v. County School Board* terminates the "with all deliberate speed" formula for desegregating southern schools under the mandate of *Brown v. Board of Education* and orders desegregation "now."

1971 In *Swann v. Charlotte-Mecklenburg County Board of Education*, the Court holds that cross-district busing, racial quotas, and redrawn school district boundaries are permissible means of ending southern school segregation.

1974 The Court rules in *Milliken v. Bradley* that a multidistrict remedy for school desegregation may involve only districts that have themselves discriminated. Hence, suburban Detroit districts cannot constitutionally be required to participate in the desegregation of the Detroit schools.

1976 In *Washington v. Davis*, the Court finds that discriminatory intent must be shown to demonstrate a constitutional violation. The appellants argued that the test for the Washington Police Department was biased against blacks and the four times as many blacks failed the tests as whites.

1977 In *United Jewish Organizations of Williamsburgh v. Carey*, the Court upholds a New York state legislative redistricting plan designed to ensure the election of black representatives in certain districts. The plan had been challenged by a group of Hasidic Jews whose community had been divided into multiple legislative districts as a consequence of the plan.

(Table continues)

Table 1-3   *(Continued)*

1978   The Supreme Court decides the *Bakke* case, the first major decision involving affirmative action. Numerical quotas are found to be illegal, but goals are not. Furthermore, race may not be the sole criterion for such programs, but it may be one of several.

1986   The Court decides in *Wygant v. Jackson Board of Education* that affirmative action plans need not be "victim specific," but that racial preferences in hiring and promotion are constitutionally preferable to layoffs.

1991   Thurgood Marshall, the first black justice, retires. He is replaced by Clarence Thomas, the second black justice, after acrimonious hearings involving alleged sexual harassment.

1992   In a unanimous ruling in *R.A.V. v. City of St. Paul*, the Court strikes down a "hate speech" ordinance as a violation of the First Amendment.

1993   In a 5–4 decision in *Shaw v. Reno*, the Court holds that it will apply standards of strict scrutiny in evaluating legislative districts constructed to contain a majority of voters from minority racial groups. Unless the state can show a compelling interest in doing so, the drawing of district boundaries only explicable by racial considerations may run afoul of the Equal Protection Clause.

1995   In the affirmative action case of *Adarand Constructors, Inc. v. Pena*, the Court holds by a 5–4 vote that all racial classifications imposed by government must be narrowly tailored and closely related to a compelling governmental purpose.

1997   In *Abrams v. Johnson*, the Court rules to uphold a Georgia redistricting map that contains only one majority-black voting district.

1999   In *Chicago v. Morales*, the Court decides that cities cannot arbitrarily prevent loitering by those suspected of being in gangs.

2000   In *Apprendi v. State of New Jersey*, the Court rules that juries, not judges, must decide whether convicted criminals should receive higher sentences because the crimes were motivated by racial hate.

2001   In *Alexander v. Sandoval*, the Court rules that, under the Civil Rights Act of 1964, only lawsuits that deal with intentional discrimination on the basis of race and national origin can be brought to enforce a ban on discrimination in programs that receive federal money.

Note: This list reflects the judgment of the authors, with guidance from Judith A. Baer and Leslie Goldstein.

Sources: Joan Biskupic and Elder Witt, *Guide to the U.S. Supreme Court*, 3d ed. (Washington, D.C.: Congressional Quarterly, 1997); Kermit L. Hall, ed., *The Oxford Companion to the Supreme Court* (New York: Oxford University Press, 1992); Robert Shnayerson, *The Illustrated History of the Supreme Court of the United States* (New York: Abrams, 1986); Mary Ann Harrell and Burnett Anderson, *Equal Justice Under Law* (Washington, D.C.: Supreme Court Historical Society, 1988); *United States Reports*, various years.

Table 1-4   Brief Overview of the Supreme Court, 2002

Contact Information	One First Street, N.E. Washington, D.C. 20543 *Phone:* (202) 479–3211 *Internet:* www.supremecourtus.gov/
Members	*Chief justice:* William H. Rehnquist *Associate justices (in order of seniority):* John Paul Stevens Sandra Day O'Connor Antonin Scalia Anthony M. Kennedy David H. Souter Clarence Thomas Ruth Bader Ginsburg Stephen G. Breyer
Information about membership	The Supreme Court is comprised of the chief justice of the United States and such number of associate justices as may be fixed by Congress. By the Act of June 25, 1948 (28 U.S.C. §1), Congress established the number of associate justices as eight. Power to nominate the J\justices is vested in the president of the United States, and appointments are made with the advice and consent of the Senate. Article III, §1, of the Constitution further provides that "[t]he Judges, both of the supreme and inferior Courts, shall hold their Offices during good Behaviour, and shall, at stated Times, receive for their Services, a Compensation, which shall not be diminished during their Continuance in Office."
Information about Court officers	Court officers assist the Court in the performance of its functions. They include the administrative assistant to the Chief Justice, the clerk, the reporter of decisions, the librarian, the marshal, the director of budget and personnel, the court counsel, the curator, the director of data systems, and the public information officer. The administrative assistant is appointed by the chief justice. The clerk, reporter of decisions, librarian, and marshal are appointed by the Court. All other Court officers are appointed by the Chief Justice in consultation with the Court.
Officers	*Administrative assistant to the chief justice:* Sally M. Rider *Clerk:* William K. Suter *Librarian:* Shelley L Dowling *Marshal:* Pamela Talkin *Reporter of decisions:* Frank D. Wagner *Director of budget and personnel:* Cyril A. Donnelly *Court counsel:* Jane E. Petkofsky

(Table continues)

Table 1-4   *(Continued)*

	Curator: Gail Galloway *Director of data systems:* Donna Clement *Public information officer:* Kathleen L. Arberg
Constitutional Origin	Article III, §1, of the Constitution provides that "[t]he judicial Power of the United States, shall be vested in one supreme Court, and in such inferior Courts as the Congress may from time to time ordain and establish." The Supreme Court of the United States was created in accordance with this provision and by authority of the Judiciary Act of September 24, 1789 (1 Stat. 73). It was organized on February 2, 1790.
Jurisdiction	According to the Constitution (Art. III, §2): "The judicial Power shall extend to all Cases, in Law and Equity, arising under this Constitution, the Laws of the United States, and Treaties made, or which shall be made, under their Authority;—to all Cases affecting Ambassadors, other public Ministers and Consuls;—to all Cases of admiralty and maritime Jurisdiction;—to Controversies to which the United States shall be a Party;—to Controversies between two or more States;—between a State and Citizens of another State;—between Citizens of different States;—between Citizens of the same State claiming Lands under Grants of different States, and between a State, or the Citizens thereof, and foreign States, Citizens or Subjects." "In all Cases affecting Ambassadors, other public ministers and Consuls, and those in which a State shall be Party, the supreme Court shall have original Jurisdiction. In all the other Cases before mentioned, the supreme Court shall have appellate jurisdiction, both as to Law and Fact, with such Exceptions, and under such Regulations as the Congress shall make." Appellate jurisdiction has been conferred upon the Supreme Court by various statutes, under the authority given Congress by the Constitution. The basic statute effective at this time in conferring and controlling jurisdiction of the Supreme Court may be found in 28 U. S. C. §1251 et seq., and various special statutes.
Rulemaking Power	Congress has from time to time conferred upon the Supreme Court power to prescribe rules of procedure to be followed by the lower courts of the United States. See 28 U. S. C. §2071 et seq.
The Building	The Supreme Court is open to the public from 9:00 A.M. to 4:30 P.M., Monday through Friday. It is closed Saturdays, Sundays, and the federal legal holidays

Table 1-4   *(Continued)*

	listed in 5 U.S.C. §6103. Unless the Court or the chief justice orders otherwise, the clerk' s office is open from 9:00 A.M. to 5:00 P.M., Monday through Friday, except on those holidays. The library is open to members of the Bar of the Court, attorneys for the various federal departments and agencies, and members of Congress.
The term	The term of the Court begins, by law, on the first Monday in October and lasts until the first Monday in October of the next year. Approximately 7,000 petitions are filed with the Court in the course of a term. In addition, some 1,200 applications of various kinds are filed each year that can be acted upon by a single justice.

Source: www.supremecourtus.gov/about/about.html (accessed July 2001).

Table 1-5   Select Congressional Legislation Relating to the
Supreme Court

Name	Cite	Description
Judiciary Act of 1789	1 Stat. 73	Provided basic appellate jurisdiction Created a three-tier judiciary staffed by Supreme Court justices and district court judges Required Supreme Court justices to ride circuit Mandated that Court consist of a chief justice and five associate justices, any four of whom would be a quorum
Judiciary Act of 1801	2 Stat. 89	Restructured the federal court system by creating independent circuit courts Eliminated circuit riding duties for Supreme Court justices
Repeal Act of 1802	2 Stat. 132	Repealed the Judiciary Act of 1801
Amendatory Act of 1802	2 Stat. 156	Revised terms of the Supreme Court, with the effect of prohibiting Court from meeting for fourteen months (December 1801 to February 1803)
Act of 1807	2 Stat. 421	Set the number of justices at seven
Judiciary Act of 1837	5 Stat. 176	Divided country into nine circuits Brought number of justices to nine Expanded the Court's jurisdiction to include appeals from new states and territories
Judiciary Act of 1863	12 Stat. 794	Added a tenth justice
Judiciary Act of 1866	14 Stat. 209	Allowed Court to fall to seven members but omitted provisions allotting the justices among the circuits
Judiciary Act of 1867	14 Stat. 433	Provided for allotment of justices to circuits
Judiciary Act of 1869	16 Stat. 44	Increased size of Court to nine Provided for a separate circuit judiciary of nine members Allowed federal judges to retire at full pay at seventy (changed to sixty-five in 1954) if they had at least ten years of service

Table 1-5   *(Continued)*

Name	Cite	Description
Act of 1873	17 Stat. 419	Formally fixed October as the start of the Court's term
Removal Act of 1875	18 Stat. 470	Greatly expanded the Court's jurisdiction over civil disputes Gave Court full review over writs of error Granted Court full federal question review of state court decisions
Judiciary Act of 1887	24 Stat. 552	Curbed access to the federal courts by raising jurisdictional amount in diversity cases Provided for writ of error in all capital cases
Judiciary Act of 1891	26 Stat. 826	Established nine Circuit Courts of Appeals (renamed Courts of Appeals in 1948) Broadened review over criminal cases Provided for limited discretionary review via writs of certiorari
Act of July 20, 1892	27 Stat. 252	Provided for *in forma pauperis* filings
Act of 1911	36 Stat. 113	Created general right of appeal from criminal convictions to the circuit court of appeals, with ultimate review power lying with the Supreme Court
Act of 1914	38 Stat. 790	Opened the door to discretionary review by allowing Court to review by certiorari state court decisions in favor of rights claimed under federal law; previously, only state court decisions denying a right had been reviewable
Act of 1915	38 Stat. 803	Substituted certiorari for appellate jurisdiction in bankruptcy cases brought up from federal courts of appeals
Act of 1916	39 Stat. 726	Confined Court's obligatory jurisdiction over state court decisions to holdings invalidating federal law or validating a state law challenged as inconsistent with federal law; all

(Table continues)

Table 1-5 *(Continued)*

Name	Cite	Description
		other state courts decisions were made reviewable by the discretionary writ of certiorari
Judiciary Act of 1925	43 Stat. 936	Greatly extended Court's discretionary jurisdiction by replacing mandatory appeals with petitions for certiorari
Act of 1946	58 Stat. 272	Mandated procedures for when Court cannot obtain a quorom of any six of the nine justices
Voting Rights Act of 1965	79 Stat. 438	Provided direct appeal of decisions of three-judge district courts in the area of voting rights
Acts of 1970, 1974, 1975, 1976	84 Stat, 1890, 88 Stat. 1706, 88 Stat. 1917, 90 Stat. 1119	Abolished most three-judge district court requirements and consequent direct appeals to the Supreme Court Expanded Court's discretionary review Eliminated direct appeals in antitrust and Interstate Commerce Commission cases
Act to Improve the Administration of Justice (1988)	102 Stat. 4642	Eliminated virtually all of the Court's nondiscretionary jurisdiction, except for appeals in reapportionment cases and suits under the Civil Rights Act, the Voting Rights Act, antitrust laws, and the Presidential Election Campaign Act
Effective Death Penalty Act of 1996	110 Stat. 1214	Limited federal court jurisdiction over habeas corpus petitions in death penalty cases.

Sources: Robert L. Stern and Eugene Gressman, *Supreme Court Practice* (Washington, D.C.: Bureau of National Affairs, various years); David M. O'Brien, *Storm Center* (New York: Norton, 1990); U.S. Senate, "Creation of the Federal Judiciary," Sen. Doc. No. 91, 75th Cong., 1st sess., July 22, 1937 (Washington, D.C.: Government Printing Office, 1938); U.S. Code.

Table 1-6   Sections of the United States Code Pertaining to the
Organization of the Supreme Court

---

§ 1. Number of justices; quorum

The Supreme Court of the United States shall consist of a Chief Justice of the
United States and eight associate justices, any six of whom shall constitute a
quorum.

§ 2. Terms of court

The Supreme Court shall hold at the seat of government a term of court com-
mencing on the first Monday in October of each year and may hold such ad-
journed or special terms as may be necessary.

§ 3. Vacancy in office of Chief Justice; disability

Whenever the Chief Justice is unable to perform the duties of his office or the
office is vacant, his powers and duties shall devolve upon the associate justice
next in precedence who is able to act, until such disability is removed or another
Chief Justice is appointed and duly qualified.

§ 4. Precedence of associate justices

Associate justices shall have precedence according to the seniority of their commissions. Justices whose commissions bear the same date shall have precedence
according to seniority in age.

§ 5. Salaries of justices

The Chief Justice and each associate justice shall each receive a salary at annual
rates determined under section 225 of the Federal Salary Act of 1967 (2 U.S.C.
351-361), as adjusted by section 461 of this title.

§ 6. Records of former court of appeals

The records and proceedings of the court of appeals, appointed previous to the
adoption of the Constitution, shall be kept until deposited with the National
Archives of the United States in the office of the clerk of the Supreme Court, who
shall furnish copies thereof to any person requiring and paying for them, in the
manner provided by law for giving copies of the records and proceedings of the
Supreme Court. Such copies shall have the same faith and credit as proceedings
of the Supreme Court.

Source: United States Code, Title 28—Judiciary and Judicial Procedure, Part I—Organization
of Courts, Chapter 1—Supreme Court. (Available at www.law.cornell.edu:80/uscode/28/
ch1.html#s6.)

Table 1-7   Sections of the United States Code Pertaining to the Jurisdiction of the Supreme Court

---

§ 1251. *Original Jurisdiction*

(a) The Supreme Court shall have original and exclusive jurisdiction of all controversies between two or more States.

(b) The Supreme Court shall have original but not exclusive jurisdiction of:

(1) All actions or proceedings to which ambassadors, other public ministers, consuls, or vice consuls of foreign states are parties;

(2) All controversies between the United States and a State;

(3) All actions or proceedings by a State against the citizens of another State or against aliens.

§ 1253. *Direct appeals from decisions of three-judge courts*

Except as otherwise provided by law, any party may appeal to the Supreme Court from an order granting or denying, after notice and hearing, an interlocutory or permanent injunction in any civil action, suit or proceeding required by any Act of Congress to be heard and determined by a district court of three judges.

§ 1254. *Courts of appeals; certiorari; appeal; certified questions*

Cases in the courts of appeals may be reviewed by the Supreme Court by the following methods:

(1) By writ of certiorari granted upon the petition of any party to any civil or criminal case, before or after rendition of judgment or decree;

(2) By certification at any time by a court of appeals of any question of law in any civil or criminal case as to which instructions are desired, and upon such certification the Supreme Court may give binding instructions or require the entire record to be sent up for decision of the entire matter in controversy.

§ 1257. *State courts; appeal; certiorari*

(a) Final judgments or decrees rendered by the highest court of a State in which a decision could be had, may be reviewed by the Supreme Court by writ of certiorari where the validity of a treaty or statute of the United States is drawn in question or where the validity of a statute of any State is drawn in question on the ground of its being repugnant to the Constitution, treaties, or laws of the United States, or where any title, right, privilege, or immunity is specially set up or claimed under the Constitution or the treaties or statutes of, or any commission held or authority exercised under, the United States.

(b) For the purposes of this section, the term "highest court of a State" includes the District of Columbia Court of Appeals.

§ 1258. *Supreme Court of Puerto Rico; certiorari*

Final judgments or decrees rendered by the Supreme Court of the Commonwealth of Puerto Rico may be reviewed by the Supreme Court by writ of certiorari where the validity of a treaty or statute of the United States is drawn in question or where the validity of a statute of the Commonwealth of Puerto Rico is drawn in question on the ground of its being repugnant to the Constitution, treaties, or laws of the United States, or where any title, right, privilege, immunity is specially set up or claimed under the Constitution or the treaties or statutes of, or any commission held or authority exercised under, the United States.

Table 1-7   *(Continued)*

§1259. Court of Appeals for the Armed Forces; certiorari

Decisions of the United States Court of Appeals for the Armed Forces may be reviewed by the Supreme Court by writ of certiorari in the following cases:

(1) Cases reviewed by the Court of Appeals for the Armed Forces under section 867(a)(1) of title 10.

(2) Cases certified to the Court of Appeals for the Armed Forces by the Judge Advocate General under section 867(a)(2) of title 10.

(3) Cases in which the Court of Appeals for the Armed Forces granted a petition for review under section 867(a)(3) of title 10.

(4) Cases, other than those described in paragraphs (1), (2), and (3) of this subsection, in which the Court of Appeals for the Armed Forces granted relief.

Source: 28 United States Code Annotated §1251–1258 (West. 1966, supp. 1992). Available at: www.law.cornell.edu/uscode/28/ch81.html.

Table 1-8 Selected Internet Sites Relating to the Supreme Court

Site (URL)	Description
FedWorld/FLITE Supreme Court Decisions (www.fedworld.gov/supcourt/index.htm)	Provides decisions from 1937 to 1975 Cases can be searched by name or keyword
FindLaw (www.findlaw.com/casecode/supreme.html)	Searchable database of Supreme Court decisions since 1893 (*U.S. Supreme Court Decisions: U.S. Reports* 150–, 1893–) Browsable by year and *U.S. Reports* volume number Searchable by citation, case title, and full text
Jurist (University of Pittsburgh Law) (jurist.law.pitt.edu/supremecourt.htm)	Provides links to other sites and general information (news and wire stories about justices and cases)
Legal Information Institute at Cornell Law School (supct.law.cornell.edu/supct)	Provides a complete listing of cases from 1990 to the present, as well as historical cases Database is searchable by topic and date
LEXIS-NEXIS (www.lexis-nexis.com)	Provides access to Court decisions and briefs
Oyez Project (Northwestern University) (oyez.nwu.edu)	Provides abstracts of the leading cases in constitutional law Allows users to download oral arguments presented before the Court
Program for Law and Politics (Michigan State University) (www.ssc.msu.edu/~pls/pljp/index.html)	Provides access to databases, developed by Harold J. Spaeth, that house information on the decisions of the Court
Supreme Court Historical Society (www.supremecourthistory.org/)	Provides information about justices and other history of the Court

Supreme Court Official Site (www.supremecourtus.gov/)	Official site of the Supreme Court. Provides current decisions, Court rules, information about the Court, docket, bar admissions, and other information
USSCPlus (www.usscplus.com)	Provides current term decisions "Top 1,000 cases" accessible without charge; other areas, such as the database of all cases, are fee-based
Villanova University Law (vls.law.vill.edu/Locator/fedcourt.html)	Provides a list of Supreme Court-related sites
Washington Post (www.washingtonpost.com/wp-srv/national/longterm/supcourt/supcourt.htm)	Provides an overview of key cases from 1996 to the present Provides links to other sites and offers news stories, history of the court, a quiz

Source: Compiled by the authors.

Table 1-9 Supreme Court Budget Appropriations, 1930–2002

Fiscal year	Salaries and expenses[a]	Building and grounds[b]	Other	Total
1930	$343,420	c		$343,420
1931	343,420	$1,000,000[d]	$50,000[e]	1,393,420
1932	343,420	3,750,000		4,093,420
1933	324,500	1,000,000		1,324,500
1934	315,173	3,490,000		3,805,173
1935	358,830	30,348		389,178
1936	486,000	49,080		535,080
1937	508,500	55,000		563,500
1938[f]	470,900	60,000		530,900
1939	479,160	61,500		540,660
1940	504,000[g]	62,500		566,500
1941	500,000	65,000		573,000
1942	601,460	70,017		671,477
1943	569,161	70,566		639,727
1944	642,214	76,600		718,814
1945	652,959	80,000		732,959
1946	668,500	104,100		772,600
1947	801,906	121,231		923,137
1948	852,920	122,800		975,720
1949	990,400	190,700		1,181,100
1950	944,100	152,000		1,096,100
1951	1,080,800	159,200		1,240,000
1952	1,152,050	172,500		1,324,550
1953	1,189,550	174,100		1,363,650
1954	1,193,236	174,100		1,367,336
1955	1,194,985	350,800		1,545,785
1956	1,294,285	367,400		1,661,685
1957	1,361,285	201,500		1,562,785
1958	1,423,835	218,200		1,642,035
1959	1,519,800	219,200		1,811,000
1960[h]	1,536,000	347,000		1,883,000
1961	1,642,000	287,000		1,929,000
1962	1,712,000	284,000		1,996,000
1963	1,752,000	323,000		2,075,000
1964	1,853,000	355,000		2,208,000
1965	2,195,000	305,000		2,500,000
1966	2,270,000	319,000		2,589,000
1967	2,305,000	324,000		2,629,000
1968	2,356,000	334,000		2,690,000
1969	2,602,000	361,000		2,963,000
1970	3,138,000	410,000		3,548,000
1971	3,746,000	502,000		4,248,000
1972	4,180,000	561,000		4,741,000
1973	4,719,000	1,014,000	95,000[i]	5,828,000
1974	5,353,000	1,493,000	75,000[i]	6,921,000
1975	5,892,000	1,004,000	372,000[i]	7,268,000
1976	6,582,000	1,454,000		8,036,000
1976[j]	1,576,000	196,000		1,772,000
1977	7,732,000	831,000		8,563,000
1978	8,691,000	1,588,000		10,279,000
1979	9,690,000	1,475,000		11,165,000

Table 1-9   *(Continued)*   37

Fiscal year	Salaries and expenses[a]	Building and grounds[b]	Other	Total
1980	10,363,000	2,182,000		12,545,000
1981	11,840,000	1,568,000	645,000[k]	14,053,000
1982	11,635,000	1,654,000		13,289,000
1983	12,675,000	2,000,000		14,675,000
1984	13,635,000	2,571,000		16,206,000
1985	14,143,000	2,242,000		16,385,000
1986	14,399,000	2,223,000		16,622,000
1987	15,513,000	2,336,000		17,849,000
1988	15,247,000	2,110,000		17,357,000
1989	15,901,000	2,131,000		18,032,000
1990	17,497,000	4,369,000		21,866,000
1991	19,083,000	3,453,000		22,536,000
1992	20,787,000	3,801,000		24,588,000
1993	22,286,000	3,320,000		25,606,000
1994	23,000,000	2,850,000		25,850,000
1995	24,000,000	3,000,000		27,000,000
1996	26,000,000	3,000,000		29,000,000
1997	27,000,000	3,000,000		30,000,000
1998	29,000,000	3,000,000		32,000,000
1999	31,000,000	4,000,000		35,000,000
2000	36,000,000	6,000,000		42,000,000
2001	39,000,000	9,000,000		48,000,000
2002 (est.)	42,000,000	68,000,000[l]		110,000,000
2003 (est.)	48,000,000	54,000,000[l]		120,000,000

[a] Include salaries for Court employees, printing and binding of decisions, purchase of books and periodicals (after 1939), committees on the preparation of rules for criminal and civil procedure (1936–1938, 1942–1954), automobile and driver for the chief justice (after 1954), and miscellaneous expenses.
[b] Include improvements, maintenance, repairs, equipment, supplies, materials, special clothing for workers, snow removal, and miscellaneous expenses.
[c] Building rental costs were part of the Department of Justice appropriations at this time and consequently are not included.
[d] Construction of the Supreme Court building began in 1931 and continued through 1934, accounting for the large expenditures for buildings and grounds.
[e] Cost of purchase of printing plates for volumes 1–265 of the *Supreme Court Reports.*
[f] Beginning in 1938 all court appropriations were included in a separate Judiciary section of the federal budget. Previously appropriations for the federal courts had been part of the budget for the Justice Department.
[g] An appropriation for books and periodicals is included in the Court's budget for the first time. Prior to 1940 such library expenses were part of the Library of Congress budget.
[h] Beginning with fiscal year 1960 budgetary figures are stated in thousands of dollars rather than actual expenditures.
[i] Additional appropriation of funds for the care of the building and grounds.
[j] In 1976 the federal government moved the end of the fiscal year from June 30 to September 30. To accomplish this a special transition fiscal quarter was necessary.
[k] Acquisition of property as an addition to the grounds of the Supreme Court.
[l] The substantial increase in funds for buildings and grounds is due to the first major renovation of the building since its construction, as well as the government's response to increased security concerns following the terrorist attacks in New York and Washington in September 2001.

Sources: Office of Management and Budget, *Budget of the United States Government* (Washington, D.C.: Government Printing Office, 1932–1962), and Office of Management and Budget, *Appendix to the Budget* (Washington, D.C.: Government Printing Office, 1963–2001).

Table 1-10 Supreme Court Budget, Fiscal Years 2001–2003

Budgetary categories	2001	2002 (est.)	2003 (est.)
Supreme Court operations			
Personnel compensation	$22,000,000	$25,000,000	$27,000,000
Civilian personnel benefits	7,000,000	8,000,000	9,000,000
Printing and reproduction	1,000,000	1,000,000	1,000,000
Other services	5,000,000	4,000,000	5,000,000
Supplies and materials	1,000,000	1,000,000	1,000,000
Equipment	3,000,000	3,000,000	5,000,000
Total operations	39,000,000	42,000,000	48,000,000
Care of buildings and grounds	9,000,000	68,000,000[a]	54,000,000[a]
Total budget authorization	48,000,000	110,000,000	102,000,000

[a] The substantial increase in funds for buildings and grounds is due to the first major renovation of the building since its construction, as well as the government's response to increased security concerns following the terrorist attacks in New York and Washington in September of 2001.

Source: Office of Management and Budget, *Appendix to the Budget* (Washington, D.C.: Government Printing Office, 2002).

Table 1-11   Salaries of the Justices, 1789–2002

Years	Chief justice	Associate justices
1789–1818	$4,000	$3,500
1819–1854	5,000	4,500
1855–1870	6,500	6,000
1871–1872	8,500	8,000
1873–1902	10,500	10,000
1903–1910	13,000	12,500
1911–1925	15,000	14,500
1926–1945	20,500	20,000
1946–1954	25,500	25,000
1955–1963	35,500	35,000
1964–1968	40,000	39,500
1969–1974	62,500	60,000
1975	65,625	63,000
1976	68,000	66,000
1977	75,000	72,000
1978	79,100	76,000
1979	84,700	81,300
1980	92,400	88,700
1981	96,800	93,000
1982–1983	100,700	96,700
1984	104,700	100,600
1985–1986	108,400	104,100
1987–1989	115,000	110,000
1990	124,000	118,000
1991	160,600	153,600
1992	166,200	159,000
1993–1998	171,500	164,100
1999	175,400	167,900
2000	181,400	173,600
2001	186,300	178,300
2002	192,600	184,400

Sources: Joan Biskupic and Elder Witt, *Guide to the U.S. Supreme Court,* 3d. ed. (Washington, D.C.: Congressional Quarterly, 1997), and *World Almanac and Book of Facts* (Mahwah, N.J.: World Almanac Books, various years); Associated Press, various years.

Table 1-12   Retirement and Pension Provisions

Year of enactment	*Provisions*
1869	The first judicial pension statute is passed. Justices having reached the age of seventy with at least ten years of service may resign their office and receive for life the same salary that was payable to them at the time of their resignation.
1909	Justices having reached the age of seventy with at least ten years of continuous service as a federal judge may resign their office and receive for life the salary that was payable at the time of their resignation for the office held ten years before the date of resignation.
1911	Justices having reached the age of seventy with at least ten years of continuous service as a federal judge may resign their office and receive for life the salary that was payable to them at the time of resignation for the office held at the time of resignation.
1929	Federal law is amended so that the ten years of judicial service required for pension eligibility need no longer be continuous.
1937	Justices having reached the age of seventy with at least ten years of service as a federal judge are allowed to retire in senior status rather than to resign. Senior justices retain the authority to perform judicial duties in any circuit when called upon by the Chief Justice. Senior justices receive the same pension benefits as resigned justices. (Lower court judges were given the "senior status" option in 1919.)
1939	The first judicial disability statute is enacted. Justices who become permanently disabled may retire regardless of age. Disabled justices who have less than ten years of service as a federal judge receive for life one-half of the annual salary being received on the date of retirement. Disabled justices with more than ten years of service as a federal judge receive for life the full annual salary being received on the date of retirement.
1948	Justices having reached the age of seventy with ten years of service as a federal judge who resign their office receive for life the full salary payable to them at the time of their resignations. Justices having reached the age of seventy with ten years of service as a federal judge who retire from office in senior status continue to receive the salary of their office for life. This includes any salary increases that might be granted to sitting justices. Disabled justices retiring receive the same benefits as other senior status justices, subject to the service provisions of the 1939 act.
1984	Federal law removes the term resignation from the pension regulations. Justices having reached the age of sixty-five may retire from office provided that the sum of their age and years of judicial

Table 1-12   *(Continued)*

Year of enactment	*Provisions*
	service equal at least eighty. Such retired justices receive for life the salary of their office at the time of their retirement. Justices having reached the age of sixty-five may retire in senior status provided that the sum of their age and years of judicial service equal at least eighty. Such senior justices will receive for life the salary of the office.
1989	Justices retiring in senior status are required to perform actual judicial duties in order to continue to receive the same salary increases as sitting members of the Court. Each year such justices must certify that during the previous twelve months they have been engaged in judicial work generally equivalent to what a regular sitting member of the judiciary would accomplish in three months.

Sources: United States Code and *Statutes at Large*, various years.

Table 1-13   Outline of the Rules of the Supreme Court of the
United States

Part I.   The Court
   Rule 1. Clerk
   Rule 2. Library
   Rule 3. Term
   Rule 4. Sessions and quorum

Part II.   Attorneys and Counselors
   Rule 5. Admission to the bar
   Rule 6. Argument pro hac vice
   Rule 7. Prohibition against practice
   Rule 8. Disbarment and disciplinary action
   Rule 9. Appearance of counsel

Part III.   Jurisdiction on Writ of Certiorari
   Rule 10. Considerations governing review on writ of certiorari
   Rule 11. Certiorari to a United States Court of Appeals before judgment
   Rule 12. Review on certiorari: how sought; parties
   Rule 13. Review on certiorari: time for petitioning
   Rule 14. Content of a petition for a writ of certiorari
   Rule 15. Briefs in opposition; reply briefs; supplemental briefs
   Rule 16. Disposition of a petition for a writ of certiorari

Part IV.   Other Jurisdiction
   Rule 17. Procedure in an original action
   Rule 18. Appeal from a United States District Court
   Rule 19. Procedure on a certified question
   Rule 20. Procedure on a petition for an extraordinary writ

Part V.   Motions and Applications
   Rule 21. Motions to the Court
   Rule 22. Applications to individual justices
   Rule 23. Stays

Part VI.   Briefs on The Merits and Oral Argument
   Rule 24. Briefs on the merits: in general
   Rule 25. Briefs on the merits: numbers of copies and time to file
   Rule 26. Joint appendix
   Rule 27. The calendar
   Rule 28. Oral argument

Part VII.   Practice and Procedure
   Rule 29. Filing and service of documents; special notifications; corporate listing
   Rule 30. Computation and extension of time
   Rule 31. Translations
   Rule 32. Models, diagrams, and exhibits
   Rule 33. Document preparation: booklet format; 8- by 11-inch paper format
   Rule 34. Document preparation: general requirements
   Rule 35. Death, substitution, and revivor; public officers
   Rule 36. Custody of Prisoners in habeas corpus proceedings

Table 1-13   *(Continued)*

Rule 37. Brief for an *amicus curiae*
Rule 38. Fees
Rule 39. Proceedings *in forma pauperis*
Rule 40. Veterans, seamen, and military cases

Part VIII.   Disposition of Cases
Rule 41. Opinions of the Court
Rule 42. Interest and damages
Rule 43. Costs
Rule 44. Rehearing
Rule 45. Process; mandates
Rule 46. Dismissing cases

Part IX.   Definitions and Effective Date
Rule 47. Reference to "state court" and "state law"
Rule 48. Effective date of rules

Note: Rules adopted January 11, 1999; effective May 3, 1999. A full text of the Court's rules is available at www.supremecourtus.gov.

Figure 1-1   The Processing of Cases

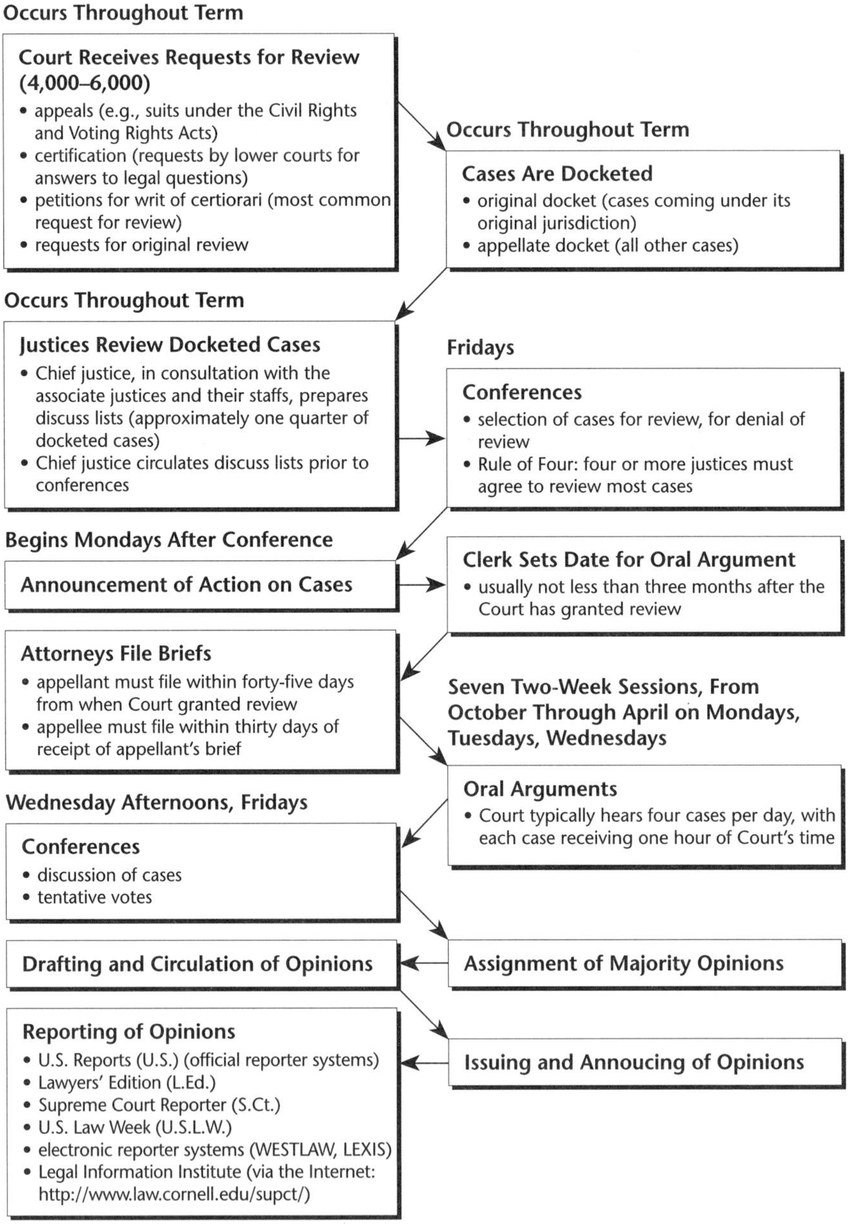

Occurs Throughout Term

Court Receives Requests for Review (4,000–6,000)
- appeals (e.g., suits under the Civil Rights and Voting Rights Acts)
- certification (requests by lower courts for answers to legal questions)
- petitions for writ of certiorari (most common request for review)
- requests for original review

Occurs Throughout Term

Cases Are Docketed
- original docket (cases coming under its original jurisdiction)
- appellate docket (all other cases)

Occurs Throughout Term

Justices Review Docketed Cases
- Chief justice, in consultation with the associate justices and their staffs, prepares discuss lists (approximately one quarter of docketed cases)
- Chief justice circulates discuss lists prior to conferences

Fridays

Conferences
- selection of cases for review, for denial of review
- Rule of Four: four or more justices must agree to review most cases

Begins Mondays After Conference

Announcement of Action on Cases

Clerk Sets Date for Oral Argument
- usually not less than three months after the Court has granted review

Attorneys File Briefs
- appellant must file within forty-five days from when Court granted review
- appellee must file within thirty days of receipt of appellant's brief

Seven Two-Week Sessions, From October Through April on Mondays, Tuesdays, Wednesdays

Oral Arguments
- Court typically hears four cases per day, with each case receiving one hour of Court's time

Wednesday Afternoons, Fridays

Conferences
- discussion of cases
- tentative votes

Drafting and Circulation of Opinions

Assignment of Majority Opinions

Reporting of Opinions
- U.S. Reports (U.S.) (official reporter systems)
- Lawyers' Edition (L.Ed.)
- Supreme Court Reporter (S.Ct.)
- U.S. Law Week (U.S.L.W.)
- electronic reporter systems (WESTLAW, LEXIS)
- Legal Information Institute (via the Internet: http://www.law.cornell.edu/supct/)

Issuing and Annoucing of Opinions

Source: Lee Epstein and Thomas G. Walker, *Constitutional Law for a Changing America: Rights, Liberties, and Justice,* 3d ed. (Washington, D.C.: CQ Press, 2001), 14.

Table 1-14   The Supreme Court's Calendar

Activity	Time
Start of term	First Monday in October
Oral argument cycle	October–April on Mondays, Tuesdays, and, Wednesdays in seven two-week sessions
Recess cycle	October–April, two or more consecutive weeks after two weeks of oral arguments and at Christmas and Easter holidays
Conferences	Wednesday afternoon following Monday oral arguments (discussion of four Monday cases)
	Friday following Tuesday and Wednesday oral arguments (discussion of eight Tuesday–Wednesday cases; certiorari petitions)
	Friday before two-week oral argument period
Majority opinion assignment	Within two weeks following oral arguments/conference
Opinion announcement	Throughout term, with bulk coming in spring/summer
Summer recess	Late June/early July until first Monday in October
Initial conference	Late September (resolve old business, consider certiorari petitions from the summer)

Source: Adapted from Lee Epstein and Thomas G. Walker, *Constitutional Law for a Changing America: Rights, Liberties, and Justice* (Washington, D.C.: CQ Press, 2001).

Table 1-15   Sections of the United States Code Pertaining to
Supreme Court Officers and Employees

---

§ 671. Clerk[a]

(a) The Supreme Court may appoint and fix the compensation of a clerk and one or more deputy clerks. The clerk shall be subject to removal by the Court. Deputy clerks shall be subject to removal by the clerk with the approval of the Court or the Chief Justice of the United States.

(b) Repealed. Pub. L. 92-310, title II, Sec. 206(c), June 6, 1972, 86 Stat. 203.

(c) The clerk may appoint and fix the compensation of necessary assistants and messengers with the approval of the Chief Justice of the United States.

(d) The clerk shall pay into the Treasury all fees, costs, and other moneys collected by him. He shall make annual returns thereof to the Court under regulations prescribed by it.

§ 672. Marshal

(a) The Supreme Court may appoint a marshal, who shall be subject to removal by the Court, and may fix his compensation.

(b) The marshal may, with the approval of the Chief Justice of the United States, appoint and fix the compensation of necessary assistants and other employees to attend the Court, and necessary custodial employees.

(c) The marshal shall:

(1) Attend the Court at its sessions;

(2) Serve and execute all process and orders issued by the Court or a member thereof;

(3) Take charge of all property of the United States used by the Court or its members;

(4) Disburse funds appropriated for work upon the Supreme Court building and ground under the jurisdiction of the Architect of the Capitol upon certified vouchers submitted by the Architect;

(5) Disburse funds appropriated for the purchase of books, pamphlets, periodicals and other publications, and for their repair, binding, and rebinding, upon vouchers certified by the librarian of the Court;

(6) Pay the salaries of the Chief Justice, associate justices, and all officers and employees of the Court and disburse other funds appropriated for disbursement, under the direction of the Chief Justice;

(7) Pay the expenses of printing briefs and travel expenses of attorneys in behalf of person whose motions to appear in forma pauperis in the Supreme Court have been approved and when counsel have been appointed by the Supreme Court, upon vouchers certified by the clerk of the Court;

(8) Oversee the Supreme Court Police.

§ 673. Reporter

(a) The Supreme Court may appoint and fix the compensation of a reporter of its decisions who shall be subject to removal by the Court.

(b) The reporter may appoint and fix the compensation of necessary professional and clerical assistants and other employees, with the approval of the Court or the Chief Justice of the United States.

(c) The reporter shall, under the direction of the Court or the Chief Justice, prepare the decisions of the Court for publication in bound volumes and advance

Table 1-15 *(Continued)*

copies in pamphlet installments. The reporter shall determine the quality and size of the paper, type, format, proofs and binding subject to the approval of the Court or the Chief Justice.

§ 674. Librarian[b]

(a) The Supreme Court may appoint a librarian, whose salary it shall fix, and who shall be subject to removal by the Court.

(b) The librarian shall, with the approval of the Chief Justice, appoint necessary assistants and fix their compensation and make rules governing the use of the library.

(c) He shall select and acquire by purchase, gift, bequest, or exchange, such books, pamphlets, periodicals, microfilm and other processed copy as may be required by the Court for its official use and for the reasonable needs of its bar.

(d) The librarian shall certify to the marshal for payment vouchers covering expenditures for the purchase of such books and other material, and for binding, rebinding and repairing the same.

§ 675. Law clerks and secretaries

The Chief Justice of the United States, and the associate justices of the Supreme Court may appoint law clerks and secretaries whose salaries shall be fixed by the Court.

§ 677. Administrative Assistant to the Chief Justice

(a) The Chief Justice of the United States may appoint an Administrative Assistant who shall serve at the pleasure of the Chief Justice and shall perform such duties as may be assigned to him by the Chief Justice. The salary payable to the Administrative Assistant shall be fixed by the Chief Justice at a rate which shall not exceed the salary payable to the Director of the Administrative Office of the United States Courts. The Administrative Assistant may elect to bring himself within the same retirement program available to the Director of the Administrative Office of the United States Courts, as provided by section 611 of this title, by filing a written election with the Chief Justice within the time and in the manner prescribed by section 611.

(b) The Administrative Assistant, with the approval of the Chief Justice, may appoint and fix the compensation of necessary employees. The Administrative Assistant and his employees shall be deemed employees of the Supreme Court.

(c)

(1) Notwithstanding section 1342 of title 31, the Administrative Assistant, with the approval of the Chief Justice, may accept voluntary personal services to assist with public and visitor programs.

(2) No person may volunteer personal services under this subsection unless the person has first agreed, in writing, to waive any claim against the United States arising out of or in connection with such services, other than a claim under chapter 81 of title 5.

(3) No person volunteering personal services under this subsection shall be considered an employee of the United States for any purpose other than for purposes of—

(A) chapter 81 of title 5; or

(B) chapter 171 of this title.

(Table continues)

Table 1-15 *(Continued)*

---

(4) In the administration of this subsection, the Administrative Assistant shall ensure that the acceptance of personal services shall not result in the reduction of pay or displacement of any employee of the Supreme Court.

---

[a] Under the Rules of the Supreme Court (Part 1, Rule 1, "Clerk"):

1. The Clerk receives documents for filing with the Court and has authority to reject any submitted filing that does not comply with these Rules.

2. The Clerk maintains the Court's records and will not permit any of them to be removed from the Court building except as authorized by the Court. Any document filed with the Clerk and made a part of the Court's records may not thereafter be withdrawn from the official Court files. After the conclusion of proceedings in this Court, original records and documents transmitted to this Court by any other court will be returned to the court from which they were received.

3. Unless the Court or the Chief Justice orders otherwise, the Clerk's office is open from 9 a.m. to 5 p.m., Monday through Friday, except on federal legal holidays listed in 5 U.S. C. §6103.

[b] Under the Rules of the Supreme Court (Part 1, Rule 2, "Library"):

1. The Court's library is available for use by appropriate personnel of this Court, members of the Bar of this Court, Members of Congress and their legal staffs, and attorneys for the United States and for federal departments and agencies.

2. The library's hours are governed by regulations made by the Librarian with the approval of the Chief Justice or the Court.

3. Library books may not be removed from the Court building, except by a Justice or a member of a Justice's staff.

Sources: United States Code, Title 28—Judiciary and Judicial Procedure, Part III—Court Officers and Employees, Chapter 45—Supreme Court. (Available at www4.law.cornell.edu/uscode/28/pIII.html.)

Table 1-16 Supreme Court Employees: Full-time Permanent Positions, 1930–2003

Year	Court employees[a]	Building employees[b]	Other employees
1930	52.5		
1931	50.8		
1932	51.8		
1933	52.8		
1934	51.8		
1935	54.5	18.4	
1936	156.9[c]	29.0[c]	7.4[d]
1937	160.5	30.2	7.4[d]
1938	172.8	32.0	0.4[d]
1939	173.8	32.0	
1940	176.8	32.0	
1941	177.8	32.0	
1942	179.0	32.4	4.7[e]
1943	172.7	29.1	5.7[e, f]
1944	144.5	28.7	3.9[e, f]
1945	144.1	29.7	3.0[e, f]
1946	133.4	31.8	2.7[e, f]
1947	142.0	34.0	
1948	151.0	34.9	
1949	157.0	36.0	
1950	159.0	36.0	
1951	162.0	37.0	
1952	162.0	37.0	
1953	163.0	37.0	
1954	163.0	37.0	
1955	162.0	38.0	1.0[g]
1956	162.0	33.0	1.0
1957	163.0	33.0	1.0
1958	163.0	33.0	1.0
1959	164.0	33.0	1.0
1960	164.0	33.0	1.0
1961	166.0	33.0	1.0
1962	168.0	33.0	1.0
1963	168.0	33.0	1.0
1964	168.0	33.0	1.0
1965	189.0	33.0	1.0
1966	189.0	33.0	1.0
1967	190.0	33.0	1.0
1968	190.0	33.0	1.0
1969	191.0	33.0	1.0
1970	204.0	33.0	1.0
1971	220.0	33.0	1.0
1972	227.0	33.0	1.0
1973	238.0	33.0	1.0
1974	243.0	33.0	1.0
1975	254.0	33.0	

(Table continues)

Table 1-16   *(Continued)*

Year	Court employees[a]	Building employees[b]	Other employees
1976	274.0	33.0	
1977	297.0	33.0	
1978	304.0	33.0	
1979	325.0	33.0	
1980	325.0	33.0	
1981	325.0	33.0	
1982	316.0	30.0	
1983	320.0	33.0	
1984	322.0	33.0	
1985	317.0	33.0	
1986	318.0	33.0	
1987	319.0	33.0	
1988	319.0	33.0	
1989	319.0	33.0	
1990	329.0	26.0	
1991	338.0	28.0	
1992[h]	340.0	28.0	
1993	341.0	45.0	
1994	345.0	34.0	
1995	345.0	28.0	
1996	364.0	26.0	
1997	361.0	26.0	
1998	367.0	26.0	
1999	371.0	21.0	
2000	383.0	26.0	
2001	396.0	32.0	
2002 (est.)	413.0	32.0	
2003 (est.)	427.0	35.0	

Note: The personnel figures shown are for the actual full-time permanent positions appropriated for the fiscal years listed with the exceptions of 2002 and 2003, where the figures are estimates.

[a] Individuals providing administrative and other services under the authority of the Supreme Court.

[b] Individuals assigned to the care of the Supreme Court building and grounds under statutory authority granted to the Architect of the Capitol.

[c] The move to the new Supreme Court building required the hiring of many additional employees, including almost 30 positions for guards and 40 janitorial positions.

[d] Advisory committee on preparation of a unified system of general rules for cases in equity and actions of law. This commission ceased to exist in 1938.

[e] Advisory committee on the preparation of rules for criminal proceedings. It was funded for personnel through 1946.

[f] Advisory committee on the preparation of rules for civil proceedings. It was funded for personnel through 1946.

[g] Beginning in 1955, the newly created position of a driver for the chief justice was placed in the "other" category. After 1974, this position was not itemized separately.

[h] Beginning with the budget for fiscal 1992 (which contains the actual figures for 1990), the government eliminated the classification "full-time permanent positions." It was replaced with the classification "total compensable work years: full-time equivalent employment."

Sources: Office of Management and Budget, *Budget of the United States Government* (Washington, D.C.: Government Printing Office, 1932–1962) and *Appendix to the Budget* (Washington, D.C.: Government Printing Office, 1963–2002).

Table 1-17   Administrative Officers of the Court, 1790–2002

Position	Officer	Years of service
Clerk of the Court[a]	John Tucker	1790–1791
	Samuel Bayard	1791–1800
	Elias B. Caldwell	1800–1825
	William Griffith	1826–1827
	William T. Carroll	1827–1863
	D. W. Middleton	1863–1880
	J. H. McKenney	1880–1913
	James D. Maher	1913–1921
	William R. Stansbury	1921–1927
	C. Elmore Cropley	1927–1952
	Harold B. Willey	1952–1956
	John T. Fey	1956–1958
	James R. Browning	1958–1961
	John F. Davis	1961–1970
	E. Robert Seaver	1970–1972
	Michael Rodak, Jr.	1972–1981
	Alexander Stevas	1981–1985
	Joseph F. Spaniol, Jr.	1985–1991
	William K. Suter	1991–
Reporter of Decisions[b]	Alexander J. Dallas	1790–1800
	William Cranch	1801–1815
	Henry Wheaton	1816–1827
	Richard Peters, Jr.	1828–1843
	Benjamin C. Howard	1843–1861
	Jeremiah S. Black	1861–1862
	John W. Wallace	1863–1875
	William T. Otto	1875–1883
	J. C. Bancroft Davis	1883–1902
	Charles Henry Butler	1902–1916
	Ernest Knaebel	1916–1946
	Walter Wyatt	1946–1963
	Henry Putzel, Jr.	1964–1979
	Henry C. Lind	1979–1987
	Frank D. Wagner	1987–
Marshal of the Court[c]	Richard C. Parsons	1867–1872
	John C. Nicolay	1872–1887
	John Montgomery Wright	1888–1915
	Frank Key Green	1915–1938
	Thomas E. Waggaman	1938–1952
	T. Perry Lippitt	1952–1972
	Frank M. Hepler	1972–1976
	Alfred Wong	1976–1994
	Dale E. Bosley	1994–2001
	Pamela Talkin	2001–
Librarian of the Court[d]	Henry Deforest Clarke	1887–1900
	Frank Key Green	1900–1915

(Table continues)

Table 1-17   *(Continued)*

Position	Officer	Years of service
	Oscar Deforest Clarke	1915–1947
	Helen C. Newman	1947–1965
	Henry Charles Hallam, Jr.	1965–1972
	Edward G. Hudon	1972–1976
	Betty H. Clowers (acting)	1976–1978
	Roger F. Jacobs	1978–1985
	Stephen G. Margeton	1985–1988
	Shelley L. Dowling	1989–

[a] Responsible for administering and processing the Court's records and paperwork, including administration of the docket, receiving case filings, distributing papers to the justices, communicating with attorneys, and preparation of orders and judgments.

[b] Responsible for editing, printing, and publishing the decisions and opinions of the Court.

[c] Initially responsible for the Court's security, but over time also assumed responsibility for maintaining the Court's building and grounds and for administering the fiscal affairs of the institution.

[d] Responsible for the acquisition and maintenance of the Court's books, periodicals, and other resources for legal research.

Sources: Joan Biskupic and Elder Witt, *Congressional Quarterly's Guide to the U.S. Supreme Court,* 3d ed. (Washington: Congressional Quarterly, 1997); *United States Reports,* various years.

2

The Supreme Court's Review Process, Caseload, and Cases

The material in this chapter provides basic information on the Court's work. We begin with the review process and the Court's rules governing the process's operations and procedures. Those rules detailing the steps litigants must take to secure Court review of their cases and the criteria the Court uses in acting on their petitions appear in Table 2-1. Note especially the criteria in Rule 10 that the Court specifies for granting a writ of certiorari. This is the most common method whereby cases reach the Supreme Court. Although the list is vague, allowing the justices to use their own discretion in granting or denying petitions, many of the reasons listed in the rule pertain to decisions in conflict with those of other courts. All things considered, a case in conflict with another appreciably enhances the likelihood that the justices will hear the matter.

Use of the writ of certiorari by the Court began with an 1891 Act of Congress, which made some types of lower court decisions "reviewable only upon the issuance" of a writ. According to one account, though, between 1891 and 1893 the Court granted only two writs. Between the mid-1890s and the end of the 1920s that figure grew and stabilized at about 16 percent. Still, the vast majority of the cases fell under the Court's obligatory jurisdiction. Accordingly (and with a good deal of prodding by the justices), Congress enacted the Judiciary Act of 1925, which greatly increased the Court's discretionary jurisdiction by replacing mandatory appeals with petitions for certiorari.[1]

The Court's caseload is considered from five different standpoints in Tables 2-2 through 2-6. The raw totals of Tables 2-5 and 2-6 show a five-fold increase in the total of docketed cases since 1880, with the number of new cases increasing tenfold. These increases suggest that the Court has difficulty remaining abreast of its docket. The data in Tables 2-3 and 2-4, however, indicate the opposite. Cases remaining on the Court's dockets at the end of the term have not appreciably increased since the mid-1960s.

Tables 2-5 and 2-6 show why: the justices simply accept for review a number of cases independent of the number filed.

After the Court agrees to review a case, it schedules it for oral argument. Table 2-7 provides a guide to oral arguments in the Court.

Tables 2-8 through 2-17 present data about the cases that the Court has decided. Table 2-8 lists the number of formally decided cases—that is, those that the Court decided after hearing oral argument. They comprise two forms: those in which the prevailing opinion is signed by an individual justice, and those in which no individual justice writes the prevailing opinion (per curiam). The Court initially decided its cases seriatim—that is, with the authoring justices identifying their individual opinions, but with no opinion constituting the opinion of the Court. Beginning in 1875 and continuing until 1925, the Court typically decided more than 200 cases per term. In 1925, Congress authorized the Court to decide for itself which cases it would hear. As a result, the Court averaged only about 125 signed opinions per term, and that figure has declined to well under 100 in recent terms.

The difference in the numbers between the first two columns of Table 2-8, signed opinions and cases disposed of by signed opinion, results because of the Court's practice of deciding related cases together under a single signed opinion. Although this practice long antedates 1926, no compilation for preceding years exists. It appears as though orally argued per curiam decisions, the subject of the third column, do not antedate 1940. An equivalent device nevertheless did exist: the practice of an individual justice announcing the Court's decision in a brief opinion without any designation other than the name of the authoring justice. Such opinions, however, are not labeled "the opinion of the Court."[2] Per curiam opinions generally address relatively uncomplicated matters that do not require more than a brief opinion.

Readers can obtain access to Court decisions, whether a signed opinion or a per curiam, in numerous places. Tables 2-9 and 2-10 provide lists of print and electronic sources. Table 2-11 breaks down the Court's formally decided cases (signed opinions and orally argued per curiams) since the beginning of the Vinson Court in 1946 into thirteen issue areas. It shows a slow decline in the number and proportion of economically based litigation and a corresponding increase in that pertaining to noneconomic rights and liberties. Thus, the proportion of economic activity cases has dropped from approximately one in three to one in five. Additionally, 59 federal income tax cases were decided during the seven terms of the Vinson Court, while only 31 were decided during the 1990 through 2000 terms. In the noneconomic sector, all categories have increased in absolute number, with the possible exception of First Amendment freedoms. Criminal procedure (overall the largest category), civil rights, due process, and the small privacy and attorney sets produce markedly more decisions currently than they did during the 1940s, 1950s, and the early 1960s. Judicial power and federalism have maintained a relatively constant number of decisions, notwithstanding the current perception that the Rehnquist Court considers decentralization a matter of some priority.

The foregoing categorization of the Court's decisions is in gross numbers and treats all cases falling within a given grouping as equally important. To rectify these shortcomings, we have compiled Tables 2-12 and 2-13, which list the Court's most important decisions chronologically. Obviously, any list of the Court's landmark decisions is a subjective venture. But the sources we have used—Joan Biskupic and Elder Witt's *Congressional Quarterly's Guide to the U.S. Supreme Court*[3] and the *New York Times*—have been deemed by scholars to be among the most reliable and comprehensive.[4]

Among the cases that have shaped modern American constitutional law are those that have made various provisions of the Bill of Rights binding on state and local governments. According to the literal language of the Constitution, and the authoritative interpretation given that language by Chief Justice John Marshall,[5] the guarantees in the Bill of Rights limit only the federal government. Accordingly, any state could, for example, deny individuals freedom of speech, impose taxes on all to support a specific religious denomination, employ cruel and unusual punishments, or deny persons a trial by jury. Not until the 1920s did the justices alter this original interpretation by reading into the due process clause of the Fourteenth Amendment, which was binding on state and local governments, various provisions of the Bill of Rights. Table 2-14 identifies these cases and the provision incorporated into the due process clause. Note that approximately half of them resulted from decisions of the Warren Court handed down between 1961 and 1969.

Tables 2-15 and 2-16 concern the exercise of the most momentous of the Court's powers: judicial review. Judicial review is the capacity of the Court to declare unconstitutional the actions of Congress, as well as the legal provisions of state and local governments. While the power to void actions of state and local governments fairly derives from the language of the supremacy clause of Article VI of the Constitution, no comparable provision authorizes the Court to declare unconstitutional actions of the other branches of the federal government. Marshall simply inferred the existence of such authority in his masterful opinion in *Marbury v. Madison* (1803).[6]

Whereas the decision of a court declaring legislation unconstitutional is upsetting to those who view the will of the people, as reflected by legislative majorities, to be the essence of democracy, the decision of a court to overrule itself is upsetting to those who view the law, and especially the Constitution, as fixed and stable. Nonetheless, as Tables 2-15 and

2-16, on the one hand, and Table 2-17, on the other, demonstrate, the Court has not been reluctant either to declare legislation unconstitutional or to overrule its own previous decisions. And though the frequency of the former is several times the frequency of the latter, by no means is the number of instances when the Court formally altered its own precedents trivial. Indeed, when one considers that in 1789 the Court had no precedents of its own at all, and very few until well after the Civil War, legal stability and fixity is at most a sometime thing.

Notes

1. Doris Marie Provine, *Case Selection in the United States Supreme Court* (Chicago: University of Chicago Press, 1980), chap. 1.
2. See, for example, *Morse v. Anderson,* 150 U.S. 156 (1893).
3. Joan Biskupic and Elder Witt, *Congressional Quarterly's Guide to the U.S. Supreme Court,* 3d ed. (Washington, D.C.: Congressional Quarterly, 1997).
4. For example, Segal and Spaeth point out that other lists often exclude statutory cases. See Jeffrey A. Segal and Harold J. Spaeth, "The Impact of *Stare Decisis* on the Votes of Supreme Court Justices," *American Journal of Political Science* 40 (1996): 971–1003. See also Beverly B. Cook, "Measuring the Significance of U.S. Supreme Court Decisions," *Journal of Politics* 55 (1993): 1127–39; Lee Epstein and Jeffrey A. Segal, "Measuring Issue Salience," *American Journal of Political Science* 44 (2000): 66–83.
5. In *Barron v. Baltimore,* 7 Pet. 243 (1833).
6. 1 Cranch 137.

Table 2-1   Supreme Court Rule 10: Considerations Governing Review on Certiorari

---

Review on a writ of certiorari is not a matter of right, but of judicial discretion. A petition for a writ of certiorari will be granted only for compelling reasons. The following, although neither controlling nor fully measuring the Court's discretion, indicate the character of the reasons the Court considers:

(a) a United States court of appeals has entered a decision in conflict with the decision of another United States court of appeals on the same important matter; has decided an important federal question in a way that conflicts with a decision by a state court of last resort; or has so far departed from the accepted and usual course of judicial proceedings, or sanctioned such a departure by a lower court, as to call for an exercise of this Court's supervisory power;

(b) a state court of last resort has decided an important federal question in a way that conflicts with the decision of another state court of last resort or of a United States court of appeals;

(c) a state court or a United States court of appeals has decided an important question of federal law that has not been, but should be, settled by this Court, or has decided an important federal question in a way that conflicts with relevant decisions of this Court.

A petition for a writ of certiorari is rarely granted when the asserted error consists of erroneous factual findings or the misapplication of a properly stated rule of law.

Note: Rule adopted January 11, 1999; effective May 3, 1999. A full text of all the Court's rules is available at: www.supremecourtus.gov.

Table 2-2   The Supreme Court's Caseload, 1880–2001 Terms

Term	New cases filed (percentage change)	Total cases on docket[a] (percentage change)
1880	417	1,212
1881	411 (−1.4)	1,254 (+3.1)
1882	434 (+5.6)	1,275 (+1.7)
1883	439 (+1.2)	1,313 (+3.0)
1884	477 (+8.7)	1,325 (+0.9)
1885	493 (+3.4)	1,348 (+1.7)
1886	499 (+1.2)	1,403 (+4.1)
1887	489 (−2.0)	1,437 (+2.4)
1888	556 (+13.7)	1,571 (+9.3)
1889	500 (−10.1)	1,648 (+4.9)
1890	636 (+27.2)	1,816 (+10.2)
1891	383 (−39.8)	1,582 (−12.9)
1892	290 (−24.3)	1,369 (−13.5)
1893	280 (−3.4)	1,224 (−10.6)
1894	341 (+21.8)	1,062 (−13.2)
1895	386 (+13.2)	1,033 (−2.7)
1896	295 (−23.6)	834 (−19.3)
1897	307 (+4.1)	689 (−17.4)
1898	523 (+70.4)	839 (+21.8)
1899	384 (−26.6)	692 (−17.5)
1900	406 (+5.7)	723 (+4.5)
1901	386 (−4.9)	732 (+1.2)
1902	391 (+1.3)	746 (+1.9)

Table 2-2   *(Continued)*

Term	New cases filed (percentage change)	Total cases on docket[a] (percentage change)
1903	430 (+9.9)	749 (+0.4)
1904	403 (−6.3)	698 (−6.8)
1905	502 (+24.6)	794 (+13.8)
1906	484 (−3.6)	801 (+0.9)
1907	480 (−0.9)	832 (+3.9)
1908	494 (+2.9)	923 (10.9)
1909	514 (+4.0)	1,000 (+8.3)
1910	516 (+0.4)	1,116 (+11.6)
1911	532 (+3.1)	1,182 (+5.9)
1912	521 (−2.1)	1,201 (+1.6)
1913	526 (+1.0)	1,142 (−4.9)
1914	530 (+0.8)	1,075 (−5.9)
1915	557 (+5.1)	1,093 (+1.7)
1916	658 (+18.1)	1,200 (+9.8)
1917	590 (−10.3)	1,145 (−4.6)
1918	593 (+0.5)	1,112 (−2.9)
1919	587 (−1.0)	1,019 (−8.4)
1920	565 (−3.7)	975 (−4.3)
1921	673 (+19.1)	1,040 (+6.7)
1922	720 (+7.0)	1,157 (+11.3)
1923	631 (−12.4)	1,123 (−2.9)
1924	909 (+44.1)	1,316 (+17.2)
1925	790 (−13.1)	1,309 (−0.5)

(Table continues)

Table 2-2   *(Continued)*

Term	New cases filed (percentage change)	Total cases on docket[a] (percentage change)
1926	718 (−9.11)	1,183 (−9.6)
1927	751 (+4.6)	1,032 (−12.8)
1928	776 (+3.3)	962 (−6.8)
1929	838 (+8.0)	981 (+2.0)
1930	845 (+0.8)	1,034 (+5.4)
1931	877 (+3.8)	1,024 (−1.0)
1932	897 (+2.3)	1,041 (+1.7)
1933	1,005 (+12.0)	1,132 (+8.7)
1934	937 (−6.8)	1,040 (−8.1)
1935	983 (+4.9)	1,092 (+5.0)
1936	950 (−3.4)	1,052 (−3.7)
1937	981 (+3.3)	1,091 (+3.7)
1938	942 (−4.0)	1,020 (−6.5)
1939	981 (+4.1)	1,078 (+5.7)
1940	977 (−0.4)	1,109 (+2.9)
1941	1,178 (+20.6)	1,302 (+17.4)
1942	984 (−16.5)	1,118 (−14.1)
1943	997 (+1.3)	1,118 (0.0)
1944	1,237 (+24.8)	1,393 (+24.6)
1945	1,316 (+6.4)	1,460 (+4.8)
1946	1,510 (+14.7)	1,678 (+14.9)
1947	1,295 (−14.2)	1,453 (−13.4)
1948	1,465 (+13.1)	1,596 (+9.8)

Table 2-2   *(Continued)*

Term	New cases filed (percentage change)	Total cases on docket[a] (percentage change)
1949	1,270 (−13.3)	1,441 (−9.7)
1950	1,181 (−7.0)	1,321 (−8.3)
1951	1,234 (+4.5)	1,353 (+2.4)
1952	1,283 (+4.0)	1,429 (+5.6)
1953	1,302 (+1.5)	1,453 (+1.7)
1954	1,397 (+7.3)	1,557 (+7.2)
1955	1,644 (+17.7)	1,849 (+18.8)
1956	1,802 (+9.6)	2,021 (+9.3)
1957	1,639 (−9.0)	1,990 (−1.5)
1958	1,819 (+11.0)	2,044 (+2.7)
1959	1,862 (+2.4)	2,143 (+4.8)
1960	1,940 (+4.2)	2,296 (+7.1)
1961	2,185 (+12.6)	2,570 (+11.9)
1962	2,373 (+8.6)	2,801 (+9.0)
1963	2,294 (−3.3)	2,768 (−1.2)
1964	2,288 (−0.3)	2,655 (−4.1)
1965	2,774 (+21.2)	3,256 (+22.6)
1966	2,752 (−0.8)	3,343 (+2.7)
1967	3,106 (+12.9)	3,559 (+6.5)
1968	3,271 (+5.3)	3,884 (+9.1)
1969	3,405 (+4.1)	4,172 (+7.4)
1970	3,419 (+0.4)	4,212 (+1.0)
1971	3,643 (+6.6)	4,533 (+7.6)

(Table continues)

Table 2-2   *(Continued)*

Term	New cases filed (percentage change)	Total cases on docket[a] (percentage change)
1972	3,749 (+2.9)	4,640 (+2.4)
1973	3,943 (+5.2)	5,079 (+9.5)
1974	3,661 (−7.2)	4,668 (−8.1)
1975	3,939 (+7.6)	4,761 (+2.0)
1976	3,873 (−1.7)	4,731 (−0.6)
1977	3,839 (−0.9)	4,704 (−0.6)
1978	3,893 (+1.4)	4,731 (+0.6)
1979	4,067 (+4.5)	4,781 (+1.1)
1980	4,252 (+4.5)	5,144 (+7.6)
1981	4,363 (+2.6)	5,311 (+3.2)
1982	4,201 (−3.7)	5,079 (−4.4)
1983	4,222 (+0.5)	5,100 (+0.4)
1984	4,046 (−4.2)	5,006 (−1.8)
1985	4,413 (+9.1)	5,158 (+3.0)
1986	4,251 (−3.7)	5,123 (−0.7)
1987	4,494 (+5.7)	5,268 (+2.8)
1988	4,776 (+6.3)	5,657 (+7.4)
1989	4,919 (+3.0)	5,746 (+1.6)
1990	5,502 (+11.9)	6,316 (+9.9)
1991	5,866 (+6.6)	6,770 (+7.2)
1992	6,303 (+7.5)	7,245 (+7.0)
1993	6,897 (+9.4)	7,786 (+7.5)
1994	6,996 (+1.4)	8,100 (+4.0)

Table 2-2   *(Continued)*

Term	New cases filed (percentage change)	Total cases on docket[a] (percentage change)
1995	6,597 (–5.7)	7,565 (–6.6)
1996	6,633 (+0.5)	7,602 (+0.5)
1997	6,781 (+2.2)	7,692 (+1.2)
1998	7,109 (+4.8)	8,083 (+5.1)
1999	7,377 (+3.8)	8,445 (+4.5)
2000	7,852 (+6.4)	8,965 (+6.2)
2001	7,924 (+0.9)	9,176 (+2.4)

Note: Consistent and reliable data not available prior to 1880.

[a] Includes all cases on all dockets in effect. The number of cases on the docket exceeds the number of cases filed because the Court carries over a certain number of cases each term.

Sources: New cases filed, 1880–1974: Gerhard Casper and Richard A. Posner, *The Workload of the Supreme Court* (Chicago: American Bar Foundation, 1976), 3; 1974–1989: Administrative Office of the United States Courts, *Annual Report of the Director of the Administrative Office of the United States Court* (Washington, D.C.: Government Printing Office, successive editions), Table A-1; 1990–2000: Clerk of the U.S. Supreme Court. Total cases on docket, 1880–1885 and 1900–1935: U.S. Department of Justice, *Annual Report of the Attorney General of the United States* (Washington, D.C.: Government Printing Office, successive editions); 1885–1900: U.S. Senate, "Creation of the Federal Judiciary," Sen. Doc. No. 91, 75th Cong., 1st Sess., July 22, 1937 (Washington, D.C.: Government Printing Office, 1938), 44; 1935–1969: Federal Judicial Center, *Report of the Study Group on the Case Load of the Supreme Court* (Washington, D.C.: Federal Judicial Center, 1972), Table A1; 1970–1989: U.S. Bureau of the Census, *Statistical Abstract of the United States* (Washington, D.C.: Government Printing Office, successive editions); 1990–2000: Clerk of the U.S. Supreme Court.

Table 2-3 Cases on the Dockets of the Supreme Court, 1935–1969 Terms

Term	Original docket			Appellate docket			Miscellaneous docket			
	Filed	Disposed[a]	Remaining[b]	Filed	Disposed[a]	Remaining[b]	Filed	Disposed[a]	Transferred	Remaining[b]
1935	3	4	12	980	986	90				
1936	1	1	12	949	941	98				
1937	10	9	13	971	1,004	65				
1938	—	1	12	942	922	85				
1939	3	4	11	978	942	121				
1940	4	6	9	973	979	115				
1941	3	2	10	1,175	1,166	124				
1942	5	5	10	979	992	111				
1943	1	2	9	996	960	147				
1944	2	—	11	1,235	1,249	133				
1945	1	—	12	1,184	1,161	156				
1946	—	—	12	1,356	1,366	146				
1947	—	—	12	733	772	107				
1948	2	1	13	773	747	142	690	677	9	16
1949	—	5	13	718	757	110	552	544	7	17
1950	—	5	8	659	687	96	522	510	14	15
1951	1	—	9	716	714	113	517	493	15	24
1952	2	—	11	742	742	121	539	536	8	19
1953	—	—	11	684	694	121	618	599	10	28
1954	—	—	11	713	721	122	684	631	9	72
1955	4	4	11	891	865	155	749	761	7	53
1956	3	3	11	974	900	260	825	767	31	80
1957	2	1	12	826	967	137	811	797	18	76
1958	3	3	12	886	886	155	930	874	18	114
1959	—	—	12	857	860	187	1,005	927	35	157
1960	—	1	11	842	887	159	1,098	1,023	17	215
1961	2	—	13	888	860	202	1,295	1,282	15	213

1962	2	7	8	957	972	210	1,414	1,348	23	256
1963	1	2	7	1,017	1,036	202	1,276	1,363	11	158
1964	4	2	9	1,038	1,027	220	1,246	1,144	7	253
1965	8	9	8	1,188	1,182	254	1,578	1,474	28	329
1966	5	5	8	1,202	1,232	237	1,545	1,653	13	208
1967	2	2	8	1,276	1,338	202	1,828	1,606	27	403
1968	1	—	9	1,323	1,288	271	1,947	1,829	34	487
1969	6	5	10	1,457	1,433	325	1,942	1,941	30	458

Note: Consistent and reliable data not available prior to 1935. Appellate docket prior to 1947 includes appeals and petitions for certiorari. Beginning in 1947, all petitions for certiorari containing motions for leave to proceed *in forma pauperis* were placed on the miscellaneous docket. If the Court granted certiorari to such a case, it was then transferred to the appellate docket. No transfer was made if the motion was granted and the case was then disposed of "on the merits by the same order."

Beginning in 1954, all appeals containing motions to proceed *in forma pauperis* were placed on the miscellaneous docket, as were "all petitions seeking the issuance of special writs," including writs of habeas corpus, mandamus, and prohibition. Petitions for certiorari containing motions for leave to proceed *in forma pauperis* continued to to be placed on the miscellaneous docket.

Beginning in 1970, the Court utilized a different numbering system (see Table 2-4).

a Includes those cases that the Court denied, dismissed, withdrew, or decided summarily.
b Cases on which the Court took no action during the term.

Sources: Administrative Office of the United States Courts, *Annual Report of the Director of the Administrative Office of the United States Court* (Washington, D.C.: Government Printing Office, successive editions), Table A-1.

Table 2-4 Cases on the Dockets of the Supreme Court, 1970–2001 Terms

| | Original cases | | Appellate cases | | | | | |
| | | | Excluding in forma pauperis | | | In forma pauperis | | |
Term	On docket	Disposed[a]	On docket	Disposed[a]	Not acted on[b]	On docket	Disposed[a]	Not acted on[b]
1970	20	7	1,903	1,399	290	2,289	1,761	487
1971	18	8	2,070	1,514	318	2,445	1,962	422
1972	21	8	2,183	1,617	349	2,436	1,947	454
1973	14	4	2,480	1,719	532	2,585	1,983	572
1974	12	4	2,308	1,732	341	2,348	1,948	372
1975	14	7	2,352	1,656	452	2,395	1,969	398
1976	8	2	2,324	1,782	305	2,398	2,053	315
1977	14	3	2,341	1,755	362	2,349	1,936	389
1978	17	0	2,383	1,813	360	2,331	1,969	335
1979	23	1	2,509	1,851	459	2,249	1,806	411
1980	24	7	2,749	2,089	425	2,371	2,000	344
1981	22	6	2,935	2,214	422	2,354	2,026	315
1982	17	3	2,710	2,005	413	2,352	2,001	339
1983	18	7	2,688	1,973	468	2,394	1,978	402
1984	15	8	2,575	2,012	322	2,416	2,064	329
1985	10	2	2,571	1,941	386	2,577	2,160	388
1986	12	1	2,547	1,947	358	2,564	2,224	314
1987	16	5	2,577	1,985	353	2,675	2,231	412
1988	14	2	2,587	2,048	316	3,056	2,609	418
1989	14	2	2,416	1,925	320	3,316	2,859	425
1990	14	3	2,351	1,883	309	3,951	3,397	515

1991	12	1	2,451	1,966	326	4,307	3,738	539
1992	12	1	2,441	2,004	301	4,792	4,234	531
1993	12	1	2,442	1,981	343	5,332	4,596	711
1994	11	2	2,515	2,068	330	5,574	4,969	591
1995	11	5	2,456	2,007	326	5,098	4,494	584
1996	7	2	2,430	2,021	306	5,165	4,597	552
1997	7	1	2,432	2,026	290	5,253	4,595	637
1998	7	2	2,387	1,984	295	5,689	4,937	738
1999	8	0	2,413	1,992	317	6,024	5,255	751
2000	9	2	2,305	1,905	281	6,651	5,719	915
2001	8	1	2,210	1,808	278	6,958	6,127	819

Note: Prior to 1970, the Court utilized a different numbering system (see Table 2-3).

[a] Includes those cases that the Court denied, dismissed, withdrew, or decided summarily.
[b] Cases on which the Court took no action during the term.

Source: 1970–1989: U.S. Bureau of the Census, *Statistical Abstract of the United States* (Washington, D.C.: Government Printing Office, successive editions); 1990–2000: Clerk of the U.S. Supreme Court.

Table 2-5 Petitions Granted Review, 1926–1969 Terms

| Term | Petitions for certiorari, excluding in forma pauperis | | Petitions for certiorari, in forma pauperis | |
	Number on docket	Number granted review (proportion granted)	Number on docket	Number granted review (proportion granted)
1926	586	117 (.20)		
1927	587	102 (.17)		
1928	649	99 (.15)		
1929	692	133 (.19)		
1930	726	159 (.22)		
1931	738	137 (.19)		
1932	797	148 (.19)		
1933	880	148 (.17)		
1934	835	165 (.20)		
1935	842	142 (.17)	59	8 (.14)
1936	809	149 (.18)	60	4 (.07)
1937	804	140 (.17)	97	15 (.16)
1938	760	125 (.16)	85	7 (.08)
1939	806	170 (.21)	117	18 (.15)
1940	814	174 (.21)	120	19 (.16)
1941	832	150 (.18)	178	16 (.09)
1942	786	158 (.20)	147	8 (.05)
1943	736	127 (.17)	214	12 (.06)
1944	865	176 (.20)	339	10 (.03)
1945	774	155 (.20)	393	15 (.04)
1946	785	148 (.19)	528	8 (.02)
1947	698	97 (.14)	426	17 (.04)
1948	733	144 (.20)	456	18 (.04)
1949	699	85 (.12)	454	7 (.02)

Table 2-5 *(Continued)*

Term	Petitions for certiorari, excluding in forma pauperis		Petitions for certiorari, in forma pauperis	
	Number on docket	*Number granted review (proportion granted)*	*Number on docket*	*Number granted review (proportion granted)*
1950	640	89 (.14)	415	17 (.04)
1951	668	94 (.14)	425	19 (.05)
1952	711	104 (.15)	454	11 (.02)
1953	669	78 (.12)	542	10 (.02)
1954	695	108 (.16)	568	12 (.02)
1955	842	123 (.15)	645	16 (.03)
1956	927	139 (.15)	689	38 (.06)
1957	840	110 (.13)	747	34 (.05)
1958	820	108 (.13)	837	24 (.03)
1959	838	122 (.15)	933	55 (.06)
1960	789	87 (.11)	1,085	22 (.02)
1961	852	103 (.12)	1,330	38 (.03)
1962	907	115 (.13)	1,412	88 (.06)
1963	972	118 (.12)	1,307	69 (.05)
1964	1,041	116 (.11)	1,170	21 (.02)
1965	1,164	124 (.12)	1,610	43 (.03)
1966	1,198	121 (.10)	1,615	56 (.04)
1967	1,269	166 (.13)	1,798	84 (.05)
1968	1,255	101 (.08)	2,121	62 (.03)
1969	1,425	108 (.08)	2,228	38 (.02)

Note: Prior to the early 1920s, petitions *in forma pauperis* were few in number. Figures for them prior to 1935 are not available. The figures listed for the 1925–1934 terms probably include all petitions.

Sources: 1926–1934: "The Supreme Court at October Term, 1930," 45 (1931): 284, and "The Supreme Court at October Term, 1934," 49 (1935): 78; 1935–1969: Administrative Office of the United States Courts, *Annual Report of the Director of the Administrative Office of the United States Courts* (Washington, D.C.: Government Printing Office, successive editions).

Table 2-6 Petitions Granted Review, 1970–2001 Terms

	Paid cases		In forma pauperis cases	
Term	Number on docket	Number granted review (proportion granted)	Number on docket	Number granted review (proportion granted)
1970	1,903	214 (.11)	2,289	41 (.02)
1971	2,070	238 (.12)	2,445	61 (.03)
1972	2,183	217 (.10)	2,436	35 (.01)
1973	2,480	229 (.09)	2,585	30 (.02)
1974	2,308	235 (.10)	2,348	28 (.01)
1975	2,352	244 (.10)	2,395	28 (.01)
1976	2,324	237 (.10)	2,398	30 (.01)
1977	2,341	224 (.10)	2,349	24 (.01)
1978	2,383	210 (.09)	2,331	27 (.01)
1979	2,509	199 (.08)	2,249	32 (.01)
1980	2,749	167 (.06)	2,371	17 (.01)
1981	2,935	203 (.07)	2,354	7 (.003)
1982	2,710	169 (.06)	2,352	10 (.004)
1983	2,688	140 (.05)	2,394	9 (.004)
1984	2,575	167 (.07)	2,416	18 (.01)
1985	2,571	166 (.07)	2,577	20 (.01)
1986	2,547	152 (.06)	2,564	15 (.02)
1987	2,577	157 (.06)	2,675	23 (.02)
1988	2,587	130 (.05)	3,056	17 (.02)
1989	2,416	103 (.04)	3,316	19 (.01)
1990	2,351	114 (.05)	3,951	27 (.007)
1991	2,451	103 (.04)	4,307	17 (.004)

Table 2-6 *(Continued)*

Term	Paid cases		In forma pauperis cases	
	Number on docket	*Number granted review (proportion granted)*	*Number on docket*	*Number granted review (proportion granted)*
1992	2,441	83 (.03)	4,792	14 (.003)
1993	2,442	78 (.03)	5,332	21 (.004)
1994	2,515	83 (.03)	5,574	10 (.002)
1995	2,456	92 (.04)	5,098	13 (.003)
1996	2,430	74 (.03)	5,165	13 (.003)
1997	2,432	75 .03	5,253	14 (.003)
1998	2,387	72 (.03)	5,689	9 (.002)
1999	2,413	78 (.03)	6,024	14 (.002)
2000	2,305	85 (.04)	6,651	14 (.002)
2001	2,210	82 (.04)	6,985	6 (.001)

Sources: 1970–1998: U.S. Bureau of the Census, *Statistical Abstract of the United States* (Washington, D.C.: Government Printing Office, successive editions); 1999–2001: Clerk of the U.S. Supreme Court.

Table 2-7   Guide to Oral Argument at the Supreme Court

Description	A case selected for argument usually involves interpretations of the U.S. Constitution or federal law. At least four justices have selected the case as being of such importance that the Supreme Court must resolve the legal issues.

An attorney for each side of a case will have an opportunity to make a presentation to the Court and answer questions posed by the justices. Prior to the argument each side has submitted a legal brief—a written legal argument outlining each party's points of law. The justices have read these briefs prior to argument and are thoroughly familiar with the case, its facts, and the legal positions that each party is advocating.

Beginning the first Monday in October, the Court is scheduled to hear up to four one-hour arguments a day, three days a week, in two-week intervals (with longer breaks in December and February), concluding the oral argument portion of the term in late April. Typically, two arguments are held in the mornings, beginning at 10:00 A.M., and two in the afternoons, beginning at 1:00 P.M. on Monday, Tuesday, and Wednesday. In the recesses between argument sessions, the justices are writing opinions, deciding which cases to hear in the future, and reading the briefs for the next argument session. They grant review in approximately 100 of the more than 7,000 petitions filed with the Court each term. No one knows exactly when a decision will be handed down by the Court in an argued case, nor is there a set time period in which the justices must reach a decision. However, all cases argued during a term of Court are decided before the summer recess begins, usually by the end of June.

During an argument week, the justices meet in a private conference, closed even to staff, to discuss the cases and to take a preliminary vote on each case. If the chief justice is in the majority on a case decision, he decides who will write the opinion. He may decide to write it himself or he may assign that duty to any other justice in the majority. If the chief justice is in the minority, the justice in the majority who has the most seniority assumes the assignment duty.

Draft opinions are privately circulated among the justices until a final draft is agreed upon. When a final decision has been reached, the justice who wrote the opinion announces the decision in a Court session and may deliver a summary of the Court's reasoning. Meanwhile, the Public Information Office releases the full text of the opinion to the public and news media.

Participants in the courtroom	**JUSTICES.** The justices enter the courtroom through three entrances behind the bench. The chief justice and two senior associate justices enter through the center, and three associate justices enter through each side. They also sit on the bench in

Table 2-7 *(Continued)*

order of seniority, with the chief justice in the middle and the others alternating from left to right, ending with the most junior associate justice on the far right, as you face the bench (see seating chart).

CLERK. The clerk of the Supreme Court or his or her representative sits to the left of the bench. The clerk's responsibilities in the courtroom include providing the justices with materials about the case, if the justices desire additional documents, and notifying the appropriate Court personnel when an opinion can be released to the public. He also swears in new members of the Supreme Court bar.

MARSHAL. The marshal or his or her representative sits to the right side of the bench. The marshal's responsibilities are to call the Court to order, maintain decorum in the courtroom, tape the audio portions of argument, and time the oral presentations so that attorneys do not exceed their one-half hour limitations.

MARSHAL'S AIDES. The marshal's aides are seated behind the justices. They often carry messages to the justices or convey messages from a justice to a member of his or her staff.

ATTORNEYS. The attorneys scheduled to argue cases are seated at the tables facing the bench. The arguing attorney will stand behind the lectern immediately in front of the chief justice. On the lectern there are two lights. When the white light goes on, the attorney has five minutes remaining to argue. The red light indicates that the attorney has used all the allotted time.

Attorneys who are admitted as members of the Supreme Court Bar may be seated in the chairs just beyond the bronze railing. Any member of the Supreme Court Bar may attend any argument, space permitting.

Others   **LAW CLERKS.** Each justice has the option of employing up to four law clerks as assistants. These clerks are law school graduates who have previously clerked for a federal judge on a lower court. The clerks often listen to oral arguments. They are seated in the chairs flanking the courtroom on the right.

SPECIAL GUESTS. Guests of justices are seated in the benches to the right of the bench and are seated in order of the seniority of the justice who invited them. The row of black chairs in front of the guest section is reserved for retired justices and officers of the Court, such as the Reporter of Decisions or the Librarian, who attend oral argument from time to time.

(Table continues)

Table 2-7   *(Continued)*

NEWS MEDIA. Members of the Supreme Court press corps sit to the left of the bench in the benches and chairs facing the guest section. The press enters the courtroom from the hallway on the left.

Courtroom seating

All oral arguments are open to the public, but seating is limited and on a first-come, first-seated basis. Before a session begins, two lines form on the plaza in front of the building. One is for those who wish to attend an entire argument, and the other, a three-minute line, is for those who wish to observe the Court in session only briefly.

Seating for the first line begins at 9:30 A.M. and 12:30 P.M. Seating for the three-minute line begins at 10:00 A.M. and 1:00 P.M. Visitors should be aware that cases might attract large crowds, with lines forming before the building opens.

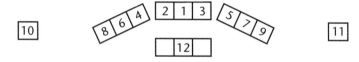

1. Chief Justice Rehnquist

2. Justice Stevens	3. Justice O'Connor
4. Justice Scalia	5. Justice Kennedy
5. Justice Souter	7. Justice Thomas
8. Justice Ginsburg	9. Justice Breyer
10. Clerk of the Court	11. Marshal of the Court

12. Counsel

Courtroom seating chart

Source: www.supremecourtus.gov/about/about.html (accessed July 2001).

Table 2-8   Signed Opinions, Cases Disposed of by Signed Opinion, and Cases Disposed of by Per Curiam Opinion, 1926–2001 Terms

Term	Number of signed opinions of the Court	Number of cases disposed of by signed opinion[a]	Number of cases disposed of by per curiam opinion after oral argument[b]
1926	199	223	
1927	175	214	
1928	129	141	
1929	134	156	
1930	166	235	
1931	150	175	
1932	168	187	
1933	158	179	
1934	156	185	
1935	145	187	
1936	149	180	
1937	152	180	
1938	139	174	
1939	137	151	
1940	165	195	20
1941	151	175	14
1942	147	196	14
1943	130	154	6
1944	156	199	7
1945	134	170	4
1946	142	190	8
1947	110	143	14
1948	114	147	18
1949	87	108	14
1950	91	114	15
1951	83	96	25
1952	104	122	10
1953	65	84	23
1954	78	86	16
1955	82	103	18
1956	100	112	23
1957	104	125	27
1958	99	116	23
1959	97	110	20
1960	110	125	22
1961	85	100	21
1962	110	129	19
1963	111	123	20
1964	91	103	17
1965	97	120	8
1966	100	132	15
1967	110	156	17
1968	99	116	14
1969	88	105	21
1970	109	137	22

(Table continues)

Table 2-8   *(Continued)*

Term	Number of signed opinions of the Court	Number of cases disposed of by signed opinion[a]	Number of cases disposed of by per curiam opinion after oral argument[b]
1971	129	140	24
1972	140	159	18
1973	141	161	8
1974	123	144	20
1975	138	160	16
1976	126	154	22
1977	129	153	8
1978	130	153	8
1979	130	143	12
1980	123	144	8
1981	141	170	10
1982	151	174	6
1983	151	174	6
1984	139	159	11
1985	146	161	10
1986	145	164	10
1987	139	151	9
1988	133	156	12
1989	129	143	3
1990	112	121	4
1991	107	120	3
1992	107	111	4
1993	84	93	6
1994	82	91	3
1995	75	87	3
1996	80	87	3
1997	91	93	1
1998	75	84	4
1999	74	79	2
2000	77	83	4
2001	76	85	3

[a] Data not available prior to 1926. Includes number of cases decided by a single opinion of the Court, not just the opinion itself.
[b] Data not available prior to 1940.

Sources: 1926: Albert P. Blaustein and Roy M Mersky, *The First One Hundred Justices* (Hamden, Conn.: Shoe String Press, 1978), 137–140; 1927–1969: Gerhard Casper and Richard A. Posner, *The Workload of the Supreme Court* (Chicago: American Bar Foundation, 1976), 76; 1970–1998: U.S. Bureau of the Census, *Statistical Abstract of the United States* (Washington, D.C.: Government Printing Office, successive editions); 1999–2001: Clerk of the U.S. Supreme Court.

Table 2-9   Reporting Systems

Reporter/publisher	Form of citation	Description
United States Reports (Washington, D.C.: Government Printing Office)	U.S. Dall. 1-4 Cranch 1-15 Wheat. 1-12 Pet. 1-16 How. 1-24 Black 1-2 Wall. 1-23	Contains the official text of opinions of the Supreme Court. Includes tables of cases reported, cases and statutes cited, miscellaneous materials, and a subject index. Includes most of the Court's decisions.
United States Supreme Court Reports, Lawyers' Edition (Rochester, N.Y.: Lawyers Co-Operative Publishing Company)	L. Ed. L. Ed. 2d	Contains official reports of opinions of the Court. Provides per curiam and other decisions not found elsewhere. Summarizes counsel briefs and individual, majority, and dissenting opinions.
Supreme Court Reporter (Saint Paul, Minn.: West Publishing Company)	S.Ct.	Contains official reports of opinions of the Court. Contains annotated reports and indexes of case names. Includes opinions of justices in chambers. Appears semimonthly.
United States Law Week (Washington, D.C.: Bureau of National Affairs)	U.S.L.W.	Weekly periodical service containing full text of Court decisions. Includes four indexes: topical, table of cases, a docket number table, and proceedings. Contains summary of cases filed recently, journal of proceedings, summary of orders, arguments before the Court, argued cases awaiting decisions, review of the Court's work, and review of the Court's docket.

Note: Citations can be read as follows: *Roe v. Wade* (1973) is 410 U.S. 113, where 410 is the volume number and 113 is the page on which the case begins. All reporters/reports listed above use the same volume/page system. See also Tables 1-8 and 2-10.

Source: Joan Biskupic and Elder Witt, *Congressional Quarterly's Guide to the U.S. Supreme Court,* 3d ed. (Washington: Congressional Quarterly, 1997).

Table 2-10   Where to Obtain Supreme Court Opinions

Sources	Contact information
Official opinions: Print United States Reports 10/16/02	Reporter of Decisions Supreme Court of the United States One First Street, N.E. Washington, D.C. 20543
Copies of recent bench and slip opinions	Public Information Office Supreme Court of the United States Washington, D.C. 20543 Phone: (202) 479–3211
Copies of recent slip opinions, preliminary prints, and bound volumes	Superintendent of Documents U.S. Government Printing Office P.O. Box 371954 Pittsburgh, Pa. 15250–7954 Phone: (202) 512–1800 Fax: (202) 512–2250
Official opinions: Electronic Project Hermes (bench opinions— by subscription only)	Director of Data Systems Supreme Court of the United States Washington, D.C. 20543
Web site (slip opinions)	Internet: www.supremecourtus.gov Public Information Officer Supreme Court of the United States Washington, D.C. 20543
Unofficial opinions: Print Reprints of *United States Reports*	William S. Hein & Co. 1285 Main Street Buffalo, N.Y. 14209 Phone: (716) 882–2600 or (800) 828–7571 Fax: (716) 883–8100 Internet: www.wshein.com
Supreme Court Reporter	Customer and Technical Service West Group 610 Opperman Drive Eagan, Minn. 55123 Phone: (800) 937–8529 or (800) 733–2889 Internet: www.westgroup.com
Supreme Court Reports, *Lawyers' Edition*	Lexis Publishing Attn.: Customer Service 1275 Broadway Albany, N.Y. 12204-2694 Phone: (800) 542–0957 Internet: www.lexis.com
United States Law Week	Bureau of National Affairs, Inc. 1231 25th Street, N.W. Washington, D.C. 20037

Table 2-10   *(Continued)*

Sources	Contact information
	Phone: (202) 452–4200 or (800) 372–1033 Fax: (800) 253–0332 Internet: www.bna.com
Unofficial opinions: Microfilm/microfiche	
Congressional Information Service	4520 East-West Highway, Suite 800 Bethesda, Md. 20814 Phone: (301) 654–1550 Internet: www.cispubs.com
William S. Hein & Co.	1285 Main Street Buffalo, N.Y. 14209 Phone: (716) 882–2600 or (800) 828–7571 Fax: (716) 883–8100 Internet: www.wshein.com
Law Library Microform Consortium	P.O. Box 1599 Kaneohe, Hawaii 96744 Phone: (800) 235–4446
Unofficial opinions: Electronic	
FedWorld: U.S. Air Force's Federal Legal Information Through Electronics	Internet: www.fedworld.gov/supcourt/index.htm
FindLaw	1235 Pear Ave., #111 Mountain View, Calif. 94043 Phone: (650) 210–1900 Fax: (650) 940–4490 Internet: www.findlaw.com/casecode/supreme.html
GPO Federal Bulletin Board (WordPerfect 5.1, Microsoft Word, PDF, and ASCII bench opinions)	GPO Access User Support Team U.S. Government Printing Office Washington, D.C. 20401 Phone: (202) 512–1530 or (888) 293–6498 Fax: (202) 512–1262 Dial-in: (202) 512–1387 FTP site: fedbbs.access.gpo.gov Telnet: fedbbs.access.gpo.gov Internet: www.access.gpo.gov/su_docs/supcrt/index.html
LEXIS-NEXIS (opinions, briefs, and secondary materials)	P.O. Box 933 Dayton, Ohio 45401-0933 Phone: (800) 227–4908 Internet: www.lexis-nexis.com
The Oyez Project, Northwestern University	Internet: oyez.nwu.edu

Source: www.supremecourtus.gov/opinions/opinions.html (accessed June 20, 2002).

Table 2-11 Formally Decided Cases, by Issue Area, 1946–2001 Terms

Term	Crim	Civ	1st	DP	Priv	Atty	Un'n	Econ	JudP	Fed	IR	FTax	Misc	Total
1946	20 (.14)	6 (.04)	8 (.06)	4 (.03)	1 (.01)	0 (.00)	15 (.11)	48 (.34)	19 (.14)	5 (.04)	4 (.03)	10 (.07)	0 (.00)	140
1947	23 (.20)	18 (.16)	5 (.04)	12 (.11)	0 (.00)	0 (.00)	4 (.04)	29 (.25)	16 (.14)	1 (.01)	2 (.02)	4 (.04)	0 (.00)	114
1948	22 (.18)	8 (.07)	3 (.03)	6 (.05)	0 (.00)	0 (.00)	8 (.07)	42 (.35)	13 (.11)	7 (.06)	2 (.02)	10 (.08)	0 (.00)	121
1949	9 (.10)	10 (.11)	7 (.08)	8 (.09)	0 (.00)	1 (.01)	2 (.02)	24 (.26)	16 (.17)	7 (.08)	0 (.00)	9 (.10)	0 (.00)	93
1950	9 (.09)	12 (.13)	8 (.08)	2 (.02)	1 (.01)	0 (.00)	4 (.04)	32 (.33)	19 (.20)	2 (.02)	2 (.02)	5 (.05)	0 (.00)	96
1951	17 (.19)	8 (.09)	6 (.07)	6 (.07)	1 (.01)	0 (.00)	2 (.02)	29 (.32)	16 (.18)	0 (.00)	2 (.02)	3 (.03)	1 (.01)	91
1952	15 (.14)	10 (.09)	6 (.06)	8 (.08)	1 (.01)	0 (.00)	8 (.08)	23 (.22)	19 (.18)	7 (.07)	0 (.00)	9 (.09)	0 (.00)	106
1953	15 (.18)	8 (.10)	4 (.05)	1 (.01)	0 (.00)	0 (.00)	6 (.07)	33 (.39)	8 (.10)	6 (.07)	0 (.00)	3 (.04)	0 (.00)	84
1954	18 (.19)	10 (.11)	5 (.05)	3 (.03)	0 (.00)	1 (.01)	4 (.04)	23 (.25)	13 (.14)	4 (.04)	0 (.00)	11 (.12)	1 (.01)	93
1955	12 (.12)	11 (.11)	5 (.05)	2 (.02)	0 (.00)	0 (.00)	10 (.10)	29 (.30)	13 (.13)	3 (.03)	3 (.03)	7 (.07)	3 (.03)	98

Year													Total
1956	20 (.17)	12 (.10)	9 (.07)	4 (.03)	0 (.00)	3 (.02)	11 (.09)	32 (.26)	17 (.14)	5 (.04)	0 (.00)	8 (.07)	0 (.00)	121
1957	32 (.25)	14 (.11)	9 (.07)	6 (.05)	1 (.01)	1 (.01)	4 (.03)	30 (.24)	16 (.13)	5 (.04)	0 (.00)	9 (.07)	0 (.00)	127
1958	26 (.22)	6 (.05)	11 (.09)	0 (.00)	0 (.00)	0 (.00)	5 (.04)	44 (.37)	13 (.11)	5 (.04)	2 (.02)	6 (.05)	0 (.00)	118
1959	16 (.14)	10 (.09)	7 (.06)	3 (.03)	0 (.00)	0 (.00)	14 (.12)	28 (.24)	16 (.14)	7 (.06)	0 (.00)	14 (.12)	0 (.00)	115
1960	30 (.23)	14 (.11)	22 (.17)	1 (.01)	0 (.00)	0 (.00)	11 (.09)	27 (.21)	11 (.09)	2 (.02)	0 (.00)	10 (.08)	0 (.00)	128
1961	17 (.17)	9 (.09)	8 (.08)	5 (.05)	0 (.00)	0 (.00)	9 (.09)	29 (.29)	11 (.11)	5 (.05)	0 (.00)	7 (.07)	1 (.01)	101
1962	21 (.17)	17 (.14)	8 (.06)	3 (.02)	0 (.00)	1 (.01)	10 (.08)	35 (.28)	12 (.10)	10 (.08)	0 (.00)	8 (.06)	0 (.00)	125
1963	22 (.17)	27 (.21)	9 (.07)	0 (.00)	0 (.00)	0 (.00)	9 (.07)	30 (.23)	16 (.12)	9 (.07)	2 (.02)	6 (.05)	0 (.00)	130
1964	16 (.15)	14 (.13)	10 (.10)	2 (.02)	1 (.01)	0 (.00)	11 (.10)	18 (.17)	19 (.18)	3 (.03)	2 (.02)	9 (.08)	0 (.00)	105
1965	16 (.16)	14 (.14)	13 (.13)	3 (.03)	0 (.00)	0 (.00)	3 (.03)	25 (.25)	15 (.15)	4 (.04)	0 (.00)	8 (.08)	0 (.00)	101
1966	28 (.25)	19 (.17)	11 (.10)	0 (.00)	0 (.00)	1 (.01)	7 (.06)	23 (.21)	18 (.16)	3 (.03)	0 (.00)	2 (.02)	0 (.00)	112

(Table continues)

Table 2-11 *(Continued)*

Term	Crim	Civ	1st	DP	Priv	Atty	Un'n	Econ	JudP	Fed	IR	FTax	Misc	Total
1967	36 (.30)	16 (.13)	13 (.11)	1 (.01)	0 (.00)	3 (.02)	9 (.07)	25 (.20)	10 (.08)	6 (.05)	0 (.00)	3 (.02)	0 (.00)	122
1968	27 (.24)	23 (.21)	10 (.09)	3 (.03)	0 (.00)	0 (.00)	4 (.04)	17 (.15)	19 (.17)	4 (.04)	0 (.00)	4 (.04)	0 (.00)	111
1969	27 (.25)	26 (.24)	10 (.09)	1 (.01)	0 (.00)	1 (.01)	6 (.06)	10 (.09)	14 (.13)	4 (.04)	1 (.01)	7 (.07)	0 (.00)	107
1970	24 (.19)	27 (.22)	22 (.18)	4 (.03)	1 (.01)	1 (.01)	9 (.07)	16 (.13)	15 (.12)	1 (.01)	0 (.00)	4 (.03)	0 (.00)	124
1971	34 (.23)	28 (.19)	16 (.11)	11 (.07)	1 (.01)	0 (.00)	7 (.05)	32 (.22)	11 (.07)	1 (.01)	2 (.01)	4 (.03)	0 (.00)	147
1972	35 (.23)	33 (.22)	18 (.12)	5 (.03)	3 (.02)	1 (.01)	6 (.04)	29 (.19)	15 (.10)	3 (.02)	2 (.01)	3 (.02)	0 (.00)	153
1973	30 (.20)	36 (.24)	14 (.09)	6 (.04)	1 (.01)	2 (.01)	8 (.05)	21 (.14)	19 (.13)	4 (.03)	1 (.01)	6 (.04)	0 (.00)	148
1974	24 (.17)	29 (.21)	8 (.06)	7 (.05)	3 (.02)	1 (.01)	6 (.04)	28 (.20)	21 (.15)	8 (.06)	0 (.00)	4 (.03)	0 (.00)	139
1975	33 (.22)	28 (.19)	13 (.09)	13 (.09)	2 (.01)	0 (.00)	5 (.03)	28 (.19)	23 (.15)	3 (.02)	2 (.01)	1 (.01)	0 (.00)	151

Year														Total
1976	30 (.21)	35 (.24)	12 (.08)	7 (.05)	5 (.03)	1 (.01)	7 (.05)	19 (.13)	15 (.10)	7 (.05)	1 (.01)	4 (.03)	0 (.00)	143
1977	29 (.21)	26 (.19)	8 (.06)	5 (.04)	1 (.01)	4 (.03)	5 (.04)	30 (.22)	14 (.10)	5 (.04)	0 (.00)	7 (.05)	1 (.01)	135
1978	29 (.22)	34 (.25)	8 (.06)	8 (.06)	4 (.03)	0 (.00)	5 (.04)	27 (.20)	12 (.09)	3 (.02)	0 (.00)	4 (.03)	0 (.00)	134
1979	32 (.23)	22 (.16)	10 (.07)	11 (.08)	6 (.04)	4 (.03)	6 (.04)	31 (.22)	13 (.09)	2 (.01)	4 (.03)	0 (.00)	0 (.00)	141
1980	25 (.20)	27 (.21)	9 (.07)	6 (.05)	1 (.01)	0 (.00)	8 (.06)	25 (.20)	17 (.13)	5 (.04)	0 (.00)	4 (.03)	1 (.01)	128
1981	19 (.13)	34 (.23)	12 (.08)	9 (.06)	4 (.03)	3 (.02)	9 (.06)	25 (.17)	23 (.16)	5 (.03)	0 (.00)	3 (.02)	2 (.01)	148
1982	30 (.19)	27 (.17)	11 (.07)	7 (.05)	4 (.03)	2 (.01)	7 (.05)	33 (.21)	16 (.10)	10 (.06)	2 (.01)	4 (.03)	2 (.01)	155
1983	40 (.26)	29 (.19)	12 (.08)	10 (.06)	2 (.01)	2 (.01)	6 (.04)	27 (.17)	13 (.08)	8 (.05)	2 (.01)	4 (.03)	0 (.00)	155
1984	33 (.23)	25 (.18)	11 (.08)	11 (.08)	1 (.01)	6 (.04)	5 (.04)	30 (.21)	8 (.06)	8 (.06)	0 (.00)	4 (.03)	0 (.00)	142
1985	43 (.28)	29 (.19)	14 (.09)	7 (.05)	1 (.01)	4 (.03)	3 (.02)	16 (.10)	20 (.13)	10 (.07)	0 (.00)	5 (.03)	1 (.01)	153
1986	41 (.27)	24 (.16)	12 (.08)	12 (.08)	1 (.01)	3 (.02)	5 (.03)	23 (.15)	15 (.10)	11 (.07)	1 (.01)	4 (.03)	1 (.01)	153

(Table continues)

Table 2-11 (*Continued*)

Term	Crim	Civ	1st	DP	Priv	Atty	Un'n	Econ	JudP	Fed	IR	FTax	Misc	Total
1987	31 (.22)	21 (.15)	12 (.08)	9 (.06)	1 (.01)	3 (.02)	7 (.05)	26 (.18)	20 (.14)	9 (.06)	0 (.00)	3 (.02)	2 (.01)	144
1988	30 (.21)	26 (.18)	15 (.11)	5 (.04)	4 (.03)	5 (.04)	5 (.04)	17 (.12)	19 (.14)	9 (.06)	0 (.00)	4 (.03)	2 (.01)	141
1989	35 (.27)	9 (.07)	14 (.11)	5 (.04)	3 (.02)	4 (.03)	4 (.03)	22 (.17)	18 (.14)	9 (.07)	1 (.01)	7 (.05)	0 (.00)	131
1990	29 (.25)	16 (.14)	5 (.04)	3 (.03)	1 (.01)	2 (.02)	8 (.07)	24 (.21)	16 (.14)	4 (.04)	2 (.02)	2 (.02)	2 (.02)	114
1991	21 (.19)	18 (.16)	8 (.07)	6 (.06)	2 (.02)	2 (.02)	1 (.01)	27 (.25)	16 (.15)	5 (.05)	0 (.00)	4 (.04)	0 (.00)	110
1992	28 (.25)	15 (.14)	8 (.07)	1 (.01)	1 (.01)	2 (.01)	2 (.02)	18 (.16)	21 (.19)	7 (.06)	2 (.02)	6 (.05)	0 (.00)	111
1993	23 (.27)	12 (.14)	4 (.05)	3 (.04)	3 (.04)	2 (.02)	1 (.01)	22 (.26)	9 (.11)	5 (.06)	0 (.00)	2 (.02)	0 (.00)	86
1994	19 (.22)	10 (.12)	8 (.09)	2 (.02)	0 (.00)	1 (.01)	0 (.00)	17 (.20)	16 (.19)	7 (.08)	2 (.02)	2 (.02)	1 (.01)	85
1995	18 (.24)	8 (.11)	5 (.07)	5 (.07)	0 (.00)	0 (.00)	4 (.05)	16 (.21)	11 (.15)	4 (.05)	1 (.01)	4 (.05)	0 (.00)	76

	Crim	Civ	1st	DP	Priv	Atty	Un'n	Econ	JudP	Fed	IR	FTax	Misc	N
1996	17 (.21)	16 (.19)	5 (.06)	5 (.06)	3 (.04)	0 (.00)	1 (.01)	16 (.19)	9 (.11)	7 (.08)	0 (.00)	3 (.04)	1 (.01)	83
1997	25 (.27)	17 (.19)	2 (.02)	4 (.04)	0 (.00)	0 (.00)	2 (.02)	15 (.16)	20 (.22)	1 (.01)	1 (.01)	3 (.03)	1 (.02)	92
1998	16 (.20)	18 (.23)	2 (.03)	4 (.05)	0 (.00)	1 (.01)	4 (.05)	14 (.18)	13 (.17)	6 (.08)	0 (.00)	0 (.00)	1 (.01)	79
1999	26 (.35)	10 (.14)	8 (.11)	2 (.03)	3 (.04)	0 (.00)	1 (.01)	10 (.14)	6 (.08)	6 (.08)	0 (.00)	2 (.03)	0 (.00)	74
2000	19 (.26)	13 (.18)	6 (.08)	5 (.07)	1 (.01)	1 (.01)	2 (.03)	9 (.12)	10 (.14)	3 (.04)	2 (.03)	3 (.04)	0 (.00)	74
2001	15 (.20)	12 (.16)	9 (.12)	3 (.04)	3 (.04)	1 (.01)	3 (.04)	10 (.13)	13 (.17)	6 (.08)	—	2 (.03)	—	77

Note: Formally decided cases include those with signed opinions and orally argued per curiams. Figures listed are the number of cases in each issue area. Figures in parentheses are the proportion of cases falling into that area each term.

The issue areas are defined as follows: Criminal procedure (Crim): the rights of persons accused of crime except for the due process rights of prisoners; Civil rights (Civ): non–First Amendment freedom cases that pertain to classifications based on race (including Native Americans), age, indigence, voting, residence, military or handicapped status, sex, or alienage; First Amendment (1st): guarantees contained therein; Due process (DP): noncriminal procedural guarantees, plus court jurisdiction over nonresident litigants and the takings clause of the Fifth Amendment; Privacy (Priv): abortion, contraception, the Freedom of Information Act and related federal statutes; Attorneys (Atty): attorneys' fees, commercial speech, admission to and removal from the bar, and disciplinary matters; Unions (Un'n): labor union activity; Economics (Econ): commercial business activity, plus litigation involving injured persons or things, employee actions vis-à-vis employers, zoning regulations, and governmental regulation of corruption other than that involving campaign spending; Judicial power (JudP): the exercise of the judiciary's own power and authority; Federalism (Fed): conflicts between the federal and state governments, excluding those between state and federal courts and those involving the priority of federal fiscal claims; Interstate relations (IR): conflicts between states, boundary disputes, and nonproperty disputes commonly arising under the full faith and credit clause of the Constitution; Federal taxation (FTax): the Internal Revenue Code and related statutes; Miscellaneous (Misc): legislative veto, separation of powers, and matters not included in any other issue area.

Source: U.S. Supreme Court Judicial Database, with analu = 0 and dec_type = 1, 6, or 7.

Table 2-12 Major Decisions of the Court: Congressional Quarterly, 1790–2002

Case name	Cite	Vote	Majority opinion writer[a]	Dissenters	Justices not participating
Chisholm v. Georgia	2 Dall. 419 (1793)	4–1	Jay[b]	Iredell	
Hylton v. United States	3 Dall. 171 (February 1796 term)	3–0	Chase, Paterson, Iredell[b]		Cushing, Wilson (but submitted an opinion), Ellsworth
Ware v. Hylton	3 Dall. 199 (1796)	4–0	Chase[b]		Iredell (but submitted an opinion)
Calder v. Bull	3 Dall. 386 (August 1798 term)	4–0	Chase[b]		
Marbury v. Madison	1 Cr. 137 (1803)	Decided without dissent	Marshall		Cushing, Moore
Bank of United States v. Deveaux	5 Cr. 61 (1809)	Decided without dissent	Marshall		Livingston
Fletcher v. Peck	6 Cr. 87 (1810)	Decided without dissent	Marshall		Chase, Cushing
Martin v. Hunter's Lessee	1 Wheat. 304 (1816)	Decided without dissent	Story		Marshall
Sturges v. Crowninshield	4 Wheat. 122 (1819)	Decided without dissent	Marshall		Todd

McCulloch v. Maryland	4 Wheat. 316 (1819)	Decided without dissent	Marshall		Todd
Dartmouth College v. Woodward	4 Wheat. 519 (1819)	5–1	Marshall	Duvall	Todd
Cohens v. Virginia	6 Wheat. 264 (1821)	Decided without dissent	Marshall		Washington
Gibbons v. Ogden	9 Wheat. 1 (1824)	Decided without dissent	Marshall		
Osborn v. Bank of the United States	9 Wheat. 738 (1824)	Decided with one dissenting vote	Marshall	Johnson	
Wayman v. Southard	10 Wheat. 1 (1825)	Decided without dissent	Marshall		Todd
Martin v. Mott	12 Wheat. 19 (January 1827 term)	Decided without dissent	Story		
Ogden v. Saunders	12 Wheat. 213 (1827)	4–3	Washington	Marshall, Story, Duvall	
Mason v. Haile	12 Wheat. 370 (January 1827 term)	6–1	Thompson	Washington	
Brown v. Maryland	12 Wheat. 419 (1827)	6–1	Marshall	Thompson	
Willson v. Blackbird Creek Marsh Co.	2 Pet. 245 (January 1829 term)	Decided without dissent	Marshall		

(Table continues)

Table 2-12 (Continued)

Case name	Cite	Vote	Majority opinion writer[a]	Dissenters	Justices not participating
Foster v. Neilson	2 Pet. 253 (January 1829 term)	Decided without dissent	Marshall		
Weston v. City Council of Charleston	2 Pet. 449 (1829)	4–2	Marshall	Johnson, Thompson	
Craig v. Missouri	4 Pet. 410 (1830)	4–3	Marshall	Johnson, Thompson, McLean	
Worcester v. Georgia	6 Pet. 515 (1832)	5–1	Marshall	Baldwin	Johnson
Barron v. Baltimore	7 Pet. 243 (January 1833 term)	Decided without dissent	Marshall		Baldwin
New York v. Miln	11 Pet. 102 (January 1837 term)	6–1	Barbour	Story	
Briscoe v. Bank of the Commonwealth of Kentucky	11 Pet. 257 (1837)	6–1	McLean	Story	
Charles River Bridge v. Warren Bridge	11 Pet. 420 (January 1837 term)	5–2	Taney	Story, Thompson	
Kendall v. United States ex rel. Stokes	12 Pet. 524 (January 1838 term)	9–0, 6–3	Thompson	Taney, Barbour, Catron (in part)	
Holmes v. Jennison	14 Pet. 540 (January 1840 term)	4–4	Taney (for Story, McLean, and Wayne); Barbour, Baldwin, Catron, and Thompson filed separate opinions		McKinley

Dobbins v. Erie County	16 Pet. 435 (January 1842 term)	Decided without dissent	Wayne			
Prigg v. Pennsylvania	16 Pet. 539 (1842)	9–0, 6–3	Story		Taney (in part), Thompson (in part), Daniel (in part)	
Louisville Railroad Company v. Letson	2 How. 497 (1844)	Decided without dissent	Wayne			Taney
Rhode Island v. Massachusetts	4 How. 591 (January 1846 term)	8–0, 7–1	McLean		Taney (in part)	
Thurlow v. Massachusetts, Fletcher v. Rhode Island, Peirce v. New Hampshire (The License Cases)	5 How. 504 (1847)	Decided without dissent	Taney, McLean, Catron, Daniel, Woodbury, and Grier all wrote separate opinions			
Luther v. Borden	7 How. 1 (1849)	5–1	Taney		Woodbury	
Smith v. Turner, Norris v. Boston (The Passenger Cases)	7 How. 283 (1849)	5–4	McLean		Taney, Daniel, Nelson, Woodbury	Catron, McKinley, Daniel
Cooley v. Board of Wardens of Port of Philadelphia	12 How. 299 (December 1851 term)	7–2	Curtis		McLean, Wayne	
Pennsylvania v. Wheeling and Belmont Bridge	13 How. 518 (1852)	7–2	McLean		Taney, Daniel	

(*Table continues*)

Table 2-12 (Continued)

Case name	Cite	Vote	Majority opinion writer[a]	Dissenters	Justices not participating
Murray's Lessee v. Hoboken Land and Improvement Co.	18 How. 272 (1856)	Decided by unanimous vote	Curtis		
Dodge v. Woolsey	18 How. 331 (1856)	6–3	Wayne	Campbell, Catron, Daniel	
Scott v. Sandford	19 How. 393 (1857)	7–2	Each justice submitted a separate opinion; Taney's is considered the formal opinion of the Court	McLean, Curtis	
Ableman v. Booth, United States v. Booth	21 How. 506 (1859)	Decided by a unanimous Court	Taney		
Kentucky v. Dennison	24 How. 66 (1861)	Decided by a unanimous Court	Taney		
The Prize Cases	2 Black 635 (1863)	5–4	Grier	Taney, Catron, Clifford, Nelson	
Ex parte Milligan	4 Wall. 2 (1866)	9–0, 5–4	Davis	Chase (in part), Miller (in part), Swayne (in part), Wayne (in part)	

Case	Citation	Vote	Opinion	Dissent
Cummings v. Missouri, Ex parte Garland	4 Wall. 277, 333 (1867)	5–4 in both cases	Field	Chase, Swayne, Davis, Miller
Mississippi v. Johnson	4 Wall. 475 (1867)	Decided by a unanimous Court	Chase	
Ex parte McCardle	7 Wall. 506 (1869)	Decided by unanimous vote	Chase	
Texas v. White	7 Wall. 700 (1869)	7–2	Chase	Swayne (in part), Grier (in part)
Woodruff v. Parham	8 Wall. 123 (1869)	Decided without dissent	Miller	
Paul v. Virginia	8 Wall. 168 (1869)	Decided by unanimous vote	Field	
Veazie Bank v. Fenno	8 Wall. 533 (1869)	7–2	Chase	Nelson, Davis
Hepburn v. Griswold (First Legal Tender Case)	8 Wall. 603 (187)	4–3	Chase	Davis, Miller, Swayne
Knox v. Lee, Parker v. Davis (Second Legal Tender Case)	12 Wall. 457 (1871)	5–4	Strong	Chase, Nelson, Clifford, Field
Low v. Austin	13 Wall. 29 (1872)	Decided by unanimous vote	Field	

(Table continues)

Table 2-12 (*Continued*)

Case name	Cite	Vote	Majority opinion writer[a]	Dissenters	Justices not participating
Bradley v. Fisher	13 Wall. 335 (1872)	7–2	Field	Davis, Clifford	
The Butchers' Benevolent Association of New Orleans v. The Crescent City Livestock Landing and Slaughterhouse Co., Esteben v. Louisiana (The Slaughterhouse Cases)	16 Wall. 36 (1873)	5–4	Miller	Chase, Field, Swayne, Bradley	
Bradwell v. State of Illinois	16 Wall. 130 (1873)	8–1	Miller	Chase	
Minor v. Happersett	21 Wall. 162 (1875)	Decided by unanimous vote	Waite		
Walker v. Sauvinet	92 U.S. 90 (1876)	7–2	Waite	Clifford, Field	
United States v. Reese	92 U.S. 214 (1876)	7–2	Waite	Hunt, Clifford	
Henderson v. Wickham, Commissioners of Immigration v. The North German Lloyd, Chy Lung v. Freeman	92 U.S. 259, 275 (1876)	Decided without dissent	Miller		

United States v. Cruikshank	92 U.S. 542 (1876)	8–1	Waite	Clifford	
Munn v. Illinois	94 U.S. 113 (1877)	7–2	Waite	Field, Strong	
Hall v. DeCuir	95 U.S. 485 (1878)	Decided without dissent	Waite		
Ex parte Siebold	100 U.S. 371 (1880)	7–2	Bradley	Field, Clifford	
Stone v. Mississippi	101 U.S. 814 (1880)	Decided without dissent	Waite		
Kilbourn v. Thompson	103 U.S. 168 (1881)	Decided by unanimous vote	Miller		
Civil Rights Cases	109 U.S. 3 (1883)	8–1	Bradley	Harlan	
Hurtado v. California	110 U.S. 516 (1884)	7–1	Matthews	Harlan	Field
Ex parte Yarbrough	110 U.S. 651 (1884)	Decided by unanimous vote	Miller		
Head Money Cases	112 U.S. 580 (1884)	Decided by unanimous vote	Miller		
Boyd v. United States	116 U.S. 616 (1886)	Decided without dissent	Bradley		

(Table continues)

Table 2-12 *(Continued)*

Case name	Cite	Vote	Majority opinion writer[a]	Dissenters	Justices not participating
Yick Wo v. Hopkins	118 U.S. 356 (1886)	Decided by unanimous vote	Matthews		
Santa Clara County v. Southern Pacific Railroad Co.	118 U.S. 394 (1886)	Decided by unanimous vote	Harlan wrote the opinion; Waite made a preliminary announcement		
Wabash, St. Louis and Pacific Railway Co. v. Illinois	118 U.S. 557 (1886)	6–3	Miller	Waite, Bradley, Gray	
Mugler v. Kansas	123 U.S. 623 (1887)	8–1	Harlan	Field	
Wisconsin v. Pelican Insurance Company	127 U.S. 265 (1888)	Decided without dissent	Gray		
Kidd v. Pearson	128 U.S. 1 (1888)	Decided without dissent	Lamar		
Chae Chan Ping v. United States (Chinese Exclusion Cases)	130 U.S. 581 (1889)	Decided by unanimous vote	Field		
Geofroy v. Riggs	133 U.S. 258 (1890)	Decided by unanimous vote	Field		

Case	Citation	Vote		
Louisville, New Orleans and Texas Railway Co. v. Mississippi	133 U.S. 587 (1890)	7–2	Brewer	Harlan, Bradley
Chicago, Milwaukee & St. Paul Railway Co. v. Minnesota	134 U.S. 418 (1890)	6–3	Blatchford	Bradley, Gray, Lamar
Counselman v. Hitchcock	142 U.S. 547 (1892)	Decided by unanimous vote	Blatchford	
United States v. Texas	143 U.S. 621 (1892)	7–2	Harlan	Fuller, Lamar
Virginia v. Tennessee	148 U.S. 503 (1893)	Decided without dissent	Field	
United States v. E. C. Knight	156 U.S. 1 (1895)	8–1	Fuller	Harlan
California v. Southern Pacific Co.	157 U.S. 229 (1895)	7–2	Fuller	Harlan, Brewer
In re Debs	158 U.S. 564 (1895)	9–0	Brewer	
Pollock v. Farmers' Loan and Trust Co.	158 U.S. 601 (1895)	5–4	Fuller	Harlan, Jackson, Brown, White
Plessy v. Ferguson	163 U.S. 537 (1896)	7–1	Brown	Harlan
Allgeyer v. Louisiana	165 U.S. 578 (1897)	Decided without dissent	Peckham	Brewer
Chicago, Burlington & Quincy Railroad Company v. Chicago	166 U.S. 226 (1897)	7–1	Harlan	Brewer

(Table continues)

Table 2-12 *(Continued)*

Case name	Cite	Vote	Majority opinion writer[a]	Dissenters	Justices not participating
Holden v. Hardy	169 U.S. 366 (1898)	7–2	Brown	Brewer, Peckham	
Smyth v. Ames	169 U.S. 466 (1898)	7–0	Harlan		Fuller, McKenna
United States v. Wong Kim Ark	169 U.S. 649 (1898)	6–2	Gray	Fuller, Harlan	McKenna
Williams v. Mississippi	170 U.S. 213 (1898)	Decided by unanimous vote	McKenna		
Maxwell v. Dow	176 U.S. 581 (1900)	8–1	Peckham	Harlan	
Knowlton v. Moore	178 U.S. 41 (1900)	5–3	White	Harlan, McKenna, Brewer (in part)	Peckham
The Insular Cases: DeLima v. Bidwell	182 U.S. 1 (1901)	5–4	Brown	Gray, McKenna, Shiras, White	
The Insular Cases: Downes v. Bidwell	182 U.S. 244 (1901)	5–4	Brown	Fuller, Harlan, Brewer, Peckham	
Champion v. Ames	188 U.S. 321 (1903)	5–4	Harlan	Fuller, Brewer Peckham, Shiras	
Northern Securities Co. v. United States	193 U.S. 197 (1904)	5–4	Harlan	Fuller, White, Holmes, Peckham	
McCray v. United States	195 U.S. 27 (1904)	6–3	White	Fuller, Brown, Peckham	

Case	Citation	Vote	Opinion	Dissenting	Not Participating
Swift and Co. v. United States	196 U.S. 375 (1905)	Decided by unanimous vote	Holmes		
Lochner v. New York	198 U.S. 45 (1905)	5–4	Peckham	Day, Harlan, Holmes, White	
Georgia v. Tennessee Copper Company	206 U.S. 230 (1907)	Decided by unanimous vote	Holmes		
Adair v. United States	208 U.S. 161 (1908)	6–2	Harlan	Holmes, McKenna	Moody
Loewe v. Lawler (Danbury Hatters Case)	208 U.S. 274 (1908)	Decided by unanimous vote	Fuller		
Muller v. Oregon	208 U.S. 412 (1908)	Decided by unanimous vote	Brewer		
Ex parte Young	209 U.S. 123 (1908)	8–1	Peckham	Harlan	
Twining v. New Jersey	211 U.S. 78 (1908)	8–1	Moody	Harlan	
Weems v. United States	217 U.S. 349 (1910)	6–2	McKenna	White, Holmes	Lurton
Muskrat v. United States	219 U.S. 346 (1911)	Decided by unanimous vote	Day		
Standard Oil Co. v. United States	221 U.S. 1 (1911)	8–1	White	Harlan (in part)	

(Table continues)

Table 2-12 (Continued)

Case name	Cite	Vote	Majority opinion writer[a]	Dissenters	Justices not participating
Gompers v. Buck's Stove and Range Co.	221 U.S. 418 (1911)	Decided by un-animous vote	Lamar		
Coyle v. Smith	221 U.S. 559 (1911)	7–2	Lurton	McKenna, Holmes	
Weeks v. United States	232 U.S. 383 (1914)	Decided by un-animous vote	Day		
Houston, East and West Texas Railway Co. v. United States, Texas and Pacific Railway Co. v. United States (Shreveport Rate Case)	234 U.S. 342 (1914)	7–2	Hughes	Lurton, Pitney	
Frank v. Mangum	237 U.S. 309 (1915)	7–2	Pitney	Holmes, Hughes	
Virginia v. West Virginia	238 U.S. 202 (1915)	Decided by un-animous vote	Hughes		
Guinn v. United States	238 U.S. 347 (1915)	8–0	White		McReynolds
United States v. Mosley	238 U.S. 383 (1915)	7–1	Holmes	Lamar	McReynolds
Hadacheck v. Los Angeles	239 U.S. 394 (1915)	Decided by un-animous vote	McKenna		

Case	Citation	Vote	Opinion	Dissenting	
Brushaber v. Union Pacific Railroad Co.	240 U.S. 1 (1916)	8–0	White	McReynolds	
Clark Distilling Co. v. Western Maryland Railway	242 U.S. 311 (1917)	7–2	White	Holmes, Van Devanter	
Bunting v. Oregon	243 U.S. 426 (1917)	5–3	McKenna	White, McReynolds, Van Devanter	Brandeis
Buchanan v. Warley	245 U.S. 60 (1917)	9–0	Day		
Selective Draft Law Cases	245 U.S. 366 (1918)	9–0	White		
Hammer v. Dagenhart	247 U.S. 251 (1918)	5–4	Day	Holmes, McKenna, Brandeis, Clarke	
Schenck v. United States	249 U.S. 47 (1919)	9–0	Holmes		
Missouri v. Holland	252 U.S. 416 (1920)	7–2	Holmes	Van Devanter, Pitney	
Duplex Printing Press Co. v. Deering	254 U.S. 443 (1921)	6–3	Pitney	Brandeis, Holmes, Clarke	
Newberry v. United States	256 U.S. 232 (1921)	5–4	McReynolds	White, (in part) Pitney, (in part) Brandeis, Clarke	
Dillon v. Gloss	256 U.S. 368 (1921)	Decided by unanimous vote	Van Devanter		
Ponzi v. Fessenden	258 U.S. 254 (1922)	Decided by unanimous vote	Taft		
Bailey v. Drexel Furniture Co.	259 U.S. 20 (1922)	8–1	Taft	Clarke	

(Table continues)

99

Table 2-12 (Continued)

Case name	Cite	Vote	Majority opinion writer[a]	Dissenters	Justices not participating
United States v. Lanza	260 U.S. 377 (1922)	8–0	Taft		
Moore v. Dempsey	261 U.S. 86 (1923)	6–2	Holmes	McReynolds, Sutherland	
Adkins v. Children's Hospital	261 U.S. 525 (1923)	5–3	Sutherland	Taft, Holmes, Sanford	Brandeis
Massachusetts v. Mellon, Frothingham v. Mellon	262 U.S. 447 (1923)	Decided by un-animous vote	Sutherland		
Carroll v. United States	267 U.S. 132 (1925)	7–2	Taft	McReynolds, Sutherland	
Pierce v. Society of Sisters	268 U.S. 510 (1925)	Decided by un-animous vote	McReynolds		
Gitlow v. New York	268 U.S. 652 (1925)	7–2	Sanford	Holmes, Brandeis	
Corrigan v. Buckley	271 U.S. 323 (1926)	Decided by un-animous vote	Sanford		
Myers v. United States	272 U.S. 52 (1926)	6–3	Taft	Holmes, Brandeis, McReynolds	

Case	Citation	Vote			
Euclid v. Ambler Realty Co.	272 U.S. 365 (1926)	6–3	Sutherland	Butler, McReynolds, Van Devanter	
Tumey v. Ohio	273 U.S. 510 (1927)	Decided by unanimous vote	Taft		
Nixon v. Herndon	273 U.S. 536 (1927)	Decided by unanimous vote	Holmes		
Buck v. Bell	274 U.S. 200 (1927)	8–1	Holmes	Butler	
Whitney v. California	274 U.S. 357 (1927)	Decided by unanimous vote	Sanford		
J. W. Hampton Jr. & Co. v. United States	276 U.S. 394 (1928)	Decided by unanimous vote	Taft		
Olmstead v. United States	277 U.S. 438 (1928)	5–4	Taft	Brandeis, Holmes, Butler, Stone	
Patton v. United States	281 U.S. 276 (1930)	7–0	Sutherland		Hughes
Stromberg v. California	283 U.S. 359 (1931)	7–2	Hughes	McReynolds, Butler	
Near v. Minnesota	283 U.S. 697 (1931)	5–4	Hughes	Butler, Van Devanter, McReynolds, Sutherland	
Nixon v. Condon	286 U.S. 73 (1932)	5–4	Cardozo	McReynolds, Butler, Sutherland, Van Devanter	

(Table continues)

Table 2-12 (*Continued*)

Case name	Cite	Vote	Majority opinion writer[a]	Dissenters	Justices not participating
Wood v. Broom	287 U.S. 1 (1932)	5–4	Hughes	Brandeis, Stone, Cardozo, Roberts	
Powell v. Alabama	287 U.S. 45 (1932)	6–2	Sutherland	Butler, McReynolds	
Home Building and Loan Assn. v. Blaisdell	290 U.S. 398 (1934)	5–4	Hughes	Sutherland, Van Devanter, Butler, McReynolds	
Nebbia v. New York	291 U.S. 502 (1934)	5–4	Roberts	McReynolds, Butler, Van Devanter, Sutherland	
Panama Refining Co. v. Ryan	293 U.S. 388 (1935)	8–1	Hughes	Cardozo	
Gold Clause Cases: Norman v. Baltimore & Ohio Railroad Co., Nortz v. United States, Perry v. United States	294 U.S. 240, 317, 330 (1935)	5–4	Hughes	McReynolds, Butler, Sutherland, Van Devanter	
Norris v. Alabama	294 U.S. 587 (1935)	8–0	Hughes		McReynolds
Railroad Retirement Board v. Alton Railroad Co.	295 U.S. 330 (1935)	5–4	Roberts	Hughes, Brandeis, Cardozo, Stone	
Grovey v. Townsend	295 U.S. 45 (1935)	Decided by un-animous vote	Roberts		

Case	Citation	Vote	Opinion	Other
Schechter Poultry Corp. v. United States	295 U.S. 495 (1935)	Decided by unanimous vote	Hughes	
Humphrey's Executor v. United States	295 U.S. 602 (1935)	Decided by unanimous vote	Sutherland	
United States v. Butler	297 U.S. 1 (1936)	6–3	Roberts	Stone, Brandeis, Cardozo
Grosjean v. American Press Co.	297 U.S. 233 (1936)	Decided by unanimous vote	Sutherland	
Brown v. Mississippi	297 U.S. 278 (1936)	Decided by a unanimous Court	Hughes	
Ashwander v. Tennessee Valley Authority	297 U.S. 288 (1936)	8–1, 5–4	Hughes	McReynolds, Brandeis, Stone, Roberts, Cardozo (all in part)
Carter v. Carter Coal Co.	298 U.S. 238 (1936)	6–3	Sutherland	Cardozo, Brandeis, Stone
Moorehead v. New York ex rel. Tipaldo	298 U.S. 587 (1936)	5–4	Butler	Hughes, Brandeis, Cardozo, Stone
United States v. Curtiss-Wright Export Corp.	299 U.S. 304 (1936)	7–1	Sutherland	McReynolds

(Table continues)

Table 2-12 (Continued)

Case name	Cite	Vote	Majority opinion writer[a]	Dissenters	Justices not participating
DeJonge v. Oregon	299 U.S. 353 (1937)	8–0	Hughes		Stone
West Coast Hotel Co. v. Parrish	300 U.S. 379 (1937)	5–4	Hughes	Butler, McReynolds, Sutherland, Van Devanter	
National Labor Relations Board v. Jones & Laughlin Steel Corp.	301 U.S. 1 (1937)	5–4	Hughes	McReynolds, Butler, Sutherland, Van Devanter	
Steward Machine Co. v. Davis	301 U.S. 548 (1937)	5–4	Cardozo	McReynolds, Butler, Sutherland, Van Devanter	
Helvering v. Davis	301 U.S. 619 (1937)	7–2	Cardozo	McReynolds, Butler	
Breedlove v. Suttles	302 U.S. 277 (1937)	Decided by unanimous vote	Butler		
Palko v. Connecticut	302 U.S. 319 (1937)	8–1	Cardozo	Butler	
Lovell v. Griffin	303 U.S. 444 (1938)	8–0	Hughes		Cardozo
Johnson v. Zerbst	304 U.S. 458 (1938)	6–2	Black	McReynolds, Butler	Cardozo
Missouri ex rel. Gaines v. Canada	305 U.S. 337 (1938)	7–2	Hughes	McReynolds, Butler	
Graves v. New York ex rel. O'Keefe	306 U.S. 466 (1939)	7–2	Stone	Butler, McReynolds	
Mulford v. Smith	307 U.S. 38 (1939)	7–2	Roberts	Butler, McReynolds	

Case	Citation	Vote	Opinion of the Court	Dissenting	Concurring
Lane v. Wilson	307 U.S. 268 (1939)	6–2	Frankfurter	McReynolds, Butler	Douglas
Coleman v. Miller	307 U.S. 433 (1939)	7–2	Hughes	Butler, McReynolds	
Hague v. C.I.O.	307 U.S. 496 (1939)	5–2	Roberts, Stone, Hughes wrote separate concurring opinions	McReynolds, Butler	Frankfurter, Douglas
Cantwell v. Connecticut	310 U.S. 296 (1940)	Decided by unanimous vote	Roberts		
Sunshine Anthracite Coal Co. v. Adkins	310 U.S. 381 (1940)	8–1	Douglas	McReynolds	
Minersville School District v. Gobitis	310 U.S. 586 (1940)	8–1	Frankfurter	Stone	
United States v. Darby Lumber Co.	312 U.S. 100 (1941)	Decided by unanimous vote	Stone		
Cox v. New Hampshire	312 U.S. 569 (1941)	Decided by unanimous vote	Hughes		
United States v. Classic	313 U.S. 299 (1941)	5–3	Stone	Black, Murphy, Douglas	Hughes
Edwards v. California	314 U.S. 160 (1941)	Decided by unanimous vote	Byrnes		

(Table continues)

Table 2-12 (Continued)

Case name	Cite	Vote	Majority opinion writer[a]	Dissenters	Justices not participating
Chaplinsky v. New Hampshire	315 U.S. 568 (1942)	Decided by unanimous vote	Murphy		
Betts v. Brady	316 U.S. 455 (1942)	6–3	Roberts	Black, Douglas, Murphy	
Skinner v. Oklahoma	316 U.S. 535 (1942)	Decided by unanimous vote	Douglas		
Ex parte Quirin	317 U.S. 1 (1942)	Decided by unanimous vote	Stone		Murphy
Wickard v. Filburn	317 U.S. 111 (1942)	Decided by unanimous vote	Jackson		
McNabb v. United States	318 U.S. 332 (1943)	7–1	Frankfurter	Reed	Rutledge
Murdock v. Pennsylvania	319 U.S. 105 (1943)	5–4	Douglas	Reed, Frankfurter, Roberts, Jackson	
West Virginia State Board of Education v. Barnette	319 U.S. 624 (1943)	6–3	Jackson	Roberts, Reed, Frankfurter	

Case	Citation	Decided by un-animous vote			
Hirabayashi v. United States	320 U.S. 81 (1943)		Stone		
Yakus v. United States	321 U.S. 414 (1944)	6–3	Stone	Roberts, Murphy, Rutledge	
Smith v. Allwright	321 U.S. 649 (1944)	8–1	Reed	Roberts	
United States v. South-Eastern Underwriters Assn.	322 U.S. 533 (1944)	4–3	Black	Stone, Frankfurter, Jackson (in part)	Roberts, Reed
Korematsu v. United States	323 U.S. 214 (1944)	6–3	Black	Roberts, Murphy, Jackson	
Girouard v. United States	328 U.S. 61 (1946)	5–3	Douglas	Stone, Reed, Frankfurter	Jackson
United States v. Lovett	328 U.S. 303 (1946)	8–0	Black		Jackson
Morgan v. Virginia	328 U.S. 373 (1946)	7–1	Reed	Burton	Jackson
Colegrove v. Green	328 U.S. 549 (1946)	4–3	Frankfurter	Black, Douglas, Murphy	Jackson
Louisiana ex rel. Francis v. Resweber	329 U.S. 459 (1947)	5–4	Reed	Burton, Douglas, Murphy, Rutledge	
Everson v. Board of Education of Ewing Township	330 U.S. 1 (1947)	5–4	Black	Jackson, Frankfurter, Rutledge, Burton	
United Public Workers v. Mitchell	330 U.S. 75 (1947)	4–3	Reed	Black, Douglas (in part), Rutledge	Murphy, Jackson

(Table continues)

Table 2-12 (Continued)

Case name	Cite	Vote	Majority opinion writer[a]	Dissenters	Justices not participating
United States v. United Mine Workers	330 U.S. 258 (1947)	Decided by a divided Court	Vinson	Murphy, Rutledge, Black, Frankfurter, Douglas, Jackson (all in part)	
United States v. California	332 U.S. 19 (1947)	6–2	Black	Frankfurter, Reed	Jackson
Fay v. New York	332 U.S. 261 (1947)	5–4	Jackson	Murphy, Black, Douglas, Rutledge	
Illinois ex rel. McCollum v. Board of Education	333 U.S. 203 (1948)	8–1	Black	Reed	
Shelley v. Kraemer	334 U.S. 1 (1948)	6–0	Vinson		Reed, Jackson, Rutledge
Terminiello v. Chicago	337 U.S. 1 (1949)	5–4	Douglas	Vinson, Frankfurter, Jackson, Burton	
Wolf v. Colorado	338 U.S. 25 (1949)	6–3	Frankfurter	Douglas, Murphy, Rutledge	
United States v. Rabinowitz	339 U.S. 56 (1950)	5–3	Minton	Frankfurter, Jackson, Black	Douglas
American Communications Assn. v. Douds	339 U.S. 382 (1950)	5–1	Vinson	Black, Jackson (in part)	Douglas, Clark, Minton
Sweatt v. Painter	339 U.S. 629 (1950)	Decided by unanimous vote	Vinson		

Case	Citation	Vote			
McLaurin v. Oklahoma State Regents for Higher Education	339 U.S. 637 (1950)	Decided by unanimous vote	Vinson		
Kunz v. New York	340 U.S. 290 (1951)	8–1	Vinson	Jackson	
Feiner v. New York	340 U.S. 315 (1951)	6–3	Vinson	Black, Douglas, Minton	
Joint Anti-Fascist Refugee Committee v. McGrath	341 U.S. 123 (1951)	5–3	Burton	Vinson, Reed, Minton	Clark
Dennis v. United States	341 U.S. 494 (1951)	6–2	Vinson	Black, Douglas	Clark
Garner v. Board of Public Works	341 U.S. 716 (1951)	5–4	Clark	Burton (in part), Frankfurter (in part), Black, Douglas	
Stack v. Boyle	342 U.S. 1 (1951)	8–0	Vinson		Minton
Rochin v. California	342 U.S. 165 (1952)	8–0	Frankfurter		Minton
Carlson v. Landon	342 U.S. 524 (1952)	5–4	Reed	Black, Frankfurter, Burton, Douglas	
Youngstown Sheet and Tube Co. v. Sawyer (The Steel Seizure Case)	343 U.S. 579 (1952)	6–3	Black	Vinson, Reed, Minton	
Terry v. Adams	345 U.S. 461 (1953)	8–1	Black	Minton	
Rosenberg v. United States	346 U.S. 273 (1953)	6–3	Vinson	Frankfurter, Black, Douglas	
Brown v. Board of Education of Topeka	347 U.S. 483 (1954)	Decided by unanimous vote	Warren		

(Table continues)

Table 2-12 (*Continued*)

Case name	Cite	Vote	Majority opinion writer[a]	Dissenters	Justices not participating
Brown v. Board of Education of Topeka	349 U.S. 294 (1955)	Decided by unanimous vote	Warren	Douglas, Black	Burton, Whittaker
Ullman v. United States	350 U.S. 422 (1955)	7–2	Frankfurter		
Pennsylvania v. Nelson	350 U.S. 497 (1956)	6–3	Warren	Reed, Minton, Burton	
Slochower v. Board of Higher Education of New York City	350 U.S. 551 (1956)	5–4	Clark	Reed, Burton, Harlan, Minton	
Watkins v. United States	354 U.S. 178 (1957)	6–1	Warren	Clark	Burton, Whittaker
Yates v. United States	354 U.S. 298 (1957)	6–1, 4–3	Harlan	Clark, Black (in part), Douglas (*in part*)	Brennan, Whittaker
Mallory v. United States	354 U.S. 449 (1957)	Decided by unanimous vote	Frankfurter		
Roth v. United States, Alberts v. California	354 U.S. 476 (1957)	7–1, 6–3	Brennan	Black, Douglas, Harlan (in part)	
Trop v. Dulles	356 U.S. 86 (1958)	5–4	Warren	Frankfurter, Burton, Clark, Harlan	
Kent v. Dulles	357 U.S. 116 (1958)	5–4	Douglas	Clark, Harlan, Burton, Whittaker	

Case	Citation	Vote	Opinion	Dissenting
Wiener v. United States	357 U.S. 349 (1958)	Decided by unanimous vote	Frankfurter	
NAACP v. Alabama ex rel. Patterson	357 U.S. 449 (1958)	Decided by unanimous vote	Harlan	
Cooper v. Aaron	358 U.S. 1 (1958)	Decided by unanimous vote	Warren (each justice personally signed it)	
Lassiter v. Northhampton County Board of Education	360 U.S. 45 (1959)	Decided by unanimous vote	Douglas	
Barenblatt v. United States	360 U.S. 109 (1959)	5–4	Harlan	Warren, Black *Brennan, Douglas*
Elkins v. United States	364 U.S. 206 (1960)	5–4	Stewart	Frankfurter, Clark, Harlan, Whittaker
Gomillion v. Lightfoot	364 U.S. 339 (1960)	Decided by unanimous vote	Frankfurter	
Communist Party v. Subversive Activities Control Board	367 U.S. 1 (1961)	5–4	Frankfurter	Warren, Black, Douglas, Brennan
Scales v. United States, Noto v. United States	367 U.S. 203, 290 (1961)	5–4	Harlan	Warren, Black, Douglas, Brennan

(Table continues)

Table 2-12 (Continued)

Case name	Cite	Vote	Majority opinion writer[a]	Dissenters	Justices not participating
Mapp v. Ohio	367 U.S. 643 (1961)	5–4	Clark	Stewart, Harlan, Frankfurter, Whittaker	Whittaker
Hoyt v. Florida	368 U.S. 57 (1961)	Decided by un-animous vote	Harlan		
Baker v. Carr	369 U.S. 186 (1962)	6–2	Brennan	Frankfurter, Harlan	Frankfurter, White
Engel v. Vitale	370 U.S. 421 (1962)	6–1	Black	Stewart	Frankfurter, White
Robinson v. California	370 U.S. 660 (1962)	6–2	Stewart	Clark, White	Frankfurter
NAACP v. Button	371 U.S. 415 (1963)	6–3	Brennan	Harlan, Clark, Stewart White (in part)	
Edwards v. South Carolina	372 U.S. 229 (1963)	8–1	Stewart	Clark	
Gideon v. Wainwright	372 U.S. 335 (1963)	Decided by un-animous vote	Black		
Gray v. Sanders	372 U.S. 368 (1963)	8–1	Douglas	Harlan	
Fay v. Noia	372 U.S. 391 (1963)	6–3	Brennan	Harlan, Clark, Stewart	
Ker v. California	374 U.S. 23 (1963)	5–4	Clark	Warren, Brennan, Douglas, Goldberg (all in part)	

Wesberry v. Sanders	376 U.S. 1 (1964)	6–3	Black	Harlan, Stewart, Clark (in part)
New York Times Co. v. Sullivan	376 U.S. 254 (1964)	Decided by unanimous vote	Brennan	
Griffin v. County School Board of Prince Edward County	377 U.S. 218 (1964)	7–2	Black	Clark, Harlan (both in part)
Reynolds v. Simms	377 U.S. 533 (1964)	8–1	Warren	Harlan
Malloy v. Hogan	378 U.S. 1 (1964)	5–4	Brennan	Harlan, Clark, White, Stewart
Murphy v. The Waterfront Commission of New York Harbor	378 U.S. 52 (1964)	Decided by unanimous vote	Goldberg	
Escobedo v. Illinois	378 U.S. 478 (1964)	5–4	Goldberg	Harlan, Stewart, White, Clark
Aptheker v. Secretary of State	378 U.S. 500 (1964)	6–3	Goldberg	Clark, Harlan, White (in part)
Heart of Atlanta Motel v. United States	379 U.S. 241 (1964)	Decided by unanimous vote	Clark	
Pointer v. Texas	380 U.S. 400 (1965)	Decided by unanimous vote	Black	

(Table continues)

Table 2-12 (Continued)

Case name	Cite	Vote	Majority opinion writer[a]	Dissenters	Justices not participating
Dombrowski v. Pfister	380 U.S. 479 (1965)	5–2	Brennan	Harlan, Clark	Black, Stewart
Harman v. Forssenius	380 U.S. 528 (1965)	Decided by unanimous vote	Warren		
Griffin v. California	380 U.S. 609 (1965)	6–2	Douglas	Stewart, White	Warren
Griswold v. Connecticut	381 U.S. 479 (1965)	7–2	Douglas	Stewart, Black	
Albertson v. Subversive Activities Control Board	382 U.S. 70 (1965)	8–0	Brennan		White
South Carolina v. Katzenbach	383 U.S. 301 (1966)	8–1	Warren	Black (in part)	
Harper v. Virginia State Board of Elections	383 U.S. 663 (1966)	6–3	Douglas	Black, Harlan, Stewart	
Elfbrandt v. Russell	384 U.S. 11 (1966)	5–4	Douglas	White, Clark, Harlan, Stewart	
Miranda v. Arizona	384 U.S. 436 (1966)	5–4	Warren	Harlan, Stewart, White, Clark (in part)	
Keyishian v. Board of Regents	385 U.S. 589 (1967)	5–4	Brennan	Clark, Harlan, Stewart, White	
Klopfer v. North Carolina	386 U.S. 213 (1967)	Decided by unanimous vote	Warren		

Case	Citation	Vote		
In re Gault	387 U.S. 1 (1967)	7–2	Fortas	Harlan (in part), Stewart
Warden v. Hayden	387 U.S. 294 (1967)	8–1	Brennan	Douglas
Loving v. Virginia	388 U.S. 1 (1967)	Decided by unanimous vote	Warren	
Washington v. Texas	388 U.S. 14 (1967)	Decided by unanimous vote	Warren	
United States v. Wade	388 U.S. 218 (1967)	5–4	Brennan	White, Harlan, Stewart, Black voted to uphold conviction
United States v. Robel	389 U.S. 258 (1967)	6–2	Warren	White, Harlan
Katz v. United States	389 U.S. 347 (1967)	7–1	Stewart	Black
Duncan v. Louisiana	391 U.S. 145 (1968)	7–2	White	Harlan, Stewart
Green v. County School Board of New Kent County, Va.	391 U.S. 430 (1968)	Decided by unanimous vote	Brennan	
Terry v. Ohio	392 U.S. 1 (1968)	8–1	Warren	Douglas
Flast v. Cohen	392 U.S. 83 (1968)	8–1	Warren	Harlan
Jones v. Alfred H. Mayer Co.	392 U.S. 409 (1968)	7–2	Stewart	Harlan, White
Tinker v. Des Moines Independent Community School District	393 U.S. 503 (1969)	7–2	Fortas	Harlan, Black

(Table continues)

Table 2-12 (*Continued*)

Case name	Cite	Vote	Majority opinion writer[a]	Dissenters	Justices not participating
Kirkpatrick v. Preisler	394 U.S. 526 (1969)	6–3	Brennan	Harlan, Stewart, White	
Shapiro v. Thompson, Washington v. Legrant, Reynolds v. Smith	394 U.S. 618 (1969)	6–3	Brennan	Warren, Black, Harlan	
Gaston County v. United States	395 U.S. 285 (1969)	7–1	Harlan	Black	
Powell v. McCormack	395 U.S. 486 (1969)	7–1	Warren	Stewart	
Chimel v. California	395 U.S. 752 (1969)	6–2	Stewart	White, Black	
Benton v. Maryland	395 U.S. 784 (1969)	6–2	Marshall	Stewart, Harlan	
In re Winship	397 U.S. 358 (1970)	5–3	Brennan	Burger, Black, Stewart	
Williams v. Florida	399 U.S. 78 (1970)	7–1	White	Marshall (in part)	Blackmun
Oregon v. Mitchell, Texas v. Mitchell, United States v. Idaho, United States v. Arizona	400 U.S. 112 (1970)	5–4 (voting age), 8–1 (residency requirements), 9–0 (literacy test ban)	Black	Burger, Harlan, Stewart, Blackmun (age), Douglas, Harlan (residency)	
Younger v. Harris	401 U.S. 37 (1971)	8–1	Black	Douglas	
Harris v. New York	401 U.S. 222 (1971)	5–4	Burger	Black, Douglas, *Brennan, Marshall*	
Griggs v. Duke Power Co.	401 U.S. 424 (1971)	8–0	Burger		Brennan

Case	Citation	Vote	Opinion author	Dissenting
Swann v. Charlotte-Mecklenburg County Board of Education	402 U.S. 1 (1971)	Decided by unanimous vote	Burger	
Graham v. Richardson	403 U.S. 365 (1971)	Decided by unanimous vote	Blackmun	
McKeiver v. Pennsylvania, In re Burris	403 U.S. 528 (1971)	6–3, 5–4	Blackmun	Douglas, Black, Marshall; Brennan dissented in Burris only
Lemon v. Kurtzman	403 U.S. 602 (1971)	Decided by unanimous vote	Burger	Marshall
New York Times Co. v. United States, United States v. The Washington Post	403 U.S. 713 (1971)	6–3	unsigned opinion (each justice wrote a separate opinion)	Burger, Blackmun, Harlan
Reed v. Reed	404 U.S. 71 (1971)	7–0	Burger	
Johnson v. Louisiana, Apodaca v. Oregon	406 U.S. 356, 404 (1972)	5–4	White	Douglas, Brennan, Marshall, Stewart
Kastigar v. United States	406 U.S. 441 (1972)	5–2	Powell	Douglas, Marshall
Argersinger v. Hamlin	407 U.S. 25 (1972)	Decided by unanimous vote	Douglas	Rehnquist, Brennan

(Table continues)

Table 2-12 (Continued)

Case name	Cite	Vote	Majority opinion writer[a]	Dissenters	Justices not participating
Furman v. Georgia, Jackson v. Georgia, Branch v. Texas	408 U.S. 238 (1972)	5–4	unsigned opinion (each justice wrote a separate opinion)	Burger, Blackmun, Powell, Rehnquist	
United States v. Brewster	408 U.S. 501 (1972)	6–3	Burger	Brennan, Douglas, White	
Branzburg v. Hayes, In re Pappas, United States v. Caldwell	408 U.S. 665 (1972)	5–4	White	Douglas, Brennan, Stewart, Marshall	
Roe v. Wade, Doe v. Bolton	410 U.S. 113, 179 (1973)	7–2	Blackmun	Rehnquist, White	
Mahan v. Howell, City of Virginia Beach v. Howell, Weinberg v. Prichard	410 U.S. 315 (1973)	5–3	Rehnquist	Brennan, Douglas, Marshall	Powell
San Antonio Independent School District v. Rodriguez	411 U.S. 1 (1973)	5–4	Powell	Marshall, Douglas, Brennan, White	
Miller v. California	413 U.S. 15 (1973)	5–4	Burger	Brennan, Stewart, Marshall, Douglas	
Keyes v. Denver School District No. 1	413 U.S. 189 (1973)	7–1	Brennan	Rehnquist	White
Edelman v. Jordan	415 U.S. 651 (1974)	5–4	Rehnquist	Brennan, Douglas, Marshall, Blackmun	
Geduldig v. Aiello	417 U.S. 484 (1974)	6–3	Stewart	Douglas, Brennan, Marshall	

United States v. Nixon	418 U.S. 683 (1974)	8–0	Burger		Rehnquist
Milliken v. Bradley	418 U.S. 717 (1974)	5–4	Burger	Douglas, Brennan, Marshall	
Taylor v. Louisiana	419 U.S. 522 (1975)	8–1	White	Rehnquist	
Weinberger v. Wiesenfeld	420 U.S. 636 (1975)	8–0	Brennan		Douglas
Bigelow v. Virginia	421 U.S. 809 (1975)	7–2	Blackmun	Rehnquist, White	
Albemarle Paper Co. v. Moody	422 U.S. 405 (1975)	7–1	Stewart	Burger (in part)	Powell
Michelin Tire Corp. v. Wages	423 U.S. 276 (1976)	8–0	Brennan		Stevens
Buckley v. Valeo	424 U.S. 1 (1976)	8–0, 7–1, 6–2 unsigned opinion	Burger (in part), Blackmun (in part), Rehnquist (in part), White (in part), Marshall (in part)	Stevens	
Washington v. Davis	426 U.S. 229 (1976)	7–2	White	Brennan, Marshall	
National League of Cities v. Usery, California v. Usery	426 U.S. 833 (1976)	5–4	Rehnquist	Brennan, White, Marshall, Stevens	
Runyon v. McCrary, Fairfax-Brewster School, Inc. v. Gonzales, Southern Independent School Association v. McCrary	427 U.S. 160 (1976)	7–2	Stewart	White, Rehnquist	
Elrod v. Burns	427 U.S. 347 (1976)	5–3	Brennan	Burger, Powell, Rehnquist	Stevens
Pasadena City Board of Education v. Spangler	427 U.S. 424 (1976)	6–2	Rehnquist	Brennan, Marshall	Stevens

(Table continues)

Table 2-12 (Continued)

Case name	Cite	Vote	Majority opinion writer[a]	Dissenters	Justices not participating
Nebraska Press Association v. Stuart	427 U.S. 539 (1976)	Decided by unanimous vote	Burger		
Gregg v. Georgia, Proffitt v. Florida, Jurek v. Texas	428 U.S. 153, 242, 262 (1976)	7–2	Stewart (Gregg), Stevens (Jurek), Powell (Proffitt)	Brennan, Marshall	
Woodson v. North Carolina, Roberts v. Louisiana	428 U.S. 280, 325 (1976)	5–4	Stewart (Woodson), Stevens, Powell (Roberts)	Burger, White, Rehnquist, Blackmun	
Stone v. Powell, Wolff v. Rice	428 U.S. 465 (1976)	6–3	Powell	Brennan, Marshall, White	
Craig v. Boren	429 U.S. 190 (1976)	7–2	Brennan	Burger, Rehnquist	
Village of Arlington Heights v. Metropolitan Housing Development Corp.	429 U.S. 252 (1977)	5–3	Powell	White, Brennan (in part), Marshall (in part)	Stevens
United Jewish Organizations of Williamsburgh v. Carey	430 U.S. 144 (1977)	7–1	White	Burger	Marshall
Complete Auto Transit Inc. v. Brady	430 U.S. 274 (1977)	Decided by unanimous vote	Blackmun		

Case	Citation	Vote	Opinion	Concurring/Dissenting
Coker v. Georgia	433 U.S. 584 (1977)	7–2	White	Burger, Rehnquist, Powell (in part)
Ballew v. Georgia	435 U.S. 223 (1978)	Decided by un-animous vote	Blackmun	
First National Bank of Boston v. Bellotti	435 U.S. 765 (1978)	5–4	Powell	White, Brennan, Marshall, Rehnquist
Zurcher v. The Stanford Daily	436 U.S. 547 (1978)	5–3	White	Stewart, Marshall, Stevens, Brennan
Monell v. Department of Social Services, City of New York	436 U.S. 658 (1978)	7–2	Brennan	Burger, Rehnquist
University of California Regents v. Bakke	438 U.S. 265 (1978)	5–4	Powell (judgment of the Court)	Stevens filed a separate opinion (joined by Burger, Rehnquist, Stewart); Brennan filed a separate opinion (joined by Marshall, White, Blackmun)
Butz v. Economou	438 U.S. 478 (1978)	5–4	White	Burger, Rehnquist, Stewart, Stevens (all in part)
Orr v. Orr	440 U.S. 268 (1979)	6–3	Brennan	Powell, Rehnquist, Burger
Burch v. Louisiana	441 U.S. 130 (1979)	Decided by un-animous vote	Rehnquist	

(Table continues)

Table 2-12 (*Continued*)

Case name	Cite	Vote	Majority opinion writer[a]	Dissenters	Justices not participating
Davis v. Passman	442 U.S. 228 (1979)	5–4	Brennan	Burger, Powell, Rehnquist, Stewart	
United States v. Helstoski	442 U.S. 477 (1979)	5–3	Burger	Brennan, Stevens (in part), Stewart (in part)	Powell
Hutchinson v. Proxmire	443 U.S. 111 (1979)	7–2	Burger	Brennan, Stewart (in part)	
United Steelworkers of America v. Weber, Kaiser Aluminum v. Weber, United States v. Weber	443 U.S. 193 (1979)	5–2	Brennan	Burger, Rehnquist	Powell, Stevens
Gannett Co, Inc. v. DePasquale	443 U.S. 368 (1979)	5–4	Stewart	Blackmun, Brennan, White, Marshall (all in part)	
Columbus Board of Education v. Penick, Dayton Board of Education v. Brinkman	443 U.S. 449 (1979)	7–2, 5–4	White	Rehnquist, Powell; Burger, Stewart (in Dayton)	
Payton v. New York, Riddick v. New York	445 U.S. 573 (1980)	6–3	Stevens	Burger, White, Rehnquist	
City of Mobile, Ala. v. Bolden	446 U.S. 55 (1980)	6–3	Stewart	Brennan, White, Marshall	
Rhode Island v. Innis	446 U.S. 291 (1980)	9–0, 6–3	Stewart	Marshall, Brennan, Stevens	

Case	Citation	Vote	Opinion author	Justices	
Harris v. McRae	448 U.S. 297 (1980)	5–4	Stewart	Brennan, Marshall, Blackmun, Stevens	
Fullilove v. Klutznick	448 U.S. 448 (1980)	6–3	Burger announced the Court's decision	Stewart, Rehnquist, Stevens	
Richmond Newspapers Inc. v. Commonwealth of Virginia	448 U.S. 555 (1980)	7–1	Burger announced the Court's decision	Rehnquist	Powell
Chandler v. Florida	449 U.S. 560 (1981)	8–0	Burger		Stevens
H. L. v. Matheson	450 U.S. 398 (1981)	6–3	Burger	Marshall, Brennan, Blackmun	
Rosker v. Goldberg	453 U.S. 57 (1981)	6–3	Rehnquist	White, Marshall, Brennan	
Dames & Moore v. Regan	453 U.S. 654 (1981)	9–0	Rehnquist		
Plyler v. Doe, Texas v. Certain Named and Unnamed Undocumented Alien Children	457 U.S. 202 (1982)	5–4	Brennan	Burger, Rehnquist, White, O'Connor	
Youngberg v. Romeo	457 U.S. 307 (1982)	9–0	Powell		
Nixon v. Fitzgerald	457 U.S. 731 (1982)	5–4	Powell	White, Brennan, Marshall, Blackmun	
Harlow v. Fitzgerald	457 U.S. 800 (1982)	8–1	Powell	Burger	
Board of Education, Island Trees Union Free School District #26 v. Pico	457 U.S. 853 (1982)	5–4	Brennan announced the Court's decision	Burger, Powell, Rehnquist, O'Connor	
Enmund v. Florida	458 U.S. 782 (1982)	5–4	White	Burger, O'Connor, Powell, Rehnquist	

(Table continues)

Table 2-12 (Continued)

Case name	Cite	Vote	Majority opinion writer[a]	Dissenters	Justices not participating
NAACP v. Claiborne Hardware Co.	458 U.S. 886 (1982)	8–0	Stevens		Marshall
Bob Jones University v. United States, Goldsboro Christian Schools v. United States	461 U.S. 574 (1983)	8–1	Burger	Rehnquist	
City of Akron v. Akron Center for Reproductive Health Inc., Akron Center for Reproductive Health Inc. v. City of Akron	462 U.S. 416 (1983)	6–3	Powell	White, Rehnquist, O'Connor	
Planned Parenthood Association of Kansas City, Missouri v. Ashcroft, Ashcroft v. Planned Parenthood Association of Kansas City, Missouri	462 U.S. 476 (1983)	5–4, 6–3	Powell	Blackmun, Brennan, Marshall, Stevens, O'Connor, White, Rehnquist (all in part)	
Karcher v. Daggett	462 U.S. 725 (1983)	5–4	Brennan	Burger, Powell, Rehnquist, White	
Brown v. Thomson	462 U.S. 835 (1983)	5–4	Powell	Brennan, White, Marshall, Blackmun	

Case	Citation	Vote	Author	Dissenting/Concurring
Immigration and Naturalization Service v. Chadha, United States House of Representatives v. Chadha, United States Senate v. Chadha	462 U.S. 919 (1983)	7–2	Burger	White, Rehnquist
Solem v. Helm	463 U.S. 277 (1983)	5–4	Powell	Burger, White, Rehnquist, O'Connor
Mueller v. Allen	463 U.S. 388 (1983)	5–4	Rehnquist	Marshall, Brennan, Blackmun, Stevens
Grove City College v. Bell	465 U.S. 555 (1984)	6–3	White	Brennan, Marshall; Stevens (in part)
Lynch v. Donnelly	465 U.S. 668 (1984)	5–4	Burger	Brennan, Marshall, Blackmun, Stevens
Schall v. Martin, Abrams v. Martin	467 U.S. 253 (1984)	6–3	Rehnquist	Brennan, Marshall, Stevens
Nix v. Williams	467 U.S. 431 (1984)	7–2	Burger	Brennan, Marshall
Firefighters Local Union #1794 v. Stotts	467 U.S. 561 (1984)	6–3	White	Brennan, Marshall, Blackmun
New York v. Quarles	467 U.S. 649 (1984)	5–4, 6–3	Rehnquist	O'Connor (in part), Stevens, Marshall, Brennan
Roberts v. U.S. Jaycees	468 U.S. 609 (1984)	7–0	Brennan	Burger, Blackmun
United States v. Leon	468 U.S. 897 (1984)	6–3	White	Brennan, Marshall, Stevens
Garcia v. San Antonio Metropolitan Transit Authority	469 U.S. 528 (1985)	5–4	Blackmun	Burger, Powell, Rehnquist, O'Connor

(Table continues)

Table 2-12 (Continued)

Case name	Cite	Vote	Majority opinion writer[a]	Dissenters	Justices not participating
Ake v. Oklahoma	470 U.S. 68 (1985)	8–1	Marshall	Rehnquist	
Federal Election Commission v. National Conservative Political Action Committee, Democratic Party of United States v. National Conservative Political Action Committee	470 U.S. 480 (1985)	6–3	Rehnquist	Marshall, White, Brennan; Stevens (in part)	
Tennessee v. Garner	471 U.S. 1 (1985)	6–3	White	O'Connor, Burger, Rehnquist	
Wallace v. Jaffree	472 U.S. 38 (1985)	6–3	Stevens	Burger, Rehnquist, White	
Aguilar v. Felton	473 U.S. 402 (1985)	5–4	Brennan	Burger, White, Rehnquist, O'Connor	
City of Cleburne, Texas v. Cleburne Living Center	473 U.S. 432 (1985)	9–0, 6–3	White	Brennan, Marshall, Blackmun (all in part)	
Vasquez v. Hillery	474 U.S. 254 (1986)	6–3	Marshall	Burger, Powell, Rehnquist	
Batson v. Kentucky	476 U.S. 79 (1986)	7–2	Powell	Burger, Rehnquist	
Lockhart v. McCree	476 U.S. 162 (1986)	6–3	Rehnquist	Brennan, Marshall, Stevens	
Wygant v. Jackson Board of Education	476 U.S. 267 (1986)	5–4	Powell announced the decision	Brennan, Marshall, Stevens, Blackmun	
Thornburgh v. American College of Obstetricians and Gynecologists	476 U.S. 747 (1986)	5–4	Blackmun	White, Rehnquist, O'Connor, Burger	

Case	Citation	Vote		
Ford v. Wainwright	477 U.S. 399 (1986)	7–2, 5–4	Marshall	Rehnquist, Burger, White (in part), O'Connor (in part)
Davis v. Bandemer	478 U.S. 109 (1986)	7–2	White	Powell (in part), Stevens (in part)
Bowers v. Hardwick	478 U.S. 186 (1986)	5–4	White	Blackmun, Brennan, Marshall, Stevens
Local #28 of the Sheet Metal Workers' International v. Equal Employment Opportunity Commission	478 U.S. 421 (1986)	5–4	Brennan	Burger, White, Rehnquist, O'Connor
Local #93, International Association of Firefighters v. City of Cleveland and Cleveland Vanguards	478 U.S. 501 (1986)	6–3	Brennan	Burger, White, Rehnquist
Bowsher v. Synar, Senate v. Synar, O'Neill v. Synar	478 U.S. 714 (1986)	7–2	Burger	White, Blackmun
Tashjian v. Republican Party of Connecticut	479 U.S. 208 (1987)	5–4	Marshall	Rehnquist, Stevens, O'Connor, Scalia
United States v. Paradise	480 U.S. 149 (1987)	5–4	Brennan	Rehnquist, O'Connor, Scalia, White
Johnson v. Transportation Agency of Santa Clara County	480 U.S. 616 (1987)	6–3	Brennan	Rehnquist, Scalia, White
Tison v. Arizona	481 U.S. 137 (1987)	5–4	O'Connor	Brennan, Marshall, Blackmun, Stevens

(Table continues)

Table 2-12 (*Continued*)

Case name	Cite	Vote	Majority opinion writer[a]	Dissenters	Justices not participating
McCleskey v. Kemp	481 U.S. 279 (1987)	5–4	Powell	Brennan, Marshall, Blackmun, Stevens	
United States v. Salerno	481 U.S. 739 (1987)	6–3	Rehnquist	Brennan, Marshall, Stevens	
Edwards v. Aguillard	482 U.S. 578 (1987)	7–2	Brennan	Rehnquist, Scalia	
South Carolina v. Baker	485 U.S. 505 (1988)	7–1	Brennan	O'Connor	Kennedy
New York State Club Association Inc. v. New York City	487 U.S. 1 (1988)	9–0	White		
Morrison v. Olson	487 U.S. 654 (1988)	7–1	Rehnquist	Scalia	Kennedy
Thompson v. Oklahoma	487 U.S. 815 (1988)	5–3	Stevens	Rehnquist, White, Scalia	Kennedy
Mistretta v. United States	488 U.S. 361 (1989)	8–0	Blackmun	Scalia	
City of Richmond v. J. A. Croson Co.	488 U.S. 469 (1989)	6–3	O'Connor	Marshall, Brennan, Blackmun	
Skinner v. Railway Labor Executives' Association	489 U.S. 602 (1989)	7–2	Kennedy	Marshall, Brennan	
National Treasury Employees Union v. Raab	489 U.S. 656 (1989)	5–4	Kennedy	Marshall, Brennan, Scalia, Stevens	
Texas v. Johnson	491 U.S. 397 (1989)	5–4	Brennan	Rehnquist, White, O'Connor, Stevens	

Case	Citation	Vote	Opinion	Concurring/Dissenting
Penry v. Lynaugh	492 U.S. 302 (1989)	5–4	O'Connor announced the Court's decision	Stevens, Blackmun, Brennan, Marshall
Stanford v. Kentucky	492 U.S. 361 (1989)	5–4	Scalia announced the Court's decision	Brennan, Marshall, Blackmun, Stevens, Scalia, Rehnquist, White, Kennedy (all in part)
Webster v. Reproductive Health Services	492 U.S. 490 (1989)	5–4	Rehnquist announced the Court's decision	Blackmun, Brennan, Marshall, Stevens (all in part)
Allegheny County v. American Civil Liberties Union, Greater Pittsburgh Chapter	492 U.S. 573 (1989)	5–4, 6–3	Blackmun	Brennan, Marshall, Stevens dissented on one point; Kennedy, Rehnquist, White, Scalia dissented on another
Wards Cove Packing Co. v. Atonio	490 U.S. 642 (1989)	5–4	White	Blackmun, Brennan, Marshall, Stevens
Employment Division, Department of Human Resources of Oregon v. Smith	494 U.S. 872 (1990)	6–3, 5–4	Scalia	Blackmun, Brennan, Marshall, O'Connor (in part)
Board of Education of the Westside Community Schools v. Mergens	496 U.S. 226 (1990)	8–1	O'Connor	Stevens
United States v. Eichman, United States v. Haggerty	496 U.S. 310 (1990)	5–4	Brennan	Rehnquist, White, Stevens, O'Connor
Michigan, Department of State Police v. Sitz	496 U.S. 444 (1990)	6–3	Rehnquist	Brennan, Marshall, Stevens

(Table continues)

Table 2-12 (*Continued*)

Case name	Cite	Vote	Majority opinion writer[a]	Dissenters	Justices not participating
Rutan v. Republican Party of Illinois, Frech v. Rutan	497 U.S. 62 (1990)	5–4	Brennan	Scalia, Rehnquist, Kennedy, O'Connor	
Cruzan v. Director, Missouri Department of Health	497 U.S. 261 (1990)	5–4	Rehnquist	Brennan, Marshall, Blackmun, Stevens	
Hodgson v. Minnesota, Minnesota v. Hodgson	497 U.S. 417 (1990)	5–4, 5–4	Stevens wrote the opinion striking down a statute that required a teenage girl to notify both biological parents of her decision to have an abortion; a separate majority found the statute ultimately constitutional because it provided for a judicial bypass	Scalia, Kennedy, Rehnquist, and White from the Stevens opinion; Brennan, Marshall, Blackmun, and Stevens from the O'Connor opinion	
Metro Broadcasting Inc. v. Federal Communications Commission, Astroline Communications Co. v. Shurberg Broadcasting of Hartford Inc.	497 U.S. 547 (1990)	5–4	Brennan	O'Connor, Rehnquist, Scalia, Kennedy	
Ohio v. Akron Center for Reproductive Health	497 U.S. 502 (1990)	6–3	Kennedy	Blackmun, Brennan, Marshall	

Case	Citation	Vote	Author	Concurring/Dissenting	
International Union, United Automobile, Aerospace & Agricultural Implement Workers of America, UAW v. Johnson Controls, Inc.	499 U.S. 187 (1991)	9–0, 5–4	Blackmun	White, Rehnquist, Kennedy, Scalia (all in part)	
Arizona v. Fulminante	499 U.S. 279 (1991)	5–4	White, Rehnquist (for separate majorities)	White, Marshall, Blackmun, Stevens, O'Connor, Rehnquist, Kennedy, Souter, Scalia (all in part)	
Rust v. Sullivan	500 U.S. 173 (1991)	5–4	Rehnquist	Blackmun, Marshall, Stevens, O'Connor	
Chisom v. Roemer, United States v. Roemer	501 U.S. 380 (1991)	6–3	Stevens	Scalia, Rehnquist, Kennedy	
Masson v. The New Yorker	501 U.S. 496 (1991)	7–2	Kennedy	White, Scalia (both in part)	
Barnes v. Glen Theatre	501 U.S. 560 (1991)	5–4	Rehnquist	White, Marshall, Blackmun, Stevens	
Cohen v. Cowles Media Co.	501 U.S. 663 (1991)	5–4	White	Souter, Marshall, Blackmun, O'Connor	
Payne v. Tennessee	501 U.S. 808 (1991)	6–3	Rehnquist	Marshall, Blackmun, Stevens	
Simon & Schuster v. Members of New York State Crime Victims Board	502 U.S. 105 (1991)	8–0	O'Connor		Thomas
R.A.V. v. City of St. Paul	505 U.S. 377 (1992)	9–0, 5–4	Scalia	White, Blackmun, O'Connor, Stevens (all in part)	

(Table continues)

Table 2-12 (Continued)

Case name	Cite	Vote	Majority opinion writer[a]	Dissenters	Justices not participating
Lee v. Weisman	505 U.S. 577 (1992)	5–4	Kennedy	Scalia, Rehnquist, White, Thomas	
United States v. Fordice, Ayers v. Fordice	505 U.S. 717 (1992)	8–1	White	Scalia	
Planned Parenthood of Southeastern Pennyslvania v. Casey	505 U.S. 833 (1992)	5–4, 7–2	O'Connor, Kennedy, and Souter wrote the opinion	Rehnquist, White, Scalia, and Thomas dissented from the part upholding a woman's right to an abortion; Blackmun and Stevens dissented from part allowing the state's abortion restrictions to stand	
Harris v. Forklift Systems	510 U.S. 17 (1993)	9–0	O'Connor		
Herrera v. Collins	506 U.S. 390 (1993)	6–3	Rehnquist	Blackmun, Stevens, Souter	
Austin v. United States	509 U.S. 390 (1993)	9–0	Blackmun		
Lamb's Chapel v. Center Moriches Union Free School District	508 U.S. 384 (1993)	9–0	White		
Zobrest v. Catalina Foothills School District	509 U.S. 1 (1993)	5–4	Rehnquist	Blackmun, Stevens, O'Connor, Souter	
Sale v. Haitian Centers Council	509 U.S. 155 (1993)	8–1	Stevens	Blackmun	

Shaw v. Reno	509 U.S. 460 (1993)	5–4	O'Connor	White, Blackmun, Stevens, Souter
Dolan v. City of Tigard	512 U.S. 374 (1994)	5–4	Rehnquist	Stevens, Blackmun, Souter, Ginsburg
J. E. B. v. Alabama ex rel. T. B.	511 U.S. 202 (1994)	6–3	Blackmun	Scalia, Rehnquist, Thomas
Turner Broadcasting System, Inc. v. Federal Communications Commission	512 U.S. 622 (1994)	8–1, 5–4	Kennedy	Stevens dissented in one part; O'Connor, Scalia, Thomas, Ginsburg dissented in another part
Board of Education of Kiryas Joel Village School District v. Grumet	512 U.S. 687 (1994)	6–3	Souter	Scalia, Rehnquist, Thomas
Madsen v. Women's Health Center, Inc.	512 U.S. 753 (1994)	6–3	Rehnquist	Scalia, Kennedy, Thomas (all in part)
Holder v. Hall	512 U.S. 874 (1994)	5–4	Kennedy	Blackmun, Stevens, Souter, Ginsburg
Adarand Constructors, Inc. v. Pena	515 U.S. 200 (1995)	5–4	O'Connor	Stevens, Souter, Ginsburg, Breyer
Missouri v. Jenkins	515 U.S. 70 (1995)	5–4	Rehnquist	Stevens, Souter, Ginsburg, Breyer
United States v. Lopez	514 U.S. 549 (1995)	5–4	Rehnquist	Breyer, Stevens, Souter, Ginsburg
McIntyre v. Ohio Elections Commission	514 U.S. 334 (1995)	7–2	Stevens	Scalia, Rehnquist
Hurley v. Irish-American Gay, Lesbian and Bisexual Group of Boston	515 U.S. 557 (1995)	9–0	Souter	

(Table continues)

Table 2-12 (*Continued*)

Case name	Cite	Vote	Majority opinion writer[a]	Dissenters	Justices not participating
Rosenberger v. Rector and Visitors of University of Virginia	515 U.S. 819 (1995)	5–4	Kennedy	Stevens, Souter, Ginsburg, Breyer	
Capitol Square Review and Advisory Board v. Pinette	515 U.S. 753 (1995)	7–2	Scalia	Stevens, Ginsburg	
Veronia School District 47J v. Acton	515 U.S. 646 (1995)	6–3	Scalia	O'Connor, Stevens, Souter	
U.S. Term Limits v. Thornton	514 U.S. 779 (1995)	5–4	Stevens	Rehnquist, O'Connor, Scalia, Thomas	
Miller v. Johnson	515 U.S. 900 (1995)	5–4	Kennedy	Stevens, Souter, Ginsburg, Breyer	
Bennis v. Michigan	516 U.S. 442 (1996)	5–4	Rehnquist	Stevens, Kennedy, Souter, Breyer	
Seminole Tribe of Florida v. Florida	517 U.S. 44 (1996)	5–4	Rehnquist	Stevens, Souter, Ginsburg, Breyer	
BMW of North America, Inc. v. Gore	517 U.S. 559 (1996)	5–4	Stevens	Rehnquist, Scalia, Thomas, Ginsburg	
Romer v. Evans	517 U.S. 620 (1996)	6–3	Kennedy	Rehnquist, Scalia, Thomas	
Shaw v. Hunt	517 U.S. 899 (1996)	5–4	Rehnquist	Stevens, Souter, Ginsburg, Breyer	

Case	Citation	Vote			
44 Liquormart, Inc. v. Rhode Island	517 U.S. 484 (1996)	9–0	Stevens	Stevens, Souter, Ginsburg, Breyer	Thomas
Bush v. Vera	517 U.S. 952 (1996)	5–4	O'Connor	Stevens	
United States v. Ursery	518 U.S. 267 (1996)	8–1	Rehnquist	Scalia	
United States v. Virginia	518 U.S. 515 (1996)	7–1	Ginsburg	Stevens, Ginsburg	
Colorado Republican Federal Campaign Committee v. Federal Election Commission	518 U.S. 604 (1996)	7–2	Breyer	Stevens, Ginsburg	
Denver Area Educational Telecommunications Consortium, Inc. v. Federal Communications Commission	518 U.S. 727 (1996)	7–2, 6–3, 5–4	Breyer	Kennedy, Ginsburg; Thomas, Rehnquist, Scalia; O'Connor,	
Turner Broadcasting System, Inc. v. Federal Communications Commission	520 U.S. 180 (1997)	5–4	Kennedy	O'Connor, Scalia, Thomas, Ginsburg	
Clinton v. Jones	520 U.S. 681 (1997)	9–0	Stevens	Stevens, Souter, Ginsburg, Breyer	
Printz v. United States	521 U.S. 98 (1997)	5–4	Scalia	Stevens, Souter, Ginsburg, Breyer	
Agostini v. Felton	521 U.S. 203 (1997)	5–4	O'Connor	Stevens, Souter, Ginsburg, Breyer	
Kansas v. Hendricks	521 U.S. 346 (1997)	5–4	Thomas		
City of Boerne v. Flores	521 U.S. 507 (1997)	6–3	Kennedy	O'Connor, Souter Breyer	

(Table continues)

Table 2-12 (Continued)

Case name	Cite	Vote	Majority opinion writer[a]	Dissenters	Justices not participating
Amchem Products, Inc. v. Windsor	521 U.S. 591 (1997)	6–2	Ginsburg	Stevens, Breyer	O'Connor
United States v. O'Hagan	521 U.S. 642 (1997)	9–0, 7–2, 6–3	Ginsburg	Rehnquist, Scalia, Thomas	
Washington v. Glucksberg	521 U.S. 702 (1997)	9–0	Rehnquist		
Vacco v. Quill	521 U.S. 793 (1997)	9–0	Rehnquist		
Reno v. American Civil Liberties Union	521 U.S. 844 (1997)	9–0, 7–2	Stevens	Rehnquist, O'Connor	
Oncale v. Sundowner Offshore Services, Inc.	523 U.S. 75 (1998)	9–0	Scalia		
Gebser v. Lago Vista Independent School District	524 U.S. 274 (1998)	5–4	O'Connor	Stevens, Souter, Ginsburg, Breyer	
United States v. Bajakajian	524 U.S. 321 (1998)	5–4	Thomas	Rehnquist, O'Connor, Scalia, Kennedy	
Swidler & Berlin v. United States	524 U.S. 399 (1998)	6–3	Rehnquist	O'Connor, Scalia, Thomas	
Clinton v. City of New York	524 U.S. 417 (1998)	6–3	Stevens	O'Connor, Scalia, Breyer	
Eastern Enterprises v. Apfel	524 U.S. 498 (1998)	5–4	O'Connor	Stevens, Souter, Ginsburg, Breyer	
National Endowments for the Arts v. Finley	524 U.S. 569 (1998)	8–1	O'Connor	Souter	

Case	Citation	Vote		Dissenters
Bragdon v. Abbott	524 U.S. 624 (1998)	5–4	Kennedy	Rehnquist, O'Connor, Scalia, Thomas
Burlington Industries, Inc. v. Ellerth	524 U.S. 742 (1998)	7–2	Kennedy	Scalia, Thomas
Faragher v. City of Boca Raton	524 U.S. 775 (1998)	7–2	Souter	Scalia, Thomas
Department of Commerce v. United States House of Representatives	525 U.S. 316 (1999)	5–4	O'Connor	Stevens, Souter, Ginsburg, Breyer
Saenz v. Roe	526 U.S. 489 (1999)	7–2	Stevens	Rehnquist, Thomas
Davis v. Monroe County Board of Education	526 U.S. 629 (1999)	5–4	O'Connor	Rehnquist, Scalia, Kennedy, Thomas
City of Chicago v. Morales	527 U.S. 41 (1999)	6–3	Stevens	Rehnquist, Scalia, Thomas
Sutton v. United Sir Lines, Inc.	527 U.S. 471 (1999)	7–2	O'Connor	Stevens, Breyer
Kolstad v. American Dental Association	527 U.S. 526 (1999)	7–2 5–4	O'Connor	Rehnquist, Thomas; Stevens, Souter, Ginsburg, Breyer
Olmstead v. L.C.	527 U.S. 581 (1999)	6–3	Ginsburg	Rehnquist, Scalia, Thomas
Florida Prepaid Postsecondary Education Expense Board v. College Savings Bank	527 U.S. 652 (1999)	5–4	Rehnquist	Stevens, Souter, Ginsburg, Breyer
College Savings Bank v. Florida Prepaid Postsecondary Education Expense Board	527 U.S. 666 (1999)	5–4	Scalia	Stevens, Souter, Ginsburg, Breyer

Table 2-12 (Continued)

Case name	Cite	Vote	Majority opinion writer[a]	Dissenters	Justices not participating
Alden v. Maine	527 U.S. 706 (1999)	5–4	Kennedy	Stevens, Souter, Ginsburg, Breyer	
Kimel v. Florida Board of Regents	528 U.S. 62 (2000)	5–4	O'Connor	Stevens, Souter, Ginsburg, Breyer	
Food and Drug Administration v. Brown & Williamson Tobacco Corp.	529 U.S. 120 (2000)	5–4	O'Connor	Stevens, Souter, Ginsburg, Breyer	
United States v. Morrison	529 U.S. 598 (2000)	5–4	Rehnquist	Stevens, Souter, Ginsburg, Breyer	
Troxel v. Granville	530 U.S. 57 (2000)	6–3	O'Connor	Stevens, Scalia, Kennedy	
Santa Fe Independent School District v. Doe	530 U.S. 290 (2000)	6–3	Stevens	Rehnquist, Scalia, Thomas	
Nixon v. Shrink Missouri Government PAC	528 U.S 377 (2000)	6–3	Souter	Scalia, Kennedy, Thomas	
Dickerson v. United States	530 U.S. 428 (2000)	7–2	Rehnquist	Scalia, Thomas	
Mitchell v. Helms	530 U.S. 793 (2000)	6–3	Thomas	Stevens, Souter, Ginsburg	
Boy Scouts of America v. Dale	530 U.S. 640 (2000)	5–4	Rehnquist	Stevens, Souter, Ginsburg, Breyer	
Stenberg v. Carhart	530 U.S. 914 (2000)	5–4	Breyer	Rehnquist, Scalia, Kennedy, Thomas	
Bush v. Gore	531 U.S. 98 (2000)	5–4	Per Curiam	Stevens, Souter, Ginsburg, Breyer	

Board of Trustees of the University of Alabama v. Garrett	531 U.S. 356 (2001)	5–4	Rehnquist	Stevens, Souter, Ginsburg, Breyer
Ferguson v. City of Charleston	532 U.S. 67 (2001)	6–3	Stevens	Rehnquist, Scalia, Thomas
Atwater v. City of Lago Vista	532 U.S. 318 (2001)	5–4	Souter	Stevens, O'Connor, Ginsburg, Breyer
PGA Tour, Inc. v. Martin	532 U.S. 661 (2001)	7–2	Stevens	Scalia, Thomas
Kyllo v. United States	533 U.S. 27 (2001)	5–4	Scalia	Rehnquist, Stevens, O'Connor, Kennedy
Good News Club v. Milford Central School	533 U.S. 98 (2001)	6–3	Thomas	Stevens, Souter, Ginsburg
Immigration and Naturalization Service v. St. Cyr	533 U.S. 289 (2001)	5–4	Stevens	Rehnquist, O'Connor, Scalia, Thomas
Federal Election Commission v. Colorado Republican Federal Campaign Committee	533 U.S. 431 (2001)	5–4	Souter	Rehnquist, Scalia, Kennedy, Thomas
Lorillard Tobacco Co. v. Reilly	533 U.S. 525 (2001)	5–4	O'Connor	Stevens, Souter, Ginsburg, Breyer
Zelman v. Simmons-Harris	2002	5–4	Rehnquist	Stevens, Souter, Ginsburg, Breyer
Atkins v. Virginia	2002	6–3	Stevens	Rehnquist, Scalia, Thomas
Ring v. Arizona	2002	7–2	Ginsburg	Rehnquist, O'Connor

(Table continues)

Table 2-12 (Continued)

Case name	Cite	Vote	Majority opinion writer[a]	Dissenters	Justices not participating
Federal Maritime Commission v. South Carolina State Ports Authority	2002		5–4	Thomas	Stevens, Souter, Ginsburg, Breyer	
Board of Education of Independent School District No. 92 of Pottawatomie County v. Earls	2002		5–4	Thomas	Stevens, O'Connor, Souter, Ginsburg	
Ashcroft v. Free Speech Coalition	2002		7–2, 6–3	Kennedy	Rehnquist, O'Connor, Scalia	
Ashcroft v. American Civil Liberties Union	2002		8–1	Thomas	Stevens	
Republican Party of Minnesota v. White	2002		5–4	Scalia	Stevens, Souter, Ginsburg, Breyer	
Toyota Motor Manufacturing v. Williams	2002		9–0	O'Connor		
Tahoe-Sierra Preservation Council, Inc. v. Tahoe Regional Planning Agency	2002		6–3	Stevens	Rehnquist, Scalia, Thomas	

a Includes writers of judgments of the Court. Concurrences not included.
b Seriatim opinion.

Sources: Joan Biskupic and Elder Witt, *Congressional Quarterly's Guide to the U.S. Supreme Court*, 3d ed. (Washington, D.C.: Congressional Quarterly, 1997); Kenneth Jost, *Supreme Court Yearbook* (Washington, D.C.: CQ Press, various editions).

Table 2-13   Major Decisions of the Supreme Court: *New York Times*
Measure, 1946–2001

Case name	Cite
United States v. Alcea Band of Indians (1946)	329 U.S. 40
Parker v. Fleming (1947)	329 U.S. 531
Everson v. Board of Education (1947)	330 U.S. 001
United Postal Workers v. Mitchell (1947)	330 U.S. 075
Oklahoma v. United States Civil Service (1947)	330 U.S. 127
United States v. UMW (1947)	330 U.S. 258
Packard Motor Car v. NLRB (1947)	330 U.S. 485
Harris v. United States (1947)	331 U.S. 145
New York v. United States (1947)	331 U.S. 284
Craig v. Harney (1947)	331 U.S. 367
United States v. Petrillo (1947)	332 U.S. 1
FCIC v. Merrill Bros. (1947)	332 U.S. 380
Patton v. Mississippi (1947)	332 U.S. 463
Sipuel v. Board of Regents (1948)	332 U.S. 631
Woods v. Miller C. (1948)	333 U.S. 138
McCullom v. Board of Education (1948)	333 U.S. 203
Winters v. New York (1948)	333 U.S. 507
Shelley v. Kramer (1948)	334 U.S. 001
Coe v. Coe (1948)	334 U.S. 378
Bay Ridge Operating v. Aaron (1948)	334 U.S. 446
Estin v. Estin (1948)	334 U.S. 541
Krieger v. Krieger (1948)	334 U.S. 555
United States v. CIO (1948)	335 U.S. 106
McDougall v. Green (1948)	335 U.S. 281
Upshaw v. United States (1948)	335 U.S. 410
Uveges v. Pennsylvania (1948)	335 U.S. 437
McDonald v. United States (1948)	335 U.S. 451
Lincoln Federal Labor v. Northwestern (1949)	335 U.S. 525
AFL v. American Sash (1949)	335 U.S. 538
Railway Express v. New York (1949)	336 U.S. 106
Algoma Plywood v. Wisconsin Employment (1949)	336 U.S. 301
Hood v. DuMond (1949)	336 U.S. 525
Rice v. Rice (1949)	336 U.S. 674
Terminiello v. Chicago (1949)	337 U.S. 001
Standard Oil v. United States (1949)	337 U.S. 293
Aero Industrial v. Campbell (1949)	337 U.S. 521
NLRB v. Pittsburgh Steamship (1949)	337 U.S. 656
Wolf v. Colorado (1949)	338 U.S. 025
Graham v. Brotherhood of Locomotive Firemen (1949)	338 U.S. 232
Kingsland v. Dorsey (1949)	338 U.S. 318
Wong Yang Sung v. McGrath (1950)	339 U.S. 033
United States v. Rabinowitz (1950)	339 U.S. 056
Morford v. United States (1950)	339 U.S. 258
Am Communications Association v. Douds (1950)	339 U.S. 382
UAW v. O'Brien (1950)	339 U.S. 454
Sweatt v. Painter (1950)	339 U.S. 629
McLaurin v. Oklahoma Regents (1950)	339 U.S. 637
United States v. Louisiana (1950)	339 U.S. 699

(Table continues)

Table 2-13   *(Continued)*

Case name	Cite
United States v. Texas (1950)	339 U.S. 707
Henderson v. United States (1950)	339 U.S. 816
Blau v. United States (1950)	340 U.S. 159
Niemotko v. Maryland (1951)	340 U.S. 268
Kunz v. New York (1951)	340 U.S. 290
Feiner v. New York (1951)	340 U.S. 315
Shepherd v. Florida (1951)	341 U.S. 050
Joint Anti-Fascist Committee v. McGrath (1951)	341 U.S. 123
Schwegmann Bros. v. Calvert Distillers (1951)	341 U.S. 384
Dennis v. United States (1951)	341 U.S. 494
Garner v. Board of Public Works (1951)	341 U.S. 716
Stack v. Boyle (1951)	342 U.S. 001
Rochin v. California (1952)	342 U.S. 165
Doremus v. Board of Education (1952)	342 U.S. 429
Carlson v. Landon (1952)	342 U.S. 524
Harisiades v. Shaughnessey (1952)	342 U.S. 580
Rutkin v. United States (1952)	343 U.S. 130
Zorach v. Clauson (1952)	343 U.S. 306
Public Utilities v. Pollak (1952)	343 U.S. 451
Burstyn v. Wilson (1952)	343 U.S. 495
Youngstown Sheet & Tube Co. v. Sawyer (1952)	343 U.S. 579
Brotherhood v. Howard (1952)	343 U.S. 768
Dixon v. Duffy (1952)	344 U.S. 143
United States v. Caltex (1952)	344 U.S. 149
United States v. Cardiff (1952)	344 U.S. 174
Wieman v. Updegraff (1952)	344 U.S. 183
United States v. Kahriger (1953)	345 U.S. 022
District of Columbia v. Thompson (1953)	346 U.S. 100
Bridges v. United States (1953)	346 U.S. 209
United States v. Grainger (1953)	346 U.S. 235
Barrows v. Jackson (1953)	346 U.S. 249
Rosenberg v. United States (1953)	346 U.S. 273
Toolson v. Yankees (1953)	346 U.S. 356
NLRB v. Local Union (1953)	346 U.S. 464
Superior Films v. Department of Education (1954)	346 U.S. 587
Irvine v. California (1954)	347 U.S. 128
Alabama v. Texas (1954)	347 U.S. 272
FCC v. ABC (1954)	347 U.S. 284
Hernandez v. Texas (1954)	347 U.S. 475
Brown v. Board of Education (1954)	347 U.S. 483
Bolling v. Sharpe (1954)	347 U.S. 497
Galvan v. Press (1954)	347 U.S. 522
Leyra v. Denno (1954)	347 U.S. 556
United States v. Harriss (1954)	347 U.S. 612
Moore v. Mead's Fine Bread (1954)	348 U.S. 115
United States v. Shubert (1955)	348 U.S. 222
National City Bank v. China (1955)	348 U.S. 356
Granville-Smith v. Granville-Smith (1955)	349 U.S.1

Table 2-13   *(Continued)*

Case name	Cite
Regan v. New York (1955)	349 U.S. 058
Quinn v. United States (1955)	349 U.S. 155
Emspak v. United States (1955)	349 U.S. 190
Bart v. United States (1955)	349 U.S. 219
Brown v. Board of Education II (1955)	349 U.S. 294
Peters v. Hobby (1955)	349 U.S. 331
United States ex rel Toth v. Quarles (1955)	350 U.S. 11
Steiner v. Mitchell (1956)	350 U.S. 247
Mitchell v. King Packing (1956)	350 U.S. 260
Ullman v. United States (1956)	350 U.S. 422
Pennsylvania v. Nelson (1956)	350 U.S. 497
Slochower v. New York City (1956)	350 U.S. 551
Railway Employees v. Hanson (1956)	351 U.S. 225
Cole v. Young (1956)	351 U.S. 536
Meat Cutters v. NLRB (1956)	352 U.S. 153
NLRB v. Lion Oil (1957)	352 U.S. 282
Butler v. Michigan (1957)	352 U.S. 380
Radovich v. NFL (1957)	352 U.S. 445
United States v. UAW (1957)	352 U.S. 567
Schware v. New Mexico Bar (1957)	353 U.S. 232
Kongisberg v. California (1957)	353 U.S. 252
Kremen v. United States (1957)	353 U.S. 346
Grunewald v. United States (1957)	353 U.S. 391
United States v. Du Pont (1957)	353 U.S. 586
Jencks v. United States (1957)	353 U.S. 657
Reid v. Covert (1957)	354 U.S. 001
Watkins v. United States (1957)	354 U.S. 178
Sweezy v. New Hampshire (1957)	354 U.S. 234
Yates v. United States (1957)	354 U.S. 298
Service v. Dulles (1957)	354 U.S. 363
Kingsley Books v. New York City (1957)	354 U.S. 436
Roth v. United States (1957)	354 U.S. 476
Girard v. Wilson (1957)	354 U.S. 524
Scales v. United States (sum rev) (1957)	355 U.S. 001
Lightfoot v. United States (1957)	355 U.S. 002
Benati v. United States (1957)	355 U.S. 096
Green v. United States (1957)	355 U.S. 184
Chicago, Milwaukee, St. Paul & Pacific R.R. v. Illinois (1958)	355 U.S. 300
Staub v. Baxley (1958)	355 U.S. 313
Detroit v. Murray Corp (1958)	355 U.S. 489
Harmon v. Brucker (1958)	355 U.S. 579
Green v. United States (1958)	356 U.S. 165
Federal Maritime Board v. Isbrandtsen (1958)	356 U.S. 481
Truax v. Gonzales (1958)	356 U.S. 617
UAW v. Russell (1958)	356 U.S. 634
United States v. Proctor and Gamble (1958)	356 U.S. 677
Local v. NLRB (1958)	357 U.S. 93
Kent v. Dulles (1958)	357 U.S. 116

(Table continues)

Table 2-13 *(Continued)*

Case name	Cite
Dayton v. Dulles (1958)	357 U.S. 144
Ivanhoe v. McCracken (1958)	357 U.S. 275
Tacoma v. Tacoma Taxpayers (1958)	357 U.S. 320
Wiener v. United States (1958)	357 U.S. 349
NAACP v. Alabama (1958)	357 U.S. 449
Cooper v. Aaron (1958)	358 U.S. 1
US Gas Pipeline v. Memphis (1958)	358 U.S. 103
Leedom v. Kyne (1958)	358 U.S. 184
International Boxing Club v. Illinois (1959)	358 U.S. 242
NW States Portland Cement Co. v. Minnesota (1959)	358 U.S. 450
Youngstown Sheet & Tube v. Bowers (1959)	358 U.S. 534
Bartkus v. Illinois (1959)	359 U.S. 121
Abbate v. United States (1959)	359 U.S. 187
SD Building Trades v. Garmon (1959)	359 U.S. 236
Frank v. Maryland (1959)	359 U.S. 360
Dick v. NY Life (1959)	359 U.S. 437
Uphaus v. Wyman (1959)	360 U.S. 72
Barenblatt v. United States (1959)	360 U.S. 109
Anonymous v. Barker (1959)	360 U.S. 287
Palermo v. United States (1959)	360 U.S. 343
Greene v. McElroy (1959)	360 U.S. 474
Kingsley International Pictures v. Regents (1959)	360 U.S. 684
USWA v. United States (1959)	361 U.S. 39
Smith v. California (1959)	361 U.S. 147
Kinsella v. United States (1960)	361 U.S. 234
Grisham v. Hagan (1960)	361 U.S. 278
McElroy v. United States (1960)	361 U.S. 281
Bates v. Little Rock (1960)	361 U.S. 516
Nelson/Globe v. Los Angeles (1960)	362 U.S. 1
United States v. Raines (1960)	362 U.S. 17
United States v. Parks Co (1960)	362 U.S. 29
United States v. Thomas (1960)	362 U.S. 58
Talley v. California (1960)	362 U.S. 60
FPC v. Tuscarora (1960)	362 U.S. 99
Thompson v. Louisville (1960)	362 U.S. 199
United States v. Louisiana et al. (1960)	363 U.S. 1
de Veau v. Braisted (1960)	363 U.S. 144
IRS v. Duberstein (1960)	363 U.S. 278
United States v. Kaiser (1960)	363 U.S. 299
Hannah v. Larche (1960)	363 U.S. 420
Elkins v. United States (1960)	364 U.S. 206
Rios v. United States (1960)	364 U.S. 253
Gomillion v. Lightfoot (1960)	364 U.S. 339
Boyton v. Virginia (1960)	364 U.S. 454
United States v. Miss. Valley Generating (1961)	364 U.S. 520
Times Film Corp. v. Chicago (1961)	365 U.S. 43
Monroe v. Pape (1961)	365 U.S. 167
Wilkinson v. United States (1961)	365 U.S. 399

Table 2-13   *(Continued)*

Case name	Cite
Braden v. United States (1961)	365 U.S. 431
Pugach v. Dollinger (1961)	365 U.S. 458
Silverman v. United States (1961)	365 U.S. 505
Carpentars Local v. NLRB (1961)	365 U.S. 651
Teamsters v. NLRB (1961)	365 U.S. 667
NLRB v. News Syndicate (1961)	365 U.S. 695
ITU v. NLRB (1961)	365 U.S. 705
Burton v. Wilmington (1961)	365 U.S. 715
Stewart v. United States (1961)	366 U.S. 1
James v. United States (1961)	366 U.S. 213
United States v. du Pont (1961)	366 U.S. 316
McGowan v. Maryland (1961)	366 U.S. 420
Two Guys v. McGinley (1961)	366 U.S. 582
Braunfeld v. Brown (1961)	366 U.S. 599
Gallagher v. Crown Kosher (1961)	366 U.S. 617
Communist Party of the US v. SACB (1961)	367 U.S. 1
Scales v. United States (1961)	367 U.S. 203
Noto v. United States (1961)	367 U.S. 290
Power Reactor v. IUE (1961)	367 U.S. 396
Torcaso v. Watkins (1961)	367 U.S. 488
Poe v. Ullman (1961)	367 U.S. 497
Mapp v. Ohio (1961)	367 U.S. 643
IAM v. Street (1961)	367 U.S. 740
Lathrop v. Donahue (1961)	367 U.S. 820
Hoyt v. Florida (1961)	368 U.S. 57
Garner v. Louisiana (1961)	368 U.S. 157
Griggs v. Alleghany County (1962)	369 U.S. 84
Teamsters v. Lucas Flour (1962)	369 U.S. 95
Fong Foo v. United States (1962)	369 U.S. 141
Baker v. Carr (1962)	369 U.S. 186
Turner v. Memphis (1962)	369 U.S. 350
California v. FPC (1962)	369 U.S. 482
Becker v. Washington (1962)	369 U.S. 541
Hutcheson v. United States (1962)	369 U.S. 599
Russell v. United States (1962)	369 U.S. 749
Sinclair Refining v. Atkinson (1962)	370 U.S. 195
Atkinson v. Sinclair Refining (1962)	370 U.S. 238
Brown Shoe v. United States (1962)	370 U.S. 294
United States v. Wise (1962)	370 U.S. 405
Engel v. Vitale (1962)	370 U.S. 421
Robinson v. California (1962)	370 U.S. 660
United States v. Loews (1962)	371 U.S. 38
NAACP v. Button (1963)	371 U.S. 415
McCulloch v. Sociedad (1963)	372 U.S. 10
Kennedy v. Mendoz-Martinez (1963)	372 U.S. 144
Edwards v. South Carolina (1963)	372 U.S. 229
Gideon v. Wainwright (1963)	372 U.S. 335
Gray v. Sanders (1963)	372 U.S. 368

(Table continues)

Table 2-13 *(Continued)*

Case name	Cite
Gibson v. Florida Legis (1963)	372 U.S. 539
Dugan v. Rank (1963)	372 U.S. 609
Colorado Anti-Discrimination v. Continental Air (1963)	372 U.S. 714
Peterson v. Greenville (1963)	373 U.S. 244
Lombard v. Louisiana (1963)	373 U.S. 267
Silver v. New York Stock Exchange (1963)	373 U.S. 341
Gober v. Birmingham (1963)	373 U.S. 374
Avent v. North Carolina (1963)	373 U.S. 375
Lopez v. United States (1963)	373 U.S. 427
Watson v. Memphis (1963)	373 U.S. 526
Arizona v. California (1963)	373 U.S. 546
Goss v. Knoxville Board (1963)	373 U.S. 683
United Association v. Borden (1963)	373 U.S. 690
Bridge Workers v. Perko (1963)	373 U.S. 701
NLRB v. General Motors Corp. (1963)	373 U.S. 734
Retail Clerks v. Schermerhorn (1963)	373 U.S. 746
Ker v. California (1963)	374 U.S. 23
Abington School District v. Schempp (1963)	374 U.S. 203
Sherbert v. Verner (1963)	374 U.S. 398
Retail Clerks v. Schermerhorn (1963)	375 U.S. 96
Anderson v. Martin (1964)	375 U.S. 399
Wesberry v. Sanders (1964)	376 U.S. 1
Wright v. Rockefeller (1964)	376 U.S. 52
Costello v. INS (1964)	376 U.S. 120
Sears & Roebuck v. Stiffel (1964)	376 U.S. 225
Compco v. Day-Brite (1964)	376 U.S. 234
New York Times v. Sullivan (1964)	376 U.S. 254
Banco Nacional v. Sabbatino (1964)	376 U.S. 398
United States v. El Paso Gas (1964)	376 U.S. 651
United States v. First National Bank (1964)	376 U.S. 665
United States v. Barnett (1964)	376 U.S. 681
Schneider v. Bush (1964)	377 U.S. 163
Griffin v. Prince Ed Board (1964)	377 U.S. 218
NAACP v. Alabama (1964)	377 U.S. 288
Hostetter v. Idlewild (1964)	377 U.S. 324
Department of Revenue v. Beam (1964)	377 U.S. 341
Reynolds v. Sims (1964)	377 U.S. 533
WMCA v. Lomenzo (1964)	377 U.S. 633
Maryland Committee v. Tawes (1964)	377 U.S. 656
Davis v. Mann (1964)	377 U.S. 678
Roman v. Sincock (1964)	377 U.S. 695
Lucas v. 44th Gen Assembly (1964)	377 U.S. 713
Malloy v. Hogan (1964)	378 U.S. 1
Murphy v. Waterfront Comm'n (1964)	378 U.S. 52
Bell v. Maryland (1964)	378 U.S. 226
Bouie v. Columbia (1964)	378 U.S. 347
Escobedo v. Illinois (1964)	378 U.S. 478
Aptheker v. Secretary of State (1964)	378 U.S. 500

Table 2-13   *(Continued)*

Case name	Cite
McLaughlin v. Florida (1964)	379 U.S. 184
Heart of Atlanta v. United States (1964)	379 U.S. 241
Katzenbach v. McClung (1964)	379 U.S. 294
Hamm v. Rock Hill (1964)	379 U.S. 306
United States v. Mississippi (1965)	380 U.S. 128
Louisiana v. United States (1965)	380 U.S. 145
United States v. Seeger (1965)	380 U.S. 163
TWUA v. Darlington (1965)	380 U.S. 263
NLRB v. Brown (1965)	380 U.S. 278
Am Ship Building v. NLRB (1965)	380 U.S. 300
FTC v. Colgate-Palmolive (1965)	380 U.S. 374
Pointer v. Texas (1965)	380 U.S. 400
Dombrowski v. Pfister (1965)	380 U.S. 479
Harman v. Forsessensius (1965)	380 U.S. 528
CIR v. Brown (1965)	380 U.S. 563
United States v. California (1965)	381 U.S. 139
Lamont v. Postmaster (1965)	381 U.S. 301
Griswold v. Connecticut (1965)	381 U.S. 479
Estes v. Texas (1965)	381 U.S. 532
Linkletter v. Walker (1965)	381 U.S. 618
Angelet v. Fay (1965)	381 U.S. 654
Albertson v. SACB (1965)	382 U.S. 70
Evans v. Newton (1966)	382 U.S. 296
South Carolina v. Katzenbach (1966)	383 U.S. 301
Book Named. . . . v. AG MA (1966)	383 U.S. 413
Ginzburg v. United States (1966)	383 U.S. 463
Mishkin v. New York (1966)	383 U.S. 502
Harper v. Virginia State Board (1966)	383 U.S. 663
United States v. Guest (1966)	383 U.S. 745
United States v. Price (1966)	383 U.S. 787
Elfbrandt v. Russell (1966)	384 U.S. 11
Seagram v. Hostetter (1966)	384 U.S. 35
United States v. General Motors (1966)	384 U.S. 127
Sheppard v. Maxwell (1966)	384 U.S. 333
Miranda v. Arizona (1966)	384 U.S. 436
Katzenbach v. Morgan (1966)	384 U.S. 641
Cardona v. Power (1966)	384 U.S. 672
Johnson v. New Jersey (1966)	384 U.S. 719
Schmerber v. California (1966)	384 U.S. 757
Adderly v. Florida (1966)	385 U.S. 39
Bond v. Floyd (1966)	385 U.S. 116
Fortson v. Morris (1966)	385 U.S. 231
Hoffa v. United States (1966)	385 U.S. 293
Time v. Hill (1967)	385 U.S. 374
Swann v. Adams (1967)	385 U.S. 440
United States v. Laub (1967)	385 U.S. 475
Travis v. United States (1967)	385 U.S. 491
Spevack v. Klein (1967)	385 U.S. 511

(Table continues)

Table 2-13   *(Continued)*

Case name	Cite
Keyishian v. Board of Regents (1967)	385 U.S. 589
Cascade Natural Gas v. El Paso (1967)	386 U.S. 129
McCray v. Illinois (1967)	386 U.S. 300
Baltimore and Ohio R.R. v. United States (1967)	386 U.S. 372
National Woodword v. NLRB (1967)	386 U.S. 612
Houston Insulation v. NLRB (1967)	386 U.S. 664
National Bellas v. Dep't of Revenue (1967)	386 U.S. 753
Redrup v. New York (1967)	386 U.S. 767
In re Gault (1967)	387 U.S. 1
Moody v. Flowers (1967)	387 U.S. 97
Dusch v. Davis (1967)	387 U.S. 112
Afroyim v. Rusk (1967)	387 U.S. 253
Warden v. Hayden (1967)	387 U.S. 294
Reitman v. Mulkey (1967)	387 U.S. 369
Camara v. Municipal Court (1967)	387 U.S. 523
See v. City of Seattle (1967)	387 U.S. 541
Loving v. Virginia (1967)	388 U.S. 1
Berger v. New York (1967)	388 U.S. 41
Curtis Pub v. Butts (1967)	388 U.S. 130
NLRB v. Allis-Chambers (1967)	388 U.S. 175
Walker v. Birmingham (1967)	388 U.S. 307
UMW v. Illinois State Bar (1967)	389 U.S. 217
United States v. Robel (1967)	389 U.S. 258
Katz v. United States (1967)	389 U.S. 347
Penn Central Merger Inclusion Cases (1968)	389 U.S. 486
Marchetti v. United States (1968)	390 U.S. 39
Haynes v. United States (1968)	390 U.S. 85
Avery v. Midland County (1968)	390 U.S. 474
United States v. Jackson (1968)	390 U.S. 570
Ginsberg v. New York (1968)	390 U.S. 629
Interstate Circuit v. Dallas (1968)	390 U.S. 676
Permian Basin Area Rate Cases (1968)	390 U.S. 747
Duncan v. Louisiana (1968)	391 U.S. 145
United States v. O'Brien (1968)	391 U.S. 367
Green v. County School Board (1968)	391 U.S. 430
Raney v. Board of Education (1968)	391 U.S. 443
Monroe v. Board of Comm'rs (1968)	391 U.S. 450
Witherspoon v. Illinois (1968)	391 U.S. 510
Terry v. Ohio (1968)	392 U.S. 1
Sibron v. New York (1968)	392 U.S. 40
Flast v. Cohen (1968)	392 U.S. 83
Board of Education v. Central School (1968)	392 U.S. 236
Assn v. Comm'r of Sanitation (1968)	392 U.S. 280
Jones v. Mayer (1968)	392 U.S. 409
Powell v. Texas (1968)	392 U.S. 514
Williams v. Rhodes (1968)	393 U.S. 23
Epperson v. Arkansas (1968)	393 U.S. 97
Carroll v. Princess Anne County (1968)	393 U.S. 175

Table 2-13   *(Continued)*

Case name	Cite
Oestereich v. Selective Service (1968)	393 U.S. 233
Presb Church v. Mary Church (1969)	393 U.S. 440
Tinker v. Des Moines (1969)	393 U.S. 503
Gregory v. City of Chicago (1969)	394 U.S. 111
Shuttlesworth v. Birmingham (1969)	394 U.S. 147
Alderman v. United States (1969)	394 U.S. 165
Orozco v. Texas (1969)	394 U.S. 324
Wells v. Rockefeller (1969)	394 U.S. 542
Stanley v. Georgia (1969)	394 U.S. 557
Shapiro v. Thompson (1969)	394 U.S. 618
Leary v. United States (1969)	395 U.S. 6
United States v. Montgomery County (1969)	395 U.S. 225
O'Callahan v. Parker (1969)	395 U.S. 258
Gaston County v. United States (1969)	395 U.S. 285
Daniel v. Paul (1969)	395 U.S. 298
Sniadach v. Family Finance (1969)	395 U.S. 337
Red Lion Broadcasting v. FCC (1969)	395 U.S. 367
Powell v. McCormack (1969)	395 U.S. 486
Kramer v. Union Free SD (1969)	395 U.S. 621
North Carolina v. Pearce (1969)	395 U.S. 711
Chimel v. California (1969)	395 U.S. 752
Benton v. Maryland (1969)	395 U.S. 784
Alexander v. Holmes County (1969)	396 U.S. 19
Gutknecht v. United States (1970)	396 U.S. 295
Evans v. Abney (1970)	396 U.S. 435
Breen v. Selective Service (1970)	396 U.S. 460
Hadley v. Junior College (1970)	397 U.S. 50
Toussie v. United States (1970)	397 U.S. 112
Wheeler v. Montgomery (1970)	397 U.S. 280
Illinois v. Allen (1970)	397 U.S. 337
Rosado v. Wyman (1970)	397 U.S. 397
Dandridge v. Williams (1970)	397 U.S. 471
Walz v. Tax Commission (1970)	397 U.S. 664
Schacht v. United States (1970)	398 U.S. 58
Boys Market v. Retail Clerks (1970)	398 U.S. 235
Maxwell v. Bishop (1970)	398 U.S. 262
Welsh v. United States (1970)	398 U.S. 333
Coleman v. Alabama (1970)	399 U.S. 1
Vale v. Louisiana (1970)	399 U.S. 30
Chambers v. Maroney (1970)	399 U.S. 42
Baldwin v. New York (1970)	399 U.S. 66
Williams v. Florida (1970)	399 U.S. 78
United States v. Sisson (1970)	399 U.S. 267
Dutton v. Evans (1970)	400 U.S. 74
Oregon v. Mitchell (1970)	400 U.S. 112
Wyman v. James (1971)	400 U.S. 309
Mayberry v. Pennsylvania (1971)	400 U.S. 455
Phillips v. Martin Marietta (1971)	400 U.S. 542

(Table continues)

Table 2-13   *(Continued)*

Case name	Cite
Younger v. Harris (1971)	401 U.S. 37
Samuels v. Mackell (1971)	401 U.S. 66
Boyle v. Landry (1971)	401 U.S. 77
Byrne v. Karalexis (1971)	401 U.S. 216
Harris v. New York (1971)	401 U.S. 222
Boddie v. Connecticut (1971)	401 U.S. 371
Tate v. Short (1971)	401 U.S. 395
Griggs v. Duke Power (1971)	401 U.S. 424
Gillette v. United States (1971)	401 U.S. 437
United States v. Freed (1971)	401 U.S. 601
Swann v. Charlotte-Mecklenburg (1971)	402 U.S. 1
United States v. Vuitch (1971)	402 U.S. 62
James v. Valtierra (1971)	402 U.S. 137
McGautha v. California (1971)	402 U.S. 183
Coates v. Cinn (1971)	402 U.S. 611
Rosenbloom v. Metromedia (1971)	403 U.S. 29
Whitcomb v. Chavis (1971)	403 U.S. 124
Abate v. Mundt (1971)	403 U.S. 182
Palmer v. Thompson (1971)	403 U.S. 217
McKeiver v. Pennsylvania (1971)	403 U.S. 528
Lemon v. Kurtzman (1971)	403 U.S. 602
Tilton v. Richardson (1971)	403 U.S. 672
Clay v. United States (1971)	403 U.S. 698
New York Times v. United States (1971)	403 U.S. 713
Reed v. Reed (1971)	404 U.S. 71
Lego v. Twomey (1972)	404 U.S. 477
Roudebush v. Hartke (1972)	405 U.S. 15
FTC v. Hutchinson (1972)	405 U.S. 233
Dunn v. Blumstein (1972)	405 U.S. 330
Stanley v. Illinois (1972)	405 U.S. 645
Wisconsin v. Yoder (1972)	406 U.S. 205
Johnson v. Louisiana (1972)	406 U.S. 356
Apodaca v. Oregon (1972)	406 U.S. 404
Kastigar v. United States (1972)	406 U.S. 441
Zicarelli v. New Jersey State Comm'n (1972)	406 U.S. 472
Jefferson v. Hackney (1972)	406 U.S. 535
Kirby v. Illinois (1972)	406 U.S. 682
Argersinger v. Hamlin (1972)	407 U.S. 25
Adams v. Williams (1972)	407 U.S. 143
Moose Lodge v. Irvis (1972)	407 U.S. 163
Flood v. Kuhn (1972)	407 U.S. 258
United States v. United States Dist Court (1972)	407 U.S. 297
United States v. Scotland Neck School (1972)	407 U.S. 484
Lloyd Corp v. Tanner (1972)	407 U.S. 551
Laird v. Tatum (1972)	408 U.S. 1
Furman v. Georgia (1972)	408 U.S. 238
United States v. Brewster (1972)	408 U.S. 501
Gravel v. United States (1972)	408 U.S. 606

Table 2-13   *(Continued)*

Case name	Cite
Branzburg v. Hayes (1972)	408 U.S. 665
Gottschalk v. Benson (1972)	409 U.S. 63
California v. LaRue (1972)	409 U.S. 109
Trafficante v. Met. Life (1972)	409 U.S. 205
Roe v. Wade (1973)	410 U.S. 113
Doe v. Bolton (1973)	410 U.S. 179
Mahan v. Howell (1973)	410 U.S. 315
Tillman v. Wheaton-Haven (1973)	410 U.S. 431
Sayler Land v. Tulare Lake Basin (1973)	410 U.S. 719
San Antonio v. Rodriguez (1973)	411 U.S. 1
Askew v. Am Waterway Operators (1973)	411 U.S. 325
Schneckloth v. Bustamonte (1973)	412 U.S. 218
Cupp v. Murphy (1973)	412 U.S. 291
Miller v. California (1973)	413 U.S. 15
New York State Department v. Dublino (1973)	413 U.S. 405
Levitt v. CPEARL (1973)	413 U.S. 472
CPEARL v. Nyquist (1973)	413 U.S. 756
United States v. Robinson (1973)	414 U.S. 218
Gustafson v. Florida (1973)	414 U.S. 260
United States v. Calandra (1974)	414 U.S. 338
Cleveland Board of Ed v. LaFleur (1974)	414 U.S. 632
Village of Belle Terres v. Boraas (1974)	416 U.S. 1
California Bankers Association v. Schultz (1974)	416 U.S. 21
Scheuer v. Rhodes (1974)	416 U.S. 232
Defunis v. Odegaard (1974)	416 U.S. 312
United States v. Giordano (1974)	416 U.S. 505
Eisen v. Carlisle (1974)	417 U.S. 156
Corning Glass v. Brennan (1974)	417 U.S. 188
Pittsburgh v. Alco (1974)	417 U.S. 369
Geduldig v. Aiello (1974)	417 U.S. 484
Parker v. Levy (1974)	417 U.S. 733
Miami Herald v. Tornillo (1974)	418 U.S. 241
Gertz v. Welch (1974)	418 U.S. 323
United States v. Maine Bancorp (1974)	418 U.S. 602
United States v. Nixon (1974)	418 U.S. 683
Milliken v. Bradley (1974)	418 U.S. 717
RR Reorganization Cases (1974)	419 U.S. 102
Jackson v. Metro Edison (1974)	419 U.S. 345
Taylor v. Louisiana (1975)	419 U.S. 522
Goss v. Lopez (1975)	419 U.S. 565
Train v. City of New York (1975)	420 U.S. 35
United States v. Bisceglia (1975)	420 U.S. 141
Wood v. Strickland (1975)	420 U.S. 308
Cox Broadcasting v. Cohn (1975)	420 U.S. 469
United States v. Florida (1975)	420 U.S. 531
Weinberger v. Wiesenfeld (1975)	420 U.S. 636
United States v. Reliable Transfer (1975)	421 U.S. 397
Connell Construct v. Plumbers (1975)	421 U.S. 616

(Table continues)

Table 2-13   *(Continued)*

Case name	Cite
Goldfarb v. Virginia State Bar (1975)	421 U.S. 773
United Housing v. Forman (1975)	421 U.S. 837
Warth v. Seldin (1975)	422 U.S. 490
O'Connor v. Donaldson (1975)	422 U.S. 563
Faretta v. California (1975)	422 U.S. 806
Michelin Tire v. Wages (1976)	423 U.S. 276
United States v. Watson (1976)	423 U.S. 411
Buckley v. Valeo (1976)	424 U.S. 1
De Canas v. Bica (1976)	424 U.S. 351
Time v. Firestone (1976)	424 U.S. 448
Paul v. Davis (1976)	424 U.S. 693
Franks v. Bowman (1976)	424 U.S. 747
Kelley v. Johnson (1976)	425 U.S. 238
Hills v. Gautreaux (1976)	425 U.S. 284
Hampton v. United States (1976)	425 U.S. 484
Virginia State Board v. VA Consumers (1976)	425 U.S. 748
Hampton v. Wong (1976)	426 U.S. 88
Washington v. Davis (1976)	426 U.S. 229
Federal Energy Admin v. Algonquin (1976)	426 U.S. 548
Roemer v. Board of Public Works (1976)	426 U.S. 736
NLC v. Usery (1976)	426 U.S. 833
Young v. Am Mini Theatres (1976)	427 U.S. 50
Runyon v. McCrary (1976)	427 U.S. 160
McDonald v. Santa Fe Trail (1976)	427 U.S. 273
Pasadena Board v. Spangler (1976)	427 U.S. 424
Andersen v. Maryland (1976)	427 U.S. 463
Nebraska Press v. Stuart (1976)	427 U.S. 539
Planned Parenthood v. Danforth (1976)	428 U.S. 52
Gregg v. Georgia (1976)	428 U.S. 153
Profitt v. Florida (1976)	428 U.S. 242
Jurek v. Texas (1976)	428 U.S. 262
Woodson v. North Carolina (1976)	428 U.S. 280
Roberts v. Louisiana (1976)	428 U.S. 325
Stone v. Powell (1976)	428 U.S. 465
General Electric v. Gilbert (1976)	429 U.S. 125
Mathews v. De Castro (1976)	429 U.S. 181
Arlington Heights v. Metro Heights (1977)	429 U.S. 252
du Pont v. Train (1977)	430 U.S. 112
UJO of Williamsburgh v. Carey (1977)	430 U.S. 144
Califano v. Goldfarb (1977)	430 U.S. 199
Complete Auto Transit v. Brady (1977)	430 U.S. 274
Brewer v. Williams (1977)	430 U.S. 387
Ingraham v. Wright (1977)	430 U.S. 651
US Trust Co v. New Jersey (1977)	431 U.S. 1
Linmark v. Willingboro (1977)	431 U.S. 85
Int'l Brotherhood v. United States (1977)	431 U.S. 324
Roberts v. Louisiana (1977)	431 U.S. 633
Beal v. Doe (1977)	432 U.S. 438

Table 2-13   *(Continued)*

Case name	Cite
Maher v. Roe (1977)	432 U.S. 464
Milliken v. Bradley (1977)	433 U.S. 267
Bates v. State Bar (1977)	433 U.S. 350
Nixon v. GSA (1977)	433 U.S. 425
Coker v. Georgia (1977)	433 U.S. 584
Nashville Gas v. Satty (1977)	434 U.S. 136
United States v. NY Telephone (1977)	434 U.S. 159
Bordenkircher v. Hayes (1978)	434 U.S. 357
Ray v. Atlantic Richfield (1978)	435 U.S. 151
Vermont Yankee v. NRDC (1978)	435 U.S. 519
Nixon v. Warner Communications (1978)	435 U.S. 589
Louisiana v. Manhart (1978)	435 U.S. 702
First National Bank v. Bellotti (1978)	435 U.S. 765
Marshall v. Barlows (1978)	436 U.S. 307
In re Primus (1978)	436 U.S. 412
Ohralik v. State Bar (1978)	436 U.S. 447
Zurcher v. Stanford Daily (1978)	436 U.S. 547
FCC v. National Citizens Comm'n (1978)	436 U.S. 775
TVA v. Hill (1978)	437 U.S. 153
Zenith Radio v. United States (1978)	437 U.S. 443
Phil v. New Jersey (1978)	437 U.S. 617
Penn Central v. New York City (1978)	438 U.S. 104
Univ. of California v. Bakke (1978)	438 U.S. 265
FCC v. Pacifica (1978)	438 U.S. 726
Orr v. Orr (1979)	440 U.S. 268
NY Telephone v. NYS Dept of Labor (1979)	440 U.S. 519
Delaware v. Prouse (1979)	440 U.S. 648
FCC v. Midwest Video (1979)	440 U.S. 689
Broadcast Music v. CBS (1979)	441 U.S. 1
Herbert v. Lando (1979)	441 U.S. 153
Dalia v. United States (1979)	441 U.S. 238
Cannon v. Univ. of Chicago (1979)	441 U.S. 677
Personnel Administration v. Feeney (1979)	442 U.S. 256
Southeastern Comm Coll v. Davis (1979)	442 U.S. 397
United States v. Helstoski (1979)	442 U.S. 477
United States v. Rutherford (1979)	442 U.S. 544
Parham v. JR (1979)	442 U.S. 584
Califano v. Westcott (1979)	443 U.S. 76
Hutchinson v. Proxmire (1979)	443 U.S. 111
Wolston v. Readers Digest (1979)	443 U.S. 157
Steelworkers v. Weber (1979)	443 U.S. 193
Gannet v. DePasquale (1979)	443 U.S. 368
Columbus Board of Education v. Penick (1979)	443 U.S. 449
Brown v. Glines (1980)	444 U.S. 348
Sec of Navy v. Huff (1980)	444 U.S. 453
NRLB v. Yeshiva (1980)	444 U.S. 672
Kissinger v. Reporters Committee (1980)	445 U.S. 136
Payton v. New York (1980)	445 U.S. 573

(Table continues)

Table 2-13   *(Continued)*

Case name	Cite
Owen v. City of Independence (1980)	445 U.S. 622
City of Mobile v. Bolden (1980)	446 U.S. 55
Rhode Island v. Innis (1980)	446 U.S. 291
Pruneyard Shopping Center v. Robins (1980)	447 U.S. 74
Diamond v. Chakrabarty (1980)	447 U.S. 303
Bryant v. Yellen (1980)	447 U.S. 352
Con Edison v. Public Service (1980)	447 U.S. 530
Central Hudson v. Public Service (1980)	447 U.S. 557
Maine v. Thiboutot (1980)	448 U.S. 1
Harris v. McCrae (1980)	448 U.S. 297
United States v. Sioux Nation (1980)	448 U.S. 371
Fullilove v. Klutznick (1980)	448 U.S. 448
Richmond Newspapers v. Virginia (1980)	448 U.S. 555
United States v. DiFranceso (1980)	449 U.S. 117
Fedorenko v. United States (1981)	449 U.S. 490
Chandler v. Florida (1981)	449 U.S. 560
H.L. v. Matheson (1981)	450 U.S. 398
Pennhurst v. Halderman (1981)	451 U.S. 1
Steagald v. United States (1981)	451 U.S. 204
Estelle v. Smith (1981)	451 U.S. 454
Edwards v. Arizona (1981)	451 U.S. 477
County of Washington v. Gunther (1981)	452 U.S. 161
Rhodes v. Chapman (1981)	452 U.S. 337
Am Textile v. Donovon (1981)	452 U.S. 490
Rostker v. Goldberg (1981)	453 U.S. 57
McCarty v. McCarty (1981)	453 U.S. 210
Haig v. Agee (1981)	453 U.S. 280
CBS v. FCC (1981)	453 U.S. 367
Commonwealth Edison v. Montana (1981)	453 U.S. 609
Dames & Moore v. Regan (1981)	453 U.S. 654
United Transportation Union v. LIRR (1982)	455 U.S. 678
United States v. MacDonald (1982)	456 U.S. 1
Am Tobacco v. Patterson (1982)	456 U.S. 63
Longshoremen v. Allied International (1982)	456 U.S. 212
United States v. Ross (1982)	456 U.S. 798
Plyler v. Doe (1982)	457 U.S. 202
Patsy v. Board of Education (1982)	457 U.S. 496
Nixon v. Fitzgerald (1982)	457 U.S. 731
Harlow v. Fitzgerald (1982)	457 U.S. 800
Board of Education v. Pico (1982)	457 U.S. 853
Board of Education v. Rowley (1982)	458 U.S. 176
New York v. Ferber (1982)	458 U.S. 747
NAACP v. Claiborne Hardware (1982)	458 U.S. 886
Pacific Gas & Electric v. Energy Resources (1983)	461 U.S. 190
Regan v. Taxation with Representation (1983)	461 U.S. 540
Bob Jones Univ. v. United States (1983)	461 U.S. 574
Akron v. Akron Center (1983)	462 U.S. 416
Planned Parenthood v. Ashcroft (1983)	462 U.S. 476

Table 2-13   *(Continued)*

Case name	Cite
Simopolous v. Virginia (1983)	462 U.S. 506
Karcher v. Daggett (1983)	462 U.S. 725
INS v. Chadha (1983)	462 U.S. 919
Motor Vehicle Manuf v. St Farm (1983)	463 U.S. 29
Container Corp v. Franchise Board (1983)	463 U.S. 159
Solem v. Helm (1983)	463 U.S. 277
Mueller v. Allen (1983)	463 U.S. 388
Dirks v. SEC (1983)	463 U.S. 646
Barefoot v. Estelle (1983)	463 U.S. 880
Arizona v. Norris (1983)	463 U.S. 1073
Sec of Interior v. California (1984)	464 U.S. 312
SONY v. Universal City Studios (1984)	464 U.S. 417
Press Enterprise v. Superior Court (1984)	464 U.S. 501
Pulley v. Harris (1984)	465 U.S. 37
NRLB v. Bildisco (1984)	465 U.S. 513
Grove City v. Bell (1984)	465 U.S. 555
Lynch v. Donnelly (1984)	465 U.S. 668
INS v. Delgado (1984)	466 U.S. 210
Bose Corp v. Consumers' Union (1984)	466 U.S. 485
Hishon v. King & Spalding (1984)	467 U.S. 69
Hawaii v. Midkiff (1984)	467 U.S. 229
Schall v. Martin (1984)	467 U.S. 253
Firefighters v. Stotts (1984)	467 U.S. 561
New York v. Quarles (1984)	467 U.S. 649
NCAA v. Board of Regents (1984)	468 U.S. 85
FCC v. LWV (1984)	468 U.S. 364
Roberts v. Jaycees (1984)	468 U.S. 609
Selective Service System v. Minnesota PIRG (1984)	468 U.S. 841
United States v. Leon (1984)	468 U.S. 897
United States v. Hensley (1985)	469 U.S. 221
New Jersey v. T.L.O. (1985)	469 U.S. 325
Garcia v. SAMTA (1985)	469 U.S. 528
Ake v. Oklahoma (1985)	470 U.S. 68
FEC v. NCPAC (1985)	470 U.S. 480
Tennessee v. Garner (1985)	471 U.S. 1
Harper & Row v. The Nation (1985)	471 U.S. 539
Wallace v. Jaffree (1985)	472 U.S. 38
Northeast Bancorp v. Board of Governors (1985)	472 U.S. 159
Thornton v. Caldor (1985)	472 U.S. 703
Pattern Makers v. NLRB (1985)	473 U.S. 95
Grand Rapids v. Ball (1985)	473 U.S. 373
Aguilar v. Felton (1985)	473 U.S. 402
City of Renton v. Playtime (1986)	475 U.S. 41
Goldman v. Weinberger (1986)	475 U.S. 503
Phil Newspapers v. Hepps (1986)	475 U.S. 767
Batson v. Kentucky (1986)	476 U.S. 79
Lockhart v. McCree (1986)	476 U.S. 162
California v. Ciraolo (1986)	476 U.S. 207

(Table continues)

Table 2-13   *(Continued)*

Case name	Cite
Dow Chemical v. United States (1986)	476 U.S. 227
Wygant v. Jackson Board of Education (1986)	476 U.S. 267
Bowen v. New York City (1986)	476 U.S. 467
Bowen v. AHA (1986)	476 U.S. 610
Thornburgh v. ACOG (1986)	476 U.S. 747
Meritor v. Vinson (1986)	477 U.S. 57
Davis v. Bandemer (1986)	478 U.S. 109
Bowers v. Hardwick (1986)	478 U.S. 186
Posadas de PR v. Tourism (1986)	478 U.S. 328
Local 28 v. EEOC (1986)	478 U.S. 421
Local 93 v. Cleveland (1986)	478 U.S. 501
Bowsher v. Synar (1986)	478 U.S. 714
Tashijan v. Republican Party (1986)	479 U.S. 208
California Federal Savings v. Guerra (1987)	479 U.S. 272
United States v. Paradise (1987)	480 U.S. 149
School Board v. Arline (1987)	480 U.S. 273
INS v. Cardoza-Fonesca (1987)	480 U.S. 421
CA Coastal v. Granite Rock (1987)	480 U.S. 572
Johnson v. Transportation Agency (1987)	480 U.S. 616
Pennzoil v. Texaco (1987)	481 U.S. 1
CTS v. Dynamics (1987)	481 U.S. 69
McCleskey v. Kemp (1987)	481 U.S. 279
Board of Directors v. Rotary Club (1987)	481 U.S. 537
St. Frances College v. Al-khazraji (1987)	481 U.S. 604
Shaare Tefilia v. Cobb (1987)	481 U.S. 615
United States v. Salerno (1987)	481 U.S. 739
Fort Halifax v. Coyne (1987)	482 U.S. 1
Shearson/Am Express v. McMahon (1987)	482 U.S. 220
First...Church v. County of Los Angeles (1987)	482 U.S. 304
Booth v. Maryland (1987)	482 U.S. 496
Edwards v. Aguillard (1987)	482 U.S. 578
McNally v. United States (1987)	483 U.S. 350
Solorio v United States (1987)	483 U.S. 435
United States v. Stanley (1987)	483 U.S. 669
Carpenter v. United States (1987)	484 U.S. 19
Hazelwood v. Kuhlmeier (1988)	484 U.S. 260
Hustler v. Falwell (1988)	485 U.S. 46
Basic v. Levinson (1988)	485 U.S. 224
Lyng v. Intl Union (1988)	485 U.S. 360
Bowen v. Kizer (1988)	485 U.S. 386
South Carolina v. Baker (1988)	485 U.S. 505
Business Electronics v. Sharp Electronics (1988)	485 U.S. 717
California v. Greenwood (1988)	486 U.S. 35
Patrick v. Burget (1988)	486 U.S. 94
K Mart v. Cartier (1988)	486 U.S. 281
Webster v. Doe (1988)	486 U.S. 592
NYS Club Assoc v. City of New York (1988)	487 U.S. 1
Boyle v. United Technologies (1988)	487 U.S. 500

Table 2-13 *(Continued)*

Case name	Cite
Morrison v. Olson (1988)	487 U.S. 654
Arizona v. Youngblood (1988)	488 U.S. 51
NCAA v. Tarkanian (1988)	488 U.S. 179
Goldberg v. Sweet (1989)	488 U.S. 252
Duquesne Light v. Barasch (1989)	488 U.S. 299
Mistretta v. United States (1989)	488 U.S. 361
City of Richmond v. Croson (1989)	488 U.S. 469
DeShaney v. Winnebago (1989)	489 U.S. 189
City of Canton v. Harris (1989)	489 U.S. 378
Skinner v. Railway Labor (1989)	489 U.S. 602
National Treasury v. Von Raab (1989)	489 U.S. 656
Board of Estimate v. Morris (1989)	489 U.S. 688
United States v. Sokolow (1989)	490 U.S. 1
California v. ARC America (1989)	490 U.S. 93
Price Waterhouse v. Hopkins (1989)	490 U.S. 228
Wards Cove v. Atonio (1989)	490 U.S. 642
Martin v. Wilks (1989)	490 U.S. 755
Patterson v. McLean (1989)	491 U.S. 164
Texas v. Johnson (1989)	491 U.S. 397
United States v. Monsanto (1989)	491 U.S. 600
Caplin & Drysdale v. United States (1989)	491 U.S. 617
Sable Commun v. FCC (1989)	492 U.S. 115
Penry v. Lynaugh (1989)	492 U.S. 302
Stanford v. Kentucky (1989)	492 U.S. 361
Webster v. RHS (1989)	492 U.S. 490
Allegheny County v. ACLU (1989)	492 U.S. 573
Univ. of Pennsylvania v. EEOC (1990)	493 U.S. 182
Spallone v. United States (1990)	493 U.S. 265
James v. Illinois (1990)	493 U.S. 307
Dole v. Steelworkers (1990)	494 U.S. 26
Washington v. Harper (1990)	494 U.S. 210
United States v. Verdugo-Urquidez (1990)	494 U.S. 259
Butler v. McKellar (1990)	494 U.S. 407
Saffle v. Parks (1990)	494 U.S. 484
Austin v. MI Chamber of Commerce (1990)	494 U.S. 652
NLRB v. Curtin Matheson (1990)	494 U.S. 775
Yellow Freight v. Donnelly (1990)	494 U.S. 820
Missouri v. Jenkins (1990)	495 U.S. 33
Osbourne v. Ohio (1990)	495 U.S. 103
California v. Am Stores (1990)	495 U.S. 271
West Side Board of Ed v. Mergens (1990)	496 U.S. 226
United States v. Eichman (1990)	496 U.S. 310
MIchigan v. Sitz (1990)	496 U.S. 444
Wilder v. VA Hospital (1990)	496 U.S. 498
Pennsylvania v. Muniz (1990)	496 U.S. 582
Pension Benefit Guaranty v. LTV (1990)	496 U.S. 633
Rutan v. Republican Party of Illinois (1990)	497 U.S. 62
Cruzan v. Director (1990)	497 U.S. 261

(Table continues)

Table 2-13   *(Continued)*

Case name	Cite
Hodgson v. Minnesota (1990)	497 U.S. 417
Ohio v. Akron Center (1990)	497 U.S. 502
Metro Broadcasting v. FCC (1990)	497 U.S. 547
Idaho v. Wright (1990)	497 U.S. 805
Maryland v. Craig (1990)	497 U.S. 836
Minnick v. Mississippi (1990)	498 U.S. 146
Board of Education v. McDowell (1991)	498 U.S. 237
McNary v. Haitian Refugee Center (1991)	498 U.S. 479
Pacific Mutual v. Haslip (1991)	499 U.S. 1
UAW v. Johnson Controls (1991)	499 U.S. 187
Arizona v. Fulimante (1991)	499 U.S. 279
Powers v. Ohio (1991)	499 U.S. 400
McCleskey v. Zant (1991)	499 U.S. 467
American Hospital Association v. NLRB (1991)	499 U.S. 606
County of Riverside v. McLaughlin (1991)	500 U.S. 44
Rust v. Sullivan (1991)	500 U.S. 173
California v. Acevedo (1991)	500 U.S. 565
Edmonson v. Leesville Concrete (1991)	500 U.S. 614
Washington Airport v. Citizens (1991)	501 U.S. 252
Wilson v. Seiter (1991)	501 U.S. 294
Chisom v. Roemer (1991)	501 U.S. 380
Houston Lawyers v. Texas (1991)	501 U.S. 419
Masson v. New Yorker (1991)	501 U.S. 496
Barnes v. Glen Theatre (1991)	501 U.S. 560
Cohen v. Cowles Media (1991)	501 U.S. 663
Coleman v. Thompson (1991)	501 U.S. 722
Payne v. Tennessee (1991)	501 U.S. 808
Simon & Schuster v. New York Crime Board (1991)	502 U.S. 105
INS v. Doherty (1992)	502 U.S. 314
Presley v. Etowah County (1992)	502 U.S. 491
Hudson v. McMillian (1992)	503 U.S. 1
Franklin v. Gwinnett County Schools (1992)	503 U.S. 60
Freeman v. Pitts (1992)	503 U.S. 467
Jacobson v. United States (1992)	503 U.S. 540
Keeney v. Tamayo Reyes (1992)	504 U.S. 1
Quill Corp v. North Dakota (1992)	504 U.S. 298
Morales v. TWA (1992)	504 U.S. 374
United States v. Alvarez-Machain (1992)	504 U.S. 655
Georgia v. McCollum (1992)	505 U.S. 42
New York v. United States (1992)	505 U.S. 144
R.A.V. v. St. Paul (1992)	505 U.S. 377
Cipollone v. Liggett (1992)	505 U.S. 504
Lee v. Weisman (1992)	505 U.S. 577
Intl Society for Krishna v. Lee (1992)	505 U.S. 672
United States v. Fordice (1992)	505 U.S. 717
Planned Parenthood v. Casey (1992)	505 U.S. 833
Bray v. Alexandria Women's Health (1993)	506 U.S. 263
Herrera v. Collins (1993)	506 U.S. 390

Table 2-13   *(Continued)*

Case name	Cite
Sullivan v. Louisiana (1993)	508 U.S. 275
Lamb's Chapel v. Center Moriches (1993)	508 U.S. 384
Wisconsin v. Mitchell (1993)	508 U.S. 476
Church of Lukumi v. Hialeah (1993)	508 U.S. 520
Zobrest v. Catalina (1993)	509 U.S. 1
Sale v. Haitian Center (1993)	509 U.S. 155
TXO Production v. Alliance (1993)	509 U.S. 443
St. Mary v. Hicks (1993)	509 U.S. 502
Alexander v United States (1993)	509 U.S. 544
Austin v. United States (1993)	509 U.S. 602
Shaw v. Reno (1993)	509 U.S. 630
Harris v. Forklift Systems (1993)	510 U.S. 17
NOW v. Scheidler (1994)	510 U.S. 249
Campbell v. Acuff-Rose (1994)	510 U.S. 569
J.E.B. v. T.B. (1994)	511 U.S. 127
Central Bank v. First Interstate Bank (1994)	511 U.S. 164
Landgraf v. USI Film (1994)	511 U.S. 244
Rivers v. Roadway Express (1994)	511 U.S. 298
Chicago v. EDF (1994)	511 U.S. 328
Carbone v. Clarkstown (1994)	511 U.S. 383
Dalton v. Specter (1994)	511 U.S. 462
Ladue v. Gilleo (1994)	512 U.S. 43
New York v. Milhelm Attea (1994)	512 U.S. 61
Dolan v. Tigard (1994)	512 U.S. 374
Kiryas Joel v. Grumet (1994)	512 U.S. 687
Madsen v. Women's Health Center (1994)	512 U.S. 753
McKennon v. Nashville Banner (1995)	513 U.S. 352
United States v. Lopez (1995)	514 U.S. 549
City of Edmond v. Oxford House (1995)	514 U.S. 725
U.S. Term Limits v. Thornton (1995)	514 U.S. 779
Missouri v. Jenkins (1995)	515 U.S. 70
Adarand v. Pena (1995)	515 U.S. 200
Hurley v. Irish-American GLIB (1995)	515 U.S. 557
Veronia School Dist v. Acton (1995)	515 U.S. 646
Rosenberger v. UVA (1995)	515 U.S. 819
Miller v. Johnson (1995)	515 U.S. 900
Wisconsin v. New York (1996)	517 U.S. 1
Seminole Tribe v. Florida (1996)	517 U.S. 44
44 Liquormart v. Rhode Island (1996)	517 U.S. 484
BMW v. Gore (1996)	517 U.S. 559
Romer v. Evans (1996)	517 U.S. 620
Smiley v. Citibank (1996)	517 U.S. 735
Lockheed v. Spink (1996)	517 U.S. 882
Shaw v. Hunt (1996)	517 U.S. 899
Bush v. Vera (1996)	517 U.S. 952
Jaffee v. Redmond (1996)	518 U.S. 1
Brown v. Pro Football (1996)	518 U.S. 231
United States v. Ursery (1996)	518 U.S. 267

(Table continues)

Table 2-13   *(Continued)*

Case name	Cite
United States v. Virginia (1996)	518 U.S. 515
Felker v. Turpin (1996)	518 U.S. 1051
Denver Area v. FCC (1996)	518 U.S. 727
United States v. Winstar (1996)	518 U.S. 839
M.L.B. v S.L.J. (1996)	519 U.S. 102
Printz v. United States (1997)	521 U.S. 98
Washington v. Glucksberg (1997)	521 U.S. 703
Vacco v. Quill (1997)	521 U.S. 793
Reno v. ACLU (1997)	521 U.S. 844
City of Boerne v. Flores (1997)	521 U.S. 507
Agostini v Felton (1997)	521 U.S. 203
Clinton v. Jones (1997)	520 U.S. 681
Turner Broadcasting System v. FCC (1997)	520 U.S. 180
Schenk v. Pro-Choice Network of NY (1997)	519 U.S. 357
State Oil Co. v. Kahn (1997)	522 U.S. 3
New Jersey v. New York (1998)	523 U.S. 767
Oncale v. Sundowner Offshore Services (1998)	523 U.S. 75
Bragdon v. Abbott (1998)	524 U.S. 624
Burlington Industries v. Ellerth (1998)	524 U.S. 742
Faragher v. City of Boca Raton (1998)	524 U.S 775
Clinton v. City of New York (1998)	524 U.S. 417
Gebser v. Lago Vista Independent School District (1998)	524 U.S. 274
Cedar Rapids Community School District v. Garret F. (1999)	523 U.S. 117
American Mfn. Mut. Ins. Co. v. Sullivan (1999)	524 U.S. 981
Dept. of Commerce v. U.S. House (1999)	525 U.S. 316
Buckley v. American Constitutional Law Foundation (1999)	525 U.S. 182
Alden v. Maine (1999)	527 U.S. 706
College Savings Bank v. Florida Prepaid Postsecondary Ed. Expense Board (1999)	527 U.S. 666
Florida Prepaid Postsecondary Ed. Expense Board v. College Savings Bank (1999)	527 U.S. 652
Sutton v. United Airlines, Inc. (1999)	527 U.S. 471
Murphy v. United Parcel Service (1999)	527 U.S. 516
Albertsons, Inc. v. Kirkingburg (1999)	527 U.S. 555
Greater New Orleans Broadcasting Assoc. Inc. v. United States (1999)	527 U.S. 173
Chicago v. Morales (1999)	527 U.S. 41
Saenz v. Roe (1999)	526 U.S. 489
Nixon v. Shrink Missouri Gov. PAC (2000)	528 U.S. 377
Illinois v. Wardlow (2000)	528 U.S. 119
Martinez v. Court of Appeals of CA 4th District (2000)	528 U.S. 152
Erie v. Pap's A.M. (2000)	529 U.S. 277
Florida v. J.L. (2000)	529 U.S. 266
Board of Regents of Univ. of Wisconsin v. Southworth (2000)	529 U.S. 217
FDA v. Brown and Williamson Tobacco (2000)	529 U.S. 120
Williams v. Taylor (2000)	529 U.S. 362
United States v. Playboy Entertainment Group (2000)	529 U.S. 803
Geier v. American Honda Motor Co. (2000)	529 U.S. 861

Table 2-13   *(Continued)*

Case name	Cite
United States v. Morrison (2000)	529 U.S. 598
Boy Scouts of America v. Dale (2000)	530 U.S. 640
Hill v. Colorado (2000)	530 U.S. 703
Stenberg v. Carhart (2000)	530 U.S. 914
Dickerson v. United States (2000)	530 U.S. 428
Apprendi v. New Jersey (2000)	530 U.S. 466
Sante Fe Independent School District v. Doe (2000)	530 U.S. 290
Troxel v. Granville (2000)	530 U.S. 57
Kimel v. Florida Board of Regents (2000)	528 U.S. 62
Bush v. Gore (2000)	531 U.S. 98
City of Indianapolis v. Edmond (2000)	531 U.S. 32
Lorillard Tobacco v. Reilly (2001)	533 U.S. 525
Zadvydas v. Davis (2001)	533 U.S. 678
Immigration and Naturalization Service v. St. Cyr (2001)	533 U.S. 289
New York Times v. Tasini (2001)	533 U.S 483
Good News Club v. Milford Central School (2001)	533 U.S. 98
Kyllo v. United States (2001)	533 U.S. 27
Penry v. Johnson (2001)	532 U.S. 782
PGA Tour v. Martin (2001)	532 U.S. 661
United States v. Oakland Cannabis Buyers' Cooperative (2001)	532 U.S. 483
Atwater v. City of Lago Vista (2001)	532 U.S. 318
Easley v. Cromartie (2001)	532 U.S. 234
Ferguson v. Charleston (2001)	532 U.S. 67
Legal Services Corporation v. Velazquez (2001)	531 U.S. 533
Whitman v. American Trucking Associations (2001)	531 U.S. 457
Alabama v. Garrett (2001)	531 U.S. 356

Note: Cases in this table (1) led to a story on the front page of the *New York Times* on the day after the Court handed it down, (2) were the lead ("headlined") cases in the story, and (3) were orally argued and decided with an opinion. For more details, see Lee Epstein and Jeffrey A. Segal, "Measuring Issue Salience," *American Journal of Political Science* 44 (2000): 66–83.

Source: Data for 1946–1996 available at www.artsci.wustl.edu/~polisci/epstein/ajps/; 1997–2001 (through July): updated by the authors. Data end with the 2000 term.

Table 2-14   Cases Incorporating Provisions of the Bill of Rights into the Due Process Clause of the Fourteenth Amendment

Provision	Case
First Amendment	
Freedom of speech and press	*Gitlow v. New York*, 268 U.S. 652 (1925)
Freedom of assembly	*DeJonge v. Oregon*, 299 U.S. 353 (1937)
Free exercise of religion	*Cantwell v. Connecticut*, 310 U.S. 296 (1940)
Establishment of religion	*Everson v. Board of Education*, 330 U.S. 1 (1947)
Fourth Amendment	
Unreasonable search and seizure	*Wolf v. Colorado*, 338 U.S. 25 (1949)
Exclusionary rule	*Mapp v. Ohio*, 367 U.S. 643 (1961)
Fifth Amendment	
Payment of compensation for the taking of private property	*Chicago, Burlington and Quincy R. Co. v. Chicago*, 166 U.S. 226 (1897)
Self-incrimination	*Malloy v. Hogan*, 378 U.S. 1 (1964)
Double jeopardy	*Benton v. Maryland*, 395 U.S. 784 (1969)
When jeopardy attaches	*Crist v. Bretz*, 437 U.S. 28 (1978)
Sixth Amendment	
Public trial	*In re Oliver*, 333 U.S. 257 (1948)
Right to counsel	*Gideon v. Wainwright*, 372 U.S. 335 (1963)
Confrontation and cross-examination of adverse witnesses	*Pointer v. Texas*, 380 U.S. 400 (1965)
Speedy trial	*Klopfer v. North Carolina*, 386 U.S. 213 (1967)
Compulsory process to obtain witnesses	*Washington v. Texas*, 388 U.S. 14 (1967)
Jury trial	*Duncan v. Louisiana*, 391 U.S. 145 (1968)
Eighth Amendment	
Cruel and unusual punishment	*Louisiana ex rel. Francis v. Resweber*, 329 U.S. 459 (1947)

Source: United States Reports.

Table 2-15   Supreme Court Decisions Holding Acts of Congress
Unconstitutional in Whole or in Part, 1789–2002

Marshall Court (January 27, 1801–March 14, 1836)

Marbury v. Madison, 1 Cr. (5 U.S.) 137 (1803)

Taney Court (March 15, 1836–December 5, 1864)

Scott v. Sandford, 19 How. (60 U.S.) 393 (1857)

Chase Court (December 6, 1864–January 20, 1874)

Gordon v. United States, 2 Wall. (69 U.S.) 561 (1865)
Ex parte Garland, 4 Wall. (71 U.S.) 333 (1867)
Reichart v. Felps, 6 Wall. (73 U.S.) 160 (1868)
The Alicia, 7 Wall. (74 U.S.) 571 (1869)
Hepburn v. Griswold, 8 Wall. (75 U.S.) 603 (1870)
The Justices v. Murray, 9 Wall. (76 U.S.) 274 (1870)
United States v. Dewitt, 9 Wall. (76 U.S.) 41 (1870)
United States v. Klein, 13 Wall. (80 U.S.) 128 (1872)

Waite Court (January 21, 1874–July 19, 1888)

United States v. Reese, 92 U.S. 214 (1876)
United States v. Fox, 95 U.S. 670 (1878)
Trade-Mark Cases, 100 U.S. 82 (1879)
United States v. Harris, 106 U.S. 629 (1883)
Civil Rights Cases, 109 U.S. 3 (1883)
Boyd v. United States, 116 U.S. 616 (1886)
Baldwin v. Franks, 120 U.S. 678 (1887)
Callan v. Wilson, 127 U.S. 540 (1888)

Fuller Court (July 20, 1888–December 11, 1910)

Monongahela Navigation Co. v. United States, 148 U.S. 312 (1893)
Pollock v. Farmers' Loan & Trust Co., 157 U.S. 429 (1895)
Wong Wing v. United States, 163 U.S. 228 (1896)
Kirby v. United States, 174 U.S. 47 (1899)
Jones v. Meehan, 175 U.S. 1 (1899)
Fairbank v United States, 181 U.S. 283 (1901)
James v. Bowman, 190 U.S. 127 (1903)
Matter of Heff, 197 U.S. 488 (1905)
Rassmussen v. United States, 197 U.S. 516 (1905)
Hodges v. United States, 203 U.S. 1 (1906)
The Employers' Liability Cases, 207 U.S. 463 (1908)
Adair v. United States, 208 U.S. 161 (1908)
Keller v. United States, 213 U.S. 138 (1909)
United States v. Evans, 213 U.S. 297 (1909)

White Court (December 12, 1910–June 29, 1921)

Coyle v. Smith, 221 U.S. 559 (1911)
Muskrat v. United States, 219 U.S. 346 (1911)
Choate v. Trapp, 224 U.S. 665 (1912)
United States v. Hvoslef, 237 U.S. 1 (1915)

(Table continues)

Table 2-15   *(Continued)*

Thames & Mersey Marine Ins. Co. v. United States, 237 U.S. 19 (1915)
Hammer v. Dagenhart, 247 U.S. 251 (1918)
Eisner v. Macomber, 252 U.S. 189 (1920)
Knickerbocker Ice Co. v. Stewart, 253 U.S. 149 (1920)
Evans v. Gore, 253 U.S. 245 (1920)
United States v. Cohen Grocery Co., 255 U.S. 81 (1921)
Weeds, Inc. v. United States, 255 U.S. 109 (1921)
Newberry v. United States, 256 U.S. 232 (1921)

Taft Court (June 30, 1921–February 12, 1930)

United States v. Moreland, 258 U.S. 433 (1922)
Bailey v. Drexel Furniture Co. (Child Labor Tax Case), 259 U.S. 20 (1922)
Hill v. Wallace, 259 U.S. 44 (1922)
Keller v. Potomac Electric Co., 261 U.S. 428 (1923)
Adkins v. Children's Hospital, 261 U.S. 525 (1923)
Washington v. Dawson & Co., 264 U.S. 219 (1924)
Miles v. Graham, 268 U.S. 501 (1925)
Trusler v. Crooks, 269 U.S. 475 (1926)
Myers v. United States, 272 U.S. 52 (1926)
Nicholds v. Coolidge, 274 U.S. 531 (1927)
Untermeyer v. Anderson, 276 U.S. 440 (1928)
National Life Insurance v. United States, 277 U.S. 508 (1928)

Hughes Court (February 13, 1930–June 11, 1941)

Heiner v. Donnan, 285 U.S. 312 (1932)
Booth v. United States, 291 U.S. 339 (1934)
Lynch v. United States, 292 U.S. 571 (1934)
Perry v. United States, 294 U.S. 330 (1935)
Panama Refining Co. v. Ryan, 293 U.S. 388 (1935)
Railroad Retirement Board v. Alton Railroad Co., 295 U.S. 330 (1935)
Schechter Corporation v. United States, 295 U.S. 495 (1935)
Louisville Bank v. Radford, 295 U.S. 555 (1935)
United States v. Constantine, 296 U.S. 287 (1935)
Hopkins Savings Association v. Cleary, 296 U.S. 315 (1935)
United States v. Butler, 297 U.S. 1 (1936)
Rickert Rice Mills v. Fontenot, 297 U.S. 110 (1936)
Ashton v. Cameron County District, 298 U.S. 513 (1936)
Carter v. Carter Coal Co., 298 U.S. 238 (1936)

Stone Court (June 12, 1941–June 19, 1946)

Tot v. United States, 319 U.S. 463 (1943)
United States v. Lovett, 328 U.S. 303 (1946)

Vinson Court (June 20, 1946–September 29, 1953)

United States v. Cardiff, 344 U.S. 174 (1952)

Warren Court (September 30, 1953–June 8, 1969)

Bolling v. Sharpe, 347 U.S. 497 (1954)
Toth v. Quarles, 350 U.S. 11 (1955)

Table 2-15   *(Continued)*

Reid v. Covert, 354 U.S. 1 (1957)
Trop v. Dulles, 356 U.S. 86 (1958)
Kinsella v. United States, 361 U.S. 234 (1960)
Grisham v. Hagan, 361 U.S. 278 (1960)
McElroy v. United States, 361 U.S. 281 (1960)
Kennedy v. Mendoza-Martinez, 372 U.S. 144 (1963)
Schneider v. Rusk, 377 U.S. 163 (1964)
Aptheker v. Secretary of State, 378 U.S. 500 (1964)
Lamont v. Postmaster General, 381 U.S. 301 (1965)
United States v. Brown, 381 U.S. 437 (1965)
Albertson v. Subversive Activities Control Board, 382 U.S. 70 (1965)
United States v. Romano, 382 U.S. 136 (1965)
Afroyim v. Rusk, 387 U.S. 253 (1967)
United States v. Robel, 389 U.S. 258 (1967)
Marchetti v. United States, 390 U.S. 39 (1968)
Grosso v. United States, 390 U.S. 62 (1968)
Haynes v. United States, 390 U.S. 85 (1968)
United States v. Jackson, 390 U.S. 570 (1968)
Shapiro v. Thompson, 394 U.S. 618 (1969)
Leary v. United States, 395 U.S. 6 (1969)
O'Callahan v. Parker, 395 U.S. 258 (1969)

Burger Court (June 9, 1969–September 16, 1986)

Turner v. United States, 396 U.S. 398 (1970)
Schacht v. United States, 398 U.S. 58 (1970)
Oregon v. Mitchell, 400 U.S. 112 (1970)
Blount v. Rizzi, 400 U.S. 410 (1971)
United States v. United States Coin & Currency, 401 U.S. 715 (1971)
Tilton v. Richardson, 403 U.S. 672 (1971)
Chief of Capitol Police v. Jeanette Rankin Brigade, 409 U.S. 972 (1972)
Richardson v. Davis, 409 U.S. 1069 (1972)
Frontiero v. Richardson, 411 U.S. 677 (1973)
U.S. Dept. of Agriculture v. Murry, 413 U.S. 508 (1973)
U.S. Dept. of Agriculture v. Moreno, 413 U.S. 528 (1973)
Jiminez v. Weinberger, 417 U.S. 628 (1974)
Weinberger v. Wiesenfeld, 420 U.S. 636 (1975)
Buckley v. Valeo, 424 U.S. 1 (1976)
National League of Cities v. Usery, 426 U.S. 833 (1976)
Califano v. Goldfarb, 430 U.S. 199 (1977)
Califano v. Silbowitz, 430 U.S. 934 (1977)
Railroad Retirement Bd. v. Kalina, 431 U.S. 909 (1977)
Marshall v. Barlow's, Inc., 436 U.S. 307 (1978)
Califano v. Westcott, 443 U.S. 76 (1979)
United States v. Will, 449 U.S. 200 (1980)
Railroad Labor Executives' Assn. v. Gibbons, 455 U.S. 457 (1982)
Northern Pipeline Construction Co. v. Marathon Pipe Line Co., 458 U.S. 50 (1982)
United States v. Grace, 461 U.S. 171 (1983)
Immigration and Naturalization Service v. Chadha, 462 U.S. 919 (1983)
Bolger v. Youngs Drug Products Corp., 463 U.S. 60 (1983)
Process Gas Consumers Group v. Comsumer Energy Council, 463 U.S. 1216 (1983)
U.S. Senate v. Federal Trade Commission, 463 U.S. 1216 (1983)

(Table continues)

Federal Communications Commission v. League of Women Voters of California, 468 U.S. 364 (1984)
Regan v. Time, Inc., 468 U.S. 641 (1984)
Federal Election Commission v. National Conservative Political Action Committee, 470 U.S. 480 (1985)
Bowsher v. Synar, 478 U.S. 714 (1986)

Rehnquist Court (September 17, 1986–)

Federal Election Commission v. Massachusetts Citizens for Life, 479 U.S. 238 (1986)
Hodel v. Irving, 481 U.S. 704 (1987)
Boos v. Barry, 485 U.S. 312 (1988)
Sable Communications of California, Inc. v. Federal Communications Commission, 492 U.S. 115 (1989)
United States v. Eichman, 496 U.S. 310 (1990)
Metro Washington Airports Authority v. Citizens for Noise Abatement, 501 U.S. 252 (1991)
New York v. United States, 505 U.S. 144 (1992)
United States v. National Treasury Employees Union, 513 U.S. 454 (1995)
Plaut v. Spendthrift Farm, Inc., 514 U.S. 211 (1995)
Rubin v. Coors Brewing Co., 514 U.S. 476 (1995)
United States v. Lopez, 514 U.S. 549 (1995)
Seminole Tribe of Florida v. Florida, 517 U.S. 44 (1996)
United States v. IBM, 517 U.S. 843 (1996)
Colorado GOP Federal Campaign Committee v. Federal Election Commission, 518 U.S. 604 (1996)
Babbitt v. Youpee, 519 U.S. 234 (1997)
Boerne v. Flores, 521 U.S. 507 (1997)
Reno v. American Civil Liberties Union, 521 U.S. 844 (1997)
Printz v. United States, 521 U.S. 898 (1997)
United States v. United States Shoe Corp., 523 U.S. 360 (1998)
United States v. Bajakajian, 524 U.S. 321 (1998)
Clinton v. New York City, 524 U.S. 417 (1998)
Eastern Enterprises v. Apfel, 524 U.S. 498 (1998)
Greater New Orleans Broadcasting Assn. v. United States, 527 U.S. 173 (1999)
Florida Education Expense Board v. College Savings Bank, 527 U.S. 627 (1999)
College Savings Bank v. Florida Education Expense Board, 527 U.S. 666 (1999)
Kimel v. Florida Board of Regents, 528 U.S. 62 (2000)
United States v. Morrison, 529 U.S. 598 (2000)
United States v. Playboy Entertainment Group, 529 U.S. 803 (2000)
Dickerson v. United States, 530 U.S. 428 (2000)
Legal Services Corp. v. Velazquez, 531 U.S. 533 (2001)
United States v. Hatter, 532 U.S. 557 (2001)
United States v. United Foods, 150 L.Ed. 2d 438 (2001)
Aschroft v. Free Speech Coalition, 152 L.Ed. 2d 403 (2002)
Thompson v. Western States Medical Center, 152 L.Ed. 2d 563 (2002)

Note: Determination of which decisions have voided acts of Congress is not a clear-cut matter. For example, the Congressional Research Service invokes criteria different from those of the Supreme Court database, which lists these decisions since the onset of the Vinson Court in 1946. The database lists only decisions in which the Court clearly indicates that it has voided a legislative enactment of some level of government; where federal law preempts state law, unconstitutionality does not result unless the Court's prevailing opinion so states.

Sources: 1789–1990: Congressional Research Service, *The Constitution of the United States of America, Analysis and Interpretation* (Washington, D.C.: U.S. Government Printing Office, 1973), 1597–1619 and supplements; 1991–2002: U.S. Supreme Court Judicial Database.

Table 2-16   Supreme Court Decisions Holding State Constitutional and Statutory Provisions and Municipal Ordinances Unconstitutional on Their Face or as Administered, 1789–2002

Marshall Court (January 27, 1801–March 14, 1836)

United States v. Peters, 5 Cranch (9 U.S.) 115 (1809)
Fletcher v. Peck, 6 Cranch (10 U.S.) 87 (1810)
New Jersey v. Wilson, 7 Cranch (11 U.S.) 164 (1812)
Terrett v. Taylor, 9 Cranch (13 U.S.) 43 (1815)
Sturges v. Crowninshield, 4 Wheat. (17 U.S.) 122 (1819)
McMillan v. McNeil, 4 Wheat. (17 U.S.) 209 (1819)
McCulloch v. Maryland, 4 Wheat. (17 U.S.) 316 (1819)
Dartmouth College v. Woodward, 4 Wheat. (17 U.S.) 518 (1819)
Farmers' & Mechanics' Bank v. Smith, 6 Wheat. (19 U.S.) 131 (1812)
Green v. Biddle, 8 Wheat. (21 U.S.) 1 (1823)
Society for the Propagation of the Gospel v. New Haven, 8 Wheat. (21 U.S.) 464 (1823)
Gibbons v. Ogden, 9 Wheat. (22 U.S.) 1 (1824)
Osborn v. Bank of the United States, 9 Wheat. (22 U.S.) 738 (1824)
Ogden v. Saunders, 12 Wheat. (25 U.S.) 213 (1827)
Brown v. Maryland, 12 Wheat. (25 U.S.) 419 (1827)
Weston v. City Council of Charleston, 2 Pet. (27 U.S.) 449 (1829)
Craig v. Missouri, 4 Pet. (29 U.S.) 410 (1830)
Worcester v. Georgia, 6 Pet. (31 U.S.) 515 (1832)
Boyle v. Zacharie & Turner, 6 Pet. (31 U.S.) 635 (1832)

Taney Court (March 15, 1836–December 5, 1864)

Dobbins v. The Commissioners of Erie County, 16 Pet. (41 U.S.) 435 (1842)
Prigg v. Pennsylvania, 16 Pet. (41 U.S.) 539 (1842)
Bronson v. Kinzie, 1 How. (42 U.S.) 311 (1843)
McCracken v. Hayward, 2 How. (43 U.S.) 608 (1844)
Gordon v. Appeal Tax Court, 3 How. (44 U.S.) 133 (1845)
Searight v. Stokes, 3 How. (44 U.S.) 151 (1845)
Neil, Moore & Co. v. Ohio, 3 How. (44 U.S.) 720 (1845)
Planters' Bank v. Sharp, 6 How. (47 U.S.) 301 (1848)
Passenger Cases, 7 How. (48 U.S.) 283 (1849)
Woodruff v. Trapnall, 10 How. (51 U.S.) 190 (1851)
Achison v. Huddleson, 12 How. (53 U.S.) 293 (1852)
Trustees for Vincennes University v. Indiana, 14 How. (55 U.S.) 269 (1853)
Curran v. Arkansas, 15 How. (56 U.S.) 304 (1854)
State Bank of Ohio v. Knoop, 16 How. (57 U.S.) 369 (1854)
Hays v. The Pacific Mail Steamship Co., 17 How. (58 U.S.) 596 (1855)
Dodge v. Woolsey, 18 How. (59 U.S.) 331 (1856)
Sinnot v. Davenport, 22 How. (63 U.S.) 227 (1860)
  accord: *Foster v. Davenport*, 22 How. (63 U.S.) 244 (1860)
Almy v. California, 24 How. (65 U.S.) 169 (1861)
Howard v. Bugbee, 24 How. (65 U.S.) 461 (1861)
Bank of Commerce v. New York City, 2 Black (67 U.S.) 620 (1863)
  accord: *Bank Tax Case*, 2 Wall. (69 U.S.) 244 (1865)

(Table continues)

Table 2-16   *(Continued)*

Chase Court (December 6, 1864–January 20, 1874)

Hawthorne v. Calef, 2 Wall. (69 U.S.) 10 (1865)
The Binghamton Bridge, 3 Wall. (70 U.S.) 51 (1866)
Van Allen v. The Assessors, 3 Wall. (70 U.S.) 573 (1866)
Bradley v. Illinois, 4 Wall. (71 U.S.) 459 (1867)
McGee v. Mathis, 4 Wall. (71 U.S.) 143 (1867)
Cummings v. Missouri, 4 Wall. (71 U.S.) 277 (1867)
The Moses Taylor, 4 Wall. (71 U.S.) 411 (1867)
Von Hoffman v. Quincy, 4 Wall. (71 U.S.) 535 (1867)
The Hine v. Trevor, 4 Wall (71 U.S.) 555 (1867)
Christmas v. Russell, 5 Wall. (72 U.S.) 290 (1867)
The Kansas Indians, 5 Wall. (72 U.S.) 737 (1867)
The New York Indians, 5 Wall. (72 U.S.) 761 (1867)
Steamship Company v. Portwardens, 6 Wall. (73 U.S.) 31 (1867)
Crandall v. Nevada, 6 Wall. (73 U.S.) 35 (1868)
Bank v. Supervisors, 7 Wall. (74 U.S.) 26 (1868)
Northern Central Ry. Co. v. Jackson, 7 Wall. (74 U.S.) 262 (1869)
The Belfast, 7 Wall. (74 U.S.) 624 (1869)
Furman v. Nichol, 8 Wall. (75 U.S.) 44 (1869)
Home of the Friendless v. Rouse, 8 Wall. (75 U.S.) 430 (1869)
The Washington University v. Rouse, 8 Wall. (75 U.S.) 439 (1869)
State Tonnage Tax Cases, 12 Wall. (79 U.S.) 204 (1871)
Ward v. Maryland, 12 Wall. (79 U.S.) 418 (1871)
Gibson v. Chouteau, 13 Wall. (80 U.S.) 92 (1872)
Wilmington Railroad v. Reid, 13 Wall. (80 U.S.) 264 (1872)
White v. Hart, 13 Wall. (80 U.S.) 646 (1872)
Osborne v. Nicholson, 13 Wall. (80 U.S.) 654 (1872)
Delmas v. Insurance Company, 14 Wall. (81 U.S.) 661 (1872)
Case of the State Freight Tax, 15 Wall. (82 U.S.) 232 (1873)
State Tax on Foreign-Held Bonds, 15 Wall. (82 U.S.) 300 (1873)
Gunn v. Barry, 15 Wall. (82 U.S.) 610 (1873)
Pierce v. Carskadon, 16 Wall. (83 U.S.) 234 (1873)
Humphrey v. Pegues, 16 Wall. (83 U.S.) 244 (1873)
Walker v. Whitehead, 16 Wall. (83 U.S.) 314 (1873)
Barings v. Dabney, 19 Wall. (86 U.S.) 1 (1873)

Waite Court (January 21, 1874–July 19, 1888)

Cannon v. New Orleans, 20 Wall. (87 U.S.) 577 (1874)
Murray v. Charleston, 96 U.S. 432 (1874)
Peete v. Morgan, 19 Wall. (86 U.S.) 581 (1874)
Pacific Railroad Company v. Maguire, 20 Wall. (87 U.S.) 36 (1874)
Insurance Company v. Morse, 20 Wall. (87 U.S.) 445 (1874)
Loan Association v. Topeka, 20 Wall. (87 U.S.) 655 (1875)
Wilmington & Weldon R. Co. v. King, 91 U.S. 3 (1875)
Welton v. Missouri, 91 U.S. 275 (1876)
Morrill v. Wisconsin, 154 U.S. 626 (1877)
Henderson v. Mayor of New York, 92 U.S. 259 (1876)
Chy Lung v. Freeman, 92 U.S. 275 (1876)

Table 2-16   *(Continued)*

Inman Steamship Co. v. Tinker, 94 U.S. 238 (1877)
Foster v. Masters of New Orleans, 94 U.S. 246 (1877)
New Jersey v. Yard, 95 U.S. 104 (1877)
Hannibal & St. Joseph R. Co. v. Husen, 95 U.S. 465 (1878)
Hall v. DeCuir, 95 U.S. 485 (1878)
Farrington v. Tennessee, 95 U.S. 679 (1878)
Pensacola Tel. Co. v. Western Union Tel Co., 96 U.S. 1 (1878)
Edwards v. Kearzey, 96 U.S. 595 (1878)
Keith v. Clark, 97 U.S. 454 (1878)
Cook v. Pennsylvania, 97 U.S. 566 (1878)
Northwestern University v. Illinois ex rel. Miller, 99 U.S. 309 (1878)
Strauder v. West Virginia, 100 U.S. 303 (1880)
Guy v. Baltimore, 100 U.S. 434 (1880)
Tiernan v. Rinker, 102 U.S. 123 (1880)
Hartman v. Greenhow, 102 U.S. 672 (1880)
Hall v. Wisconsin, 103 U.S. 5 (1880)
Webber v. Virginia, 103 U.S. 344 (1881)
United States ex rel. Wolff v. New Orleans, 103 U.S. 358 (1881)
  accord: *Louisiana v. Pilsbury*, 105 U.S. 278 (1881)
Asylum v. New Orleans, 105 U.S. 362 (1881)
Western Union Telegraph Co. v. Texas, 105 U.S. 460 (1881)
Ralls County Court v. United States, 105 U.S. 733 (1881)
Parkersburg v. Brown, 106 U.S. 487 (1882)
New York v. Compagnie Gén. Transatlantique, 107 U.S. 59 (1882)
Kring v. Missouri, 107 U.S. 221 (1883)
Nelson v. St. Martin's Parish, 111 U.S. 716 (1884)
Moran v. New Orleans, 112 U.S. 69 (1884)
Cole v. La Grange, 113 U.S. 1 (1885)
Gloucester Ferry Co. v. Pennsylvania, 114 U.S. 196 (1885)
Virginia Coupon Cases, 114 U.S. 269 (1885)
New Orleans Gas Co. v. Louisiana Light Co., 115 U.S. 650 (1885)
New Orleans Water-Works Co. v. Rivers, 115 U.S. 674 (1885)
Effinger v. Kenney, 115 U.S. 566 (1885)
Louisville Gas Co. v. Citizens' Gas Co., 115 U.S. 683 (1885)
Fiske v. Jefferson Police Jury, 116 U.S. 131 (1885)
Mobile v. Watson, 116 U.S. 289 (1886)
Walling v. Michigan, 116 U.S. 446 (1886)
Royall v. Virginia, 116 U.S. 572 (1886)
Pickard v. Pullman Southern Car Co., 117 U.S. 34 (1886)
Van Brocklin v. Tennessee, 117 U.S. 151 (1886)
Sprague v. Thompson, 118 U.S 90 (1886)
Wabash, St. Louis & P. Ry. Co. v. Illinois, 118 U.S. 557 (1886)
Yick Wo v. Hopkins, 118 U.S. 356 (1886)
Robbins v. Shelby Taxing District, 120 U.S. 489 (1887)
Corson v. Maryland, 120 U.S. 502 (1887)
Barron v. Burnside, 121 U.S. 186 (1887)
Fargo v. Michigan, 121 U.S. 230 (1887)
Seibert v. Lewis, 122 U.S. 284 (1887)
Philadelphia Steamship Co. v. Pennsylvania, 122 U.S. 326 (1887)
Western Union Telegraph Co. v. Pendleton, 122 U.S. 347 (1887)

(Table continues)

Table 2-16   *(Continued)*

Bowman v. Chicago & Nw. Ry. Co., 125 U.S. 465 (1888)
Western Union Telegraph Co. v. Massachusetts, 125 U.S. 530 (1888)
California v. Pacific Railroad Co., 127 U.S. 1 (1888)
Ratterman v. Western Union Tel. Co., 127 U.S. 411 (1888)
Leloup v. Port of Mobile, 127 U.S. 640 (1888)

Fuller Court (July 20, 1888–December 11, 1910)

Asher v. Texas, 128 U.S. 129 (1888)
Stoutenburgh v. Hennick, 129 U.S. 141 (1889)
Western Union Telegraph Co. v. Alabama, 132 U.S. 472 (1889)
Medley, Petitioner, 134 U.S. 160 (1890)
Chicago, Minneapolis & St. Paul Ry. Co. v. Minnesota, 134 U.S. 418 (1890)
Leisy v. Hardin, 135 U.S. 100 (1890)
Lyng v. Michigan, 135 U.S. 161 (1890)
McGahey v. Virginia, 135 U.S. 662 (1890)
Norfolk & Western R. Co. v. Pennsylvania, 136 U.S. 114 (1890)
Minnesota v. Barber, 136 U.S. 313 (1890)
McCall v. California, 136 U.S. 104 (1890)
Brimmer v. Rebman, 138 U.S. 78 (1891)
Pennoyer v. McConnaughy, 140 U.S. 1 (1891)
Crutcher v. Kentucky, 141 U.S. 47 (1891)
Voight v. Wright, 141 U.S. 62 (1891)
Harman v. Chicago, 147 U.S. 396 (1893)
Brennan v. Titusville, 153 U.S. 289 (1894)
Mobile & Ohio Railroad v. Tennessee, 153 U.S. 486 (1894)
New York, L.E. & W.R. Co. v. Pennsylvania, 153 U.S. 628 (1894)
Covington & Cincinnati Bridge Co. v. Kentucky, 154 U.S. 204 (1894)
Gulf, C. & S.F. Ry. Co. v. Hefley, 158 U.S. 98 (1896)
Bank of Commerce v. Tennessee, 161 U.S. 134 (1896)
Barnitz v. Beverly, 163 U.S. 118 (1896)
Illinois Central Ry. v. Illinois, 163 U.S. 142 (1896)
Missouri Pacific Railway v. Nebraska, 164 U.S. 403 (1896)
Scott v. Donald, 165 U.S. 58 (1897)
Gulf, C. & S.F. Ry. Co. v. Ellis, 165 U.S. 150 (1897)
Allgeyer v. Louisiana, 165 U.S. 578 (1897)
Smyth v. Ames, 169 U.S. 466 (1898)
Houston & Texas Central Ry. v. Texas, 170 U.S. 243 (1898)
Thompson v. Utah, 170 U.S. 343 (1898)
Walla Walla v. Walla Walla Water Co., 172 U.S. 1 (1898)
Schollenberger v. Pennsylvania, 171 U.S. 1 (1898)
Collins v. New Hampshire, 171 U.S. 30 (1898)
Blake v. McClung, 172 U.S. 239 (1898)
Norwood v. Baker, 172 U.S. 269 (1898)
Dewey v. Des Moines, 173 U.S. 193 (1899)
Ohio v. Thomas, 173 U.S. 276 (1899)
Lake Shore & Mich. S. Ry. Co. v. Smith, 173 U.S. 684 (1899)
Houston & Texas Central R. Co. v. Texas, 177 U.S. 66 (1900)
Cleveland, C.C. & St. Louis Ry. Co. v. Illinois, 177 U.S. 514 (1900)
Stearns v. Minnesota, 179 U.S. 223 (1900)

Table 2-16   *(Continued)*

Duluth & I.R.R. Co. v. Kentucky, 179 U.S. 302 (1900)
Los Angeles v. Los Angeles Water Co., 177 U.S. 558 (1900)
Cotting v. Kansas City Stock Yards Co., 183 U.S. 79 (1901)
Louisville & Nashville R. Co. v. Eubank, 184 U.S. 27 (1902)
Connolly v. Union Sewer Pipe Co., 184 U.S. 540 (1902)
Detroit v. Detroit Citizens' St. Ry. Co., 184 U.S. 368 (1902)
Stockard v. Morgan, 185 U.S. 27 (1902)
Louisville & J. Ferry Co. v. Kentucky, 188 U.S. 385 (1903)
The Roanoke, 189 U.S. 185 (1903)
The Robert W. Parsons, 191 U.S. 17 (1903)
Allen v. Pullman Company, 191 U.S. 171 (1903)
Caldwell v. North Carolina, 187 U.S. 622 (1903)
Postal Telegraph-Cable Co. v. Taylor, 192 U.S. 64 (1904)
Cleveland v. Cleveland City Ry. Co., 194 U.S. 517 (1904)
Bradley v. Lightcap, 195 U.S. 1 (1904)
Dobbins v. Los Angeles, 195 U.S. 223 (1904)
Central of Georgia Ry. Co. v. Murphey, 196 U.S. 194 (1905)
Lochner v. New York, 198 U.S. 45 (1905)
Union Transit Co. v. Kentucky, 199 U.S. 194 (1905)
Houston & Texas Central Railroad v. Mayes, 201 U.S. 321 (1906)
Powers v. Detroit & Grand Haven Ry., 201 U.S. 543 (1906)
Vicksburg v. Waterworks Co., 202 U.S. 453 (1906)
Cleveland v. Cleveland Electric Ry., 201 U.S. 529 (1906)
Rearick v. Pennsylvania, 203 U.S. 507 (1906)
American Smelting Co. v. Colorado, 204 U.S. 103 (1907)
Home Savings Bank v. Des Moines, 205 U.S. 503 (1907)
Adams Express Co. v. Kentucky, 206 U.S. 129 (1907)
  accord: *American Express Co. v. Kentucky*, 206 U.S. 139 (1907)
Vicksburg v. Vicksburg Waterworks Co., 206 U.S. 496 (1907)
Central of Georgia Ry. v. Wright, 207 U.S. 127 (1907)
Darnell & Son v. Memphis, 208 U.S. 113 (1908)
Ex parte Young, 209 U.S. 123 (1908)
Londoner v. Denver, 210 U.S. 373 (1908)
Galveston, Houston & San Antonio Ry. Co. v. Texas, 210 U.S. 217 (1908)
Willcox v. Consolidated Gas Co., 212 U.S. 19 (1909)
Louisville & Nashville R. Co. v. Stock Yards Co., 212 U.S. 132 (1909)
Nielson v. Oregon, 212 U.S. 315 (1909)
Adams Express Co. v. Kentucky, 214 U.S. 218 (1909)
Louisiana ex rel. Hubert v. New Orleans, 215 U.S. 170 (1909)
Minneapolis v. Street Railway Co., 215 U.S. 417 (1910)
North Dakota ex rel. Flaherty v. Hanson, 215 U.S. 515 (1910)
Western Union Tel. Co. v. Kansas, 216 U.S. 1 (1910)
Ludwig v. Western Union Tel. Co., 216 U.S. 146 (1910)
Southern Railway Co. v. Greene, 216 U.S. 400 (1910)
International Textbook Co. v. Pigg, 217 U.S. 91 (1910)
St. Louis S.W. Ry. v. Arkansas, 217 U.S. 136 (1910)
Missouri Pacific Ry. v. Nebraska, 217 U.S. 196 (1910)
Dozier v. Alabama, 218 U.S. 124 (1910)
Herndon v. Chicago, R.I. & P. R. Co., 218 U.S. 135 (1910)

(Table continues)

Table 2-16   *(Continued)*

White Court (December 12, 1910–June 29, 1921)

Bailey v. Alabama, 219 U.S. 219 (1911)
Oklahoma v. Kansas Nat. Gas Co., 221 U.S. 229 (1911)
Berryman v. Whitman College, 222 U.S. 334 (1912)
Northern Pacific Ry. Co. v. Washington, 222 U.S. 370 (1912)
Southern Ry. Co. v. Reid, 222 U.S. 424 (1912)
  accord: *Southern Ry. Co. v. Reil & Beam*, 222 U.S. 444 (1912)
  accord: *Southern Ry. Co. v. Burlington Lumber Co.*, 225 U.S. 99 (1912)
Louisville & Nashville R. v. Cook Brewing Co., 223 U.S. 70 (1912)
Atchison Topeka & Santa Fe Ry. Co. v. O'Connor, 223 U.S. 280 (1912)
Oklahoma v. Wells, Fargo & Co., 223 U.S. 298 (1912)
Haskell v. Kansas Natural Gas Co., 224 U.S. 217 (1912)
St. Louis, I.M. & S. Ry. Co. v. Wynne, 224 U.S. 354 (1912)
Bucks Stove Co. v. Vickers, 226 U.S. 205 (1912)
Eubank v. Richmond, 226 U.S. 137 (1912)
Williams v. Talladega, 226 U.S. 404 (1912)
Chicago R.I. & P. Ry. Co. v. Hardwick Elevator Co., 226 U.S. 426 (1913)
  accord: *St. Louis, Iron Mt. & S. Ry. v. Edwards*, 227 U.S. 265 (1913)
Adams Express Co. v. Croninger, 226 U.S. 491 (1913)
  accord: *Chicago, B. & Q. Ry. v. Miller*, 226 U.S. 513 (1913)
  accord: *Chicago, St. Paul, Minneapolis, & Omaha Ry. Co. v. Latta*, 226 U.S. 519 (1913)
New York Central Railroad Co. v. Hudson County, 227 U.S. 248 (1913)
Grand Trunk Western Ry. v. South Bend, 227 U.S. 544 (1913)
Crenshaw v. Arkansas, 227 U.S. 389 (1913)
  accord: *Rogers v. Arkansas*, 227 U.S. 401 (1913)
  accord: *Stewart v. Michigan*, 232 U.S. 665 (1914)
McDermott v. Wisconsin, 228 U.S. 115 (1913)
Missouri, K. & T. Ry. v. Harriman Bros., 227 U.S. 657 (1914)
Ettor v. Tacoma, 228 U.S. 148 (1913)
St. Louis, S.F. & T. Ry. Co. v. Seale, U.S. 156 (1913)
Chicago, B. & Q. R. v. Hall, 229 U.S. 511 (1913)
Owensboro v. Cumberland Telephone Co., 230 U.S. 58 (1913)
Boise Water Co. v. Boise City, 230 U.S. 84 (1913)
Old Colony Trust Co. v. Omaha, 230 U.S. 100 (1913)
Missouri Pacific Ry. Co. v. Tucker, 230 U.S. 340 (1913)
Chicago, Minneapolis & St. Paul Ry. Co. v. Polt, 232 U.S. 165 (1914)
  accord: *Chicago, M. & St. P. Ry. Co. v. Kennedy*, 232 U.S. 626 (1914)
Harrison v. St. Louis, S.F. & T.R. Co., 232 U.S. 318 (1914)
Foote v. Maryland, 232 U.S. 495 (1914)
Farmers Bank v. Minnesota, 232 U.S. 516 (1914)
Russell v. Sebastian, 233 U.S. 195 (1914)
Singer Sewing Machine Co. v. Brickell, 233 U.S. 304 (1914)
Tennessee Coal Co. v. George, 233 U.S. 354 (1914)
Carondelet Canal Co. v. Louisiana, 233 U.S. 362 (1914)
Smith v. Texas, 233 U.S. 630 (1914)
Erie R.R. Co. v. New York, 233 U.S. 671 (1914)
International Harvester Co. v. Kentucky, 234 U.S. 216 (1914)
  accord: *International Harvester v. Kentucky*, 234 U.S. 579 (1914)
  accord: *Collins v. Kentucky*, 234 U.S. 634 (1914)
  accord: *American Machine Co. v. Kentucky*, 236 U.S. 660 (1915)

Table 2-16   *(Continued)*

Missouri Pacific Ry. Co. v. Larabee, 234 U.S. 459 (1914)
Western Union Telegraph Co. v. Brown, 234 U.S. 542 (1914)
United States v. Reynolds, 235 U.S. 133 (1914)
McCabe v. Atchison, Topeka & Santa Fe Ry. Co., 235 U.S. 151 (1914)
Sioux Remedy Co. v. Cope, 235 U.S. 197 (1914)
Choctaw & Gulf R.R. v. Harrison, 235 U.S. 292 (1914)
Adams Express Co. v. New York, 232 U.S. 12 (1914)
U.S. Express Co. v. New York, 232 U.S. 35 (1914)
Sault Ste. Marie v. International Transit Co., 234 U.S. 333 (1914)
South Covington Ry. v. Covington, 235 U.S. 537 (1915)
Coppage v. Kansas, 236 U.S. 1 (1915)
Heyman v. Hays, 236 U.S. 178 (1915)
  accord: *Southern Operating Co. v. Hayes,* 236 U.S. 188 (1915)
Globe Bank v. Martin, 236 U.S. 288 (1915)
Southern Ry. Co. v. R.R. Comm., 236 U.S. 439 (1915)
Kirmeyer v. Kansas, 236 U.S. 568 (1915)
Northern Pac. Ry. v. North Dakota ex rel. McCue, 236 U.S. 585 (1915)
Norfolk & West Ry. v. Conley, 236 U.S. 605 (1915)
Wright v. Central of Georgia Ry., 236 U.S. 674 (1915)
  accord: *Wright v. Louisville & Nashville R.,* 236 U.S. 687 (1915)
Davis v. Virginia, 236 U.S. 697 (1915)
Chicago B. & Q. Ry. v. Wisconsin R.R. Com., 237 U.S. 220 (1915)
Coe v. Armour Fertilizer Works, 237 U.S. 413 (1915)
Charleston & W.C. Ry. Co. v. Varnville Co., 237 U.S. 597 (1915)
Atchison, Topeka & Santa Fe Ry. Co. v. Vosburg, 238 U.S. 56 (1915)
Rossi v. Pennsylvania, 238 U.S. 62 (1915)
Guinn v. United States, 238 U.S. 347 (1915)
  accord: *Mayers v. Anderson,* 238 U.S. 368 (1915)
Southwestern Tel. Co. v. Danaher, 238 U.S. 482 (1915)
Chicago, Minneapolis & St. Paul R. v. Wisconsin, 238 U.S. 491 (1915)
Traux v. Raich, 239 U.S. 33 (1915)
Provident Savings Assn. v. Kentucky, 239 U.S. 103 (1915)
Gast Realty Co. v. Schneider Granite Co., 240 U.S. 55 (1916)
Indian Oil Co. v. Oklahoma, 240 U.S. 522 (1916)
Rosenberger v. Pacific Express Co., 241 U.S. 48 (1916)
McFarland v. American Sugar Co., 241 U.S. 79 (1916)
Wisconsin v. Philadelphia & Reading Coal Co., 241 U.S. 329 (1916)
Detroit United Ry. v. Michigan, 242 U.S. 238 (1916)
Buchanan v. Warley, 245 U.S. 60 (1917)
  accord: *Harmon v. Tyler,* 273 U.S. 668 (1927)
  accord: *City of Richmond v. Deans,* 281 U.S. 704 (1930)
Rowland v. Boyle, 244 U.S. 106 (1917)
New York Central R. Co. v. Winfield, 244 U.S. 147 (1917)
  accord: *Erie R.R. Co. v. Winfield,* 244 U.S. 170 (1917)
Southern Pacific Co. v. Jensen, 244 U.S. 205 (1917)
  accord: *Clyde S.S. Co. v. Walker,* 244 U.S. 255 (1917)
  accord: *Steamship Bowdoin Co. v. Indust. Accident Comm. of California,* 246 U.S. 648
  (1918)

(Table continues)

Table 2-16   *(Continued)*

Seaboard Air Line Ry. v. Blackwell, 244 U.S. 310 (1917)
Western Oil Refg. Co. v. Lipscomb, 244 U.S. 346 (1917)
Adams v. Tanner, 244 U.S. 590 (1917)
American Express Company v. Caldwell, 244 U.S. 617 (1917)
Hendrickson v. Apperson, 245 U.S. 105 (1917)
  accord: *Hendrickson v. Creager*, 245 U.S. 115 (1917)
Looney v. Crane Co., 245 U.S. 178 (1917)
Crew Levick v. Pennsylvania, 245 U.S. 292 (1917)
International Paper Co. v. Massachusetts, 246 U.S. 135 (1918)
  accord: *Locomobile Co. v. Massachusetts*, 246 U.S. 146 (1918)
Cheney Brothers Co. v. Massachusetts, 246 U.S. 147 (1918)
New York Life Ins. Co. v. Dodge, 246 U.S. 357 (1918)
Georgia v. Cincinnati So. Ry., 248 U.S. 26 (1918)
Union Pac. R. Co. v. Pub. Service Comm., 248 U.S. 67 (1918)
Northern Ohio Traction & Light Co. v. Ohio ex rel. Pontius, 245 U.S. 574 (1918)
Denver v. Denver Union Water Co., 246 U.S. 178 (1918)
Covington v. South Covington St. Ry. Co., 246 U.S. 413 (1918)
Detroit United Railway v. Detroit, 248 U.S. 429 (1919)
Los Angeles v. Los Angeles Gas Corp., 251 U.S. 32 (1919)
Flexner v. Farson, 248 U.S. 289 (1919)
Central of Georgia Ry. Co. v. Wright, 248 U.S. 525 (1919)
Union Tank Line Co. v. Wright, 249 U.S. 275 (1919)
Standard Oil Co. v. Graves, 249 U.S. 389 (1919)
Chalker v. Birmingham & N.W. Ry. Co., 249 U.S. 522 (1919)
New Orleans & N.E.R.R. Co. v. Scarlet, 249 U.S. 528 (1919)
  accord: *Yazoo & M.V.R.R. Co. v. Mullins*, 249 U.S. 531 (1919)
Pennsylvania R. Co. v. Public Service Comm., 250 U.S. 566 (1919)
Postal Tel.-Cable Co. v. Warren-Godwin Co., 251 U.S. 27 (1919)
Western Union Telegraph Co. v. Boegli, 251 U.S. 315 (1920)
Travis v. Yale & Towne Mfg. Co., 252 U.S. 60 (1920)
Oklahoma Operating Co. v. Love, 252 U.S. 331 (1920)
  accord: *Oklahoma Gin Co. v. Oklahoma*, 252 U.S. 339 (1920)
Askren v. Continental Oil Co., 252 U.S. 444 (1920)
Wallace v. Hines, 253 U.S. 66 (1920)
Hawke v. Smith (No. 1), 253 U.S. 221 (1920)
  accord: *Hawke v. Smith (No. 2)*, 253 U.S. 221 (1920)
Ohio Valley Co. v. Ben Avon Borough, 253 U.S. 287 (1920)
Royster Guano Co. v. Virginia, 253 U.S. 412 (1920)
Johnson v. Maryland, 254 U.S. 51 (1920)
Turner v. Wade, 254 U.S. 64 (1920)
Bank of Minden v. Clement, 256 U.S. 126 (1921)
Bethlehem Motors Co. v. Flynt, 256 U.S. 421 (1921)
Merchant's National Bank v. Richmond, 256 U.S. 635 (1921)
Bowman v. Continental Oil Co., 256 U.S. 642 (1921)
Kansas City So. Ry. v. Road Imp. Dist. No. 6, 256 U.S. 658 (1921)

Taft Court (June 30, 1921–February 12, 1930)

Eureka Pipe Line Co. v. Hallanan, 257 U.S. 265 (1921)
United Fuel Gas Co. v. Hallanan, 257 U.S. 277 (1921)

Table 2-16   *(Continued)*

Dahnke-Walker Co. v. Bondurant, 257 U.S. 282 (1921)
Truax v. Corrigan, 257 U.S. 312 (1921)
Gillespie v. Oklahoma, 257 U.S. 501 (1922)
Terral v. Burke Constr. Co., 257 U.S. 529 (1922)
Lemke v. Farmers Grain Co., 258 U.S. 50 (1922)
  accord: *Lemke v. Homer Farmers Elevator Co.*, 258 U.S. 65 (1922)
Newton v. Consolidated Gas Co., 258 U.S. 165 (1922)
  accord: *Newton v. New York Gas Co.*, 258 U.S. 178 (1922)
  accord: *Newton v. Kings County Lighting Co.*, 258 U.S. 180 (1922)
  accord: *Newton v. Brooklyn Union Gas Co.*, 258 U.S. 604 (1922)
  accord: *Newton v. Consolidated Gas Co.*, 259 U.S. 101 (1922)
Forbes Pioneer Boat Line v. Everglades Drainage Dist., 258 U.S. 338 (1922)
Texas Co. v. Brown, 258 U.S. 466 (1922)
Chicago & N.W. Ry. v. Nye Schneider Fowler Co., 260 U.S. 35 (1922)
St. Louis Compress Co. v. Arkansas, 260 U.S. 346 (1922)
Champlain Co. v. Brattleboro, 260 U.S. 366 (1922)
Pennsylvania Coal Co. v. Mahon, 260 U.S. 393 (1922)
Houston v. Southwestern Tel. Co., 259 U.S. 318 (1922)
Paducah v. Paducah Ry., 261 U.S. 267 (1923)
Columbia R., Gas & Electric Co. v. South Carolina, 261 U.S. 236 (1923)
Federal Land Bank v. Crosland, 261 U.S. 374 (1923)
Phipps v. Cleveland Refg. Co., 261 U.S. 449 (1923)
Thomas v. Kansas City So. Ry., 261 U.S. 481 (1923)
Davis v. Farmers Co-operative Co., 262 U.S. 313 (1923)
First National Bank v. California, 262 U.S. 366 (1923)
Meyer v. Nebraska, 262 U.S. 390 (1923)
Bartels v. Iowa, 262 U.S. 404 (1923)
Bohning v. Ohio, 262 U.S. 404 (1923)
Georgia Ry. Co. v. Decatur, 262 U.S. 432 (1923)
  accord: *Georgia Ry. Co. v. College Park*, 262 U.S. 441 (1923)
Wolff Packing Co. v. Industrial Court, 262 U.S. 522 (1923)
  accord: *Dorchy v. Kansas*, 264 U.S. 286 (1924)
  accord: *Wolff Packing Co. v. Industrial Court*, 267 U.S. 552 (1925)
Kentucky Co. v. Paramount Exch., 262 U.S. 544 (1923)
Pennsylvania v. West Virginia, 262 U.S. 553 (1923)
Bunch v. Cole, 263 U.S. 250 (1923)
Clallam County v. United States, 263 U.S. 341 (1923)
Texas Transp. Co. v. New Orleans, 264 U.S. 150 (1924)
Asakura v. Seattle, 265 U.S. 332 (1924)
Sperry Oil Co. v. Chisholm, 264 U.S. 488 (1924)
Burns Baking Co. v. Bryan, 264 U.S. 504 (1924)
Missouri ex rel. Burnes National Bank v. Duncan, 265 U.S. 17 (1924)
Atchison, Topeka & Santa Fe Ry. Co. v. Wells, 265 U.S. 101 (1924)
Air-Way Corp. v. Day, 266 U.S. 71 (1924)
Aetna Life Ins. Co. v. Dunken, 266 U.S. 389 (1924)
Real Silk Mills v. Portland, 268 U.S. 325 (1925)
Tampa Interocean Steamship Co. v. Louisiana, 266 U.S. 594 (1925)
Ozark Pipe Line v. Monier, 266 U.S. 555 (1925)
Michigan Commission v. Duke, 266 U.S. 570 (1925)
Flanagan v. Federal Coal Co., 267 U.S. 222 (1925)

(Table continues)

Table 2-16   *(Continued)*

Buck v. Kuykendall, 267 U.S. 307 (1925)
  accord: *Bush Co. v. Maloy*, 267 U.S. 317 (1925)
  accord: *Allen v. Galveston Truck Line Corp.*, 289 U.S. 708 (1933)
Missouri Pacific R. Co. v. Stroud, 267 U.S. 404 (1925)
Lancaster v. McCarty, 267 U.S. 427 (1925)
Shafer v. Farmers Grain Co., 268 U.S. 189 (1925)
Alpha Cement Co. v. Massachusetts, 268 U.S. 203 (1925)
Frick v. Pennsylvania, 268 U.S. 473 (1925)
Pierce v. Society of Sisters, 268 U.S. 510 (1925)
Davis v. Cohen, 268 U.S. 638 (1925)
Lee v. Osceola Imp. Dist., 268 U.S. 643 (1925)
First National Bank v. Anderson, 269 U.S. 341 (1926)
Connally v. General Const. Co., 269 U.S. 385 (1926)
Browning v. Hooper, 269 U.S. 396 (1926)
Rhode Island Trust Co. v. Doughton, 270 U.S. 69 (1926)
Oregon-Washington Co. v. Washington, 270 U.S. 87 (1926)
Schlesinger v. Wisconsin, 270 U.S. 230 (1926)
  accord: *Uihlein v. Wisconsin*, 273 U.S. 642 (1926)
Weaver v. Palmer Bros. Co., 270 U.S. 402 (1926)
Fidelity & Deposit Co. v. Tafoya, 270 U.S. 426 (1926)
Childers v. Beaver, 270 U.S. 555 (1926)
Appleby v. City of New York, 271 U.S. 365 (1926)
Appleby v. Delaney, 271 U.S. 403 (1926)
Frost Trucking Co. v. Railroad Comm., 271 U.S. 583 (1926)
Jaybird Mining Co. v. Wier, 271 U.S. 609 (1926)
Hughes Bros. Co. v. Minnesota, 272 U.S. 469 (1926)
Hanover Ins. Co. v. Harding, 272 U.S. 494 (1926)
Wachovia Trust Co. v. Doughton, 272 U.S. 567 (1926)
Ottinger v. Consolidated Gas Co., 272 U.S. 576 (1926)
  accord: *Ottinger v. Brooklyn Union Co.*, 272 U.S. 579 (1926)
Napier v. Atlantic Coast Line, 272 U.S. 605 (1926)
Miller v. Milwaukee, 272 U.S. 713 (1927)
DiSanto v. Pennsylvania, 273 U.S. 34 (1927)
Missouri Pacific v. Porter, 273 U.S. 341 (1927)
Tyson & Brother v. Banton, 273 U.S. 418 (1927)
Tumey v. Ohio, 273 U.S. 510 (1927)
Nixon v. Herndon, 273 U.S. 536 (1927)
First National Bank v. Hartford, 273 U.S. 548 (1927)
  accord: *Minnesota v. First National Bank*, 273 U.S. 561 (1927)
  accord: *Commercial National Bank v. Custer County*, 275 U.S. 502 (1927)
  accord: *Keating v. Public National Bank*, 284 U.S. 587 (1932)
Fairmont Co. v. Minnesota, 274 U.S. 1 (1927)
Ohio Pub. Serv. Co. v. Ohio ex rel. Fritz, 274 U.S. 12 (1927)
Southern Ry. Co. v. Kentucky, 274 U.S. 76 (1927)
Road Improvement Dist. v. Missouri Pacific R. Co., 274 U.S. 188 (1927)
Fiske v. Kansas, 274 U.S. 380 (1927)
Cline v. Frink Dairy Co., 274 U.S. 445 (1927)
Power Mfg. Co. v. Saunders, 274 U.S. 490 (1927)
Northwestern Ins. Co. v. Wisconsin, 275 U.S. 136 (1927)
Mayor of Vidalia v. McNeely, 274 U.S. 676 (1927)

Table 2-16   *(Continued)*

Delaware L. & W. R.R. v. Morristown, 276 U.S. 182 (1928)
Sprout v. South Bend, 277 U.S. 163 (1928)
Nectow v. Cambridge, 277 U.S. 183 (1928)
Washington ex rel. Seattle Trust Co. v. Roberge, 278 U.S. 116 (1928)
Wuchter v. Pizzutti, 276 U.S. 13 (1928)
  accord: *Consolidated Flour Mills Co. v. Muegge*, 278 U.S. 559 (1928)
Missouri ex rel. Robertson v. Miller, 276 U.S. 174 (1928)
Montana National Bank v. Yellowstone County, 276 U.S. 479 (1928)
New Brunswick v. United States, 276 U.S. 547 (1928)
Brooke v. Norfolk, 277 U.S. 27 (1928)
Louisville Gas Co. v. Coleman, 277 U.S. 32 (1928)
Long v. Rockwood, 277 U.S. 142 (1928)
Standard Pipe Line v. Highway Dist., 277 U.S. 160 (1928)
Panhandle Oil Co. v. Missouri ex rel. Knox, 277 U.S. 218 (1928)
  accord: *Graysburg Oil Co. v. Texas*, 278 U.S. 582 (1929)
Ribnik v. McBride, 277 U.S. 350 (1928)
Quaker City Cab Co. v. Pennsylvania, 277 U.S. 389 (1928)
Foster-Fountain Packing Co. v. Haydel, 278 U.S. 1 (1928)
  accord: *Johnson v. Haydel*, 278 U.S. 16 (1928)
Hunt v. United States, 278 U.S. 96 (1928)
Louis K. Liggett Co. v. Baldridge, 278 U.S. 105 (1928)
Williams v. Standard Oil Co., 278 U.S. 235 (1929)
International Shoe Co. v. Pinkus, 278 U.S. 261 (1929)
Cudahy Co. v. Hinkle, 278 U.S. 460 (1929)
Frost v. Corporation Commission, 278 U.S. 515 (1929)
Manley v. Georgia, 279 U.S. 1 (1929)
Nielsen v. Johnson, 279 U.S. 47 (1929)
Carson Petroleum Co. v. Vial, 279 U.S. 95 (1929)
London Guarantee & Accident Co. v. Industrial Comm., 279 U.S. 109 (1929)
Helson v. Kentucky, 279 U.S. 245 (1929)
Macallen Co. v. Massachusetts, 279 U.S. 620 (1929)
Western & Atlantic Ry. Co. v. Henderson, 279 U.S. 639 (1929)
Safe Deposit & T. Co. v. Virginia, 280 U.S. 83 (1929)
Farmers Loan Co. v. Minnesota, 280 U.S. 204 (1930)
New Jersey Tel. Co. v. Tax Board, 280 U.S. 338 (1930)
Carpenter v. Shaw, 280 U.S. 363 (1930)

Hughes Court (February 13, 1930–June 11, 1941)

Moore v. Mitchell, 281 U.S. 18 (1930)
Lindgren v. United States, 281 U.S. 38 (1930)
Baizley Iron Works v. Span, 281 U.S. 222 (1930)
  accord: *Employers' Liability Assurance Co. v. Cook*, 281 U.S. 233 (1930)
Missouri ex rel. Missouri Ins. Co. v. Gehner, 281 U.S. 313 (1930)
Home Ins. Co. v. Dick, 281 U.S. 397 (1930)
Baldwin v. Missouri, 281 U.S. 586 (1930)
Surplus Trading Co. v. Cook, 281 U.S. 647 (1930)
Beidler v. South Carolina Tax Comm., 282 U.S. 1 (1930)
Chicago, St. Paul, Minneapolis & P. Ry. v. Holmberg, 282 U.S. 162 (1930)
Furst v. Brewster, 282 U.S. 493 (1931)

(Table continues)

Table 2-16   *(Continued)*

Coolidge v. Long, 282 U.S. 582 (1931)
Hans Rees' Sons v. North Carolina ex rel. Maxwell, 283 U.S. 123 (1931)
Interstate Transit, Inc. v. Lindsey, 283 U.S. 183 (1931)
Stromberg v. California, 283 U.S. 359 (1931)
Smith v. Cahoon, 283 U.S. 553 (1931)
Near v. Minnesota ex rel. Olsen, 283 U.S. 697 (1931)
Santovincenzo v. Egan, 284 U.S. 30 (1931)
State Tax Comm. v. Interstate Natural Gas Co., 284 U.S. 41 (1931)
Hoeper v. Tax Commission, 284 U.S. 206 (1931)
Van Huffel v. Harkelrode, 284 U.S. 225 (1931)
First National Bank v. Maine, 284 U.S. 312 (1932)
Henkel v. Chicago, St. Paul, Minneapolis & O. Ry. Co., 284 U.S. 444 (1932)
New State Ice Co. v. Liebmann, 285 U.S. 262 (1932)
Coombes v. Getz, 285 U.S. 434 (1932)
Nixon v. Condon, 286 U.S. 73 (1932)
Champlin Rfg. Co. v. Corporation Comm., 286 U.S. 210 (1932)
Anglo-Chilean Corp. v. Alabama, 288 U.S. 218 (1933)
Louis K. Liggett Co. v. Lee, 288 U.S. 517 (1933)
Consolidated Textile Co. v. Gregory, 289 U.S. 85 (1933)
Johnson Oil Co. v. Oklahoma ex rel. Mitchell, 290 U.S. 158 (1933)
Southern Ry. Co. v. Virginia, 290 U.S. 190 (1933)
Morrison v. California, 291 U.S. 82 (1934)
Standard Oil Co. v. California, 291 U.S. 242 (1934)
Murray v. Gerrick & Co., 291 U.S. 315 (1934)
Hartford Accident & Insurance Co. v. Delta Pine Land Co., 292 U.S. 143 (1934)
McKnett v. St. Louis & S. F. Ry. Co., 292 U.S. 230 (1934)
W.B. Worthen Co. v. Thomas, 292 U.S. 426 (1934)
Concordia Ins. Co. v. Illinois, 292 U.S. 535 (1934)
Jennings v. United States Fidelity & Guaranty Co., 294 U.S. 216 (1935)
   accord: Old Company's Lehigh v. Meeker, 294 U.S. 227 (1935)
Cooney v. Mountain States Tel. Co., 294 U.S. 384 (1935)
Baldwin v. G.A.F. Seelig, 294 U.S. 511 (1935)
Stewart Dry Goods Co. v. Lewis, 294 U.S. 550 (1935)
   accord: Valentine v. A. & P. Tea Co., 299 U.S. 32 (1936)
Panhandle Co. v. Highway Comm., 294 U.S. 613 (1935)
Broderick v. Rosner, 294 U.S. 629 (1935)
Worthen Co. v. Kavanaugh, 295 U.S. 56 (1935)
Georgia Ry. & Electric Co. v. Decatur, 295 U.S. 165 (1935)
Senior v. Braden, 295 U.S. 422 (1935)
Schuylkill Trust Co. v. Pennsylvania, 296 U.S. 113 (1935)
Colgate v. Harvey, 296 U.S. 404 (1935)
Oklahoma v. Barnsdall Corp., 296 U.S. 521 (1936)
Treigle v. Acme Homestead Assn., 297 U.S. 189 (1936)
Grosjean v. American Press Co., 297 U.S. 233 (1936)
   accord: Arizona Publishing Co. v. O'Neil, 304 U.S. 543 (1938)
Mayflower Farms v. Ten Eyck, 297 U.S. 266 (1936)
Bingaman v. Golden Eagle Lines, 297 U.S. 626 (1936)
Fisher's Blend Station v. State Tax Comm., 297 U.S. 650 (1936)
International Steel & I. Co. v. National Surety Co., 297 U.S. 657 (1936)
Graves v. Texas Company, 298 U.S. 393 (1936)

Table 2-16   *(Continued)*

Morehead v. New York ex rel. Tipaldo, 298 U.S. 587 (1936)
Binney v. Long, 299 U.S. 280 (1936)
De Jonge v. Oregon, 299 U.S. 353 (1937)
New York ex rel. Rogers v. Graves, 299 U.S. 401 (1937)
Lawrence v. Shaw, 300 U.S. 245 (1937)
Ingles v. Morf, 300 U.S. 290 (1937)
Herndon v. Lowry, 301 U.S. 242 (1937)
Lindsey v. Washington, 301 U.S. 397 (1937)
Hartford Ins. Co. v. Harrison, 301 U.S. 459 (1937)
Puget Sound Co. v. Tax Commission, 302 U.S. 90 (1937)
James v. Dravo Contracting Co., 302 U.S. 134 (1937)
Connecticut General Life Ins. Co. v. Johnson, 303 U.S. 77 (1938)
Indiana ex rel. Anderson v. Brand, 303 U.S. 95 (1938)
Indiana ex rel. Valentine v. Marker, 303 U.S. 628 (1938)
Adams Mfg. Co. v. Storen, 304 U.S. 307 (1938)
Collins v. Yosemite Park Co., 304 U.S. 518 (1938)
Missouri ex rel. Gaines v. Canada, 305 U.S. 337 (1938)
Lovell v. Griffin, 303 U.S. 444 (1938)
Hague v. C.I.O., 307 U.S. 496 (1939)
Schneider v. City of Irvington, 308 U.S. 147 (1939)
Gwin, White & Prince, Inc. v. Henneford, 305 U.S. 434 (1939)
Hale v. Bimco Trading Co., 306 U.S. 375 (1939)
Lanzetta v. New Jersey, 306 U.S. 451 (1939)
Lane v. Wilson, 307 U.S. 268 (1939)
Thornhill v. Alabama, 310 U.S. 88 (1940)
Cantwell v. Connecticut, 310 U.S. 296 (1940)
McCarroll v. Dixie Lines, 309 U.S. 176 (1940)
Best v. Maxwell, 311 U.S. 454 (1940)
McGoldrick v. Gulf Oil Corp., 309 U.S. 414 (1940)
Carlson v. California, 310 U.S. 106 (1940)
Hines v. Davidowitz, 312 U.S. 52 (1941)
Wood v. Lovett, 313 U.S. 362 (1941)

Stone Court (June 12, 1941–June 19, 1946)

Federal Land Bank v. Bismarck Co., 314 U.S. 95 (1941)
Edwards v. California, 314 U.S. 160 (1941)
Taylor v. Georgia, 315 U.S. 25 (1942)
Cloverleaf Butter Co. v. Patterson, 315 U.S. 148 (1942)
Tulee v. Washington, 315 U.S. 681 (1942)
Skinner v. Oklahoma ex rel. Wilwinson, 316 U.S. 535 (1942)
Pacific Coast Dairy v. Dept. of Agriculture, 318 U.S. 285 (1943)
Jones v. Opelika, 319 U.S. 103 (1943)
Mayo v. United States, 319 U.S. 441 (1943)
Taylor v. Mississippi, 319 U.S. 583 (1943)
Jamison v. Texas, 318 U.S. 413 (1943)
Largent v. Texas, 318 U.S. 418 (1943)
Murdock v. Pennsylvania, 319 U.S. 105 (1943)
Martin v. Struthers, 319 U.S. 141 (1943)
Follett v. McCormick, 321 U.S. 573 (1944)

(Table continues)

Table 2-16   *(Continued)*

Pollack v. Williams, 322 U.S. 4 (1944)
United States v. Allegheny County, 322 U.S. 174 (1944)
McLeod v. Dilworth Co., 322 U.S. 327 (1944)
Thomas v. Collins, 323 U.S. 516 (1945)
Hoover & Allison Co. v. Evatt, 324 U.S. 652 (1945)
Hill v. Florida ex rel. Watson, 325 U.S. 538 (1945)
Southern Pacific Co. v. Arizona, 325 U.S. 761 (1945)
Marsh v. Alabama, 326 U.S. 501 (1946)
Tucker v. Texas, 326 U.S. 517 (1946)
Republic Pictures Corp. v. Kappler, 327 U.S. 757 (1946)
First Iowa Hydro-Electric Coop. v. FPC, 328 U.S. 152 (1946)
Morgan v. Virginia, 328 U.S. 373 (1946)

Vinson Court (June 20, 1946–September 29, 1953)

Richfield Oil Corp. v. State Board, 329 U.S. 69 (1946)
Freeman v. Hewit, 329 U.S. 239 (1946)
Nippert v. Richmond, 327 U.S. 416 (1946)
Joseph v. Carter & Weekes Co., 330 U.S. 422 (1947)
Bethlehem Steel Co. v. New York Employment Relations Board, 330 U.S. 767 (1947)
  accord: *Plankington Packing Co. v. WERB*, 338 U.S. 953 (1950)
Rice v. Sante Fe Elevator Corp., 331 U.S. 218 (1947)
Order of Travelers v. Wolfe, 331 U.S. 586 (1947)
United States v. California, 332 U.S. 19 (1947)
Sipuel v. Board of Regents, 332 U.S. 631 (1948)
Oyama v. California, 332 U.S. 633 (1948)
Seaboard R. Co. v. Daniel, 333 U.S. 118 (1948)
Winters v. New York, 333 U.S. 507 (1948)
Toomer v. Witsell, 334 U.S. 385 (1948)
Takahaski v. Fish Comm., 334 U.S. 410 (1948)
Greyhound Lines v. Mealey, 334 U.S. 653 (1948)
Saia v. New York, 334 U.S. 558 (1948)
Terminiello v. Chicago, 337 U.S. 1 (1949)
La Crosse Tel. Corp. v. WERB, 336 U.S. 18 (1949)
Hood & Sons v. Du Mond, 336 U.S. 525 (1949)
Schnell v. Davis, 336 U.S. 933 (1949)
Union National Bank v. Lamb, 337 U.S. 38 (1949)
Wheeling Steel Corp. v. Glander, 337 U.S. 562 (1949)
Treichler v. Wisconsin, 338 U.S. 251 (1949)
Wissner v. Wissner, 338 U.S. 655 (1950)
New Jersey Insurance Co. v. Div. of Tax Appeals, 338 U.S. 665 (1950)
Mullane v. Central Hanover Bank & Trust Co., 339 U.S. 306 (1950)
United Automobile Workers v. O'Brien, 339 U.S. 454 (1950)
Sweatt v. Painter, 339 U.S. 629 (1950)
United States v. Louisiana, 339 U.S. 699 (1950)
United States v. Texas, 339 U.S. 707 (1950)
McLaurin v. Oklahoma State Regents, 339 U.S. 637 (1950)
Bus Employees v. WERB, 340 U.S. 383 (1951)
Norton Co. v. Dept. of Revenue, 340 U.S. 534 (1951)
Spector Motor Service v. O'Connor, 340 U.S. 602 (1951)

Table 2-16   *(Continued)*

Hughes v. Fetter, 341 U.S. 609 (1951)
Kunz v. New York, 340 U.S. 290 (1951)
Dean Milk Co. v. Madison, 340 U.S. 349 (1951)
Gelling v. Texas, 343 U.S. 960 (1952)
Carson v. Roane-Anderson Co., 342 U.S. 232 (1952)
  accord: *General Electric Co. v. Washington*, 347 U.S. 909 (1954)
Standard Oil Co. v. Peck, 342 U.S. 382 (1952)
Memphis Steam Laundry v. Stone, 342 U.S. 389 (1952)
First National Bank v. United Air Lines, 342 U.S. 396 (1952)
Joseph Burstyn, Inc. v. Wilson, 343 U.S. 495 (1952)
Kedroff v. St. Nicholas Cathedral, 344 U.S. 94 (1952)
Wieman v. Updegraff, 344 U.S. 183 (1952)
Fowler v. Rhode Island, 345 U.S. 67 (1953)
Dameron v. Brodhead, 345 U.S. 322 (1953)

Warren Court (September 30, 1953–June 8, 1969)

Kern-Limerick, Inc. v. Scurlock, 347 U.S. 110 (1954)
Michigan-Wisconsin Pipe Line Co. v. Calvert, 347 U.S. 157 (1954)
Miller Bros. Co. v. Maryland, 347 U.S. 340 (1954)
Railway Express Agency v. Virginia, 347 U.S. 359 (1954)
Franklin National Bank v. New York, 347 U.S. 373 (1954)
Brown v. Board of Education, 347 U.S. 483 (1954)
Castle v. Hayes Freight Lines, 348 U.S. 61 (1954)
Society for Savings v. Bowers, 349 U.S. 143 (1955)
Pennsylvania v. Nelson, 350 U.S. 497 (1956)
Holmes v. City of Atlanta, 350 U.S. 879 (1955)
Indiana Dept. of Revenue v. Nebeker, 348 U.S. 933 (1955)
Slochower v. Board of Higher Education, 350 U.S. 551 (1956)
Griffin v. Illinois, 351 U.S. 12 (1956)
Covey v. Town of Somers, 351 U.S. 141 (1956)
Railway Employees' Dept. v. Hansen, 351 U.S. 225 (1956)
Walker v. Hutchinson City, 352 U.S. 112 (1956)
Leslie Miller, Inc. v. Arkansas, 352 U.S. 187 (1956)
Butler v. Michigan, 352 U.S. 380 (1957)
Gayle v. Browder, 352 U.S. 903 (1956)
Guss v. Utah Labor Board, 353 U.S. 1 (1957)
West Point Wholesale Grocery Co. v. Opelika, 354 U.S. 390 (1957)
Morey v. Doud, 354 U.S. 457 (1957)
Lambert v. California, 355 U.S. 225 (1957)
Staub v. Baxley, 355 U.S. 313 (1958)
Public Utility Commission v. United States, 355 U.S. 534 (1958)
Eskridge v. Washington Prison Bd., 357 U.S. 214 (1958)
Chicago v. Atchison, Topeka & Santa Fe R. Co., 357 U.S. 77 (1958)
Speiser v. Randall, 357 U.S. 513 (1958)
First Unitarian Church v. Los Angeles, 357 U.S. 545 (1958)
Teamsters Union v. Oliver, 358 U.S. 283 (1959)
Bibb v. Navajo Freight Lines, Inc., 359 U.S. 520 (1959)
San Diego Unions v. Garmon, 359 U.S. 236 (1959)
  accord: *Devries v. Baumgartner's Electric Co.*, 359 U.S. 498 (1959)

(Table continues)

Table 2-16   *(Continued)*

---

accord: *Superior Court v. Washington ex rel. Yellow Cab*, 361 U.S. 373 (1960)
accord: *Bogle v. Jakes Foundry Co.*, 362 U.S. 401 (1960)
accord: *McMahon v. Milam Manufacturing Company*, 368 U.S. 7 (1961)
accord: *Marine Engineers v. Interlake Co.*, 370 U.S 173 (1962)
accord: *Waxman v. Virginia*, 371 U.S. 4 (1962)
accord: *Construction Laborers v. Curry*, 371 U.S. 542 (1963)
accord: *Journeymen & Plumbers' Union v. Borden*, 373 U.S. 690 (1962)
accord: *Iron Workers v. Perko*, 373 U.S. 701 (1963)
State Athletic Comm. v. Dorsey, 359 U.S. 533 (1959)
Kingsley Pictures Corp. v. Regents, 360 U.S. 684 (1959)
Smith v. California, 361 U.S. 147 (1959)
Faubus v. Aaron, 361 U.S. 197 (1959)
Phillips Chemical Co. v. Dumas Independent School District, 361 U.S. 376 (1960)
Rohr Corp. v. San Diego County, 362 U.S. 628 (1960)
Bates v. Little Rock, 361 U.S. 516 (1960)
Talley v. California, 362 U.S. 60 (1960)
Gomillion v. Lightfoot, 364 U.S. 339 (1960)
Boynton v. Virginia, 364 U.S. 454 (1960)
Shelton v. Tucker, 364 U.S. 479 (1960)
Bush v. Orleans School Board, 364 U.S. 500 (1961)
Orleans Parish School Board v. Bush, 365 U.S. 569 (1961)
Ferguson v. Georgia, 365 U.S. 570 (1961)
Louisiana v. N.A.A.C.P. ex rel. Gremillion, 366 U.S. 293 (1961)
United States v. Oregon, 366 U.S. 643 (1961)
United States v. Shimer, 367 U.S. 374 (1961)
Torcaso v. Watkins, 367 U.S. 488 (1961)
Marcus v. Search Warrant, 367 U.S. 717 (1961)
Tugwell v. Bush, 367 U.S. 907 (1961)
Legislature of Louisiana v. United States, 367 U.S. 908 (1961)
Federal Land Bank v. Kiowa County, 368 U.S. 146 (1961)
Cramp v. Board of Public Instruction, 368 U.S. 278 (1961)
United States v. Union Central Life Ins. Co., 368 U.S. 291 (1961)
Campbell v. Hussey, 368 U.S. 297 (1961)
St. Helena Parish School Board v. Hall, 368 U.S. 515 (1962)
Bailey v. Patterson, 369 U.S. 31 (1962)
Turner v. Memphis, 369 U.S. 350 (1962)
Free v. Bland, 369 U.S. 663 (1962)
State Board of Ins. v. Todd Shipyards, 370 U.S. 451 (1962)
Central R. Co. v. Pennsylvania, 370 U.S. 607 (1962)
Robinson v. California, 370 U.S. 660 (1962)
Lassiter v. United States, 371 U.S. 10 (1962)
United States v. Buffalo Savings Bank, 371 U.S. 228 (1963)
Paul v. United States, 371 U.S. 245 (1963)
Schroeder v. New York City, 371 U.S. 208 (1962)
N.A.A.C.P. v. Button, 371 U.S. 415 (1963)
Gideon v. Wainwright, 372 U.S. 335 (1963)
Gray v. Sanders, 372 U.S. 368 (1963)
Lane v. Brown, 372 U.S. 477 (1963)
Michigan National Bank v. Robertson, 372 U.S. 591 (1963)
accord: *Mercantile Nat. Bank v. Langdeau*, 371 U.S. 555 (1963)

Table 2-16   *(Continued)*

Halliburton Oil Well Cementing Co. v. Reily, 373 U.S. 64 (1963)
Willner v. Committee on Character & Fitness, 373 U.S. 96 (1963)
Peterson v. Greenville, 373 U.S. 244 (1963)
  accord: *Gober v. Birmingham*, 373 U.S. 374 (1963)
Lombard v. Louisiana, 373 U.S. 267 (1963)
Wright v. Georgia, 373 U.S. 284 (1963)
Sperry v. Florida ex rel. Florida Bar, 373 U.S. 379 (1963)
Bus Employees v. Missouri, 374 U.S. 74 (1963)
Abington Township School District v. Schempp, 374 U.S. 203 (1963)
Sherbert v. Verner, 374 U.S. 398 (1963)
Polar Ice Cream & Creamery Co. v. Andrews, 375 U.S. 361 (1964)
Anderson v. Martin, 375 U.S. 399 (1964)
Wesberry v. Sanders, 376 U.S. 1 (1964)
  accord: *Martin v. Bush*, 376 U.S. 222 (1964)
City of New Orleans v. Barthe, 376 U.S. 189 (1964)
Sears, Roebuck & Co. v. Stiffel Co., 376 U.S. 225 (1964)
Hostetter v. Idlewild Bon Voyage Liquor Corp., 377 U.S. 324 (1964)
  accord: *Dept. of Alcoholic Beverage Control of Cal. v. Ammex Warehouse Co.*, 378 U.S. 124 (1964)
Dept. of Revenue v. James B. Beam Distilling Co., 377 U.S. 341 (1964)
Baggett v. Bullitt, 377 U.S. 360 (1964)
Chamberlin v. Dade County Board of Public Instruction, 377 U.S. 402 (1964)
Reynolds v. Sims, 377 U.S. 533 (1964)
  accord: *WMCA, Inc. v. Lomenzo*, 377 U.S. 633 (1964)
  accord: *Maryland Committee for Fair Representation v. Tawes*, 377 U.S. 656 (1964)
  accord: *Davis v. Mann*, 377 U.S. 678 (1964)
  accord: *Roman v. Sincock*, 377 U.S. 695 (1964)
  accord: *Lucas v. Forty-Fourth General Assembly of Colorado*, 377 U.S. 713 (1964)
  accord: *Meyers v. Thigpen*, 378 U.S. 554 (1964)
  accord: *Williams v. Moss*, 378 U.S. 558 (1964)
  accord: *Pinney v. Butterworth*, 378 U.S. 564 (1964)
  accord: *Hill v. Davis*, 378 U.S. 565 (1964)
A Quantity of Copies of Books v. Kansas, 378 U.S. 205 (1964)
Tancil v. Woolls; Virginia Board of Elections v. Hamm, 379 U.S. 19 (1964)
Garrison v. Louisiana, 379 U.S. 64 (1964)
McLauglin v. Florida, 379 U.S. 184 (1964)
Stanford v. Texas, 379 U.S. 476 (1965)
Cox v. Louisiana, 379 U.S. 536 (1965)
Freedman v. Maryland, 380 U.S. 51 (1965)
Carrington v. Rash, 380 U.S. 89 (1965)
Louisiana v. United States, 380 U.S. 145 (1965)
Reserve Life Insurance Co. v. Bowers, 380 U.S. 258 (1965)
American Oil Co. v. Neill, 380 U.S. 451 (1965)
Dombrowski v. Pfister, 380 U.S. 479 (1965)
Harman v. Forssenius, 380 U.S. 528 (1965)
Corbett v. Stergios, 381 U.S. 124 (1965)
Jordan v. Silver, 381 U.S. 415 (1965)
Griswold v. Connecticut, 381 U.S. 479 (1965)
Giaccio v. Pennsylvania, 382 U.S. 399 (1966)
Baxstrom v. Herold, 383 U.S. 107 (1966)

(Table continues)

Table 2-16   *(Continued)*

Harper v. Virginia Board of Elections, 383 U.S. 663 (1966)
  accord: *Texas v. United States*, 384 U.S. 155 (1966)
Elfbrandt v. Russell, 384 U.S. 11 (1966)
Mills v. Alabama, 384 U.S. 214 (1966)
Rinaldi v. Yeager, 384 U.S. 305 (1966)
Alton v. Tawes, 384 U.S. 315 (1966)
Carr v. City of Altus, 385 U.S. 35 (1966)
Swann v. Adams, 385 U.S. 440 (1967)
  accord: *Kirkpatrick v. Preisler*, 385 U.S. 450 (1967)
Short v. Ness Produce Co., 385 U.S. 537 (1967)
Keyishian v. Board of Regents, 385 U.S. 589 (1967)
National Bellas Hess, Inc. v. Dept. of Revenue of Illinois, 386 U.S. 753 (1967)
Holding v. Blankenship, 387 U.S. 94 (1967)
Reitman v. Mulkey, 387 U.S. 369 (1967)
Camara v. Municipal Court, 387 U.S. 523 (1967)
See v. Seattle, 387 U.S. 541 (1967)
Loving v. Virginia, 388 U.S. 1 (1967)
Washington v. Texas, 388 U.S. 14 (1967)
Berger v. New York, 388 U.S. 41 (1967)
Whitehill v. Elkins, 389 U.S. 54 (1967)
Lucas v. Rhodes, 389 U.S. 212 (1967)
Nash v. Florida Industrial Commission, 389 U.S. 235 (1967)
Rockefeller v. Wells, 389 U.S. 421 (1967)
Zschernig v. Miller, 389 U.S. 429 (1968)
Dinis v. Volpe, 389 U.S. 570 (1968)
Louisiana Financial Assistance Comm. v. Poindexter, 389 U.S. 571 (1968)
Kirk v. Gong, 389 U.S. 572 (1968)
James v. Gilmore, 389 U.S. 572 (1968)
Tietel Film Corp. v. Cusack, 390 U.S. 139 (1968)
Lee v. Washington, 390 U.S. 333 (1968)
Avery v. Midland County, 390 U.S. 474 (1968)
Interstate Circuit, Inc. v. Dallas, 390 U.S. 676 (1968)
Scafati v. Greenfield, 390 U.S. 713 (1968)
Levy v. Louisiana, 391 U.S. 68 (1968)
  accord: *Glona v. American Guarantee Liability Insurance Co.*, 391 U.S. 73 (1968)
Rabeck v. New York, 391 U.S. 462 (1968)
Witherspoon v. Illinois, 391 U.S. 510 (1968)
Louisiana Education Comm. for Needy Children v. Poindexter, 393 U.S. 17 (1968)
Williams v. Rhodes, 393 U.S. 23 (1968)
Epperson v. Arkansas, 393 U.S. 97 (1968)
WHYY, Inc. v. Glassboro, 393 U.S. 117 (1968)
South Carolina State Board of Education v. Brown, 393 U.S. 222 (1968)
Hunter v. Erickson, 393 U.S. 385 (1969)
Kirkpatrick v. Preisler, 394 U.S. 526 (1969)
  accord: *Wells v. Rockefeller*, 394 U.S. 542 (1969)
Stanley v. Georgia, 394 U.S. 557 (1969)
Street v. New York, 394 U.S. 576 (1969)
Shapiro v. Thompson, 394 U.S. 618 (1969)
Moore v. Ogilvie, 394 U.S. 814 (1969)
Sniadach v. Family Finance Corp. 395 U.S. 337 (1969)
Brandenburg v. Ohio, 395 U.S. 444 (1969)

Table 2-16   *(Continued)*

Kramer v. Union Free School District, 395 U.S. 621 (1969)
Cipriano v. City of Houma, 395 U.S. 701 (1969)

Burger Court (June 9, 1969–September 16, 1986)

Turner v. Fouche, 396 U.S. 346 (1970)
Wyman v. Bowens, 397 U.S. 49 (1970)
Hadley v. Junior College District, 397 U.S. 50 (1970)
In re Winship, 397 U.S. 358 (1970)
Rosado v. Wyman, 397 U.S. 397 (1970)
Lewis v. Martin, 397 U.S. 552 (1970)
Baldwin v. New York, 399 U.S. 66 (1970)
Phoenix v. Kolodziejski, 399 U.S. 204 (1970)
Williams v. Illinois, 399 U.S. 235 (1970)
Wisconsin v. Constantineau, 400 U.S. 433 (1971)
Groppi v. Wisconsin, 400 U.S. 505 (1971)
Rockefeller v. Socialist Workers Party, 400 U.S. 806 (1970)
Parish School Board v. Stewart, 400 U.S. 884 (1970)
Bower v. Vaughan, 400 U.S. 884 (1970)
Rafferty v. MacKay, 400 U.S. 954 (1970)
Boddie v. Connecticut, 401 U.S. 371 (1971)
Tate v. Short, 401 U.S. 395 (1971)
North Carolina State Board of Education v. Swann, 402 U.S. 43 (1971)
California Dept. of Human Resources Development v. Java, 402 U.S. 121 (1971)
Bell v. Burson, 402 U.S. 535 (1971)
Coates v. Cincinnati, 402 U.S. 611 (1971)
Perez v. Campbell, 402 U.S. 637 (1971)
Nyquist v. Lee, 402 U.S. 935 (1971)
Whitcomb v. Chavis, 403 U.S. 124 (1971)
Connell v. Higginbotham, 403 U.S. 207 (1971)
Graham v. Richardson, 403 U.S. 365 (1971)
Sailer v. Leger, 403 U.S. 365 (1971)
Lemon v. Kurtzman, 403 U.S. 602 (1971)
  accord: *Sanders v. Johnson*, 403 U.S. 955 (1971)
Pease v. Hansen, 404 U.S. 70 (1971)
Reed v. Reed, 404 U.S. 71 (1971)
Townsend v. Swank, 404 U.S. 282 (1971)
Dunn v. Rivera, 404 U.S. 1054 (1972)
Wyman v. Lopez, 404 U.S. 1055 (1972)
Lindsey v. Normet, 405 U.S. 56 (1972)
Bullock v. Carter, 405 U.S. 134 (1972)
Papachristou v. Jacksonville, 405 U.S. 156 (1972)
Dunn v. Blumstein, 405 U.S. 330 (1972)
  accord: *Caniffe v. Burg*, 405 U.S. 1034 (1972)
  accord: *Davis v. Kohn*, 405 U.S. 1034 (1972)
  accord: *Cody v. Andrews*, 405 U.S. 1034 (1972)
  accord: *Donovan v. Keppel*, 405 U.S. 1034 (1972)
  accord: *Whitcomb v. Affeldt*, 405 U.S. 1034 (1972)
  accord: *Amos v. Hadnott*, 405 U.S. 1035 (1972)
  accord: *Virginia State Board of Elections v. Bufford*, 405 U.S. 1035 (1972)

(Table continues)

Table 2-16 *(Continued)*

Eisenstadt v. Baird, 405 U.S. 438 (1972)
Gooding v. Wilson, 405 U.S. 518 (1972)
Stanley v. Illinois, 405 U.S. 645 (1972)
Weber v. Aetna Casualty & Surety Co. 406 U.S. 164 (1972)
Wisconsin v. Yoder, 406 U.S. 205 (1972)
Brooks v. Tennessee, 406 U.S. 605 (1972)
Jackson v. Indiana, 406 U.S. 715 (1972)
Fuentes v. Shevin, 406 U.S. 67 (1972)
James v. Strange, 406 U.S. 128 (1972)
United States v. Scotland Neck City Board of Education, 406 U.S. 484 (1972)
State Dept. of Health & Rehab. Services v. Zarate, 407 U.S. 918 (1972)
Police Dept. of Chicago v. Mosley, 408 U.S. 92 (1972)
Furman v. Georgia, 408 U.S. 238 (1972)
Ward v. Village of Monroeville, 409 U.S. 57 (1972)
Evco v. Jones, 409 U.S. 91 (1972)
Philpott v. Essex County Welfare Board, 409 U.S. 413 (1973)
Gomez v. Perez, 409 U.S. 535 (1973)
Georges v. McCellan, 409 U.S. 535 (1973)
Texas Board of Barber Examiners v. Bolton, 409 U.S. 807 (1972)
Essex v. Wolman, 409 U.S. 808 (1972)
Sterrett v. Mothers' and Children's Rights Organization, 409 U.S. 809 (1972)
Cason v. City of Columbia, 409 U.S. 1053 (1972)
Robinson v. Hanrahan, 409 U.S. 38 (1972)
Amos v. Sims, 409 U.S. 942 (1972)
Fugate v. Potomac Electric Power Co., 409 U.S. 942 (1972)
Roe v. Wade, 410 U.S. 113 (1973)
Doe v. Bolton, 410 U.S. 179 (1973)
Mahan v. Howell, 410 U.S. 315 (1973)
Whitcomb v. Communist Party of Indiana, 410 U.S. 976 (1973)
Mescalero Apache Tribe v. Jones, 411 U.S. 145 (1973)
McClanahan v. Arizona State Tax Commission, 411 U.S. 164 (1973)
New Jersey Welfare Rights Organization v. Cahill, 411 U.S. 619 (1973)
City of Burbank v. Lockheed Air Terminal, Inc., 411 U.S. 624 (1973)
Parker v. Levy, 411 U.S. 978 (1973)
Gagnon v. Scarpelli, 411 U.S. 778 (1973)
Vlandis v. Kline, 412 U.S. 441 (1973)
Wardius v. Oregon, 412 U.S. 470 (1973)
White v. Regester, 412 U.S. 755 (1973)
White v. Weiser, 412 U.S. 783 (1973)
Miller v. Gomez, 412 U.S. 914 (1973)
Levitt v. Committee for Public Education & Religious Liberty, 413 U.S. 472 (1973)
Sugarman v. Dougall, 413 U.S. 634 (1973)
Committee for Public Education & Religious Liberty v. Nyquist, 413 U.S. 756(1973)
Sloan v. Lemon, 413 U.S. 825 (1973)
   accord: *Grit v. Wolman*, 413 U.S. 902 (1973)
Stevenson v. West, 413 U.S. 902 (1973)
Nelson v. Miranda, 413 U.S. 902 (1973)
Department of Game v. Puyallup Tribe, 414 U.S. 44 (1973)
Kusper v. Pontikes, 414 U.S. 51 (1973)
Lefkowitz v. Turley, 414 U.S. 70 (1973)

Table 2-16   *(Continued)*

Communist Party of Indiana v. Whitcomb, 414 U.S. 441 (1974)
O'Brien v. Skinner, 414 U.S. 524 (1974)
Texas v. Pruett, 414 U.S. 802 (1973)
Danforth v. Rodgers, 414 U.S. 1035 (1973)
Lewis v. New Orleans, 415 U.S. 130 (1974)
Memorial Hospital v. Maricopa County, 415 U.S. 250 (1974)
Davis v. Alaska, 415 U.S. 308 (1974)
Smith v. Goguen, 415 U.S. 566 (1974)
Lubin v. Panish, 415 U.S. 709 (1974)
Wallace v. Sims, 415 U.S. 902 (1974)
Beasley v. Food Fair, 416 U.S. 653 (1974)
Schwegmann Bros. Giant Super Markets v. Louisiana Milk Comm., 416 U.S. 922 (1974)
Indiana Real Estate Comm. v. Satoskar, 417 U.S. 938 (1974)
Marburger v. Public Funds for Public Schools, 417 U.S. 961 (1974)
Miami Herald Publishing Co. v. Tornillo, 418 U.S. 241 (1974)
Letter Carriers v. Austin, 418 U.S. 264 (1974)
Spence v. Washington, 418 U.S. 405 (1974)
  accord: *Cahn v. Long Island Vietnam Moratorium Committee*, 418 U.S. 906 (1974)
Taylor v. Louisiana, 419 U.S. 522 (1975)
Goss v. Lopez, 419 U.S. 565 (1975)
North Georgia Finishing, Inc. v. Di-Chem, Inc., 419 U.S. 601 (1975)
Franchise Tax Board v. United Americans, 419 U.S. 890 (1974)
Cox Broadcasting Corp. v. Cohn, 420 U.S. 469 (1975)
Austin v. New Hampshire, 420 U.S. 656 (1975)
Stanton v. Stanton, 421 U.S. 7 (1975)
Hill v. Stone, 421 U.S. 289 (1975)
Meek v. Pittenger, 421 U.S. 349 (1975)
Bigelow v. Virginia, 421 U.S. 809 (1975)
Erznoznik v. Jacksonville, 422 U.S. 205 (1975)
Herring v. New York, 422 U.S. 853 (1975)
Turner v. Department of Employment Security, 423 U.S. 44 (1975)
Schwartz v. Vanasco, 423 U.S. 1041 (1976)
Tucker v. Salera, 424 U.S. 959 (1976)
Moe v. Salish & Kootenai Tribes, 425 U.S. 463 (1976)
Hynes v. Mayor & Council of Oradell, 425 U.S. 610 (1976)
Virginia State Board of Pharmacy v. Virginia Citizens Consumer Council, Inc., 425 U.S. 748 (1976)
  accord: *California State Board of Pharmacy v. Terry*, 426 U.S. 913 (1976)
Kleppe v. New Mexico, 425 U.S. 529 (1976)
Bryan v. Itasca County, 426 U.S. 373 (1976)
Planned Parenthood of Central Missouri v. Danforth, 427 U.S. 52 (1976)
  accord: *Gerstein v. Coe*, 428 U.S. 901 (1976)
Machinists & Aerospace Workers v. WERC, 427 U.S. 132 (1976)
Woodson v. North Carolina, 427 U.S. 280 (1976)
  accord: *Roberts v. Louisiana*, 427 U.S. 325 (1976)
  accord: *Williams v. Oklahoma*, 428 U.S. 907 (1976)
Craig v. Boren, 429 U.S. 190 (1976)
Boston Stock Exchange v. State Tax Commission, 429 U.S. 318 (1977)
Sendak v. Arnold, 429 U.S. 968 (1976)
Exon v. McCarthy, 429 U.S. 972 (1976)

(Table continues)

Table 2-16   *(Continued)*

Lefkowitz v. C.D.R. Enterprises, 429 U.S. 1031 (1977)
Guste v. Weeks, 429 U.S. 1056 (1977)
Bowen v. Women's Services, 429 U.S. 1067 (1977)
Jones v. Rath Packing Co., 430 U.S. 519 (1977)
Wooley v. Maynard, 430 U.S. 705 (1977)
Trimble v. Gordon, 430 U.S. 762 (1977)
United States Trust Co. v. New Jersey, 431 U.S. 1 (1977)
Linmark Associates v. Willingboro, 431 U.S. 85 (1977)
Chapelle v. Greater Baton Rouge Airport Dist., 431 U.S. 159 (1977)
Douglas v. Seacoast Products, 431 U.S. 265 (1977)
Moore v. East Cleveland, 431 U.S. 494 (1977)
Roberts v. Louisiana, 431 U.S. 633 (1977)
Carey v. Population Services International, 431 U.S. 678 (1977)
Lefkowitz v. Cunningham, 431 U.S. 801 (1977)
Nyquist v. Mauclet, 432 U.S. 1 (1977)
Hunt v. Washington State Apple Advertising Commission, 432 U.S. 333 (1977)
Shaffer v. Heitner, 433 U.S. 186 (1977)
Wolman v. Walter, 433 U.S. 229 (1977)
Dothard v. Rawlinson, 433 U.S. 321 (1977)
Coker v. Georgia, 433 U.S. 584 (1977)
Jernigan v. Lendall, 433 U.S. 901 (1977)
New York v. Cathedral Academy, 434 U.S. 125 (1977)
Carter v. Miller, 434 U.S. 356 (1978)
Zablocki v. Redhail, 434 U.S. 374 (1978)
Maher v. Buckner, 434 U.S. 898 (1977)
Ray v. Atlantic Richfield Co., 435 U.S. 151 (1978)
Ballew v. Georgia, 435 U.S. 223 (1978)
McDaniel v. Paty, 435 U.S. 618 (1978)
First National Bank of Boston v. Bellotti, 435 U.S. 765 (1978)
Landmark Communications v. Virginia, 435 U.S. 839 (1978)
Hicklin v. Orbeck, 437 U.S. 518 (1978)
City of Philadelphia v. New Jersey, 437 U.S. 617 (1978)
Allied Structural Steel Co. v. Spannaus, 438 U.S. 234 (1978)
Lockett v. Ohio, 438 U.S. 586 (1978)
Duren v. Missouri, 439 U.S. 357 (1979)
Colautti v. Franklin, 439 U.S. 379 (1979)
Hisquierdo v. Hisquierdo, 439 U.S. 572 (1979)
Miller v. Youakim, 440 U.S. 125 (1979)
Illinois State Board of Elections v. Socialist Workers Party, 440 U.S. 173 (1979)
Orr v. Orr, 440 U.S. 268 (1979)
Ashcroft v. Freiman, 440 U.S. 941 (1979)
Quern v. Hernandez, 440 U.S. 951 (1979)
Burch v. Louisiana, 441 U.S. 130 (1979)
Arizona Public Service Co. v. Snead, 441 U.S. 141 (1979)
Hughes v. Oklahoma, 441 U.S. 322 (1979)
Caban v. Mohammed, 441 U.S. 380 (1979)
Japan Line, Ltd. v. Los Angeles County, 441 U.S. 434 (1979)
Torres v. Puerto Rico, 442 U.S. 465 (1979)
Beggans v. Public Funds for Public Schools, 442 U.S. 907 (1979)
Smith v. Daily Mail Publishing Co., 443 U.S. 97 (1979)

Table 2-16   *(Continued)*

Bellotti v. Baird, 443 U.S. 622 (1979)
Village of Schaumberg v. Citizens for a Better Environment, 444 U.S. 620 (1980)
California Retail Liquor Dealers Assn. v. Midcal Aluminum, Inc., 445 U.S. 97 (1980)
Vance v. Universal Amusement Co., Inc., 445 U.S. 308 (1980)
Vitek v. Jones, 445 U.S. 480 (1980)
Payton v. New York, 445 U.S. 573 (1980)
Ventura County v. Gulf Oil Corp., 445 U.S. 947 (1980)
Wengler v. Druggists Mutual Insurance Co., 446 U.S. 142 (1980)
Lewis v. BT Investment Managers, Inc., 447 U.S. 27 (1980)
Washington v. Confederated Tribes, 447 U.S. 134 (1980)
Carey v. Brown, 447 U.S. 455 (1980)
Beck v. Alabama, 447 U.S. 625 (1980)
White Mountain Apache Tribe v. Bracker, 448 U.S. 136 (1980)
Central Machinery Co. v. Arizona State Tax Comm., 448 U.S. 160 (1980)
Minnesota v. Planned Parenthood, 448 U.S. 901 (1980)
Stone v. Graham, 449 U.S. 39 (1980)
Democratic Party of United States v. Wisconsin, 449 U.S. 107 (1981)
Webb's Fabulous Pharmacies, Inc. v. Beckwith, 449 U.S. 155 (1980)
Kirchberg v. Feenstra, 449 U.S. 455 (1981)
Kassel v. Consolidated Freightways Corp., 449 U.S. 662 (1981)
Edwards v. Service Machine & Shipbuilding Corp., 449 U.S. 913 (1980)
Town of Southampton v. Troyer, 449 U.S. 988 (1980)
Weaver v. Graham, 450 U.S. 24 (1981)
Chicago & North Western Transp. Co. v. Kalo Brick & Tile Co., 450 U.S. 311 (1981)
Jefferson County v. United States, 450 U.S. 901 (1981)
Alessi v. Raybestos-Manhattan, Inc., 451 U.S. 504 (1981)
Maryland v. Louisiana, 451 U.S. 725 (1981)
Little v. Streater, 452 U.S. 1 (1981)
Schad v. Borough of Mount Ephraim, 452 U.S. 61 (1981)
McCarty v. McCarty, 453 U.S. 210 (1981)
Metromedia, Inc. v. San Diego, 453 U.S. 490 (1981)
Campbell v. John Donnelly & Sons, 453 U.S. 916 (1981)
Citizens Against Rent Control v. Berkeley, 454 U.S. 290 (1981)
Agsalud v. Standard Oil Co., 454 U.S. 801 (1981)
Louisiana Dairy Stabilization Bd. v. Dairy Fresh Corp., 454 U.S. 884 (1981)
Brockett v. Spokane Arcades, 454 U.S. 1022 (1981)
Firestone v. Let's Help Florida, 454 U.S. 1130 (1981)
Santosky v. Kramer, 455 U.S. 745 (1982)
Treen v. Karen B., 455 U.S. 912 (1982)
Brown v. Hartlage, 456 U.S. 45 (1982)
Mills v. Habluetzel, 456 U.S. 91 (1982)
California State Bd. of Equalization v. United States, 456 U.S. 141 (1982)
Larson v. Valente, 456 U.S. 228 (1982)
Greene v. Lindsay, 456 U.S. 444 (1982)
Rusk v. Espinosa, 456 U.S. 951 (1982)
Zobel v. Williams, 457 U.S. 55 (1982)
Blum v. Bacon, 457 U.S. 132 (1982)
Plyler v. Doe, 457 U.S. 202 (1982)
Globe Newspaper Co. v. Superior Court, 457 U.S. 596 (1982)
Edgar v. Mite Corp., 457 U.S. 624 (1982)

(Table continues)

Table 2-16   *(Continued)*

Fidelity Federal Savings & Loan Assn. v. De la Cuesta, 458 U.S. 141 (1982)
Loretto v. Teleprompter Manhattan CATV Corp., 458 U.S. 419 (1982)
Washington v. Seattle School Disrict No. 1, 458 U.S. 457 (1982)
Enmund v. Florida, 458 U.S. 782 (1982)
Ramah Navajo School Bd. v. Bureau of Revenue, 458 U.S. 832 (1982)
Sporhase v. Nebraska ex rel. Douglas, 458 U.S. 941 (1982)
Brown v. Socialist Workers '74 Campaign Committee, 459 U.S. 87 (1982)
Larkin v. Grendel's Den, Inc., 459 U.S. 116 (1982)
Memphis Bank & Trust Co. v. Garner, 459 U.S. 392 (1983)
King v. Sanchez, 459 U.S. 801 (1982)
Giacabbe v. Andrews, 459 U.S. 801 (1982)
Busbee v. Georgia, 459 U.S. 1166 (1983)
Minneapolis Star & Tribune Co. v. Minnesota Commissioner of Revenue, 460 U.S. 575
  (1983)
Anderson v. Celebrezze, 460 U.S. 780 (1983)
Kolender v. Lawson, 461 U.S. 352 (1983)
Pennsylvania Public Utility Comm'n v. CONRAIL, 461 U.S. 912 (1983)
Pickett v. Brown, 462 U.S. 1 (1983)
Exxon Corp. v. Eagerton, 462 U.S. 176 (1983)
Philco Aviation v. Shacket, 462 U.S. 406 (1983)
Akron v. Akron Center for Reproductive Health, Inc., 462 U.S. 416 (1983)
Planned Parenthood Association v. Ashcroft, 462 U.S. 476 (1983)
Karcher v. Daggett, 462 U.S. 725 (1983)
Mennonite Board of Missions v. Adams, 462 U.S. 791 (1983)
Shaw v. Delta Airlines, 463 U.S. 85 (1983)
American Bank & Trust Co. v. Dallas County, 463 U.S. 855 (1983)
Arcudi v. Stone & Webster Engineering, 463 U.S. 1220 (1983)
Aloha Airlines v. Director of Taxation, 464 U.S. 7 (1983)
Healy v. United States Brewers Ass'n, 464 U.S. 909 (1983)
Southland Corp. v. Keating, 465 U.S. 1 (1984)
Texas v. KVUE-TV, 465 U.S. 1092 (1984)
Westinghouse Electric Corp. v. Tully, 466 U.S. 388 (1984)
Wallace v. Jaffree, 466 U.S. 924 (1984)
Bernal v. Fainter, 467 U.S. 216 (1984)
Michigan Canners & Freezers Ass'n v. Agricultural Marketing and Bargaining Bd., 467
  U.S. 461 (1984)
Armco Inc. v. Hardesty, 467 U.S. 638 (1984)
Capital Cities Cable v. Crisp, 467 U.S. 691 (1984)
Brown v. Brandon, 467 U.S. 1223 (1984)
Secretary of State of Maryland v. Joseph H. Munson Co., 467 U.S. 947 (1984)
Bacchus Imports, Ltd. v. Dias, 468 U.S. 263 (1984)
Lawrence County v. Lead-Deadwood School District, 469 U.S. 256 (1985)
Deukmejian v. National Meat Ass'n, 469 U.S. 1100 (1985)
Westhafer v. Worrell Newspapers, 469 U.S. 1200 (1985)
Metropolitan Life Insurance Co. v. Ward, 470 U.S. 869 (1985)
Oklahoma City Board of Education v. National Gay Task Force, 470 U.S. 903 (1985)
Hunter v. Underwood, 471 U.S. 222 (1985)
Williams v. Vermont, 472 U.S. 14 (1985)
Wallace v. Jaffree, 472 U.S. 38 (1985)
Jensen v. Quaring, 472 U.S. 478 (1985)

Table 2-16   *(Continued)*

Brockett v. Spokane Arcades, 472 U.S. 491 (1985)
Hooper v. Bernalillo County Assessor, 472 U.S. 612 (1985)
Estate of Thornton v. Caldor, Inc., 472 U.S. 703 (1985)
City of Cleburne v. Cleburne Living Center, Inc., 473 U.S. 432 (1985)
Gerace v. Grocery Mfrs. of America, 474 U.S. 801 (1985)
Wisconsin Dep't of Industry v. Gould, Inc., 475 U.S. 282 (1986)
Exxon Corp. v. Hunt, 475 U.S. 355 (1986)
Philadelphia Newspapers, Inc. v. Hepps, 475 U.S. 767 (1986)
Hudnut v. American Booksellers Ass'n, 475 U.S. 1001 (1986)
Brown-Foreman Distillers Corp. v. New York State Liquor Authority, 476 U.S. 573 (1986)
Thornburgh v. American College of Obstetricians & Gynecologists, 476 U.S. 747 (1986)
Three Affiliated Tribes v. World Engineering, 476 U.S. 877 (1986)
Attorney General of New York v. Soto-Lopez, 476 U.S. 898 (1986)
Offshore Logistics v. Tallentire, 477 U.S. 207 (1986)
Roberts v. Burlington Industries, 477 U.S. 901 (1986)
Brooks v. Burlington Industries, 477 U.S. 901 (1986)
Thornburg v. Gingles, 478 U.S. 30 (1986)

Rehnquist Court (September 17, 1986–)

Rose v. Arkansas State Police, 479 U.S. 1 (1986)
Tashjian v. Republican Party of Connecticut, 479 U.S. 208 (1986)
324 Liquor Corp. v. Duffy, 479 U.S. 335 (1987)
Babbitt v. Planned Parenthood, 479 U.S. 925 (1986)
California v. Cabazon Band of Mission Indians, 480 U.S. 202 (1987)
Wilkinson v. Jones, 480 U.S. 926 (1987)
Arkansas Writers' Project, Inc. v. Ragland, 481 U.S. 221 (1987)
Miller v. Florida, 482 U.S. 423 (1987)
City of Houston v. Hill, 482 U.S. 451 (1987)
Perry v. Thomas, 482 U.S. 483 (1987)
Booth v. Maryland, 482 U.S. 496 (1987)
Board of Airport Commissioners for the City of Los Angeles v. Jews for Jesus, Inc., 482 U.S. 569 (1987)
Edwards v. Aguillard, 482 U.S. 578 (1987)
Sumner v. Shuman, 483 U.S. 66 (1987)
Tyler Pipe Industries, Inc. v. Washington Dept. of Revenue, 483 U.S. 232 (1987)
American Trucking Associations, Inc. v. Scheiner, 483 U.S. 266 (1987)
Hartigan v. Zbaraz, 484 U.S. 171 (1987)
Montana v. Crow Tribe of Indians, 484 U.S. 997 (1988)
Schneidewind v. ANR Pipeline Co., 485 U.S. 293 (1988)
Bennett v. Arkansas, 485 U.S. 395 (1988)
City of Manassas v. United States, 485 U.S. 1017 (1988)
New Energy Company of Indiana v. Limbach, 486 U.S. 269 (1988)
Maynard v. Cartwright, 486 U.S. 356 (1988)
Meyer v. Grant, 486 U.S. 414 (1988)
Clark v. Jeter, 486 U.S. 456 (1988)
Shapero v. Kentucky Bar Assn., 486 U.S. 466 (1988)
Lakewood v. Plain Dealer Publishing Co., 486 U.S. 750 (1988)
Bendix Autolite Corp. v. Midwesco Enterprises, Inc., 486 U.S. 888 (1988)
Riley v. National Federation of the Blind, 487 U.S. 781 (1988)

(Table continues)

Table 2-16   *(Continued)*

Mackey v. Lanier Collection Agency and Service, Inc., 486 U.S. 888 (1988)
Supreme Court of Virginia v. Friedman, 487 U.S. 59 (1988)
Felder v. Casey, 487 U.S. 131 (1988)
Boyle v. United Technologies Corp., 487 U.S. 500 (1988)
Thompson v. Oklahoma, 487 U.S. 815 (1988)
Coy v. Iowa, 487 U.S. 1012 (1988)
City of Richmond v. J.A. Croson Co., 488 U.S. 469 (1989)
Texas Monthly, Inc. v. Bullock, 489 U.S. 1 (1989)
Bonito Boats, Inc. v. Thunder Craft Boats, Inc., 489 U.S. 141 (1989)
Eu v. San Francisco County Democratic Central Committee, 489 U.S. 214 (1989)
Board of Estimate of New York City v. Morris, 489 U.S. 688 (1989)
Davis v. Michigan Dept. of Treasury, 489 U.S. 803 (1989)
Quinn v. Millsap, 491 U.S. 95 (1989)
Healy v. Beer Institute, Inc., 491 U.S. 324 (1989)
Texas v. Johnson, 491 U.S. 397 (1989)
Allegheny Pittsburgh Coal Co. v. Webster County Comm'n., 488 U.S. 336 (1989)
Barnard v. Thorstenn, 489 U.S. 546 (1989)
The Florida Star v. B.J.F., 491 U.S. 524 (1989)
FW/PBS, Inc. v. Dallas, 493 U.S. 215 (1990)
McKoy v. North Carolina, 494 U.S. 433 (1990)
Butterworth v. Smith, 494 U.S. 624 (1990)
Peel v. Attorney Registration & Disciplinary Commission, 496 U.S. 91 (1990)
Hodgson v. Minnesota, 497 U.S. 417 (1990)
Connecticut v. Doehr, 501 U.S. 1 (1991)
Gentile v. Nevada State Bar, 501 U.S. 1030 (1991)
Simon and Schuster v. Crime Victims Board, 502 U.S. 105 (1991)
Norman v. Reed, 502 U.S. 279 (1992)
Wyoming v. Oklahoma, 502 U.S. 437 (1992)
Foucha v. Louisiana, 504 U.S. 71 (1992)
Chemical Waste Management v. Hunt, 504 U.S. 334 (1992)
Fort Gratiot Landfill v. Michigan Dep't, 504 U.S. 353 (1992)
Kraft General Food v. Iowa Dep't, 505 U.S. 71 (1992)
Forsyth County v. The Nationalist Movement, 505 U.S. 123 (1992)
R.A.V. v. St. Paul, 507 U.S. 377 (1992)
Lee v. Krishna Society, 505 U.S. 830 (1992)
Planned Parenthood v. Casey, 505 U.S. 833 (1992)
Cincinnati v. Discovery Network, 507 U.S. 410 (1993)
El Vocero De Puerto Rico v. Puerto Rico, 508 U.S. 117 (1993)
Lamb's Chapel v. Center Moriches School Dist., 508 U.S. 384 (1993)
Church of Lukumi Babalu v. Hialeah, 508 U.S. 520 (1993)
Harper v. Virginia Department of Taxation, 509 U.S. 86 (1993)
Oregon Waste Systems v. Oregon Dep't., 511 U.S. 93 (1994)
C&A Carbone, Inc. v. Town of Clarkston, 511 U.S. 383 (1994)
Associated Industries v. Lohman, 511 U.S. 641 (1994)
Montana Dep't v. Kurth Ranch, 511 U.S. 767 (1994)
Ladue v. Galleo, 512 U.S. 43 (1994)
West Lynn Creamery v. Healy, 512 U.S. 186 (1994)
Kiryas Joel Board of Education v. Grumet, 512 U.S. 687 (1994)
Honda Motor Co. v. Oberg, 512 U.S. 415 (1994)
Reich v. Collins, 513 U.S. 106 (1994)

Table 2-16   *(Continued)*

McIntyre v. Ohio Elections Commission, 514 U.S. 334 (1995)
U.S. Term Limits, Inc. v. Thornton, 514 U.S. 779 (1995)
Miller v. Johnson, 515 U.S. 900 (1995)
Fulton Corp. v. Faulkner, 516 U.S. 325 (1996)
Cooper v. Oklahoma, 517 U.S. 348 (1996)
44 Liquormart, Inc. v. Rhode Island, 517 U.S. 484 (1996)
Romer v. Evans, 517 U.S. 620 (1996)
Shaw v. Hunt, 517 U.S. 899 (1996)
Bush v. Vera, 517 U.S. 952 (1996)
M.L.B. v. S.L.J., 519 U.S. 102 (1996)
Lynce v. Mathis, 519 U.S. 433 (1997)
Chandler v Miller, 520 U.S. 305 (1997)
Camps Newfound/Owatonna v. Town of Harrison, 520 U.S. 564 (1997)
Foster v. Love, 522 U.S. 67 (1997)
Buckley v. American Constitutional Law Foundation, 525 U.S. 182 (1999)
Saenz v. Roe, 526 U.S. 489 (1999)
Chicago v. Morales, 527 U.S. 41 (1999)
Hunt-Wesson, Inc. v. California Franchise Tax Board, 528 U.S. 458 (2000)
Rice v. Cayetano, 528 U.S. 495 (2000)
Troxel v. Granville, 530 U.S. 57 (2000)
Crosby v. National Foreign Trade Council, 530 U.S. 363 (2000)
California Democratic Party v. Jones, 530 U.S. 567 (2000)
Steinberg v. Carhart, 530 U.S. 914 (2000)
City of Indianapolis v. Edmond, 531 U.S. 32 (2000)
Cook v. Gralike, 531 U.S. 510 (2001)

Note: Determination of which decisions have declared state and local legislation unconstitutional is not a clear-cut matter. For example, the Congressional Research Service invokes criteria different from those of the Supreme Court database, which lists these decisions since the onset of the Vinson Court in 1946. The Congressional Research Service includes "decisions in which provisions of state constitutions, statutes, and municipal ordinances were found to be unconstitutional either in substance or as enforced, including provisions which conflicted with federal legislative acts and were therefore void because of the supremacy clause" (p. 1623). The database, by contrast, lists only decisions in which the Court clearly indicates that it has voided a legislative enactment of some level of government; where federal law preempts state law, unconstitutionality does not result unless the Court's prevailing opinion so states.

Sources: 1789–1990: Congressional Research Service, *The Constitution of the United States of America, Analysis and Interpretation* (Washington, D.C.: Government Printing Office, 1973), 1623–1785 and supplements; 1991–2000: U.S. Supreme Court Judicial Database.

Table 2-17 Supreme Court Decisions Overruled by Subsequent
Decisions, 1789–2002

Court	Overruling case	Overruled case
Marshall Court (January 27, 1801– March 14, 1836)	*Hudson v. Guestier*, 6 Cr. (10 U.S.) 281 (1810)	*Rose v. Himley*, 4 Cr. (8 U.S.) 241 (1808)
Taney Court (March 15, 1836– December 5, 1864)	*The Genesse Chief,* 12 How. (53 U.S.) 443 (1851)	*The Thomas Jefferson,* 10 Wheat. (23 U.S.) 428 (1825) *The Orleans v. Phoebus,* 11 Pet. (36 U.S.) 175 (1837)
	Gazzam v. Phillip's Lessee, 20 How. (61 U.S.) 372 (1858)	*Brown's Lessee v. Clements,* 3 How. (44 U.S. 650 (1845)
Chase Court (December 6, 1864– January 20, 1874)	*Mason v. Eldred*, 6 Wall. (73 U.S.) 231 (1868)	*Sheehy v. Mandeville,* 6 Cr. (10 U.S.) 253 (1810)
Waite Court (January 21, 1874– July 19, 1888)	*Hornbuckle v. Toombs,* 18 Wall. (85 U.S.) 648 (1874)	*Noonan v. Lee*, 2 Bl. (67 U.S.) 499 (1863) *Orchard v. Hughes*, 1 Wall. (68 U.S.) 73 (1864) *Dunphy v. Kleinsmith,* 11 Wall. (78 U.S.) 610 (1871)
	Union Pac. R. Co. v. McShane, 22 Wall. (89 U.S.) 444 (1874)	*Kansas Pac. R. Co. v. Prescott*, 16 Wall. (83 U.S.) 803 (1873) (in part)
	County of Cass v. Johnston, 95 U.S. 360 (1877)	*Harshman v. Bates County*, 92 U.S. 569 (1875)
	Fairfield v. County of Gallatin, 100 U.S. 47 (1879)	*Town of Concord v. Savings-Bank*, 92 U.S. 625 (1875)
	Tilghman v. Proctor, 102 U.S. 707 (1880)	*Mitchell v. Tilghman,* 19 Wall. (86 U.S.) 287 (1873)
	United States v. Phelps, 107 U.S. 320 (1883)	*Shelton v. The Collector,* 5 Wall. (72 U.S.) 113 (1867)
	Kountze v. Omaha Hotel Co., 107 U.S. 378 (1883)	*Stafford v. The Union Bank of Louisiana*, 16 How. (57 U.S.) 135 (1853)
	Morgan v. United States, 113 U.S. 476 (1885)	*Texas v. White*, 7 Wall. (74 U.S.) 700 (1869)
	Leloup v. Port of Mobile, 127 U.S. 640 (1888)	*Osbourne v. Mobile*, 16 Wall. (83 U.S.) 479 (1873)
Fuller Court (July 20, 1888– December 11, 1910)	*Leisy v. Hardin*, 135 U.S. 100, 118 (1890)	*Peirce v. New Hampshire,* 5 How. (46 U.S.) 504 (1847)
	Brenham v. German-American Bank, 144 U.S. 173 (1892)	*Rogers v. Burlington,* 3 Wall. (10 U.S.) 654 (1866)

Table 2-17   *(Continued)*

Court	Overruling case	Overruled case
		Mitchell v. Burlington, 4 Wall. (71 U.S.) 270 (1867)
	Roberts v. Lewis, 153 U.S. 367(1894)	*Giles v. Little,* 104 U.S. 291 (1881)
White Court (December 12, 1910– June 29, 1921)	*Garland v. Washington,* 232 U.S. 642 (1914)	*Crain v. United States,* 162 U.S. 625 (1896)
	United States v. Nice, 241 U.S. 591 (1916)	*Matter of Heff,* 197 U.S. 488 (1905)
	Rosen v. United States, 245 U.S. 467 (1918)	*United States v. Reid,* 12 How. (53 U.S.) 361 (1851)
	Boston Store v. American Graphophone Co., 246 U.S. 8 (1918) and *Motion Picture Co. v. Universal Film Co.,* 243 U.S. 502 (1917)	*Henry v. Dick Co.,* 224 U.S. 1 (1912)
Taft Court (June 30, 1921– February 12, 1930)	*Terrel v. Burke Constr. Co.,* 257 U.S. 529 (1922)	*Doyle v. Continental Ins. Co.,* 94 U.S. 535 (1877) *Security Mutual Life Ins. Co. v. Prewitt,* 202 U.S. 246 (1906)
	Lee v. Chesapeake & Ohio Ry., 260 U.S. 653 (1923)	*Ex Parte Wisner,* 203 U.S. 449 (1906) and qualifying, *In re Moore,* 209 U.S. 490 (1908)
	Alpha Cement Co. v. Massachusetts, 268 U.S. 203 (1925)	*Baltic Mining Co. v. Massachusetts,* 231 U.S. 68 (1913)
	Gleason v. Seaboard Ry., 278 U.S. 349 (1929)	*Friedlander v. Texas & Railway Co.,* 130 U.S. 416 (1889)
	Farmers Loan Co. v. Minnesota, 280 U.S. 204 (1930)	*Blackstone v. Miller,* 188 U.S. 189 (1903)
Hughes Court (February 13, 1930– June 11, 1941)	*East Ohio Gas Co. v. Tax Comm.,* 283 U.S. 465 (1931)	*Penna. Gas Co. v. Pub. Service Comm.,* 292 U.S. 23 (1920)
	Chicago & E.I.R. Co. v. Commission, 284 U.S. 296 (1932)	*Erie R.R. Co. v. Collins,* 253 U.S. 77 (1920) *Erie R.R. Co., v. Szary,* 253 U.S. 86 (1920)
	Funk v. United States, 290 U.S. 371 (1933); *see also Hawkins v. United States,* 358 U.S. 74 (1958)	*Stein v. Bowman,* 13 Pet. (38 U.S.) 209 (1839) (in part) *Hendrix v. United States,* 219 U.S. 79 (1911)

(Table continues)

Table 2-17 *(Continued)*

Court	Overruling case	Overruled case
		Jin Fuey Moy v. United States, 254 U.S. 189 (1920)
	West Coast Hotel Co. v. Parrish, 300 U.S. 379 (1937)	*Adkins v. Children's Hospital*, 261 U.S. 525 (1923)
	Helvering v. Producers Corp., 303 U.S. 376 (1938)	*Gillespie v. Oklahoma*, 257 U.S. 501 (1922)
		Burnet v. Coronado Oil & Gas Co., 285 U.S. 393 (1932)
	Erie R. Co. v. Tompkins, 304 U.S. 64 (1938)	*Swift v. Tyson*, 16 Pet. (41 U.S.) 1 (1842)
	Graves v. N.Y. ex rel. O'Keefe, 306 U.S. 466 (1939)	*Collector v. Day*, 11 Wall. (78 U.S.) 113 (1871)
		N.Y. ex rel. Rogers v. Graves, 299 U.S. 401 (1937)
	O'Malley v. Woodrough, 307 U.S. 277 (1939)	*Miles v. Graham*, 268 U.S. 501 (1925)
	Madden v. Kentucky, 309 U.S. 83 (1940)	*Colgate v. Harvey*, 296 U.S. 404 (1935)
	Helvering v. Hallock, 309 U.S. 106 (1940)	*Helvering v. St. Louis Trust Co.*, 296 U.S. 48 (1935)
		Becker v. St. Louis Trust Co., 296 U.S. 48 (1935)
	United States v. Darby, 312 U.S. 100 (1941)	*Hammer v. Dagenhart*, 247 U.S. 251 (1918)
		Carter v. Carter Coal Co., 298 U.S. 238 (1936) (limited)
	United States v. Chicago, M. St. P. & P.R. Co., 312 U.S. 592 (1941)	*United States v. Lynah*, 188 U.S. 445 (1903) (in part)
	Nye v. United States, 313 U.S. 33 (1941)	*Toledo Newspaper v. Heyward*, 250 U.S. 633 (1918)
	California v. Thompson, 313 U.S. 109 (1941)	*Di Santo v. Pennsylvania*, 273 U.S. 34 (1927)
	Olson v. Nebraska, 313 U.S. 236 (1941)	*Ribnik v. McBride*, 277 U.S. 350 (1928)
Stone Court (June 12, 1941– June 19, 1946)	*Alabama v. King & Boozer*, 314 U.S. 1 (1941)	*Panhandle Oil Co. v. Knox*, 277 U.S. 218 (1928)
		Graves v. Texas Co., 298 U.S. 393 (1936)
	State Tax Comm. v. Aldrich, 316 U.S. 174 (1942)	*First National Bank v. Maine*, 284 U.S. 312 (1932)
	Williams v. North Carolina, 317 U.S. 287 (1942)	*Haddock v. Haddock*, 201 U.S. 562 (1906)

Table 2-17   *(Continued)*

Court	Overruling case	Overruled case
	Brady v. Roosevelt S.S. Co., 317 U.S. 575 (1943)	*Johnson v. Fleet Corp.,* 280 U.S. 320 (1930)
	Jones v. Opelika, 319 U.S. 103 (1943) (reargument)	*Jones v. Opelika,* 316 U.S. 584 (1942)
	Board of Education v. Barnette, 319 U.S. 624 (1943)	*Minersville District v. Gobitis,* 310 U.S. 586 (1940)
	Smith v. Allwright, 321 U.S. 649 (1944)	*Grovey v. Townsend,* 295 U.S. 45 (1935)
	Girouard v. United States, 328 U.S. 61 (1946)	*United States v. MacIntosh,* 283 U.S. 605 (1931) *United States v. Bland,* 283 U.S. 636 (1931)
Vinson Court (June 20, 1946– September 29, 1953)	*Angel v. Buelington,* 330 U.S. 183 (1947)	*David Lupton's Sons v. Auto Club of Am.,* 225 U.S. 489 (1912) (rendered obsolete by previous law)
	Comr. v. Estate of Church, 335 U.S. 632 (1949)	*May v. Heiner,* 281 U.S. 238 (1930)
	Oklahoma Tax Comm. v. Texas Co., 336 U.S. 342 (1949)	*Choctaw & Gulf R.R. v. Harrison,* 235 U.S. 292 (1914) *Indian Oil Co. v. Oklahoma,* 240 U.S. 522 (1916) *Howard v. Gipsy Oil Co.,* 247 U.S. 503 (1918) *Large Oil Co. v. Howard,* 248 U.S. 549 (1919) *Oklahoma v. Barnsdall Corp.,* 296 U.S. 521 (1936)
	Cosmopolitan Co. v. McAllister, 337 U.S. 783 (1949)	*Hust v. Moore-McCormack Lines,* 328 U.S. 707 (1946)
	United States v. Rabinowitz, 339 U.S. 56 (1950)	*Trupiano v. United States,* 334 U.S. 699 (1948) *McDonald v. United States,* 335 U.S. 451 (1948)
	Joseph Burstyn, Inc. v. Wilson, 343 U.S. 495 (1952)	*Mutual Film Corp., v. Ohio Indus'l Comm.,* 236 U.S. 230 (1915)
Warren Court (September 30, 1953– June 8, 1969)	*Brown v. Board of Education,* 347 U.S. 483 (1954)	*Cumming v. Board of Education,* 175 U.S. 528 (1899) *Gong Lum v. Rice,* 275 U.S. 78 (1927)

(Table continues)

Table 2-17   *(Continued)*

Court	Overruling case	Overruled case
	Reid v. Covert, 354 U.S. 1 (1957)	*Kinsella v. Krueger*, 351 U.S. 470 (1956) *Reid v. Covert*, 351 U.S. 487 (1956)
	Vanderbilt v. Vanderbilt, 354 U.S. 416 (1957); see also *Armstrong v. Armstrong*, 350 U.S. 568 (1956)	*Thompson v. Thompson*, 226 U.S. 551 (1913)
	Ladner v. United States, 358 U.S. 169 (1958) (on rehearing)	*Ladner v. United States*, 355 U.S. 282 (1958)
	United States v. Raines, 362 U.S. 17 (1960)	*United States v. Reese*, 92 U.S. 214 (1876)
	Elkins v. United States, 364 U.S. 206 (1960) and *Rios v. United States*, 364 U.S. 253 (1960)	*Weeks v. United States*, 232 U.S. 383 (1914) (in part) *Center v. United States*, 267 U.S. 575 (1925) *Byars v. United States*, 273 U.S. 28 (1927) (in part) *Feldman v. United States*, 322 U.S. 487 (1944) (in part)
	James v. United States, 366 U.S. 213 (1961)	*CIR v. Wilcox*, 327 U.S. 404 (1946)
	Mapp v. Ohio, 367 U.S. 643 (1961); see also *Ker v. California*, 374 U.S. 23 (1963)	*Wolf v. Colorado*, 338 U.S. 25 (1949) (in part) *Irvine v. California*, 347 U.S. 128 (1954)
	Baker v. Carr, 369 U.S. 186 (1962)	*Colegrove v. Green*, 328 U.S. 549 (1946) (in part)
	Wesberry v. Sanders, 376 U.S. 1 (1964)	*Colegrove v. Green*, 328 U.S. 549 (1946)
	Smith v. Evening News Association, 371 U.S. 195 (1962); see also *Truck Drivers Union v. Riss & Co.*, 372 U.S. 517 (1923)	*Westinghouse Employees v. Westinghouse Corp.*, 348 U.S. 437 (1955) (in part)
	Construction & General Laborers' Union v. Curry, 371 U.S. 542 (1962)	*Building Union v. Ledbetter Co.*, 344 U.S. 178 (1952) (in part)
	Gideon v. Wainwright, 372 U.S. 335 (1963)	*Betts v. Brady*, 316 U.S. 455 (1942)
	Gray v. Sanders, 372 U.S. 368 (1963)	*Cook v. Fortson*, 329 U.S. 675 (1946) *South v. Peters*, 339 U.S. 276 (1950)

Table 2-17   *(Continued)*

Court	Overruling case	Overruled case
		Cox v. Peters, 342 U.S. 936 (1952) *Hartsfield v. Sloan*, 357 U.S. 916 (1958)
	Fay v. Noia, 372 U.S. 391 (1963)	*Darr v. Burford*, 339 U.S. 200 (1950) (in part)
	Ferguson v. Skrupa, 372 U.S. 726 (1963)	*Adams v. Tanner*, 244 U.S. 590 (1917)
	Malloy v. Hogan, 378 U.S. 1 (1964)	*Twining v. New Jersey*, 211 U.S. 78 (1908) *Adamson v, California*, 332 U.S. 46 (1947)
	Murphy v. Waterfront Commission, 378 U.S. 52 (1964)	*Jack v. Kansas*, 199 U.S. 372 (190) *United States v. Murdock*, 284 U.S. 141 (1931) *Feldman v. United States*, 332 U.S. 487 (1944) *Knapp v. Schweitzer*, 357 U.S. 371 (1958) *Mills v. Louisiana*, 360 U.S. 230 (1959)
	Jackson v. Denno, 378 U.S. 368 (1964)	*Stein v. New York*, 346 U.S. 156 (1953)
	Pointer v. Texas, 380 U.S. 400 (1965)	*West v. Louisiana*, 194 U.S. 258 (1904)
	Swift & Co. v. Wickham, 382 U.S. 111 (1965)	*Kesler v. Dep't of Public Safety*, 369 U.S. 153 (1962)
	Harris v. United States, 382 U.S. 162 (1965)	*Brown v. United States*, 359 U.S. 41 (1959)
	Harper v. Virginia Board of Elections, 383 U.S. 663 (1966)	*Breedlove v. Suttles*, 302 U.S. 277 (1937) *Butler v. Thompson*, 341 U.S. 937 (1937)
	Spevack v. Klein, 385 U.S. 511 (1967)	*Cohen v. Hurley*, 366 U.S. 177 (1961)
	Afroyim v. Rusk, 387 U.S. 253 (1967)	*Perez v. Brownell*, 356 U.S. 44 (1958)
	Warden v. Hayden, 387 U.S. 294 (1967)	*Gouled v. United States*, 255 U.S. 298 (1921)
	Camara v. Municipal Court, 387 U.S. 523 (1967)	*Frank v. Maryland*, 359 U.S. 360 (1959)
	Katz v. United States, 389 U.S. 347 (1967)	*Olmstead v. United States*, 277 U.S. 438 (1928)

(Table continues)

Table 2-17 *(Continued)*

Court	Overruling case	Overruled case
	Peyton v. Rowe, 391 U.S. 54 (1968)	*McNally v. Hill*, 293 U.S. 131 (1934)
	Bruton v. United States, 391 U.S. 123 (1968)	*Delli Paoli v. United States*, 352 U.S. 232 (1957)
	Carafas v. LaVallee, 391 U.S. 234 (1968)	*Parker v. Ellis*, 362 U.S. 574 (1960)
	Lee v. Florida, 392 U.S. 378 (1968)	*Schwartz v. Texas*, 344 U.S. 199 (1952)
	Jones v. Alfred H. Mayer Co., 392 U.S. 409 (1968)	*Hodges v. United States*, 203 U.S. 1 (1906)
	Moore v. Ogilvie, 394 U.S. 814 (1969)	*MacDougall v. Green*, 335 U.S. 281 (1958)
	Brandenburg v. Ohio, 395 U.S. 444 (1969)	*Whiteny v. California*, 274 U.S. 357 (1927)
	Chimel v. California, 395 U.S. 752 (1969)	*Harris v. United States*, 331 U.S. 145 (1947) *United States v. Rabinowitz*, 339 U.S. 56 (1950)
	Benton v. Maryland, 395 U.S. 784 (1969)	*Palko v. Connecticut*, 302 U.S. 319 (1937)
Burger Court (June 9, 1969– September 16, 1986)	*Boys Markets v. Retail Clerks*, 398 U.S. 235 (1970)	*Sinclair v. Refining Co. v. Atkinson*, 370 U.S. 195 (1962)
	Prince v. Georgia, 398 U.S. 323, (1970)	*Brantley v. Georgia*, 217 U.S. 284 (1910)
	Moragne v. States Marine Lines, Inc., 398 U.S. 375 (1970)	*The Harrisburg*, 119 U.S. 199 (1886)
	Blonder-Tongue Laboratories, Inc. v. University of Illinois Foundation, 402 U.S. 313 (1971)	*Triplett v. Lowell*, 297 U.S. 638 (1936)
	Perez v. Campbell, 402 U.S. 637 (1971)	*Kesler v. Dep't of Public Safety*, 369 U.S. 153 (1962)
	Griffin v. Breckenridge, 403 U.S. 88 (1971)	*Collins v. Hardyman*, 341 U.S. 651 (1951) (in part)
	Andrews v. Louisville & Nashville R. Co., 406 U.S. 320 (1972)	*Moore v. Ill. Cent. R. Co.*, 312 U.S. 630 (1941)
	Lehnhausen v. Lake Shore Auto Parts Co., 410 U.S. 356 (1973)	*Quaker City Cab v. Pennsylvania*, 277 U.S. 389 (1928)

Table 2-17 *(Continued)*

Court	Overruling case	Overruled case
	Braden v. 30th Judicial Circuit Court, 410 U.S. 484 (1973)	*Ahrens v. Clark*, 335 U.S. 188 (1948)
	Miller v. California, 413 U.S. 15 (1973)	*A Book Named "John Cleland's Memoirs of a Woman of Pleasure" v. Attorney General*, 383 U.S. 413 (1966)
	North Dakota Pharmacy Board v. Snyder's Drug Stores, 414 U.S. 156 (1973)	*Liggett Co. v. Baldridge*, 278 U.S. 105 (1929)
	Edelman v. Jordan, 415 U.S. 651 (1974)	*Shapiro v. Thompson*, 394 U.S. 618 (1969) (in part) *State Dept' of Health & Rehabilitation Services v. Zarate*, 407 U.S. 918 (1972) *Sterett v. Mothers' & Chil dren's Rights Organization*, 409 U.S. 67 (1972)
	Mitchell v. W.T. Grant Co., 416 U.S. 600 (1974)	*Fuentes v. Shevin*, 407 U.S. 67 (1972)
	Taylor v. Louisiana, 419 U.S. 522 (1975)	*Hoyt v. Florida*, 368 U.S. 57 (1971) (in effect)
	United States v. Reliable Transfer Co., 421 U.S. 397 (1975)	*Schooner Catherine v. Dickinson*, 17 How. (58 U.S.) 170 (1854)
	Michelin Tire Co. v. Wages, 423 U.S. 276 (1976); *Dove v. United States*, 423 U.S. 325 (1976)	*Low v. Austin*, 13 Wall. (80 U.S.) 29 (1871) *Durham v. United States*, 401 U.S. 481 (1971)
	Hudgens v. National Labor Relations Board, 424 U.S. 507 (1976)	*Amalgamated Food Employees Union v. Logan Valley Plaza*, 391 U.S. 308 (1968)
	Virginia Board of Pharmacy v. Virginia Citizens Consumer Council, 425 U.S. 748 (1976)	*Valentine v. Chrestensen*, 316 U.S. 52 (1942)
	National League of Cities v. Usery, 426 U.S. 833 (1976)	*Maryland v. Wirtz*, 392 U.S. 183 (1968)
	Machinists & Aerospace Workers v. Wisconsin Employment Relations Commission, 427 U.S. 132 (1976)	*UAW v. WERB*, 336 U.S. 245 (1957)
	New Orleans v. Dukes, 427 U.S. 297 (1976)	*Morey v. Doud*, 354 U.S. 457 (1957)

(Table continues)

Table 2-17 *(Continued)*

Court	Overruling case	Overruled case
	Gregg v. Georgia, 428 U.S. 153 (1976)	*McGautha v. California*, 402 U.S. 183 (1971)
	Craig v. Boren, 429 U.S. 190 (1976)	*Goesaert v. Cleary*, 335 U.S. 464 (1948)
	Oregon ex rel. State Land Board v. Corvallis Sand Gravel Co., 429 U.S. 363 (1976)	*Bonelli Cattle Co. v. Arizona*, 414 U.S. 313 (1973)
	Complete Auto Transit, Inc. v. Brady, 430 U.S. 274 (1977)	*Spector Motor Service v. O'Connor*, 340 U.S. 602 (1951)
	Continental T. V., Inc. v. GTE Sylvania Inc., 433 U.S. 36 (1977)	*United States v. Arnold, Schwinn & Co.*, 388 U.S. 365 (1967)
	Shaffer v. Heitner, 433 U.S. 186 (1977)	*Pennoyer v. Neff*, 95 U.S. 714 (1878)
	Revenue Dept. v. Washington Stevedoring Cos, 435 U.S. 734 (1978)	*Puget Sound Stevedoring Co. v. State Tax Comm'n*, 302 U.S. 90 (1937) *Joseph v. Carter & Weeks Stevedoring Co.*, 330 U.S. 422 (1947)
	Monell v. Dept. of Social Services, 436 U.S. 658 (1978)	*Monroe v. Pape*, 365 U.S. 167 (1961)(in part) *City of Kenosha v. Bruno*, 412 U.S. 507 (1973) (in part) *Morr v. County of Almeda*, 411 U.S. 693 (1973)
	Burks v. United States, 437 U.S. 1 (1978)	*Bryan v. United States*, 338 U.S. 552 (1950) (in part) *Sapir v. United States*, 348 U.S. 373 (1955) (in part) *Yates v. United States*, 354 U.S. 298 (1957) (in part) *Forman v. United States*, 361 U.S. 416 (1960) (in part)
	United States v. Scott, 437 U.S. 82 (1978)	*United States v. Jenkins*, 420 U.S. 358 (1975)
	Hughes v. Oklahoma, 441 U.S. 322 (1979)	*Geer v. Connecticut*, 161 U.S. 519 (1896)
	Illinois v. Gates, 462 U.S. 213 (1983)	*Aquilar v. Texas*, 378 U.S. 108 (1964) *Spinelli v. United States*, 393 U.S. 410 (1969)
	Pennhurst State School & Hosp. v. Halderman 465 U.S. 89 (1984)	*Rolston v. Missouri Fund Comm'rs*, 120 U.S. 390 (1887) (in part)

Table 2-17   *(Continued)*

Court	Overruling case	Overruled case
		Siler v. Louisville & Nashville R.R. Co., 213 U.S. 175 (1909) (in part) *Atchison, T. & S.F. Ry. Co. v. O'Connor*, 223 U.S. 280 (1912) (in part) *Greene v. Louisville & Interurban R.R. Co.*, 244 U.S. 499 (1917) (in part) *Johnson v. Lankford*, 245 U.S. 541 (1918) (in part) Numerous other cases fall more or less under the *Pennhurst* doctrine. See 465 U.S. 109–111 nn.17–21, 117–121 (maj. op.) and id., 130–37, 159–163, 165–166 nn.50 & 52 (dissent) (listing 28 cases)
	United States v. One Assortment of 89 Firearms, 465 U.S. 354 (1984)	*Coffey v. United States*, 116 U.S. 436 (1886)
	Limbach v. Hooven & Allison Co., 466 U.S. 353 (1984)	*Hooven & Allison Co. v. Evatt*, 324 U.S. 652 (1945)
	Copperweld Corp. v. Independence Tube Corp. 467 U.S. 752 (1984)	*United States v. Yellow Cab Co.*, 332 U.S. 218 (1947) *Kiefer-Stewart Co. v. Jos. E. Seagram & Sons*, 340 U.S. 211 (1951)
	Garcia v. San Antonio Metropolitan Transit Authority, 469 U.S. 528 (1985)	*National League of Cities v. Usery*, 426 U.S. 833 (1976)
	United States v. Miller, 471 U.S. 130 (1985)	*Ex parte Bain*, 121 U.S. 1 (1887) (in part)
	Daniels v. Williams, 474 U.S. 327 (1986)	*Parratt v. Taylor*, 451 U.S. 527 (1981) (in part)
	U.S. v. Lane, 474 U.S. 438 (1986)	*McElroy v. United States*, 164 U.S. 76 (1896)
	Batson v. Kentucky, 476 U.S. 79 (1986)	*Swain v. Alabama*, 380 U.S. 202 (1965) (in part)
Rehnquist Court (September 17, 1986–2002)	*Puerto Rico v. Bransted*, 483 U.S. 219 (1987)	*Kentucky v. Dennison*, 65 U.S. (24 How.) 66 (1861)
	Solorio v. United States, 483 U.S. 435 (1987)	*O'Callahan v. Parker*, 395 U.S. 258 (1969)

(Table continues)

Table 2-17   *(Continued)*

Court	Overruling case	Overruled case
	Welch v. Texas Dept. of Highways and Public Transportation, 483 U.S. 468 (1987)	*Parden v. Terminal Ry.*, 377 U.S. 84 (1964) (in part)
	Gulfstream Aerospace Corp. v. Mayacamus Corp., 485 U.S. 271 (1988)	*Enelow v. New York Life Ins. Co.*, 293 U.S. 379 (1935); *Ettelson v. Metropolitan Life Ins. Co.*, 317 U.S. 188 (1942)
	South Carolina v. Baker, 485 U.S. 505 (1988)	*Pollock v. Farmers' Loan & Trust Co.*, 157 U.S. 429 (1895)
	Thornburgh v. Abbott, 490 U.S. 401 459 (1989)	*Procunier v. Martinez*, 416 U.S. 396 (1974) (in part)
	Rodriguez de Quijas v. Shearson/American Express, Inc., 490 U.S. 477 (1989)	*Wilko v. Swann*, 346 U.S. 427 (1953)
	Alabama v. Smith, 490 U.S. 794 (1989)	*Simpson v. Rice*, 395 U.S. 711 (1969)
	Healy v. Beer Institute, 491 U.S. 324 (1989)	*Joseph E. Seagram & Sons v. Hostetter*, 384 U.S. 35 (1966)
	W.S. Kirkpatrick & Co. v. Environmental Tectronics Corp., 493 U.S. 400 (1990)	*American Banana Co. v. United Fruit Co.*, 213 U.S. 347 (1909)
	Collins v. Youngblood, 497 U.S. 37 (1990)	*Kring v. Missouri*, 107 U.S. 221 (1883); *Thompson v. Utah*, 170 U.S. 343 (1898)
	California v. Acevedo, 500 U.S. 565 (1991)	*Arkansas v. Sanders*, 442 U.S. 753 (1979)
	Coleman v. Thompson, 501 U.S. 722 (1991)	*Fay v. Noia*, 372 U.S. 391 (1963)
	Payne v. Tennessee, 501 U.S. 808 (1991)	*Booth v. Maryland*, 482 U.S. 496 (1987); *South Carolina v. Gathers*, 490 U.S. 805 (1989)
	Keeney v. Tamayo-Reyes, 504 U.S. 1 (1992)	*Townsend v. Sain*, 372 U.S. 293 (1963)
	Quill Corp. v. North Dakota, 504 U.S. 298 (1992)	*National Bellas Hess v. Illinois Dep't. of Revenue*, 386 U.S. 753 (1967)
	Planned Parenthood v. Casey, 505 U.S. 833 (1992)	*Akron v. Akron Center for Reproductive Health*, 462 U.S. 416 (1983); *Thornburgh v. American College*, 476 U.S. 747 (1986)

Table 2-17   *(Continued)*

Court	Overruling case	Overruled case
	Harper v. Virginia Tax Dep't, 509 U.S. 86 (1993)	*Chevron Oil Co. v. Huson,* 404 U.S. 97 (1971)
	Nichols v. United States, 511 U.S. 738 (1994)	*Baldasar v. Illinois,* 446 U.S. 222 (1980)
	OWCP v. Greenwich Collieries, 512 U.S. 267 (1994)	*NLRB v. Transportation Management Corp.,* 462 U.S. 393 (1983)
	Hubbard v. United States, 514 U.S. 695 (1995)	*United States v. Bramblett,* 348 U.S. 503 (1955)
	Adarand Constructors v.Pena, 515 U.S. 200 (1995)	*Fullilove v. Klutznick,* 448 U.S. 448 (1980); *Metro Broadcasting v. FCC,* 497 U.S. 547 (1990)
	United States v. Gaudin, 515 U.S. 506 (1995)	*Sinclair v. United States,* 279 U.S. 263 (1929)
	Seminole Tribe of Florida v. Florida, 517 U.S. 44 (1996)	*Pennsylvania v. Union Gas Co.,* 491 U.S. 1 (1989)
	44 Liquormart, Inc. v. Rhode Island, 517 U.S. 484 (1996)	*California v. LaRue,* 409 U.S. 109 (1972)
	Quackenbush v. Allstate Insurance Co., 517 U.S. 706 (1996)	*Thermtron Products, Inc. v. Hermansdorfer,* 423 U.S. 336 (1976)
	Lewis v. Casey, 518 U.S. 343 (1996)	*Bounds v. Smith,* 430 U.S. 817 (1977)
	State Oil Co. v. Khan, 522 U.S. 3 (1997)	*Albrecht v. Herald Co.,* 390 U.S. 145 (1968)
	Hudson v. United States, 522 U.S. 93 (1997)	*United States v. Halper,* 490 U.S. 435 (1989)
	Hohn v. United States, 524 U.S. 23 (1998)	*House v. Mayo,* 324 U.S. 42 (1945)
	College Savings Bank v. Florida Education Expense Board, 527 U.S. 666 (1999)	*Parden v. Terminal Railroad Co.,* 377 U.S. 184 (1964)
	Mitchell v. Helms, 530 U.S. 793 (2000)	*Meek v. Pittenger,* 421 U.S. 349 (1975) *Wolman v. Walter,* 433 U.S. 229 (1977)
	United States v. Hatter, 532 U.S. 557 (2001)	*Evans v. Gore,* 253 U.S. 245 (1920)
	Lapides v. Board of Regents, 152 L.Ed. 2d 806 (2002)	*Ford Motor Co. v. Department of Treasury of Indiana,* 323 U.S. 459 (1945)

United States v. Cotton, 152 L.Ed. 2d 860 (2002)	*Ex parte Bain,* 121 U.S. 1 (1897)
Atkins v. Virginia, 153 L.Ed. 2d 335 (2002)	*Penry v. Lynaugh,* 492 U.S. 302 (1989)

Note: The determination of whether the Court has formally altered one of its own precedents is a subjective judgment, as acknowledged by the Congressional Research Service, which includes only "reversals stated in express terms by the Supreme Court." The Supreme Court Judicial Database, in contrast, defines such wording as "overruled," "disapproved," "no longer good law," "can no longer be considered controlling," or "modify and narrow" as evidence of overruling. It excludes cases in which the Court "distinguishes" a precedent.

Sources: 1789–1990: Congressional Research Service, *The Constitution of the United States of America, Analysis and Interpretation* (Washington, D.C.: U.S. Government Printing Office, 1973) and supplements; 1991–2000: U.S. Supreme Court Judicial Database.

3

The Supreme Court's Opinion, Decision, and Outcome Trends

This chapter provides longitudinal data on several aspects of the Court's opinions, decisions, and outcomes. The information contained in the tables that follow deals primarily with the *institutional output of the Court as a whole*, not with that of particular justices. Readers interested in the voting behavior of the Court's members should refer to Chapter 5.

We begin with information on the Court's opinion trends. Tables 3-1 through 3-4 provide the number and proportion of cases that were decided unanimously, with dissenting opinions, with concurring opinions, and by 4–3 or 5–4 votes. As noted in the introduction to the book, the accuracy of the data that antedate 1946 cannot be confirmed as the sources from which they have been culled do not report reliability. It is also important to note that, given the varied data sources used to compile these tables, some inconsistency may arise as the result of differing definitions of unanimity and dissent. Results are simply reported, with no attempt to impose consistency on the data.

These data show that unanimity remained high throughout the nineteenth century, notwithstanding the small number of cases decided in many terms. Not until the 1940s does substantial dissent appear. Since then, the trend has been essentially flat, with approximately two-fifths of the cases decided unanimously and the other three-fifths with dissent. By the same token, prior to 1940 the proportion of cases decided by a one-vote margin never exceeded 10 percent. Since then, it has ranged between 2 percent and 28 percent.

Although numerous closely divided decisions may belie judicial objectivity, most of these cases have produced an authoritative result: a decision backed by an opinion with which a majority of the participating justices agree. Markedly more embarrassing are cases in which a majority is unable to agree on the reasons for its decision. These are termed judgments of the Court and are the subject of Table 3-5. Although they have reached double digits in only four terms since 1946, they most often occur in highly salient issue areas, such as civil rights and civil liberties. They result because one or more of the justices in the majority decision coalition specially concurs—that is, agrees with the result the majority has reached, but refuses to agree with the reasoning sustaining that outcome.

Unlike other federal and most state courts, the justices are free to determine which of the cases brought to their attention by losing litigants they will decide. Table 3-6 shows that, overall, the justices accept cases from lower courts that they wish to overturn. In only six terms since 1946 have the justices affirmed more cases than they have reversed.

Tables 3-7 and 3-8 divide the cases the Court has chosen to decide into broad issue areas and specify the proportion that were decided in a liberal direction. Although these data indicate increases in the conservative proportion across the issue areas since the heyday of the Warren Court, marked variation in the conservative proportion exists from one issue to the next. These results may reflect the changes in the Court's membership and the attitudes of the more recently appointed justices—to name just two possibilities.

Finally, Tables 3-9 through 3-12 provide, among other information, data on the (ideological) medians of the Court. The first three tables in this group are based on actual voting patterns in the areas of civil liberties, criminal procedure, and economics, respectively. Tables 3-11 and 3-12 contain the medians, as calculated from various measures and models scholars have developed.

Table 3-1   Unanimous Decisions, 1900–2001 Terms

Term	Number of unanimous decisions	Total number of cases[a]	Proportion of cases that were unanimous
1900	151	197	.766
1910	150	168	.893
1920	178	217	.820
1930	148	166	.892
1931	124	150	.827
1932	141	168	.839
1933	132	158	.835
1934	134	156	.859
1935	119	145	.821
1936	118	149	.792
1937	106	152	.697
1938	89	139	.640
1939	95	137	.693
1940	118	165	.715
1941	92	151	.609
1942	72	147	.490
1943	50	130	.385
1944	62	156	.397
1945	57	134	.425
1946	54	142	.380
1947	28	110	.255
1948	23	114	.202
1949	22	87	.253
1950	29	91	.319
1951	16	83	.193
1952	17	104	.163
1953	30	84	.357
1954	41	93	.441
1955	42	98	.429
1956	35	121	.289
1957	37	127	.291
1958	49	118	.415
1959	30	115	.261
1960	41	128	.320
1961	37	101	.366
1962	48	125	.384
1963	57	130	.438
1964	44	106	.415
1965	42	102	.412
1966	37	112	.330
1967	47	122	.385
1968	41	111	.369
1969	39	107	.364

(Table continues)

Table 3-1   *(Continued)*

Term	Number of unanimous decisions	Total number of cases[a]	Proportion of cases that were unanimous
1970	44	125	.355
1971	56	147	.381
1972	43	153	.281
1973	47	148	.318
1974	53	139	.381
1975	61	151	.404
1976	49	143	.343
1977	46	135	.341
1978	51	134	.381
1979	39	141	.277
1980	46	128	.359
1981	54	148	.365
1982	62	155	.400
1983	71	155	.458
1984	63	142	.444
1985	51	153	.333
1986	48	153	.314
1987	64	144	.444
1988	59	140	.421
1989	44	131	.336
1990	44	114	.386
1991	44	110	.400
1992	53	111	.477
1993	34	86	.395
1994	37	85	.435
1995	34	76	.447
1996	42	83	.506
1997	47	92	.511
1998	32	78	.410
1999	30	75	.400
2000	35	79	.443
2001	29	77	.377

[a] For 1953–1994, the total number of cases includes those with signed opinions and orally argued per curiams; for earlier terms, includes signed opinions of the Court only.

Sources: Number of unanimous decisions, 1900, 1910, 1920, 1930, 1935–1944: C. Herman Pritchett, "The Divided Supreme Court," *Michigan Law Review* 44 (1945): 428; 1931–1934: Karl M. Zobell, "Dissenting Opinions," *Cornell Law Quarterly* 44 (1949): 205; 1945–1952: C. Herman Pritchett, *Civil Liberties and the Vinson Court* (Chicago: University of Chicago Press, 1954), 21; 1953–1994: U.S. Supreme Court Judicial Database, with orally argued citation as unit of analysis (analu = 0; dec_type = 1, 6, or 7). Total number of cases and proportions therefrom, 1900–1926: Albert P. Blaustein and Roy M. Mersky, *The First One Hundred Justices* (Hamden, Conn.: Shoe String Press, 1978), 137–140; 1927–1952: Gerhard Casper and Richard A. Posner, *The Workload of the Supreme Court* (Chicago: American Bar Foundation, 1976), 76; 1953–2001: U.S. Supreme Court Judicial Database, with analu = 0; dec_type = 1, 6, or 7.

Table 3-2 Dissenting Opinions, 1800–2001 Terms

Term[a]	Number of cases with dissenting opinions	Total number of cases[b]	Proportion of cases with at least one dissenting opinion[c]
1800	0	0	.000
1801	0	4	.000
1803	0	11	.000
1804	0	15	.000
1805	1	10	.100
1806	0	17	.000
1807	0	10	.000
1808	4	21	.190
1809	4	37	.108
1810	1	27	.037
1812	1	31	.032
1813	3	39	.077
1814	5	46	.109
1815	2	39	.051
1816	3	40	.075
1817	1	40	.025
1818	2	36	.056
1819	0	32	.000
1820	3	26	.115
1821	1	33	.030
1822	1	29	.034
1823	2	27	.074
1824	4	39	.103
1825	0	27	.000
1826	0	29	.000
1827	1	45	.022
1828	3	53	.057
1829	2	42	.048
1830	7	51	.137
1831	7	40	.175
1832	5	50	.100
1833	2	38	.053
1834	2	59	.034
1835	3	38	.079
1836	1	48	.021
1837	5	19	.263
1838	5	40	.125
1839	5	51	.098
1840	3	41	.073
1841	0	31	.000
1842	2	42	.048
1843	4	26	.154
1844	3	39	.077
1845	13	49	.265
1846	2	46	.043

(Table continues)

Table 3-2   *(Continued)*

Term[a]	Number of cases with dissenting opinions	Total number of cases[b]	Proportion of cases with at least one dissenting opinion[c]
1847	5	35	.143
1848	3	35	.086
1849	8	40	.200
1850	25	156	.160
1851	10	94	.106
1852	12	53	.226
1853	16	80	.200
1854	15	71	.211
1855	14	90	.156
1856	8	63	.127
1857	9	70	.129
1858	6	69	.087
1859	4	115	.035
1860	3	64	.047
1861	2	74	.027
1862	7	41	.171
1863	4	75	.053
1864	5	55	.091
1865	7	70	.100
1866	6	128	.047
1867	7	96	.073
1868	13	114	.114
1869	14	169	.083
1870	15	151	.099
1871	21	148	.142
1872	23	157	.146
1873	21	193	.109
1874	17	186	.091
1875	23	200	.115
1876	16	219	.073
1877	21	248	.085
1878	23	198	.116
1879	18	205	.088
1880	9	221	.041
1881	11	232	.047
1882	17	267	.064
1883	14	277	.051
1884	11	271	.041
1885	18	280	.064
1886	12	298	.040
1887	13	287	.045
1888	6	242	.025
1889	16	282	.057
1890	14	297	.047
1891	20	252	.115

Table 3-2   *(Continued)*

Term[a]	Number of cases with dissenting opinions	Total number of cases[b]	Proportion of cases with at least one dissenting opinion[c]
1892	22	231	.095
1893	23	280	.082
1894	23	225	.102
1895	25	257	.097
1896	12	228	.053
1897	16	184	.087
1898	14	173	.081
1899	15	214	.070
1900	22	197	.112
1901	12	179	.067
1902	18	213	.085
1903	20	208	.096
1904	17	194	.088
1905	22	168	.131
1906	12	205	.059
1907	15	176	.085
1908	14	181	.077
1909	9	175	.051
1910	13	168	.077
1911	9	230	.039
1912	10	271	.037
1913	5	285	.018
1914	16	257	.062
1915	5	235	.021
1916	16	207	.077
1917	13	208	.062
1918	14	213	.066
1919	23	168	.137
1920	16	217	.074
1921	24	171	.140
1922	15	223	.067
1923	12	212	.057
1924	10	232	.043
1925	12	210	.057
1926	24	199	.121
1927	32	175	.183
1928	14	129	.109
1929	14	134	.104
1930	13	166	.078
1931	16	150	.107
1932	17	168	.101
1933	18	158	.114
1934	11	156	.071
1935	20	145	.138
1936	17	149	.114

(Table continues)

Table 3-2 *(Continued)*

Term[a]	Number of cases with dissenting opinions	Total number of cases[b]	Proportion of cases with at least one dissenting opinion[c]
1937	26	152	.171
1938	35	139	.252
1939	20	137	.146
1940	27	165	.164
1941	44	151	.291
1942	63	147	.429
1943	68	130	.523
1944	79	156	.506
1945	67	134	.500
1946	80	142	.563
1947	70	110	.636
1948	86	114	.754
1949	56	87	.644
1950	56	91	.615
1951	69	83	.831
1952	90	104	.865
1953	47	84	.560
1954	43	93	.462
1955	49	98	.500
1956	82	121	.678
1957	84	127	.661
1958	63	118	.534
1959	83	115	.722
1960	84	128	.656
1961	60	101	.594
1962	71	125	.568
1963	70	130	.538
1964	58	106	.547
1965	57	102	.559
1966	75	112	.670
1967	74	122	.607
1968	69	111	.622
1969	64	107	.598
1970	81	125	.648
1971	92	147	.626
1972	107	153	.699
1973	101	148	.682
1974	81	139	.583
1975	91	151	.603
1976	94	143	.657
1977	89	135	.659
1978	83	134	.619
1979	105	141	.745
1980	83	128	.648
1981	94	148	.635

Table 3-2   *(Continued)*

Term[a]	Number of cases with dissenting opinions	Total number of cases[b]	Proportion of cases with at least one dissenting opinion[c]
1982	94	155	.606
1983	85	155	.548
1984	79	142	.556
1985	101	153	.660
1986	106	153	.693
1987	80	144	.556
1988	84	141	.596
1989	84	131	.641
1990	70	114	.614
1991	65	110	.591
1992	58	111	.526
1993	53	86	.616
1994	47	85	.553
1995	42	76	.553
1996	41	83	.494
1997	45	92	.489
1998	46	78	.590
1999	45	75	.600
2000	44	79	.557
2001	48	77	.623

[a] Court did not meet during 1802 or 1811.

[b] For 1953 to 2000, total number of cases includes those with signed opinions and orally argued per curiams; for earlier terms, includes signed opinions of the Court only.

[c] Due to ambiguity in the description of data prior to the 1953 term, we cannot determine whether data represent the number of dissenting opinions or the number of cases with dissenting opinions. Hence, the proportion may not be comparable across all terms.

Sources: Number of dissenting opinions, 1800–1952: Albert P. Blaustein and Roy M. Mersky, *The First One Hundred Justices* (Hamden, Conn.: Shoe String Press, 1978), 137–140; 1953–2000: U.S. Supreme Court Judicial Database, with orally argued citation as unit of analysis (analu = 0; dec_type = 1, 6, or 7). Total number of cases and proportions therefrom, 1800–1926: Blaustein and Mersky, *The First One Hundred Justices,* 137–140; 1927–1952: Gerhard Casper and Richard A. Posner, *The Workload of the Supreme Court* (Chicago: American Bar Foundation, 1976), 76; 1953–2000: U.S. Supreme Court Judicial Database, with analu = 0; dec_type = 1, 6, or 7.

Table 3-3   Concurring Opinions, 1800–2001 Terms

Term[a]	Number of cases with concurring opinions	Total number of cases[b]	Proportion of cases with at least one concurring opinion[c]
1800	0	0	.000
1801	0	4	.000
1803	0	11	.000
1804	1	15	.067
1805	1	10	.100
1806	0	17	.000
1807	0	10	.000
1808	2	21	.095
1809	0	37	.000
1810	1	27	.037
1812	1	31	.032
1813	3	39	.077
1814	0	46	.000
1815	2	39	.051
1816	1	40	.025
1817	0	40	.000
1818	0	36	.000
1819	0	32	.000
1820	0	26	.000
1821	0	33	.000
1822	0	29	.000
1823	0	27	.000
1824	1	39	.026
1825	1	27	.037
1826	0	29	.000
1827	1	45	.022
1828	1	53	.019
1829	1	42	.024
1830	1	51	.020
1831	2	40	.050
1832	1	50	.020
1833	0	38	.000
1834	0	59	.000
1835	1	38	.026
1836	0	48	.000
1837	2	19	.105
1838	3	40	.075
1839	2	51	.039
1840	4	41	.098
1841	0	31	.000
1842	6	42	.143
1843	0	26	.000
1844	1	39	.026
1845	0	49	.000
1846	2	46	.043

Table 3-3   *(Continued)*

Term[a]	Number of cases with concurring opinions	Total number of cases[b]	Proportion of cases with at least one concurring opinion[c]
1847	4	35	.114
1848	1	35	.029
1849	0	40	.000
1850	0	156	.000
1851	3	94	.032
1852	0	53	.000
1853	7	80	.087
1854	5	71	.070
1855	7	90	.078
1856	7	63	.111
1857	2	70	.029
1858	1	69	.014
1859	0	115	.000
1860	0	64	.000
1861	2	74	.027
1862	0	41	.000
1863	4	75	.053
1864	1	55	.018
1865	1	70	.014
1866	2	128	.016
1867	0	96	.000
1868	3	114	.026
1869	0	169	.000
1870	3	151	.020
1871	0	148	.000
1872	7	157	.045
1873	9	193	.047
1874	2	186	.011
1875	1	200	.005
1876	3	219	.014
1877	4	248	.016
1878	5	198	.025
1879	1	205	.005
1880	2	221	.009
1881	0	232	.000
1882	3	267	.011
1883	4	277	.014
1884	2	271	.007
1885	4	280	.014
1886	1	298	.003
1887	4	287	.014
1888	1	242	.004
1889	3	282	.011
1890	2	297	.007
1891	3	252	.012

(Table continues)

Table 3-3   *(Continued)*

Term[a]	Number of cases with concurring opinions	Total number of cases[b]	Proportion of cases with at least one concurring opinion[c]
1892	0	231	.000
1893	1	280	.004
1894	1	225	.004
1895	1	257	.004
1896	0	228	.000
1897	3	184	.016
1898	1	173	.006
1899	4	214	.019
1900	5	197	.025
1901	3	179	.017
1902	4	213	.019
1903	3	208	.014
1904	7	194	.036
1905	5	168	.030
1906	4	205	.020
1907	5	176	.028
1908	3	181	.017
1909	7	175	.040
1910	1	168	.006
1911	0	230	.000
1912	1	271	.004
1913	3	285	.011
1914	1	257	.004
1915	1	235	.004
1916	1	207	.005
1917	1	208	.005
1918	0	213	.000
1919	3	168	.018
1920	7	217	.032
1921	1	171	.006
1922	1	223	.004
1923	3	212	.014
1924	0	232	.000
1925	0	210	.000
1926	8	199	.040
1927	2	175	.011
1928	2	129	.016
1929	2	134	.015
1930	2	166	.012
1931	1	150	.007
1932	1	168	.006
1933	4	158	.025
1934	7	156	.045
1935	4	145	.028
1936	2	149	.013

Table 3-3   *(Continued)*

Term[a]	Number of cases with concurring opinions	Total number of cases[b]	Proportion of cases with at least one concurring opinion[c]
1937	11	152	.072
1938	11	139	.079
1939	5	137	.036
1940	5	165	.030
1941	17	151	.113
1942	24	147	.163
1943	16	130	.123
1944	31	156	.199
1945	36	134	.269
1946	31	142	.218
1947	31	110	.282
1948	32	114	.281
1949	10	87	.115
1950	22	91	.242
1951	17	83	.205
1952	24	104	.231
1953	14	84	.167
1954	15	93	.161
1955	17	98	.173
1956	21	121	.174
1957	24	127	.189
1958	29	118	.246
1959	32	115	.278
1960	34	128	.266
1961	33	101	.327
1962	36	125	.288
1963	39	130	.300
1964	40	106	.377
1965	32	102	.314
1966	32	112	.286
1967	59	122	.484
1968	52	111	.468
1969	44	107	.411
1970	62	125	.496
1971	56	147	.381
1972	49	153	.320
1973	51	148	.345
1974	43	139	.309
1975	70	151	.464
1976	67	143	.469
1977	56	135	.415
1978	63	134	.470
1979	58	141	.411
1980	66	128	.516
1981	70	148	.473

(Table continues)

Table 3-3   *(Continued)*

Term[a]	Number of cases with concurring opinions	Total number of cases[b]	Proportion of cases with at least one concurring opinion[c]
1982	58	155	.374
1983	55	155	.355
1984	53	142	.373
1985	64	153	.418
1986	61	153	.399
1987	53	144	.368
1988	68	140	.486
1989	58	131	.443
1990	40	114	.351
1991	47	109	.431
1992	49	112	.438
1993	47	87	.540
1994	37	84	.440
1995	27	76	.355
1996	27	83	.325
1997	35	92	.380
1998	33	78	.423
1999	34	75	.453
2000	28	79	.354
2001	29	77	.377

[a] Court did not meet during 1802 or 1811.
[b] For 1953 to 1994, total number of cases includes those with signed opinions and orally argued per curiams; for earlier terms, includes signed opinions of the Court only.
[c] Due to ambiguity in the description of data prior to the 1953 term, we cannot determine whether data represent the number of concurring opinions or the number of cases with concurring opinions. Hence, the proportion may not be comparable across all terms.

Sources: Number of concurring opinions, 1800–1952: Albert P. Blaustein and Roy M. Mersky, *The First One Hundred Justices* (Hamden, Conn.: Shoe String Press, 1978), 137–140; 1953–2000: U.S. Supreme Court Judicial Database, with orally argued citation as unit of analysis (analu = 0; dec_type = 1, 6, or 7). Total number of cases and proportions therefrom, 1800–1926: Blaustein and Mersky, *The First One Hundred Justices,* 137–140; 1927–1952: Gerhard Casper and Richard A. Posner, *The Workload of the Supreme Court* (Chicago: American Bar Foundation, 1976), 76; 1953–2000: U.S. Supreme Court Judicial Database, with analu = 0; dec_type = 1, 6, or 7.

Table 3-4   Cases Decided by a 5–4 or 4–3 Vote, 1800–2001 Terms

Term[a]	Number of cases decided by a one-vote margin[b]	Total number of cases[c]	Proportion of cases decided by a one-vote margin[b, d]
1800	0	0	.000
1801	0	4	.000
1803	0	11	.000
1804	0	15	.000
1805	0	10	.000
1806	0	17	.000
1807	1	10	.100
1808	2	21	.095
1809	0	37	.000
1810	3	27	.111
1812	0	31	.000
1813	0	39	.000
1814	1	46	.022
1815	0	39	.000
1816	0	40	.000
1817	0	40	.000
1818	1	36	.028
1819	0	32	.000
1820	0	26	.000
1821	1	33	.030
1822	1	29	.034
1823	0	27	.000
1824	0	39	.000
1825	0	27	.000
1826	1	29	.034
1827	1	45	.022
1828	1	53	.019
1829	0	42	.071
1830	0	51	.000
1831	3	40	.075
1832	0	50	.000
1833	0	38	.000
1834	0	59	.000
1835	0	38	.000
1836	0	48	.000
1837	1	19	.053
1838	3	40	.075
1839	0	51	.000
1840	1	41	.024
1841	0	31	.000
1842	1	42	.024
1843	0	26	.000
1844	0	39	.000
1845	0	49	.000
1846	0	46	.000
1847	0	35	.000

(Table continues)

Table 3-4   *(Continued)*

Term[a]	Number of cases decided by a one-vote margin[b]	Total number of cases[c]	Proportion of cases decided by a one-vote margin[b, d]
1848	0	35	.000
1849	2	40	.050
1850	7	156	.045
1851	0	94	.000
1852	1	53	.019
1853	3	80	.037
1854	1	71	.014
1855	1	90	.011
1856	0	63	.000
1857	2	70	.029
1858	0	69	.000
1859	0	115	.000
1860	0	64	.000
1861	0	74	.000
1862	1	41	.024
1863	0	75	.000
1864	2	55	.036
1865	1	70	.014
1866	3	128	.023
1867	0	96	.000
1868	0	114	.000
1869	1	169	.006
1870	0	151	.000
1871	1	148	.007
1872	6	157	.038
1873	3	193	.016
1874	3	186	.016
1875	2	200	.010
1876	3	219	.014
1877	2	248	.008
1878	1	198	.005
1879	0	205	.000
1880	0	221	.000
1881	0	232	.000
1882	3	267	.007
1883	0	277	.004
1884	3	271	.011
1885	7	280	.020
1886	2	298	.007
1887	2	287	.007
1888	0	242	.000
1889	0	282	.000
1890	1	297	.003
1891	2	252	.008
1892	1	231	.004
1893	2	280	.007

Table 3-4 *(Continued)*

Term[a]	Number of cases decided by a one-vote margin[b]	Total number of cases[c]	Proportion of cases decided by a one-vote margin[b, d]
1894	3	225	.013
1895	2	257	.008
1896	6	228	.026
1897	3	184	.016
1898	6	173	.035
1899	7	214	.033
1900	15	197	.076
1901	7	179	.039
1902	3	213	.014
1903	10	208	.048
1904	7	194	.036
1905	9	168	.054
1906	2	205	.010
1907	3	176	.017
1908	1	181	.006
1909	6	175	.034
1910	2	168	.012
1911	3	230	.013
1912	5	271	.018
1913	1	285	.004
1914	6	257	.023
1915	0	235	.000
1916	8	207	.039
1917	4	208	.019
1918	9	213	.042
1919	10	168	.060
1920	6	217	.028
1921	2	171	.012
1922	0	223	.000
1923	0	212	.000
1924	2	232	.009
1925	1	210	.005
1926	4	199	.020
1927	6	175	.034
1928	1	129	.008
1929	0	134	.000
1930	6	166	.036
1931	2	150	.013
1932	3	168	.018
1933	6	158	.038
1934	8	156	.051
1935	7	145	.048
1936	13	149	.087
1937	3	152	.020
1938	6	139	.043
1939	4	137	.029

(Table continues)

Table 3-4   *(Continued)*

Term[a]	Number of cases decided by a one-vote margin[b]	Total number of cases[c]	Proportion of cases decided by a one-vote margin[b, d]
1940	5	165	.030
1941	15	151	.099
1942	10	147	.068
1943	17	130	.131
1944	30	156	.192
1945	6	134	.045
1946	25	142	.176
1947	25	110	.227
1948	31	114	.272
1949	5	87	.057
1950	12	91	.132
1951	11	83	.133
1952	8	104	.077
1953	11	84	.131
1954	2	93	.022
1955	13	98	.133
1956	13	121	.107
1957	29	127	.228
1958	22	118	.186
1959	25	115	.217
1960	27	128	.211
1961	9	101	.089
1962	13	125	.104
1963	12	130	.092
1964	6	106	.057
1965	11	101	.109
1966	20	112	.179
1967	2	122	.016
1968	5	111	.045
1969	2	107	.019
1970	28	124	.226
1971	30	147	.204
1972	30	153	.196
1973	30	148	.203
1974	16	139	.115
1975	14	151	.093
1976	24	143	.168
1977	20	135	.148
1978	24	134	.179
1979	27	141	.191
1980	17	128	.133
1981	34	148	.230
1982	31	155	.200
1983	27	155	.174
1984	20	142	.141
1985	35	153	.229

Table 3-4 *(Continued)*

Term[a]	Number of cases decided by a one-vote margin[b]	Total number of cases[c]	Proportion of cases decided by a one-vote margin[b, d]
1986	42	153	.275
1987	16	144	.111
1988	33	141	.234
1989	37	131	.282
1990	22	114	.193
1991	14	110	.127
1992	19	111	.171
1993	13	86	.151
1994	16	85	.188
1995	12	76	.158
1996	17	83	.205
1997	15	92	.163
1998	15	78	.192
1999	19	75	.253
2000	24	79	.304
2001	20	77	.260

[a] Court did not meet during 1802 or 1811.

[b] Includes only cases decided by a 5–4 or 4–3 vote. We are aware that the outcome of 5–3 or 4–2 to reverse votes depends on a single vote, but we exclude them to keep the data consistent across all sources beginning with the 1800 term.

[c] For 1953–2000, the total number of cases includes those with signed opinions and orally argued per curiams; for earlier terms, includes signed opinions of the Court only.

[d] Due to ambiguity in the description of data prior to the 1953 term, we cannot determine whether data represent the number of concurring opinions or the number of cases with concurring opinions. Hence, the proportion may not be comparable across all terms.

Sources: Number of cases decided by a one-vote margin: 1800–1923: U.S. Senate, "Creation of the Federal Judiciary," Sen. Doc. No. 91, 75th Cong., 1st Sess., July 22, 1937 (Washington, D.C.: U.S. Government Printing Office, 1938), 260–272; 1923–1952: "Five-Four Decisions of the United States Supreme Court—Resurrection of the Extraordinary Majority," *Suffolk University Law Review* 7 (1973): 916; 1953–2000: U.S. Supreme Court Judicial Database, with citation as the unit of analysis (analu = 0; dec_type = 1, 6, or 7). Total number of cases and proportions therefrom, 1800–1926: Albert P. Blaustein and Roy M. Mersky, *The First One Hundred Justices* (Hamden, Conn.: Shoe String Press, 1978), 137–140; 1927–1952: Gerhard Casper and Richard A. Posner, *The Workload of the Supreme Court* (Chicago: American Bar Foundation, 1976), 76; 1953–2000: U.S. Supreme Court Judicial Database, with analu = 0; dec_type = 1, 6, or 7.

Table 3-5   Cases Decided by a Judgment of the Court,
1946–2001 Terms

Term	Number of cases decided by judgment	Total number of cases	Proportion of cases decided by a judgment
1946	3	190	.016
1947	7	143	.049
1948	8	149	.054
1949	3	108	.028
1950	6	113	.053
1951	1	97	.010
1952	3	124	.024
1953	5	89	.056
1954	1	86	.012
1955	1	104	.010
1956	4	112	.036
1957	1	125	.008
1958	2	116	.017
1959	2	109	.018
1960	9	123	.073
1961	4	102	.039
1962	0	129	.000
1963	2	123	.016
1964	1	103	.010
1965	3	121	.025
1966	4	132	.030
1967	1	158	.006
1968	2	114	.018
1969	3	105	.029
1970	16	120	.133
1971	7	139	.050
1972	6	158	.038
1973	3	160	.019
1974	0	141	.000
1975	10	159	.063
1976	7	157	.045
1977	8	153	.052
1978	6	152	.039
1979	12	140	.086
1980	6	144	.042
1981	4	169	.024
1982	8	179	.045
1983	1	171	.006
1984	2	157	.013
1985	5	160	.031
1986	6	163	.037
1987	3	152	.020
1988	10	156	.064
1989	5	142	.035
1990	3	119	.025
1991	3	118	.025

Table 3-5 *(Continued)*

1992	2	109	.018
1993	4	97	.041
1994	0	90	.000
1995	7	89	.079
1996	1	91	.011
1997	3	94	.032
1998	0	81	.000
1999	3	81	.037
2000	0	87	.000
2001	2	89	.022

Note: A judgment is a decision of the Court, the opinion in support of which is joined by less than a majority of the participating justices. Only those decisions that the Court clearly labels as a judgment are counted as such. If reference is made to a judgment and an opinion of the Court, it is counted as an opinion. Only signed opinion cases may produce a judgment of the Court. Count is by docket number. We include *Ker v. California,* 374 U.S. 23 (1963), wherein a majority agreed on the standard whereby state searches and seizures are to be evaluated, but only a plurality agreed on the application of that standard. We also include two of the three docket numbers of *County of Allegheny v. American Civil Liberties Union,* 492 U.S. 573 (1989) that were decided by a judgment of the Court. Total number of cases excludes original jurisdiction cases.

Source: U.S. Supreme Court Judicial Database, with analu = 0 or 1; dec_type = 1 or 7; jur ~ = 9.

Table 3-6 Disposition of Cases, 1946–2001 Terms

Term	Number of cases[a]	Percentage reversed[b]
1946	191	45.5
1947	147	56.5
1948	155	59.4
1949	121	52.9
1950	120	55.8
1951	107	36.4
1952	125	52.0
1953	111	47.7
1954	102	64.7
1955	118	53.4
1956	134	64.2
1957	151	56.3
1958	135	59.3
1959	127	59.8
1960	143	53.1
1961	122	68.9
1962	143	74.8
1963	142	76.1
1964	118	72.0
1965	126	72.2
1966	146	69.9
1967	170	67.6
1968	127	71.7
1969	123	65.0
1970	136	58.8
1971	159	61.6
1972	170	68.8
1973	168	67.3
1974	157	68.2
1975	172	66.9
1976	175	64.0
1977	158	69.0
1978	156	66.7
1979	150	60.7
1980	149	66.4
1981	176	65.3
1982	185	63.2
1983	175	72.6
1984	160	64.4
1985	167	58.1
1986	171	61.4
1987	157	50.3
1988	165	50.3
1989	144	55.6
1990	121	62.8
1991	121	64.5
1992	113	61.1

Table 3-6 *(Continued)*

Term	Number of cases[a]	Percentage reversed[b]
1993	99	44.4
1994	93	60.2
1995	89	58.4
1996	91	65.9
1997	94	53.2
1998	81	65.4
1999	81	58.0
2000	87	57.5
2001	89	70.8

[a] Includes all orally argued docket numbers excluding cases affirmed by an equally divided vote and cases arising under original jurisdiction.
[b] Any decision in which the petitioning party prevailed.

Source: U.S. Supreme Court Judicial Database, with analu = 0 or 1; dec_type = 1, 6, or 7; jur ~ = 9.

Table 3-7 Direction of Court Decisions, by Issue Area and Chief Justice, 1946–2000 Terms

Issue area	Vinson (1946–1952)		Warren (1953–1968)		Burger (1969–1985)		Rehnquist (1986–2001)	
	% liberal	N cases	% liberal	N cases	% liberal	N cases	% liberal	N cases
Civil liberties	45.6	355	67.9	781	43.7	1,418	43.3	891
Criminal procedure	40.3	144	59.0	351	34.1	516	35.4	393
Civil rights	56.3	80	76.4	225	52.0	494	51.2	246
First Amendment	27.8	54	69.7	155	48.6	208	51.6	112
Due process	62.0	71	86.5	37	44.5	128	43.2	74
Privacy	0.0	5	66.7	3	27.5	40	44.8	29
Attorneys	0.0	1	90.0	10	53.1	32	48.1	27
Unions	48.1	54	70.1	127	56.5	108	44.0	50
Economic activity	61.5	291	72.0	443	51.5	429	47.0	287
Judicial power	31.9	144	40.5	232	27.7	271	40.1	232
Federalism	46.2	39	68.3	82	64.0	86	54.5	99
Federal taxation	73.9	69	76.3	114	72.1	68	71.2	52

Note: The issue areas are defined as follows: Civil liberties: combines criminal procedure, civil rights, First Amendment, due process, privacy, and attorneys issue areas; Criminal procedure: the rights of persons accused of crime except for the due process rights of prisoners; Civil rights: non–First Amendment freedom cases that pertain to classifications based on race (including Native Americans), age, indigence, voting, residence, military or handicapped status, sex, or alienage; First Amendment: guarantees contained therein; Due process: noncriminal procedural guarantees, plus court jurisdiction over nonresident litigants and the takings clause of the Fifth Amendment; Privacy: abortion, contraception, the Freedom of Information Act and related federal statutes; Attorneys: attorneys' fees, commercial speech, admission to and removal from the bar, and disciplinary matters; Unions: labor union activity; Economic activity: commercial business activity, plus litigation involving injured persons or things, employee actions vis-à-vis employers, zoning regulations, and governmental regulation of corruption other than that involving campaign spending; Judicial power: the exercise of the judiciary's own power and authority; Federalism: conflicts between the federal and state governments, excluding those between state and federal courts, and those involving the priority of federal fiscal claims; Federal taxation: the Internal Revenue Code and related statutes.

The term *liberal* represents the voting direction of the justices across the various issue areas. It is most appropriate in the areas of civil liberties, criminal procedure, civil rights, First Amendment, due process, privacy, and attorneys where it signifies pro-defendant votes in criminal procedure cases, pro-women or -minorities in civil rights cases, pro-individual against the government in First Amendment, due process, and privacy cases, and pro-attorney in attorneys' fees and bar membership cases. In takings clause cases, however, a pro-government/anti-owner vote is considered liberal. The use of the term is perhaps less appropriate in union cases, where it represents pro-union votes against individuals and the government, and in economic cases, where it represents pro-government votes against challenges to federal regulatory authority and pro-competition, anti-business, pro-liability, pro-injured person, and pro-bankruptcy votes. In federalism and federal taxation, liberal indicates pro-national government positions; in judicial power cases, the term represents pro-judiciary positions.

Source: U.S. Supreme Court Judicial Database, with orally argued citation as unit of analysis, with analu = 0; dec_type = 1, 6, or 7.

Table 3-8 Direction of Court Decisions (Percentage Liberal), by Issue Area, 1946–2001 Terms

Term	CL	Crim	Civ	1st A	DP	Priv	Atty	Un'n	Econ	JudP	Fed	FTax
1946	25.9 (39)	15.0 (20)	50.0 (6)	25.0 (8)	50.0 (4)	0.0 (1)	—	53.3 (15)	68.8 (48)	42.1 (19)	60.0 (5)	70.0 (10)
1947	67.1 (58)	60.9 (23)	72.2 (18)	60.0 (5)	66.7 (12)	—	—	25.0 (4)	62.1 (29)	43.8 (16)	100.0 (1)	100.0 (4)
1948	70.7 (39)	59.1 (22)	50.0 (8)	33.3 (3)	50.0 (6)	—	—	50.0 (8)	57.1 (42)	30.8 (13)	14.3 (7)	100.0 (10)
1949	45.2 (35)	22.2 (9)	60.0 (10)	0.0 (7)	50.0 (8)	—	0.0 (1)	100.0 (2)	58.3 (24)	18.8 (16)	71.4 (7)	55.6 (18)
1950	57.6 (32)	55.6 (9)	50.0 (12)	25.0 (8)	0.0 (2)	0.0 (1)	—	25.0 (4)	59.4 (32)	21.1 (19)	50.0 (2)	60.0 (5)
1951	39.5 (38)	47.1 (17)	50.0 (8)	16.7 (6)	33.3 (6)	0.0 (1)	—	0.0 (2)	55.2 (29)	25.0 (16)	—	66.7 (3)
1952	41.3 (40)	52.9 (15)	50.0 (10)	66.7 (6)	87.5 (8)	0.0 (1)	—	50.0 (8)	43.5 (23)	36.8 (19)	28.6 (7)	77.8 (9)
1953	50.0 (28)	40.0 (15)	62.5 (8)	50.0 (4)	100.0 (1)	—	—	66.7 (6)	45.5 (33)	37.5 (8)	66.7 (6)	100.0 (3)
1954	64.9 (37)	50.0 (18)	70.0 (10)	80.0 (5)	100.0 (3)	—	100.0 (1)	100.0 (4)	73.9 (23)	30.8 (13)	100.0 (4)	90.9 (11)
1955	60.0 (30)	41.7 (12)	63.6 (11)	80.0 (5)	100.0 (2)	—	—	80.0 (10)	83.3 (30)	57.1 (14)	66.7 (3)	57.1 (7)
1956	60.4 (48)	65.0 (20)	33.3 (12)	55.6 (9)	100.0 (4)	—	100.0 (3)	72.7 (11)	87.1 (31)	44.4 (18)	80.0 (5)	75.0 (8)
1957	58.7 (63)	40.6 (32)	71.4 (14)	77.8 (9)	100.0 (6)	0.0 (1)	100.0 (1)	50.0 (4)	72.4 (29)	31.3 (16)	50.0 (6)	55.6 (9)

(Table continues)

Table 3-8 (*Continued*)

Term	CL	Crim	Civ	1st A	DP	Priv	Atty	Un'n	Econ	JudP	Fed	FTax
1958	57.8 (43)	44.4 (27)	66.7 (6)	81.8 (11)	—	—	—	80.0 (5)	65.9 (44)	3.3 (12)	100.0 (5)	100.0 (6)
1959	51.4 (36)	46.7 (15)	70.0 (10)	42.9 (7)	33.3 (3)	—	—	64.3 (14)	81.5 (27)	44.4 (8)	42.9 (7)	57.1 (14)
1960	55.2 (67)	66.7 (30)	57.1 (14)	36.4 (22)	100.0 (1)	—	—	90.0 (11)	51.9 (27)	27.3 (11)	50.0 (2)	90.0 (10)
1961	77.5 (39)	70.6 (17)	88.9 (9)	87.5 (8)	60.0 (5)	100.0 (1)	—	88.9 (9)	63.0 (27)	50.0 (12)	80.0 (5)	85.7 (7)
1962	84.0 (50)	71.4 (21)	94.1 (17)	100.0 (8)	66.7 (3)	—	100.0 (1)	70.0 (10)	80.0 (35)	58.3 (12)	60.0 (10)	100.0 (8)
1963	82.8 (58)	68.2 (22)	92.6 (27)	88.9 (9)	—	—	—	66.7 (9)	76.7 (30)	31.3 (16)	77.8 (9)	50.0 (6)
1964	75.0 (44)	56.3 (16)	85.7 (14)	81.8 (11)	100.0 (2)	100.0 (1)	—	54.5 (11)	72.2 (18)	31.6 (19)	100.0 (3)	77.8 (9)
1965	71.7 (46)	56.3 (16)	85.7 (14)	69.2 (13)	100.0 (3)	—	—	33.3 (3)	80.0 (25)	46.7 (15)	0.0 (4)	62.5 (8)
1966	62.7 (59)	64.3 (28)	68.4 (19)	54.5 (11)	—	—	0.0 (1)	71.4 (7)	78.3 (23)	44.4 (18)	66.7 (3)	50.0 (2)
1967	77.9 (68)	77.1 (35)	81.3 (16)	69.2 (13)	100.0 (1)	—	100.0 (3)	44.4 (9)	72.0 (25)	54.5 (11)	100.0 (6)	100.0 (3)
1968	79.4 (63)	63.0 (27)	87.0 (23)	100.0 (10)	100.0 (3)	—	—	75.0 (4)	76.5 (17)	31.6 (19)	50.0 (4)	100.0 (4)
1969	56.9 (65)	44.4 (27)	69.2 (26)	60.0 (10)	0.0 (1)	—	100.0 (1)	33.3 (6)	70.0 (10)	21.4 (14)	25.0 (4)	85.7 (7)

Year												
1970	48.1 (79)	29.2 (24)	51.9 (27)	54.5 (22)	100.0 (4)	0.0 (1)	100.0 (1)	66.7 (9)	56.3 (16)	6.7 (15)	0.0 (1)	75.0 (4)
1971	52.2 (90)	41.2 (34)	64.3 (28)	43.8 (16)	63.6 (11)	100.0 (1)	—	28.6 (7)	53.1 (32)	27.3 (11)	100.0 (1)	50.0 (4)
1972	40.0 (95)	31.4 (35)	54.5 (33)	22.2 (18)	40.0 (5)	66.7 (3)	100.0 (1)	50.0 (6)	69.0 (29)	13.3 (15)	100.0 (3)	66.7 (3)
1973	43.8 (89)	33.3 (30)	47.2 (36)	64.3 (14)	33.3 (6)	0.0 (1)	50.0 (2)	37.5 (8)	52.4 (21)	42.1 (19)	50.0 (4)	83.3 (6)
1974	55.6 (72)	54.2 (24)	58.6 (29)	62.5 (8)	71.4 (7)	0.0 (3)	0.0 (1)	66.7 (6)	50.0 (28)	23.8 (21)	87.5 (8)	100.0 (4)
1975	37.5 (88)	18.2 (33)	53.6 (28)	53.8 (13)	23.1 (13)	100.0 (2)	—	40.0 (5)	42.9 (28)	25.0 (24)	100.0 (3)	100.0 (1)
1976	37.8 (90)	36.7 (30)	42.9 (35)	33.3 (12)	28.6 (7)	20.0 (5)	100.0 (1)	57.1 (7)	36.8 (19)	13.3 (15)	57.1 (7)	75.0 (4)
1977	50.7 (73)	58.6 (29)	38.5 (26)	62.5 (8)	60.0 (5)	0.0 (1)	50.0 (4)	60.0 (5)	66.7 (30)	21.4 (14)	40.0 (5)	57.1 (7)
1978	41.0 (83)	37.9 (29)	44.1 (34)	25.0 (8)	37.5 (8)	75.0 (4)	—	60.0 (5)	44.4 (27)	25.0 (12)	66.7 (3)	50.0 (4)
1979	49.4 (85)	37.5 (32)	59.1 (22)	70.0 (10)	54.5 (11)	0.0 (6)	100.0 (4)	33.3 (6)	54.8 (31)	46.2 (13)	100.0 (2)	—
1980	35.3 (68)	40.0 (25)	33.3 (27)	44.4 (9)	16.7 (6)	0.0 (1)	—	75.0 (8)	56.0 (25)	29.4 (17)	60.0 (5)	25.0 (4)
1981	46.9 (81)	26.3 (19)	55.9 (34)	75.0 (12)	33.3 (9)	0.0 (4)	66.7 (3)	88.9 (9)	53.8 (26)	30.4 (23)	100.0 (5)	66.7 (3)
1982	39.5 (81)	26.7 (30)	55.6 (27)	45.5 (11)	42.9 (7)	25.0 (4)	0.0 (2)	57.1 (7)	54.5 (33)	43.8 (16)	60.0 (10)	75.0 (4)
1983	35.8 (95)	20.0 (40)	58.6 (29)	33.3 (12)	40.0 (10)	0.0 (2)	50.0 (2)	66.7 (6)	35.7 (28)	23.1 (13)	57.1 (7)	75.0 (4)

(Table continues)

Table 3-8 (Continued)

Term	CL	Crim	Civ	1st A	DP	Priv	Atty	Un'n	Econ	JudP	Fed	FTax
1984	41.4 (87)	30.3 (33)	60.0 (25)	45.5 (11)	36.4 (11)	0.0 (1)	33.3 (6)	60.0 (5)	43.3 (30)	37.5 (8)	50.0 (8)	100.0 (4)
1985	37.1 (97)	26.2 (42)	41.4 (29)	42.9 (14)	71.4 (7)	100.0 (1)	25.0 (4)	66.7 (3)	37.5 (16)	38.1 (21)	60.0 (10)	80.0 (5)
1986	44.1 (93)	34.1 (41)	58.3 (24)	50.0 (12)	50.0 (12)	100.0 (1)	0.0 (3)	80.0 (5)	39.1 (23)	20.0 (15)	63.6 (11)	75.0 (4)
1987	49.4 (77)	45.2 (31)	47.6 (21)	50.0 (12)	66.7 (9)	0.0 (1)	66.7 (3)	14.3 (7)	61.5 (26)	40.0 (20)	66.7 (9)	66.7 (3)
1988	38.8 (85)	23.3 (30)	50.0 (26)	46.7 (15)	20.0 (5)	25.0 (4)	80.0 (5)	0.0 (5)	52.9 (17)	36.8 (19)	44.4 (9)	75.0 (4)
1989	35.7 (70)	25.7 (35)	55.6 (9)	35.7 (14)	50.0 (4)	33.3 (3)	75.0 (4)	75.0 (4)	50.0 (22)	55.6 (18)	55.6 (9)	85.7 (7)
1990	41.1 (56)	31.0 (29)	68.8 (16)	40.0 (5)	33.3 (3)	0.0 (1)	0.0 (2)	50.0 (8)	45.8 (24)	62.5 (16)	75.0 (4)	0.0 (2)
1991	49.1 (56)	42.9 (21)	55.6 (18)	75.0 (8)	33.3 (6)	50.0 (2)	0.0 (2)	0.0 (1)	48.1 (27)	50.0 (16)	60.0 (5)	75.0 (4)
1992	40.0 (54)	39.3 (28)	33.3 (15)	50.0 (8)	0.0 (1)	100.0 (1)	50.0 (2)	50.0 (2)	44.4 (18)	42.9 (21)	71.4 (7)	83.3 (6)
1993	44.7 (47)	39.1 (23)	33.3 (12)	50.0 (4)	33.3 (3)	100.0 (3)	100.0 (2)	0.0 (1)	50.0 (22)	11.1 (9)	20.0 (5)	100.0 (2)
1994	44.7 (40)	47.4 (19)	40.0 (10)	75.0 (8)	50.0 (2)	—	0.0 (1)	—	47.1 (17)	31.3 (16)	42.9 (7)	50.0 (2)
1995	44.4 (36)	38.9 (18)	50.0 (8)	80.0 (5)	40.0 (5)	—	—	75.0 (4)	25.0 (16)	54.5 (11)	75.0 (4)	75.0 (4)

Year	CL	Crim	Civ	1st A	DP	Priv	Atty	Un'n	Econ	Fed	JudP	FTax
1996	34.8 (46)	29.4 (17)	43.8 (16)	20.0 (5)	40.0 (5)	50.0 (4)	—	0.0 (1)	62.5 (16)	22.2 (9)	42.9 (7)	66.7 (3)
1997	39.6 (48)	32.0 (25)	64.7 (17)	0.0 (2)	0.0 (4)	—	—	0.0 (2)	53.3 (15)	35.0 (20)	100.0 (1)	33.3 (3)
1998	46.3 (41)	31.3 (16)	55.6 (18)	100.0 (2)	50.0 (4)	—	0.0 (1)	100.0 (4)	21.4 (14)	38.5 (13)	16.7 (6)	—
1999	49.0 (49)	38.5 (26)	54.5 (11)	42.9 (7)	100.0 (2)	100.0 (3)	—	0.0 (1)	40.0 (10)	50.0 (6)	66.7 (6)	100.0 (2)
2000	47.9 (48)	42.9 (21)	61.5 (13)	66.7 (6)	33.3 (6)	0.0 (1)	0.0 (1)	0.0 (2)	70.0 (10)	40.0 (10)	100.0 (3)	50.0 (4)
2001	39.5 (43)	33.3 (15)	33.3 (12)	55.6 (9)	66.7 (3)	0.0 (3)	100.0 (1)	66.7 (3)	30.0 (10)	38.5 (13)	33.3 (6)	100.0 (2)

Note: Figures listed are the percent liberal in each issue area. Figures in parentheses are the total number of cases falling into that area each term. "—" indicates no cases in issue area. Readers should take care in interpreting the percentages as some of the figures on which they are based are quite small.

The issue areas are defined as follows: Civil liberties (CL): combines criminal procedure, civil rights, First Amendment, due process, privacy, and attorney issue areas; Criminal procedure (Crim): the rights of persons accused of crimes except for the due process rights of prisoners; Civil rights (Civ): non–First Amendment freedom cases that pertain to classifications based on race (including Native American), age, indigence, voting, residence, military or handicapped status, sex, or alienage; First Amendment (1st A): guarantees contained therein; Due process (DP): noncriminal procedural guarantees, plus court jurisdiction over nonresident litigants and the takings clause of the Fifth Amendment; Privacy (Priv): abortion, contraception, the Freedom of Information Act and related federal statutes; Attorneys (Atty): attorneys' fees, commercial speech, admission to and removal from the bar, and disciplinary matters; Unions (Un'n): labor union activity; Economics (Econ): commercial business activity, plus litigation involving injured persons or things, employees actions vis-à-vis employers, zoning regulations, and governmental regulation of corruption other than that involving campaign spending; Judicial power (JudP): the exercise of the judiciary's own power and authority; Federalism (Fed): conflicts between the federal and state governments, excluding those between state and federal courts, and those involving the priority of federal fiscal claims; Federal taxation (FTax): the Internal Revenue Code and related statutes.

The term *liberal* represents the voting direction of the justices across the various issue areas. It is most appropriate in the areas of civil liberties, criminal procedure, civil rights, First Amendment, due process, privacy, and attorneys where it signifies pro-defendant votes in criminal procedure cases, pro-women or -minorities in civil rights cases, pro-individual against the government in First Amendment, due process, and privacy cases and pro-attorney in attorneys' fees and bar membership cases. In takings clause cases, however, a pro-government/anti-owner vote is considered liberal. The use of the term is perhaps less appropriate in union cases, where it represents pro-union votes against both individuals and the government, and in economic cases, where it represents pro-government votes against challenges to federal regulatory authority and pro-competition, anti-business, pro-liability, pro-injured person, and pro-bankruptcy votes. In federalism and federal taxation, liberal indicates pro-national government positions; in judicial federal power cases, the term represents pro-judiciary positions.

Source: U.S. Supreme Court Judicial Database, with analu = 0; dec_type = 1, 6, or 7.

Table 3-9   Means and Medians in Civil Liberties Cases, 1946–2001 Terms

Term	Mean[a]	Standard deviation	Median[b]	Median justice
1946	0.401	0.154	0.333	Frankfurter
1947	0.640	0.152	0.559	Frankfurter
1948	0.525	0.251	0.487	Frankfurter
1949	0.473	0.170	0.400	Jackson
1950	0.518	0.130	0.500	Clark
1951	0.503	0.204	0.395	Burton
1952	0.522	0.190	0.425	Burton
1953	0.523	0.190	0.444	Clark
1954	0.609	0.193	0.622	Clark
1955	0.575	0.235	0.517	Clark
1956	0.596	0.252	0.509	Reed/Frankfurter
1957	0.613	0.254	0.525	Frankfurter
1958	0.624	0.248	0.465	Whittaker
1959	0.583	0.261	0.417	Stewart
1960	0.593	0.256	0.530	Stewart
1961	0.709	0.196	0.667	Stewart
1962	0.708	0.215	0.843	Brennan
1963	0.758	0.205	0.860	Brennan
1964	0.700	0.142	0.705	Brennan
1965	0.676	0.172	0.717	Black
1966	0.617	0.213	0.569	Black
1967	0.688	0.150	0.739	Warren
1968	0.698	0.144	0.771	Fortas
1969	0.552	0.172	0.504	White/Black
1970	0.558	0.205	0.481	Stewart
1971	0.564	0.259	0.495	White
1972	0.527	0.285	0.389	Blackmun
1973	0.544	0.252	0.449	White
1974	0.584	0.201	0.529	Powell
1975	0.469	0.236	0.378	White
1976	0.423	0.234	0.351	White
1977	0.526	0.191	0.527	Stevens
1978	0.484	0.212	0.464	Blackmun
1979	0.507	0.233	0.459	Stewart
1980	0.459	0.187	0.441	White
1981	0.474	0.204	0.457	White
1982	0.468	0.245	0.366	White
1983	0.449	0.192	0.347	Powell
1984	0.459	0.200	0.407	Powell
1985	0.464	0.238	0.347	O'Connor
1986	0.513	0.298	0.375	Powell
1987	0.534	0.208	0.457	Kennedy
1988	0.503	0.256	0.333	O'Connor
1989	0.461	0.295	0.271	White
1990	0.495	0.250	0.397	O'Connor
1991	0.483	0.201	0.474	Kennedy
1992	0.484	0.187	0.411	White

Table 3-9   *(Continued)*

Term	Mean[a]	Standard deviation	Median[b]	Median justice
1993	0.459	0.182	0.447	Kennedy
1994	0.518	0.216	0.488	O'Connor
1995	0.503	0.182	0.550	Kennedy
1996	0.415	0.166	0.362	O'Connor
1997	0.428	0.194	0.333	Kennedy
1998	0.474	0.192	0.381	O'Connor
1999	0.526	0.247	0.385	O'Connor
2000	0.459	0.261	0.417	O'Connor
2001	0.387	0.218	0.418	O'Connor

Note: Civil Liberties includes criminal procedure, civil rights, first amendment, due process, privacy, and attorneys.

[a] The mean is the average percent liberal score for the justices who served during that term.
[b] The median is the median percent liberal score for the justices who served during that term.

Source: U.S. Supreme Court Judicial Database, with analu = 0 or 1; dec_type = 1, 6, or 7.

Table 3-10   Means and Medians in Criminal Cases, 1946–2001 Terms

Term	Mean[a]	Standard deviation	Median[b]	Median justice
1946	0.361	0.195	0.200	Burton
1947	0.597	0.187	0.583	Frankfurter
1948	0.561	0.270	0.636	Frankfurter
1949	0.430	0.314	0.222	Burton
1950	0.598	0.148	0.556	Burton
1951	0.545	0.228	0.471	Burton
1952	0.335	0.298	0.143	Vinson
1953	0.419	0.190	0.357	Jackson
1954	0.489	0.193	0.500	Harlan
1955	0.467	0.235	0.455	Clark
1956	0.669	0.252	0.742	Frankfurter/ Brennan
1957	0.557	0.254	0.469	Frankfurter
1958	0.570	0.248	0.385	Harlan
1959	0.507	0.261	0.375	Stewart
1960	0.628	0.256	0.586	Stewart
1961	0.678	0.196	0.600	Whittaker
1962	0.626	0.215	0.773	Brennan
1963	0.707	0.205	0.773	Brennan
1964	0.567	0.142	0.500	Brennan
1965	0.550	0.172	0.563	Brennan
1966	0.632	0.213	0.536	Black
1967	0.675	0.150	0.743	Warren
1968	0.576	0.144	0.615	Fortas
1969	0.469	0.172	0.472	White/Black
1970	0.440	0.205	0.417	Black
1971	0.450	0.259	0.412	White
1972	0.441	0.285	0.265	White
1973	0.445	0.252	0.267	Blackmun
1974	0.629	0.201	0.542	Powell
1975	0.319	0.236	0.182	Powell
1976	0.396	0.234	0.355	Powell
1977	0.602	0.191	0.607	Stevens
1978	0.496	0.212	0.448	White
1979	0.409	0.233	0.375	Blackmun
1980	0.474	0.187	0.440	Blackmun
1981	0.332	0.204	0.316	White
1982	0.361	0.245	0.233	White
1983	0.336	0.192	0.200	White
1984	0.381	0.200	0.240	Powell
1985	0.424	0.238	0.279	White
1986	0.476	0.298	0.268	Powell
1987	0.503	0.208	0.355	White
1988	0.416	0.256	0.300	Scalia
1989	0.438	0.295	0.229	White
1990	0.428	0.250	0.300	Scalia
1991	0.399	0.201	0.381	White

Table 3-10   *(Continued)*

Term	Mean[a]	Standard deviation	Median[b]	Median justice
1992	0.441	0.187	0.379	White
1993	0.401	0.182	0.435	Kennedy
1994	0.409	0.216	0.421	Breyer
1995	0.401	0.182	0.389	Kennedy
1996	0.346	0.166	0.294	Kennedy
1997	0.387	0.194	0.280	Scalia
1998	0.403	0.192	0.375	Scalia
1999	0.481	0.247	0.333	Kennedy
2000	0.473	0.238	0.421	O'Connor
2001	0.333	0.271	0.367	O'Connor

Note: Criminal cases involve the rights of persons accused of crime except for the due process rights of prisoners.

[a] The mean is the average percent liberal score for the justices who served during that term.

[b] The median is the median percent liberal score for the justices who served during that term.

Source: U.S. Supreme Court Judicial Database, with analu = 0 or 1; dec_type = 1, 6, or 7.

Table 3-11   Means and Medians in Economic Liberties Cases, 1946–2001
Terms

Term	Mean[a]	Standard deviation	Median[b]	Median justice
1946	0.630	0.126	0.597	Reed
1947	0.577	0.242	0.515	Reed
1948	0.584	0.192	0.510	Reed
1949	0.543	0.250	0.583	Minton
1950	0.572	0.106	0.559	Minton
1951	0.503	0.110	0.467	Jackson
1952	0.509	0.162	0.464	Clark
1953	0.523	0.190	0.513	Minton
1954	0.609	0.193	0.704	Minton
1955	0.575	0.235	0.725	Minton
1956	0.652	0.252	0.654	Whittaker/ Brennan
1957	0.613	0.254	0.656	Clark
1958	0.662	0.248	0.696	Clark
1959	0.583	0.261	0.690	Clark
1960	0.593	0.256	0.541	Clark
1961	0.688	0.196	0.697	Brennan/ Clark
1962	0.708	0.215	0.778	Douglas
1963	0.758	0.205	0.675	Brennan
1964	0.700	0.142	0.655	Brennan
1965	0.676	0.172	0.769	Black
1966	0.617	0.213	0.759	Warren
1967	0.688	0.150	0.667	Douglas
1968	0.698	0.144	0.714	Fortas
1969	0.552	0.172	0.613	Brennan/ White
1970	0.558	0.205	0.500	Marshall
1971	0.564	0.259	0.474	Blackmun
1972	0.527	0.285	0.571	White
1973	0.544	0.252	0.464	Blackmun
1974	0.584	0.201	0.559	Marshall
1975	0.498	0.236	0.484	Powell
1976	0.423	0.234	0.429	Rehnquist
1977	0.526	0.191	0.633	Blackmun
1978	0.484	0.212	0.484	Stewart
1979	0.507	0.233	0.568	Blackmun
1980	0.459	0.187	0.531	Stewart
1981	0.474	0.204	0.545	Stevens
1982	0.468	0.245	0.500	Rehnquist
1983	0.449	0.192	0.438	Rehnquist
1984	0.459	0.200	0.472	Stevens
1985	0.464	0.238	0.474	Stevens
1986	0.513	0.298	0.519	Blackmun
1987	0.534	0.208	0.486	White
1988	0.503	0.256	0.455	White

Table 3-11   *(Continued)*

Term	Mean[a]	Standard deviation	Median[b]	Median justice
1989	0.461	0.295	0.462	Rehnquist
1990	0.495	0.250	0.469	Rehnquist
1991	0.483	0.201	0.500	Rehnquist
1992	0.484	0.187	0.524	Rehnquist
1993	0.459	0.182	0.652	Rehnquist
1994	0.518	0.216	0.467	Breyer
1995	0.503	0.182	0.350	Souter
1996	0.415	0.166	0.588	Souter
1997	0.428	0.194	0.526	Scalia
1998	0.474	0.192	0.444	Souter
1999	0.526	0.247	0.364	Scalia
2000	0.789	0.061	0.800	Rehnquist/ O'Connor/ Scalia, Kennedy/ Souter/ Thomas
2001	0.387	0.176	0.500	Rehnquist/ Kennedy/ Thomas

Note: Economic liberties cases involve commercial business activity, plus litigation involving injured persons or things, employee actions vis-à-vis employers, zoning regulations, and governmental regulation of corruption other than that involving campaign spending.

[a] The mean is the average percent liberal score for the justices who served during that term.

[b] The median is the median percent liberal score for the justices who served during that term.

Source: U.S. Supreme Court Judicial Database, with analu = 0 or 1; dec_type = 1, 6, or 7.

Table 3-12   Means and Medians of Segal-Cover Scores, 1946–2001 Terms

Term	Mean[a]	Standard deviation	Median[b]	Median justice
1946	0.561	0.434	0.500	Vinson
1947	0.561	0.434	0.500	Vinson
1948	0.561	0.434	0.500	Vinson
1949	0.388	0.390	0.450	Reed
1950	0.388	0.390	0.450	Reed
1951	0.388	0.390	0.450	Reed
1952	0.388	0.390	0.450	Reed
1953	0.388	0.390	0.450	Reed
1954	0.360	0.353	0.450	Reed
1955	0.360	0.353	0.450	Reed
1956	0.380	0.406	0.455	Warren/ Douglas
1957	0.372	0.427	0.460	Douglas
1958	0.477	0.316	0.500	Warren
1959	0.477	0.316	0.500	Warren
1960	0.477	0.316	0.500	Warren
1961	0.477	0.316	0.500	Warren
1962	0.551	0.259	0.500	Warren
1963	0.551	0.259	0.500	Warren
1964	0.551	0.259	0.500	Warren
1965	0.607	0.293	0.500	Warren
1966	0.607	0.293	0.500	Warren
1967	0.718	0.224	0.750	Black
1968	0.718	0.224	0.750	Black
1969	0.524	0.529	0.625	Black/White
1970	0.391	0.624	0.500	White
1971	0.049	0.746	0.460	Douglas
1972	0.049	0.746	0.460	Douglas
1973	0.049	0.746	0.460	Douglas
1974	0.049	0.746	0.460	Douglas
1975	−0.058	0.748	−0.500	Stevens
1976	−0.058	0.748	−0.500	Stevens
1977	−0.058	0.748	−0.500	Stevens
1978	−0.058	0.748	−0.500	Stevens
1979	−0.058	0.748	−0.500	Stevens
1980	−0.058	0.748	−0.500	Stevens
1981	−0.132	0.722	−0.500	Stevens
1982	−0.132	0.722	−0.500	Stevens
1983	−0.132	0.722	−0.500	Stevens
1984	−0.132	0.722	−0.500	Stevens
1985	−0.132	0.722	−0.500	Stevens
1986	−0.158	0.748	−0.500	Stevens
1987	−0.113	0.727	−0.270	Kennedy
1988	−0.113	0.727	−0.270	Kennedy
1989	−0.113	0.727	−0.270	Kennedy
1990	−0.262	0.612	−0.340	Souter
1991	−0.449	0.427	−0.500	Stevens

Table 3-12   *(Continued)*

Term	Mean[a]	Standard deviation	Median[b]	Median justice
1992	−0.449	0.427	−0.500	Stevens
1993	−0.464	0.394	−0.500	Stevens
1994	−0.396	0.406	−0.340	Souter
1995	−0.396	0.406	−0.340	Souter
1996	−0.396	0.406	−0.340	Souter
1997	−0.396	0.406	−0.340	Souter
1998	−0.396	0.406	−0.340	Souter
1999	−0.396	0.406	−0.340	Souter
2000	−0.396	0.406	−0.340	Souter
2001	−0.396	0.406	−0.340	Souter

Note: The Segal-Cover scores are from 1.00 (most liberal) to −1.00 (most conservative); they were derived from content analyses of newspaper editorials prior to confirmation.

[a] The mean is the average Segal-Cover score for the justices who served during that term.

[b] The median is the median Segal-Cover score for the justices who served during that term.

Sources: Jeffrey A. Segal and Albert D. Cover, "Ideological Values and the Votes of U.S. Supreme Court Justices," *American Political Science Review* 83 (1989): 560; Jeffrey A. Segal, Lee Epstein, Charles M. Cameron, and Harold J. Spaeth, "Ideological Values and the Votes of U.S. Supreme Court Justices Revisited," *Journal of Politics* 57 (1995): 816.

Table 3-13 Martin and Quinn's Estimated Locations of the Most
Liberal, Median, and Most Conservative Ideal Points,
1937–2000 Terms

Term	Minimum	Median	Maximum	Justice	Probability
1937	−2.911	−0.459	3.118	Hughes	0.409
1938	−3.230	−0.633	3.141	Stone	0.400
1939	−3.335	−0.977	2.989	Reed	0.526
1940	−3.375	−0.568	2.661	Reed	0.517
1941	−3.274	−0.130	1.897	Byrnes	0.416
1942	−3.000	0.092	2.165	Reed	0.479
1943	−2.668	−0.029	2.542	Reed	0.619
1944	−2.503	−0.211	2.900	Reed	0.981
1945	−2.149	−0.020	0.857	Reed	0.929
1946	−2.012	0.217	1.153	Reed	0.739
1947	−1.976	0.481	1.222	Reed	0.504
1948	−1.999	0.561	1.349	Frankfurter	0.529
1949	−1.776	0.885	1.403	Burton	0.239
1950	−1.703	0.915	1.484	Burton	0.315
1951	−1.717	0.907	1.581	Burton	0.479
1952	−2.203	1.016	1.539	Clark	0.248
1953	−2.719	0.559	1.511	Clark	0.517
1954	−3.214	0.322	1.462	Frankfurter	0.585
1955	−3.540	0.509	1.185	Frankfurter	0.529
1956	−3.787	0.128	1.258	Clark	0.485
1957	−4.176	0.512	1.357	Clark	0.967
1958	−4.477	0.506	1.704	Clark	0.931
1959	−4.671	0.410	1.917	Clark	0.860
1960	−4.835	0.525	2.049	Stewart	0.857
1961	−4.976	0.156	2.307	White	0.470
1962	−5.094	−0.762	2.495	Goldberg	0.762
1963	−5.229	−0.791	2.522	Brennan	0.590
1964	−5.428	−0.524	2.344	Goldberg	0.568
1965	−5.596	−0.578	2.215	Black	0.788
1966	−5.738	−0.324	1.901	Black	0.938
1967	−5.875	−0.832	1.342	Marshall	0.532
1968	−5.997	−0.766	0.887	Marshall	0.336
1969	−6.087	0.180	1.993	Black	0.489
1970	−6.186	0.462	2.290	Harlan	0.366
1971	−6.265	0.779	3.581	White	0.990
1972	−6.288	1.024	3.953	White	0.814
1973	−6.338	0.655	4.205	White	0.586
1974	−6.399	0.611	4.276	White	0.721
1975	−2.498	0.556	4.368	Stewart	0.521
1976	−2.832	0.464	4.344	Stewart	0.510
1977	−3.011	0.207	4.305	Blackmun	0.425
1978	−3.182	0.126	4.316	Blackmun	0.755
1979	−3.382	0.154	4.335	White	0.809
1980	−3.542	0.084	4.190	White	0.831
1981	−3.666	0.012	4.047	White	0.916
1982	−3.843	0.461	3.958	White	0.997

Table 3-13   *(Continued)*

Term	Minimum	Median	Maximum	Justice	Probability
1983	−3.905	0.721	3.881	White	0.790
1984	−3.989	0.659	3.695	Powell	0.864
1985	−4.074	0.783	3.491	Powell	0.917
1986	−4.263	0.754	3.245	Powell	0.961
1987	−4.420	0.902	2.838	White	0.712
1988	−4.497	1.010	2.695	White	0.860
1989	−4.496	0.795	2.523	White	0.965
1990	−4.293	0.858	2.344	Souter	0.413
1991	−2.162	0.668	2.823	Souter	0.280
1992	−2.345	0.713	3.036	O'Connor	0.532
1993	−2.573	0.695	3.362	Kennedy	0.684
1994	−2.918	0.576	3.562	O'Connor	0.536
1995	−3.149	0.522	3.690	Kennedy	0.666
1996	−3.262	0.644	3.833	Kennedy	0.672
1997	−3.238	0.623	3.914	Kennedy	0.825
1998	−3.207	0.656	3.990	Kennedy	0.577
1999	−3.142	0.740	4.068	O'Connor	0.709
2000	−3.031	0.549	4.185	O'Connor	0.767

Note: The ideal points for each justice in each term are estimated using the dynamic ideal point model of Martin and Quinn (2002). The ideal points for each justice in each term are available at adm.wustl.edu/supct.html. This table contains the estimated location of the minimum (most liberal), median, and maximum (most conservative) ideal point. These quantities differ slightly from the estimated ideal point of the minimum, median, and maximum justice because we are accounting for the posterior uncertainty in the ideal points of all justices to estimate this quantity. The justice column contains the identity of the justice with the highest posterior probability of being the median justice. These probabilities are reported in the final column.

Source: Andrew D. Martin and Kevin M. Quinn, "Dynamic Ideal Point Estimation via Markov Chain Monte Carlo for the U.S. Supreme Court, 1953–1999," *Political Analysis* 10 (2002): 134–153.

4

The Justices: Backgrounds, Nominations, and Confirmations

From its inception through the 1995 term, 108 individuals have served on the United States Supreme Court. Their names and dates of service are listed in Table 4-1. These men and women have participated in crucial legal and political decisions that have shaped the powers of our government and determined our personal rights. Yet little is known about them. In this chapter we will shed some light on the individuals who have sat on the highest bench of the land.

We first take a look at what kinds of people have been tapped for Supreme Court service. Tables 4-2 through 4-11 present personal and background information on the justices. The data from these tables demonstrate that the justices have tended to be drawn from the ranks of the nation's political and social elites. Table 4-2 shows that the justices have largely come from economically secure families. With the exception of the Jacksonian era, members of elite families dominated the Court from its beginning until the aftermath of the Great Depression. Relatively few of the justices prior to the mid-twentieth century emerged from humble family origins. In the more recent period, however, individuals chosen for Court service have appeared from the middle and lower socioeconomic classes. Yet the tilt in favor of the upper classes remains. Most were reared in childhood environments that reflected the lifestyle of the economic elite. In the early periods, this frequently meant being raised on plantations or large farms. Later, it meant spending childhood years in comfortable surroundings in large metropolitan areas.

The justices have also tended to come from the ethnic and religious traditions of mainstream America. During the earlier periods of Court history, religious and ethnic factors were quite important in the appointment process, reflecting their significance in American politics generally. In the modern era, however, ethnic and religious distinctions have become less important. Tables 4-2 and 4-3 illustrate that most of the justices trace their family roots to northern European countries, most frequently the British

Isles. After the initial years, only three individuals were appointed to the Court who were born in foreign lands: David Brewer, born in Asia Minor to American missionaries; George Sutherland, born in England; and Felix Frankfurter, born in Austria. No person of African descent had ever been selected until Thurgood Marshall broke that barrier in 1967; no woman until Sandra Day O'Connor in 1981; no person of Italian background had been appointed before Antonin Scalia in 1986. A justice of Latin American or Asian origins has yet to be selected. In matters of religious preference, Episcopalians and Presbyterians have dominated the Court. This is not surprising given that these denominations historically have attracted the nation's social and economic elite. The first Catholic did not reach the High Court until Roger Taney was appointed in 1836, and it took more than a half century before a second member of that church (Edward White) was nominated. Louis Brandeis became the first Jewish justice in 1916, and only six others (Cardozo, Frankfurter, Goldberg, Fortas, Ginsburg, and Breyer) have followed. The Court remains overwhelmingly Protestant.

One of the reasons the elite have dominated the Court is that a sound education is a prerequisite for judicial service. Over a good portion of our history, education, especially education that included legal training, was available only to the upper classes, who could afford to send their children to the appropriate schools or tutors. Individuals from the lower socioeconomic groups rarely had the opportunity to obtain the proper training and experience to qualify for the Court. Table 4-4 summarizes the educational records of the justices. As a group, the justices represent the highest in educational attainment, most having attended highly prestigious educational institutions or studied under renowned private tutors. Similarly exceptional has been the justices' legal training. During the colonial period and the first century after independence, it was customary for legal aspirants to study law privately under the direction of established attorneys. Those who reached the Supreme Court frequently were privileged to have had some of the nation's most prestigious private practitioners as their mentors. Later, when law school became the customary route to acquiring a legal education, Supreme Court justices frequently had attended the elite Ivy League law schools.

As the future justices reached adulthood, most married and had families (Table 4-5). Only Benjamin Cardozo, John Clarke, James McReynolds, William Moody, Frank Murphy, and David Souter remained single. The early careers of the justices normally included a period of private practice, and sometimes a law professorship (Table 4-6). One-third served in the armed forces when the nation was drawn into war (Table 4-7). Almost all of the justices were involved in some form of political activity prior to their appointment. Table 4-8 shows that many were state or federal legislators, governors, or cabinet officials. One, William Howard Taft, had even been president. A majority of the justices also served as judges in the lower state or federal courts. A surprising one-third of the members, how-ever, had had absolutely no judicial experience before putting on the robe of a Supreme Court justice (Table 4-9; see Table 4-10 for a summary of background characteristics). Finally, Table 4-11 evidences the high eco-nomic status the justices maintain while serving on the Court.

The remaining tables deal with the nomination process. Table 4-12 lists all Supreme Court nominees, along with information on their ages, home states, and occupational positions when nominated. Table 4-13 supplies comparative data concerning justices whom nominees were set to replace. A number of factors influencing the president's selection of a nominee have remained important over the years. First, the president prefers to nominate an individual from the ranks of his own political party. This allows the chief executive to reward political supporters as well as to select individuals who have an acceptable political ideology. This partisan tradition was started by George Washington, who ap-pointed only Federalists to the High Court. When presidents select from outside their own political party, they tend to do so only when the nomi-nee has a similar ideological stance. Second, the president considers the qualifications of the nominee. These extend both to questions of personal character and of legal competence. No president wants to be remem-bered for having selected an unqualified justice, or wishes to nominate those whose qualifications may make confirmation difficult. Third, repre-sentational concerns often come into play. In the period prior to the Civil War, regional representation was a major factor in the nomination process. As time went on, regional considerations declined in importance to be replaced by ethnic and religious factors. Today, representation of racial minorities and women is a significant issue.

After nomination to a seat on the Court, a successful candidate must obtain Senate confirmation. As Table 4-14 illustrates, approximately 20 percent of all Supreme Court nominees have failed to be confirmed by the Senate. Although this means that most candidates are successful, Supreme Court nominations have a higher rejection rate than those of any other federal office. Most of the rejections have been clustered at cer-tain points in history. President John Tyler suffered the most rebuffs from the Senate. During his short tenure in office, Tyler submitted six Supreme Court nominations. Only one (Samuel Nelson) achieved favorable Senate action. The twentieth century has witnessed five rejections—John Parker in 1930, Abe Fortas in 1968, Clement Haynsworth in 1969, Harrold Car-swell in 1970, and Robert Bork in 1987. Often nominees' qualifications, ideological orientations, and interest group reactions affect these nomina-tion outcomes. Table 4-15 and 4-16 provide data on these factors. Finally, Table 4-17 describes some nomination anomalies, such as individuals who have been nominated for the Court more than once or those who have been nominated and confirmed, but never served.

Table 4-1 The Justices of the United States Supreme Court

Appointment number/justice[a]	Position	Appointing president	Years of service[b]
1. John Jay	Chief justice	Washington	1789–1795
2. John Rutledge[c]	Associate justice	Washington	1789–1791
3. William Cushing	Associate justice	Washington	1789–1810
4. James Wilson	Associate justice	Washington	1789–1798
5. John Blair, Jr.	Associate justice	Washington	1789–1796
6. James Iredell	Associate justice	Washington	1790–1799
7. Thomas Johnson	Associate justice	Washington	1791–1793
8. William Paterson	Associate justice	Washington	1793–1806
9. John Rutledge[d]	Chief justice	Washington	1795
10. Samuel Chase	Associate justice	Washington	1796–1811
11. Oliver Ellsworth	Chief justice	Washington	1796–1800
12. Bushrod Washington	Associate justice	J. Adams	1798–1829
13. Alfred Moore	Associate justice	J. Adams	1799–1804
14. John Marshall	Chief justice	J. Adams	1801–1835
15. William Johnson	Associate justice	Jefferson	1804–1834
16. Henry Brockholst Livingston	Associate justice	Jefferson	1806–1823
17. Thomas Todd	Associate justice	Jefferson	1807–1826
18. Gabriel Duvall	Associate justice	Madison	1811–1835
19. Joseph Story	Associate justice	Madison	1811–1845
20. Smith Thompson	Associate justice	Monroe	1823–1843
21. Robert Trimble	Associate justice	J. Q. Adams	1826–1828
22. John McLean	Associate justice	Jackson	1829–1861
23. Henry Baldwin	Associate justice	Jackson	1830–1844
24. James Moore Wayne	Associate justice	Jackson	1835–1867

Table 4-1   *(Continued)*

Appointment number/justice[a]	Position	Appointing president	Years of service[b]
25. Roger Brooke Taney	Chief justice	Jackson	1836–1864
26. Philip Pendleton Barbour	Associate justice	Jackson	1836–1841
27. John Catron	Associate justice	Jackson	1837–1865
28. John McKinley	Associate justice	Van Buren	1837–1852
29. Peter Vivian Daniel	Associate justice	Van Buren	1841–1860
30. Samuel Nelson	Associate justice	Tyler	1845–1872
31. Levi Woodbury	Associate justice	Polk	1846–1851
32. Robert Cooper Grier	Associate justice	Polk	1846–1870
33. Benjamin Robbins Curtis	Associate justice	Fillmore	1851–1857
34. John Archibald Campbell	Associate justice	Pierce	1853–1861
35. Nathan Clifford	Associate justice	Buchanan	1858–1881
36. Noah Haynes Swayne	Associate justice	Lincoln	1862–1881
37. Samuel Freeman Miller	Associate justice	Lincoln	1862–1890
38. David Davis	Associate justice	Lincoln	1862–1877
39. Stephen Johnson Field	Associate justice	Lincoln	1863–1897
40. Salmon Portland Chase	Chief justice	Lincoln	1864–1873
41. William Strong	Associate justice	Grant	1870–1880
42. Joseph P. Bradley	Associate justice	Grant	1870–1892
43. Ward Hunt	Associate justice	Grant	1872–1882
44. Morrison Remick Waite	Chief justice	Grant	1874–1888
45. John Marshall Harlan	Associate justice	Hayes	1877–1911
46. William Burnham Woods	Associate justice	Hayes	1880–1887
47. Stanley Matthews	Associate justice	Garfield	1881–1889
48. Horace Gray	Associate justice	Arthur	1881–1902

(Table continues)

Table 4-1   *(Continued)*

Appointment number/justice[a]	Position	Appointing president	Years of service[b]
49. Samuel Blatchford	Associate justice	Arthur	1882–1893
50. Lucius Quintus Cincinnatus Lamar	Associate justice	Cleveland	1888–1893
51. Melville Weston Fuller	Chief justice	Cleveland	1888–1910
52. David Josiah Brewer	Associate justice	Harrison	1889–1910
53. Henry Billings Brown	Associate justice	Harrison	1890–1906
54. George Shiras, Jr.	Associate justice	Harrison	1892–1903
55. Howell Edmunds Jackson	Associate justice	Harrison	1893–1895
56. Edward Douglass White[c]	Associate justice	Cleveland	1894–1910
57. Rufus Wheeler Peckham	Associate justice	Cleveland	1895–1909
58. Joseph McKenna	Associate justice	McKinley	1898–1925
59. Oliver Wendell Holmes, Jr.	Associate justice	T. Roosevelt	1902–1932
60. William Rufus Day	Associate justice	T. Roosevelt	1903–1922
61. William Henry Moody	Associate justice	T. Roosevelt	1906–1910
62. Horace Harmon Lurton	Associate justice	Taft	1909–1914
63. Charles Evans Hughes[c]	Associate justice	Taft	1910–1916
64. Edward Douglass White[d]	Chief justice	Taft	1910–1921
65. Willis Van Devanter	Associate justice	Taft	1910–1937
66. Joseph Rucker Lamar	Associate justice	Taft	1910–1916
67. Mahlon Pitney	Associate justice	Taft	1912–1922
68. James Clark McReynolds	Associate justice	Wilson	1914–1941
69. Louis Dembitz Brandeis	Associate justice	Wilson	1916–1939
70. John Hessin Clarke	Associate justice	Wilson	1916–1922
71. William Howard Taft	Chief justice	Harding	1921–1930
72. George Sutherland	Associate justice	Harding	1922–1938

Table 4-1   *(Continued)*

Appointment number/justice[a]	Position	Appointing president	Years of service[b]
73. Pierce Butler	Associate justice	Harding	1922–1939
74. Edward Terry Sanford	Associate justice	Harding	1923–1930
75. Harlan Fiske Stone[c]	Associate justice	Coolidge	1925–1941
76. Charles Evans Hughes[d]	Chief justice	Hoover	1930–1941
77. Owen Josephus Roberts	Associate justice	Hoover	1930–1945
78. Benjamin Nathan Cardozo	Associate justice	Hoover	1932–1938
79. Hugo Lafayette Black	Associate justice	F. Roosevelt	1937–1971
80. Stanley Forman Reed	Associate justice	F. Roosevelt	1938–1957
81. Felix Frankfurter	Associate justice	F. Roosevelt	1939–1962
82. William Orville Douglas	Associate justice	F. Roosevelt	1939–1975
83. Francis William (Frank) Murphy	Associate justice	F. Roosevelt	1940–1949
84. Harlan Fiske Stone[d]	Chief justice	F. Roosevelt	1941–1946
85. James Francis Byrnes	Associate justice	F. Roosevelt	1941–1942
86. Robert Houghwout Jackson	Associate justice	F. Roosevelt	1941–1954
87. Wiley Blount Rutledge	Associate justice	F. Roosevelt	1943–1949
88. Harold Hitz Burton	Associate justice	Truman	1945–1958
89. Fred Moore Vinson	Chief justice	Truman	1946–1953
90. Tom Campbell Clark	Associate justice	Truman	1949–1967
91. Sherman Minton	Associate justice	Truman	1949–1956
92. Earl Warren	Chief justice	Eisenhower	1953–1969
93. John Marshall Harlan	Associate justice	Eisenhower	1955–1971
94. William Joseph Brennan, Jr.	Associate justice	Eisenhower	1956–1990
95. Charles Evans Whittaker	Associate justice	Eisenhower	1957–1962

(Table continues)

Table 4-1 *(Continued)*

Appointment number/justice[a]	Position	Appointing president	Years of service[b]
96. Potter Stewart	Associate justice	Eisenhower	1958–1981
97. Byron Raymond White	Associate justice	Kennedy	1962–1993
98. Arthur Joseph Goldberg	Associate justice	Kennedy	1962–1965
99. Abe Fortas	Associate justice	Johnson	1965–1969
100. Thurgood Marshall	Associate justice	Johnson	1967–1991
101. Warren Earl Burger	Chief justice	Nixon	1969–1986
102. Harry Andrew Blackmun	Associate justice	Nixon	1970–1994
103. Lewis Franklin Powell, Jr.	Associate justice	Nixon	1971–1987
104. William Hubbs Rehnquist[c]	Associate justice	Nixon	1971–1986
105. John Paul Stevens	Associate justice	Ford	1975–
106. Sandra Day O'Connor	Associate justice	Reagan	1981–
107. William Hubbs Rehnquist[d]	Chief justice	Reagan	1986–
108. Antonin Scalia	Associate justice	Reagan	1986–
109. Anthony McLeod Kennedy	Associate justice	Reagan	1988–
110. David H. Souter	Associate justice	Bush	1990–
111. Clarence Thomas	Associate justice	Bush	1991–
112. Ruth Bader Ginsburg	Associate justice	Clinton	1993–
113. Stephen G. Breyer	Associate justice	Clinton	1994–

[a] Ordered according to date of appointment.
[b] Begin with date of Senate confirmation or date of recess appointment (whichever occurred first); end with date of service termination.
[c] Served subsequently as chief justice.
[d] Served previously as associate justice.

Source: Joan Biskupic and Elder Witt, *Congressional Quarterly's Guide to the U.S. Supreme Court,* 3d ed. (Washington, D.C.: Congressional Quarterly, 1997).

Table 4-2 Birth and Childhood Statistics for the Justices

Justice (appointment number)	Date of birth	Place of birth	Childhood locations[a]	Childhood surroundings[b]	Family status[c]	Judicial family[d]
Baldwin, Henry (23)	January 14, 1780	New Haven, Connecticut	Same	Family farm	Lower-middle	No
Barbour, Philip P. (26)	May 25, 1783	Orange County, Virginia	Same	Family farm	Upper	Yes
Black, Hugo L. (79)	February 27, 1886	Harlan, Alabama	Ashland, Alabama	Small town	Lower-middle	No
Blackmun, Harry A. (102)	November 12, 1908	Nashville, Illinois	Minneapolis, Minnesota	Urban	Middle	No
Blair, John, Jr. (5)	1732	Williamsburg, Virginia	Same	Family plantation	Upper	No
Blatchford, Samuel (49)	March 9, 1820	New York City, New York	Same	Urban	Upper	No
Bradley, Joseph P. (42)	March 14, 1813	Berne, New Hampshire	Same	Family farm	Lower-middle	No
Brandeis, Louis D. (69)	November 13, 1856	Louisville, Kentucky	Same	Urban	Upper	No
Brennan, William J., Jr. (94)	April 25, 1906	Newark, New Jersey	Same	Urban	Middle	No

(Table continues)

Table 4-2 (*Continued*)

Justice (appointment number)	Date of birth	Place of birth	Childhood locations[a]	Childhood surroundings[b]	Family status[c]	Judicial family[d]
Brewer, David J. (52)	June 20, 1837	Smyrna, Asia Minor (Turkey)	Wethersfield, Connecticut	Small town	Upper-middle	Yes
Breyer, Stephen G. (113)	August 15, 1938	San Francisco, California	Same	Urban	Upper-middle	No
Brown, Henry B. (53)	March 2, 1836	South Lee, Massachusetts	Same	Small town	Upper-middle	No
Burger, Warren E. (101)	September 17, 1907	St. Paul, Minnesota	Same	Urban	Lower-middle	No
Burton, Harold H. (88)	June 22, 1888	Jamaica Plain, Massachusetts	Same	Urban	Middle	No
Butler, Pierce (73)	March 17, 1866	Northfield, Minnesota	Pine Bend, Minnesota	Family farm	Lower-middle	No
Byrnes, James F. (85)	May 2, 1879	Charleston, South Carolina	Same	Urban	Lower	No
Campbell, John A. (34)	June 24, 1811	Washington, Georgia	Same	Small town	Middle	Yes
Cardozo, Benjamin (78)	May 24, 1870	New York City, New York	Same	Urban	Upper	Yes

Catron, John (27)	1786[e]	Pennsylvania[e]	Virginia and Kentucky	Rural	Lower	No
Chase, Salmon P. (40)	January 13, 1808	Cornish, New Hampshire	Keene, New Hampshire	Small town	Middle	No
Chase, Samuel (10)	April 17, 1741	Somerset County, Maryland	Baltimore, Maryland	Urban	Upper-middle	No
Clark, Tom C. (90)	September 23, 1899	Dallas, Texas	Same	Urban	Upper-middle	No
Clarke, John H. (70)	September 18, 1857	Lisbon, Ohio	Same	Small town	Upper-middle	Yes
Clifford, Nathan (35)	August 18, 1803	Rumney, New Hampshire	Western New Hampshire	Rural	Lower	No
Curtis, Benjamin R. (33)	November 4, 1809	Watertown, Massachusetts	Same	Small town	Middle	Yes
Cushing, William (3)	March 1, 1732	Scituate, Massachusetts	Same	Small town	Upper	Yes
Daniel, Peter V. (29)	April 24, 1784	Stafford County, Virginia	Same	Family plantation	Upper	No
Davis, David (38)	March 9, 1815	Cecil County, Maryland	Same	Rural	Middle	No
Day, William R. (60)	April 17, 1849	Ravenna, Ohio	Same	Small town	Upper	Yes

(Table continues)

Table 4-2 (Continued)

Justice (appointment number)	Date of birth	Place of birth	Childhood locations[a]	Childhood surroundings[b]	Family status[c]	Judicial family[d]
Douglas, William O. (82)	October 16, 1898	Maine, Minnesota	Yakima, Washington	Small town	Lower	No
Duvall, Gabriel (18)	December 6, 1752	Prince Georges County, Maryland	Buena Vista, Maryland	Family plantation	Upper	No
Ellsworth, Oliver (11)	April 29, 1745	Windsor, Connecticut	Same	Family farm	Upper	No
Field, Stephen J. (39)	November 4, 1816	Haddam, Connecticut	Stockbridge, Massachusetts	Small town	Upper middle	No
Fortas, Abe (99)	June 19, 1910	Memphis, Tennessee	Same	Urban	Lower-middle	No
Frankfurter, Felix (81)	November 15, 1882	Vienna, Austria	Vienna, Austria; New York City	Urban	Lower-middle	No
Fuller, Melville W. (51)	February 11, 1833	Augusta, Maine	Same	Small city	Upper	Yes
Ginsburg, Ruth Bader (112)	March 15, 1933	Brooklyn, New York	Same	Urban	Middle	No

Goldberg, Arthur J. (98)	August 8, 1908	Chicago, Illinois	Same	Urban	Lower	No
Gray, Horace (48)	March 24, 1828	Boston, Massachusetts	Same	Urban	Upper	Yes
Grier, Robert C. (32)	March 5, 1794	Cumberland County, Pennsylvania	Lycoming County, Pennsylvania	Rural	Middle	No
Harlan, John Marshall I (45)	June 1, 1833	Boyle County, Kentucky	Same	Rural	Upper	No
Harlan, John Marshall II (93)	May 20, 1899	Chicago, Illinois	Same	Urban	Upper	Yes
Holmes, Oliver W., Jr. (59)	March 8, 1841	Boston, Massachusetts	Same	Urban	Upper	Yes
Hughes, Charles Evans (63, 76)	April 11, 1862	Glens Falls, New York	Same	Small town	Middle	No
Hunt, Ward (43)	June 14, 1810	Utica, New York	Same	Small city	Upper-middle	No
Iredell, James (6)	October 5, 1751	Lewes, England	England	Urban	Upper	No
Jackson, Howell E. (55)	April 8, 1832	Paris, Tennessee	Jackson, Tennessee	Small town	Middle	No
Jackson, Robert H. (86)	February 13, 1892	Spring Creek, Pennsylvania	Frewsburg, New York	Small town	Middle	No

(Table continues)

Table 4-2 (*Continued*)

Justice (appointment number)	Date of birth	Place of birth	Childhood locations[a]	Childhood surroundings[b]	Family status[c]	Judicial family[d]
Jay, John (1)	December 12, 1745	New York, New York	Rye, New York	Family farm	Upper	No
Johnson, Thomas (7)	November 4, 1732	Calvert County, Maryland	Same	Family plantation	Upper	No
Johnson, William (15)	December 27, 1771	Charleston, South Carolina	Same	Urban	Upper-middle	No
Kennedy, Anthony (109)	July 23, 1936	Sacramento, California	Same	Urban	Upper-middle	No
Lamar, Joseph R. (66)	October 14, 1857	Elbert County, Georgia	Ruckersville, Georgia	Family plantation	Upper-middle	Yes
Lamar, Lucius Q.C. (50)	September 17, 1825	Eatonton, Georgia	Eatonton, Georgia	Family plantation	Upper	Yes
Livingston, Henry Brockholst (16)	November 25, 1757	New York, New York	New York City; Elizabethtown, New Jersey	Urban	Upper	Yes
Lurton, Horace (62)	February 26, 1844	Newport, Kentucky	Clarksville, Tennessee	Small town	Upper-middle	No
Marshall, John (14)	September 24, 1755	Germantown, Virginia	Same	Rural	Middle	No

Name	Birth date	Birthplace	Residence	Setting	Social class	
Marshall, Thurgood (100)	July 2, 1908	Baltimore, Maryland	Same	Urban	Lower-middle	No
Matthews, Stanley (47)	July 21, 1824	Cincinnati, Ohio	Same	Urban	Middle	No
McKenna, Joseph (58)	August 10, 1843	Philadelphia, Pennsylvania	Same	Urban	Lower-middle	No
McKinley, John (28)	May 1, 1780	Culpepper County, Virginia	Lincoln County, Kentucky	Rural	Upper-middle	No
McLean, John (22)	March 11, 1785	Morris County, New Jersey	Virginia, Kentucky, Ohio	Rural	Lower-middle	No
McReynolds, James C. (68)	February 3, 1862	Elkton, Kentucky	Same	Family farm	Upper-middle	No
Miller, Samuel (37)	April 5, 1816	Richmond, Kentucky	Madison County, Kentucky	Family farm	Lower-middle	No
Minton, Sherman (91)	October 20, 1890	Georgetown, Indiana	New Albany, Indiana	Family farm	Lower-middle	No
Moody, William H. (61)	December 23, 1853	Newbury, Massachusetts	Same	Family farm	Upper	Yes
Moore, Alfred (13)	May 21, 1755	Brunswick County, North Carolina	Same	Rural	Upper	Yes

(Table continues)

Table 4-2 (*Continued*)

Justice (appointment number)	Date of birth	Place of birth	Childhood locations[a]	Childhood surroundings[b]	Family status[c]	Judicial family[d]
Murphy, Frank (83)	April 13, 1890	Harbor Beach, Michigan	Same	Small town	Middle	No
Nelson, Samuel (30)	November 10, 1792	Hebron, New York	Washington County, New York	Family farm	Upper-middle	No
O'Connor, Sandra Day (106)	March 26, 1930	El Paso, Texas	Same	Urban	Upper	No
Paterson, William (8)	December 24, 1745	County Antrim, Ireland	Princeton, New Jersey	Small town	Upper	No
Peckham, Rufus W. (57)	November 8, 1838	Albany, New York	Same	Urban	Upper	Yes
Pitney, Mahlon (67)	February 5, 1858	Morristown, New Jersey	Same	Family farm	Upper	Yes
Powell, Lewis F., Jr. (103)	September 19, 1907	Suffolk, Virginia	Norfolk, Virginia	Urban	Upper	No
Reed, Stanley F. (80)	December 31, 1884	Minerva, Kentucky	Same	Small town	Upper-middle	No
Rehnquist, William (104, 107)	October 1, 1924	Milwaukee, Wisconsin	Same	Urban	Upper-middle	No

Roberts, Owen J. (77)	May 2, 1875	Germantown, Pennsylvania	Philadelphia, Pennsylvania	Urban	Middle	No
Rutledge, John (2, 9)	September, 1739	Charleston, South Carolina	Same	Urban	Upper	No
Rutledge, Wiley B. (87)	July 20, 1894	Cloverport, Kentucky	Same	Small town	Middle	No
Sanford, Edward T. (74)	July 23, 1865	Knoxville, Tennessee	Same	Small city	Upper	No
Scalia, Antonin (108)	March 11, 1936	Trenton, New Jersey	Queens, New York	Urban	Middle	No
Shiras, George, Jr. (54)	January 26, 1832	Pittsburgh, Pennsylvania	Western Pennsylvania	Family farm	Upper	Yes
Souter, David H. (110)	September 17, 1939	Melrose, Massachusetts	Weare, New Hampshire	Small town	Middle	No
Stevens, John Paul (105)	April 20, 1920	Chicago, Illinois	Same	Urban	Upper	No
Stewart, Potter (96)	January 23, 1915	Jackson, Michigan	Cincinnati, Ohio	Urban	Upper	Yes
Stone, Harlan Fiske (75, 84)	October 11, 1872	Chesterfield, New Hampshire	Same	Family farm	Middle	No
Story, Joseph (19)	September 18, 1779	Marblehead, Massachusetts	Same	Small town	Upper	Yes

(Table continues)

Table 4-2 (*Continued*)

Justice (appointment number)	Date of birth	Place of birth	Childhood locations[a]	Childhood surroundings[b]	Family status[c]	Judicial family[d]
Strong, William (41)	May 6, 1808	Somers, Connecticut	Same	Small town	Upper-middle	No
Sutherland, George (72)	March 25, 1862	Buckinghamshire, England	Provo, Utah	Small town	Lower-middle	No
Swayne, Noah H. (36)	December 7, 1804	Frederick County, Virginia	Same	Rural	Upper-middle	No
Taft, William H. (71)	September 15, 1857	Cincinnati, Ohio	Same	Urban	Upper	Yes
Taney, Roger B. (25)	March 17, 1777	Calvert County, Maryland	Same	Family plantation	Upper	No
Thomas, Clarence (111)	June 23, 1948	Savannah, Georgia	Pin Point, Georgia	Small town	Lower	No
Thompson, Smith (20)	January 17, 1768	Dutchess County, New York	Same	Rural	Upper-middle	No
Todd, Thomas (17)	January 23, 1765	King and Queen County, Virginia	Same	Rural	Lower-middle	No
Trimble, Robert (21)	November 17, 1776	Augusta County, Virginia	Jefferson County, Kentucky	Rural	Lower-middle	No

Name	Birth date	Birthplace		Setting	Class	
Van Devanter, Willis (65)	April 17, 1859	Marion, Indiana	Same	Small town	Upper-middle	No
Vinson, Fred M. (89)	January 22, 1890	Louisa, Kentucky	Same	Small town	Lower-middle	No
Waite, Morrison (44)	November 29, 1816	Lyme, Connecticut	Same	Small town	Upper	Yes
Warren, Earl (92)	March 19, 1891	Los Angeles, California	Bakersfield, California	Small town	Lower-middle	No
Washington, Bushrod (12)	June 5, 1762	Westmoreland County, Virginia	Same	Family plantation	Upper	No
Wayne, James M. (24)	1790	Savannah, Georgia	Same	Family plantation	Upper	No
White, Byron R. (97)	June 8, 1917	Fort Collins, Colorado	Wellington, Colorado	Small town	Middle	No
White, Edward D. (56, 64)	November 3, 1845	Lafourche Parish, Louisiana	Same	Family plantation	Upper	Yes
Whittaker, Charles E. (95)	February 22, 1901	Troy, Kansas	Same	Family farm	Lower-middle	No
Wilson, James (4)	September 14, 1742	Caskardy, Scotland	Scotland	Rural	Lower	No
Woodbury, Levi (31)	December 22, 1789	Francestown, New Hampshire	Same	Family farm	Upper-middle	No
Woods, William B. (46)	August 3, 1824	Newark,	Same	Small town	Upper-middle	No

(Table continues)

Table 4-2 (*Continued*)

[a] "Same" indicates that the location of the justice's childhood was the same as his or her place of birth.

[b] Refers to the general environment in which the justice spent his or her formative years. In several cases a justice's family moved one or more times during the justice's childhood. In such cases, the more prominent childhood experience is listed.

[c] Indicates general socioeconomic status of the justice's family during his or her childhood. The families of some of the justices, especially in the earlier years of the nation, experienced major upward or downward shifts in their economic status. In such cases the justices are categorized according to the status that best describes the largest segment of their childhood.

[d] Indicates whether the justice grew up in a family with a tradition of judicial service.

[e] Both the date and place of John Catron's birth are unclear. Some scholars estimate it to have been as early as 1778, and there is some evidence that it may have occurred in Virginia.

Sources: Joan Biskupic and Elder Witt, *Congressional Quarterly's Guide to the U.S. Supreme Court*, 3d ed. (Washington: Congressional Quarterly, 1997); Leon Friedman and Fred L. Israel, eds., *The Justices of the United States Supreme Court: Their Lives and Major Opinions* (New York: R.R. Bowker, 1969–1978); Harold W. Chase et al., *Biographical Dictionary of the American Judiciary* (Detroit: Gale Research, 1976); *Judges of the United States* 2d ed. (Washington: Judicial Conference of the United States, 1983); *The National Cyclopaedia of American Biography* (New York: James T. White, various years); *Dictionary of American Biography* (New York: Charles Scribner's Sons, various editions); John R. Schmidhauser, *Supreme Court Justices Biographical Data 1958* (Ann Arbor, Mich.: Inter-University Consortium for Political Research, 1972).

Table 4-3 Family Background of the Justices

Justice (appointment number)	Religion	Ethnic background	Father/ mother	Father's occupation	Political offices held by father
Baldwin, Henry (23)	Episcopalian	English	Michael Baldwin Theodora Wolcott	Small farmer; skilled craftsman	None
Barbour, Philip P. (26)	Episcopalian	Scotch	Thomas Barbour Mary P. Thomas	Plantation owner	Virginia legislator
Black, Hugo L. (79)	Baptist	Scotch/Irish	William L. Black Martha A. Toland	Storekeeper; farmer	None
Blackmun, Harry A. (102)	Methodist	English/German	Corwin Blackmun Theo Reuter	Businessman	None
Blair, John, Jr. (5)	Episcopalian[a]	Scotch/Irish	John Blair Mary Monro	Plantation owner	Virginia legislator; governor's council, acting governor
Blatchford, Samuel (49)	Episcopalian[a]	English	Richard Blatchford Julia Ann Mumford	Lawyer; banker	New York legislator
Bradley, Joseph P. (42)	Dutch Reform[b]	English	Philo Bradley Mercy Gardiner	Small farmer; teacher	None
Brandeis, Louis D. (69)	Jewish	German	Adolph Brandeis Fredericka Dembitz	Grain merchant	None
Brennan, William J., Jr. (94)	Roman Catholic	Irish	William J. Brennan Agnes McDermott	Labor organizer; brewery worker	New Jersey local official

(Table continues)

Table 4-3 *(Continued)*

Justice (appointment number)	Religion	Ethnic background	Father/ mother	Father's occupation	Political offices held by father
Brewer, David J. (52)	Congregational	English	Josiah Brewer Emilia Field	Congregational minister	None
Breyer, Stephen G. (113)	Jewish	German/ Romanian/ Prussian/Polish	Irving G. Breyer Anne Roberts	Lawyer	Attorney for public school district
Brown, Henry B. (53)	Congregational	English	Billings Brown Mary Tyler	Merchant; manufacturer	None
Burger, Warren E. (101)	Presbyterian	Swiss/German	Charles J. Burger Katharine Schnittger	Railroad cargo inspector; small farmer; salesman	None
Burton, Harold H. (88)	Unitarian	English/Swiss	Alfred E. Burton Gertrude Hitz	Professor	None
Butler, Pierce (73)	Roman Catholic	Irish	Patrick Butler Mary Gaffney	Small farmer	None
Byrnes, James F. (85)[c]	Episcopalian[d]	Irish	James Byrnes Elizabeth McSweeney	Municipal clerk	None
Campbell, John A. (34)	Episcopalian[a]	Scotch/Irish	Duncan Campbell Mary Williamson	Lawyer; teacher	Georgia legislator
Cardozo, Benjamin (78)	Jewish	Spanish	Albert Cardozo Rebecca Nathan	Lawyer	New York judge

Name (age)	Religion	Ethnicity	Parents	Father's occupation	Prior position
Catron, John (27)	Presbyterian	German	Peter Catron Unknown	Small farmer	None
Chase, Salmon P. (40)[e]	Episcopalian	English/Scotch	Ithamar Chase Janette Ralston	Tavern owner	New Hampshire local official
Chase, Samuel (10)	Episcopalian	English	Thomas Chase Martha Walker	Episcopal clergy	None
Clark, Tom C. (90)	Presbyterian	Scotch	William H. Clark Jennie Falls	Lawyer	Texas local official
Clarke, John H. (70)	Protestant	Scotch/Irish	John Clarke Melissa Hessin	Lawyer	Ohio judge
Clifford, Nathan (35)	Unitarian[f]	English	Nathaniel Clifford Lydia Simpson	Small farmer	None
Curtis, Benjamin R. (33)[g]	Episcopalian[h]	English	Benjamin Curtis Lois Robbins	Ship captain	None
Cushing, William (3)	Congregational[i]	English	John Cushing Mary Cotton	Lawyer	Massachusetts judge
Daniel, Peter V. (29)	Episcopalian	English	Travers Daniel Frances Moncure	Plantation owner	Virginia legislator
Davis, David (38)[j]	Presbyterian[a]	English/Welsh	David Davis Ann Mercer	Physician	None
Day, William R. (60)	Lutheran	English	Luther Day Emily Spalding	Lawyer	Ohio chief justice

(Table continues)

Table 4-3 (*Continued*)

Justice (appointment number)	Religion	Ethnic background	Father/ mother	Father's occupation	Political offices held by father
Douglas, William O. (82)[k]	Presbyterian	Scotch	William Douglas Julia F. Bickford	Presbyterian minister	None
Duvall, Gabriel (18)	Episcopalian	French	Benjamin Duvall Susanna Tyler	Plantation owner	Unknown
Ellsworth, Oliver (11)	Congregational	English	David Ellsworth Jemima Leavitt	Farm owner; captain, Connecticut militia	Connecticut local official
Field, Stephen J. (39)	Episcopalian	English	David Dudley Field Submit Dickinson	Congregational minister	None
Fortas, Abe (99)	Jewish	English	William Fortas Ray Berson	Cabinetmaker	None
Frankfurter, Felix (81)	Jewish[l]	Austrian	Leopold Frankfurter Emma Winter	Merchant	None
Fuller, Melville W. (51)[m]	Episcopalian	English	Frederick A. Fuller Catherine Weston	Lawyer	Maine local official
Ginsburg, Ruth Bader (112)	Jewish	German	Nathan Bader Celia Amster	Merchant	None
Goldberg, Arthur J. (98)	Jewish	Russian	Joseph Goldberg Rebecca Perlstein	Carter, peddler	None

Name	Religion	Nationality	Parents	Father's Occupation	Prior Office
Gray, Horace (48)	Unitarian	English	Horace Gray Harriet Upham	Businessman	None
Grier, Robert C. (32)	Presbyterian	Scotch	Issac Grier Elizabeth Cooper	Presbyterian minister; farmer; teacher	None
Harlan, John Marshall I (45)	Presbyterian	English	James Harlan Eliza S. Davenport	Lawyer	Kentucky attorney general, secretary of state; U.S. representative
Harlan, John Marshall II (93)	Presbyterian	English	John M. Harlan Elizabeth Flagg	Lawyer	Illinois local official
Holmes, Oliver W., Jr. (59)	Unitarian	English	Oliver W. Holmes Amelia Lee Jackson	Professor; poet; physician	None
Hughes, Charles E. (63, 76)	Baptist	English	David C. Hughes Mary C. Connelly	Baptist minister	None
Hunt, Ward (43)	Episcopalian	English	Montgomery Hunt Elizabeth Stringham	Banker	None
Iredell, James (6)	Episcopalian	English/Irish	Francis Iredell Margaret McCulloch	Merchant	None
Jackson, Howell E. (55)	Baptist	Scotch	Alexander Jackson Mary Hurt	Physician	None
Jackson, Robert H. (86)	Episcopalian	Scotch	William E. Jackson Angelina Houghwout	Farm owner; livery stable owner	None

(Table continues)

Table 4-3 *(Continued)*

Justice *(appointment number)*	Religion	Ethnic background	Father/ mother	Father's occupation	Political offices held by father
Jay, John (1)	Episcopalian[n]	French/Dutch	Peter Jay Mary Van Cortlandt	Merchant	None
Johnson, Thomas (7)	Episcopalian	English	Thomas Johnson Dorcas Sedgwick	Plantation owner	Maryland legislator
Johnson, William (15)	Presbyterian[a]	English/Dutch	William Johnson Sarah Nightingale	Blacksmith; landowner	South Carolina legislator
Kennedy, Anthony (109)	Roman Catholic	Irish	Anthony Kennedy Gladys McLeod	Lawyer; lobbyist	None
Lamar, Joseph R. (66)[o]	Disciples of Christ	French	James S. Lamar Mary Rucker	Lawyer; Disciples of Christ minister	None
Lamar, Lucius Q. C. (50)[p]	Methodist	French	Lucius Q. C. Lamar Sarah Bird	Plantation owner; lawyer	Georgia judge
Livingston, H. Brockholst (16)	Presbyterian	Scotch/Dutch	William Livingston Susanna French	Landowner	New Jersey governor
Lurton, Horace (62)	Episcopalian	English	Lycurgus Lurton Sarah Ann Harmon	Physician; Episcopal minister	None
Marshall, John (14)	Episcopalian	English/Welsh	Thomas Marshall Mary Randolph Keith	Farmer; surveyor; land speculator	Virginia revenue collector, legislator

Name	Religion	Ethnicity	Parents	Occupation	
Marshall, Thurgood (100)	Episcopalian	African	William Marshall / Norma Williams	Club steward	None
Matthews, Stanley (47)	Presbyterian	English	Thomas J. Matthews / Isabella Brown	Professor	None
McKenna, Joseph (58)q	Roman Catholic	Irish	John McKenna / May Ann Johnson	Baker	None
McKinley, John (28)	Protestant	Scotch	Andrew McKinley / Mary Logan	Physician	None
McLean, John (22)	Methodistr	Scotch/Irish	Fergus McLean / Sophia Blackford	Weaver; small farmer	None
McReynolds, James C. (68)	Disciples of Christ	Scotch/Irish	John McReynolds / Ellen Reeves	Physician; farmer	None
Miller, Samuel (37)	Unitarian	German	Frederick Miller / Patsy Freeman	Small farmer	None
Minton, Sherman (91)	Protestant	English	John E. Minton / Emma Lyvers	Small farmer	None
Moody, William H. (61)	Episcopalian	English	Henry Moody / Melissa Emerson	Businessman; farmer	None
Moore, Alfred (13)	Episcopalian	English/Irish	Maurice Moore / Anne Grange	Lawyer	North Carolina judge
Murphy, Frank (83)	Roman Catholic	Irish	John Murphy / Mary Brennan	Lawyer	None

(Table continues)

Table 4-3 (*Continued*)

Justice (appointment number)	Religion	Ethnic background	Father/ mother	Father's occupation	Political offices held by father
Nelson, Samuel (30)	Episcopalian	Scotch/Irish	John Rogers Nelson Jane McCarters	Farm owner	None
O'Connor, Sandra Day (106)	Episcopalian	English	Harry A. Day Ada Mae Wilkey	Rancher	None
Paterson, William (8)	Presbyterian	Scotch/Irish	Richard Paterson Mary	Manufacturer of tin plate; merchant; real estate investor	None
Peckham, Rufus W. (57)	Episcopalian	English	Rufus W. Peckham Isabella Lacey	Lawyer	New York judge, district attorney; U.S. representative
Pitney, Mahlon (67)	Presbyterian	English	Henry C. Pitney Sarah L. Halsted	Lawyer	New Jersey judge
Powell, Lewis F., Jr. (103)	Presbyterian	English/Welsh	Lewis F. Powell Mary Gwathmey	Businessman	None
Reed, Stanley F. (80)	Protestant	English	John A. Reed Frances Forman	Physician	None
Rehnquist, William (104, 107)	Lutheran	Scandinavian	William B. Rehnquist Margery Peck	Sales	None
Roberts, Owen J. (77)	Episcopalian	Welsh/Dutch/ Scotch/Irish	Josephus Roberts Emma Laferty	Businessman	Pennsylvania local official

Name	Religion	Ethnicity	Parents	Father's occupation	Prior office
Rutledge, John (2, 9)	Episcopalian	Scotch/English	John Rutledge Sarah Hext	Physician	None
Rutledge, Wiley B. (87)	Unitarian	English	Wiley Rutledge Mary Lou Wigginton	Baptist minister	None
Sanford, Edward T. (74)	Episcopalian	English/Swiss	Edward J. Sanford Emma Chavannes	Lumber and construction business	None
Scalia, Antonin (108)	Roman Catholic	Italian	Eugene Scalia Catherine Panaro	Professor	None
Shiras, George, Jr. (54)	Presbyterian[t]	Scotch	George Shiras Eliza Herron	Brewer; peach farmer	None
Souter, David H. (110)	Episcopalian	English	Joseph A. Souter Helen A. Hackett	Banker	None
Stevens, John Paul (105)	Protestant	English	Ernest J. Stevens Elizabeth Street	Businessman	None
Stewart, Potter (96)	Episcopalian	English	James G. Stewart Harriet L. Potter	Lawyer	Cincinnati mayor; Ohio supreme court
Stone, Harlan Fiske (75, 84)	Episcopalian	English	Frederick L. Stone Ann Sophia Butler	Farm owner	New Hampshire local official
Story, Joseph (19)	Unitarian[u]	English	Elisha Story Mehitable Pedrick	Physician	None

(Table continues)

Table 4-3 (*Continued*)

Justice (appointment number)	Religion	Ethnic background	Father/ mother	Father's occupation	Political offices held by father
Strong, William (41)	Presbyterian	English	William L. Strong Harriet Deming	Presbyterian minister	None
Sutherland, George (72)	Episcopalian	Scotch/English	Alexander Sutherland Frances Slater	Lawyer; postman; prospector	None
Swayne, Noah H. (36)[v]	Quaker	English	Joshua Swayne Rebecca Smith	Farm owner	None
Taft, William H. (71)	Unitarian	Scotch/English	Alphonso Taft Louisa M. Torrey	Lawyer	Ohio judge; U.S. secretary of war; U.S. attorney general
Taney, Roger B. (25)	Roman Catholic	English	Michael Taney Monica Brooke	Tobacco planter; plantation owner	Virginia legislator
Thomas, Clarence (111)[w]	Roman Catholic[x]	African	M. C. Thomas Leola Anderson	Farm worker	None
Thompson, Smith (20)	Presbyterian	English	Ezra Thompson Rachel Smith	Farm owner	New York local official
Todd, Thomas (17)[y]	Presbyterian[a]	English	Richard Todd Elizabeth Richards	Plantation owner	Local official
Trimble, Robert (21)	Presbyterian	Scotch	William Trimble Mary McMillan	Pioneer settler; farmer	Kentucky local official

Name	Religion	Ethnicity	Parents	Father's Occupation	Political Office
Van Devanter, Willis (65)	Episcopalian	Dutch	Isaac Van Devanter / Violetta Spencer	Lawyer	None
Vinson, Fred M. (89)	Methodist	English	James Vinson / Virginia Ferguson	County jailer	Kentucky local official
Waite, Morrison (44)	Episcopalian	English	Henry Matson Waite / Maria Selden	Lawyer; farmer	Connecticut chief justice
Warren, Earl (92)	Protestant	Scandinavian	Methias Warren / Chrystal Hernlund	Railroad car mechanic	None
Washington, Bushrod (12)	Episcopalian	English	John A. Washington / Hannah Bushrod	Plantation owner	Virginia legislator; county judge
Wayne, James M. (24)	Episcopalian	English	Richard Wayne / Elizabeth Clifford	Plantation owner	Georgia local official
White, Byron R. (97)	Episcopalian	English	Alpha A. White / Maude Burger	Lumber company manager	Mayor of Wellington, Colorado
White, Edward D. (56, 64)[z]	Roman Catholic	Irish	Edward White / Catherine Ringgold	Plantation owner; lawyer	Louisiana judge, governor; U.S. representative
Whittaker, Charles E. (95)	Methodist	English	Charles Whittaker / Ida Miller	Farm owner	None
Wilson, James (4)	Episcopalian	Scotch	William Wilson / Alison Lansdale	Small farmer	None

(Table continues)

Table 4-3 (*Continued*)

Justice (appointment number)	Religion	Ethnic background	Father/mother	Father's occupation	Political offices held by father
Woodbury, Levi (31)	Presbyterian[a]	English	Peter Woodbury Mary Woodbury	Merchant; farmer	New Hampshire legislator
Woods, William B. (46)	Protestant	Scotch/English	Ezekiel Woods Sarah J. Burnham	Farm owner; merchant	None

Note: During the historical period in which all but the most recent justices were reared, families tended to depend upon the father for financial support and mothers generally remained at home to administer the household and care for the children. Similarly, politics was a sphere of activity almost exclusively reserved for men. Consequently, listed here are the occupations of the fathers as an indicator of the economic and social status of the family. Also listed are the political offices held by the fathers as an indicator of the political atmosphere in the home. Specific notes (see below) indicate family situations in which these traditional roles were not in place.

a For a number of justices there is some confusion as to whether they belonged to the Presbyterian Church or the Episcopal Church. Both strains of Protestantism traditionally have attracted individuals from the upper socioeconomic groups. Here we list the affiliation most commonly cited in the literature, but some sources identify the justice with membership in the other church.

b Some sources claim that as an adult Bradley affiliated with either the Lutheran or Presbyterian churches.

c Byrnes's father died several weeks before he was born. His mother supported the family as a dressmaker.

d Byrnes converted from Roman Catholicism.

e Chase's father died when he was nine. He spent the rest of his childhood with an uncle in Ohio.

f Clifford converted from the Congregational Church.

g When Curtis was five years old his father died at sea while on a voyage to Chile. He was raised by his mother, who supported the family by running a boardinghouse and library.

h Curtis converted from Unitarianism.

i Some sources claim that Cushing became affiliated with the Unitarian faith.

j Davis's father died before his birth. He was raised by his mother, who remarried when Davis was five years old. Davis's stepfather was a bookseller and stationer.

k Douglas's father died when he was six. He was raised by his mother.

l Frankfurter's religious faith was largely agnostic.

m When Fuller was still an infant, his mother won divorce from his father on grounds of adultery. His mother moved in with her father and supported herself and two children as a piano teacher. When she remarried, the eleven-year-old Fuller decided to remain with his grandfather.

[n] Jay was raised in the French Huguenot religious tradition.

[o] When Lamar was eight his mother died. His father remarried two years later and moved the family to Augusta, Georgia.

[p] Lamar's father committed suicide when he was nine. He was raised by his mother with the help of other family members.

[q] McKenna's father died when he was fifteen. The eldest of six children, McKenna aided his mother in raising the family.

[r] McLean converted from Presbyterianism.

[s] Listed as Jean McArthur by some sources.

[t] Shiras became an agnostic in his advanced years.

[u] Some scholars claim Story to have been a member of the Congregational Church.

[v] Swayne's father died when he was four. He was raised by his mother.

[w] When Thomas was a young child his father deserted the family. His mother worked as a crab picker. Shortly thereafter he went to live with his grandparents who played a major role in his upbringing.

[x] Thomas was born into a Baptist family, but was raised by his grandparents as a Roman Catholic and studied for the Catholic priesthood. In his later adult years he regularly attended a charismatic Episcopal church. In 1996 Thomas returned to the Roman Catholic church.

[y] Todd's father died when he was an infant. His mother ran a boardinghouse and raised him until she died several years later. Todd was entrusted to guardians until he reached maturity.

[z] White was two when his father died. His mother remarried not long thereafter. White spent much of his childhood in boarding schools.

Sources: Joan Biskupic and Elder Witt, *Congressional Quarterly's Guide to the U.S. Supreme Court,* 3d ed. (Washington, D.C.: Congressional Quarterly, 1997); Leon Friedman and Fred L. Israel, eds., *The Justices of the United States Supreme Court: Their Lives and Major Opinions* (New York: R.R. Bowker, 1969–1978); Harold W. Chase et al., *Biographical Dictionary of the American Judiciary* (Detroit: Gale Research, 1976); *Judges of the United States,* 2d ed. (Washington, D.C.: Judicial Conference of the United States, 1983); John R. Schmidhauser, *Supreme Court Justices Biographical Data 1958* (Ann Arbor, Mich.: Inter-University Consortium for Political Research, 1972); *The National Cyclopaedia of American Biography* (New York: James T. White, various years); and *Dictionary of American Biography* (New York: Charles Scribner's Sons, various editions). Updated by the authors.

Table 4-4 Education and Legal Training of the Justices

Justice (appointment number)	Undergraduate education		Graduate education		Law school		Read the law[a]	
	School	Status/ dates	School	Status/ dates	School	Status/ dates	Mentor state	Dates studied
Baldwin, Henry (23)	Yale	Graduated 1797					Alexander Dallas (Pennsylvania)	1798
Barbour, Philip P. (26)	William and Mary	Attended 1801					Self-taught (Virginia)	1800
Black, Hugo L. (79)	Birmingham Medical	Attended 1903–04			Alabama	Graduated 1906		
Blackmun, Harry A. (102)	Harvard	B.A. 1929			Harvard	Graduated 1932		
Blair, John, Jr. (5)	William and Mary	Graduated 1754			Middle Temple (England)	Attended 1755–56		
Blatchford, Samuel (49)	Columbia	B.A. 1837					William H. Seward (New York)	1837–41
Bradley, Joseph P. (42)	Rutgers	Graduated 1836					Archer Gifford (New Jersey)	1836–39
Brandeis, Louis D. (69)	Annen Real Schule (Germany)	Attended 1873–75			Harvard	Graduated 1877		

Name	Undergraduate	Degree	Scholar	Law school	Status	Read law	Years
Brennan, William J., Jr. (94)	Pennsylvania	B.S. 1928		Harvard	Graduated 1931		
Brewer, David J. (52)	Wesleyan / Yale	Attended 1852–53 / B.A. 1856		Albany	Graduated 1858	David Dudley Field (New York)	1856–57
Breyer, Stephen G. (113)	Stanford	B.A. 1959	Oxford / Marshall scholar 1959–61	Harvard	Graduated 1964		
Brown, Henry B. (53)	Yale	B.A. 1856		Yale / Harvard	Attended 1858–59 / Attended 1859	Local attorneys (Michigan)	1859–60
Burger, Warren E. (101)	Minnesota	Attended 1925–27		St. Paul	Graduated 1931		
Burton, Harold H. (88)	Bowdoin	B.A. 1909		Harvard	Graduated 1912		
Butler, Pierce (73)	Carleton	B.A., B.S. 1887				J. W. Pinch and John Twohy (Minnesota)	1887–88
Byrnes, James F. (85)	None					Self-taught (South Carolina)	1896–1903
Campbell, John A. (34)	Georgia / West Point	Graduated 1825 / Attended 1825–28				Self-taught (Georgia)	1829

(Table continues)

Table 4-4 (Continued)

Justice (appointment number)	Undergraduate education		Graduate education		Law school		Read the law[a]	
	School	Status/dates	School	Status/dates	School	Status/dates	Mentor state	Dates studied
Cardozo, Benjamin (78)	Columbia	B.A. 1889	Columbia	M.A. 1890	Columbia	Attended 1890–91		
Catron, John (27)	None						Self-taught (Tennessee)	1813–14
Chase, Salmon P. (40)	Dartmouth	Graduated 1826					William Wirt (Washington, D.C.)	1827–30
Chase, Samuel (10)	None						John Hammond and John Hall (Maryland)	1759–61
Clark, Tom C. (90)	Virginia Military Texas	Attended 1917–18 B.A. 1921			Texas	Graduated 1922		
Clarke, John H. (70)	Western Reserve	B.A. 1877	Western Reserve	M.A. 1880			John Clarke (Ohio)	1877–78
Clifford, Nathan (35)	None						Josiah Quincy (New Hampshire)	1826–27

Name	College		College		Read law with (State)	Years
Curtis, Benjamin R. (33)	Harvard	Graduated 1829	Harvard	Graduated 1832		
Cushing, William (3)	Harvard	Graduated 1751			Jeremiah Gridley (Massachusetts)	1753–55
Daniel, Peter V. (29)	Princeton	Attended 1802–03			Edmund Randolph (Virginia)	1805–08
Davis, David (38)	Kenyon	Graduated 1832	Yale	Attended 1835	Henry W. Bishop (Massachusetts)	1833–34
Day, William R. (60)	Michigan	B.S. 1870	Michigan	Attended 1871–72	George Robinson (Ohio)	1871
Douglas, William O. (82)	Whitman	B.A. 1920	Columbia	Graduated 1925		
Duvall, Gabriel (18)	None				Local lawyers (Maryland)	1775–78
Ellsworth, Oliver (11)	Yale	Attended 1762–64	Princeton	Graduated 1766	Self-taught (Connecticut)	1767–71
Field, Stephen J. (39)	Williams	Graduated 1837			David Dudley Field and John Van Buren (New York)	1838–40

(Table continues)

Table 4-4 (*Continued*)

Justice (appointment number)	Undergraduate education		Graduate education		Law school		Read the law[a]	
	School	Status/dates	School	Status/dates	School	Status/dates	Mentor state	Dates studied
Fortas, Abe (99)	Southwestern	B.A. 1930			Yale	Graduated 1933		
Frankfurter, Felix (81)	College of the City of New York	B.A. 1902			Harvard	Graduated 1906		
Fuller, Melville W. (51)	Bowdoin	B.A. 1853			Harvard	Attended 1854-55	Family members (Maine)	1853-54
Ginsburg, Ruth Bader (112)	Cornell	B.A. 1954			Harvard / Columbia	Attended 1956-58 / Graduated 1959		
Goldberg, Arthur J. (98)	Crane Jr. College / DePaul / Northwestern	Attended 1924-26 / Attended 1924-26 / B.S.L. 1929			North-western	Graduated 1930		
Gray, Horace (48)	Harvard	B.A. 1845			Harvard	Graduated 1849	John Lowell (Massachusetts)	1849-51
Grier, Robert C. (32)	Dickinson	Graduated 1812					Self-taught (Pennsylvania)	1815-17

Name	College	Degree	Second School	Detail	Law School	Law Date	Read Law Under	Dates
Harlan, John Marshall I (45)	Centre	Graduated 1850			Transylvania	Attended 1851–53	James Harlan, Thomas Marshal, and George Robertson (Kentucky)	1853
Harlan, John Marshall II (93)	Princeton	B.A. 1920	Oxford	Rhodes Scholar 1920–23	New York	Graduated 1925		
Holmes, Oliver W., Jr. (59)	Harvard	B.A. 1861			Harvard	Graduated 1866		
Hughes, Charles E. (63, 76)	Colgate Brown	Attended 1876–78 B.A. 1881	Brown	M.A.	Columbia	Graduated 1884	William Gleason (New York)	1881–82
Hunt, Ward (43)	Union	Graduated 1828			Litchfield	Attended 1831	Hiram Denio (New York)	1829–31
Iredell, James (6)	None						Samuel Johnston (North Carolina)	1768–70
Jackson, Howell E. (55)	West Tennessee Virginia	B.A. 1849 Attended 1851–52			Cumberland	Graduated 1856	A. W. O. Totten and Milton Brown (Tennessee)	1851–54
Jackson, Robert H. (86)	None				Albany	Attended 1912		
Jay, John (1)	Columbia	Graduated 1764					Benjamin Kissam (New York)	1765–68

(Table continues)

Table 4-4 (*Continued*)

Justice (appointment number)	Undergraduate education		Graduate education		Law school		Read the law[a]	
	School	Status/dates	School	Status/dates	School	Status/dates	Mentor/state	Dates studied
Johnson, Thomas (7)	None						Stephen Bordley (Maryland)	1759–60
Johnson, William (15)	Princeton	Graduated 1790					Charles Pinckney (South Carolina)	1790–93
Kennedy, Anthony (109)	Stanford	B.A. 1958	London School of Economics	Attended 1957–58	Harvard	Graduated 1961		
Lamar, Joseph R. (66)	Georgia Bethany	Attended 1874–75 B.A. 1877			Washington and Lee	Attended 1877	Henry Clay Foster (Georgia)	1878
Lamar, Lucius Q. C. (50)	Emory	B.A. 1845					Absalom Chappell (Georgia)	1845–47
Livingston, H. Brockholst (16)	Princeton	Graduated 1774					Peter Yates (New York)	1782–83
Lurton, Horace (62)	Chicago	Attended 1859–60			Cumberland	Graduated 1867		
Marshall, John (14)	None				William and Mary	Attended 1780	Self-taught (Virginia)	1780

Name	College	Degree	Law school	Law degree	Read law under	Years
Marshall, Thurgood (100)	Lincoln	B.A. 1930	Howard	Graduated 1933		
Matthews, Stanley (47)	Kenyon	B.A. 1840			Self-taught (Ohio)	1840–42
McKenna, Joseph (58)	Benicia Institute	Graduated 1865	Columbia	Attended 1897	Self-taught (California)	1864–65
McKinley, John (28)	None				Self-taught (Kentucky)	1798–1800
McLean, John (22)	None				John Gano and Arthur St. Clair, Jr. (Ohio)	1804–06
McReynolds, James C. (68)	Vanderbilt	B.S. 1882	Virginia	Graduated 1884		
Miller, Samuel (37)	Transylvania	M.D. 1838			Self-taught (Kentucky)	1846–47
Minton, Sherman (91)	None		Indiana Yale	Graduated 1915 LL.M. 1917		
Moody, William H. (61)	Harvard	B.A. 1876	Harvard	Attended 1876–77	Richard H. Dana (Massachusetts)	1877–78
Moore, Alfred (13)	None				Maurice Moore (North Carolina)	1754–55

(Table continues)

Table 4-4 (*Continued*)

Justice (appointment number)	Undergraduate education		Graduate education		Law school		Read the law[a]	
	School	Status/dates	School	Status/dates	School	Status/dates	Mentor state	Dates studied
Murphy, Frank (83)	Michigan	B.A. 1912			Michigan	Graduated 1914		
					Lincoln's Inn (England)	Attended 1919		
					Trinity College (Ireland)	Attended 1919		
Nelson, Samuel (30)	Middlebury	Graduated 1813					Law offices of Savage and Woods (New York)	1814–17
O'Connor, Sandra Day (106)	Stanford	B.A. 1950			Stanford	Graduated 1952		
Paterson, William (8)	Princeton	Graduated 1763	Princeton	M.A. 1766			Richard Stockton (New Jersey)	1766–69
Peckham, Rufus W. (57)	None						Rufus Peckham (New York)	1857–59
Pitney, Mahlon (67)	Princeton	B.A. 1879	Princeton	M.A. 1882			Henry C. Pitney (New Jersey)	1879–82

Name	College	Degree	Graduate School	Graduate Degree	Law/Professional School	Law Study	Read Law Under
Powell, Lewis F., Jr. (103)	Washington and Lee	B.S. 1929			Washington and Lee	Graduated 1931	
					Harvard	LL.M 1932	
Reed, Stanley F. (80)	Kentucky Wesleyan	B.A. 1902			Virginia	Attended 1906–07	
	Yale	B.A. 1906			Columbia	Attended 1908–09	
					University of Paris	Attended 1909–10	
Rehnquist, William (104, 107)	Stanford	B.A. 1948	Stanford	M.A. 1948	Stanford	Graduated 1952	
			Harvard	M.A. 1950			
Roberts, Owen J. (77)	Pennsylvania	B.A. 1895			Pennsylvania	Graduated 1898	
Rutledge, John (2, 9)	None				Middle Temple (England)	Attended 1758–60	Andrew Rutledge (South Carolina) 1753–55
							James Parsons (South Carolina) 1755–57
Rutledge, Wiley B. (87)	Maryville	Attended 1910–12			Indiana	Attended 1914–15	
	Wisconsin	B.A. 1914			Colorado	Graduated 1922	
Sanford, Edward T. (74)	Tennessee	B.A., Ph.B. 1883	Tennessee	M.A. 1889	Harvard	Graduated 1889	
	Harvard	B.A. 1884					

(Table continues)

Table 4-4 (*Continued*)

Justice (appointment number)	Undergraduate education		Graduate education		Law school		Read the law[a]	
	School	Status/dates	School	Status/dates	School	Status/dates	Mentor state	Dates studied
Scalia, Antonin (108)	Georgetown	B.A. 1957	Fribourg (Switzerland)	Attended 1957	Harvard	Graduated 1960		
Shiras, George, Jr. (54)	Ohio Yale	Attended 1849–51 B.A. 1853			Yale	Attended 1853–54	Hopewell Hepburn (Pennsylvania)	1854–55
Souter, David H. (110)	Harvard	B.A. 1961	Oxford	Scholar Rhodes 1961–63	Harvard	Graduated 1966		
Stevens, John Paul (105)	Chicago	B.A. 1941			North-western	Graduated 1947		
Stewart, Potter (96)	Yale	B.A. 1937	Cambridge	Fellow 1937–38	Yale	Graduated 1941		
Stone, Harlan Fiske (75, 84)	Amherst	B.A. 1894	Amherst	M.A. 1897	Columbia	Graduated 1898		
Story, Joseph (19)	Harvard	Graduated 1798					Samuel Sewall and Samuel Putnam (Massachusetts)	1798–1801

Name	College	Undergraduate	Graduate School	Graduate Degree	Law School	Law School Status	Read Law Under	Years
Strong, William (41)	Yale	B.A. 1828	Yale	M.A. 1831	Yale	Attended 1832	Local lawyers (New Jersey)	1829–32
Sutherland, George (72)	Brigham Young	Attended 1878–1881			Michigan	Attended 1883		
Swayne, Noah H. (36)	None						John Scott and Francis Brooks (Virginia)	1821–23
Taft, William H. (71)	Yale	B.A. 1878			Cincinnati	Graduated 1880		
Taney, Roger B. (25)	Dickinson	Graduated 1795					Jeremiah Chase (Maryland)	1796–98
Thomas, Clarence (111)	Immaculate Conception Holy Cross	Attended 1967–68 B.A. 1971			Yale	Graduated 1974		
Thompson, Smith (20)	Princeton	Graduated 1788					Gilbert Livingston and James Kent (New York)	1789–92
Todd, Thomas (17)	Washington and Lee	Graduated 1783					Harry Innes (Virginia)	1784–88
Trimble, Robert (21)	Transylvania	Attended 1796–97					George Nicholas and James Brown (Kentucky)	1801–03
Van Devanter, Willis (65)	DePauw	B.A. 1878			Cincinnati	Graduated 1881		

(Table continues)

Table 4-4 (*Continued*)

Justice (appointment number)	Undergraduate education		Graduate education		Law school		Read the law[a]	
	School	Status/dates	School	Status/dates	School	Status/dates	Mentor state	Dates studied
Vinson, Fred M. (89)	Centre	B.A. 1909			Centre	Graduated 1911		
Waite, Morrison (44)	Yale	Graduated 1837					Samuel Young (Ohio)	1838–39
Warren, Earl (92)	California	B.A. 1912			California	Graduated 1914		
Washington, Bushrod (12)	William and Mary	Graduated 1778					James Wilson (Pennsylvania)	1782–84
Wayne, James M. (24)	Princeton	Graduated 1808					John Noel (Georgia) Charles Chauncey (Connecticut)	1808–09 1809–1810
White, Byron R. (97)	Colorado	B.A. 1938	Oxford	Rhodes Scholar 1939	Yale	Graduated 1946		
White, Edward D. (56, 64)	Mount St. Mary's Georgetown	Attended 1856 Attended 1857–61			Louisiana	Attended 1866–68	Edward Bermudez (Louisiana)	1866–68

Name	College/University		Law school		Read law under	
Whittaker, Charles E. (95)	None		Kansas City	Graduated 1924		
Wilson, James (4)	St. Andrews (Scotland)	Attended 1756–60			John Dickinson (Pennsylvania)	1766–67
Woodbury, Levi (31)	Dartmouth	Graduated 1809	Tapping-Reeve	Attended 1810	Samuel Dana and Jeremiah Smith (Massachusetts)	1810–12
Woods, William B. (46)	Western Reserve / Yale	Attended 1841–44 Graduated 1845			S. D. King (Ohio)	1845–47

Note: Colleges and universities listed by names used today. During earlier periods, some institutions had different names. For example, Columbia University was known as King's College and Princeton as the College of New Jersey. In the earlier historical periods, colleges and universities often "graduated" students without conferring degrees. In later periods, graduates were given degrees (e.g., bachelor of arts, bachelor of science) indicating the course of study taken. Also, in the earlier historical periods an undergraduate education frequently took less time than the standard four-year curriculum of today.

[a] During the early years of the nation's history it was common for lawyers to be trained by "reading the law" rather than attending law school. This was accomplished through self-study or by serving as an apprentice under an experienced lawyer. Only in the more modern period have justices trained in a formal law school setting. Benjamin Curtis, appointed in 1851, was the first justice with an earned degree from an American law school.

Sources: Joan Biskupic and Elder Witt, *Congressional Quarterly's Guide to the U.S. Supreme Court*, 3d ed. (Washington, D.C.: Congressional Quarterly, 1997); Leon Friedman and Fred L. Israel, eds., *The Justices of the United States Supreme Court: Their Lives and Major Opinions* (New York: R.R. Bowker, 1969–1978); Harold W. Chase et al., *Biographical Dictionary of the American Judiciary* (Detroit: Gale Research, 1976); *Judges of the United States*, 2d ed. (Washington, D.C.: Judicial Conference of the United States, 183); *The National Cyclopaedia of American Biography* (New York: James T. White, various years); and *Dictionary of American Biography* (New York: Charles Scribner's Sons, various editions); John R. Schmidhauser, *Supreme Court Justices Biographical Data 1958* (Ann Arbor, Mich.: Inter-University Consortium for Political Research, 1972).

Table 4-5   Marriages and Children of the Justices

Justice (appointment number)	Spouse (date of marriage)	Children[a]
Baldwin, Henry (23)	Marianna Norton (1802, d. 1803); Sally Ellicott (1805)	1
Barbour, Philip P. (26)	Frances Todd Johnson (1804)	7
Black, Hugo L. (79)	Josephine Foster (1921, d. 1951); Elizabeth Seay DeMerritte (1957)	3
Blackmun, Harry A. (102)	Dorothy E. Clark (1941)	3
Blair, John, Jr. (5)	Jean Blair (1756)	Unknown
Blatchford, Samuel (49)	Caroline Appleton (1844)	2
Bradley, Joseph P. (42)	Mary Hornblower (1844)	7
Brandeis, Louis D. (69)	Alice Goldmark (1891)	2
Brennan, William J., Jr. (94)	Marjorie Leonard (1928, d. 1982); Mary Fowler (1983)	3
Brewer, David J. (52)	Louisa R. Landon (1861, d. 1898); Emma Miner Mott (1901)	4
Breyer, Stephen G. (113)	Joanna Freda Hare (1967)	3
Brown, Henry B. (53)	Caroline Pitts (1864, d. 1901); Josephine Tyler (1904)	Unknown
Burger, Warren E. (101)	Elvera Stromberg (1933)	2
Burton, Harold H. (88)	Selma Florence Smith (1912)	4
Butler, Pierce (73)	Annie M. Cronin (1891)	8
Byrnes, James F. (85)	Maude Busch (1906)	0
Campbell, John A. (34)	Anna Esther Goldthwaite (1830s)	5
Cardozo, Benjamin (78)	Unmarried	
Catron, John (27)	Mary Childress (1807)	0
Chase, Salmon P. (40)	Katharine Jane Garniss (1834, d. 1835); Eliza Ann Smith (1839, d. 1845); Sarah Belle Dunlop Ludlow (1846)	6

Table 4-5 *(Continued)*

Justice (appointment number)	Spouse (date of marriage)	Children[a]
Chase, Samuel (10)	Anne Baldwin (1762, d.); Hannah Kitty Giles (1784)	7
Clark, Tom C. (90)	Mary Jane Ramsey (1924)	3
Clarke, John H. (70)	Unmarried	
Clifford, Nathan (35)	Hannah Ayer (1828)	6
Curtis, Benjamin R. (33)	Eliza Maria Woodward (1833, d. 1844); Anna Wroe Curtis (1846, d. 1860); Maria Malleville Allen (1861)	12
Cushing, William (3)	Hannah Phillips (1774)	0
Daniel, Peter V. (29)	Lucy Randolph (1809, d. 1847); Elizabeth Harris (1853)	5
Davis, David (38)	Sarah Walker Woodruff (1838, d. 1879); Adeline Burr (1883)	2
Day, William R. (60)	Mary Elizabeth Schaefer (1875)	4
Douglas, William O. (82)	Mildred Riddle (1923, divorced 1954); Mercedes Hester (1954, divorced 1963); Joan Martin (1963, divorced 1966); Cathleen Heffernan (1966)	2
Duvall, Gabriel (18)	Mary Bryce (1787, d. 1790); Jane Gibbon (1795)	1
Ellsworth, Oliver (11)	Abigale Wolcott (1772)	7
Field, Stephen J. (39)	Virginia Swearingen (1859)	0
Fortas, Abe (99)	Carolyn Eugenia Agger (1935)	0
Frankfurter, Felix (81)	Marion A. Denman (1919)	0
Fuller, Melville W. (51)	Calista Ophelia Reynolds (1858, d. 1864); Mary E. Coolbaugh (1866)	8
Ginsburg, Ruth Bader (112)	Martin D. Ginsburg (1954)	2
Goldberg, Arthur J. (98)	Dorothy Kurgans (1931)	2

(Table continues)

Table 4-5   *(Continued)*

Justice (appointment number)	Spouse (date of marriage)	Children[a]
Gray, Horace (48)	Jane Matthews (1889)	0
Grier, Robert C. (32)	Isabella Rose (1829)	2
Harlan, John Marshall I (45)	Malvina F. Shanklin (1856)	6
Harlan, John Marshall II (93)	Ethel Andrews (1928)	1
Holmes, Oliver W., Jr. (59)	Fanny Bowdich Dixwell (1872)	0
Hughes, Charles E. (63, 76)	Antoinette Carter (1888)	4
Hunt, Ward (43)	Mary Ann Savage (1837, d. 1845); Marie Taylor (1853)	3
Iredell, James (6)	Hannah Johnston (1773)	3
Jackson, Howell E. (55)	Sophia Malloy (1859, d. 1873); Mary E. Harding (1874)	7
Jackson, Robert H. (86)	Irene Gerhardt (1916)	2
Jay, John (1)	Sarah Van Brugh Livingston (1774)	7
Johnson, Thomas (7)	Ann Jennings (1766)	8
Johnson, William (15)	Sarah Bennett (1794)	10
Kennedy, Anthony (109)	Mary Davis (1963)	3
Lamar, Joseph R. (66)	Clarinda Huntington Pendleton (1879)	3
Lamar, Lucius Q. C. (50)	Virginia Longstreet (1847, d. 1884); Henrietta Dean Holt (1887)	4
Livingston, H. Brockholst (16)	Catharine Keteltas; Ann Ludlow; Catharine Kortright (marriage dates unknown)	11
Lurton, Horace (62)	Mary Francis Owen (1867)	4
Marshall, John (14)	Mary Willis Ambler (1783)	10
Marshall, Thurgood (100)	Vivian Burey (1929, d. 1955); Cecilia Suyat (1955)	2

Table 4-5 *(Continued)*

Justice (appointment number)	Spouse (date of marriage)	Children[a]
Matthews, Stanley (47)	Mary Ann Black (1843, d. 1885); Mary Theaker (1887)	8
McKenna, Joseph (58)	Amanda F. Bornemann (1869)	4
McKinley, John (28)	Juliana Bryan; Elizabeth Armistead (marriage dates unknown)	Unknown
McLean, John (22)	Rebecca Edwards (1807, d. 1840); Sarah Bellow Ludlow Garrard (1843)	8
McReynolds, James C. (68)	Unmarried	
Miller, Samuel (37)	Lucy Ballinger (1839, d. 1854); Elizabeth Winter Reeves (1857)	5
Minton, Sherman (91)	Gertrude Gurtz (1917)	3
Moody, William H. (61)	Unmarried	
Moore, Alfred (13)	Susanna Eagles (1775)	4
Murphy, Frank (83)	Unmarried	
Nelson, Samuel (30)	Pamela Woods (1819, d. 1822); Catherine Ann Russell (1825)	4
O'Connor, Sandra Day (106)	John O'Connor (1952)	3
Paterson, William (8)	Cornelia Bell (1779, d. 1783); Euphemia White (1785)	3
Peckham, Rufus W. (57)	Harriette M. Arnold (1866)	2
Pitney, Mahlon (67)	Florence T. Shelton (1891)	3
Powell, Lewis F., Jr. (103)	Josephine M. Rucker (1936)	4
Reed, Stanley F. (80)	Winifred Elgin (1908)	2
Rehnquist, William (104, 107)	Natalie Cornell (1953)	3
Roberts, Owen J. (77)	Elizabeth Caldwell Rogers (1904)	1
Rutledge, John (2, 9)	Elizabeth Grimke (1763)	10

(Table continues)

Table 4-5   *(Continued)*

Justice (appointment number)	*Spouse (date of marriage)*	*Children*[a]
Rutledge, Wiley B. (87)	Annabel Person (1917)	3
Sanford, Edward T. (74)	Lutie Mallory Woodruff (1891)	2
Scalia, Antonin (108)	Maureen McCarthy (1960)	9
Shiras, George, Jr. (54)	Lillie E. Kennedy (1857)	2
Souter, David H. (110)	Unmarried	
Stevens, John Paul (105)	Elizabeth Jane Sheeren (1942, divorced 1979); Maryan Mulholland Simon (1980)	4
Stewart, Potter (96)	Mary Ann Bertles (1943)	3
Stone, Harlan F. (75, 84)	Agnes Harvey (1899)	2
Story, Joseph (19)	Mary Lynde Oliver (1804, d. 1805); Sarah Waldo Wetmore (1808)	7
Strong, William (41)	Priscilla Lee Mallery (1836, d. 1844); Rachel Davies Bull (1849)	7
Sutherland, George (72)	Rosamund Lee (1883)	3
Swayne, Noah H. (36)	Sarah Ann Wager (1832)	5
Taft, William H. (71)	Helen Herron (1886)	3
Taney, Roger B. (25)	Anne P. C. Key (1806)	7
Thomas, Clarence (111)	Kate Ambush (1971, divorced, 1984); Virginia Lamp (1987)	1
Thompson, Smith (20)	Sarah Livingston (1794, d. 1833); Eliza Livingston (1836)	7
Todd, Thomas (17)	Elizabeth Harris (1788, d. 1811); Lucy Payne (1812)	8
Trimble, Robert (21)	Nancy Timberlake (1803)	10
Van Devanter, Willis (65)	Dellice Burhans (1883)	2
Vinson, Fred M. (89)	Roberta Dixson (1923)	2

Table 4-5   *(Continued)*

Justice (appointment number)	Spouse (date of marriage)	Children[a]
Waite, Morrison (44)	Amelia C. Warner (1840)	5
Warren, Earl (92)	Nina P. Meyers (1925)	6
Washington, Bushrod (12)	Julia Ann Blackburn (1785)	0
Wayne, James M. (24)	Mary Johnson Campbell (1813)	3
White, Byron R. (97)	Marion Stearns (1946)	2
White, Edward D. (56, 64)	Virginia Montgomery Kent (1894)	0
Whittaker, Charles E. (95)	Winifred R. Pugh (1928)	3
Wilson, James (4)	Rachel Bird (1771, d. 1786); Hannah Gray (1793)	7
Woodbury, Levi (31)	Elizabeth Williams Clapp (1819)	5
Woods, William B. (46)	Anne E. Warner (1855)	2

[a] Because infant mortality rates were high in the early periods of American history, sources often vary as to number of children credited to each justice. Some sources count all live births, while others count only those children who survived infancy. Here, the most commonly cited figures in the biographical literature are used.

Sources: John Biskupic and Elder Witt, *Congressional Quarterly's Guide to the U.S. Supreme Court*, 3d ed. (Washington, D.C.: Congressional Quarterly, 1997); Leon Friedman and Fred L. Israel, eds., *The Justices of the United States Supreme Court: Their Lives and Major Opinions* (New York: R.R. Bowker, 1969–1978); Harold W. Chase et al., *Biographical Dictionary of the American Judiciary* (Detroit: Gale Research, 1976); *Judges of the United States*, 2d ed. (Washington, D.C.: Judicial Conference of the United States, 1983); *The National Cyclopaedia of American Biography* (New York: James T. White, various years); and *Dictionary of American Biography* (New York: Charles Scribner's Sons, various editions).

Table 4-6 Private Practice and Law Professorships of the Justices

Justice (appointment number)	Bar admission, state/year	Private law practice, location/years[a]	Law school	Rank	Years of service
Baldwin, Henry (23)	Pennsylvania, 1798	Pennsylvania, 1798–1816, 1822–29			
Barbour, Philip P. (26)	Virginia, 1800	Kentucky, 1800; Virginia, 1802–13			
Black, Hugo L. (79)	Alabama, 1906	Alabama, 1906–15, 1918–26			
Blackmun, Harry A. (102)	Minnesota, 1932	Minnesota, 1933–59	Mitchell College of Law University of Minnesota	Instructor Instructor	1935–41 1945–47
Blair, John, Jr. (5)	Virginia, 1756	Virginia, 1756–77			
Blatchford, Samuel (49)	New York, 1842	New York, 1842–67			
Bradley, Joseph P. (42)	New Jersey, 1839	New Jersey, 1839–70			
Brandeis, Louis D. (69)	Massachusetts, 1878	Missouri, 1878–79; Massachusetts, 1879–1916			
Brennan, William J., Jr. (94)	New Jersey, 1931	New Jersey, 1931–42, 1946–49			
Brewer, David J. (52)	New York, 1858; Kansas, 1859	Kansas, 1859–61	George Washington University	Lecturer	1890s

Name				Position	
Breyer, Stephen G. (113)	District of Columbia, 1966; California, 1966; Massachusetts, 1971		Harvard University Harvard University	Assistant professor Professor	1967–70 1970–80
Brown, Henry B. (53)	Michigan, 1860	Michigan, 1860–61, 1868–75	University of Michigan Detroit Medical College	Lecturer Lecturer	1860s 1868–71
Burger, Warren E. (101)	Minnesota, 1931	Minnesota, 1931–53	Mitchell College of Law	Lecturer	1931–48
Burton, Harold H. (88)	Ohio, 1912; Utah, 1914	Ohio, 1912–14, 1918–35; Utah, 1914–16; Idaho, 1916–17	Western Reserve University	Instructor	1923–25
Butler, Pierce (73)	Minnesota, 1888	Minnesota, 1888–91, 1897–1922			
Byrnes, James F. (85)	South Carolina, 1903	South Carolina, 1925–30, 1947–50			
Campbell, John A. (34)	Georgia, 1829	Alabama, 1830–52; Louisiana, 1865–89			
Cardozo, Benjamin (78)	New York, 1891	New York, 1891–1914			
Catron, John (27)	Tennessee, 1815	Tennessee, 1815–24, 1834–37			
Chase, Salmon P. (40)	Ohio, 1830	Ohio, 1830–49			
Chase, Samuel (10)	Maryland, 1761	Maryland, 1761–87			
Clark, Tom C. (90)	Texas, 1922	Texas, 1922–27, 1932–37			
Clarke, John H. (70)	Ohio, 1878	Ohio, 1878–1914			

(Table continues)

Table 4-6 (*Continued*)

Justice (appointment number)	Bar admission, state/year	Private law practice, location/years[a]	Law school	Rank	Years of service
Clifford, Nathan (35)	New Hampshire, 1827	Maine, 1827–34, 1843–46, 1849–57			
Curtis, Benjamin R. (33)	Massachusetts, 1832	Massachusetts, 1832–51, 1857–74			
Cushing, William (3)	Massachusetts, 1755	Massachusetts, 1755–72			
Daniel, Peter V. (29)	Virginia, 1808	Virginia, 1808–18			
Davis, David (38)	Illinois, 1835	Illinois, 1835–48			
Day, William R. (60)	Ohio, 1872	Ohio, 1872–86, 1890–97			
Douglas, William O. (82)	New York, 1925	New York, 1925–26; Washington, 1927–28	Columbia University Yale University	Assistant professor Professor	1928 1929–36
Duvall, Gabriel (18)	Maryland, 1778	Maryland, 1778–94			
Ellsworth, Oliver (11)	Connecticut, 1771	Connecticut, 1771–84			
Field, Stephen J. (39)	New York, 1841	New York, 1841–48; California, 1849–57			
Fortas, Abe (99)	Connecticut, 1934; District of Columbia, 1945	District of Columbia, 1947–65	Yale University	Associate professor Professor	1933–37 1946–47

Frankfurter, Felix (81)	New York, 1905	New York, 1905–06	Harvard University	Professor	1914–41
Fuller, Melville W. (51)	Maine, 1855; Illinois, 1856	Maine, 1855–56; Illinois, 1856–88			
Ginsburg, Ruth Bader (112)	New York, 1959; District of Columbia, 1975		Rutgers University Rutgers University Rutgers University Columbia University	Assistant professor Associate professor Professor Professor	1963–66 1966–69 1969–72 1972–80
Goldberg, Arthur J. (98)	Illinois, 1929	Illinois, 1929–42, 1945–61	John Marshall Law School	Professor	1945–48
Gray, Horace (48)	Massachusetts, 1851	Massachusetts, 1851–64			
Grier, Robert C. (32)	Pennsylvania, 1817	Pennsylvania, 1817–33			
Harlan, John Marshall I (45)	Kentucky, 1853	Kentucky, 1853–61, 1867–77	George Washington University	Lecturer	1889–1910
Harlan, John Marshall II (93)	New York, 1925	New York, 1925, 1927, 1931–42, 1946–51			
Holmes, Oliver W., Jr. (59)	Massachusetts, 1867	Massachusetts, 1867–82	Harvard University Lowell Institute Harvard University	Instructor Lecturer Professor	1870–71 1880 1882
Hughes, Charles Evans (63, 76)	New York, 1884	New York, 1884–91, 1893–1906, 1917–21, 1925–30	Cornell University New York University	Professor Lecturer Lecturer	1891–93 1893–95 1893–1900

(Table continues)

Table 4-6 *(Continued)*

Justice *(appointment number)*	Bar admission, state/year	Private law practice, location/years[a]	Law school	Rank	Years of service
Hunt, Ward (43)	New York, 1831	New York, 1831–66			
Iredell, James (6)	North Carolina, 1770	North Carolina, 1770–77, 1782–90			
Jackson, Howell E. (55)	Tennessee, 1856	Tennessee, 1856–61, 1865–80	Southwest Baptist University	Professor	1875–80
Jackson, Robert H. (86)	New York, 1913	New York, 1913–34			
Jay, John (1)	New York, 1768	New York, 1768–74			
Johnson, Thomas (7)	Maryland, 1760	Maryland, 1760–76			
Johnson, William (15)	South Carolina, 1793	South Carolina, 1793–99			
Kennedy, Anthony (109)	California, 1961	California, 1961–76	University of the Pacific	Lecturer	1965–88
Lamar, Joseph R. (66)	Georgia, 1878	Georgia, 1880–1903, 1906–10			
Lamar, Lucius Q. C. (50)	Georgia, 1847	Georgia, 1847–48, 1852–55; Mississippi, 1849–52, 1855–56, 1866–72	University of Mississippi	Professor	1867–70
Livingston, H. Brockholst (16)	New York, 1783	New York, 1783–1802			
Lurton, Horace (62)	Tennessee, 1867	Tennessee, 1867–75, 1878–86	Vanderbilt University	Professor Dean	1898–1905 1905–09

Marshall, John (14)	Virginia, 1780	Virginia, 1780–97			
Marshall, Thurgood (100)	Maryland, 1933	Maryland, 1933–36			
Matthews, Stanley (47)	Tennessee, 1842; Ohio, 1844	Tennessee, 1842–44; Ohio, 1844–51, 1854–58, 1865–77, 1879–81			
McKenna, Joseph (58)	California, 1865	California, 1865–66, 1870–85			
McKinley, John (28)	Kentucky, 1800	Kentucky, 1800–18; Alabama, 1818–26			
McLean, John (22)	Ohio, 1807	Ohio, 1807–11			
McReynolds, James C. (68)	Tennessee, 1884	Tennessee, 1884–1903, 1907–12	Vanderbilt University	Lecturer	1900–03
Miller, Samuel (37)	Kentucky, 1847	Kentucky, 1847–50; Iowa, 1850–62			
Minton, Sherman (91)	Indiana, 1915	Indiana, 1915–16, 1919–25, 1928–33; Florida, 1925–28			
Moody, William H. (61)	Massachusetts, 1878	Massachusetts, 1878–88			
Moore, Alfred (13)	North Carolina, 1775	North Carolina, 1775–76, 1777–82, 1791–99			

(Table continues)

Table 4-6 (*Continued*)

Justice (*appointment number*)	Bar admission, state/year	Private law practice, location/years[a]	Law school	Rank	Years of service
Murphy, Frank (83)	Michigan, 1914	Michigan, 1914–17, 1920–23	University of Detroit	Lecturer	1914–17, 1922–27
Nelson, Samuel (30)	New York, 1817	New York, 1817–20			
O'Connor, Sandra Day (106)	California, 1952; Arizona, 1957	Arizona, 1959–65, 1969–75			
Paterson, William (8)	New Jersey, 1769	New Jersey, 1769–76, 1783–88			
Peckham, Rufus W. (57)	New York, 1859	New York, 1859–69, 1872–81			
Pitney, Mahlon (67)	New Jersey, 1882	New Jersey, 1882–94, 1899–1901			
Powell, Lewis F., Jr. (103)	Virginia, 1933	Virginia, 1933–71			
Reed, Stanley F. (80)	Kentucky, 1910	Kentucky, 1910–29			
Rehnquist, William (104, 107)	Arizona, 1953	Arizona, 1953–69			
Roberts, Owen J. (77)	Pennsylvania, 1898	Pennsylvania, 1898–1901, 1905–24	University of Pennsylvania	Lecturer / Dean	1898–1919 / 1948–51
Rutledge, John (2, 9)	England, 1760	South Carolina, 1761–74			

Rutledge, Wiley B. (87)	Colorado, 1922	Colorado, 1922–24	University of Colorado	Professor	1924–26
			Washington University	Professor	1926–35
				Dean	1930–35
			University of Iowa	Professor and dean	1935–39
Sanford, Edward T. (74)	Tennessee, 1888	Tennessee, 1890–1906	University of Tennessee	Lecturer	1898–1906
Scalia, Antonin (108)	Ohio, 1962; Virginia, 1970	Ohio, 1961–67	University of Virginia	Professor	1967–74
			University of Chicago	Professor	1977–82
Shiras, George, Jr. (54)	Pennsylvania, 1855	Iowa, 1855–58; Pennsylvania, 1858–92			
Souter, David H. (110)	New Hampshire, 1966	New Hampshire, 1966–68			
Stevens, John Paul (105)	Illinois, 1949	Illinois, 1948–51; 1952–70	Northwestern University	Lecturer	1950–54
			University of Chicago	Lecturer	1977–82
Stewart, Potter (96)	Ohio, 1942; New York, 1942	New York, 1941–42, 1945–47; Ohio, 1947–54			
Stone, Harlan Fiske (75, 84)	New York, 1898	New York, 1899–1924	Columbia University	Professor	1899–1905
				Dean	1910–23
Story, Joseph (19)	Massachusetts, 1801	Massachusetts, 1801–08, 1810–11	Harvard University	Professor	1829–45
Strong, William (41)	Pennsylvania, 1832	Pennsylvania, 1832–46, 1868–70			

(Table continues)

Table 4-6 (*Continued*)

Justice (appointment number)	Bar admission, state/year	Private law practice, location/years[a]	Law school	Rank	Years of service
Sutherland, George (72)	Michigan, 1883; Utah, 1883	Utah, 1883–1900, 1903–05; District of Columbia, 1917–22			
Swayne, Noah H. (36)	Virginia, 1823	Ohio, 1825–30, 1841–61			
Taft, William H. (71)	Ohio, 1880	Ohio, 1880–81, 1883–85	University of Cincinnati Yale University	Professor and dean Professor	1896–1900 1913–21
Taney, Roger B. (25)	Maryland, 1799	Maryland, 1799–1826			
Thomas, Clarence (111)	Missouri, 1974	Missouri, 1977–79			
Thompson, Smith (20)	New York, 1792	New York, 1793–1802			
Todd, Thomas (17)	Virginia, 1788	Kentucky, 1788–1801			
Trimble, Robert (21)	Kentucky, 1803	Kentucky, 1803–06, 1809–13			
Van Devanter, Willis (65)	Indiana, 1881	Indiana, 1881–83; Wyoming; 1884–88, 1890–97	George Washington University	Lecturer	1898–1903
Vinson, Fred M. (89)	Kentucky, 1911	Kentucky, 1911–21, 1929–30			

Justice					
Waite, Morrison (44)	Ohio, 1839	Ohio, 1839–74			
Warren, Earl (92)	California, 1914	California, 1914–17			
Washington, Bushrod (12)	Virginia, 1784	Virginia, 1784–98			
Wayne, James M. (24)	Georgia, 1810	Georgia, 1810–19			
White, Byron R. (97)	Colorado, 1947	Colorado, 1947–61			
White, Edward D. (56, 64)	Louisiana, 1868	Louisiana, 1868–78, 1880–90			
Whittaker, Charles E. (95)	Missouri, 1923	Missouri, 1923–54			
Wilson, James (4)	Pennsylvania, 1767	Pennsylvania, 1768–89	University of Pennsylvania	Professor	1789–90
Woodbury, Levi (31)	New Hampshire, 1812	New Hampshire, 1812–16			
Woods, William B. (46)	Ohio, 1847	Ohio, 1847–62; Alabama, 1866–67			

[a]Legal practice may have been combined with activities such as farming, business ventures, teaching, or part-time political positions. Includes work as a solo practitioner, in a law firm, or with a corporation. Does not include full-time employment with the government or interest groups, or those years the justices may have practiced law on an irregular or part-time basis while holding a major public office. The years of private practice for justices during the early periods of American history are difficult to identify accurately because law was often practiced on a less formal basis than in later years.

Sources: John Biskupic and Elder Witt, Congressional Quarterly's Guide to the U.S. Supreme Court, 3d ed. (Washington, D.C.: Congressional Quarterly, 1997); Leon Friedman and Fred L. Israel, eds., The Justices of the United States Supreme Court: Their Lives and Major Opinions (New York: R.R. Bowker, 1969–1978); Harold W. Chase et al., Biographical Dictionary of the American Judiciary (Detroit: Gale Research, 1976); Judges of the United States, 2d ed. (Washington, D.C.: Judicial Conference of the United States, 1983); The National Cyclopaedia of American Biography (New York: James T. White, various years); and Dictionary of American Biography (New York: Charles Scribner's Sons, various editions). Updated by the authors.

Table 4-7 Military Experience of the Justices

Justice (appointment number)	Service	Dates	Rank	Wars
Black, Hugo L. (79)	Army	1917–18	Captain	World War I
Brennan, William J., Jr. (94)	Army	1942–46	Colonel	World War II
Breyer, Stephen G. (113)	Army Reserve	1957–65	Corporal	
Burton, Harold H. (88)	Army	1917–18	Captain	World War I
Catron, John (27)	Army	1812	Enlisted soldier	War of 1812
Clark, Tom C. (90)	Army	1918	Infantryman	World War I
Douglas, William O. (82)	Army	1918	Private	World War I
Duvall, Gabriel (18)	Continental Army	1776–81	Private, mustermaster	Revolution
Goldberg, Arthur J. (98)	Army	1942–44	Captain, major	World War II
Harlan, John Marshall I (45)	Union Army	1861–63	Colonel	Civil War
Harlan, John Marshall II (93)	Army Air Force	1943–45	Colonel	World War II
Holmes, Oliver W., Jr. (59)	Union Army	1861–64	Lieutenant, captain	Civil War
Jay, John (1)	New York Militia	1776–78	Colonel	Revolution
Johnson, Thomas (7)	Maryland Militia	1776–77	Brigadier general	Revolution
Kennedy, Anthony (109)	National Guard	1961	Private first class	
Lamar, Lucius Q. C. (50)	Confederate Army	1861–65	Colonel, judge advocate	Civil War
Livingston, H. Brockholst (16)	Continental Army	1776–79	Lt. colonel	Revolution
Lurton, Horace (62)	Confederate Army	1861–65	Sgt. major	Civil War
Marshall, John (14)	Continental Army	1776–81	Captain	Revolution
Matthews, Stanley (47)	Union Army	1861–63	Colonel	Civil War
Minton, Sherman (91)	Army	1917–18	Captain	World War I
Moore, Alfred (13)	Continental Army	1776–77	Captain	Revolution
Murphy, Frank (83)	Army	1917–18	Lieutenant, captain	World War I
	Army	1942	Lt. colonel	World War II
Paterson, William (8)	Minutemen[a]	1776–78	Officer	Revolution
Powell, Lewis F., Jr. (103)	Army Air Force	1942–46	Colonel	World War II
Reed, Stanley F. (80)	Army	1917–18	Lieutenant	World War I
Rehnquist, William (104, 107)	Army Air Force	1943–46	Sergeant	World War II

Stevens, John Paul (105)	Navy	1942–45	Lt. commander	World War II
Stewart, Potter (96)	Navy	1942–45	Lieutenant	World War II
Todd, Thomas (17)	Continental Army	1781	Private	Revolution
Warren, Earl (92)	Army	1917–18	Lieutenant	World War I
Washington, Bushrod (12)	Continental Army	1780–81	Private	Revolution
Wayne, James M. (24)	Georgia Militia	1812	Captain	War of 1812
White, Byron R. (97)	Navy	1942–46	Lieutenant	World War II
White, Edward D. (56, 64)	Confederate Army	1861–65	Private, lieutenant	Civil War
Woods, William B. (46)	Union Army	1862–66	Brigadier general	Civil War

[a] American citizen army at the time of the Revolution whose members volunteered to be ready for military service at a minute's notice.

Sources: John Biskupic and Elder Witt, *Congressional Quarterly's Guide to the U.S. Supreme Court*, 3d ed. (Washington, D.C.: Congressional Quarterly, 1997); Leon Friedman and Fred L. Israel, eds., *The Justices of the United States Supreme Court: Their Lives and Major Opinions* (New York: R.R. Bowker, 1969–1978); Harold W. Chase et al., *Biographical Dictionary of the American Judiciary* (Detroit: Gale Research, 1976); *Judges of the United States*, 2d ed. (Washington, D.C.: Judicial Conference of the United States, 1983); *The National Cyclopaedia of American Biography* (New York: James T. White, various years); and *Dictionary of American Biography* (New York: Charles Scribner's Sons, various editions). Updated by the authors.

Table 4-8 Political Experience of the Justices

Justice (appointment number)	Political experience[a]	
	State	Federal
Baldwin, Henry (23)		House of Representatives (Pennsylvania), 1817–22
Barbour, Philip P. (26)	Virginia House of Delegates, 1812–14; president, Virginia Constitutional Convention, 1829–30	House of Representatives (Virginia), 1814–25, 1827–30; Speaker of the House, 1821–23
Black, Hugo L. (79)	Solicitor, Jefferson County, Alabama, 1915–17	Senate (Alabama), 1927–37
Blair, John, Jr. (5)	Virginia House of Burgesses, 1766–70; clerk, Virginia Governor's Council, 1770–75; member, Virginia Governor's Council, 1776; delegate, Virginia constitutional convention, 1776	Delegate, Constitutional Convention, 1787
Brewer, David J. (52)	County attorney, Leavenworth, Kansas, 1869–70	
Breyer, Stephen G. (113)		Antitrust attorney, Justice Department, 1965–67; Watergate Special Prosecution Force, Justice Department, 1973; Counsel, Senate Judiciary Committee, 1974–80; Commissioner, U.S. Sentencing Commission, 1985–89
Brown, Henry B. (53)		Deputy marshal, Eastern District of Michigan, 1861; assistant U.S. attorney, Eastern District of Michigan, 1863–68
Burger, Warren E. (101)		Assistant attorney general, 1953–56
Burton, Harold H. (88)	Ohio House of Representatives, 1929; director of law, Cleveland,	Senate (Ohio), 1941–45

Table 4-8   *(Continued)*

Justice (appointment number)	Political experience[a]	
	State	*Federal*
	Ohio, 1929–32; acting mayor, Cleveland, Ohio, 1931–32; mayor, Cleveland, Ohio, 1935–40	
Butler, Pierce (73)	Assistant county attorney, Ramsey County, Minnesota, 1891–93; county attorney, Ramsey County, Minnesota, 1893–97; Board of Regents, University of Minnesota, 1907–24	
Byrnes, James F. (85)	Circuit court solicitor, South Carolina, 1908–10	House of Representatives (South Carolina), 1911–25; Senate (South Carolina), 1931–41
Campbell, John A. (34)	Alabama House of Representatives, 1837, 1843	
Chase, Salmon P. (40)	Governor, Ohio, 1856–60	Senate (Ohio), 1849–55; secretary of the Treasury, 1861–64
Chase, Samuel (10)	Maryland General Assembly, 1764–84; member, Maryland Committee of Correspondence, 1774; member, Maryland Convention and Council of Safety, 1775; delegate, Maryland convention to ratify the U.S. Constitution, 1788	Continental Congress (Maryland), 1774–78; signed Declaration of Independence, 1776; Congress (Maryland), 1784–85
Clark, Tom C. (90)	Civil district attorney, Dallas, Texas, 1927–32	Special assistant, Justice Department, 1937–43; assistant attorney general, 1943–45; attorney general, 1945–49
Clifford, Nathan (35)	Maine House of Representatives, 1830–34; speaker, Maine House of Representatives, 1832–34; attorney general, Maine, 1834–38	House of Representatives (Maine), 1839–43; attorney general, 1846–48; minister to Mexico, 1848–49

(Table continues)

Table 4-8   *(Continued)*

| Justice | Political experience[a] | |
(appointment number)	State	Federal
Curtis, Benjamin R. (33)	Massachusetts House of Representatives, 1849–51	
Cushing, William (3)	Member, Massachusetts convention to ratify the U.S. Constitution, 1788; member, Massachusetts constitutional convention, 1779	Presidential elector, 1788
Daniel, Peter V. (29)	Virginia House of Delegates, 1809–12; Privy Council, Virginia, 1812–35; lieutenant governor, Virginia, 1818–35	
Davis, David (38)	Illinois House of Representatives, 1845–47; member, Illinois constitutional convention, 1847	
Day, William R. (60)		Assistant secretary of state, 1897–98; secretary of state, 1898; delegate, Paris Peace Conference, 1898–99
Douglas, William O. (82)		Member, Securities and Exchange Commission, 1936–39; chairman, Securities and Exchange Commission, 1937–39
Duvall, Gabriel (18)	Clerk, Maryland Convention, 1775–77; clerk, Maryland House of Delegates, 1777–1787; member, Maryland State Council, 1782–85; Maryland House of Delegates, 1787–94	House of Representatives (Maryland), 1794–96; presidential elector, 1796, 1800; comptroller of the Treasury, 1802–11
Ellsworth, Oliver (11)	Connecticut General Assembly, 1773–76; state's attorney, Hartford County, Connecticut, 1777–85; Governor's Council, Connecticut, 1780–85	Continental Congress (Connecticut), 1777–82; Congress (Connecticut), 1782–84; delegate, Constitutional Convention, 1787; Senate (Connecticut), 1789–96

Table 4-8   *(Continued)*

| Justice | Political experience[a] | |
(appointment number)	State	Federal
Field, Stephen J. (39)	Alcalde, Marysville, California, 1850; California House of Representatives, 1850–51	
Fortas, Abe (99)		Assistant director, Securities and Exchange Commission, 1937–39; general counsel, Public Works Administration, 1939–40; director, division of power, Interior Department, 1941–42; under secretary, Interior Department, 1942–46
Frankfurter, Felix (81)		Assistant U.S. attorney, Southern District of New York, 1906–09; law officer, War Department, 1910–14; secretary and counsel, President's Mediation Commission, 1917; assistant to secretary of labor, 1917–18
Fuller, Melville W. (51)	City council, Augusta, Maine, 1856; member, Illinois constitutional convention, 1861; Illinois House of Representatives, 1863–64	
Goldberg, Arthur J. (98)		Secretary of labor, 1961–62
Harlan, John Marshall I (45)	Adjutant general, Kentucky, 1851; attorney general, Kentucky, 1863–67	Member, Louisiana Reconstruction Commission, 1877
Harlan, John Marshall II (93)	Special assistant attorney general, New York, 1928–30; chief counsel, New York State Crime Commission, 1951–53	Assistant U.S. attorney, southern district of New York, 1925–27
Hughes, Charles Evans (63, 76)	Special counsel, New York House of Representatives, 1905–06; governor, New York, 1907–10	Secretary of state, 1921–25

(Table continues)

Table 4-8   *(Continued)*

| Justice | Political experience[a] | |
(appointment number)	State	Federal
Hunt, Ward (43)	New York General Assembly, 1839; mayor, Utica, New York, 1844	
Iredell, James (6)	Attorney general, North Carolina, 1779–81; member, North Carolina Council of State, 1787; delegate, North Carolina convention to ratify the U.S. Constitution, 1788	Comptroller of customs, Edenton, North Carolina, 1768–74[b]; collector of customs, North Carolina, 1774–76[b]
Jackson, Howell E. (55)	Tennessee House of Representatives, 1880	Receiver of alien property, 1861–64[c]; Senate (Tennessee), 1881–86
Jackson, Robert H. (86)		General counsel, Internal Revenue Bureau, 1934–36; special counsel, Securities and Exchange Commission, 1935; assistant attorney general, 1936–38; solicitor general, 1938–39; attorney general, 1940–41
Jay, John (1)	New York provincial Congress, 1776–77	Continental Congress (New York), 1774–79; minister to Spain, 1779; secretary of foreign affairs, 1784–89
Johnson, Thomas (7)	Maryland Provincial Assembly, 1762; delegate, Maryland constitutional convention, 1776; governor, Maryland, 1777–79; Maryland House of Delegates, 1780, 1786, 1787; member, Maryland convention to ratify the U.S. Constitution, 1788	Delegate, Annapolis Convention, 1774; Continental Congress (Maryland), 1774–77
Johnson, William (15)	South Carolina House of Representatives, 1794–98; South Carolina Speaker of the House, 1798; founder and trustee, University of South Carolina	

Table 4-8 *(Continued)*

Justice (appointment number)	Political experience[a]	
	State	*Federal*
Lamar, Joseph R. (66)	Georgia House of Representatives, 1886–89; member, commission to codify Georgia laws, 1893	
Lamar, Lucius Q. C. (50)	Georgia House of Representatives, 1853	Delegate, Mississippi secession convention, 1861[c]; special envoy to Russia, 1862[c]; House of Representatives (Mississippi), 1857–60, 1873–77; Senate (Mississippi), 1877–85; secretary of interior, 1885–88
Livingston, H. Brockholst (16)	New York General Assembly, 1786, 1800–02	
Marshall, John (14)	Executive Council of State, Virginia, 1782–84; Virginia House of Delegates, 1782–85, 1787–90, 1795–96; delegate, Virginia convention to ratify the U.S. Constitution, 1788	Minister to France, 1797–98; House of Representatives (Virginia), 1799–1800; secretary of state, 1800–01
Marshall, Thurgood (100)		Solicitor general, 1965–67
Matthews, Stanley (47)	Assistant prosecutor, Hamilton County, Ohio, 1845; clerk, Ohio House of Representatives, 1848–49; Ohio Senate, 1855–58	U.S. attorney, Southern District of Ohio, 1858–61; presidential elector, 1864, 1868; counsel, Hayes-Tilton electoral commission, 1877; Senate (Ohio), 1877–79
McKenna, Joseph (58)	District attorney, Solano County, California, 1866–70; California House of Representatives, 1875–76	House of Representatives (California), 1885–92; attorney general, 1897
McKinley, John (28)	Alabama House of Representatives, 1820, 1831, 1836	Senate (Alabama), 1826–31, 1837; House of Representatives (Alabama), 1833–35

(Table continues)

Table 4-8   *(Continued)*

Justice (appointment number)	Political experience[a]	
	State	*Federal*
McLean, John (22)		Examiner, U.S. Land Office, 1811–12; House of Representatives (Ohio), 1813–16; commissioner, General Land Office, 1822–23; postmaster general, 1823–29
McReynolds, James C. (68)		Assistant attorney general, 1903–07; attorney general, 1913–14
Minton, Sherman (91)	Counselor, Indiana Public Service Commission, 1933–34	Senate (Indiana), 1935–41; administrative assistant to the president, 1941
Moody, William H. (61)	City solicitor, Haverhill, Massachusetts, 1888–90; district attorney, Eastern district of Massachusetts, 1890–95	House of Representatives (Massachusetts), 1895–1902; secretary of the Navy, 1902–04; attorney general, 1904–06
Moore, Alfred (13)	North Carolina Senate, 1782; attorney general, North Carolina, 1782–91; North Carolina House of Commons, 1792	
Murphy, Frank (83)	Mayor, Detroit, Michigan, 1930–33; governor, Michigan, 1937–39	Assistant U.S. attorney, Eastern District of Michigan, 1919–20; governor of the Philippines, 1933–35; high commission to the Philippines, 1935–36; attorney general, 1939–40
Nelson, Samuel (30)	Delegate, New York state constitutional convention, 1821	Presidential elector, 1820; postmaster, Cortland, New York, 1820–23
O'Connor, Sandra Day (106)	Deputy county attorney, San Mateo, California, 1952–53; assistant attorney general, Arizona, 1965–69; Arizona Senate, 1969–75; majority leader, Arizona Senate, 1973–74	

Table 4-8   *(Continued)*

Justice (appointment number)	Political experience[a]	
	State	*Federal*
Paterson, William (8)	New Jersey Provincial Congress, 1775–76; delegate, New Jersey state constitutional convention, 1776; attorney general, New Jersey, 1776–83; governor, New Jersey, assistant, 1790–93	Delegate, Constitutional Convention, 1787; Senate (New Jersey), 1789–90
Peckham, Rufus W. (57)	District attorney, Albany County, New York, 1869–72; city attorney, Albany, New York, 1881–83	
Pitney, Mahlon (67)	New Jersey Senate, 1899–1901; president, New Jersey Senate, 1901	House of Representatives (New Jersey), 1895–99
Powell, Lewis F., Jr. (103)	President, Richmond, Virginia, school board, 1952–61; member, Virginia state school board, 1961–69; president, Virginiastate school board, 1968–69	
Reed, Stanley F. (80)	Kentucky House of Representatives, 1912–16	General counsel, Federal Farm Board, 1929–32; general counsel, Reconstruction Finance Corporation, 1932–35; special assistant to the attorney general, 1935; solicitor general, 1935–38
Rehnquist, William (104, 107)		Assistant attorney general, 1969–71
Roberts, Owen J. (77)	Assistant district attorney, Philadelphia, Pennsylvania, 1901–04	Special deputy attorney general, 1918; special U.S. attorney, 1924–30
Rutledge, John (2, 9)	South Carolina Assembly, 1761–76; attorney general pro tem, South Carolina, 1764–65; president, Republic of South Carolina, 1776–78; governor, South Carolina,	Continental Congress (South Carolina), 1774–76; Congress (South Carolina), 1782–83; delegate, Constitutional Convention, 1787

(Table continues)

Table 4-8   *(Continued)*

Justice	Political experience[a]	
(appointment number)	*State*	*Federal*
	1779–82; member, South Carolina convention to ratify the U.S. Constitution, 1788	
Sanford, Edward T. (74)	Trustee, University of Tennessee, 1897–1923	Special assistant to attorney general, 1906–07; assistant attorney general, 1907–08
Scalia, Antonin (108)		General counsel, White House Office of Telecommunications Policy, 1971–72; chairman, Administrative Conference of the United States, 1972–74; assistant attorney general, 1974–77
Shiras, George, Jr. (54)		Presidential elector, 1888
Souter, David H. (110)	Assistant attorney general, New Hampshire, 1968–71; deputy attorney general, New Hampshire, 1971–76; attorney general, New Hampshire, 1976–78	
Stevens, John Paul (105)		Associate counsel, House Judiciary Committee, 1951; attorney general's committee to study antitrust laws, 1953–55
Stewart, Potter (96)	City council, Cincinnati, Ohio, 1950–53; vice mayor, Cincinnati, Ohio, 1952–53	
Stone, Harlan Fiske (75, 84)		Attorney general, 1924–25
Story, Joseph (19)	Massachusetts House of Representatives, 1805–08, 1811; Massachusetts Speaker of the House, 1811	House of Representatives (Massachusetts), 1808–09
Strong, William (41)		House of Representatives (Pennsylvania), 1847–51
Sutherland, George (72)	Utah Senate, 1896–1900	House of Representatives (Utah), 1901–03; Senate

Table 4-8 *(Continued)*

Justice (appointment number)	Political experience[a]	
	State	*Federal*
		(Utah), 1905–17; counsel, Norway-United States arbitration, 1921–22
Swayne, Noah H. (36)	Prosecuting attorney, Coshocton County, Ohio, 1826–29; Ohio House of Representatives, 1830, 1836; city council, Columbus, Ohio, 1834	U.S. attorney for the district of Ohio, 1830–41
Taft, William H. (71)	Assistant prosecutor, Hamilton County, Ohio, 1881–83; assistant solicitor, Hamilton County, Ohio, 1885–87	Solicitor general, 1890–92; chairman, the Philippine Commission, 1900–01; governor, Philippine Islands, 1901–04; secretary of war, 1904–08; president, 1909–13; joint chairman, National War Labor Board, 1918–19
Taney, Roger B. (25)	Maryland House of Delegates, 1799–1800; Maryland Senate, 1816–21; attorney general, Maryland, 1827–31	Attorney general, 1831–33; acting secretary of war, 1831; secretary of the Treasury (confirmation rejected), 1833–34
Thomas, Clarence (111)	Assistant attorney general, Missouri, 1974–77	Legislative assistant, Senate, 1979–81; assistant secretary for civil rights, Department of Education, 1981–82; chairman, Equal Employment Opportunity Commission, 1982–90
Thompson, Smith (20)	New York House of Representatives, 1800; member, New York constitutional convention, 1801; member, New York State Board of Regents, 1813	Secretary of the Navy, 1819–23
Todd, Thomas (17)	Clerk, Kentucky House of Representatives, 1792–1801	
Trimble, Robert (21)	Kentucky House of Representatives, 1802	U.S. attorney for the district of Kentucky, 1813–17

(Table continues)

Table 4-8   *(Continued)*

Justice (appointment number)	Political experience[a]	
	State	*Federal*
Van Devanter, Willis (65)	City attorney, Cheyenne, Wyoming, 1887–88; Wyoming territorial legislature, 1888	Assistant attorney general, 1897–03
Vinson, Fred M. (89)	City attorney, Louisa, Kentucky, 1913; commonwealth attorney, Kentucky, 1921–24	House of Representatives (Kentucky), 1923–29, 1931–38; director, Office of Economic Stabilization, 1943–45; administrator, Federal Loan Agency, 1945; director, Office of War Mobilization and Reconversion, 1945; secretary of the Treasury, 1945–46
Waite, Morrison (44)	Ohio House of Representatives, 1850–52; president, Ohio constitutional convention, 1873–74	Member, U.S. delegation to Geneva Arbitration Convention, 1871
Warren, Earl (92)	Deputy city attorney, Oakland, California, 1919–20; deputy assistant district attorney, Alameda County, California, 1920–23; chief deputy district attorney, Alameda County, California, 1923–25; district attorney, Alameda County, California, 1925–39; attorney general, California, 1939–43; governor, California, 1943–53	Republican vice-presidential nominee, 1948
Washington, Bushrod (12)	Virginia House of Delegates, 1787–88; member, Virginia convention to ratify the U.S. Constitution, 1788	
Wayne, James M. (24)	Georgia House of Representatives, 1815–16; mayor, Savannah, Georgia, 1817–19	House of Representatives (Georgia), 1829–35
White, Byron R. (97)		Deputy attorney general, 1961–62

Table 4-8   *(Continued)*

Justice	Political experience[a]	
(appointment number)	State	Federal
White, Edward D. (56, 64)	Louisiana Senate, 1874	Senate (Louisiana), 1891–94
Wilson, James (4)	Member, Pennsylvania convention to ratify the U.S. Constitution, 1787	Continental Congress (Pennsylvania), 1775–77; signed Declaration of Independence, 1776; delegate, Constitutional Convention, 1787; Congress (Pennsylvania), 1783, 1785–87
Woodbury, Levi (31)	Clerk, New Hampshire Senate, 1816; governor, New Hampshire, 1823–24; speaker, New Hampshire House of Representatives, 1825	Senate (New Hampshire), 1825–31, 1841–45; secretary of the Navy, 1831–34; secretary of the Treasury, 1834–41
Woods, William B. (46)	Mayor, Newark, Ohio, 1856; Ohio House of Represen- tatives, 1858–62; speaker, Ohio House of Represen- tatives, 1858–60	

Note: The names of justices who held no state or federal offices prior to taking seat on the Supreme Court have been omitted.

[a] Includes nonjudicial governmental positions held by justice prior to taking seat on the Supreme Court.
[b] Office held under colonial English government.
[c] Office held under Confederate States of America.

Sources: Joan Biskupic and Elder Witt, *Congressional Quarterly's Guide to the U.S. Supreme Court,* 3d ed. (Washington, D.C.: Congressional Quarterly, 1997); Leon Friedman and Fred L. Israel, eds., *The Justices of the United States Supreme Court: Their Lives and Major Opinions* (New York: R.R. Bowker, 1969–1978); Harold W. Chase et al., *Biographical Dictionary of the American Judiciary* (Detroit: Gale Research, 1976); *Judges of the United States,* 2d ed. (Washington, D.C.: Judicial Conference of the United States, 1983); *The National Cyclopaedia of American Biography* (New York: James T. White, various years); and *Dictionary of American Biography* (New York: Charles Scribner's Sons, various editions). Updated by the authors.

Table 4-9   Prior Judicial Experience of the Justices

Justice (appointment number)	Judicial experience[a]	
	State	Federal
Barbour, Philip P. (26)	Judge, General Court, Virginia, 1825–27	Judge, Eastern District of Virginia, 1830–36
Black, Hugo L. (79)	Judge, Police Court, Birmingham, Alabama, 1910–11	
Blackmun, Harry A. (102)		Law clerk, Court of Appeals for the Eighth Circuit, 1932–33; Judge, Court of Appeals for the Eighth Circuit, 1959–70
Blair, John, Jr. (5)	Judge, General Court, Virginia, 1777–78; Chief judge, General Court, Virginia, 1779; Judge, Court of Appeals, Virginia, 1780–89; Judge, Supreme Court of Appeals, Virginia, 1789	
Blatchford, Samuel (49)		Judge, Southern District of New York, 1867–72; Judge, Second Judicial Circuit, 1872–82
Brennan, William J., Jr. (94)	Judge, Superior Court, New Jersey, 1949–50; Judge, Superior Court, Appellate Division, New Jersey, 1950–52; Judge, Supreme Court, New Jersey, 1952–56	
Brewer, David J. (52)	Judge, County Probate and Criminal Courts, Kansas, 1863–64; Judge, District Court, Kansas, 1865–69; Justice, Supreme Court, Kansas, 1870–84	Commissioner, Circuit Court, Kansas Division, 1861–62; Judge, Eighth Judicial Circuit, 1884–89
Breyer, Stephen G. (113)		Law clerk, Justice Arthur Goldberg, 1964–65; Judge, Court of Appeals for the First Circuit, 1980–90

Table 4-9 *(Continued)*

Justice (appointment number)	Judicial experience[a]	
	State	*Federal*
Brown, Henry B. (53)	Judge, Circuit Court, Michigan, 1868	Judge, Eastern District of Michigan, 1875–90
Burger, Warren E. (101)		Judge, Court of Appeals for the District of Columbia Circuit, 1956–69
Byrnes, James F. (85)	Reporter, Circuit Court, South Carolina, 1900–08	
Cardozo, Benjamin (78)	Justice, Supreme Court, New York, 1914; Judge, Court of Appeals, New York, 1914–26; Chief Judge, Court of Appeals, New York, 1926–32	
Catron, John (27)	Judge, Supreme Court, Tennessee, 1824–31; Chief Justice, Supreme Court, Tennessee, 1831–34	
Chase, Samuel (10)	Judge, Criminal Court, Baltimore, Maryland, 1788–96; Chief Judge, General Court, Maryland, 1791–96	
Clarke, John H. (70)		Judge, Northern District of Ohio, 1914–16
Cushing, William (3)	Judge, Probate Court, Massachusetts, 1760–61; Judge, Superior Court, Massachusetts, 1772–77; Chief Justice, Superior Court, Massachusetts, 1777–80; Judge, Supreme Court, Massachusetts, 1780–89	
Daniel, Peter V. (29)		Judge, Eastern District of Virginia, 1836–41
Davis, David (38)	Judge, Circuit Court, Illinois, 1848–62	

(Table continues)

Table 4-9   *(Continued)*

Justice	Judicial experience[a]	
(appointment number)	*State*	*Federal*
Day, William R. (60)	Judge, Court of Common Pleas, Ohio, 1886–90	Judge, Court of Appeals for the Sixth Circuit, 1899–1903
Duvall, Gabriel (18)	Chief Justice, General Court, Maryland, 1796–1802	
Ellsworth, Oliver (11)	Judge, Superior Court, Connecticut, 1785–89	
Field, Stephen J. (39)	Justice, Supreme Court, California, 1857–59; Chief Justice, Supreme Court, California, 1859–63	
Ginsburg, Ruth Bader (112)		Law clerk, Judge Edmund Palmieri, Southern District of New York, 1959–61; Judge, Court of Appeals for the District of Columbia, 1980–93
Gray, Horace (48)	Reporter, Supreme Court, Massachusetts, 1854–64; Associate Justice, Supreme Court, Massachusetts, 1864–73; Chief Justice, Supreme Court, Massachusetts, 1873–81	
Grier, Robert C. (32)	Presiding Judge, District Court, Pennsylvania, 1833–46	
Harlan, John Marshall I (45)	Judge, Franklin County Court, Kentucky, 1858–59	
Harlan, John Marshall II (93)		Judge, Court of Appeals for the Second Circuit, 1954–55
Holmes, Oliver W., Jr. (59)	Associate Justice, Supreme Court, Massachusetts, 1882–99; Chief Justice, Supreme Court, Massachusetts, 1899–1902	

Table 4-9 *(Continued)*

Justice	Judicial experience[a]	
(appointment number)	*State*	*Federal*
Hughes, Charles Evans (63, 76)		Judge, Permanent Court of Arbitration and International Court of Justice, 1926–30[b]
Hunt, Ward (43)	Judge, Court of Appeals, New York, 1866–68; Chief Judge, Court of Appeals, New York, 1868–69; Commissioner of Appeals, New York, 1869–73	
Iredell, James (6)	Judge, Superior Court, North Carolina, 1778	
Jackson, Howell E. (55)	Judge, Court of Arbitration, Tennessee, 1875–79	Judge, Sixth Judicial Circuit, 1886–91; Judge, Court of Appeals for the Sixth Circuit, 1891–93
Jay, John (1)	Chief Justice, Supreme Court, New York, 1777–78	
Johnson, Thomas (7)	Chief Judge, General Court, Maryland, 1790–91	
Johnson, William (15)	Judge, Court of Common Pleas, South Carolina, 1799–1804	
Kennedy, Anthony (109)		Judge, Court of Appeals for the Ninth Circuit, 1976–88
Lamar, Joseph R. (66)	Associate Justice, Supreme Court, Georgia, 1903–05	
Livingston, H. Brockholst (16)	Judge, Supreme Court, New York, 1802–07	
Lurton, Horace (62)	Chancellor in Equity, Tennessee, 1875–78; Judge, Supreme Court, Tennessee, 1886–93	Judge, Court of Appeals for the Sixth Circuit, 1893–1909

(Table continues)

Table 4-9   *(Continued)*

Justice (appointment number)	Judicial experience[a]	
	State	*Federal*
Marshall, Thurgood (100)		Judge, Court of Appeals for the Second Circuit, 1961–65
Matthews, Stanley (47)	Judge, Court of Common Pleas, Ohio, 1851–53; Judge, Superior Court, Ohio, 1863–65	
McKenna, Joseph (58)		Judge, Court of Appeals for the Ninth Circuit, 1892–97
McLean, John (22)	Judge, Supreme Court, Ohio, 1816–22	
Miller, Samuel (37)	Justice of the Peace, Kentucky, 1844	
Minton, Sherman (91)		Judge, Court of Appeals for the Seventh Circuit, 1941–49
Moore, Alfred (13)	Judge, Superior Court, North Carolina, 1799	
Murphy, Frank (83)	Judge, Recorder's Court, Detroit, Michigan, 1923–30	
Nelson, Samuel (30)	Judge, Circuit Court, New York, 1823–31; Associate Justice, Supreme Court, New York, 1831–37; Chief Justice, Supreme Court, New York, 1837–45	
O'Connor, Sandra Day (106)	Judge, Superior Court, Arizona, 1975–79; Judge, Court of Appeals, Arizona, 1979–81	
Peckham, Rufus W. (57)	Judge, Supreme Court, New York, 1883–86; Judge, Court of Appeals, New York, 1886–95	

Table 4-9 *(Continued)*

Justice (appointment number)	Judicial experience[a]	
	State	*Federal*
Pitney, Mahlon (67)	Associate Justice, Supreme Court, New Jersey, 1901–08; Chancellor, New Jersey, 1908–12	
Rehnquist, William (104, 107)		Law Clerk, Justice Robert Jackson, 1952–53
Rutledge, John (2, 9)	Chief Judge, Chancery Court, South Carolina, 1784–91	
Rutledge, Wiley B. (87)		Judge, Court of Appeals for the District of Columbia Circuit, 1939–43
Sanford, Edward T. (74)		Judge, Middle and Eastern Districts of Tennessee, 1908–23
Scalia, Antonin (108)		Judge, Court of Appeals for the District of Columbia Circuit, 1982–86
Souter, David H. (110)	Judge, Superior Court, New Hampshire, 1978–83; Judge, Supreme Court, New Hampshire, 1983–90	Judge, Court of Appeals for the First Circuit, 1990
Stevens, John Paul (105)		Law Clerk, Justice Wiley Rutledge, 1947–48; Judge, Court of Appeals for the Seventh Circuit, 1970–75
Stewart, Potter (96)		Judge, Court of Appeals for the Sixth Circuit, 1954–58
Strong, William (41)	Justice, Supreme Court, Pennsylvania, 1857–68	
Taft, William H. (71)	Judge, Superior Court, Ohio, 1887–90	Judge, Court of Appeals for the Sixth Circuit, 1892–1900

(Table continues)

Table 4-9   *(Continued)*

Justice *(appointment number)*	*Political experience*[a]	
	State	*Federal*
Thomas, Clarence (111)		Judge, Court of Appeals for the District of Columbia Circuit, 1990–91
Thompson, Smith (20)	Associate Justice, Supreme Court, New York, 1802–14; Chief Justice, Supreme Court, New York, 1814–18	
Todd, Thomas (17)	Clerk, Court of Appeals, Kentucky, 1799–1801; Judge, Court of Appeals, Kentucky, 1801–06; Chief Justice, Court of Appeals, Kentucky, 1806–07	Clerk, District of Kentucky, 1792–1801
Trimble, Robert (21)	Judge, Court of Appeals, Kentucky, 1807–09	Judge, District of Kentucky, 1817–26
Van Devanter, Willis (65)	Chief Justice, Supreme Court, Wyoming Territory, 1889–90	Judge, Court of Appeals for the Eighth Circuit, 1903–10
Vinson, Fred M. (89)		Judge, Court of Appeals for the District of Columbia Circuit, 1938–43
Wayne, James M. (24)	Judge, Court of Common Pleas, Savannah, Georgia, 1820–22; Judge, Superior Court, Georgia, 1822–28	
White, Byron R. (97)		Law Clerk, Chief Justice Fred M. Vinson, 1946–47
White, Edward D. (56, 64)	Associate Justice, Supreme Court, Louisiana, 1878–80	
Whittaker, Charles E. (95)		Judge, Western District of Missouri, 1954–56; Judge, Court of Appeals for the Eighth Circuit, 1956–57

Table 4-9   *(Continued)*

Justice	Political experience[a]	
(appointment number)	*State*	*Federal*
Woodbury, Levi (31)	Associate Justice, Superior Court, New Hampshire, 1817–23	
Woods, William B. (46)	Chancellor, Chancery Court, Alabama, 1868–69	Judge, Fifth Judicial Circuit, 1869–80

Note: The names of justices who held no local, state, or federal judicial branch position prior to taking seat on the Supreme Court have been omitted.

[a] Includes local, state, and federal judicial branch positions held by justice prior to taking seat on the Supreme Court.

[b] International jurisdiction; Hughes served in this capacity after his tenure on the Court as an associate justice, but prior to his second term on the Court as chief justice.

Sources: Joan Biskupic and Elder Witt, *Congressional Quarterly's Guide to the U.S. Supreme Court,* 3d ed. (Washington, D.C.: Congressional Quarterly, 1997); Leon Friedman and Fred L. Israel, eds., *The Justices of the United States Supreme Court: Their Lives and Major Opinions* (New York: R.R. Bowker, 1969–1978); Harold W. Chase et al., *Biographical Dictionary of the American Judiciary* (Detroit: Gale Research, 1976); *Judges of the United States,* 2d ed. (Washington, D.C.: Judicial Conference of the United States, 1983); *The National Cyclopaedia of American Biography* (New York: James T. White, various years); and *Dictionary of American Biography* (New York: Charles Scribner's Sons, various editions). Updated by the authors.

Table 4-10   Summary of Background Characteristics of the Justices of the United States

Characteristic	Number	Percentage
Family socioeconomic class background		
Upper class	35	32.4
Upper-middle class	28	25.9
Middle class	20	18.5
Lower-middle class	18	16.7
Lower class	7	6.5
Nationality background		
English, Irish, Scottish	89	82.4
German, Austrian, Russian	8	7.4
Spanish, French, Dutch, Italian	7	6.5
African	2	1.9
Scandinavian	2	1.9
Race		
Caucasian	106	98.1
African American	2	1.9
Sex		
Male	106	98.1
Female	2	1.9
Religion		
Protestant	92	85.2
Catholic	9	8.3
Jewish	7	6.5
Political party affiliation at time of appointment		
Democrat	43	39.8
Republican	43	39.8
Federalist	13	12.0
Democratic-Republican	7	6.5
Independent	1	0.9
Whig	1	0.9
Political experience prior to appointment		
Justices with judicial experience	73	67.6
Justices with legislative experience[a]	56	51.9
Justices with executive experience[b]	68	63.0
Age at time of appointment[c]		
30–39 years	4	3.6
40–49 years	28	25.0
50–59 years	59	52.7
60–69 years	21	18.8

Table 4-10   *(Continued)*

Characteristic	Number	Percentage
Length of tenure[d]		
30+ years	12	12.1
25–29 years	9	9.1
20–24 years	14	14.1
15–19 years	18	18.2
10–14 years	12	12.1
5–9 years	22	22.2
Less than 5 years	12	12.1

[a] Representatives sitting in local, state, colonial, territorial, and federal legislatures. Staff positions not included.
[b] Includes presidents, governors and their immediate staff; lieutenant governors; administrative and regulatory officials; justice department officials, prosecutors; school system administrators; mayors; postmasters; ambassadors.
[c] Includes both appointments for Justices White, Hughes, Stone, and Rehnquist who were successfully nominated, confirmed, and served as associate justice and chief justice.
[d] Excludes justices sitting in 2001.

Source: Compiled by the authors.

Table 4-11   Net Worth of the Justices, 2001

Justice (appointment number)	Net worth[a]
Ruth Bader Ginsburg (112)	$7,700,000–33,700,000
Stephen G. Breyer (113)	4,200,000–15,200,000
Sandra Day O'Connor (106)	2,800,000–6,400,000
John Paul Stevens (105)	1,300,000–2,700,000
David H. Souter (110)	1,000,000–5,100,000
Antonin Scalia (108)	500,000–1,300,000
William H. Rehnquist (104, 107)	510,000–1,200,000
Clarence Thomas (111)	150,000–410,000
Anthony M. Kennedy (109)	45,000–180,000

[a] Federal legislation requires Supreme Court justices to file periodic financial disclosure statements. The forms ask the justices to list their assets and liabilities within specified ranges, thus making the final totals somewhat vague. The reported figures may significantly underestimate the actual net worth of the justices because not all assets need to be disclosed. For example, the justices are not required to report the worth of their primary residences, personal property, and certain retirement funds. The financial reports are available to the general public.

Sources: Ethics in Government Act financial disclosure forms for 2001; *Atlanta Journal-Constitution,* June 1, 2002; *Washington Post,* June 1, 2002.

Table 4-12 Supreme Court Nominees

President/nominee	Year	Position at time of nomination	Age	Home state
George Washington:				
John Jay[a]	1789	U.S. secretary of foreign affairs	43	New York
John Rutledge	1789	South Carolina Chancery Court judge	50	South Carolina
William Cushing	1789	Massachusetts Supreme Court judge	57	Massachusetts
Robert H. Harrison[b]	1789	Maryland General Court judge	44	Maryland
James Wilson	1789	Lawyer, business speculator	47	Pennsylvania
John Blair, Jr.	1789	Virginia Supreme Court judge	57	Virginia
James Iredell	1790	Lawyer	38	North Carolina
Thomas Johnson	1791	Maryland General Court judge	58	Maryland
William Paterson[b]	1793	New Jersey governor	47	New Jersey
William Paterson	1793	New Jersey governor	47	New Jersey
John Rutledge[a, b]	1795	South Carolina chief justice	55	South Carolina
William Cushing[a, b]	1796	Sitting associate justice	63	Massachusetts
Samuel Chase	1796	Maryland General Court judge	54	Maryland
Oliver Ellsworth[a]	1796	U.S. senator	50	Connecticut
John Adams:				
Bushrod Washington	1798	Lawyer	36	Virginia
Alfred Moore	1799	North Carolina Superior Court judge	44	North Carolina
John Jay[a, b]	1800	New York governor	55	New York
John Marshall[a]	1801	U.S. secretary of state	45	Virginia
Thomas Jefferson:				
William Johnson	1804	South Carolina Common Pleas judge	33	South Carolina
H. Brockholst Livingston	1806	New York Supreme Court judge	49	New York
Thomas Todd	1807	Kentucky chief justice	42	Kentucky

(Table continues)

Table 4-12 (*Continued*)

President/nominee	Year	Position at time of nomination	Age	Home state
James Madison:				
Levi Lincoln[b]	1811	Massachusetts Governor's Council	61	Massachusetts
Alexander Wolcott[b]	1811	U.S. revenue collector	52	Connecticut
John Quincy Adams[b]	1811	U.S. minister to Russia	43	Massachusetts
Gabriel Duvall	1811	U.S. controller of the Treasury	58	Maryland
Joseph Story	1811	Speaker of the Massachusetts House	32	Massachusetts
James Monroe:				
Smith Thompson	1823	U.S. secretary of the Navy	55	New York
John Quincy Adams:				
Robert Trimble	1826	U.S. District Court judge	49	Kentucky
John Crittenden[b]	1828	U.S. attorney	41	Kentucky
Andrew Jackson:				
John McLean	1829	U.S. postmaster general	43	Ohio
Henry Baldwin	1830	Lawyer, businessman	49	Pennsylvania
James M. Wayne	1835	U.S. representative	45	Georgia
Roger Brooke Taney[b]	1835	Lawyer	57	Maryland
Roger Brooke Taney[a]	1835	Lawyer	58	Maryland
Philip P. Barbour	1835	U.S. District Court judge	51	Virginia
William Smith[b]	1837	Alabama state representative	75	Alabama
John Catron	1837	Lawyer	51	Tennessee
Martin Van Buren:				
John McKinley	1837	U.S. senator	57	Alabama
Peter V. Daniel	1841	U.S. District Court judge	56	Virginia

John Tyler:				
John C. Spencer[b]	1844	U.S. secretary of the Treasury	56	New York
Reuben H. Walworth[b]	1844	New York chancellor	55	New York
Edward King[b]	1844	Pennsylvania Common Pleas judge	50	Pennsylvania
Edward King[b]	1844	Pennsylvania Common Pleas judge	50	Pennsylvania
Samuel Nelson	1845	New York Supreme Court judge	52	New York
John M. Read[b]	1845	Lawyer	47	Pennsylvania
James K. Polk:				
George W. Woodward[b]	1845	Pennsylvania District Court judge	36	Pennsylvania
Levi Woodbury	1845	U.S. senator	56	New Hampshire
Robert C. Grier	1846	U.S. District Court judge	52	Pennsylvania
Millard Fillmore:				
Benjamin R. Curtis	1851	Massachusetts state representative	42	Massachusetts
Edward A. Bradford[b]	1852	Lawyer	38	Louisiana
George E. Badger[b]	1853	U.S. senator	57	North Carolina
William C. Micou[b]	1853	Lawyer	47	Louisiana
Franklin Pierce:				
John A. Campbell	1853	Lawyer	41	Alabama
James Buchanan:				
Nathan Clifford	1857	Lawyer	54	Maine
Jeremiah S. Black[b]	1861	U.S. secretary of state	51	Pennsylvania
Abraham Lincoln:				
Noah H. Swayne	1862	Lawyer	56	Ohio
Samuel F. Miller	1862	Lawyer	46	Iowa
David Davis	1862	Illinois Circuit Court judge	47	Illinois
Stephen J. Field	1863	California Supreme Court judge	46	California
Salmon P. Chase[a]	1864	U.S. secretary of the Treasury	56	Ohio

(Table continues)

Table 4-12 *(Continued)*

President/nominee	Year	Position at time of nomination	Age	Home state
Andrew Johnson:				
Henry Stanbery[b]	1866	Lawyer	63	Ohio
Ulysses S. Grant:				
Ebenezer R. Hoar[b]	1869	U.S. attorney general	53	Massachusetts
Edwin M. Stanton[b]	1869	Lawyer	54	Ohio
William Strong	1870	Lawyer	61	Pennsylvania
Joseph P. Bradley	1870	Lawyer	57	New Jersey
Ward Hunt	1872	New York commissioner of appeals	62	New York
George H. Williams[a, b]	1873	U.S. attorney general	50	Oregon
Caleb Cushing[a, b]	1874	U.S. minister to Spain	73	Massachusetts
Morrison R. Waite[a]	1874	Ohio Constitutional Convention, lawyer	57	Ohio
Rutherford B. Hayes:				
John Marshall Harlan I	1877	Louisiana Reconstruction Commission	44	Kentucky
William B. Woods	1880	U.S. Circuit Court judge	56	Georgia
Stanley Matthews[b]	1881	Lawyer	56	Ohio
James Garfield:				
Stanley Matthews	1881	Lawyer	56	Ohio
Chester Arthur:				
Horace Gray	1881	Massachusetts chief justice	53	Massachusetts
Roscoe Conkling[b]	1882	Lawyer	52	New York
Samuel Blatchford	1882	U.S. Circuit Court judge	62	New York

Grover Cleveland:				
Lucius Q. C. Lamar	U.S. secretary of the Interior	1887	62	Mississippi
Melville W. Fuller[a]	Lawyer	1888	55	Illinois
Benjamin Harrison:				
David J. Brewer	U.S. Circuit Court judge	1889	52	Kansas
Henry B. Brown	U.S. District Court judge	1890	54	Michigan
George Shiras, Jr.	Lawyer	1892	60	Pennsylvania
Howell E. Jackson	U.S. Court of Appeals judge	1893	60	Tennessee
Grover Cleveland:				
Willia B. Hornblower[b]	Lawyer	1893	42	New York
Wheeler H. Peckham[b]	Lawyer	1894	61	New York
Edward D. White	U.S. senator	1894	48	Louisiana
Rufus W. Peckham	New York Court of Appeals judge	1895	57	New York
William McKinley:				
Joseph McKenna	U.S. attorney general	1897	54	California
Theodore Roosevelt:				
Oliver W. Holmes, Jr.	Massachusetts chief justice	1902	61	Massachusetts
William Rufus Day	U.S. Court of Appeals judge	1903	53	Ohio
William H. Moody	U.S. attorney general	1906	52	Massachusetts
William Howard Taft:				
Horace H. Lurton	U.S. Court of Appeals judge	1909	65	Tennessee
Charles E. Hughes	New York governor	1910	48	New York
Edward D. White[a]	Sitting associate justice	1910	65	Louisiana
Willis Van Devanter	U.S. Court of Appeals judge	1910	51	Wyoming
Joseph Rucker Lamar	Lawyer	1910	53	Georgia
Mahlon Pitney	New Jersey chancellor	1912	54	New Jersey

(Table continues)

Table 4-12 (*Continued*)

President/nominee	Year	Position at time of nomination	Age	Home state
Woodrow Wilson:				
James C. McReynolds	1914	U.S. attorney general	52	Tennessee
Louis D. Brandeis	1916	Lawyer	59	Massachusetts
John H. Clarke	1916	U.S. District Court judge	58	Ohio
Warren Harding:				
William H. Taft[a]	1921	Law school professor	63	Ohio
George Sutherland	1922	Lawyer	60	Utah
Pierce Butler	1922	Lawyer	56	Minnesota
Edward T. Sanford	1923	U.S. District Court judge	57	Tennessee
Calvin Coolidge:				
Harlan Fiske Stone	1925	Law school dean	52	New York
Herbert Hoover:				
Charles E. Hughes[a]	1930	International Court of Justice judge	67	New York
John J. Parker[b]	1930	U.S. Court of Appeals judge	44	North Carolina
Owen J. Roberts	1930	U.S. special prosecutor	55	Pennsylvania
Benjamin N. Cardozo	1932	New York Court of Appeals judge	61	New York
Franklin Roosevelt:				
Hugo L. Black	1937	U.S. senator	51	Alabama
Stanley F. Reed	1938	U.S. solicitor general	53	Kentucky
Felix Frankfurter	1939	Law school professor	56	Massachusetts
William O. Douglas	1939	Securities and Exchange Commission	40	Connecticut
Frank Murphy	1940	U.S. attorney general	49	Michigan
Harlan Fiske Stone[a]	1941	Sitting associate justice	68	New York
James Francis Byrnes	1941	U.S. senator	62	South Carolina

Name	Year	Previous position	Age	State
Robert H. Jackson	1941	U.S. attorney general	49	New York
Wiley B. Rutledge	1943	U.S. Court of Appeals judge	48	Iowa
Harry S. Truman:				
Harold H. Burton	1945	U.S. senator	57	Ohio
Fred M. Vinson[a]	1946	U.S. secretary of the Treasury	56	Kentucky
Tom C. Clark	1949	U.S. attorney general	49	Texas
Sherman Minton	1949	U.S. Court of Appeals judge	58	Indiana
Dwight Eisenhower:				
Earl Warren[a]	1953	California governor	62	California
John Marshall Harlan II	1954	U.S. Court of Appeals judge	55	New York
William J. Brennan, Jr.	1956	New Jersey Supreme Court judge	50	New Jersey
Charles E. Whittaker	1957	U.S. Court of Appeals judge	56	Missouri
Potter Stewart	1959	U.S. Court of Appeals judge	43	Ohio
John Kennedy:				
Byron R. White	1962	U.S. deputy attorney general	44	Colorado
Arthur J. Goldberg	1962	U.S. secretary of Labor	54	Illinois
Lyndon Johnson:				
Abe Fortas	1965	Lawyer	55	Tennessee
Thurgood Marshall	1967	U.S. solicitor general	58	New York
Abe Fortas[a,b]	1968	Sitting associate justice	58	Tennessee
Homer Thornberry[b]	1968	U.S. Court of Appeals judge	59	Texas
Richard Nixon:				
Warren E. Burger[a]	1969	U.S. Court of Appeals judge	61	Minnesota
Clement Haynsworth, Jr.[b]	1969	U.S. Court of Appeals judge	56	South Carolina
G. Harrold Carswell[b]	1970	U.S. Court of Appeals judge	50	Florida
Harry A. Blackmun	1970	U.S. Court of Appeals judge	61	Minnesota
Lewis F. Powell, Jr.	1971	Lawyer	64	Virginia
William H. Rehnquist	1971	U.S. assistant attorney general	47	Arizona

(Table continues)

Table 4-12 (*Continued*)

President/nominee	Year	Position at time of nomination	Age	Home state
Gerald Ford:				
John Paul Stevens	1975	U.S. Court of Appeals judge	55	Illinois
Ronald Reagan:				
Sandra Day O'Connor	1981	Arizona Appeals Court judge	51	Arizona
William H. Rehnquist[a]	1986	Sitting associate justice	61	Arizona
Antonin Scalia	1986	U.S. Court of Appeals judge	50	Virginia
Robert H. Bork[b]	1987	U.S. Court of Appeals judge	60	D.C.
Anthony M. Kennedy	1987	U.S. Court of Appeals judge	51	California
George Bush:				
David H. Souter	1990	U.S. Court of Appeals judge	50	New Hampshire
Clarence Thomas	1991	U.S. Court of Appeals judge	43	Georgia
Bill Clinton:				
Ruth Bader Ginsburg	1993	U.S. Court of Appeals judge	60	New York
Stephen G. Breyer	1994	U.S. Court of Appeals judge	55	Massachusetts

Note: Nominees are ordered chronologically according to the dates of their nominations or recess appointments, whichever came first. Only names of those officially nominated and sent to the Senate for confirmation are included. For example, Daniel Ginsburg, nominated by Ronald Reagan in 1987, is not included because his nomination was withdrawn before official submission to the Senate.

[a] Nomination for chief justice.
[b] Unsuccessful nomination. The nominee either failed to obtain Senate confirmation or did not serve after being confirmed.

Sources: Joan Biskupic and Elder Witt, *Congressional Quarterly's Guide to the U.S. Supreme Court*, 3d ed. (Washington, D.C.: Congressional Quarterly, 1997); Leon Friedman and Fred L. Israel, eds., *The Justices of the United States Supreme Court: Their Lives and Major Opinions* (New York: R.R. Bowker, 1969–1978); Harold W. Chase et al., *Biographical Dictionary of the American Judiciary* (Detroit: Gale Research, 1976); *Judges of the United States*, 2d ed. (Washington, D.C.: Judicial Conference of the United States, 1983); *The National Cyclopaedia of American Biography* (New York: James T. White, various years); and *Dictionary of American Biography* (New York: Charles Scribner's Sons, various editions). Updated by the authors.

Table 4-13 Supreme Court Nominees and the Vacancies To Be Filled

President/nominee	State	Party at time of appointment[a]	Previous party affiliations[a]	Justice to be replaced Name	Justice to be replaced State	Justice to be replaced Party[a]
George Washington (Fed):						
John Jay[b]	NY	Fed		c	—	—
John Rutledge	SC	Fed		c	—	—
William Cushing	MA	Fed		c	—	—
Robert H. Harrison[d]	MD	Fed		c	—	—
James Wilson	PA	Fed		c	—	—
John Blair, Jr.	VA	Fed		c	—	—
James Iredell	NC	Fed		—	—	—
Thomas Johnson	MD	Fed		John Rutledge	SC	Fed
William Paterson[d]	NJ	Fed		Thomas Johnson	MD	Fed
William Paterson	NJ	Fed		Thomas Johnson	MD	Fed
John Rutledge[b, d]	SC	Fed		John Jay	NY	Fed
William Cushing[b, d]	MA	Fed		John Jay	NY	Fed
Samuel Chase	MD	Fed		John Blair	VA	Fed
Oliver Ellsworth[b]	CT	Fed		John Jay	NY	Fed
John Adams (Fed):						
Bushrod Washington	VA	Fed		James Wilson	PA	Fed
Alfred Moore	NC	Fed		James Iredell	NC	Fed
John Jay[b, d]	NY	Fed		Oliver Ellsworth	CT	Fed
John Marshall[b]	VA	Fed		Oliver Ellsworth	CT	Fed
Thomas Jefferson (Dem-Rep):						
William Johnson	SC	Dem-Rep		Alfred Moore	NC	Fed
H. Brockholst Livingston	NY	Dem-Rep	Fed	William Paterson	NJ	Fed
Thomas Todd	KY	Dem-Rep		e	—	—

(Table continues)

Table 4-13 *(Continued)*

President/nominee	State	Party at time of appointment[a]	Previous party affiliations[a]	Justice to be replaced		
				Name	State	Party[a]
James Madison (Dem-Rep):						
Levi Lincoln[d]	MA	Dem-Rep		William Cushing	MA	Fed
Alexander Wolcott[d]	CT	Dem-Rep		William Cushing	MA	Fed
John Quincy Adams[d]	MA	Dem-Rep		William Cushing	MA	Fed
Gabriel Duvall	MD	Dem-Rep		Samuel Chase	MD	Fed
Joseph Story	MA	Dem-Rep		William Cushing	MA	Fed
James Monroe (Dem-Rep):						
Smith Thompson	NY	Dem-Rep		H. Brockholst Livingston	NY	Dem-Rep
John Quincy Adams (Dem-Rep):						
Robert Trimble	KY	Dem-Rep		Thomas Todd	KY	Dem-Rep
John Crittenden[d]	KY	Dem-Rep		Robert Trimble	KY	Dem-Rep
Andrew Jackson (Dem):						
John McLean	OH	Dem	Dem-Rep	Robert Trimble	KY	Dem-Rep
Henry Baldwin	PA	Dem	Fed	Bushrod Washington	VA	Fed
James M. Wayne	GA	Dem		William Johnson	SC	Dem-Rep
Roger Brooke Taney[d]	MD	Dem	Fed	Gabriel Duvall	MD	Dem-Rep
Roger Brooke Taney[b]	MD	Dem	Fed	John Marshall	VA	Fed
Philip P. Barbour	VA	Dem	Dem-Rep	Gabriel Duvall	MD	Dem-Rep
William Smith[d]	AL	Dem		[e]	—	—
John Catron	TN	Dem		[e]	—	—
Martin Van Buren (Dem):						
John McKinley	AL	Dem		[e]	—	—
Peter V. Daniel	VA	Dem	Dem-Rep	Philip Barbour	VA	Dem

John Tyler (Dem):						
John C. Spencer	NY	Whig		Smith Thompson	NY	Dem-Rep
Reuben H. Walworth[d]	NY	Dem		Smith Thompson	NY	Dem-Rep
Edward King[d]	PA	Dem		Henry Baldwin	PA	Dem
Edward King[d]	PA	Dem		Henry Baldwin	PA	Dem
Samuel Nelson	NY	Dem	Dem-Rep	Smith Thompson	NY	Dem-Rep
John M. Read[d]	PA	Dem		Henry Baldwin	PA	Dem
James K. Polk (Dem):						
George W. Woodward[d]	PA	Dem		Henry Baldwin	PA	Dem
Levi Woodbury	NH	Dem	Dem-Rep	Joseph Story	MA	Dem-Rep
Robert C. Grier	PA	Dem		Henry Baldwin	PA	Dem
Millard Fillmore (Whig):						
Benjamin R. Curtis	MA	Whig		Levi Woodbury	NH	Dem
Edward A. Bradford[d]	LA	Whig		John McKinley	AL	Dem
George E. Badger[d]	NC	Whig		John McKinley	AL	Dem
William C. Micou[d]	LA	Whig		John McKinley	AL	Dem
Franklin Pierce (Dem):						
John A. Campbell	AL	Dem		John McKinley	AL	Dem
James Buchanan (Dem):						
Nathan Clifford	ME	Dem		Benjamin Curtis	MA	Whig
Jeremiah S. Black[d]	PA	Dem		Peter Daniel	VA	Dem
Abraham Lincoln (Rep):						
Noah H. Swayne	OH	Rep	Dem	John McLean	OH	Dem
Samuel F. Miller	IA	Rep	Whig	Peter Daniel	VA	Dem
David Davis	IL	Rep	Whig	John Campbell	AL	Dem

(Table continues)

Table 4-13 (Continued)

President/nominee	State	Party at time of appointment[a]	Previous party affiliations[a]	Justice to be replaced		
				Name	State	Party[a]
Stephen J. Field	CA	Dem		e	—	—
Salmon P. Chase	OH	Rep	Whig, Anti-Slavery, Liberty, Free Soil	Roger Taney	MD	Dem
Reuben H. Walworth[d]	NY	Dem		Smith Thompson	NY	Dem-Rep
Andrew Johnson (Dem):						
Henry Stanbery[d]	OH	Rep		John Catron	TN	Dem
Ulysses S. Grant (Rep):						
Ebenezer R. Hoar[d]	MA	Rep		f	—	—
Edwin M. Stanton[d]	OH	Rep		Robert Grier	PA	Dem
William Strong	PA	Rep	Dem	Robert Grier	PA	Dem
Joseph P. Bradley	NJ	Rep	Whig	f	—	—
Ward Hunt	NY	Rep	Dem, Free Soil	Samuel Nelson	NY	Dem
George H. Williams[b, d]	OR	Rep		Salmon Chase	OH	Rep
Caleb Cushing[b, d]	MA	Rep		Salmon Chase	OH	Rep
Morrison R. Waite[c]	OH	Rep	Whig	Salmon Chase	OH	Rep

Nominee	State	Party		Justice Replaced	State	Party
Rutherford B. Hayes (Rep):						
John Marshall Harlan I	KY	Rep	Whig, Know-Nothing, Union	David Davis	IL	Rep
William B. Woods	GA	Rep	Dem	William Strong	PA	Rep
Stanley Matthews[d]	OH	Rep	Dem	Noah Swayne	OH	Rep
James Garfield (Rep):						
Stanley Matthews	OH	Rep		Noah Swayne	OH	Rep
Chester Arthur (Rep):						
Horace Gray	MA	Rep	Free Soil	Nathan Clifford	ME	Dem
Roscoe Conkling[d]	NY	Rep		Ward Hunt	NY	Rep
Samuel Blatchford	NY	Rep		Ward Hunt	NY	Rep
Grover Cleveland (Dem):						
Lucius Q. C. Lamar	MS	Dem		William Woods	GA	Rep
Melville W. Fuller[b]	IL	Dem		Morrison Waite	OH	Rep
Benjamin Harrison (Rep):						
David J. Brewer	KS	Rep		Stanley Matthews	OH	Rep
Henry B. Brown	MI	Rep		Samuel Miller	IA	Rep
George Shiras, Jr.	PA	Rep		Joseph Bradley	NJ	Rep
Howell E. Jackson	TN	Dem	Whig	Lucius Q. C. Lamar	MS	Dem
Grover Cleveland (Dem):						
William B. Hornblower[d]	NY	Dem		Samuel Blatchford	NY	Rep
Wheeler H. Peckham[d]	NY	Dem		Samuel Blatchford	NY	Rep
Edward D. White	LA	Dem		Samuel Blatchford	NY	Rep
Rufus W. Peckham	NY	Dem		Howell Jackson	TN	Dem

(Table continues)

Table 4-13 (*Continued*)

President/nominee	State	Party at time of appointment[a]	Previous party affiliations[a]	Justice to be replaced		
				Name	State	Party[a]
William McKinley (Rep):						
Joseph McKenna	CA	Rep	Dem	Stephen Field	CA	Dem
Theodore Roosevelt (Rep):						
Oliver W. Holmes, Jr.	MA	Rep		Horace Gray	MA	Rep
William Rufus Day	OH	Rep		George Shiras	PA	Rep
William H. Moody	MA	Rep		Henry B. Brown	MI	Rep
William Howard Taft (Rep):						
Horace H. Lurton	TN	Dem		Rufus Peckham	NY	Dem
Charles E. Hughes	NY	Rep		David Brewer	KS	Rep
Edward D. White[c]	LA	Dem		Melville Fuller	IL	Dem
Willis Van Devanter	WY	Rep		Edward White	LA	Dem
Joseph Rucker Lamar	GA	Dem		William Moody	MA	Rep
Mahlon Pitney	NJ	Rep		John M. Harlan I	KY	Rep
Woodrow Wilson (Dem):						
James C. McReynolds	TN	Dem		Horace Lurton	TN	Dem
Louis D. Brandeis	MA	Rep[g]		Joseph Rucker Lamar	GA	Dem
John H. Clarke	OH	Dem		Charles E. Hughes	NY	Rep
Warren Harding (Rep):						
William H. Taft[b]	OH	Rep		Edward White	LA	Dem
George Sutherland	UT	Rep		John H. Clarke	OH	Dem
Pierce Butler	MN	Dem		William Rufus Day	OH	Rep
Edward T. Sanford	TN	Rep		Mahlon Pitney	NJ	Rep

Nominee	State	Party	Replaced	State	Party
Calvin Coolidge (Rep)					
Harlan Fiske Stone	NY	Rep	Joseph McKenna	CA	Rep
Herbert Hoover (Rep):					
Charles E. Hughes[b]	NY	Rep	William H. Taft	OH	Rep
John J. Parker[d]	NC	Rep	Edward T. Sanford	TN	Rep
Owen J. Roberts	PA	Rep	Edward T. Sanford	TN	Rep
Benjamin N. Cardozo	NY	Dem	Oliver W. Holmes	MA	Rep
Franklin Roosevelt (Dem):					
Hugo L. Black	AL	Dem	Willis Van Devanter	WY	Rep
Stanley F. Reed	KY	Dem	George Sutherland	UT	Rep
Felix Frankfurter	MA	Ind	Benjamin Cardozo	NY	Dem
William O. Douglas	CT	Dem	Louis D. Brandeis	MA	Rep[g]
Frank Murphy	MI	Dem	Pierce Butler	MN	Dem
Harlan Fiske Stone[b]	NY	Rep	Charles E. Hughes	NY	Rep
James Francis Byrnes	SC	Dem	James McReynolds	TN	Dem
Robert H. Jackson	NY	Dem	Harlan Fiske Stone	NY	Rep
Wiley B. Rutledge	IA	Dem	James F. Byrnes	SC	Dem
Harry S Truman (Dem):					
Harold H. Burton	OH	Rep	Owen Roberts	PA	Rep
Fred M. Vinson[b]	KY	Dem	Harlan Fiske Stone	NY	Rep
Tom C. Clark	TX	Dem	Frank Murphy	MI	Dem
Sherman Minton	IN	Dem	Wiley B. Rutledge	IA	Dem
Dwight Eisenhower (Rep):					
Earl Warren[c]	CA	Rep	Fred Vinson	KY	Dem
John Marshall Harlan II	NY	Rep	Robert Jackson	NY	Dem
William J. Brennan, Jr.	NJ	Dem	Sherman Minton	IN	Dem
Charles E. Whittaker	MO	Rep	Stanley Reed	KY	Dem
Potter Stewart	OH	Rep	Harold Burton	OH	Rep

(Table continues)

Table 4-13 (Continued)

President/nominee	State	Party at time of appointment[a]	Previous party affiliations[a]	Justice to be replaced		
				Name	State	Party[a]
John Kennedy (Dem):						
Byron R. White	CO	Dem		Charles Whittaker	MO	Rep
Arthur J. Goldberg	IL	Dem		Felix Frankfurter	MA	Ind
Lyndon Johnson (Dem):						
Abe Fortas	TN	Dem		Arthur Goldberg	IL	Dem
Thurgood Marshall	NY	Dem		Tom C. Clark	TX	Dem
Abe Fortas[b,d]	TN	Dem		Earl Warren	CA	Rep
Homer Thornberry[d]	TX	Dem		Abe Fortas	TN	Dem
Richard Nixon (Rep):						
Warren E. Burger	MN	Rep		Earl Warren	CA	Rep
Clement Haynsworth, Jr.[d]	SC	Dem		Abe Fortas	TN	Dem
G. Harrold Carswell[d]	FL	Rep		Abe Fortas	TN	Dem
Harry A. Blackmun	MN	Rep		Abe Fortas	TN	Dem
Lewis F. Powell, Jr.	VA	Dem		Hugo Black	AL	Dem
William H. Rehnquist	AZ	Rep		John M. Harlan II	NY	Rep
Gerald Ford (Rep):						
John Paul Stevens	IL	Rep		William O. Douglas	CT	Dem
Ronald Reagan (Rep):						
Sandra Day O'Connor	AZ	Rep		Potter Stewart	OH	Rep
William H. Rehnquist[b]	AZ	Rep		Warren E. Burger	MN	Rep
Antonin Scalia	VA	Rep		William Rehnquist	AZ	Rep
Robert H. Bork[d]	DC	Rep		Lewis Powell	VA	Dem
Anthony M. Kennedy	CA	Rep		Lewis Powell	VA	Dem

George Bush (Rep):					
David H. Souter	NH	Rep	William J. Brennan	NJ	Dem
Clarence Thomas	GA	Rep	Thurgood Marshall	NY	Dem
Bill Clinton (Dem):					
Ruth Bader Ginsburg	NY	Dem	Byron White	CO	Dem
Stephen G. Breyer	MA	Dem	Harry A. Blackmun	MN	Rep

Note: Nominees are ordered chronologically according to the dates of their nominations or recess appointments, whichever came first. Only names of those officially nominated and sent to the Senate for confirmation are included.

[a] "Fed" indicates Federalist, "Dem-Rep" indicates Democratic Republican, "Dem" indicates Democrat, "Rep" indicates Republican, "Ind" indicates independent.

[b] Nomination for chief justice.

[c] Indicates original appointment.

[d] Unsuccessful nomination. The nominee either failed to obtain Senate confirmation or did not serve after being confirmed.

[e] Newly created seat.

[f] This seat was temporarily abolished upon the death of Justice James Wayne in 1867 as part of a congressional strategy to remove any opportunity for President Andrew Johnson to appoint a justice to the Court. Shortly after Ulysses Grant captured the presidency, the Republican Congress reestablished the seat. As part of the same strategy, Congress also abolished the seat held by James Catron. The Catron seat was not reestablished.

[g] Early in his career, Louis Brandeis registered as a Republican and officially remained so at the time of his nomination. Many scholars, however, classify him as a Democrat because he underwent a significant change in political identification in his later adult years and openly supported some Democratic candidates.

Sources: Joan Biskupic and Elder Witt, *Congressional Quarterly's Guide to the U.S. Supreme Court*, 3d ed. (Washington, D.C.: Congressional Quarterly, 1997); Leon Friedman and Fred L. Israel, eds., *The Justices of the United States Supreme Court: Their Lives and Major Opinions* (New York: R.R. Bowker, 1969–1978); Harold W. Chase et al., *Biographical Dictionary of the American Judiciary* (Detroit: Gale Research, 1976); *Judges of the United States*, 2d ed. (Washington, D.C.: Judicial Conference of the United States, 1983); John R. Schmidhauser, *Supreme Court Justices Biographical Data 1958* (Ann Arbor, Mich.: Inter-University Consortium for Political Research, 1972); *The National Cyclopaedia of American Biography* (New York: James T. White, various years); and *Dictionary of American Biography* (New York: Charles Scribner's Sons, various editions). Updated by the authors. We depart from CQ and follow the coding of Robert Scigliano, *The Supreme Court and the Presidency* (New York: Free Press, 1971), for John Tyler's and Andrew Johnson's political party.

Table 4-14 Senate Action on Supreme Court Nominees

President	Party	Nominee	Date of appointment	Confirmation or other action	Vote
Washington	Fed	John Jay[a]	Sept. 24, 1789	Sept. 26, 1789	Voice
		John Rutledge	Sept. 24, 1789	Sept. 26, 1789	Voice
		William Cushing	Sept. 24, 1789	Sept. 26, 1789	Voice
		Robert H. Harrison	Sept. 24, 1789	Sept. 26, 1789	Declined
		James Wilson	Sept. 24, 1789	Sept. 26, 1789	Voice
		John Blair	Sept. 24, 1789	Sept. 26, 1789	Voice
		James Iredell	Feb. 8, 1790	Feb. 10, 1790	Voice
		Thomas Johnson	Nov. 1, 1791	Nov. 7, 1791	Voice
		William Paterson	Feb. 27, 1793	Feb. 28, 1793	Withdrawn
		William Paterson	March 4, 1793	March 4, 1793	Voice
		John Rutledge[a]	July 1, 1795	Dec. 15, 1795	Rejected, 10–14
		William Cushing[a]	Jan. 26, 1796	Jan. 27, 1796	Declined
		Samuel Chase	Jan. 26, 1796	Jan. 27, 1796	Voice
		Oliver Ellsworth[a]	March 3, 1796	March 4, 1796	21–1
J. Adams	Fed	Bushrod Washington	Dec. 19, 1798	Dec. 20, 1798	Voice
		Alfred Moore	Dec. 6, 1799	Dec. 10, 1799	Voice
		John Jay[a]	Dec. 18, 1800	Dec. 19, 1800	Declined
		John Marshall[a]	Jan. 20, 1801	Jan. 27, 1801	Voice
Jefferson	D-R	William Johnson	March 22, 1804	March 24, 1804	Voice
		H. Brockholst Livingston	Dec. 13, 1806	Dec. 17, 1806	Voice
		Thomas Todd	Feb. 28, 1807	March 3, 1807	Voice
Madison	D-R	Levi Lincoln	Jan. 2, 1811	Jan. 3, 1811	Declined
		Alexander Walcott	Feb. 4, 1811	Feb. 13, 1811	Rejected, 9–24

President	Party	Nominee			
		John Quincy Adams	Feb. 21, 1811	Feb. 22, 1811	Declined
		Joseph Story	Nov. 15, 1811	Nov. 18, 1811	Voice
		Gabriel Duvall	Nov. 15, 1811	Nov. 18, 1811	Voice
Monroe	D-R	Smith Thompson	Dec. 8, 1823	Dec. 19, 1823	Voice
J.Q. Adams	D-R	Robert Trimble	April 11, 1826	May 9, 1826	27–5
		John J. Crittendon	Dec. 17, 1828	Feb. 12, 1829	Postponed
Jackson	Dem	John McLean	March 6, 1829	March 7, 1829	Voice
		Henry Baldwin	Jan. 4, 1830	Jan. 6, 1830	41–2
		James Wayne	Jan. 7, 1835	Jan. 9, 1835	Voice
		Roger B. Taney	Jan. 15, 1835	March 15, 1835	Postponed
		Roger B. Taney[a]	Dec. 28, 1835	March 15, 1836	29–15
		Philip P. Barbour	Dec. 28, 1835	March 15, 1836	30–11
		William Smith	March 3, 1837	March 8, 1837	23–16, declined
		John Catron	March 3, 1837	March 8, 1837	28–15
Van Buren	Dem	John McKinley	Sept. 18, 1837	Sept. 25, 1837	Voice
		Peter V. Daniel	Feb. 26, 1841	March 2, 1841	22–5
Tyler	Dem	John Spencer	Jan. 9, 1844	Jan. 31, 1844	Rejected, 21–26
		Reuben H. Walworth	March 13, 1844	June 17, 1844	Withdrawn
		Edward King	June 5, 1844	June 15, 1844	Postponed
		Edward King	Dec. 4, 1844	Feb. 7, 1845	Withdrawn
		Samuel Nelson	Feb. 4, 1845	Feb. 14, 1845	Voice
		John M. Read	Feb. 7, 1845	No action	
Polk	Dem	George G. Woodward	Dec. 23, 1845	Jan. 22, 1846	Rejected, 20–29
		Levi Woodbury	Dec. 23, 1845	Jan. 3, 1846	Voice
		Robert C. Grier	Aug. 3, 1846	Aug. 4, 1846	Voice

(Table continues)

Table 4-14 (*Continued*)

President	Party	Nominee	Date of appointment	Confirmation or other action	Vote
Fillmore	Whig	Benjamin Curtis	Dec. 11, 1851	Dec. 29, 1851	Voice
		Edward A. Bradford	Aug. 16, 1852	No action	
		George E. Badger	Jan. 10, 1853	Feb. 11, 1853	Postponed
		William Micou	Feb. 24, 1853	No action	
Pierce	Dem	John A. Campbell	March 22, 1853	March 25, 1853	Voice
Buchanan	Dem	Nathan Clifford	Dec. 9, 1857	Jan. 12, 1858	26–23
		Jeremiah S. Black	Feb. 5, 1861	Feb. 21, 1861	Rejected, 25–26
Lincoln	Rep	Noah H. Swayne	Jan. 21, 1862	Jan. 24, 1862	38–1
		Samuel F. Miller	July 16, 1862	July 16, 1862	Voice
		David Davis	Dec. 1, 1862	Dec. 8, 1862	Voice
		Stephen J. Field	March 6, 1863	March 10, 1863	Voice
		Salmon P. Chase	Dec. 6, 1864	Dec. 6, 1864	Voice
A. Johnson	Dem	Henry Stanbery	April 16, 1866	No action	
Grant	Rep	Ebenezer R. Hoar	Dec. 15, 1869	Feb. 3, 1870	Rejected, 24–33
		Edwin M. Stanton	Dec. 20, 1869	Dec. 20, 1869	46–11
		William Strong	Feb. 7, 1870	Feb. 18, 1870	46–11
		Joseph P. Bradley	Feb. 7, 1870	March 21, 1870	46–9
		Ward Hunt	Dec. 3, 1872	Dec. 11, 1872	Voice
		George H. Williams[a]	Dec. 1, 1873	Jan. 8, 1874	Withdrawn
		Caleb Cushing[a]	Jan. 9, 1874	Jan. 13, 1874	Withdrawn
		Morrison R. Waite[a]	Jan. 19, 1874	Jan. 21, 1874	63–0

President	Party	Nominee	Date nominated	Date confirmed or action	Vote
Hayes	Rep	John M. Harlan	Oct. 17, 1877	Nov. 29, 1877	Voice
		William B. Woods	Dec. 15, 1880	Dec. 21, 1880	39–8
		Stanley Matthews	Jan. 26, 1881	No action	
Garfield	Rep	Stanley Matthews	March 14, 1881	May 12, 1881	24–23
Arthur	Rep	Horace Gray	Dec. 19, 1881	Dec. 20, 1881	51–5
		Roscoe Conkling	Feb. 24, 1882	March 2, 1882	39–12, declined
		Samuel Blatchford	March 13, 1882	March 27, 1882	Voice
Cleveland	Dem	Lucius Q. C. Lamar	Dec. 6, 1887	Jan. 16, 1888	32–28
		Melville W. Fuller[a]	April 30, 1888	July 20, 1888	41–20
B. Harrison	Rep	David J. Brewer	Dec. 4, 1889	Dec. 18, 1889	53–11
		Henry B. Brown	Dec. 23, 1890	Dec. 29, 1890	Voice
		George Shiras, Jr.	July 19, 1892	July 26, 1892	Voice
		Howell E. Jackson	Feb. 2, 1893	Feb. 18, 1893	Voice
Cleveland	Dem	William B. Hornblower	Sept. 19, 1893	Jan. 15, 1894	Rejected, 24–30
		Wheeler H. Peckham	Jan. 22, 1894	Feb. 16, 1894	Rejected, 32–41
		Edward D. White	Feb. 19, 1894	Feb. 19, 1894	Voice
		Rufus W. Peckham	Dec. 3, 1895	Dec. 9, 1895	Voice
McKinley	Rep	Joseph McKenna	Dec. 16, 1897	Jan. 21, 1898	Voice
T. Roosevelt	Rep	Oliver W. Holmes	Dec. 2, 1902	Dec. 4, 1902	Voice
		William R. Day	Feb. 19, 1903	Feb. 23, 1903	Voice
		William H. Moody	Dec. 3, 1906	Dec. 12, 1906	Voice
Taft	Rep	Horace H. Lurton	Dec. 13, 1909	Dec. 20, 1909	Voice
		Charles E. Hughes	April 25, 1910	May 2, 1910	Voice
		Edward D. White[a]	Dec. 12, 1910	Dec. 12, 1910	Voice

(Table continues)

Table 4-14 (*Continued*)

President	Party	Nominee	Date of appointment	Confirmation or other action	Vote
		Willis Van Devanter	Dec. 12, 1910	Dec. 15, 1910	Voice
		Jospeh R. Lamar	Dec. 12, 1910	Dec. 15, 1910	Voice
		Mahlon Pitney	Feb. 19, 1912	March 13, 1912	50–26
Wilson	Dem	James C. McReynolds	Aug. 19, 1914	Aug. 29, 1914	44–6
		Louis D. Brandeis	Jan. 28, 1916	June 1, 1916	47–22
		John H. Clarke	July 14, 1916	July 24, 1916	Voice
Harding	Rep	William H. Taft[a]	June 30, 1921	June 30, 1921	Voice
		George Sutherland	Sept. 5, 1922	Sept. 5, 1922	Voice
		Pierce Butler	Nov. 23, 1922	Dec. 21, 1922	61–8
		Edward T. Sanford	Jan. 24, 1923	Jan. 29, 1923	Voice
Coolidge	Rep	Harlan F. Stone	Jan. 25, 1925	Feb. 5, 1925	71–6
Hoover	Rep	Charles E. Hughes[a]	Feb. 3, 1930	Feb. 13, 1930	52–26
		John J. Parker	March 21, 1930	May 7, 1930	Rejected, 39–41
		Owen J. Roberts	May 9, 1930	May 20, 1930	Voice
		Benjamin N. Cardozo	Feb. 15, 1932	Feb. 24, 1932	Voice
F. Roosevelt	Dem	Hugo L. Black	Aug. 12, 1937	Aug. 17, 1937	63–16
		Stanley F. Reed	Jan. 15, 1938	Jan. 25, 1938	Voice
		Felix Frankfurter	Jan. 5, 1939	Jan. 17, 1939	Voice
		William O. Douglas	March 20, 1939	April 4, 1939	62–4
		Frank Murphy	Jan. 4, 1940	Jan. 15, 1940	Voice
		Harlan F. Stone[a]	June 12, 1941	June 27, 1941	Voice
		James F. Byrnes	June 12, 1941	June 12, 1941	Voice

President	Party	Nominee	Date of nomination	Date of confirmation	Vote
		Robert H. Jackson	June 12, 1941	July 7, 1941	Voice
		Wiley B. Rutledge	Jan. 11, 1943	Feb. 8, 1943	Voice
Truman	Dem	Harold H. Burton	Sept 19, 1945	Sept. 19, 1945	Voice
		Fred M. Vinson[a]	June 6, 1946	June 20, 1946	Voice
		Tom C. Clark	Aug. 2, 1949	Aug. 18, 1949	73–8
		Sherman Minton	Sept. 15, 1949	Oct. 4, 1949	48–16
Eisenhower	Rep	Earl Warren[a]	Sept. 30, 1953	March 1, 1954	Voice
		John M. Harlan	Jan. 10, 1955	March 16, 1955	71–11
		William J. Brennan, Jr.	Jan. 14, 1957	March 19, 1957	Voice
		Charles E. Whittaker	March 2, 1957	March 19, 1957	Voice
		Potter Stewart	Jan. 17, 1959	May 5, 1959	70–17
Kennedy	Dem	Byron White	March 3, 1962	April 11, 1962	Voice
		Arthur J. Goldberg	Aug. 29, 1962	Sept. 25, 1962	Voice
L. Johnson	Dem	Abe Fortas	July 28, 1965	Aug. 11, 1965	Voice
		Thurgood Marshall	June 13, 1967	Aug. 30, 1967	69–11
		Abe Fortas[a]	June 26, 1968	Oct. 4, 1968	Withdrawn
		Homer Thornberry	June 26, 1968	No action	
Nixon	Rep	Warren E. Burger[a]	May 21, 1969	June 9, 1969	74–3
		Clement Haynsworth, Jr.	Aug. 18, 1969	Nov. 21, 1969	Rejected, 45–55
		G. Harrold Carswell	Jan. 19, 1970	April 8, 1970	Rejected, 45–51
		Harry A. Blackmun	April 14, 1970	May 12, 1970	94–0
		Lewis F. Powell, Jr.	Oct. 21, 1971	Dec. 6, 1971	89–1
		William H. Rehnquist	Oct. 21, 1971	Dec. 10, 1971	68–26
Ford	Rep	John Paul Stevens	Nov. 28, 1975	Dec. 17, 1975	98–0

(Table continues)

Table 4-14 (*Continued*)

President	Party	Nominee	Date of appointment	Confirmation or other action	Vote
Reagan	Rep	Sandra Day O'Connor	Aug. 19, 1981	Sept. 21, 1981	99–0
		William H. Rehnquist[a]	June 20, 1986	Sept. 17, 1986	65–33
		Antonin Scalia	June 24, 1986	Sept. 17, 1986	98–0
		Robert H. Bork	July 1, 1987	Oct. 23, 1987	Rejected, 42–58
		Anthony Kennedy	Nov. 11, 1987	Feb. 3, 1988	97–0
Bush	Rep	David Souter	July 25, 1990	Oct. 2, 1990	90–9
		Clarence Thomas	July 1, 1991	Oct. 15, 1991	52–48
Clinton	Dem	Ruth Bader Ginsburg	June 14, 1993	Aug. 3, 1993	96–3
	Dem	Stephen G. Breyer	May 13, 1994	July 29, 1994	87–9

Note: "Fed" indicates Federalist, "D-R" indicates Democratic Republican, "Dem" indicates Democrat, "Rep" indicates Republican.

[a] Nominated for chief justice.

Sources: Updated from Elder Witt, *Guide to the U.S. Supreme Court*, 2d ed. (Washington, D.C.: Congressional Quarterly, 1990), and Congressional Quarterly, *Presidential Elections Since 1789*, 4th ed. (Washington, D.C.: Congressional Quarterly, 1987). We depart from CQ and follow the coding of Robert Scigliano, *The Supreme Court and the Presidency* (New York: Free Press, 1971), for John Tyler's and Andrew Johnson's political party.

Table 4-15   American Bar Association Rating of Supreme Court
Nominees, 1956–2000

Nominee	Year	ABA rating (vote)
William Brennan	1956	Eminently qualified (unanimous)
Charles Whitaker	1957	Eminently qualified (unanimous)
Potter Stewart	1959	Exceptionally well qualified (10–1)
Byron White	1962	Exceptionally well qualified (unanimous)
Arthur Goldberg	1962	Highly acceptable from the standpoint of professional qualifications
Abe Fortas	1965	Highly acceptable from the viewpoint of professional qualifications
Thurgood Marshall	1967	Highly acceptable from the viewpoint of professional qualifications
Abe Fortas (Chief Justice)	1968	Highly acceptable from the viewpoint of professional qualifications
Homer Thornberry	1968	Highly acceptable from the viewpoint of professional qualifications (unanimous)
Warren Burger	1969	Highly acceptable from the viewpoint of professional qualifications (unanimous)
Clement Haynsworth, Jr.	1969	Highly acceptable from the viewpoint of professional qualifications (unanimous)
G. Harrold Carswell	1970	Qualified (unanimous)
Harry Blackmun	1970	Meeting high standards of professional competence, temperament and integrity (unanimous)
Lewis Powell, Jr.	1971	In an exceptional degree meets high standards of professional competence, judicial temperament and integrity, and is one of the best qualified lawyers available for appointment to the Supreme Court (unanimous)
William Rehnquist	1971	Unanimously qualified (9 well qualified, 3 not opposed)
John Paul Stevens	1975	Meets high standards of professional competence, judicial temperament and integrity (unanimous)

(Table continues)

Table 4-15   *(Continued)*

Nominee	Year	ABA rating (vote)
Sandra Day O'Connor	1981	The committee is of the opinion that Judge O'Connor meets the highest standards of judicial temperament and integrity. Her professional experience to date has not been as extensive or challenging as that of some other persons who might be available for appointment to the Supreme Court of the United States. Nevertheless, after considering her outstanding academic record, her demonstrated intelligence and her service as a legislator, a lawyer, and a trial and appellate judge, the committee is of the opinion that she is qualified from the standpoint of professional competence for appointment to the Supreme Court of the United States.
William Rehnquist (Chief Justice)	1986	Well qualified (unanimous)
Antonin Scalia	1986	Well qualified (unanimous)
Robert Bork	1987	Well qualified (10 well qualified, 1 not opposed, 4 not qualified)
Anthony Kennedy	1987	Well qualified (unanimous)
David Souter	1990	Well qualified (unanimous)
Clarence Thomas	1991	Qualified (12 qualified, 2 not qualified, 1 recusal)
Ruth Bader Ginsburg	1993	Well qualified (unanimous)
Stephen Breyer	1994	Well qualified (unanimous)

Note: The American Bar Association's Committee on the Federal Judiciary began rating Supreme Court nominees in 1956. At various points in its history, the committee altered its rating categories, making comparisons across time difficult. This table includes the unofficial ratings given to Supreme Court nominees. The American Bar Association does not issue an official list of such ratings. Committee votes are provided when such data are available.

Sources: The American Bar Association and numerous secondary sources.

Table 4-16   Confirmation Factors, 1953–2002

Nominee	Perceived ideology	Perceived qualifications	Interest group support	Interest group opposition
Warren	.75	.74	0	2
Harlan	.88	.86	4	4
Brennan	1.00	1.00	0	0
Whittaker	.50	1.00	0	0
Stewart	.75	1.00	0	0
White	.50	.50	2	0
Goldberg	.75	.92	1	0
Fortas (1)	1.00	1.00	0	0
Marshall	1.00	.84	0	1
Fortas (2)[a]	.85	.64	7	4
Burger	.12	.96	3	0
Haynsworth[a]	.16	.34	5	16
Carswell[a]	.04	.11	1	3
Blackmun	.12	.97	5	0
Powell	.17	1.00	0	1
Rehnquist (1)	.05	.89	1	9
Stevens	.25	.96	11	3
O'Connor	.48	1.00	7	4
Scalia	.00	1.00	10	14
Rehnquist (2)	.05	.40	20	8
Bork[a]	.10	.79	21	17
Kennedy	.37	.89	10	14
Souter	.33	.77	20	17
Thomas	.16	.41	21	32
Ginsburg	.68	1.00	4	6
Breyer	.48	.55	3	3

Note: Nominee ideology: 1 = most liberal, 0 = most conservative; nominee qualifications: 1 = most qualified, 0 = least qualified. Interest group support and interest group opposition represent the number of groups presenting oral or written testimony for or against each nominee.

[a] Unsuccessful nomination.

Sources: Nominee ideology and nominee qualifications are derived from a content analysis of editorial judgments in the *New York Times, Washington Post, Chicago Tribune,* and *Los Angeles Times*. Interest group support and opposition are derived from the Senate Judiciary Committee hearings for each nominee. See Jeffrey A. Segal, Charles M. Cameron, and Albert D. Cover, "A Spatial Model of Roll Call Voting: Senators, Constituents, Presidents and Interest Groups in Supreme Court Confirmations," *American Journal of Political Science* 36 (1992): 96.

Table 4-17   Appointment Anomalies

Justices Who Served Without Being Confirmed

Article II, section 2, of the Constitution authorizes the president to fill vacancies when the Senate is in recess. The individual nominated may serve in office until the Senate returns to session and acts on the nomination. A number of justices, especially in the Court's early history, received recess appointments but did not take their seats until after the Senate had confirmed their nominations. Five justices, however, received recess appointments and served a period of time without the benefit of Senate confirmation:

John Rutledge served as chief justice for four months in 1795.

Benjamin Curtis served as associate justice for two months in 1851.

Earl Warren served as chief justice for five months in 1953–54.

William Brennan served as associate justice for five months in 1956–57.

Potter Stewart served as associate justice for seven months in 1958–59.

Of these justices, all were later confirmed except Rutledge, whom the Senate rejected by a 10–14 vote in December of 1795.

Individuals Who Did Not Serve After Receiving Senate Confirmation

Eight individuals were nominated by the president and confirmed by the Senate and yet did not serve:

Robert H. Harrison was nominated to be associate justice by President George Washington and confirmed by the Senate in 1789. Because of health considerations and his selection to be Chancellor of Maryland, he declined the Supreme Court post to serve at the state level.

William Cushing, a sitting associate justice, was nominated to be chief justice by President Washington and confirmed by the Senate in 1796. Cushing declined the post because of age and health considerations, but he continued to serve as an associate justice.

John Jay, who had resigned the chief justiceship in 1795, was nominated again to be chief justice by President John Adams and was confirmed by the Senate in 1800. Jay declined to return to the federal bench.

Levi Lincoln, a former attorney general, was nominated to be associate justice by President James Madison and was confirmed by the Senate in 1811. Lincoln declined, citing poor health and age.

John Quincy Adams, then minister to Russia, was nominated to be associate justice by President Madison and was confirmed by the Senate in 1811. Adams declined the post, preferring to pursue his political ambitions that ultimately led to the White House.

Table 4-17 *(Continued)*

William Smith was nominated to be associate justice by President Andrew Jackson and confirmed by the Senate in 1837. He declined, preferring to engage in activities that offered higher remuneration.

Edwin Stanton, former secretary of war, received President Ulysses S. Grant's nomination to be associate justice and was confirmed by the Senate in 1869. Four days later, before he could take his seat, Stanton died.

Roscoe Conkling, a former senator from New York, received President Chester Arthur's nomination to be associate justice and was confirmed in 1882. He decided not to accept the position.

Justices Confirmed by the Senate Following a Previous Rejection

Three individuals attained a position on the Court after an unsuccessful first nomination:

William Paterson of New Jersey was nominated associate justice by President Washington on February 27, 1793. The nomination was withdrawn the next day because of a constitutional technicality. Paterson had been a member of the United States Senate and had participated in the development of the Supreme Court in the Judiciary Act of 1789. Article I, section 6, of the Constitution stipulates that no member of Congress "during the time for which he was elected" can be appointed to any office created during his term. Although Paterson was no longer a senator (he resigned in 1790 to become governor of New Jersey), the Senate term to which he was originally elected would not expire until March 4, 1793. Washington waited four more days and resubmitted the nomination. Paterson was confirmed the same day.

Roger Taney received President Jackson's nomination to be associate justice in 1835, but confirmation was indefinitely postponed by the Senate. Later that year, with a new Congress having been seated, Jackson nominated Taney to replace John Marshall as chief justice. In March of 1836 the Senate confirmed Taney by a 29–15 margin.

Stanley Matthews was nominated to be associate justice by Rutherford Hayes in January of 1881. Because of Matthews's close ties to unpopular railroad interests, the Senate killed the nomination by inaction. The newly inaugurated James Garfield then renominated Matthews, and he was confirmed by a 24–23 vote in May of 1881.

Justices Who Served Under Two Successful Nominations and Confirmations

Six individuals who had already served on the Court received a second nomination and were confirmed. Two, William Cushing and John Jay, as described above, declined to serve. The remaining four, however, accepted service under the second appointment:

(Table continues)

Table 4-17 *(Continued)*

Edward White was confirmed as associate justice in 1894, and in 1910 was successfully promoted to chief justice, a position he held until his death in 1921.

Charles Evans Hughes served as associate justice from 1910 to 1916, when he resigned to seek the presidency. In 1930 he was confirmed as chief justice and served in that capacity until his retirement in 1941.

Harlan Fiske Stone was appointed associate justice in 1925 and after 16 years of service was promoted by Franklin Roosevelt to chief justice where he served until his death in 1946.

William Rehnquist became associate justice in 1971 and was later confirmed as chief justice in 1986.

Justices Whose Second Nominations Were Rejected by the Senate

Two individuals were successfully confirmed as associate justices, but later were rejected when nominated to become chief justice:

John Rutledge served as associate justice for eighteen months during Washington's first administration. He resigned to become chief justice of South Carolina. Four years later, in 1795, Washington gave Rutledge a recess appointment to be chief justice. He served for four months before the Senate returned to session and rejected the nomination.

Abe Fortas was successfully appointed associate justice by Lyndon Johnson in 1965. Three years later Johnson attempted to elevate Fortas to replace Earl Warren as chief justice. Because of charges of ethical impropriety, the Senate refused to confirm and the nomination was withdrawn.

Rejected Twice

In the history of the Court, only one person has been nominated twice and rejected both times:

Edward King, a distinguished Philadelphia legal scholar and judge, was nominated by President John Tyler to be associate justice in 1844. Tyler, who had assumed the presidency upon William Henry Harrison's death, was extremely unpopular in the Senate. The Senate killed the King nomination by voting to postpone action on it. Six months later Tyler once again submitted King's name, and once again the Senate refused to confirm. Before Tyler's term ended the Senate rejected a total of five of his nominations to the Supreme Court.

Sources: Joan Biskupic and Elder Witt, *Congressional Quarterly's Guide to the U.S. Supreme Court*, 3d ed. (Washington, D.C.: Congressional Quarterly, 1997); Henry J. Abraham, *Justices and Presidents*, 2d ed. (New York: Oxford University Press, 1985); and Albert P. Blaustein and Roy M. Mersky, *The First One Hundred Justices* (Hamden, Conn.: Archon Books, 1978).

5

The Justices: Post-Confirmation
Activities and Departures
from the Court

Tables in the preceding chapter depict aspects of the justices' lives prior to their confirmation proceedings. In this chapter, we focus on the careers of the justices after their ascent to the bench. These data begin in Table 5-1 with the justices' lengths of service. Justice William O. Douglas served the longest, with a tenure in excess of 36 years. At the opposite extreme, Thomas Johnson sat on the Court for little more than a year. Table 5-2 divides the Supreme Court's history into its component natural courts, a term used to identify periods of time in which the same set of justices served continuously. Such periods could vary greatly in length, from as long as 12 years to as short as one month. The average span, however, ran to just 24 months. A few natural court periods were too brief to allow much judicial activity. For example, the Court comprising Vinson 2 decided only one minor matter, *Telefilm v. Superior Court* (1949).[1]

Career data next extend to the justices' service on the various circuit courts (Tables 5-3 and 5-4). At the creation of the federal judicial system, Supreme Court justices were required to serve as circuit court judges. During the first years of the operation of the federal judiciary no official assignments of individual judges to specific circuits occurred. There appears to have been a disagreement over who should make such assignments, Congress or the Court itself. The Judiciary Act of 1801, passed as the Federalists were leaving power, created six circuits, but did not require the justices to sit on the circuit courts. Consequently, the act did not provide for circuit court assignments by the justices. The act was repealed by the Jeffersonians in 1802, who subsequently assigned the justices to specific circuits (Table 5-3).

Much time was spent "riding circuit," traveling throughout a multistate jurisdiction, often on horseback, hearing cases. In the earliest years, riding circuit demanded more time and effort from the justices than did their Supreme Court duties. The justices disliked this obligation and frequently petitioned Congress to eliminate it. Each justice was assigned a circuit for which he was responsible. Assignments were made at various times, either by Congress or by the Court. Usually a justice was assigned a circuit that included his home state. Congress periodically altered the number and composition of the circuits. This was prompted by westward expansion, political maneuvering, and the Civil War. The most significant of those circuit alterations are reflected in Table 5-3. After Congress revamped the structure of the circuits following the Civil War (Table 5-4), no major geographical changes in the configuration of the circuits occurred. The division of the Eighth Circuit in 1929 and the division of the Fifth in 1981 were the only significant alterations, and they were accomplished with no changes elsewhere. When new states were admitted or territories acquired, they were simply assigned to existing circuits. In 1891 Congress created the federal courts of appeals. This reform eliminated the justices' circuit riding responsibilities. Today the justices retain jurisdiction over one or more circuits assigned them by the Court. They are empowered to issue injunctions and stays of execution as well as handle emergency matters that arise out of their respective circuits. This is especially important when the Supreme Court is not in session and an urgent matter must be decided. The justices also perform an important, but largely informal, function of acting as a liaison between the Supreme Court and the lower federal court judges in the circuits.

Table 5-5 examines the nonjudicial activities of the justices while sitting on the Court. Participation in extrajudicial activities, commonplace and generally accepted during most of the Court's history, is unusual today. Since 1969, when Justice Abe Fortas was forced to resign under fire for ethical violations stemming from extrajudicial activities, members of the judiciary have been much more sensitive to the problems associated with becoming involved in pursuits not directly connected to their federal court duties. Failure to heed ethical considerations can lead to the threat of impeachment proceedings as in the case of Justice Fortas. Table 5-6 describes the occasions on which serious attempts to remove a justice by impeachment occurred. Two of these centered on the justiceship of William O. Douglas. It is notable that all were unsuccessful.

We next explore the justices' departures from the Court and their lives after judicial service. Table 5-7 outlines the circumstances surrounding each justice's termination of service. Slightly less than half died in office, while another large proportion retired after suffering debilitating health problems. After justices leave the Court (or sometimes while they are still on the bench), scholars and legal analysts rate their performances. The primary objective of such efforts has been to identify the truly great justices. A sample of these studies and their findings appear in Table 5-8. We include this because some readers might be interested in how observers of the Court have viewed the contributions of its members over time. Readers should be aware, however, that these rankings are, for the most part, quite subjective.

Many justices continued to be active in public affairs even after their Court service. Table 5-9 reviews the postjudicial activities of those members surviving their Court tenures. Table 5-10 lists the date and place of death of the justices, as well as the location of interment.

We conclude this chapter with four tables that provide the reader with further resources with which to investigate more fully the work and lives of the justices. Table 5-11 is a listing of the libraries or other public depositories for scholarly study where the personal papers of the justices are located. Table 5-12 lists prominent books and articles written by the members of the Court, and Table 5-13 provides a sample of classic statements that can be found in the written opinions of the justices. Finally, for those who wish to read more about the lives of those individuals who have held the highest judicial post in the nation, Table 5-14 lists published biographical material on each of the justices.

Note

1. 338 U.S. 801.

Table 5-1   Length of Service (Ranked)

Justice (appointment number)[a]	Length of tenure[b]
1. Douglas, William O. (82)	36 years, 7 months
2. Field, Stephen J. (39)	34 years, 8 months
3. Marshall, John (14)	34 years, 5 months
4. Black, Hugo L. (79)	34 years, 1 month
5. Harlan, John Marshall I (45)	33 years, 10 months
6. Story, Joseph (19)	33 years, 9 months
7. Brennan, William J., Jr. (94)	33 years, 9 months
8. Wayne, James M. (24)	32 years, 5 months
9. McLean, John (22)	32 years, 2 months
10. White, Bryon R. (97)	31 years, 2 months
11. Washington, Bushrod (12)	30 years, 11 months
12. Johnson, William (15)	30 years, 4 months
13. Holmes, Oliver W., Jr. (59)	29 years, 1 month
14. Taney, Roger B. (25)	28 years, 6 months
15. Miller, Samuel (37)	28 years, 2 months
16. Catron, John (27)	28 years, 2 months
17. Nelson, Samuel (30)	27 years, 9 months
18. White, Edward D. (56, 64)	27 years, 3 months
19. McKenna, Joseph (58)	26 years, 11 months
20. Van Devanter, Willis (65)	26 years, 5 months
21. McReynolds, James C. (68)	26 years, 5 months
22. Blackmun, Harry A.	24 years, 2 months
23. Marshall, Thurgood (100)	24 years, 1 month
24. Frankfurter, Felix (81)	23 years, 7 months
25. Grier, Robert C. (32)	23 years, 6 months
26. Clifford, Nathan (35)	23 years, 6 months
27. Duvall, Gabriel (18)	23 years, 1 month
28. Stewart, Potter (96)	22 years, 8 months
29. Brandeis, Louis D. (69)	22 years, 8 months
30. Fuller, Melville W. (51)	21 years, 11 months
31. Bradley, Joseph P. (42)	21 years, 10 months
32. Stone, Harlan Fiske (75, 84)	21 years, 2 months
33. Cushing, William (3)	20 years, 11 months
34. Gray, Horace (48)	20 years, 8 months
35. Brewer, David J. (52)	20 years, 3 months
36. Thompson, Smith (20)	19 years, 11 months
37. Day, William R. (60)	19 years, 8 months
38. Daniel, Peter V. (29)	19 years, 2 months
39. Reed, Stanley F. (80)	19 years, 1 month
40. Swayne, Noah H. (36)	19 years
41. Todd, Thomas (17)	18 years, 11 months
42. Clark, Tom C. (90)	17 years, 9 months
43. Hughes, Charles Evans (63, 76)	17 years, 5 months
44. Burger, Warren E. (101)	17 years, 3 months
45. Butler, Pierce (73)	16 years, 10 months
46. Harlan, John Marshall II (93)	16 years, 6 months
47. Livingston, H. Brockholst (16)	16 years, 3 months
48. Warren, Earl (92)	15 years, 8 months

Table 5-1   *(Continued)*

Justice (appointment number)[a]	Length of tenure[b]
49. Powell, Lewis F., Jr. (103)	15 years, 6 months
50. Brown, Henry B. (53)	15 years, 4 months
51. Chase, Samuel (10)	15 years, 4 months
52. Sutherland, George (72)	15 years, 4 months
53. Roberts, Owen J. (77)	15 years, 2 months
54. McKinley, John (28)	14 years, 9 months
55. Baldwin, Henry (23)	14 years, 3 months
56. Davis, David (38)	14 years, 2 months
57. Waite, Morrison (44)	14 years, 2 months
58. Peckham, Rufus W. (57)	13 years, 10 months
59. Paterson, William (8)	13 years, 6 months
60. Jackson, Robert H. (86)	13 years, 3 months
61. Burton, Harold H. (88)	13 years
62. Blatchford, Samuel (49)	11 years, 3 months
63. Strong, William (41)	10 years, 9 months
64. Pitney, Mahlon (67)	10 years, 9 months
65. Shiras, George, Jr. (54)	10 years, 6 months
66. Iredell, James (6)	9 years, 8 months
67. Murphy, Frank (83)	9 years, 6 months
68. Hunt, Ward (43)	9 years, 1 month
69. Wilson, James (4)	8 years, 10 months
70. Taft, William H. (71)	8 years, 7 months
71. Chase, Salmon P. (40)	8 years, 5 months
72. Campbell, John A. (34)	8 years, 1 month
73. Matthews, Stanley (47)	7 years, 10 months
74. Vinson, Fred M. (89)	7 years, 2 months
75. Sanford, Edward T. (74)	7 years, 1 month
76. Minton, Sherman (91)	7 years
77. Rutledge, Wiley B. (87)	6 years, 7 months
78. Woods, William B. (46)	6 years, 4 months
79. Cardozo, Benjamin (78)	6 years, 4 months
80. Blair, John, Jr. (5)	6 years, 4 months
81. Clarke, John H. (70)	6 years, 1 month
82. Curtis, Benjamin R. (33)	5 years, 9 months
83. Jay, John (1)	5 years, 9 months
84. Woodbury, Levi (31)	5 years, 8 months
85. Lamar, Joseph R. (66)	5 years
86. Whittaker, Charles E. (95)	5 years
87. Lamar, Lucius Q.C. (50)	5 years
88. Barbour, Philip P. (26)	4 years, 11 months
89. Ellsworth, Oliver (11)	4 years, 6 months
90. Lurton, Horace (62)	4 years, 6 months
91. Moore, Alfred (13)	4 years, 1 month
92. Moody, William H. (61)	3 years, 11 months
93. Fortas, Abe (99)	3 years, 9 months
94. Goldberg, Arthur J. (98)	2 years, 10 months
95. Jackson, Howell E. (55)	2 years, 5 months
96. Trimble, Robert (21)	2 years, 3 months

(Table continues)

Table 5-1   *(Continued)*

Justice (appointment number)[a]	*Length of tenure*[b]
97. Rutledge, John (2, 9)	1 year, 10 months
98. Byrnes, James F. (85)	1 year, 3 months
99. Johnson, Thomas (7)	1 year, 2 months

[a] Only those justices who had departed the Court by the end of the 2001 term are included.
[b] Length of tenure measured from the date of confirmation to the date of departure, plus any time served under a recess appointment. Data are presented to the nearest completed month. Ties are broken by the number of days served beyond the last completed month.

Source: Joan Biskupic and Elder Witt, *Congressional Quarterly's Guide to the U.S. Supreme Court,* 3d ed. (Washington, D.C.: Congressional Quarterly, 1997).

Table 5-2 Natural Courts

Natural court[a]	Justices[b]	Dates	U.S. Reports[c]
Jay 1	Jay (o October 19, 1789), J. Rutledge (o February 15, 1790), Cushing (o February 2, 1790), Wilson (o October 5, 1789), Blair (o February 2, 1790)	October 5, 1789–May 12, 1790	2
Jay 2	Jay, Rutledge (r March 5, 1791), Cushing, Wilson, Blair, Iredell (o May 12, 1790)	May 12, 1790–August 6, 1792	2
Jay 3	Jay, Cushing, Wilson, Blair, Iredell, T. Johnson (o August 6, 1792; r January 16, 1793)	August 6, 1792–March 11, 1793	2
Jay 4	Jay (r June 29, 1795), Cushing, Wilson, Blair, Iredell, Paterson (o March 11, 1793)	March 11, 1793–August 12, 1795	2–3
Rutledge 1	J. Rutledge (o August 12, 1795; rj December 15, 1795), Cushing, Wilson, Blair (r January 27, 1796), Iredell, Paterson	August 12, 1795–February 4, 1796	3
No chief justice	Cushing, Wilson, Iredell, Paterson, S. Chase (o February 4, 1796)	February 4, 1796–March 8, 1796	3
Ellsworth 1	Ellsworth (o March 8, 1796), Cushing, Wilson (d August 21, 1798), Iredell, Paterson, S. Chase	March 8, 1796–February 4, 1799	3
Ellsworth 2	Ellsworth, Cushing, Iredell (d October 20, 1799), Paterson, S. Chase, Washington (o February 4, 1799)	February 4, 1799–April 21, 1800	3–4
Ellsworth 3	Ellsworth (r December 15, 1800), Cushing, Paterson, S. Chase, Washington, Moore (o April 21, 1800)	April 21, 1800–February 4, 1801	4
Marshall 1	Marshall (o February 4, 1801), Cushing, Paterson, S. Chase, Washington, Moore (r January 26, 1804)	February 4, 1801–May 7, 1804	5–6

(*Table continues*)

Table 5-2 (Continued)

Natural court[a]	Justices[b]	Dates	U.S. Reports[c]
Marshall 2	Marshall, Cushing, Paterson (d September 9, 1806), S. Chase, Washington, W. Johnson (o May 7, 1804)	May 7, 1804– January 20, 1807	6–7
Marshall 3	Marshall, Cushing, S. Chase, Washington, W. Johnson, Livingston (o January 20, 1807)	January 20, 1807– May 4, 1807	8
Marshall 4	Marshall, Cushing (d September 13, 1810), S. Chase (d June 19, 1811), Washington, W. Johnson, Livingston, Todd (o May 4, 1807)	May 4, 1807– November 23, 1811	8–10
Marshall 5	Marshall, Washington, W. Johnson, Livingston, Todd, Duvall (o November 23, 1811)	November 23, 1811– February 3, 1812	11
Marshall 6	Marshall, Washington, W. Johnson, Livingston (d March 18, 1823), Todd, Duvall, Story (o February 3, 1812)	February 3, 1812– February 10, 1824	11–21
Marshall 7	Marshall, Washington, W. Johnson, Todd (d February 7, 1826), Duvall, Story, Thompson (o February 10, 1824)	February 10, 1824– June 16, 1826	22–24
Marshall 8	Marshall, Washington (d November 26, 1829), W. Johnson, Duvall, Story, Thompson, Trimble (o June 16, 1826; d August 25, 1828)	June 16, 1826– January 11, 1830	25–27
Marshall 9	Marshall, W. Johnson (d August 4, 1834), Duvall (r January 14, 1835), Story, Thompson, McLean (o January 11, 1830), Baldwin (o January 18, 1830)	January 11, 1830– January 14, 1835	28–33
Marshall 10	Marshall (d July 6, 1835), Story, Thompson, McLean, Baldwin, Wayne (o January 14, 1835)	January 14, 1835– March 28, 1836	34–35
Taney 1	Taney (o March 28, 1836), Story, Thompson, McLean, Baldwin, Wayne	March 28, 1836– May 12, 1836	35

Taney 2	Taney, Story, Thompson, McLean, Baldwin, Wayne, Barbour (o May 12, 1836)	May 12, 1836–May 1, 1837	35–36
Taney 3	Taney, Story, Thompson, McLean, Baldwin, Wayne, Barbour, Catron (o May 1, 1837)	May 1, 1837–January 9, 1838	36
Taney 4	Taney, Story, Thompson, McLean, Baldwin, Wayne, Barbour, Catron, McKinley (o January 9, 1838)	January 9, 1838–January 10, 1842	37–40
Taney 5	Taney, Story, Thompson, McLean, Baldwin, Wayne, Barbour (d February 25, 1841), Catron, McKinley, Daniel (o January 10, 1842)	January 10, 1842–February 27, 1845	40–44
Taney 6	Taney, Story, Thompson (d December 18, 1843), McLean, Baldwin (d April 21, 1844), Wayne, Catron, McKinley, Daniel, Nelson (o February 27, 1845)	February 27, 1845–September 23, 1845	44
Taney 7	Taney, Story (d September 10, 1845), McLean, Wayne, Catron, McKinley, Daniel, Nelson, Woodbury (o September 23, 1845)	September 23, 1845–August 10, 1846	44–45
Taney 8	Taney, McLean, Wayne, Catron, McKinley, Daniel, Nelson, Woodbury (d September 4, 1851), Grier (o August 10, 1846)	August 10, 1846–October 10, 1851	46–52
Taney 9	Taney, McLean, Wayne, Catron, McKinley (d July 19, 1852), Daniel, Nelson, Grier, Curtis (o October 10, 1851)	October 10, 1851–April 11, 1853	53–55
Taney 10	Taney, McLean, Wayne, Catron, Daniel, Nelson, Grier, Curtis (r September 30, 1857), Campbell (o April 11, 1853)	April 11, 1853–January 21, 1858	56–61
Taney 11	Taney, McLean (d April 4, 1861), Wayne, Catron, Daniel (d May 31, 1860), Nelson, Grier, Campbell (r April 30, 1861), Clifford (o January 21, 1858)	January 21, 1858–January 27, 1862	61–66
Taney 12	Taney, Wayne, Catron, Nelson, Grier, Clifford, Swayne (o January 27, 1862)	January 27, 1862–July 21, 1862	66

(Table continues)

Table 5-2 (*Continued*)

Natural court[a]	Justices[b]	Dates	U.S. Reports[c]
Taney 13	Taney, Wayne, Catron, Nelson, Grier, Clifford, Swayne, Miller (*o* July 21, 1862)	July 21, 1862–December 10, 1862	67
Taney 14	Taney, Wayne, Catron, Nelson, Grier, Clifford, Swayne, Miller, Davis (*o* December 10, 1862)	December 10, 1862–May 20, 1863	67
Taney 15	Taney (*d* October 12, 1864) Wayne, Catron, Nelson, Grier, Clifford, Swayne, Miller, Davis, Field (*o* May 20, 1863)	May 20, 1863–December 15, 1864	67–68
Chase 1	S. P. Chase (*o* December 15, 1864), Wayne (*d* July 5, 1867), Catron (*d* May 30, 1865), Nelson, Grier (*r* January 31, 1870), Clifford, Swayne, Miller, Davis, Field	December 15, 1864–March 14, 1870	69–76
Chase 2	S. P. Chase, Nelson (*r* November 28, 1872), Clifford, Swayne, Miller, Davis, Field, Strong (*o* March 14, 1870), Bradley (*o* March 23, 1870)	March 14, 1870–January 9, 1873	76–82
Chase 3	S. P. Chase (*d* May 7, 1873), Clifford, Swayne, Miller, Davis, Field, Strong, Bradley, Hunt (*o* January 9, 1873)	January 9, 1873–March 4, 1874	82–86
Waite 1	Waite (*o* March 4, 1874), Clifford, Swayne, Miller, Davis (*r* March 4, 1877), Field, Strong, Bradley, Hunt	March 4, 1874–December 10, 1877	86–95
Waite 2	Waite, Clifford, Swayne, Miller, Field, Strong (*r* December 14, 1880), Bradley, Hunt, Harlan I (*o* December 10, 1877)	December 10, 1877–January 5, 1881	95–103
Waite 3	Waite, Clifford, Swayne (*r* January 24, 1881), Miller, Field, Bradley, Hunt, Harlan I, Woods (*o* January 5, 1881)	January 5, 1881–May 17, 1881	103
Waite 4	Waite, Clifford (*d* July 25, 1881), Miller, Field, Bradley, Hunt, Harlan I, Woods, Matthews (*o* May 17, 1881)	May 17, 1881–January 9, 1882	103–104

Waite 5	Waite, Miller, Field, Bradley, Hunt (*r* January 27, 1882), Harlan I, Woods, Matthews, Gray (*o* January 9, 1882)	January 9, 1882–April 3, 1882	104–105
Waite 6	Waite, Miller, Field, Bradley, Harlan I, Woods (*d* May 14, 1887), Matthews, Gray, Blatchford (*o* April 3, 1882)	April 3, 1882–January 18, 1888	105–124
Waite 7	Waite (*d* March 23, 1888), Miller, Field, Bradley, Harlan I, Matthews, Gray, Blatchford, L. Lamar (*o* January 18, 1888)	January 18, 1888–October 8, 1888	124–127
Fuller 1	Fuller (*o* October 8, 1888), Miller, Field, Bradley, Harlan I, Matthews (*d* March 22, 1889), Gray, Blatchford, L. Lamar	October 8, 1888–January 6, 1890	128–132
Fuller 2	Fuller, Miller (*d* October 13, 1890), Field, Bradley, Harlan I, Gray, Blatchford, L. Lamar, Brewer (*o* January 6, 1890)	January 6, 1890–January 5, 1891	132–137
Fuller 3	Fuller, Field, Bradley (*d* January 22, 1892), Harlan I, Gray, Blatchford, L. Lamar, Brewer, Brown (*o* January 5, 1891)	January 5, 1891–October 10, 1892	137–145
Fuller 4	Fuller, Field, Harlan I, Gray, Blatchford, L. Lamar (*d* January 23, 1893), Brewer, Brown, Shiras (*o* October 10, 1892)	October 10, 1892–March 4, 1893	146–148
Fuller 5	Fuller, Field, Harlan I, Gray, Blatchford (*d* July 7, 1893), Brewer, Brown, Shiras, H. Jackson (*o* March 4, 1893)	March 4, 1893–March 12, 1894	148–151
Fuller 6	Fuller, Field, Harlan I, Gray, Brewer, Brown, Shiras, H. Jackson (*d* August 8, 1895), E. White (*o* March 12, 1894)	March 12, 1894–January 6, 1896	152–160
Fuller 7	Fuller, Field (*r* December 1, 1897), Harlan I, Gray, Brewer, Brown, Shiras, E. White, Peckham (*o* January 6, 1896)	January 6, 1896–January 26, 1898	160–169
Fuller 8	Fuller, Harlan I, Gray (*d* September 15, 1902), Brewer, Brown, Shiras, E. White, Peckham, McKenna (*o* January 26, 1898)	January 26, 1898–December 8, 1902	169–187

(Table continues)

Table 5-2 *(Continued)*

Natural court[a]	Justices[b]	Dates	U.S. Reports[c]
Fuller 9	Fuller, Harlan I, Brewer, Brown, Shiras (r February 23, 1903), E. White, Peckham, McKenna, Holmes (o December 8, 1902)	December 8, 1902–March 2, 1903	187–188
Fuller 10	Fuller, Harlan I, Brewer, Brown (r May 28, 1906), E. White, Peckham, McKenna, Holmes, Day (o March 2, 1903)	March 2, 1903–December 17, 1906	188–203
Fuller 11	Fuller, Harlan I, Brewer, E. White, Peckham (d October 24, 1909), McKenna, Holmes, Day, Moody (o December 17, 1906)	December 17, 1906–January 3, 1910	203–215
Fuller 12	Fuller (d July 4, 1910), Harlan I, Brewer (d March 28, 1910), E. White, McKenna, Holmes, Day, Moody, Lurton (o January 3, 1910)	January 3, 1910–October 10, 1910	215–217
No chief justice	Harlan I, E. White (p December 18, 1910), McKenna, Holmes, Day, Moody (r November 20, 1910), Lurton, Hughes (o October 10, 1910)	October 10, 1910–December 19, 1910	218
White 1	E. White (o December 19, 1910), Harlan I (d October 14, 1911), McKenna, Holmes, Day, Lurton, Hughes, Van Devanter (o January 3, 1911), J. Lamar (o January 3, 1911)	December 19, 1910–March 18, 1912	218–223
White 2	E. White, McKenna, Holmes, Day, Lurton (d July 12, 1914), Hughes, Van Devanter, J. Lamar, Pitney (o March 18, 1912)	March 18, 1912–October 12, 1914	223–234
White 3	E. White, McKenna, Holmes, Day, Hughes, Van Devanter, J. Lamar (d January 2, 1916), Pitney, McReynolds (o October 12, 1914)	October 12, 1914–June 5, 1916	235–241
White 4	E. White, McKenna, Holmes, Day, Hughes (r June 10, 1916), Van Devanter, Pitney, McReynolds, Brandeis (o June 5, 1916)	June 5, 1916–October 9, 1916	235–241
White 5	E. White (d May 19, 1921), McKenna, Holmes, Day, Van Devanter, Pitney, McReynolds, Brandeis, Clarke (o October 9, 1916)	October 9, 1916–July 11, 1921	242–256

Court	Composition	Dates	Pages
Taft 1	Taft (o July 11, 1921), McKenna, Holmes, Day, Van Devanter, Pitney, McReynolds, Brandeis, Clarke (r September 18, 1922)	July 11, 1921–October 2, 1922	257–259
Taft 2	Taft, McKenna, Holmes, Day (r November 13, 1922), Van Devanter, Pitney (r December 31, 1922), McReynolds, Brandeis, Sutherland (o October 2, 1922)	October 2, 1922–January 2, 1923	260
Taft 3	Taft, McKenna, Holmes, Van Devanter, McReynolds, Brandeis, Sutherland, Butler (o January 2, 1923)	January 2, 1923–February 19, 1923	260
Taft 4	Taft, McKenna (r January 5, 1925), Holmes, Van Devanter, McReynolds, Brandeis, Sutherland, Butler, Sanford (o February 19, 1923)	February 19, 1923–March 2, 1925	260–267
Taft 5	Taft (r February 3, 1930), Holmes, Van Devanter, McReynolds, Brandeis, Sutherland, Butler, Sanford, Stone (o March 2, 1925)	March 2, 1925–February 24, 1930	267–280
Hughes 1	Hughes (o February 24, 1930), Holmes, Van Devanter, McReynolds, Brandeis, Sutherland, Butler, Sanford (d March 8, 1930), Stone	February 24, 1930–June 2, 1930	280–281
Hughes 2	Hughes, Holmes (r January 12, 1932), Van Devanter, McReynolds, Brandeis, Sutherland, Butler, Stone, Roberts (o June 2, 1930)	June 2, 1930–March 14, 1932	281–285
Hughes 3	Hughes, Van Devanter (r June 2, 1937), McReynolds, Brandeis, Sutherland, Butler, Stone, Roberts, Cardozo (o March 14, 1932)	March 14, 1932–August 19, 1937	285–301
Hughes 4	Hughes, McReynolds, Brandeis, Sutherland (r January 17, 1938), Butler, Stone, Roberts, Cardozo, Black (o August 19, 1937)	August 19, 1937–January 31, 1938	302–303
Hughes 5	Hughes, McReynolds, Brandeis, Butler, Stone, Roberts, Cardozo (d July 9, 1938), Black, Reed (o January 31, 1938)	January 31, 1938–January 30, 1939	303–305
Hughes 6	Hughes, McReynolds, Brandeis (r February 13, 1939), Butler, Stone, Roberts, Black, Reed, Frankfurter (o January 30, 1939)	January 30, 1939–April 17, 1939	306
Hughes 7	Hughes, McReynolds, Butler (d November 16, 1939), Stone, Roberts, Black, Reed, Frankfurter, Douglas (o April 17, 1939)	April 17, 1939–February 5, 1940	306–308

(Table continues)

Table 5-2 *(Continued)*

Natural court[a]	Justices[b]	Dates	U.S. Reports[c]
Hughes 8	Hughes (*r* July 1, 1941), McReynolds (*r* January 31, 1941), Stone (*p* July 2, 1941), Roberts, Black, Reed, Frankfurter, Douglas, Murphy (*o* February 5, 1940)	February 5, 1940–July 3, 1941	308–313
Stone 1	Stone (*o* July 3, 1941), Roberts, Black, Reed, Frankfurter, Douglas, Murphy, Byrnes (*o* July 8, 1941; *r* October 3, 1942), R. Jackson (*o* July 11, 1941)	July 3, 1941–February 15, 1943	314–318
Stone 2	Stone, Roberts (*r* July 31, 1945), Black, Reed, Frankfurter, Douglas, Murphy, R. Jackson, W. Rutledge (*o* February 15, 1943)	February 15, 1943–October 1, 1945	318–226
Stone 3	Stone (*d* April 22, 1946), Black, Reed, Frankfurter, Douglas, Murphy, R. Jackson, W. Rutledge, Burton (*o* October 1, 1945)	October 1, 1945–June 24, 1946	326–328
Vinson 1	Vinson (*o* June 24, 1946), Black, Reed, Frankfurter, Douglas, Murphy (*d* July 19, 1949), R. Jackson, W. Rutledge, Burton	June 24, 1946–August 24, 1949	329–338
Vinson 2	Vinson, Black, Reed, Frankfurter, Douglas, R. Jackson, W. Rutledge (*d* September 10, 1949), Burton, Clark (*o* August 24, 1949)	August 24, 1949–October 12, 1949	338
Vinson 3	Vinson (*d* September 8, 1953), Black, Reed, Frankfurter, Douglas, R. Jackson, Burton, Clark, Minton (*o* October 12, 1949)	October 12, 1949–October 5, 1953	338–346
Warren 1	Warren (*o* October 5, 1953), Black, Reed, Frankfurter, Douglas, R. Jackson (*d* October 9, 1954), Burton, Clark, Minton	October 5, 1953–March 28, 1955	346–348
Warren 2	Warren, Black, Reed, Frankfurter, Douglas, Burton, Clark, Minton (*r* October 15, 1956), Harlan II (*o* March 28, 1955)	March 28, 1955–October 16, 1956	348–352
Warren 3	Warren, Black, Reed (*r* February 25, 1957), Frankfurter, Douglas, Burton, Clark, Harlan II, Brennan (*o* October 16, 1956)	October 16, 1956–March 25, 1957	352
Warren 4	Warren, Black, Frankfurter, Douglas, Burton (*r* October 13, 1958), Clark, Harlan II, Brennan, Whittaker (*o* March 25, 1957)	March 25, 1957–October 14, 1958	352–358

Court	Members	Dates	Pages
Warren 5	Warren, Black, Frankfurter, Douglas, Clark, Harlan II, Brennan, Whittaker (r March 31, 1962), Stewart (o October 14, 1958)	October 14, 1958–April 16, 1962	358–369
Warren 6	Warren, Black, Frankfurter (r August 28, 1962), Douglas, Clark, Harlan II, Brennan, Stewart, B. White (o April 16, 1962)	April 16, 1962–October 1, 1962	369–370
Warren 7	Warren, Black, Douglas, Clark, Harlan II, Brennan, Stewart, B. White, Goldberg (o October 1, 1962; r July 25, 1965)	October 1, 1962–October 4, 1965	371–381
Warren 8	Warren, Black, Douglas, Clark (r June 12, 1967), Harlan II, Brennan, Stewart, B. White, Fortas (o October 4, 1965)	October 4, 1965–October 2, 1967	382–388
Warren 9	Warren (r June 23, 1969), Black, Douglas, Harlan II, Brennan, Stewart, B. White, Fortas (r May 14, 1969), T. Marshall (o October 2, 1967)	October 2, 1967–June 23, 1969	389–395
Burger 1	Burger (o June 23, 1969), Black, Douglas, Harlan II, Brennan, Stewart, B. White, T. Marshall	June 23, 1969–June 9, 1970	395–397
Burger 2	Burger, Black (r September 17, 1971) Douglas, Harlan II (r September 23, 1971), Brennan, Stewart, B. White, T. Marshall, Blackmun (o June 9, 1970)	June 9, 1970–January 7, 1972	397–404
Burger 3	Burger, Douglas (r November 12, 1975), Brennan, Stewart, B. White, T. Marshall, Blackmun, Powell (o January 7, 1972), Rehnquist (o January 7, 1972)	January 7, 1972–December 19, 1975	404–423
Burger 4	Burger, Brennan, Stewart (r July 3, 1981), B. White, T. Marshall, Blackmun, Powell, Rehnquist, Stevens (o December 19, 1975)	December 19, 1975–September 25, 1981	423–453
Burger 5	Burger (r September 26, 1986), Brennan, B. White, T. Marshall, Blackmun, Powell, Rehnquist (p September 26, 1986), Stevens, O'Connor (o September 25, 1981)	September 25, 1981–September 26, 1986	453–478
Rehnquist 1	Rehnquist (o September 26, 1986), Brennan, B. White, T. Marshall, Blackmun, Powell (r June 26, 1987), Stevens, O'Connor, Scalia (o September 26, 1986)	September 26, 1986–February 18, 1988	478–484

(Table continues)

Table 5-2 (*Continued*)

Natural court[a]	Justices[b]	Dates	U.S. Reports[c]
Rehnquist 2	Rehnquist, Brennan (r July 20, 1990), B. White, T. Marshall, Blackmun, Stevens, O'Connor, Scalia, Kennedy (o February 18, 1988)	February 18, 1988– October 9, 1990	484–498
Rehnquist 3	Rehnquist, B. White, T. Marshall (r October 1, 1991), Blackmun, Stevens, O'Connor, Scalia, Kennedy, Souter (o October 9, 1990)	October 9, 1990– October 23, 1991	498–501
Rehnquist 4	Rehnquist, B. White (r July 1, 1993), Blackmun, Stevens, O'Connor, Scalia, Kennedy, Souter, Thomas (o October 23, 1991)	October 23, 1991– August 10, 1993	502–509
Rehnquist 5	Rehnquist, Blackmun, (r August 3, 1994), Stevens, O'Connor, Scalia, Kennedy, Souter, Thomas, Ginsburg (o August 10, 1993)	August 10, 1993– August 3, 1994	510–512
Rehnquist 6	Rehnquist, Stevens, O'Connor, Scalia, Kennedy, Souter, Thomas, Ginsburg, Breyer (o August 3, 1994)	August 3, 1994–	513–

Note: The term *natural court* refers to a period of time during which the membership of the Court remains stable. There are a number of ways to determine the beginning and ending of a natural court. Here a natural court begins when a new justice takes the oath of office and continues until the next new justice takes the oath. When two or more justices join the Court within a period of fifteen or fewer days we treat it as the beginning of a single natural court (for example, Marshall 9, Chase 2, White 1, Stone 1).

[a] Numbered sequentially within the tenure of each chief justice.

[b] The name of the chief justice appears first, with associate justices following in order of descending seniority. In addition, the date a justice left the Court, creating a vacancy for the next justice to be appointed, is given, as well as the date the new justice took the oath of office. o = oath of office taken, d = died, r = resigned or retired, rj = recess appointment rejected by Senate, p = promoted from associate justice to chief justice.

[c] Volumes of *United States Reports* in which the actions of each natural court generally may be found. Because of the manner in which decisions were published prior to the twentieth century, these volume numbers may not contain all of the decisions of a given natural court. They do, however, provide a general guide to the location of each natural court's published decisions. Natural courts of short duration may have little business published in the reports.

Sources: Clare Cushman, ed., *The Supreme Court Justices: Illustrated Biographies 1789–1993* (Washington, D.C.: Supreme Court Historical Society and Congressional Quarterly, 1993); Kermit Hall, ed., *The Oxford Companion to the Supreme Court* (New York: Oxford University Press, 1992); Commission on the Bicentennial of the United States Constitution, *The Supreme Court of the United States: Its Beginnings and Its Justices, 1790–1991* (Washington, D.C.: Supreme Court Historical Society, 1992); Administrative Office of the United States Courts, various reports; and *United States Reports*, various years.

Table 5-3   Circuit Justice Assignments, 1802–1867

Circuit	Justice assigned	Dates of service
First Circuit 1802–1820: Massachusetts, New Hampshire, Rhode Island; 1820–1867: Maine, Massachusetts, New Hampshire, Rhode Island	William Cushing Joseph Story Levi Woodbury Benjamin Curtis Nathan Clifford	1802–1810 1811–1845 1845–1851 1851–1857 1858–1867
Second Circuit 1802–1867: Connecticut, New York, Vermont	William Paterson H. Brockholst Livingston Smith Thompson Vacant Samuel Nelson	1802–1806 1806–1823 1823–1843 1844 1845–1867
Third Circuit 1802–1867: New Jersey, Pennsylvania	Bushrod Washington Henry Baldwin Robert Grier	1802–1829 1830–1844 1846–1867
Fourth Circuit 1802–1842: Delaware, Maryland; 1842–1863: Delaware, Maryland, Virginia; 1863–1867: Delaware, Maryland, North Carolina, South Carolina, Virginia, West Virginia	Samuel Chase Gabriel Duvall Roger B. Taney Salmon P. Chase	1802–1811 1811–1835 1836–1864 1864–1867
Fifth Circuit 1802–1842: North Carolina, Virginia; 1842–1863: Alabama, Louisiana; 1863–1867: Alabama, Florida, Georgia, Mississippi	John Marshall Philip Barbour Peter Daniel John McKinley John Campbell Vacant James Wayne	1802–1835 1836–1841 1841–1845 1845–1852 1853–1861 1862 1863–1867
Sixth Circuit 1802–1842: Georgia, South Carolina; 1842–1862: Georgia, North Carolina, South Carolina; 1862–1867: Arkansas, Kentucky, Louisiana, Tennessee, Texas	Alfred Moore William Johnson James Wayne John Catron Vacant	1802–1804 1804–1834 1835–1863 1863–1865 1866–1867
Seventh Circuit 1807–1837: Kentucky, Ohio, Tennessee; 1837–1862: Illinois, Indiana, Michigan, Ohio; 1862–1867: Indiana, Ohio	Thomas Todd Robert Trimble Vacant John McLean Noah Swayne	1807–1826 1826–1828 1829 1830–1861 1862–1867

(Table continues)

Table 5-3   *(Continued)*

Circuit	Justice assigned	Dates of service
Eighth Circuit 1837–1862: Kentucky, Missouri, Tennessee; 1862–1867: Illinois, Michigan, Wisconsin	John Catron David Davis	1837–1863 1863–1867
Ninth Circuit 1837–1842: Alabama, Arkansas, Louisiana, Mississippi; 1842–1862: Arkansas, Mississippi; 1862–1867: Iowa, Kansas, Minnesota, Missouri	John McKinley Peter Daniel Samuel Miller	1837–1845 1845–1860 1862–1867
Tenth Circuit 1863–1865: California, Oregon; 1865–1867: California, Nevada, Oregon	Stephen Field	1863–1867
California Circuit 1855–1863	No assignment	

Source: The Federal Cases Comprising Cases Argued and Determined in the Circuit and District Courts of the United States, Vol. I (St. Paul, Minn.: West Publishing, 1894), x–xvii.

Table 5-4   Circuit Justice Assignments, 1867–2002

Circuit	Justice assigned	Dates of service
First Circuit		
Maine, Massachusetts, New	Nathan Clifford	1867–1881
Hampshire, Rhode Island,	John Marshall Harlan I	1881
Puerto Rico[a]	Horace Gray	1882–1902
	Rufus Peckham	1902
	Oliver Wendell Holmes	1902–1932
	Louis Brandeis	1932–1939
	Felix Frankfurter	1939–1962
	Arthur Goldberg	1962–1965
	William Brennan	1969–1990
	David Souter	1990–
Second Circuit		
Connecticut, New York,	Samuel Nelson	1867–1872
Vermont	Ward Hunt	1873–1882
	Stephen Field	1882
	Samuel Blatchford	1882–1893
	Horace Gray	1893–1894
	Henry Brown	1894–1896
	Rufus Peckham	1896–1909
	Horace Lurton	1910–1911
	Charles Evans Hughes	1911–1916
	Louis Brandeis	1916–1925
	Harlan Fiske Stone	1925–1941
	Robert Jackson	1941–1945
	Stanley Reed	1945–1946
	Robert Jackson	1946–1954
	Felix Frankfurter	1954–1955
	John Marshall Harlan II	1955–1971
	Thurgood Marshall	1972–1991
	Clarence Thomas	1991–1994
	Ruth Bader Ginsburg	1994–
Third Circuit		
Delaware, New Jersey,	Robert Grier	1867–1870
Pennsylvania, Virgin Islands[b]	William Strong	1870–1880
	Joseph Bradley	1881–1892
	John Marshall Harlan I	1892
	George Shiras	1892–1903
	Henry Brown	1903–1906
	Edward D. White	1906
	William Moody	1906–1910
	Horace Lurton	1911
	Mahlon Pitney	1911–1922
	Pierce Butler	1923–1925
	Louis Brandeis	1925–1930
	Owen Roberts	1930–1945
	Harold Burton	1945–1956
	William Brennan	1956–1990
	David Souter	1990–

(Table continues)

Table 5-4   *(Continued)*

Circuit	Justice assigned	Dates of service
Fourth Circuit[c]		
Maryland, North Carolina,	Salmon P. Chase	1867–1873
South Carolina, Virginia, West	Morrison Waite	1874–1888
Virginia	Melville Fuller	1888–1910
	Edward D. White	1911–1921
	William Howard Taft	1921–1930
	Charles Evans Hughes	1930–1941
	Harlan Fiske Stone	1941–1946
	Fred Vinson	1946–1953
	Earl Warren	1953–1969
	Warren Burger	1969–1986
	William Rehnquist	1986–
Fifth Circuit		
Alabama,[d] Florida,[d] Georgia,[d]	James Wayne	1867
Louisiana, Mississippi, Texas,	Vacant	1868
Canal Zone[e]	Noah Swayne	1869
	Joseph Bradley	1870–1880
	William Woods	1881–1887
	John Marshall Harlan I	1887
	Lucius Q. C. Lamar	1888–1893
	Howell Jackson	1893–1894
	Edward D. White	1894–1911
	Joseph Lamar	1911–1916
	Edward D. White	1916
	James McReynolds	1916–1923
	Edward Sanford	1923–1930
	Louis Brandeis	1930–1932
	Benjamin Cardozo	1932–1937
	Hugo Black	1937–1971
	Lewis Powell	1972–1981
	Byron White	1981–1987
	William Rehnquist	1987
	Byron White	1987–1990
	Antonin Scalia	1990–
Sixth Circuit		
Kentucky, Michigan, Ohio,	Noah Swayne	1867–1881
Tennessee	Stanley Matthews	1881–1889
	John Marshall Harlan I	1889–1890
	David Brewer	1890–1891
	Henry Brown	1892–1894
	Howell Jackson	1894–1896
	John Marshall Harlan I	1896–1911
	William Day	1911–1922
	James McReynolds	1922–1941
	Frank Murphy	1941
	Stanley Reed	1941–1957
	Harold Burton	1957–1958
	Potter Stewart	1958–1981
	Byron White	1981

Table 5-4   *(Continued)*

Circuit	Justice assigned	Dates of service
	Sandra Day O'Connor	1981–1986
	Antonin Scalia	1986–1990
	John Paul Stevens	1990–
Seventh Circuit		
Illinois, Indiana, Wisconsin	David Davis	1867–1877
	John Marshall Harlan I	1878–1892
	Melville Fuller	1892–1894
	John Marshal Harlan I	1894–1896
	Henry Brown	1896–1903
	William Day	1903–1911
	Horace Lurton	1911–1914
	James McReynolds	1914–1916
	John Clarke	1916–1922
	George Sutherland	1922–1925
	Pierce Butler	1925–1929
	Willis Van Devanter	1929–1937
	Benjamin Cardozo	1937–1938
	Felix Frankfurter	1939
	William O. Douglas	1939–1940
	Frank Murphy	1940–1941
	James Byrnes	1941–1942
	Frank Murphy	1943–1949
	Sherman Minton	1949–1956
	Harold Burton	1956–1957
	Tom Clark	1957–1967
	Thurgood Marshall	1967–1972
	William Rehnquist	1972–1975
	John Paul Stevens	1975–
Eighth Circuit[f]		
Arkansas, Colorado, Iowa,	Samuel Miller	1867–1890
Kansas, Minnesota, Missouri,	David Brewer	1890–1910
Nebraska, New Mexico, North	Willis Van Devanter	1911–1929
Dakota, Oklahoma, South	Pierce Butler	1929–1939
Dakota, Utah, Wyoming	Stanley Reed	1940–1941
	Frank Murphy	1941–1943
	Wiley Rutledge	1943–1949
	Tom Clark	1949–1957
	Charles Whittaker	1957–1962
	Tom Clark	1962
	Byron White	1962–1970
	Harry Blackmun	1970–1994
	Clarence Thomas	1994–
Ninth Circuit[g]		
Alaska, Arizona, California,	Stephen Field	1867–1897
Guam, Hawaii, Idaho, Montana,	David Brewer	1897–1898
Nevada, Northern Mariana	Joseph McKenna	1898–1925
Islands, Oregon, Washington	George Sutherland	1925–1938
	Stanley Reed	1938–1940

(Table continues)

Table 5-4   *(Continued)*

Circuit	Justice assigned	Dates of service
	William Douglas	1940–1975
	William Rehnquist	1975–1986
	Sandra Day O'Connor	1986–
Tenth Circuit		
Colorado, Kansas, New Mexico,	Willis Van Devanter	1929–1937
Oklahoma, Utah, Wyoming	Pierce Butler	1937–1939
	Stanley Reed	1940–1941
	Frank Murphy	1941–1943
	Wiley Rutledge	1943–1949
	Tom Clark	1949–1957
	Charles Whittaker	1957–1962
	William Douglas	1962
	Byron White	1962–1993
	Ruth Bader Ginsburg	1993–1994
	Stephen Breyer	1994–
Eleventh Circuit		
Alabama, Georgia, Florida	Lewis Powell	1981–1987
	Sandra Day O'Connor	1987
	John Paul Stevens	1987–1988
	Anthony Kennedy	1988–
District of Columbia Circuit[h]	Charles Evans Hughes	1938–1941
	Harlan Fiske Stone	1941–1946
	Fred Vinson	1946–1953
	Earl Warren	1953–1969
	Warren Burger	1969–1986
	William Rehnquist	1986–
Federal Circuit[i]	Warren Burger	1982–1986
	William Rehnquist	1986–

[a] Added in 1915.

[b] Added in 1938.

[c] Traditionally, the chief justice has served as circuit justice for the Fourth Circuit.

[d] Moved to the newly created Eleventh Circuit in 1981.

[e] Added in 1922, but removed from the circuit in 1979 with the implementation of the Panama Canal treaty that transferred the Canal Zone back to Panama.

[f] In 1867 the Eighth Circuit included only Arkansas, Iowa, Kansas, Minnesota, and Missouri. The states of Colorado, Nebraska, New Mexico, North Dakota, Oklahoma, South Dakota, Utah, and Wyoming were added as they achieved statehood. Colorado, Kansas, New Mexico, Oklahoma, Utah, and Wyoming were split off from the Eighth Circuit and combined to make a new Tenth Circuit in 1929.

[g] The Ninth Circuit contained only California, Nevada, and Oregon in 1867. As they attained statehood, Arizona, Idaho, Montana, and Washington were added. Alaska and Hawaii were added while still territories. Guam was included in 1966, and the Northern Mariana Islands in 1978.

[h] Became a full circuit in 1938. The chief justice traditionally serves as its circuit justice.

[i] Created in 1981. This court has no geographical jurisdiction but hears appeals concerning customs, patents, and special claims against the federal government. The chief justice has served as its circuit justice.

Sources: 1867–1891: *The Federal Courts Comprising Cases Argued and Determined in the Circuit and District Courts of the United States,* Vol. I (St. Paul, Minn.: West Publishing, 1894), x–xvii; 1891–2001: *The Supreme Court Reporter* (St. Paul, Minn.: West Publishing, annual volumes).

Table 5-5   Extrajudicial Activities While Sitting on the Court

Justice (appointment number)[a]	*Activity*[b]
Blatchford, Samuel (49)	Trustee, Columbia University, 1882–1893
Bradley, Joseph P. (42)	Member, commission to decide disputed Tilden-Hayes presidential election, 1877
Brandeis, Louis D. (69)	Adviser to President Woodrow Wilson; aided the development of the University of Louisville; active in Zionist causes
Brennan, William J., Jr. (94)	Participant, annual appellate judges seminar, New York University
Brewer, David J. (52)	President, Venezuela–British Guiana Border Commission, 1899; lecturer at Yale University and George Washington University; president, Associated Charities of Washington
Burger, Warren E. (101)	Participant, annual appellate judges seminar, New York University; lobbied for judicial reform
Butler, Pierce (73)	Trustee, Catholic University; member, Board of Regents, University of Minnesota
Byrnes, James F. (85)	Active in Franklin Roosevelt's administration, including drafting legislation, advising on appointments, and mediating disagreements among administrative agencies
Campbell, John A. (34)	Served as a mediator between Southern states and the incoming Lincoln administration, 1860–1861
Catron, John (27)	Openly supported James Buchanan for president in 1856
Chase, Salmon P. (40)	Presided over impeachment trial of President Andrew Johnson, 1868; considered a possible presidential candidate, 1868 and 1872
Chase, Samuel (10)	Remained active in Federalist Party politics, including openly campaigning for the election of John Adams in 1800; campaigned for passage of Alien and Sedition acts
Clarke, John H. (70)	Active in promoting world peace and U.S. entry into the League of Nations

(Table continues)

Table 5-5 *(Continued)*

Justice (appointment number)[a]	*Activity*[b]
Clifford, Nathan (35)	Chair, commission to decide disputed Tilden-Hayes presidential election, 1877
Cushing, William (3)	Ran for governor of Massachusetts, 1794
Davis, David (38)	Nominee of Labor Reform Party for president, 1872
Douglas, William O. (82)	Adviser to Franklin Roosevelt; considered for Democratic vice-presidential nomination, 1944 and 1948; director, Parvin Foundation; executive, Center for the Study of Democratic Institutions; active in political, legal, and environmental writing
Ellsworth, Oliver (11)	Commissioner to France, 1799–1800
Field, Stephen J. (39)	Member, commission to decide disputed Tilden-Hayes presidential election, 1877; considered a possible Democratic presidential candidate, 1880 and 1884
Fortas, Abe (99)	Adviser to President Lyndon Johnson; instructor, American University Law School; consultant, Wolfson Foundation
Frankfurter, Felix (81)	Adviser to Franklin Roosevelt; active in scholarly writing
Fuller, Melville W. (51)	Member, Venezuela–British Guiana Border Commission, 1899; member, Permanent Court of Arbitration at the Hague, 1900–1910
Grier, Robert C. (32)	Advised President James Buchanan of decision in *Dred Scott* case before it was announced
Harlan, John Marshall I (45)	Member, Bering Sea Tribunal of Arbitration, 1893
Hughes, Charles E. (63, 76)	Member, federal postal rate commission; president, tribunal to arbitrate Guatemala–Honduras border dispute, 1930; extensive writing activities
Jackson, Robert H. (86)	Chief prosecutor, Nuremberg war crimes trial, 1945–1946; active in legal and political writing

Table 5-5   *(Continued)*

Justice (appointment number)[a]	*Activity*[b]
Jay, John (1)	Secretary of foreign affairs, 1789; envoy to Great Britain, 1794–1795; adviser to President George Washington and Treasury Secretary Alexander Hamilton throughout term of office
Johnson, Thomas (7)	Board of Commissioners of the Federal City, 1791–1793
Johnson, William (15)	Adviser to President James Monroe; political writings
Lamar, Joseph R. (66)	Member, mediation conference on United States–Mexico relations, Niagara Falls, Canada, 1914
Livingston, H. Brockholst (16)	Trustee, Columbia University, 1806–1823
Marshall, John (14)	Secretary of state, 1801; delegate, Virginia constitutional convention, 1829; member, Washington Historical Monument Society
McLean, John (22)	Honorary president, American Sunday School Union, 1849; several informal attempts to become a candidate for president
Miller, Samuel (37)	Member, commission to decide disputed Tilden–Hayes presidential election, 1877; considered a possible presidential candidate, 1880 and 1884; active in scholarly writing
Moody, William H. (61)	Adviser to Theodore Roosevelt
Moore, Alfred (13)	Trustee, University of North Carolina, 1799–1804
Murphy, Frank (83)	Lieutenant colonel, U.S. army, 1942
Nelson, Samuel (30)	Received support for 1860 Democratic presidential nomination; member, Alabama Claims Commission, 1871
Reed, Stanley F. (80)	Chair, President's Commission on Civil Service Improvement, 1939–1941
Roberts, Owen J. (77)	Trustee, University of Pennsylvania; chair, Pearl Harbor Inquiry Board, 1941–1942; member, Commission for the Protection and Salvage of Artistic and Historic Monuments in Europe, 1943–1945

(Table continues)

Table 5-5   *(Continued)*

Justice (appointment number)[a]	*Activity*[b]
Rutledge, John (2, 9)	Chancery judge, South Carolina, 1789–1791
Sanford, Edward T. (74)	Trustee, George Peabody College for Teachers, 1923–1930
Stewart, Potter (96)	Active in American Bar Association committees
Stone, Harlan Fiske (75, 84)	Adviser to Herbert Hoover and Franklin Roosevelt; trustee, Amherst College; member of the boards of directors of several literary, artistic, and educational organizations
Story, Joseph (19)	Harvard University Board of Overseers, 1819–1829; delegate, Massachusetts constitutional convention, 1820; fellow of the Harvard Corporation; professor of law, Harvard University, 1829–1845; drafted federal statutes; member, Massachusetts Codification Commission, 1836–1837; active in legal writing and publication
Strong, William (41)	Member, commission to decide disputed Tilden-Hayes presidential election, 1877
Swayne, Noah H. (36)	Campaigned for ratification of the Fifteenth Amendment
Taft, William H. (71)	Presidential and congressional adviser; active in the American Bar Association; diplomatic mission to Great Britain; trustee, Hampton Institute; lobbied bar and government groups for judicial reform
Taney, Roger B. (25)	Adviser to Presidents Andrew Jackson and Martin Van Buren; informally involved in Maryland politics
Thompson, Smith (20)	Unsuccessful campaign for governor of New York, 1828
Todd, Thomas (17)	Stockholder in companies attempting to develop public roads in Kentucky; real estate investments in Kentucky
Van Devanter, Willis (65)	Arbitrated Great Britain–United States dispute over a ship seizure
Vinson, Fred M. (89)	Adviser to President Harry Truman

Table 5-5 *(Continued)*

Justice (appointment number)[a]	Activity[b]
Waite, Morrison (44)	Trustee, Peabody Education Fund, 1874–1888; member, Yale Corporation, 1882–1888
Warren, Earl (92)	Chair, commission to investigate the assassination of President John F. Kennedy
Washington, Bushrod (12)	Executor of President George Washington's estate; president, American Colonization Society, 1816
Wayne, James M. (24)	Active in developing transportation systems in Georgia; chair, Georgia State Railroad Convention, 1836; officer in various historical societies
White, Edward D. (56, 64)	Arbitrator of Panama–Costa Rica border dispute
Wilson, James (4)	Trustee, College of Philadelphia; unsuccessful business activities; jailed briefly for unsatisfied debts
Woodbury, Levi (31)	Contended for 1848 Democratic presidential nomination

[a] Justices without significant extrajudicial activities are not included.

[b] Refers to service beyond those activities normally expected. Lectures speeches, short courses at law schools, etc., are not included. The years listed for each activity are only those concurrent with Supreme Court service.

Sources: Robert B. McKay, "The Judiciary and Nonjudicial Activities," *Law and Contemporary Problems* 35 (Winter 1970): 9–36; Elder Witt, *Guide to the U.S. Supreme Court,* 2d ed. (Washington, D.C.: Congressional Quarterly, 1990); Leon Friedman and Fred L. Israel, eds., *The Justices of the United States Supreme Court: Their Lives and Major Opinions* (New York: R.R. Bowker, 1969–1978); Harold W. Chase et al., *Biographical Dictionary of the American Judiciary* (Detroit: Gale Research, 1976); *Judges of the United States,* 2d ed. (Washington, D.C.: Judicial Conference of the United States, 1983); *The National Cyclopaedia of American Biography* (New York: James T. White, various years); and *Dictionary of American Biography* (New York: Charles Scribner's Sons, various editions).

Table 5-6   Impeachment Actions Against Supreme Court Justices

Justice	Attempt	Outcome
Samuel Chase	On March 12, 1804, the House voted eight articles of impeachment by a 72–32 vote. Six of these called into question Chase's actions "while presiding on circuit at treason and sedition trials." The other two centered on "addresses delivered to grand juries."	The Senate acquitted Chase of all charges on March 1, 1805.
William O. Douglas	On June 18, 1953, Rep. W. M. Wheeler (D-Ga.) introduced a resolution of impeachment against Douglas. The resolution came the day after Douglas had temporarily stayed the execution of Julius and Ethel Rosenberg. The Judiciary Committee created a subcommittee of "inquiry."	On June 19, the Supreme Court overruled Douglas. The Judiciary Committee tabled the resolution of impeachment on July 7.
	On April 15, 1970, Rep. Gerald Ford (R-Mich.), in a speech on the House floor, raised five charges against Douglas, centering on ethical violations (e.g., providing legal advice, failing to recuse). Ford called for the creation of a special committee, but the matter went to the House Judiciary Committee, which, on April 21, established a subcommittee to look into Ford's charges.	On April 21, the House subcommittee voted (3-1-1) that no grounds existed for impeachment.
Abe Fortas	On May 11, 1969, Rep. H. R. Gross (R-Iowa) stated that he had prepared articles of impeachment against Fortas, charging him with various ethical violations. Gross's announcement came a week after *Life* magazine had reported on Fortas's involvement with the Wolfson Foundation. On May 13, Rep. Clark MacGregor (R-Minn.) proposed that the House Judiciary Committee begin preliminary investigations.	Fortas resigned from the Court on May 14.

Source: Elder Witt, *Guide to the U.S. Supreme Court,* 2d ed. (Washington, D.C.: Congressional Quarterly, 1990), 654–657.

Table 5-7 Departure from the Court

Justice (appointment number)	Year	Reason[a]	Age	Replacement
Baldwin, Henry (23)	1844	Died in office	64	Robert Grier
Barbour, Philip P. (26)	1841	Died in office	57	Peter Daniel
Black, Hugo L. (79)	1971	Declining health; stroke	85	Lewis Powell
Blackmun, Harry A. (102)	1994	Advanced age	85	Stephen G. Breyer
Blair, John, Jr. (5)	1796	General decline in health; chronic headaches, weakness, decreased mental abilities; difficulties riding circuit	64	Samuel Chase
Blatchford, Samuel (49)	1893	Died in office	73	Edward White
Bradley, Joseph P. (42)	1892	Died in office	78	George Shiras
Brandeis, Louis D. (69)	1939	Advanced age	82	William O. Douglas
Brennan, William J., Jr. (94)	1990	Advanced age	84	David Souter
Brewer, David J. (52)	1910	Died in office	72	Charles E. Hughes
Brown, Henry B. (53)	1906	Declining health; blindness	70	William Moody
Burger, Warren E. (101)[b]	1986	Advanced age; desire to spend time chairing the Commission for the Bicentennial of the Constitution	79	William Rehnquist
Burton, Harold H. (88)	1958	Declining physical abilities due to Parkinson's disease	70	Potter Stewart

(Table continues)

Table 5-7 *(Continued)*

Justice (appointment number)	Year	Reason[a]	Age	Replacement
Butler, Pierce (73)	1939	Died in office	73	Frank Murphy
Byrnes, James F. (85)	1942	Resigned to assist war effort as director of the Office of Economic Stabilization	63	Wiley Rutledge
Campbell, John A. (34)	1861	Resigned to join the Confederacy	49	David Davis
Cardozo, Benjamin (78)	1938	Died in office	68	Felix Frankfurter
Catron, John (27)	1865	Died in office	79	Seat abolished
Chase, Salmon P. (40)[b]	1873	Died in office	65	Morrison Waite
Chase, Samuel (10)	1811	Died in office	70	Gabriel Duvall
Clark, Tom C. (90)	1967	Retired to remove possible conflicts of interest that might arise with his son's appointment as attorney general	67	Thurgood Marshall
Clarke, John H. (70)	1922	Resigned to campaign for U.S. participation in the League of Nations and other peace efforts	65	George Sutherland
Clifford, Nathan (35)	1881	Died in office	77	Horace Gray
Curtis, Benjamin R. (33)	1857	Resigned due to dissatisfaction with judicial salaries, circuit riding responsibilities, and strained relations on the Court	47	Nathan Clifford
Cushing, William (3)	1810	Died in office	78	Joseph Story

Daniel, Peter V. (29)	1860	Died in office	76	Samuel Miller
Davis, David (38)	1877	Resigned to take seat in U.S. Senate	61	John M. Harlan I
Day, William R. (60)	1922	Advanced age; declining health	73	Pierce Butler
Douglas, William O. (82)	1975	Effects of a stroke	77	John Paul Stevens
Duvall, Gabriel (18)	1835	Advanced age; declining health; deafness	82	Philip Barbour
Ellsworth, Oliver (11)[b]	1800	Health problems aggravated by rigors of a lengthy diplomatic mission to Europe	55	John Marshall
Field, Stephen J. (39)	1897	Declining mental abilities	81	Joseph McKenna
Fortas, Abe (99)	1969	Resigned under criticism for unethical behavior	58	Harry Blackmun
Frankfurter, Felix (81)	1962	Effects of a stroke	79	Arthur Goldberg
Fuller, Melville W. (51)[b]	1910	Died in office	77	Edward White
Goldberg, Arthur J. (98)	1965	Resigned to accept position as U.S. ambassador to the United Nations	56	Abe Fortas
Gray, Horace (48)	1902	Died in office	74	Oliver W. Holmes
Grier, Robert C. (32)	1870	Severe decline in mental and physical abilities	75	William Strong
Harlan, John Marshall I (45)	1911	Died in office	78	Mahlon Pitney
Harlan, John Marshall II (93)	1971	Declining health	72	William Rehnquist

(Table continues)

Table 5-7 (*Continued*)

Justice (appointment number)	Year	Reason[a]	Age	Replacement
Holmes, Oliver W., Jr. (59)	1932	Advanced age	90	Benjamin Cardozo
Hughes, Charles E. (63)	1916	Resigned to run for president	54	John H. Clarke
Hughes, Charles E. (76)[b]	1941	Advanced age; declining health	79	Harlan F. Stone
Hunt, Ward (43)	1882	Decline in ability due to a stroke; special retirement bill passed by Congress made him eligible for pension	71	Samuel Blatchford
Iredell, James (6)	1799	Died in office	48	Alfred Moore
Jackson, Howell E. (55)	1895	Died in office	63	Rufus Peckham
Jackson, Robert H. (86)	1954	Died in office	62	John M. Harlan II
Jay, John (1)[b]	1795	Resigned to become governor of New York	49	Oliver Ellsworth[c]
Johnson, Thomas (7)	1793	Health considerations; difficulties of riding circuit	60	William Paterson
Johnson, William (15)	1834	Died in office	63	James M. Wayne
Lamar, Joseph R. (66)	1916	Died in office	58	Louis Brandeis
Lamar, Lucius Q. C. (50)	1893	Died in office	67	Howell Jackson
Livingston, H. Brockholst (16)	1823	Died in office	65	Smith Thompson
Lurton, Horace (62)	1914	Died in office	70	James McReynolds

Name	Year	Reason	Age	Successor
Marshall, John (14)[b]	1835	Died in office	79	Roger B. Taney
Marshall, Thurgood (100)	1991	Advanced age; declining health	83	Clarence Thomas
Matthews, Stanley (47)	1889	Died in office	64	David Brewer
McKenna, Joseph (58)	1925	Advanced age; declining mental abilities	81	Harlan F. Stone
McKinley, John (28)	1852	Died in office	72	John Campbell
McLean, John (22)	1861	Died in office	76	Noah Swayne
McReynolds, James C. (68)	1941	Advanced age; realization that further opposition to New Deal would be unsuccessful	78	James Byrnes
Miller, Samuel (37)	1890	Died in office	74	Henry Brown
Minton, Sherman (91)	1956	Debilitating effects of pernicious anemia	65	William J. Brennan
Moody, William H. (61)	1910	Severe arthritis	56	Joseph Lamar
Moore, Alfred (13)	1804	Declining health	48	William Johnson
Murphy, Frank (83)	1949	Died in office	59	Tom C. Clark
Nelson, Samuel (30)	1872	Advanced age; declining health aggravated by demands of serving on the Alabama Claims Commission	80	Ward Hunt
Paterson, William (8)	1806	Died in office	60	H. B. Livingston
Peckham, Rufus W. (57)	1909	Died in office	70	Horace Lurton

(Table continues)

Table 5-7 (Continued)

Justice (appointment number)	Year	Reason[a]	Age	Replacement
Pitney, Mahlon (67)	1922	Decreased ability due to stroke	64	Edward Sanford
Powell, Lewis F., Jr. (103)	1987	Advanced age	79	Anthony Kennedy
Reed, Stanley F. (80)	1957	Health considerations required reduced workload	72	Charles Whittaker
Rehnquist, William (104)	1986	Promoted to chief justice	61	Antonin Scalia
Roberts, Owen J. (77)	1945	Retired to pursue other activities, including the deanship of the University of Pennsylvania law school	70	Harold Burton
Rutledge, John (2)	1791	Resigned to become chief justice of South Carolina	51	Thomas Johnson
Rutledge, John (9)[b]	1795	Recess appointment rejected by Senate	56	Oliver Ellsworth
Rutledge, Wiley B. (87)	1949	Died in office	55	Sherman Minton
Sanford, Edward T. (74)	1930	Died in office	64	Owen Roberts
Shiras, George, Jr. (54)	1903	Retired in good health in order to enjoy retirement with family	71	William R. Day
Stewart, Potter (96)	1981	Retired in good health in order to enjoy retirement years and spend time with family	66	Sandra D. O'Connor
Stone, Harlan Fiske (75)	1941	Promoted to chief justice	68	Robert Jackson
Stone, Harlan Fiske (84)[b]	1946	Died in office	73	Fred Vinson
Story, Joseph (19)	1845	Died in office	65	Levi Woodbury

Justice	Age	Reason	Year	Replacement
Strong, William (41)	72	Retired to set an example for others to step down before suffering a decline in physical and mental abilities	1880	William Woods
Sutherland, George (72)	75	Advanced age; improved judicial retirement provisions; realization that further opposition to New Deal would be unsuccessful	1938	Stanley Reed
Swayne, Noah H. (36)	76	Declining mental abilities; a promise from President Rutherford B. Hayes to appoint his friend Stanley Matthews as his replacement	1881	Stanley Matthews
Taft, William H. (71)[b]	72	Declining health	1930	Charles E. Hughes
Taney, Roger B. (25)[b]	87	Died in office	1864	Salmon P. Chase
Thompson, Smith (20)	75	Died in office	1843	Samuel Nelson
Todd, Thomas (17)	61	Died in office	1826	Robert Trimble
Trimble, Robert (21)	51	Died in office	1828	John McLean
Van Devanter, Willis (65)	78	Advanced age; enactment of improved judicial retirement statute; realization that further opposition to New Deal would be unsuccessful	1937	Hugo Black
Vinson, Fred M. (89)[b]	63	Died in office	1953	Earl Warren
Waite, Morrison (44)[b]	71	Died in office	1888	Melville Fuller
Warren, Earl (92)[b]	78	Advanced age	1969	Warren Burger
Washington, Bushrod (12)	67	Died in office	1829	Henry Baldwin

(Table continues)

Table 5-7 *(Continued)*

Justice (appointment number)	Year	Reason[a]	Age	Replacement
Wayne, James M. (24)	1867	Died in office	77	Joseph Bradley[d]
White, Byron R. (97)	1993	Retired in good health to spend time with family and allow the appointment of a younger justice	76	Ruth Bader Ginsburg
White, Edward D. (56)	1910	Promoted to chief justice	65	Willis Van Devanter
White, Edward D. (64)[b]	1921	Died in office	75	William H. Taft
Whittaker, Charles E. (95)	1962	Health problems aggravated by Court's workload	61	Byron White
Wilson, James (4)	1798	Died in office	55	Bushrod Washington
Woodbury, Levi (31)	1851	Died in office	61	Benjamin Curtis
Woods, William B. (46)	1887	Died in office	62	Lucius Q. C. Lamar

[a] Lists factors cited at the time of departure. Other motives may also be involved. One of the more important is political timing. For example, a justice of advanced age enjoying relatively good health may be more prone to retire if the incumbent president is likely to appoint an acceptable replacement. Conversely, a justice of advanced age suffering health problems may attempt to postpone retirement if the incumbent president is likely to appoint a replacement whose political or legal views are at odds with his own.
[b] Chief justice.
[c] Jay was first replaced by John Rutledge, who received a recess appointment from George Washington. Rutledge served as chief justice only four months before the Senate reconvened and rejected the nomination.
[d] Bradley replaced Wayne after a three-year period during which the seat was temporarily abolished by Congress.

Sources: Elder Witt, *Guide to the U.S. Supreme Court*, 2d ed. (Washington, D.C.: Congressional Quarterly, 1990); Leon Friedman and Fred L. Israel, eds., *The Justices of the United States Supreme Court: Their Lives and Major Opinions* (New York: R.R. Bowker, 1969–1978); Harold W. Chase et al., *Biographical Dictionary of the American Judiciary* (Detroit: Gale Research, 1976); *Judges of the United States*, 2d ed. (Washington, D.C.: Judicial Conference of the United States, 1983); *The National Cyclopaedia of American Biography* (New York: James T. White, various years); and *Dictionary of American Biography* (New York: Charles Scribner's Sons, various editions). Updated by the authors.

Table 5-8 Justices Rated "Great," Selected Studies

Hughes (1928)	Pound (1938)[a]	Frankfurter (1957)	Frank (1958)	Currie (1964)	Nagel (1970)
J. Marshall	J. Marshall	J. Marshall	J. Marshall	J. Marshall	J. Marshall
Story	Story	W. Johnson	W. Johnson	W. Johnson	W. Johnson
Curtis	Holmes	Story	Story	Story	Story
Miller	Cardozo	Taney	McLean	Taney	Taney
Field		Curtis	Taney	Miller	Curtis
Bradley		Campbell	Curtis	Bradley	Campbell
Gray		Miller	Campbell	Holmes	Miller
Brewer		Field	Miller	Brandeis	Field
		Bradley	Davis	Hughes	Bradley
		Matthews	Field		Harlan I
		E. White	Bradley		Brewer
		Holmes	Waite		Holmes
		Moody	Harlan I		Moody
		Hughes	Brewer		Hughes
		Brandeis	Holmes		Brandeis
		Cardozo	Moody		Cardozo
			Hughes		Black
			Brandeis		Frankfurter
			Taft		Douglas
			Sutherland		R. Jackson
			Butler		Warren
			Stone		
			Cardozo		

Asch (1971)	Blaustein and Mersky (1972)[b]	Schwartz (1979)[c]	Hambleton (1983)	Congressional Quarterly (1990)	Bradley (1990)[d]
Jay	J. Marshall	J. Marshall	J. Marshall	W. Johnson	J. Marshall
J. Marshall	Story	Story	Story	Curtis	Holmes
Taney	Taney	Holmes	Taney	Harlan I	Warren
Miller	Harlan I	Cardozo	Holmes	Holmes	Brandeis
Harlan I	Holmes	Black	Cardozo	Brandeis	Black
Holmes	Hughes	Warren	Brandeis	Cardozo	Brennan
Brandeis	Brandeis		Hughes	Stone	Cardozo
Hughes	Stone		Black	Frankfurter	Frankfurter
Stone	Cardozo		Warren	Brennan	Douglas
Cardozo	Black			T. Marshall	Rehnquist
Frankfurter	Frankfurter				
R. Jackson	Warren				
Black					
Douglas					
Warren					

(Table continues)

Table 5-8   *(Continued)*

Pederson and Provize (1993)[e]	*Pederson and Provize (1993)*[f]	*Pederson and Provize (1993)*[g]	*Pederson and Provize (1993)*[h]	*Pederson and Provize (1993)*[i]
J. Marshall	J. Marshall	J. Marshall	J. Marshall	J. Marshall
Holmes	Holmes	Holmes	Rehnquist	Holmes
Warren	Cardozo	Brandeis	O'Connor	Warren
Brandeis	Brandeis	Cardozo	Brger	Brandeis
Brennan	Warren	Frankfurter	Warren	Black
Black	Black	Warren	Brennan	Brennan
Harlan I	Frankfurter	Douglas	Holmes	Cardozo
Douglas	Brennan	Black	Blackmun	Farnkfurter
Frankfurter	Douglas	Taney	T. Marshall	Douglas
Cardozo	Taft	Story	Black	Rehnquist
		Harlan II		
		Rehnquist		

Note: All studies list justices chronologically, with the exception of Bradley's and the Pederson and Provize studies, which list in order of perceived greatness. Readers should be aware that these rankings are, for the most part, quite subjective. With the exceptions of the Blaustein and Mersky and Bradley studies, authors used their own judgments in devising their rankings.

[a] Pound's study also listed jurists who did not serve on the Supreme Court, including James Kent, John Bannister Gibson, Lemuel Shaw, Thomas Ruffin, Thomas McIntyre Cooley, and Charles Doe.

[b] Blaustein and Mersky asked 65 scholars to "grade" the justices in a continuum from A to E, where A is great, B is near great, C is average, D is below average, and E is failure. Included here are those rated A. (See source listed below for listings rated B through E.)

[c] Schwartz's study also listed jurists who did not serve on the Supreme Court, including James Kent, Lemuel Shaw, Arthur T. Vanderbilt, and Roger John Traynor.

[d] Bradley sent surveys to 493 lawyers, judges, and scholars. His response rates ranged from 37 percent (scholars) to 12 percent (judges).

[e] According to scholars surveyed by Bradley.

[f] According to judges surveyed by Bradley.

[g] According to attorneys surveyed by Bradley.

[h] According to students surveyed by Bradley.

[i] According to all respondents surveyed by Bradley.

Sources: Lists of great judges were compiled by Robert C. Bradley, "The Supreme Court: Who Are the Great Justices and What Criteria Did They Meet?," unpublished paper on record with the author, 1991, Appendix A. We supplemented those lists from the original sources: Sidney H. Asch, *The Supreme Court and its Great Justices* (New York: Arco, 1971); Albert P. Blaustein and Roy M. Mersky, *The First One Hundred Justices* (Hamden, Conn.: Archon Books, 1978); George R. Currie, "A Judicial All-star Nine," *Wisconsin Law Review* (1964): 3–31; John P. Frank, *Marble Palace* (New York: Alfred A. Knopf, 1958); Felix Frankfurter, "The Supreme Court in the Mirror of Justices," *University of Pennsylvania Law Review* 105 (1957): 781–796; James E. Hambleton, "The All-Time All-Star All-Era Supreme Court," *American Bar Association Journal* 69 (1983): 463–464; Charles Evans Hughes, *The Supreme Court of the United States* (New York: Columbia University Press, 1928); Stuart S. Nagel, "Characteristics of Supreme Court Greatness," *Journal of the American Bar Association* 56 (1970): 957–959; Roscoe Pound, *The Formative Era of American Law* (Boston: Little, Brown, 1938); Bernard Schwartz, "The Judicial Ten: America's Greatest Judges," *Southern Illinois University Law Review* (1979): 405–447; and William D. Pederson and Norman W. Provizer, *Great Justices of U.S. Supreme Court* (New York: Peter Lang, 1993), which contains the results of Bradley's survey.

Table 5-9 Post-Court Activities

Justice (appointment number)[a]	Post-Court years	Post-Court activities
Black, Hugo L. (79)	1 week	Retired in poor health
Blackmun, Harry A. (102)	5	Retired in declining health
Blair, John, Jr. (5)	4	Retired in declining health at his home in Williamsburg, Virginia
Brandeis, Louis D. (69)	2	Devoted his retirement years to the support of Zionist causes
Brennan, William J., Jr. (94)	7	Retired in poor health in Washington, D.C.
Brown, Henry B. (53)	7	Retired in declining health in New York; active in promoting legal reform
Burger, Warren E. (101)	9	Retired in Washington, D.C.; chaired Commission for the Bicentennial of the Constitution
Burton, Harold H. (88)	6	Retired in poor health in Washington, D.C.
Byrnes, James F. (85)	29	Director, Office of Economic Stabilization, 1942–1943; director, Office of War Mobilization and Reconversion, 1943–1945; secretary of state, 1945–1947; private practice, Washington, D.C. and South Carolina, 1947–1951; governor, South Carolina, 1951–1955; retirement in South Carolina
Campbell, John A. (34)	27	Assistant secretary of war, Confederate States of America, 1862–1865; built prosperous law practice, New Orleans, 1866–1889; argued several appeals before the Supreme Court, including the *Slaughterhouse Cases* (1873)
Clark, Tom C. (90)	10	Chair, Board of Directors, American Judicature Society, 1967–1969; judge, United States court of appeals, by designation, 1967–1977; director, Federal Judicial Center, 1968–1970

(Table continues)

Table 5-9   *(Continued)*

Justice (appointment number)[a]	Post-Court years	Post-Court activities
Clarke, John H. (70)	22	Retired in San Diego; worked for the cause of peace: president, League of Nations' Non-Partisan Association of the United States, 1922–1930; trustee, World Peace Foundation, 1923–1931
Curtis, Benjamin R. (33)	17	Operated successful law practice in Boston, 1857–1874; Andrew Johnson's lead attorney in his 1868 impeachment proceedings; declined Johnson nomination to be attorney general
Davis, David (38)	9	United States senator from Illinois, 1877–1883; president pro tem of the Senate, 1881–1883; administrator of the Lincoln family estate; retirement in Bloomington, Illinois
Day, William R. (60)	7 months	Umpire, commission to settle World War I claims, 1922–1923
Douglas, William O. (82)	4	Retired in poor health in Washington, D.C.
Duvall, Gabriel (18)	9	Retired in declining health to Marietta, his estate in Maryland; wrote a family history
Ellsworth, Oliver (11)	7	Governor's council of Connecticut, 1801–1807; promoted agricultural development; retired at Elmwood, his estate in Windsor, Connecticut
Field, Stephen J. (39)	1	Retired in ill health
Fortas, Abe (99)	13	Private practice, Washington, D.C., 1969–1982
Frankfurter, Felix (81)	2	Retired in poor health in Washington, D.C.
Goldberg, Arthur J. (98)	24	Ambassador to the United Nations, 1965–1968; Democratic nominee for governor of New York, 1970; private practice

Table 5-9   *(Continued)*

Justice (appointment number)[a]	Post-Court years	Post-Court activities
Grier, Robert C. (32)	7 months	Retired in ill health in Philadelphia
Harlan, John Marshall II (93)	3 months	Retired in poor health in Washington, D.C.
Holmes, Oliver W., Jr. (59)	3	Divided his retirement years between Washington, D.C., and Massachusetts
Hughes, Charles Evans (63, 76)	13; 7	Following initial resignation as associate justice in 1916: Republican presidential nominee, 1916; secretary of state, 1921–1925; president of the American Bar Association, 1924–1925; judge, Permanent Court of International Justice, 1928–1930; chair, New York State Reorganization Commission; lawyer in private practice. Following retirement as chief justice in 1941: retirement in declining health
Hunt, Ward (43)	4	Retired in poor health
Jay, John (1)	33	Governor of New York, 1795–1801; nominated and confirmed to be chief justice in 1800, but declined to serve; president of American Bible Society, 1821; retirement on his 800-acre estate in Westchester County, New York; conducted agricultural experiments; active in peace groups
Johnson, Thomas (7)	26	Board of commissioners to plan the development of nation's capitol in Washington, D.C., 1791–1794; declined offer to serve as secretary of state, 1795; retirement in Frederick, Maryland
Marshall, Thurgood (100)	1	Retired in poor health in Washington, D.C.
McKenna, Joseph (58)	2	Retired in poor health in Washington, D.C.
McReynolds, James C. (68)	5	Retired in Washington, D.C.

(Table continues)

Table 5-9   *(Continued)*

Justice (appointment number)[a]	Post-Court years	Post-Court activities
Minton, Sherman (91)	8	Retired in poor health in New Albany, Indiana
Moody, William H. (61)	6	Retired in poor health due to crippling arthritis in Haverhill, Massachusetts
Moore, Alfred (13)	6	Retired to North Carolina; devoted his efforts to establishing the University of North Carolina, which he served as a trustee from 1789–1807
Nelson, Samuel (30)	1	Retired in declining health to his home in Cooperstown, New York
Pitney, Mahlon (67)	2	Retired in Washington, D.C., in poor health
Powell, Lewis F., Jr. (103)	11	Retired in Virginia; sat by designation as court of appeals judge
Reed, Stanley F. (80)	23	Chair, U.S. Civil Rights Commission, 1957; served by designation as a judge on the courts of appeals and the court of claims
Roberts, Owen J. (77)	10	Member, Amnesty Board, 1945–1947; president, Pennsylvania Bar Association, 1947; dean, University of Pennsylvania Law School, 1948–1951; trustee, University of Pennsylvania, 1943–1955; president, American Philosophical Society, 1952; chair, Fund for the Advancement of Education, 1953; active in world federalist movement
Rutledge, John (2, 9)	9	Chief justice of South Carolina, 1791–1795; nominated to be chief justice, served four months as recess appointment, confirmation rejected by Senate, 1795; South Carolina Assembly, 1798–1799; unsuccessful suicide attempt
Shiras, George, Jr. (54)	21	Retired in good health spending time with family in Florida, Michigan, and Pennsylvania

Table 5-9   *(Continued)*

Justice (appointment number)[a]	Post-Court years	Post-Court activities
Stewart, Potter (96)	4	Retired in good health
Strong, William (41)	14	Retired in good health in Washington, D.C.; vice president, American Bible Society, 1871–1895; president, American Tract Society, 1873–1895; president, American Sunday School Union, 1883–1895
Sutherland, George (72)	4	Retired in declining health
Swayne, Noah H. (36)	3	Retired in poor health
Taft, William H. (71)	1 month	Retired in poor health
Van Devanter, Willis (65)	3	Retired to New York; served by designation as a United States district judge
Warren, Earl (92)	5	Retired in Washington, D.C.; wrote memoirs
White, Byron R. (97)	9	Retired in good health in Washington, D.C.; sat by designation as a court of appeals judge; chaired Commission on Structural Alternatives for the Federal Courts of Appeal
Whittaker, Charles E. (95)	11	Legal staff, General Motors Corporation, 1965; special counsel, Senate Committee on Standards and Conduct, to develop ethics code, 1966; law practice, Kansas City

[a] Justices who died in office and those sitting in 1996 are not included.

Sources: Elder Witt, *Guide to the U.S. Supreme Court,* 2d ed. (Washington, D.C.: Congressional Quarterly, 1990); Leon Friedman and Fred L. Israel, eds., *The Justices of the United States Supreme Court: Their Lives and Major Opinions* (New York: R.R. Bowker, 1969–1978); Harold W. Chase et al., *Biographical Dictionary of the American Judiciary* (Detroit: Gale Research, 1976); *Judges of the United States,* 2d ed. (Washington, D.C.: Judicial Conference of the United States, 1983); *The National Cyclopaedia of American Biography* (New York: James T. White, various years); and *Dictionary of American Biography* (New York: Charles Scribner's Sons, various editions). Updated by the authors.

Table 5-10 The Deaths of the Justices

Justice (appointment number)	Date/place of death	Age	Resting place/Memorial[a]
Baldwin, Henry (23)	April 21, 1844 Philadelphia, Pa.	64	Greendale Cemetery[a] Meadville, Pa.
Barbour, Philip P. (26)	February 25, 1841 Washington, D.C.	57	Congressional Cemetery Washington, D.C.
Black, Hugo L. (79)	September 25, 1971 Washington, D.C.	85	Arlington National Cemetery Arlington, Va.
Blackmun, Harry A. (102)	March 4, 1999 Arlington, Va.	90	Arlington National Cemetery Arlington, Va.
Blair, John, Jr. (5)	August 31, 1800 Williamsburg, Va.	68	Bruton Parish Church Williamsburg, Va.
Blatchford, Samuel (49)	July 7, 1893 Newport, R.I.	73	Green Wood Cemetery Brooklyn, N.Y.
Bradley, Joseph P. (42)	January 22, 1892 Washington, D.C.	78	Mount Pleasant Cemetery Newark, N.J.
Brandeis, Louis D. (69)	October 5, 1941 Washington, D.C.	84	University of Louisville Law School Louisville, Ky.
Brennan, William J., Jr. (94)	July 24, 1997 Arlington, Va.	91	Arlington National Cemetery Arlington, Va.
Brewer, David J. (52)	March 28, 1910 Washington, D.C.	72	Mount Muncie Cemetery Leavenworth, Kan.

Name (Age)	Date and place of death	Age	Cemetery and location
Brown, Henry B. (53)	September 4, 1913 Bronxville, N.Y.	77	Elmwood Cemetery Detroit, Mich.
Burger, Warren E. (101)	June 25, 1995 Washington, D.C.	87	Arlington National Cemetery Arlington, Va.
Burton, Harold H. (88)	October 28, 1964 Washington, D.C.	76	Highland Park Cemetery Cleveland, Ohio
Butler, Pierce (73)	November 16, 1939 Washington, D.C.	73	Calvary Cemetery St. Paul, Minn.
Byrnes, James F. (85)	April 9, 1972 Columbia, S.C.	92	Trinity Cathedral Graveyard Columbia, S.C.
Campbell, John A. (34)	March 12, 1889 Baltimore, Md.	77	Green Mount Cemetery Baltimore, Md.
Cardozo, Benjamin (78)	July 9, 1938 Port Chester, N.Y.	68	Cypress Hills Cemetery Brooklyn, N.Y.
Catron, John (27)	May 30, 1865 Nashville, Tenn.	79	Mount Olivet Cemetery Nashville, Tenn.
Chase, Salmon P. (40)	May 7, 1873 New York, N.Y.	65	Spring Grove Cemetery Cincinnati, Ohio
Chase, Samuel (10)	June 19, 1811 Baltimore, Md.	70	St. Paul's Cemetery Baltimore, Md.
Clark, Tom C. (90)	June 13, 1977 New York, N.Y.	77	Restland Memorial Park Dallas, Texas

(Table continues)

Table 5-10 (*Continued*)

Justice (appointment number)	Date/place of death	Age	Resting place/Memorial
Clarke, John H. (70)	March 22, 1945 San Diego, Calif.	87	Lisbon Cemetery Lisbon, Ohio
Clifford, Nathan (35)	July 25, 1881(63, 76) Cornish, Maine	77	Evergreen Cemetery Portland, Maine
Curtis, Benjamin R. (33)	September 15, 1874 Newport, R.I.	64	Mount Auburn Cemetery Cambridge, Mass.
Cushing, William (3)	September 13, 1810 Scituate, Mass.	78	Family Cemetery Scituate, Mass.
Daniel, Peter V. (29)	May 31, 1860 Richmond, Va.	76	Hollywood Cemetery Richmond, Va.
Davis, David (38)	June 26, 1886 Bloomington, Ill.	71	Evergreen Memorial Cemetery Bloomington, Ill.
Day, William R. (60)	July 9, 1923 Mackinac Island, Mich.	74	West Lawn Cemetery Canton, Ohio
Douglas, William O. (82)	January 19, 1980 Washington, D.C.	81	Arlington National Cemetery Arlington, Va.
Duvall, Gabriel (18)	March 6, 1844 Prince George's Co., Md.	91	Family estate Prince George's Co., Md.
Ellsworth, Oliver (11)	November 26, 1807 Windsor, Conn.	62	Palisado Cemetery Windsor, Conn.

Name	Date and place of death	Age	Place of burial
Field, Stephen J. (39)	April 9, 1899 Washington, D.C.	82	Rock Creek Cemetery Washington, D.C.
Fortas, Abe (99)	April 5, 1982 Washington, D.C.	71	Cremated, no interment
Frankfurter, Felix (81)	February 22, 1965 Washington, D.C.	82	Mount Auburn Cemetery Cambridge, Mass.
Fuller, Melville W. (51)	July 4, 1910 Sorrento, Maine	77	Graceland Cemetery Chicago, Ill.
Goldberg, Arthur J. (98)	January 19, 1990 Washington, D.C.	81	Arlington National Cemetery Arlington, Va.
Gray, Horace (48)	September 15, 1902 Nahant, Mass.	74	Mount Auburn Cemetery Cambridge, Mass.
Grier, Robert C. (32)	September 25, 1870 Philadelphia, Pa.	76	West Laurel Hill Cemetery Bala-Cynwyd, Pa.
Harlan, John Marshall I (45)	October 14, 1911 Washington, D.C.	78	Rock Creek Cemetery Washington, D.C.
Harlan, John Marshall II (93)	December 29, 1971 Washington, D.C.	72	Emmanuel Church Cemetery Weston, Conn.
Holmes, Oliver W., Jr. (59)	March 6, 1935 Washington, D.C.	93	Arlington National Cemetery Arlington, Va.
Hughes, Charles E. (63, 76)	August 27, 1948 Osterville, Mass.	86	The Woodlawn Cemetery Bronx, N.Y.

(Table continues)

Table 5-10 *(Continued)*

Justice (appointment number)	Date/place of death	Age	Resting place/Memorial
Hunt, Ward (43)	March 24, 1886 Washington, D.C.	75	Forest Hill Cemetery Utica, N.Y.
Iredell, James (6)	October 20, 1799 Edenton, N.C.	48	Hayes Plantation Edenton, N.C.
Jackson, Howell E. (55)	August 8, 1895 West Meade, Tenn.	63	Mount Olivet Cemetery Nashville, Tenn.
Jackson, Robert H. (86)	October 9, 1954 Washington, D.C.	62	Mapel Grove Cemetery Frewsburg, N.Y.
Jay, John (1)	May 17, 1829 Bedford, N.Y.	83	Family Cemetery Rye, N.Y.
Johnson, Thomas (7)	October 26, 1819 Frederick, Md.	86	Mount Olivet Cemetery Frederick, Md.
Johnson, William (15)	August 4, 1834 Brooklyn, N.Y.	62	Unknown[b]
Lamar, Joseph R. (66)	January 2, 1916 Washington, D.C.	58	Summerville Cemetery Augusta, Ga.
Lamar, Lucius Q. C. (50)	January 23, 1893 Vineville, Ga.	67	St. Peter's Cemetery[c] Oxford, Miss.
Livingston, H. Brockholst (16)	March 18, 1823 Washington, D.C.	65	Green Wood Cemetery Brooklyn, N.Y.

Lurton, Horace (62)	July 12, 1914 Atlantic City, N.J.	70	Greenwood Cemetery Clarksville, Tenn.
Marshall, John (14)	July 6, 1835 Philadelphia, Pa.	79	Shockoe Hill Cemetery Richmond, Va.
Marshall, Thurgood (100)	January 24, 1993 Washington, D.C.	84	Arlington National Cemetery Arlington, Va.
Matthews, Stanley (47)	March 22, 1889 Washington, D.C.	64	Spring Grove Cemetery Cincinnati, Ohio
McKenna, Joseph (58)	November 21, 1926 Washington, D.C.	83	Mount Olivet Cemetery Washington, D.C.
McKinley, John (28)	July 19, 1852 Louisville, Ky.	72	Cave Hill Cemetery Louisville, Ky.
McLean, John (22)	April 4, 1861 Cincinnati, Ohio	76	Spring Grove Cemetery Cincinnati, Ohio
McReynolds, James C. (68)	August 24, 1946 Washington, D.C.	84	Glenwood Cemetery Elkton, Ky.
Miller, Samuel (37)	October 13, 1890 Washington, D.C.	74	Oakland Cemetery Keokuk, Iowa
Minton, Sherman (91)	April 9, 1965 New Albany, Ind.	74	Holy Trinity Catholic Cemetery New Albany, Ind.
Moody, William H. (61)	July 2, 1917 Haverhill, Mass.	63	Byfield Parish Churchyard Georgetown, Mass.

(Table continues)

Table 5-10 (*Continued*)

Justice (appointment number)	Date/place of death	Age	Resting place/Memorial
Moore, Alfred (13)	October 15, 1810 Bladen County, N.C.	55	St. Philip's Churchyard Southport, N.C.
Murphy, Frank (83)	July 19, 1949 Detroit, Mich.	59	Our Lady of Lake Huron Cemetery Harbor Beach, Mich.
Nelson, Samuel (30)	December 13, 1873 Cooperstown, N.Y.	81	Lakewood Cemetery Cooperstown, N.Y.
Paterson, William (8)	September 9, 1806 Albany, N.Y.	60	Albany Rural Cemetery Menands, N.Y.
Peckham, Rufus W. (57)	October 24, 1909 Altamont, N.Y.	70	Albany Rural Cemetery Menands, N.Y.
Pitney, Mahlon (67)	December 9, 1924 Washington, D.C.	66	Evergreen Cemetery Morristown, N.J.
Powell, Lewis F., Jr. (103)	August 25, 1998 Richmond, Va.	90	Hollywood Cemetery Richmond, Va.
Reed, Stanley F. (80)	April 2, 1980 Huntington, N.Y.	95	Maysville Cemetery Maysville, Ky.
Roberts, Owen J. (77)	May 17, 1955 West Vincent, Pa.	80	St. Andrew's Cemetery West Vincent, Pa.
Rutledge, John (2, 9)	July 18, 1800 Charleston, S.C.	60	St. Michael's Cemetery Charleston, S.C.

Rutledge, Wiley B. (87)	September 10, 1949 York, Maine	55	Green Mountain Cemetery Boulder, Colo.
Sanford, Edward T. (74)	March 8, 1930 Washington, D.C.	64	Greenwood Cemetery Knoxville, Tenn.
Shiras, George, Jr. (54)	August 2, 1924 Pittsburgh, Pa.	92	Allegheny Cemetery Pittsburgh, Pa.
Stewart, Potter (96)	December 7, 1985 Hanover, N.H.	70	Arlington National Cemetery Arlington, Va.
Stone, Harlan Fiske (75, 84)	April 22, 1946 Washington, D.C.	73	Rock Creek Cemetery Washington, D.C.
Story, Joseph (19)	September 10, 1845 Cambridge, Mass.	65	Mount Auburn Cemetery Cambridge, Mass.
Strong, William (41)	August 19, 1895 Lake Minnewassa, N.Y.	87	Charles Evans Cemetery Reading, Pa.
Sutherland, George (72)	July 18, 1942 Stockbridge, Mass.	80	Cedar Hill Cemetery Suitland, Md.
Swayne, Noah H. (36)	June 8, 1884 New York, N.Y.	79	Oak Hill Cemetery Washington, D.C.
Taft, William H. (71)	March 8, 1930 Washington, D.C.	72	Arlington National Cemetery Arlington, Va.
Taney, Roger B. (25)	October 12, 1864 Washington, D.C.	87	St. John the Evangelist Cemetery Frederick, Md.

(Table continues)

Table 5-10 *(Continued)*

Justice (appointment number)	Date/place of death	Age	Resting place/Memorial
Thompson, Smith (20)	December 18, 1843 Poughkeepsie, N.Y.	75	Poughkeepsie Cemetery Poughkeepsie, N.Y.
Todd, Thomas (17)	February 7, 1826 Frankfort, Ky.	61	Frankfort Cemetery Frankfort, Ky.
Trimble, Robert (21)	August 25, 1828 Paris, Ky.	51	Paris Cemetery Paris, Ky.
Van Devanter, Willis (65)	February 8, 1941 Washington, D.C.	81	Rock Creek Cemetery Washington, D.C.
Vinson, Fred M. (89)	September 8, 1953 Washington, D.C.	63	Pinehill Cemetery Louisa, Ky.
Waite, Morrison (44)	March 23, 1888 Washington, D.C.	71	Woodlawn Cemetery Toledo, Ohio
Warren, Earl (92)	July 9, 1974 Washington, D.C.	83	Arlington National Cemetery Arlington, Va.
Washington, Bushrod (12)	November 26, 1829 Philadelphia, Pa.	67	Family vault Mount Vernon, Va.
Wayne, James M. (24)	July 5, 1867 Washington, D.C.	77	Laurel Grove Cemetery Savannah, GA
White, Byron R. (97)	April 15, 2002 Denver, Co.	84	Saint Johns Episcopal Cathedral Denver, Co.

Name	Date of death	Age	Burial place
White, Edward D. (56, 64)	May 19, 1921 Washington, D.C.	75	Oak Hill Cemetery Washington, D.C.
Whittaker, Charles E. (95)	November 26, 1973 Kansas City, Mo.	72	Calvary Cemetery Kansas City, Mo.
Wilson, James (4)	August 21, 1798 Edenton, N.C.	55	Christ Churchyard Philadelphia, Pa.
Woodbury, Levi (31)	September 4, 1851 Portsmouth, N.H.	61	Harmony Grove Cemetery Portsmouth, N.H.
Woods, William B. (46)	May 14, 1887 Washington, D.C.	62	Cedar Hill Cemetery Newark, Ohio

[a] Baldwin originally was buried in Oak Hill Cemetery in Washington, D.C.

[b] Justice William Johnson died from complications of surgery in New York where he had gone for medical care. His body was to be shipped for burial in St. Philip's churchyard in Charleston, S.C. However, there is evidence that, although a monument to Johnson was erected at St. Philip's, the body never arrived. What happened to Johnson's body remains a mystery. See the Christensen source for a full account.

[c] Lamar originally was buried in Riverside Cemetery in Macon, Ga.

Sources: George A. Christensen, "Here Lies the Supreme Court: Gravesites of the Justices," *1983 Supreme Court Historical Society Yearbook* (1983): 17–30; Elder Witt, *Guide to the U.S. Supreme Court*, 2d ed. (Washington, D.C.: Congressional Quarterly, 1990); Leon Friedman and Fred L. Israel, eds., *The Justices of the United States Supreme Court: Their Lives and Major Opinions* (New York: R.R. Bowker, 1969–1978); Harold W. Chase et al., *Biographical Dictionary of the American Judiciary* (Detroit: Gale Research, 1976); *Judges of the United States*, 2d ed. (Washington, D.C.: Judicial Conference of the United States, 1983); *The National Cyclopaedia of American Biography* (New York: James T. White, various years); *Dictionary of American Biography* (New York: Charles Scribner's Sons, various editions); findagrave.com; and politicalgraveyard.com. Updated by the authors.

Table 5-11 Locations of Justices' Personal Papers

Justice (appointment number)[a]	Size of collection[b]	Location of collection[c]
Baldwin, Henry (23)	Medium	National Archives Washington, D.C. Crawford County Historical Society Meadville, Penn.
Barbour, Philip P. (26)	Medium	Virginia Historical Society Richmond, Va. University of Virginia Charlottesville, Va.
Black, Hugo L. (79)	Large	Library of Congress, Manuscript Division Washington, D.C.
Blackmun, Harry A. (102)	Large	Library of Congress Washington, D.C.
Blair, John, Jr. (5)	Very small	College of William and Mary Library Williamsburg, Va.
Blatchford, Samuel (49)	None	
Bradley, Joseph P. (42)	Medium	New Jersey Historical Society Newark, N.J.
Brandeis, Louis D. (69)	Large	University of Louisville Law School Louisville, Ky. Brandeis University Library Waltham, Mass. Harvard Law School Library Cambridge, Mass. American Jewish Archives Cincinnati, Ohio
Brennan, William J., Jr. (94)	Large	Library of Congress, Manuscript Division Washington, D.C.
Brewer, David J. (52)	Medium	Yale University Library New Haven, Conn. Library of Congress, Manuscript Division Washington, D.C.
Brown, Henry B. (53)	Small	Detroit Public Library Detroit, Mich. Yale University New Haven, Conn.

Table 5-11   *(Continued)*

Justice (appointment number)[a]	*Size of collection*[b]	*Location of collection*[c]
Burger, Warren E. (101)	None	
Burton, Harold H. (88)	Large	Library of Congress, Manuscript Division Washington, D.C.
Butler, Pierce (73)	Very small	Minnesota Historical Society St. Paul, Minn.
Byrnes, James F. (85)	Large	Robert Muldrow Cooper Library Clemson University, S.C.
Campbell, John A. (34)	Small	Southern Historical Collection University of North Carolina Chapel Hill, N.C.
Cardozo, Benjamin (78)	Small	Columbia University Libraries New York, N.Y.
		American Jewish Archives Cincinnati, Ohio
		American Jewish Historical Society Waltham, Mass.
Catron, John (27)	None	
Chase, Salmon P. (40)	Large	Historical Society of Pennsylvania Philadelphia, Pa.
		Library of Congress, Manuscript Division Washington, D.C.
		Ohio Historical Society Columbus, Ohio
Chase, Samuel (10)	Small	Maryland Historical Society Library Baltimore, Md.
Clark, Tom C. (90)	Large	University of Texas Law Library Austin, Texas
		Harry S Truman Library Independence, Mo.
Clarke, John H. (70)	Small	Case Western Reserve University Cleveland, Ohio
Clifford, Nathan (35)	Small	Maine Historical Society Portland, Maine
Curtis, Benjamin R. (33)	Small	Library of Congress, Manuscript Division Washington, D.C.

(Table continues)

Table 5-11   *(Continued)*

Justice (appointment number)[a]	Size of collection[b]	Location of collection[c]
Cushing, William (3)	Small	Massachusetts Historical Society Boston, Mass.
		Scituate Historical Society Scituate, Mass.
		Library of Congress, Manuscript Division Washington, D.C.
Daniel, Peter V. (29)	Small	Virginia Historical Society Richmond, Va.
		University of Virginia Library Charlottesville, Va.
Davis, David (38)	Large	Illinois State Historical Society Library Springfield, Ill.
		Chicago Historical Society Chicago, Ill.
		Illinois Historical Survey Collection University of Illinois Urbana, Ill.
Day, William R. (60)	Large	Library of Congress, Manuscript Division Washington, D.C.
Douglas, William O. (82)	Large	Library of Congress, Manuscript Division Washington, D.C.
Duvall, Gabriel (18)	Small	Library of Congress, Manuscript Division Washington, D.C.
Ellsworth, Oliver (11)	Small	Library of Congress Washington, D.C.
		New York Public Library New York, N.Y.
Field, Stephen J. (39)	Small	Bancroft Library, Manuscript Division University of California Berkeley, Calif.
Fortas, Abe (99)	Large	Sterling Memorial Library Yale University New Haven, Conn.

Table 5-11   *(Continued)*

Justice (appointment number)[a]	*Size of collection*[b]	*Location of collection*[c]
Frankfurter, Felix (81)	Large	Harvard Law School Library Cambridge, Mass.
		Library of Congress, Manuscript Division Washington, D.C.
Fuller, Melville W. (51)	Large	Library of Congress, Manuscript Division Washington, D.C.
		Chicago Historical Society Library Chicago, Ill.
		Bowdoin College Brunswick, Maine
Goldberg, Arthur J. (98)	Large	John F. Kennedy Library Boston, Mass.
		Library of Congress Washington, D.C.
		University of Notre Dame Notre Dame, Ind.
Gray, Horace (48)	Small	Library of Congress, Manuscript Division Washington, D.C.
Grier, Robert C. (32)	Very small	Historical Society of Pennsylvania Philadelphia, Penn.
Harlan, John Marshall I (45)	Large	Library of Congress, Manuscript Division Washington, D.C.
		University of Louisville Law Library Louisville, Ky.
Harlan, John Marshall II (93)	Large	Seeley G. Mudd Manuscript Library Princeton University Princeton, N.J.
Holmes, Oliver W., Jr. (59)	Large	Harvard Law School Library Cambridge, Mass.
		Library of Congress, Manuscript Division Washington, D.C.
Hughes, Charles Evans (63, 76)	Large	Library of Congress, Manuscript Division Washington, D.C.
		Columbia University New York N.Y.
		Brown University Providence, R.I.

(Table continues)

Table 5-11   *(Continued)*

Justice (appointment number)[a]	*Size of collection*[b]	*Location of collection*[c]
Hunt, Ward (43)	None	
Iredell, James (6)	Medium	North Carolina State Office of Archives and History Raleigh, N.C. Southern Historical Collection University of North Carolina Chapel Hill, N.C. Duke University Durham, N.C.
Jackson, Howell E. (55)	Small	Tennessee State Library and Archives Memphis, Tenn. Southern Historical Collection University of North Carolina Chapel Hill, N.C.
Jackson, Robert H. (86)	Large	Library of Congress, Manuscript Division Washington, D.C.
Jay, John (1)	Medium	Columbia University New York, N.Y. New York Historical Society New York, N.Y. Library of Congress Washington, D.C.
Johnson, Thomas (7)	Small	C. Burr Artz Library Frederick, Md.
Johnson, William (15)	None	
Lamar, Joseph R. (66)	Medium	University of Georgia Library Athens, Ga.
Lamar, Lucius Q. C. (50)	Small	Mississippi Department of Archives and History Jackson, Miss. Southern Historical Collection University of North Carolina Chapel Hill, N.C.
Livingston, H. Brockholst (16)	None	

Table 5-11   *(Continued)*

Justice (appointment number)[a]	*Size of collection*[b]	*Location of collection*[c]
Lurton, Horace (62)	Small	Library of Congress, Manuscript Division Washington, D.C.
Marshall, John (14)	Small	American Philosophical Society Philadelphia, Pa.
		Library of Congress, Manuscript Division Washington, D.C.
		College of William and Mary Williamsburg, Pa.
Marshall, Thurgood (100)	Large	Library of Congress, Manuscript Division Washington, D.C.
Matthews, Stanley (47)	Small	Cincinnati Historical Society Cincinnati, Ohio
		Rutherford B. Hayes Library Fremont, Ohio
McKenna, Joseph (58)	None	
McKinley, John (28)	None	
McLean, John (22)	Medium	Library of Congress, Manuscript Division Washington, D.C.
		Ohio Historical Society Columbus, Ohio
McReynolds, James C. (68)	Small	University of Virginia Library Charlottesville, Va.
Miller, Samuel (37)	Very small	Library of Congress Washington, D.C.
Minton, Sherman (91)	Small	Harry S Truman Library Independence, Mo.
		Indiana University Bloomington, Ind.
Moody, William H. (61)	Large	Library of Congress, Manuscript Division Washington, D.C.
		Haverhill Historical Society Haverhill, Mass.
		Essex Institute Salem, Mass.

(Table continues)

Table 5-11   *(Continued)*

Justice (appointment number)[a]	*Size of collection*[b]	*Location of collection*[c]
Moore, Alfred (13)	Very small	North Carolina State Office of Archives and History Raleigh, N.C.
Murphy, Frank (83)	Large	Michigan Historical Collection University of Michigan Ann Arbor, Mich.
		Detroit Public Library Burton Historical Collection Detroit, Mich.
Nelson, Samuel (30)	None	
Paterson, William (8)	Medium	Princeton University Library Princeton, N.J.
		New York Public Library New York, N.Y.
		Library of Congress, Manuscript Division Washington, D.C.
		Rutgers University Library New Brunswick, N.J.
Peckham, Rufus W. (57)	Small	Library of Congress, Manuscript Division Washington, D.C.
Pitney, Mahlon (67)	None	
Powell, Lewis F., Jr.	Large	Washington and Lee University Lexington, Va.
Reed, Stanley F. (80)	Large	University of Kentucky Library Lexington, Ky.
Roberts, Owen J. (77)	None	
Rutledge, John (2, 9)	Small	Duke University Durham, N.C.
		Charleston Library Society Charleston, S.C.
		South Carolina Historical Society Charleston, S.C.
Rutledge, Wiley B. (87)	Large	Library of Congress, Manuscript Division Washington, D.C.

Table 5-11 *(Continued)*

Justice (appointment number)[a]	Size of collection[b]	Location of collection[c]
Sanford, Edward T. (74)	Small	University of Tennessee Library Knoxville, Tenn.
Shiras, George, Jr. (54)	None	
Stewart, Potter (96)	Large	Sterling Memorial Library Yale University New Haven, Conn.
Stone, Harlan Fiske (75, 84)	Large	Library of Congress, Manuscript Division Washington, D.C. Columbia University Libraries New York, N.Y.
Story, Joseph (19)	Medium	Library of Congress, Manuscript Division Washington, D.C. William Clements Library University of Michigan Ann Arbor, Mich. New York Historical Society New York, N.Y. Massachusetts Historical Society Boston, Mass. Humanities Research Center University of Texas Austin, Texas
Strong, William (41)	Very small	Historical Society of Pennsylvania Philadelphia, Pa.
Sutherland, George (72)	Medium	Library of Congress, Manuscript Division Washington, D.C.
Swayne, Noah H. (36)	Small	Ohio Historical Society Columbus, Ohio
Taft, William H. (71)	Large	Library of Congress, Manuscript Division Washington, D.C. Cincinnati Historical Society Cincinnati, Ohio

(Table continues)

Table 5-11   *(Continued)*

Justice (appointment number)[a]	Size of collection[b]	Location of collection[c]
Taney, Roger B. (25)	Small	Library of Congress, Manuscript Division Washington, D.C.
		Dickinson College Library Carlisle, Pa.
Thompson, Smith (20)	Small	Library of Congress, Manuscript Division Washington, D.C.
		New York Historical Society New York, N.Y.
		Princeton University Princeton, N.J.
Todd, Thomas (17)	Very small	Cincinnati Historical Society Cincinnati, Ohio
		Filson Club Historical society Louisville, Ky.
Trimble, Robert (21)	None	
Van Devanter, Willis (65)	Large	Library of Congress, Manuscript Division Washington, D.C.
		Case Western Reserve University Library Cleveland, Ohio
Vinson, Fred M. (89)	Large	University of Kentucky Library Lexington, Ky.
Waite, Morrison (44)	Large	Library of Congress, Manuscript Division Washington, D.C.
Warren, Earl (92)	Large	Library of Congress, Manuscript Division Washington, D.C.
		California State Archives Sacramento, Calif.
Washington, Bushrod (12)	Small	Duke University Durham, N.C.
		Mount Vernon Ladies Association of the Union Mount Vernon, Va.
Wayne, James M. (24)	Very small	Georgia Historical Society Savannah, Ga.

Table 5-11 *(Continued)*

Justice *(appointment number)*[a]	*Size of collection*[b]	*Location of collection*[c]
White, Byron R. (97)	Large	Library of Congress Washington, D.C.
White, Edward D. (56, 64)	None	
Whitaker, Charles E. (95)	None	
Wilson, James (4)	Small	Historical Society of Pennsylvania Philadelphia, Pa. Dickinson College Library Carlisle, Pa.
Woodbury, Levi (31)	Large	Library of Congress, Manuscript Division Washington, D.C. New Hampshire Historical Society Concord, N.H. Dartmouth College Hanover, N.H.
Woods, William B. (46)	None	

Note: This table lists collections of private papers deposited in libraries and other public institutions. Many of these collections have restrictions on use, and some have limited numbers of items dealing with the justices' Supreme Court years. The personal papers of other individuals may also hold scattered items linked to the various justices. Consult the sources for this table for a more complete listing of collections of other individuals that may have items of relevance to Supreme Court justices.

[a] Recent Supreme Court justices not included as their personal papers are not yet available for public or scholarly use.

[b] Refers to combined holdings in all locations. Large = over 5,000 items; Medium = up to 5,000 items; Small = up to 1,000 items; Very small = scattered items; None = no known collections.

[c] Where more than one location listed, appear in descending order of collection size.

Sources: Alexandra K. Wigdor, *The Personal Papers of Supreme Court Justices: A Descriptive Guide* (New York: Garland Publishing, 1986), and Peter A. Wonders, *Directory of Manuscript Collections Related to Federal Judges, 1789–1997* (Washington, D.C.: Federal Judicial Center, 1998). Updated by the authors.

Table 5-12   Selected Books and Articles Written by the Justices

Justice (appointment number)[a]	*Books and articles*[b]
Baldwin, Henry (23)	*A General View of the Origin and Nature of the Constitution and Government of the United States.* Philadelphia: American Constitutional and Legal History Service, 1837.
Black, Hugo L. (79)	"The Lawyer and Individual Freedom." *Tennessee Law Review* 21 (December 1950): 461–471.
	"The Bill of Rights." *New York University Law Review* 35 (April 1960): 865–881.
	A Constitutional Faith. New York: Alfred A. Knopf, 1968.
Blackmun, Harry A. (102)	"Marital Deduction and Its Use in Minnesota." *Minnesota Law Review* 36 (December 1951): 50–64.
	"Thoughts about Ethics." *Emory Law Journal* 24 (Winter 1975): 3–20.
	"Section 1983 and Federal Protection of Individual Rights: Will the Statute Remain Alive or Fade Away?" *New York University Law Review* 60 (April 1985): 1–29.
Blatchford, Samuel (49)	*Blatchford's Circuit Court Reports*, 1852.
	Blatchford's and Howland's Reports, 1855.
Bradley, Joseph P. (42)	*Family Notes Respecting the Bradley Family of Fairfield.* Newark, N.J.: A. Pierson, 1894.
	Miscellaneous Writings of the Late Honorable Joseph P. Bradley and a Review of His Judicial Record. Edited by Charles Bradley. Newark, N.J.: L.J. Hardham, 1902.
Brandeis, Louis D. (69)	"The Right to Privacy" (with Samuel D. Warren). *Harvard Law Review* 4 (December 15, 1890): 193–220.
	Business: A Profession. Boston: Small, Maynard, 1914.
	Other People's Money: And How the Bankers Use It. New York: Stokes, 1914.
	"The Living Law." *Illinois Law Review* 10 (February 1916): 461–471.

Table 5-12   *(Continued)*

Justice (appointment number)[a]	*Books and articles*[b]
Brennan, William J., Jr. (94)	"The Bill of Rights and the States." *New York University Law Review* 36 (April 1961): 761–778.
	"Constitutional Adjudication." *Notre Dame Lawyer* 40 (August 1965): 559–569.
	An Affair with Freedom. New York: Atheneum, 1967.
	"State Constitutions and the Protection of Individual Rights." *Harvard Law Review* 90 (1977): 489–504.
	"Constitutional Adjudication and the Death Penalty: A View from the Court." *Harvard Law Review* 100 (December 1986): 313–331.
Brewer, David J. (52)	*The Income Tax Cases and Some Comments Thereon.* Iowa City: University of Iowa Press, 1895.
	The United States as a Christian Nation. Philadelphia: J.C. Winston Co., 1905.
	American Citizenship. New Haven, Conn.: Yale University Press, 1911.
Breyer, Stephen G. (113)	*The Federal Power Commission and the Regulation of Energy* (with Paul MacAvoy). Washington, D.C.: Brookings, 1974.
	Administrative Law and Regulatory Policy (with Richard Stewart). Boston: Little, Brown, 1979 and subsequent revisions.
	Regulation and Reform. Cambridge, Mass. Harvard University Press, 1982.
	Breaking the Vicious Cycle: Toward Effective Risk Regulation. Cambridge, Mass.: Harvard University Press, 1993.
Brown, Henry B. (53)	"The Dissenting Opinions of Mr. Justice Daniel." *American Law Review* 21 (November/December 1887): 869–900.
	"Judicial Independence." *American Bar Association Reports* 12 (1889): 265–288.
	"The Distribution of Property." *American Bar Association Reports* 16 (1893): 213–242.

(Table continues)

Table 5-12   *(Continued)*

Justice (appointment number)[a]	*Books and articles*[b]
Burger, Warren E. (101)	"New Chief Justice's Philosophy of Law in America." *New York State Bar Journal* 41 (October 1969): 454–479.
	"Thinking the Unthinkable." *Loyola Law Review* 31 (Spring 1985): 205–220.
	"The Time is Now for the Intercircuit Panel." *American Bar Association Journal* 71 (April 1985): 86–91.
Burton, Harold H. (88)	*The Story of the Place Where First and A Streets Formerly Met at What Is Now the Site of the Supreme Court Building.* Washington, D.C.: Library of Congress, 1952.
	"Unsung Services of the Supreme Court of the United States." *Fordham Law Review* 24 (Summer 1955): 169–177.
	"Judging Is Also Administration: An Appreciation of Constructive Leadership." *Temple Law Quarterly* 21 (October 1947): 77–90.
Butler, Pierce (73)	"Some Opportunities and Duties of Lawyers." *American Bar Association Journal* 9 (September 1923): 583–587.
Byrnes, James F. (85)	*Speaking Frankly.* New York: Harper, 1947.
	All in One Lifetime. New York: Harper, 1958.
	"The Supreme Court and States Rights." *Alabama Lawyer* 20 (October 1959): 396–403.
Cardozo, Benjamin (78)	*The Nature of the Judicial Process.* New Haven, Conn.: Yale University Press, 1921.
	The Growth of the Law. New Haven, Conn.: Yale University Press, 1924.
	The Paradoxes of Legal Science. New York: Columbia University Press, 1928.
Chase, Salmon P. (40)	*Inside Lincoln's Cabinet: The Civil War Diaries of Salmon P. Chase.* Edited by David Donald. New York: Longman's Green, 1954.
Clark, Tom C. (90)	"Administrative Law." *Journal of the Bar Association of the District of Columbia* 18 (July 1951): 254–261.

Table 5-12   *(Continued)*

Justice (appointment number)[a]	*Books and articles*[b]
	"Constitutional Adjudication and the Supreme Court." *Drake Law Review* 9 (May 1960): 59–65.
	"American Bar Association Standards for Criminal Justice: Prescription for an Ailing System." *Notre Dame Lawyer* 47 (February 1972): 429–441.
Clarke, John H. (70)	"Practice Before the Supreme Court." *Virginia Law Register* 8 (August 1922): 241–252.
	"Reminiscences of the Courts and Law." *Proceedings of the California State Bar Association* 5 (1932): 20–31.
Curtis, Benjamin R. (33)	*Executive Power.* Cambridge, Mass.: Houghton, 1862.
	A Memoir of Benjamin Robbins Curtis. Boston: Little, Brown, 1879
Douglas, William O. (82)	*An Almanac of Liberty.* Garden City, N.Y.: Doubleday, 1954.
	Freedom of the Mind. Garden City, N.Y.: Doubleday, 1962.
	The Bible and the Schools. Boston: Little, Brown, 1966.
	Points of Rebellion. New York: Random House, 1970.
	Go East Young Man. New York: Random House, 1974.
	The Court Years, 1939–1975: The Autobiography of William O. Douglas. New York: Random House, 1980.
Ellsworth, Oliver (11)	*Essays on the Constitution of the United States, Published During Its Discussion by the People, 1787–1788.* Brooklyn, N.Y.: Historical Printing Club, 1892.
Field, Stephen J. (39)	"The Centenary of the Supreme Court of the United States." *American Law Review* 24 (May/June 1890): 351–368.

(Table continues)

Table 5-12   *(Continued)*

Justice (appointment number)[a]	*Books and articles*[b]
	Personal Reminiscences of Early Days in California with other Sketches. Washington, D.C., 1893. Reprint. New York: Da Capo Press, 1968.
Fortas, Abe (99)	*Concerning Dissent and Civil Disobedience.* New York: New American Library, 1968.
	"Criminal Justice 'Without Pity.' " *Trial Lawyers Quarterly* 9 (Summer 1973): 9–14.
Frankfurter, Felix (81)	*The Case of Sacco and Vanzetti: A Critical Analysis for Lawyers and Laymen.* Boston: Little, Brown, 1927.
	The Business of the Supreme Court: A Study in the Federal Judicial System (with James M. Landis). New York: Macmillan, 1928.
	The Commerce Clause Under Marshall, Taney and Waite. Chapel Hill: University of North Carolina Press, 1937.
	Mr. Justice Holmes and the Constitution. Cambridge, Mass.: Harvard University Press, 1938.
	The Public and Its Government. Boston: Beacon Press, 1964.
Ginsburg, Ruth Bader (112)	*Civil Procedure in Sweden* (with Anders Bruzelius). The Hague: M. Nijhoff, 1965.
	Text, Cases and Materials on Sex-based Discrimination (with Kenneth M. Davidson and Herma Hill Kay). St. Paul, Minn.: West Publishing, 1974.
	"Some Thoughts on Autonomy and Equality in Relation to *Roe v. Wade.*" *North Carolina Law Review* 63 (January 1985): 375–386.
	"Speaking in a Judicial Voice." *New York University Law Review* 67 (December 1992): 1185–1209.
Goldberg, Arthur J. (98)	*AFL/CIO: Labor United.* New York: McGraw-Hill, 1956.
	"Declaring the Death Penalty Unconstitutional" (with Alan Dershowitz). *Harvard Law Review* 83 (June 1970): 1773–1819.

Table 5-12   *(Continued)*

Justice (appointment number)[a]	*Books and articles*[b]
	Equal Justice: The Warren Era of the Supreme Court. Evanston, Ill.: Northwestern University Press, 1971.
Harlan, John Marshall I (45)	"The Supreme Court of the United States and Its Work." *American Law Review* 30 (November/December 1896): 900–902.
	"James Wilson and the Formation of the Constitution." *American Law Review* 34 (July/August 1900): 481–504.
Harlan, John Marshall II (93)	"Some Aspects of the Judicial Process in the Supreme Court of the United States." *Australian Law Journal* 33 (August 1959): 108–125.
	"The Bill of Rights and the Constitution." *American Bar Association Journal* 50 (October 1964): 918–920.
Holmes, Oliver W., Jr. (59)	*The Common Law.* Boston: Little, Brown, 1881.
	The Holmes-Pollock Letters. Edited by Mark D. Howe. Cambridge, Mass.: Harvard University Press, 1941.
	The Holmes-Laski Letters. Edited by Mark D. Howe. Cambridge, Mass.: Harvard University Press, 1953.
	The Holmes-Einstein Letters. Edited by James B. Peabody. New York: St. Martin's Press, 1964.
Hughes, Charles E. (63, 76)	*Conditions of Progress in Democratic Government.* New Haven, Conn.: Yale University Press, 1910.
	Pathways of Peace. New York: Harper, 1925.
	The Supreme Court of the United States. New York: Columbia University Press, 1928.
	Pan American Peace Plans. New Haven, Conn.: Yale University Press, 1929.
Iredell, James (6)	"Letter of James Iredell to Johnson." *Massachusetts Historical Society Proceedings* 53 (1920): 27–28.
Jackson, Robert H. (86)	*The Struggle for Judicial Supremacy.* New York: Alfred A. Knopf, 1941.

(Table continues)

Table 5-12   *(Continued)*

Justice (appointment number)[a]	*Books and articles*[b]
	Full Faith and Credit: The Lawyer's Clause of the Constitution. New York: Columbia University Press, 1945.
	The Case Against the Nazi War Criminals. New York: Alfred A. Knopf, 1946.
	The Supreme Court in the American System of Government. Cambridge, Mass.: Harvard University Press, 1955.
Jay, John (1)	*An Address to the People of the State of New York on the Subject of the Constitution, Agreed upon at Philadelphia, September 17, 1787.* New York: Loudon, 1788.
	The Federalist Papers (with James Madison and Alexander Hamilton), ed. Garry Wills (New York: Bantam, 1982).
Johnson, William (15)	*Sketches of the Life and Correspondence of Nathanael Greene.* Charleston, S.C.: A.E. Miller, 1822.
Kennedy, Anthony M. (109)	"Judicial Ethics and the Rule of Law." *St. Louis University Law Journal* 40 (Summer 1996): 1067–1077.
	"Law and Belief." *Trial* 34 (July 1998): 22–26.
Lamar, Joseph R. (66)	*A Century's Progress in Law.* Augusta, Ga.: Richards and Shaver, 1900.
	"History of the Establishment of the Supreme Court of Georgia." *Report of the Georgia Bar Association* 24 (1907): 85–103.
Lurton, Horace (62)	"Evolution of the Right of Trial." *Ohio Law Bulletin* 52 (1907): 442.
Marshall, John (14)	*The Life of George Washington,* 5 vols. Philadelphia: C. P. Wayne, 1804–1807.
	A History of the Colonies Planted by the English on the Continent of North America, from Their Settlement, to the Commencement of That War Which Terminated in Their Independence. Philadelphia: A. Small, 1824.
	The Writing of John Marshall upon the Federal Constitution. Boston: J. Munroe, 1839.

Table 5-12 *(Continued)*

Justice (appointment number)[a]	*Books and articles*[b]
Marshall, Thurgood (100)	"The Supreme Court as Protector of Civil Rights: Equal Protection of the Laws." *Annals of the American Academy of Political and Social Sciences* 275 (May 1951): 101–110.
	"The Continuing Challenge of the Fourteenth Amendment." *Georgia Law Review* 3 (Fall 1968): 1–10.
	"Financing Public Interest Law Practice: The Role of the Organized Bar." *American Bar Association Journal* 61 (December 1975): 1487–1491.
Matthews, Stanley (47)	*The Function of the Legal Profession in the Progress of Civilization.* Cincinnati: R. Clarke, 1881.
McLean, John (22)	*The Letters of John McLean to John Teesdale.* Edited by William Salter. Oberlin, Ohio: Bibliotheca Sacra, 1899.
Miller, Samuel (37)	*The Supreme Court of the United States.* Washington, D.C.: W. H. Barnes, 1877.
	The Constitution and the Supreme Court of the United States of America. New York: D. Appleton, 1889.
O'Connor, Sandra Day (106)	"The Changing of the Circuit Justice." *University of Toledo Law Review* 17 (Spring 1986): 521–526.
	The Life of the Law: Principles of Logic and Experience from the United States. Washington, D.C.: National Legal Center, 1996.
Powell, Lewis F., Jr. (103)	"Myths and Misconceptions about the Supreme Court." *American Bar Association Journal* 61 (November 1975): 1344–1347.
	"Of Politics and the Court." *Supreme Court Historical Society Yearbook, 1982* (1982): 23–26.
	"The Burger Court." *Washington and Lee Law Review* 44 (Winter 1987): 1–10.
Reed, Stanley F. (80)	"Our Constitutional Philosophy: Concerning the Significance of Judicial Review in the Evolution of American Democracy." *Kentucky State Bar Journal* 2 (June 1961): 136–146.

(Table continues)

Table 5-12   *(Continued)*

Justice (appointment number)[a]	Books and articles[b]
Rehnquist, William (104, 107)	*The Supreme Court: The Way It Was, The Way It Is.* New York: Morrow, 1987.
	Grand Inquests: The Historic Impeachments of Justice Samuel Chase and President Andrew Johnson. New York: Morrow, 1992.
	Civil Liberty and the Civil War. Washington, D.C.: National Legal Center, 1997.
	All the Laws but One: Civil Liberties in Wartime. New York: Knopf, 1998.
Roberts, Owen J. (77)	*The Court and the Constitution.* Cambridge, Mass.: Harvard University Press, 1951.
Rutledge, Wiley B. (87)	*A Declaration of Legal Faith.* Lawrence: University of Kansas Press, 1947.
Sanford, Edward T. (74)	*Blount College and the University of Tennessee.* Knoxville: University of Tennessee Press, 1894.
Scalia, Antonin (108)	"Vermont Yankee: The APA, the D.C. Circuit, and the Supreme Court." *Supreme Court Review,* 1978 (1978): 345–409.
	"Historical Anomalies in Administrative Law." *Supreme Court Historical Society Yearbook,* 1985 (1985): 101–111.
	A Matter of Interpretation. Princeton, N.J.: Princeton University Press, 1997.
Souter, David H. (110)	"A Tribute to Justice Harry Blackmun." *Yale Law Journal* 104 (October 1994): 5–6.
Stevens, John Paul (105)	*Mr. Justice Rutledge.* Chicago: University of Chicago Press, 1956.
	"Some Thoughts on Judicial Restraint." *Judicature* 66 (November 1983): 177–183.
	"The Freedom of Speech." *Yale Law Journal* 102 (April 1993): 1293–1313.
	The Bill of Rights: A Century of Progress. Chicago: University of Chicago Press, 1992.

Table 5-12   *(Continued)*

Justice (appointment number)[a]	*Books and articles*[b]
Stewart, Potter (96)	"The Nine of Us: 'Guardians of the Constitution'." *Florida Bar Journal* 41 (October 1967): 1090–1097.
	"A View From Inside the Court." *Cleveland Bar Association Journal* 39 (January 1968): 69–92.
	"Or of the Press." *Hastings Law Journal* 26 (January 1975): 631–637.
Stone, Harlan Fiske (75, 84)	*Law and Its Administration.* New York: Columbia University Press, 1915.
	"The Public Influence of the Bar." *Harvard Law Review* 48 (November 1934): 1–14.
	"The Common Law in the United States." *Harvard Law Review* 50 (November 1936): 4–26.
	"Dissenting Opinions Are Not without Value." *Journal of the American Judicature Society* 26 (October 1942): 78.
Story, Joseph (19)	*Commentaries on the Constitution of the United States.* Boston: Hilliard, Gray, 1833.
	Commentaries on the Law, 9 vols., published between 1832–1845.
	Discourse upon the Life, Character and Services of the Honorable John Marshall. Boston: J. Munroe, 1835.
Strong, William (41)	*Two Lectures upon the Relations of Civil Law to Church Polity, Discipline, and Property.* New York: Dodd, Mead, 1875.
	"The Needs of the Supreme Court." *North American Review* 132 (May 1881): 437–450.
	"Relief for the Supreme Court." *North American Review* 151 (November 1890): 567–575.
Sutherland, George (72)	*Private Rights and Government Control.* Washington, D.C.: Government Printing Office, 1917.
	Constitutional Power and World Affairs. New York: Columbia University Press, 1919.

(Table continues)

Table 5-12   *(Continued)*

Justice (appointment number)[a]	*Books and articles*[b]
Taft, William H. (71)	*Four Aspects of Civic Duty.* New York: Charles Scribner's Sons, 1906.
	Popular Government: Its Essence, Its Permanence, and Its Perils. New Haven, Conn.: Yale University Press, 1913.
	The Anti-Trust Act and the Supreme Court. New York: Harper and Row, 1914.
	The President and His Powers. New York: Columbia University Press, 1916.
	Liberty Under Law: An Interpretation of the Principles of Our Constitutional Government. New Haven, Conn.: Yale University Press, 1922.
Taney, Roger B. (25)	*The Decision in the Merryman Case, upon the Writ of Habeas Corpus.* Philadelphia: John Campbell, 1862.
Thomas, Clarence (111)	"Transition from Policymaker to Judge—A Matter of Deference." *Creighton Law Review* 26 (Fall 1993): 241–253.
	The Virtue of Defeat: *Plessy v. Ferguson* in Retrospect." *Journal of Supreme Court History* 2 (1997): 15–24.
	"Why Federalism Matters." *Drake Law Review* 48 (2000): 231–238.
Van Devanter, Willis (65)	"The Supreme Court of the United States." *Indiana Law Journal* 5 (May 1930): 553–562.
Vinson, Fred M. (89)	"Our Enduring Constitution." *Washington and Lee Law Review* 6 (1949): 1–11.
	"Supreme Court Work: Opinion on Dissents." *Oklahoma Bar Association Journal* 20 (September 1949): 1269–1275.
Waite, Morrison (44)	"The Supreme Court of the United States." *Albany Law Journal* 36 (October 15, 1887): 315–318.
Warren, Earl (92)	*Hughes and the Court.* Hamilton, N.Y.: Colgate University, 1962.

Table 5-12   *(Continued)*

Justice (appointment number)[a]	*Books and articles*[b]
	"The Bill of Rights and the Military." *New York University Law Review* 37 (April 1962): 181–203.
	"All Men Are Created Equal." *Record of the Association of the Bar of the City of New York* 25 (June 1970): 351–364.
	A Republic, if You Can Keep It. New York: Quadrangle Books, 1972.
	Memoirs. New York: Doubleday, 1977.
White, Byron R. (97)	"Supreme Court Review of Agency Decisions." *Administrative Law Review* 26 (Winter 1974): 107–112.
	"Challenges for the U. S. Supreme Court and the Bar: Contemporary Reflections." *Antitrust Law Journal* 51 (August 1982): 275–282.
	"Work of the Supreme Court: A Nuts and Bolts Description." *New York State Bar Journal* 54 (October 1982): 346–349.
White, Edward D. (56, 64)	"Supreme Court of the United States." *American Bar Association Journal* 7 (July 1921): 341–343.
Whittaker, Charles E. (95)	"Role of the Supreme Court." *Arizona Law Review* 17 (Fall 1963): 292–301.
Wilson, James (4)	*Commentaries on the Constitution of the United States* (with Thomas Mikean). Philadelphia: T. Lloyd, 1792.
	Works. Philadelphia: Lorenzo Press, 1804.
	Selected Political Essays. Edited by Randolph Adams. New York: Alfred A. Knopf, 1930.
Woodbury, Levi (31)	*Writings of Levi Woodbury, LL.D., Political, Judicial, and Literary.* Boston: Little, Brown, 1852.

[a] Justices with no significant books or articles credited to them not listed.

[b] Books and articles included should not be considered exhaustive. Several members of the Court were quite prolific authors. Where a justice published numerous books or articles, the more significant of those works are listed.

Sources: Fenton S. Martin and Robert U. Goehlert, *The United States Supreme Court: A Bibliography* (Washington, D.C.: Congressional Quarterly, 1990); Leon Friedman and Fred L. Israel, eds., *The Justices of the United States Supreme Court: Their Lives and Major Opinions* (New York: R. R. Bowker, 1969–1978). Updated by the authors.

Table 5-13   Classic Statements from the Bench

Abortion

This right of privacy, whether it be founded in the Fourteenth Amendment's concept of personal liberty and restrictions upon state action, as we feel it is, or, as the District Court determined, in the Ninth Amendment's reservation of rights to the people, is broad enough to encompass a woman's decision whether or not to terminate her pregnancy.

Harry Blackmun, for the Court, *Roe v. Wade*, 410 U.S. 113 (1973), at 152.

Just as improvements in medical technology will move *forward* at the point at which the State may regulate for reasons of maternal health, different technological improvements will move *backward* the point of viability at which the State may proscribe abortions. . . . [T]he Roe framework . . . is clearly on a collision course with itself.

Sandra Day O'Connor, dissenting, *Akron* v. *Akron Center for Reproductive Health*, 462 U.S. 416 (1983), at 456–458.

Today, *Roe v. Wade* (1973) and the fundamental constitutional right of women to decide whether to terminate a pregnancy survive but are not secure. . . .

I fear for the future. I fear for the liberty and equality of the millions of women who have lived and come of age in the 16 years since *Roe* was decided. I fear for the integrity of, and public esteem for, this Court.

I dissent.

Harry Blackmun, concurring in part and dissenting in part, *Webster v. Reproductive Health Services*, 492 U.S. 490 (1989), at 537–538.

Avoidance of constitutional questions

When the validity of an act of the Congress is drawn in question, and even if a serious doubt of constitutionality is raised, it is a cardinal principle that this Court will first ascertain whether a construction of the statute is fairly possible by which the question may be avoided.

Louis D. Brandeis, dissenting, *Ashwander v. Tennessee Valley Authority*, 297 U.S. 288 (1936), at 348.

Balancing of freedoms

. . . I do not agree that laws directly abridging First Amendment freedoms can be justified by a congressional or judicial balancing process. . . .

To apply the Court's balancing test under such circumstances is to read the First Amendment to say "Congress shall pass no law abridging freedom of speech, press, assembly and petition unless Congress and the Supreme Court reach the joint conclusion that on balance the interest of the Government in stifling these freedoms is greater than the interest of the people in having them exercised.". . .

. . . For no number of laws against communism can have as much effect as the personal conviction which comes from having heard its arguments and rejected them, or from having once accepted its tenets and later recognized their worthlessness. . . .

Ultimately all the questions in this case really boil down to one—whether we as a people will try fearfully and futilely to preserve democracy by adopting to-

Table 5-13   *(Continued)*

talitarian methods, or whether in accordance with our traditions and our Constitution we will have the confidence and courage to be free.

Hugo L. Black, dissenting, *Barenblatt v. United States,* 360 U.S. 109 (1959), at 141, 143–144, 162.

Bill of Rights, criteria governing applicability to the states

The Commonwealth of Massachusetts is free to regulate the procedure of its courts in accordance with its own conception of policy and fairness unless in doing so it offends some principle of justice so rooted in the traditions and conscience of our people as to be ranked as fundamental.

Benjamin N. Cardozo, for the Court, *Snyder v. Massachusetts,* 291 U.S. 97 (1934), at 105.

. . . of the very essence of a scheme of ordered liberty.

Benjamin N. Cardozo, for the Court, *Palko v. Connecticut,* 302 U.S. 319 (1937), at 325.

. . . the proceedings by which this conviction was obtained do more than offend some fastidious squeamishness or private sentimentalism about combatting crime too energetically. This is conduct that shocks the conscience.

Felix Frankfurter, for the Court, *Rochin v. California,* 342 U.S. 165 (1952), at 172.

Bill of Rights, purpose of

The very purpose of a Bill of rights was to withdraw certain subjects from the vicissitudes of political controversy, to place them beyond the reach of majorities and officials and to establish them as legal principles to be applied by the courts. One's right to life, liberty, and property, to free speech, a free press, freedom of worship and assembly, and other fundamental rights may not be submitted to vote; they depend on the outcome of no election.

Robert H. Jackson, for the Court, *West Virginia State Board of Education v. Barnette,* 319 U.S. 624 (1943), at 638.

Business affected with a public interest

Property does become clothed with a public interest when used in a manner to make it of public consequence, and affect the community at large. When, therefore, one devotes his property to a use in which the public has an interest, he, in effect, grants to the public an interest in that use, and must submit to be controlled by the public for the common good, to the extent of the interest he has thus created.

Morrison R. Waite, for the Court, *Munn v. Illinois,* 94 U.S. 113 (1877), at 126.

Capital punishment

These death sentences are cruel and unusual in the same way that being struck by lightening is cruel and unusual. For, of all the people convicted of . . . murders . . . many just as reprehensible, the petitioners are among the capriciously

(Table continues)

Table 5-13   *(Continued)*

---

selected random handful. . . . I simply conclude that the Eighth and Fouteenth Amendments cannot . . . permit this unique penalty to be so wantonly and freakishly administered.

Potter Stewart, concurring, *Furman v. Georgia*, 408 U.S. 238 (1972), at 309–310.

Sixteen years ago, this Court decreed—by a sheer act of will . . . —that the People (as in We, the People) cannot decree the death penalty, absolutely and categorically, for *any* criminal act, even (presumably) genocide; the jury must always be given the option of extending mercy. . . . Today, obscured within the fog of confusion that is our annually improvised . . . "death is different" jurisprudence, the Court strikes a further blow against the People. . . . Not only must mercy be allowed, but now only the merciful may be permitted to sit in judgment. Those who agree with the author of Exodus . . . must be banished from American juries—not because the People have so decreed, but because such jurors do not share the . . . penological preferences of this Court.

Antonin Scalia, dissenting, *Morgan v. Illinois*, 504 U.S. 719 (1992), at 751–752.

Perhaps one day this Court will develop procedural rules or verbal formulas that actually will provide consistency, fairness, and reliability in a capital-sentencing scheme. I am not optimistic that such a day will come. I am more optimistic, though, that this Court eventually will conclude that the effort to eliminate arbitrariness, while preserving fairness "in the infliction of (death) is so plainly doomed to failure that it and the death penalty must be abandoned altogether." I may not live to see that day, but I have faith that eventually it will arrive. The path the Court has chosen lessens all of us. I dissent.

Harry A. Blackmun, dissenting from the Court's denial of review, *Callins v. Collins* (1994).

Church and state, wall of separation between

Neither a state nor the Federal Government can set up a church. Neither can pass laws which aid one religion, aid all religions, or prefer one religion over another. Neither can force nor influence a person to go to or to remain away from church against his will or force him to profess a belief or disbelief in any religion. No person can be punished for entertaining or professing religious beliefs or disbeliefs, for church attendance or non-attendance. No tax in any amount, large or small, can be levied to support any religious activities or institutions, whatever they may be called, or whatever form they may adopt to teach or practice religion. Neither a state nor the Federal Government can, openly or secretly, participate in the affairs of any religious organizations or groups and vice versa. In the words of Jefferson, the clause against establishment of religion by law was intended to erect "a wall of separation between Church and State."

Hugo L. Black, for the Court, *Everson v. Board of Education*, 330 U.S. 1 (1947), at 15–16.

Clear and present danger doctrine

The question in every case is whether the words used are used in such circumstances and are of such a nature as to create a clear and present danger that they will bring about the substantive evils that Congress has a right to prevent. It is a question of proximity and degree. When a nation is at war many things that

Table 5-13   *(Continued)*

might be said in time of peace are such a hindrance to its effort that their utterance will not be endured so long as men fight, and that no court could regard them as protected by any constitutional right.

   Oliver Wendell Holmes, for the Court, *Schenck v. United States*, 249 U.S. 47 (1919), at 52.

. . . the constitutional guarantees of free speech and free press do not permit a State to forbid or prescribe advocacy of the use of force or of law violation except where such advocacy is directed to inciting or producing imminent lawless action and is likely to incite or produce such action.

   per curiam, *Brandenburg v. Ohio*, 395 U.S. 444 (1969), at 447.

Commander in chief, president as

   If a war be made by invasion of a foreign nation, the President is not only authorized but bound to resist force, by force. He does not initiate the war, but is bound to accept the challenge without waiting for any special legislative authority. And whether the hostile party be a foreign invader, or States organized in rebellion, it is none the less a war. . . .

   Robert C. Grier, for the Court, *The Prize Cases*, 2 Black 635 (1863), at 668.

Commerce, definition of

Commerce, undoubtedly, is traffic, but it is something more; it is intercourse. It describes the commercial intercourse between nations, and parts of nations, in all its branches, and is regulated by prescribing rules for carrying on that intercourse.

   John Marshall, for the Court, *Gibbons v. Ogden*, 9 Wheat. 1 (1824), at 189–190.

Commercial speech

The level of discourse reaching a mailbox simply cannot be limited to that which would be suitable for a sandbox.

   Thurgood Marshall, for the Court, *Bolger v. Youngs Drug Products Corp.*, 463 U.S. 60 (1983), at 74.

Common law

   The common law is not a brooding omnipresence in the sky, but the articulate voice of some sovereign or quasi sovereign that can be identified.

   Oliver Wendell Holmes, dissenting, *Southern Pacific Co. v. Jensen*, 244 U.S. 205 (1917), at 222.

Common law, federal

Except in matters governed by the Federal Constitution or by Acts of Congress, the law to be applied in any case is the law of the State. And whether the law of the State shall be declared by its Legislature in a statute or by its highest court in a decision is not a matter of federal concern. There is no federal general common law.

   Louis D. Brandeis, for the Court, *Erie R. Co. v. Tompkins*, 304 U.S. 62 (1938), at 78.

(Table continues)

Table 5-13   *(Continued)*

Communist Party, members of

. . . they are miserable merchants of unwanted ideas; their wares remain unsold. The fact that their ideas are abhorrent does not make them powerful.
  William O. Douglas, dissenting, *Dennis v. United States,* 341 U.S. 494 (1951), at 589.

The Constitution

There is no war between the Constitution and common sense.
  Tom Clark, for the Court, *Mapp v. Ohio,* 367 U.S. 643 (1961), at 657.

Constitutional gloss

  The Court is forever adding new stories to the temples of constitutional law, and the temples have a way of collapsing when one story too many is added.
  Robert H. Jackson, concurring in the result, *Douglas v. Jeannette,* 319 U.S. 157 (1943), at 181.

Contraception

  Since 1879, Connecticut has had on its books a law which forbids the use of contraceptives by anyone. I think this is an uncommonly silly law.
  Potter Stewart, dissenting, *Griswold v. Connecticut,* 381 U.S. 479 (1965), at 527.

Contract, freedom of

The liberty mentioned in [the Fourteenth A]mendment . . . is deemed to embrace the right of the citizen to be free in the enjoyment of all his faculties; to be free to use them in all lawful ways; to live and work where he will; to earn his livelihood by any lawful calling; to pursue any livelihood or avocation; and for that purpose to enter into all contracts which may be proper, necessary, and essential to his carrying out to a successful conclusion the purposes above mentioned.
  Rufus W. Peckham, for the Court, *Allgeyer v. Louisiana,* 165 U.S. 578 (1897), at 589.

It might safely be affirmed that almost all occupations more or less affect the health. . . . But are we all, on that account, at the mercy of legislative majorities?
  . . . The act is . . . but . . . an illegal interference with the rights of individuals, both employers and employees, to make contracts regarding labor upon such terms as they may think best. . . . Statutes of the nature of that under review, limiting the hours in which grown and intelligent men may labor to earn their living, are mere meddlesome interferences with the rights of the individual. . . .
  Rufus W. Peckham, for the Court, *Lochner v. New York,* 198 U.S. 45 (1905), at 59, 61.

What is this freedom? The Constitution does not speak of freedom of contract. It speaks of liberty and prohibits the deprivation of liberty without due process of law. In prohibiting that deprivation the Constitution does not recognize an absolute and uncontrollable liberty. . . . Liberty under the Constitution is thus

Table 5-13   *(Continued)*

necessarily subject to the restraints of due process, and regulation which is reasonable in relation to its subject and is adopted in the interests of the community is due process.

Charles Evans Hughes, for the Court, *West Coast Hotel Co. v. Parrish*, 300 U.S. 379 (1937), at 391.

Counsel, right to

The right to be heard would be, in many cases, of little avail if it did not comprehend the right to be heard by counsel. Even the intelligent and educated layman has small and sometimes no skill in the science of the law. . . . He requires the guiding hand of counsel at every step in the proceedings against him. Without it, though he be not guilty, he faces the danger of conviction because he does not know how to establish his innocence.

George Sutherland, for the Court, *Norris v. Alabama*, 287 U.S. 45 (1932), at 68–69.

. . . reason and reflection require us to recognize that in our adversary system of criminal justice, any person haled into court, who is too poor to hire a lawyer, cannot be assured a fair trial unless counsel is provided for him. . . . That government hires lawyers to prosecute and defendants who have money hire lawyers to defend are the strongest indications of the widespread belief that lawyers in criminal courts are necessities, not luxuries. The right of one charged with a crime to counsel may not be deemed fundamental and essential to fair trials in some countries, but it is in ours.

Hugo L. Black, for the Court, *Gideon v. Wainwright*, 372 U.S. 335 (1963), at 344.

Debate on public issues

. . . debate on public issues should be uninhibited, robust, and wide-open, and that it may well include vehement, caustic, and sometimes unpleasantly sharp attacks on government and public officials.

William J. Brennan, Jr., for the Court, *New York Times Co. v. Sullivan*, 376 U.S. 254 (1964), at 270.

Die, right to

It cannot be disputed that the Due Process Clause protects an interest in life as well as an interest in refusing life-sustaining medical treatment.

William H. Rehnquist, for the Court, *Cruzan v. Director, Missouri Health Department*, 497 U.S. 261 (1990), at 281.

Disclosure of news sources

. . . we cannot seriously entertain the notion that the First Amendment protects a newsman's agreement to conceal the criminal conduct of his source, or evidence thereof, on the theory that it is better to write about crime than to do something about it.

Byron R. White, for the Court, *Branzburg v. Hayes*, 408 U.S. 665 (1972), at 692.

(Table continues)

Table 5-13   *(Continued)*

Dissent

Dissent is essential to an effective judiciary in a democratic society, and especially for a tribunal exercising the powers of this Court.
  Felix Frankfurter, dissenting, *Ferguson v. Moore McCormack Lines,* 352 U.S. 521 (1957), at 528.

Eavesdropping

  The price of lawful public dissent must not be a dread of subjection to an unchecked surveillance power. Nor must the fear of unauthorized official eavesdropping deter vigorous citizen dissent and discussion of Government action in private conversation. For private dissent, no less than open public discourse, is essential to our free society.
  Lewis F. Powell, Jr., for the Court, *United States v. United States District Court,* 407 U.S. 297 (1972), at 314.

Emergency

  While emergency does not create power, emergency may furnish the occasion for the exercise of power.
  Charles Evans Hughes, for the Court, *Home Building & Loan Assn. v. Blaisdell,* 290 U.S. 398 (1934), at 426.

Equal protection, violation of

In the area of economics and social welfare, a State does not violate the Equal Protection Clause merely because the classifications made by its laws are imperfect. If the classification has some "reasonable basis," it does not offend the Constitution simply because the classification "is not made with mathematical nicety or because in practice it results in some inequality."
  Potter Stewart, for the Court, *Dandridge v. Williams,* 397 U.S. 471 (1970), at 485.

Establishment of religion

Every analysis in this area must begin with consideration of the cumulative criteria developed by the Court over many years. Three such tests may be gleaned from our cases. First, the statute must have a secular legislative purpose; second, its principal or primary effect must be one that neither advances nor inhibits religion; finally, the statute must not foster "an excessive government entanglement with religion."
  Warren Burger, for the Court, *Lemon v. Kurtzman,* 403 U.S. 602 (1971), at 612–613.

Exclusionary rule

  . . . our holding that the exclusionary rule is an essential part of both the Fourth and the Fourteenth Amendments is not only the logical dictate of prior cases, but it also makes very good sense. . . . Presently, a federal prosecutor may make no

Table 5-13   *(Continued)*

---

use of evidence illegally seized, but a State's attorney across the street may, although he is operating under the enforcement prohibitions of the same Amendment. Thus, the State, by admitting evidence unlawfully seized, serves to encourage disobedience to the Federal Constitution which it is bound to uphold.

Tom C. Clark, for the Court, *Mapp v. Ohio*, 367 U.S. 643 (1961), at 657.

Extraordinary conditions, constitutional power over

Extraordinary conditions do not create or enlarge constitutional power.

Charles Evan Hughes, for the Court, *Schechter Poultry v. United States*, 295 U.S. 495 (1935), at 528.

Federalism

It is one of the happy incidents of the federal system that a single courageous State may, if its citizens choose, serve as a laboratory; and try novel social and economic experiments without risk to the rest of the country.

Louis D. Brandeis, dissenting, *New State Ice Co. v. Liebmann*, 285 U.S. 262 (1932), at 311.

The [Tenth] amendment states but a truism that all is retained which has not been surrendered. There is nothing in the history of its adoption to suggest that it was more than declaratory of the relationship between the national and state governments as it had been established by the Constitution before the amendment or that its purpose was other than to allay fears that the new national government might seek to exercise powers not granted, and that the states might not be able to exercise fully their reserved powers.

Harlan Fiske Stone, for the Court, *United States v. Darby*, 312 U.S. 100 (1941), at 124.

It is illuminating for purposes of reflection, if not for argument, to note that one of the greatest "fictions" of our federal system is that the Congress exercises only those powers delegated to it, while the remainder are reserved to the States or to the people.

William Rehnquist, concurring, *Hodel v. Virginia Surface Mining and Reclamation Association*, 452 U.S. 264 (1981), at 307.

Fighting words

There are certain well-defined and narrowly limited classes of speech, the prevention and punishment of which have never been thought to raise any Constitutional problem. These include . . . "fighting" words—those which by their very utterance inflict injury or tend to incite an immediate breach of the peace.

Frank Murphy, for the Court, in *Chaplinsky v. New Hampshire*, 315 U.S. 568 (1942), at 571–572.

First Amendment

If the First Amendment means anything, it means that a State has no business telling a man, sitting alone in his own house, what books he may read or what films he may watch.

Thurgood Marshall, for the Court, *Stanley v. Georgia*, 394 U.S. 557 (1969), at 565.

(Table continues)

Table 5-13   *(Continued)*

First Amendment, principle underlying

If there is a bedrock principle underlying the First Amendment, it is that the Government may not prohibit the expression of an idea simply because society finds the idea itself offensive or disagreeable.
    William J. Brennan, Jr., for the Court, *Texas v. Johnson*, 491 U.S. 397 (1989), at 414.

Foreign affairs, conduct of

. . . the President . . . [is] the sole organ of the Federal government in the field of international relations—a power which does not require as a basis for its exercise an act of Congress, but which, of course, like every other governmental power, must be exercised in subordination to the applicable provisions of the Constitution.
    George Sutherland, for the Court, *United States v. Curtiss-Wright Export Corp.*, 299 U.S. 304 (1936), at 320.

Fourteenth Amendment and substantive due process

The Fourteenth Amendment does not enact Mr. Herbert Spencer's *Social Statics.*
    Oliver Wendell Holmes, dissenting, *Lochner v. New York*, 198 U.S. 45 (1905) at 75.

Fundamental rights, freedom of speech and press as

. . . freedom of speech and of the press—which are protected by the 1st Amendment from abridgment by Congress—are among the fundamental rights and "liberties" protected by the due process clause of the 14th Amendment from impairment by the States.
    Edward Terry Sanford, for the Court, *Gitlow v. New York*, 268 U.S. 652 (1925), at 666.

Great cases and bad law

Great cases, like hard cases, make bad law. For great cases are called great, not by reason of the real importance in shaping the law of the future, but because of some accident of immediate overwhelming interest which appeals to the feelings and distorts the judgment. These immediate interests exercise a kind of hydraulic pressure which makes what previously was clear seem doubtful, and before which even well settled principles of law will bend.
    Oliver Wendell Holmes, dissenting, *Northern Security Co. v. United States*, 193 U.S. 197 (1904), at 400–401.

Ideas, free trade in

Persecution for the expression of opinions seems to me perfectly logical. If you have no doubt of your premises or your power and want a certain result with all your heart you naturally express your wishes in law and sweep away all opposition. To allow opposition by speech seems to indicate that you think the

Table 5-13   *(Continued)*

speech impotent, as when a man says that he has squared the circle. . . . But when men have realized that time has upset many fighting faiths, they may come to believe even more than they believe the foundations of their own conduct that the ultimate good desired is better reached by free trade in ideas,—that the best test of truth is the power of the thought to get itself accepted in the competition of the market; and that truth is the only ground upon which their wishes safely can be carried out. That, at any rate, is the theory of our Constitution. It is an experiment, as all life is an experiment. Every year, if not every day, we have to wager our salvation upon some prophecy based upon imperfect knowledge. While that experiment is part of our system I think that we should be eternally vigilant against attempts to check the expression of opinions that we loathe and believe to be fraught with death, unless they so imminently threaten interference with the lawful and pressing purposes of the law that an immediate check is required to save the country.

Oliver Wendell Holmes, dissenting, *Abrams v. United States*, 250 U.S. 616 (1919), at 630.

Implied powers

We admit, as all must admit, that the powers of the government are limited, and that its limits are not to be transcended. But we think the sound construction of the constitution must allow to the national legislature that discretion, with respect to the means by which the powers it confers are to be carried into execution, which will enable that body to perform the high duties assigned to it, in the manner most beneficial to the people. Let the end be legitimate, let it be within the scope of the constitution, and all means which are appropriate, which are plainly adapted to that end, which are not prohibited, but consist with the letter and spirit of the constitution, are constitutional.

John Marshall, for the Court, *McCulloch v. Maryland*, 4 Wheat. 316 (1819), at 421.

. . . we must never forget it is a constitution we are expounding. . . . a constitution intended to endure for ages to come, and, consequently, to be adapted to the various crises of human affairs.

John Marshall, for the Court, *McCulloch v. Maryland*, 4 Wheat. 316 (1819), at 407, 415.

Intent, legislative

Just what our forefathers did envision, or would have envisioned had they foreseen modern conditions must be divined from materials almost as enigmatic as the dreams Joseph was called upon to interpret for Pharoah. A century and half of partisan debate and scholarly specification yields no net result but only supplies more or less apt quotations from respected sources on each side of any question. They largely cancel each other.

Robert H. Jackson, concurring, *Youngstown Sheet and Tube Co. v. Sawyer*, 343 U.S. 579 (1952), at 634–635.

The number of possible motivations, to begin with, is not binary, or indeed even finite. In the present case, for example, a particular legislator need not have voted

(Table continues)

Table 5-13 *(Continued)*

for the Act either because he wanted to foster religion or because he wanted to improve education. He may have thought the bill would provide jobs for his district, or may have wanted to make amends with a faction of his party he had alienated on another vote, or he may have been a close friend of the bill's sponsor, or he may have been repaying a favor he owed the Majority Leader, or he may have hoped the Governor would appreciate his vote and make a fundraising appearance for him, or he may have been pressured to vote for a bill he disliked by a wealthy contributor or a flood of constituent mail, or he may have been seeking favorable publicity, or he may have been reluctant to hurt the feelings of a loyal staff member who worked on the bill, or he may have been mad at his wife who opposed the bill, or he may have been intoxicated and entirely *un*motivated when the vote was called, or he may have accidentally voted "yes" instead of "no," or, of course, he may have had (and very likely did have) a combination of some of the above and many other motivations. To look for *the sole purpose* of even a single legislator is probably to look for something that does not exist.

Putting that problem aside, however, where ought we to look for the individual legislator's purpose? We cannot . . . assume that every member present . . . agreed with the motivation expressed in a particular legislator's pre-enactment floor or committee statement. . . . Can we assume . . . that they all agree with the motivation expressed in the staff-prepared committee reports . . . [or] post-enactment floor statements? Or post-enactment testimony from legislators, obtained expressly for the lawsuit? . . . media reports on . . . legislative bargaining? All these sources, of course, are eminently manipulable.

. . . If a state senate approves a bill by a vote of 26 to 25, and only one intended solely to advance religion, is the law unconstitutional? What if 13 of 26 had that intent? What if 3 of the 26 had the impermissible intent, but 3 of the 25 voting against the bill were motivated by religious hostility or were simply attempting to "balance" the votes of their impermissibly motivated colleagues? Or is it possible that the intent of the bill's sponsor is alone enough to invalidate it— on a theory, perhaps, that even though everyone else's intent was pure, what they produced was the fruit of a forbidden tree.

Antonin Scalia, dissenting, *Edwards v. Aguillard,* 482 U.S. 578 (1987), at 636–638.

Interrogation versus investigation

. . . interrogation under *Miranda* refers not only to express questioning, but also to any words or actions on the part of the police (other than those normally attendant to arrest and custody) that the police should know are reasonably likely to elicit an incriminating response from the suspect. . . . A practice that the police should know is reasonably likely to evoke an incriminating response from a suspect amounts to interrogation.

Potter Stewart, *Rhode Island v. Innis,* 446 U.S. 291 (1980), at 301.

Investigation, congressional

There is no general authority to expose the private affairs of individuals without justification in terms of the functions of the Congress. . . . No inquiry is an end in itself; it must be related to, and in furtherance of, a legitimate task of the Con-

Table 5-13   *(Continued)*

gress. Investigations conducted solely for the personal aggrandizement of the investigators or to "punish" those investigated are indefensible.

Earl Warren, for the Court, *Watkins v. United States,* 354 U.S. 178 (1957), at 187.

Judicial policy making

The Court is most vulnerable and comes nearest to illegitimacy when it deals with judge-made constitutional law having little or no cognizable roots in the language or design of the Constitution.

Byron R. White, for the Court, *Bowers v. Hardwick,* 478 U.S. 186 (1986), at 194.

I am not so naive (nor do I think our forbears were) as to be unaware that judges in a real sense "make" law. But they make it *as judges make it,* which is to say *as though* they were "finding" it—discerning what the law is, rather than decreeing what it is today *changed to,* or what it will *tomorrow* be.

Antonin Scalia, concurring in the judgment, *James M. Beam Distilling Co. v. Georgia,* 501 U.S. 529 (1991), at 549.

. . . even though the Justice is not naive enough (nor does he think the Framers were naive enough) to be unaware that judges in a real sense "make" law, he suggests that judges (in an unreal sense, I suppose) should never concede that they do and must claim that they do no more than discover it, hence suggesting that there are citizens naive enough to believe them.

Byron R. White, concurring in the judgment, *James M. Beam Distilling Co. v. Georgia,* 501 U.S. 529 (1991), at 546.

Judicial power

It is emphatically the province and duty of the judicial department to say what the law is.

John Marshall, for the Court, *Marbury v. Madison,* 1 Cranch 137 (1803), at 177.

Judicial power, as contradistinguished from the power of the laws, has no existence. Courts are the mere instruments of the law, and can will nothing. When they are said to exercise a discretion, it is a mere legal discretion, a discretion to be exercised in discerning the course prescribed by law; and, when that is discerned, it is the duty of the court to follow it. Judicial power is never exercised for the purpose of giving effect to the will of the judge; always for the purpose of giving effect to the will of the legislature. . . .

John Marshall, for the Court, *Osborn v. Bank of the United States,* 9 Wheat. 738 (1824), at 866.

. . . the only check upon our own exercise of power is our own sense of self-restraint. For the removal of unwise laws from the statute books appeal lies not to the courts but to the ballot and the processes of democratic government.

Harlan Fiske Stone, dissenting, *United States v. Butler,* 297 U.S. 1 (1936), at 79.

. . . the interpretation of the Fourteenth Amendment enunciated by this Court . . . is the supreme law of the land, and Art. VI of the Constitution makes it of binding effect on the States any Thing in the Constitution or Laws of any State to the Contrary notwithstanding.

per curiam, *Cooper v. Aaron,* 358 U.S. 1 (1958), at 18.

(Table continues)

Table 5-13   *(Continued)*

Judicial restraint

. . . a Constitution is not intended to embody a particular economic theory, whether of paternalism and the organic relation of the citizen to the state or of *laissez faire*. It is made for people of fundamentally differing views, and the accident of our finding certain opinions natural and familiar, or novel, and even shocking, ought not to conclude our judgment upon the question whether statutes embodying them conflict with the Constitution of the United States.

General propositions do not decide concrete cases. The decision will depend on a judgment or intuition more subtle than any articulate major premise. But I think that the proposition just stated, if it is accepted, will carry us far toward the end. Every opinion tends to become a law. I think that the word "liberty" in the Fourteenth Amendment is perverted when it is held to prevent the natural outcome of a dominant opinion, unless it can be said that a rational and fair man necessarily would admit that the statute proposed would infringe fundamental principles as they have been understood by the traditions of our people and our law.

Oliver Wendell Holmes, dissenting, *Lochner v. New York*, 198 U.S. 45 (1905), at 75–76.

One who belongs to the most vilified and persecuted minority in history is not likely to be insensible to the freedoms guaranteed by our Constitution. Were my purely personal attitude relevant I should wholeheartedly associate myself with the general libertarian views in the Court's opinion, representing as they do the thought and action of a lifetime. But as judges we are neither Jew nor Gentile, neither Catholic nor agnostic. We owe equal attachment to the Constitution and are equally bound by our judicial obligations whether we derive our citizenship for the earliest or the latest immigrants to these shores.

Felix Frankfurter, dissenting, *West Virginia v. Barnette*, 319 U.S. 624 (1943), at 646–647.

The Court's authority—possessed of neither the purse nor the sword—ultimately rests on sustained public confidence in its moral sanction. Such feeling must be nourished by the Court's complete detachment, in fact and in appearance, from political entanglements and by abstention from injecting itself into the clash of political forces in political settlements.

Felix Frankfurter, dissenting, *Baker v. Carr*, 369 U.S. 186 (1962), at 267.

Judicial review

It is a proposition too plain to be contested, that the constitution controls any legislative act repugnant to it; or, that the legislature may alter the constitution by an ordinary act.

John Marshall, for the Court, *Marbury v. Madison*, 1 Cranch 137 (1803), at 177.

To hold a governmental act to be unconstitutional is not to announce that we forbid it, but that the *Constitution* forbids it. . . .

Antonin Scalia, concurring in the result, *American Trucking Assns. v. Smith*, 496 U.S. 167 (1990), at 201.

Table 5-13   *(Continued)*

Judicial review, exercise of

When an act of Congress is appropriately challenged in the courts as not conforming to the constitutional mandate, the judicial branch of government has only one duty,—to lay the article of the Constitution which is invoked beside the statute which is challenged and to decide whether the latter squares with the former. All the Court does, or can do, is to announce its considered judgment upon the question. The only power it has, if such it may be called, is the power of judgment. The court neither approves nor condemns any legislative policy. Its delicate and difficult office is to ascertain and declare whether the legislation is in accordance with, or in contravention of, the provisions of the Constitution; and, having done that, its duty ends.

Owen J. Roberts, for the Court, *United States v. Butler*, 297 U.S. 1 (1936), at 62–63.

Jurisdiction

Without jurisdiction the court cannot proceed at all in any cause. Jurisdiction is power to declare the law, and when it ceases to exist, the only function remaining to the court is that of announcing the fact and dismissing the cause. And this is not less clear upon authority than upon principle.

Salmon P. Chase, for the Court, *Ex parte McCardle*, 7 Wall. 506 (1869), at 514.

Laws, faithful execution of

To contend that the obligation imposed on the President to see the laws faithfully executed implies a power to forbid their execution, is a novel construction of the Constitution, and entirely inadmissible.

Smith Thompson, for the Court, *Kendall v. United States*, 12 Pet. 524 (1838), at 613.

Left alone, right to be

The makers of our Constitution undertook to secure conditions favorable to the pursuit of happiness. They recognized the significance of man's spiritual nature, of his feelings and of his intellect. They knew that only a part of the pain, pleasure and satisfactions of life are to be found in material things. They sought to protect Americans in their beliefs, their thoughts, their emotions and their sensations. They conferred, as against the government, the right to be let alone—the most comprehensive of rights and the right most valued by civilized men.

Louis D. Brandeis, dissenting, *Olmstead v. United States*, 277 U.S. 438 (1928), at 478.

Letter of the law

It is a familiar rule that a thing may be within the letter of the statute and yet not within the statute, because not within its spirit, nor within the intention of its makers.

David J. Brewer, for the Court, *Holy Trinity Church v. United States*, 143 U.S. 457 (1892), at 459.

(Table continues)

Table 5-13   *(Continued)*

Libel

The constitutional guarantees require, we think, a federal rule that prohibits a public official from recovering damages for a defamatory falsehood relating to his conduct unless he proves that the statement was made with "actual malice"—that is, with knowledge that it was false or with reckless disregard of whether it was false or not.

William J. Brennan, Jr., for the Court, *New York Times v. Sullivan,* 376 U.S. 254 (1964), at 279–280.

Liberty, protection of

Experience should teach us to be most on our guard to protect liberty when the government's purposes are beneficent. Men born to freedom are naturally alert to repel invasion of their liberty by evil-minded rulers. The greatest dangers to liberty lurk in the insidious encroachment by men of zeal, well-meaning, but without understanding.

Louis D. Brandeis, dissenting, *Olmstead v. United States,* 277 U.S. 438 (1928), at 479.

Liberty versus property

. . . the dichotomy between personal liberty and property rights is a false one. Property does not have rights. People have rights. The right to enjoy property without unlawful deprivation, no less than the right to travel, is, in truth, a personal right. In fact, a fundamental interdependence exists between the right to liberty and the personal right to property. Neither can have meaning without the other.

Potter Stewart, for the Court, *Lynch v. Household Finance Co.,* 405 U.S. 538 (1972), at 552.

Marriage

We deal with a right of privacy older than the Bill of Rights—older than our political parties, older than our school system. Marriage is a coming together for better or for worse, hopefully enduring, and intimate to the degree of being sacred. It is an association that promotes a way of life, not causes; a harmony in living, not political faiths; a bilateral loyalty, not commercial or social projects. Yet it is an association for as noble a purpose as any involved in our prior decisions.

William O. Douglas, for the Court, *Griswold v. Connecticut,* 381 U.S. 479 (1965), at 486.

Martial law

Martial law cannot arise from a threatened invasion. The necessity must be actual and present; the invasion real, such as effectually closes the courts and deposes the civil administration.

David Davis, for the Court, *Ex parte Milligan,* 4 Wall. 2 (1866), at 127.

Table 5-13   *(Continued)*

Military necessity

It is said that we are dealing here with the case of imprisonment of a citizen in a concentration camp solely because of his ancestry, without evidence or inquiry concerning his loyalty and good disposition towards the United States. . . . To cast this case into outlines of racial prejudice, without reference to the real military dangers which were presented, merely confuses the issue. Korematsu was not excluded because of hostility to him or his race. He *was* excluded because we are at war with the Japanese Empire, because the properly constituted military authorities feared an invasion of our West Coast and felt constrained to take proper security measures. . . .

Hugo L. Black, for the Court, *Korematsu v. United States,* 323 U.S. 214 (1944), at 223.

This exclusion of "all persons of Japanese ancestry, both alien and non-alien," from the Pacific Coast area on a plea of military necessity in the absence of martial law . . . goes over "the very brink of constitutional power" and falls into the ugly abyss of racism.

Frank Murphy, dissenting, *Korematsu v. United States,* 323 U.S. 214 (1944), at 233.

. . . [This] is the case of convicting a citizen as a punishment for not submitting to imprisonment in a concentration camp, based on his ancestry, and solely because of his ancestry. . . .

Owen J. Roberts, dissenting, *Korematsu v. United States,* 323 U.S. 214 (1944), at 226.

. . . if any fundamental assumption underlies our system, it is that guilt is personal and not inheritable. . . . But here is an attempt to make an otherwise innocent act a crime merely because this prisoner is the son of parents as to whom he had no choice, and belongs to a race from which there is no way to resign. . . .

But if we cannot confine military expedients by the Constitution, neither would I distort the Constitution to approve all that the military may deem expedient.

Robert H. Jackson, dissenting, *Korematsu v. United States,* 323 U.S. 214 (1944), at 243–245.

Minority groups

Groups which find themselves unable to achieve their objectives through the ballot frequently turn to the courts. Just as it was true of the opponents of New Deal legislation during the 1930s, for example, no less is it true of the Negro minority today. And, under the conditions of modern government, litigation may well be the sole practicable avenue open to a minority to petition for redress of grievances.

William J. Brennan, Jr., for the Court, *NAACP v. Button,* 371 U.S. 415 (1963), at 429–430.

Miranda warnings

. . . we hold that when an individual is taken into custody or otherwise deprived of his freedom by the authorities in any significant way and is subject to questioning,

(Table continues)

Table 5-13   *(Continued)*

---

the privilege against self-incrimination is jeopardized. Procedural safeguards must be employed to protect the privilege, and unless other fully effective means are adopted to notify the person of his right of silence and to assure that the exercise of the right will be scrupulously honored, the following measures are required. He must be warned prior to any questioning that he has the right to remain silent, that anything he says can be used against him in a court of law, that he has the right to the presence of an attorney, and that if he cannot afford an attorney one will be appointed for him prior to any questioning if he so desires. Opportunity to exercise these rights must be afforded to him throughout the interrogation. After such warnings have been given, and such opportunity afforded him, the individual may knowingly and intelligently waive these rights and agree to answer questions or make a statement. But unless and until such warnings and waiver are demonstrated by the prosecution at trial, no evidence obtained as a result of interrogation can be used against him.

Earl Warren, for the Court, *Miranda v. Arizona*, 384 U.S. 436 (1966), at 478–479.

Miscegenation

The Fourteenth Amendment requires that the freedom of choice to marry not be restricted by invidious racial discrimination. Under our Constitution, the freedom to marry, or not to marry, a person of another race resides with the individual and cannot be infringed by the State.

Earl Warren, for the Court, *Loving v. Virginia*, 388 U.S. 1 (1967) at 12.

National supremacy

Judges of equal learning and integrity, in different states, might differently interpret a statute, or a treaty of the United States, or even the constitution itself. If there were no revising authority to control these jarring and discordant judgments, and harmonize them into uniformity, the laws, the treaties, the constitution of the United States would be different in different states, and might, perhaps, never have . . . the same construction, obligation, or efficacy, in any two states. The public mischiefs that would attend such a state of things would be truly deplorable . . . the appellate jurisdiction must continue to be the only adequate remedy for such evils.

John Marshall, for the Court, *Martin v. Hunter's Lessee*, 1 Wheat. 304 (1816), at 348.

One person, one vote

. . . the command of Art. I, Sec. 2, that Representatives be chosen "by the People of the several States" means that as nearly as is practicable one man's vote in a congressional election is to be worth as much as another's.

Hugo L. Black, for the Court, *Wesberry v. Sanders*, 376 U.S. 1 (1964), at 7–8.

Political patronage

Today the Court establishes the constitutional principle that party membership is not a permissible factor in the dispensation of government jobs, except

Table 5-13   *(Continued)*

those jobs for the performance of which party affiliation is an "appropriate requirement." . . . if there is any category of jobs for whose performance party affiliation is not an appropriate requirement, it is the job of being a judge, where partisanship is not only unneeded but positively undesirable. It is, however, rare that a federal administration of one party will appoint a judge from another party. And it has always been so. See Marbury v. Madison . . . . Thus, the new principle that the Court today announces will be enforced by a corps of judges (the members of this Court included) who overwhelmingly owe their office to its violation. Something must be wrong here, and I suggest it is the Court.

Antonin Scalia, dissenting, *Rutan v. Republican Party of Illinois*, 497 U.S. 62 52 (1990), at 92.

Political questions

Prominent on the surface . . . is found a textually demonstrable constitutional commitment of the issue to a coordinate political department; or a lack of judicially discoverable and manageable standards for resolving it; or the impossibility of deciding without an initial policy determination of a kind clearly for nonjudicial discretion; or the impossibility of a court's undertaking independent resolution without expressing lack of the respect due coordinate branches of government; or an unusual need for unquestioning adherence to a political decision already made; or the potentiality of embarrassment from multifarious pronouncements by various departments on one question.

William J. Brennan, Jr., for the Court, *Baker v. Carr*, 369 U.S. 186 (1962), at 217.

Political speech

. . . the opportunity for free political discussion to the end that government may be responsive to the will of the people and that changes may be obtained by lawful means, an opportunity essential to the security of the Republic, is a fundamental principle of our constitutional system.

Charles Evans Hughes, for the Court, *Stromberg v. California*, 283 U.S. 359 (1931), at 369.

Pornography

. . . hard-core pornography. I shall not . . . attempt . . . to define the kinds of material I understand to be embraced within that shorthand description; and perhaps I could never succeed in intelligibly doing so. But I know it when I see it. . . .

Potter Stewart, concurring, *Jacobellis v. Ohio*, 378 U.S. 184 (1964), at 197.

Prayer

. . . it is no part of the business of government to compose official prayers for any group of the American people to recite as part of a religious program carried on by government.

Hugo L. Black, for the Court, *Engel v. Vitale*, 370 U.S. 421 (1962), at 425.

Precedent, adherence to

If there is any inconsistency or illogic in all this, it is an inconsistency and illogic of long standing that is to be remedied by the Congress and not by this Court. . . .

(Table continues)

Table 5-13   *(Continued)*

---

there is merit in consistency even though some might claim that beneath that consistency is a layer of inconsistency.

Harry A. Blackmun, for the Court, *Flood v. Kuhn,* 407 U.S. 258 (1972), at 284.

Adherence to precedent is, in the usual case, a cardinal and guiding principal of adjudication, and "[c]onsiderations of stare decisis have special force in the area of statutory interpretation, for here, unlike in the context of constitutional interpretation, the legislative power is implicated, and Congress remains free to alter what we have done."

Sandra Day O'Connor, for the Court, *California v. Federal Energy Regulatory Commission,* 495 U.S. 490 (1990), at 499.

Preferred freedoms doctrine

There may be narrower scope for operation of the presumption of constitutionality when legislation appears on its face to be within a specific prohibition of the Constitution, such as those of the first ten amendments, which are deemed equally specific when held to be embraced within the Fourteenth. . . .

It is unnecessary to consider now whether legislation which restricts those political processes which can ordinarily be expected to bring about repeal of undesirable legislation, is to be subjected to more exacting judicial scrutiny. . . .

Nor need we enquire whether similar considerations enter into the review of statutes directed at particular religions or racial minorities: whether prejudice against discrete and insular minorities may be a special condition, which tends seriously to curtail the operations of those political processes ordinarily to be relied upon to protect minorities, and which may call for a correspondingly more searching judicial inquiry.

Harlan Fiske Stone, for the Court, *United States v. Carolene Products Co.,* 304 U.S. 144 (1938), at 152–153, note 4.

Preferred precedents doctrine

Considerations in favor of stare decisis are at their acme in cases involving property and contract rights, where reliance interests are involved . . . the opposite is true in cases . . . involving procedural and evidentiary rules.

William H. Rehnquist, for the Court, *Payne v. Tennessee,* 501 U.S. 808 (1991), at 828.

Principle, qualification of

. . . we learned long ago that broad statements of principle, no matter how correct in the context in which they are made, are sometimes qualified by contrary decisions before the absolute limit of the stated principle is reached.

John Paul Stevens, for the Court, *Young v. American Mini Theatres, Inc.,* 427 U.S. 50 (1976), at 65.

Privacy

. . . specific guarantees in the Bill of Rights have penumbras, formed by emanations from those guarantees that help give them life and substance. . . . Various guarantees create zones of privacy.

William O. Douglas, for the Court, *Griswold v. Connecticut,* 381 U.S. 479 (1965), at 484.

Table 5-13   *(Continued)*

It would betray our whole plan for a tranquil and orderly society to say that a citizen, because of his personal prejudices, habits, attitudes, or beliefs, is cast outside the law's protection and cannot call for the aid of officers sworn to uphold the law and preserve the peace. The worst citizen no less than the best is entitled to equal protection of the laws of his State and of his Nation.

Hugo L. Black, dissenting, *Bell v. Maryland,* 378 U.S. 226 (1964), at 327–328.

. . . the Fourth Amendment protects people, not places. What a person knowingly exposes to the public, even in his own home or office, is not a subject of Fourth Amendment protection. . . . But what he seeks to preserve as private, even if an area accessible to the public, may be constitutionally protected.

Potter Stewart, for the Court, *Katz v. United States,* 389 U.S. 347 (1967), at 351–352.

Probable cause

In dealing with probable cause . . . as the very name implies, we deal with probabilities. These are not technical; they are the factual and practical considerations of every day life on which reasonable and prudent men, not legal technicians, act.

Wiley Rutledge, for the Court, *Brinegar v. United States,* 338 U.S. 160 (1949), at 175.

Religious people, Americans as

We are a religious people whose institutions presuppose a Supreme Being.

William O. Douglas, for the Court, *Zorach v. Clauson,* 343 U.S. 306 (1952), at 313.

Rights of students and teachers, First Amendment

First Amendment rights, applied in the light of the special characteristics of the school environment, are available to teachers and students. It can hardly be argued that either students or teachers shed their constitutional rights to freedom of speech or expression at the schoolhouse gate.

Abe Fortas, for the Court, *Tinker v. Des Moines Independent School District,* 393 U.S. 503 (1969), at 506.

Role of the Court

It is the province of a court to expound the law, not to make it.

Roger B. Taney, for the Court, *Luther v. Borden,* 7 How. 1 (1849), at 41.

Segregation

We consider the underlying fallacy of the plaintiff's argument to consist in the assumption that the enforced segregation of the two races stamps the colored race with a badge of inferiority. If this be so, it is not by reason of anything found

(Table continues)

Table 5-13 *(Continued)*

in the act, but solely because the colored race chooses to put that construction on it.

Henry Billings Brown, for the Court, *Plessy v. Ferguson*, 163 U.S. 537 (1896), at 551.

Our Constitution is color blind, and neither knows nor tolerates classes among citizens. In respect of civil rights, all citizens are equal before the law. The humblest is the peer of the most powerful. The law . . . takes no account of his surroundings or of his color when his civil rights . . . are involved.

. . . the judgment this day rendered will, in time, prove to be quite as pernicious as the decision made by this tribunal in the *Dred Scott Case*. . . . The destinies of the two races in this country are indissolubly linked together, and the interests of both require that the common government of all shall not permit the seeds of race hate to be planted under the sanction of law. What can more certainly arouse race hate, what more certainly create and perpetuate a feeling of distrust between these races, than state enactments which in fact proceed on the ground that colored citizens are so inferior and degraded that they cannot be allowed to sit in public coaches occupied by white citizens?

John Marshall Harlan, dissenting, *Plessy v. Ferguson*, 163 U.S. 537 (1896), at 559–560.

We conclude that in the field of public education the doctrine of "separate but equal" has no place. Separate educational facilities are inherently unequal.

Earl Warren, for the Court, *Brown v. Board of Education*, 347 U.S. 483 (1954), at 495.

. . . continued operation of segregated schools under a standard of allowing "all deliberate speed" for desegregation is no longer constitutionally permissible. . . . the obligation of every school district is to terminate dual school systems at once and to operate now and hereafter only unitary schools.

per curiam, *Alexander v. Holmes County Board of Education*, 396 U.S. 19 (1969), at 20.

Self-incrimination

. . . the American system of criminal prosecution is accusatorial, not inquisitorial, and . . . the Fifth Amendment privilege is its essential mainstay.

William J. Brennan, Jr., for the Court, *Malloy v. Hogan*, 378 U.S. 1 (1964), at 7.

Sex discrimination

Man is, or should be, woman's protector and defender. The natural and proper timidity and delicacy which belongs to the female sex evidently unfits it for many of the occupations of civil life. The constitution of the family organization, which is founded in the divine ordinance, as well as in the nature of things, indicates the domestic sphere as that which properly belongs to the domain and functions of womanhood. The harmony, not to say identity, of interests and views which belong, or should belong, to the family institution, is repugnant to the ideas of a woman adopting a distinct and independent career from that of her husband. . . .

Table 5-13   *(Continued)*

. . . The paramount destiny and mission of woman are to fulfil the noble and benign offices of wife and mother. This is the law of the Creator.

Joseph P. Bradley, concurring in the judgment, *Bradwell v. Illinois,* 16 Wall. 130 (1873), at 141.

Despite the enlightened emancipation of women from the restrictions and protections of bygone years, and their entry into many parts of community life formerly considered to be reserved to men, woman is still regarded as the center of home and family life. We cannot say that it is constitutionally impermissible for a State, acting in pursuit of the general welfare, to conclude that a woman should be relieved from the civic duty of jury service unless she herself determines that such service is consistent with her own special responsibilities.

John M. Harlan, for the Court, *Hoyt v. Florida,* 368 U.S. 57 (1961), at 61–62.

If it was ever the case that women were unqualified to sit on juries or were so situated that none of them should be required to perform jury service, that time has long since passed.

Byron R. White, for the Court, *Taylor v. Louisiana,* 419 U.S. 522 (1975), at 537.

To withstand constitutional challenge . . . classifications by gender must serve important governmental objectives and must be substantially related to achievement of those objectives.

William J. Brennan, Jr., for the Court, *Craig v. Boren,* 429 U.S. 190 (1976), at 197.

Slavery

. . . [Blacks] had for more than a century before been regarded as beings of an inferior order; and altogether unfit to associate with the white race, either in social or political relations; and so far inferior, that they had no rights which the white man was bound to respect; and that the negro might justly and lawfully be reduced to slavery for his benefit. He was bought and sold, and treated as an ordinary article of merchandise and traffic, whenever a profit could be made by it. This opinion was at that time fixed and universal in the civilized portion of the white race.

Roger B. Taney, for the Court, *Scott v. Sandford,* 19 How. 393 (1857), at 407.

Speech

We cannot accept the view that an apparently limitless variety of conduct can be labeled "speech" whenever the person engaging in the conduct intends thereby to express an idea.

Earl Warren, for the Court, *United States v. O'Brien,* 391 U.S. 367 (1968), at 376.

Standing

Have the appellants alleged such a personal stake in the outcome of the controversy as to assure that concrete adverseness which sharpens the presentation of issues upon which the court so largely depends for illumination of difficult constitutional questions? This is the gist of the question of standing.

William J. Brennan, Jr., for the Court, *Baker v. Carr,* 369 U.S. 186 (1962), at 204.

(Table continues)

Table 5-13   *(Continued)*

Stare decisis

Ordinarily it is sound policy to adhere to prior decisions but this practice has quite properly never been a blind, inflexible rule. Courts are not omniscient. Like every other human agency, they too can profit from trial and error, from experience and reflection. As others have demonstrated, the principle commonly referred to as *stare decisis* has never been thought to extend so far as to prevent the courts from correcting their own errors. . . . Indeed, the Court has a special responsibility where questions of constitutional law are involved to review its decisions from time to time and where compelling reasons present themselves to refuse to follow erroneous precedents; otherwise its mistakes in interpreting the Constitution are extremely difficult to alleviate and needlessly so.

Hugo L. Black, dissenting, *Green v. United States,* 356 U.S. 165 (1958), at 195.

Sterilization

We have seen more than once that the public welfare may call upon the best citizens for their lives. It would be strange if it could not call upon those who already sap the strength of the state for these lesser sacrifices, often not felt to be such by those concerned, in order to prevent our being swamped with incompetence. It is better for all the world, if instead of waiting to execute degenerate offspring for their crime, or to let them starve for their imbecility, society can prevent those who are manifestly unfit from continuing their kind. The principle that sustains compulsory vaccination is broad enough to cover cutting the Fallopian tubes. . . . Three generations of imbeciles are enough.

Oliver Wendell Holmes, for the Court, *Buck v. Bell,* 274 U.S. 200 (1927), at 207.

Taxation, power of

. . . the power to tax involves the power to destroy. . . .

John Marshall, for the Court, *McCulloch v. Maryland,* 4 Wheat. 316 (1919), at 431.

Tenth Amendment

Our conclusion is unaffected by the Tenth Amendment which provides: "The powers not delegated to the United States by the Constitution nor prohibited by it to the states are reserved to the states respectively or to the people." The amendment states but a truism that all is retained which has not been surrendered.

Harlan Fiske Stone, for the Court, *United States v. Darby,* 312 U.S. 100 (1941), at 123–124.

Thought, freedom of

. . . if there is any principle of the Constitution that more imperatively calls for attachment than any other it is the principle of free thought—not free thought for those who agree with us but freedom for the thought we hate.

Oliver Wendell Holmes, dissenting, *United States v. Schwimmer,* 279 U.S. 644 (1929), at 654–655.

Table 5-13   *(Continued)*

Time of war, constitutional rights in

When peace prevails, and the authority of the government is undisputed, there is no difficulty of preserving the safeguards of liberty . . . ; but if society is disturbed by civil commotion—if the passions of men are aroused and the restraints of law weakened, if not disregarded—these safeguards need, and should receive, the watchful care of those intrusted with the guardianship of the Constitution and laws.

> David Davis, for the Court, *Ex parte Milligan*, 4 Wall. 2 (1866), at 123–124.

Union, nature of

The Constitution, in all its provisions, looks to an indestructible Union, composed of indestructible States.

> Salmon P. Chase, for the Court, *Texas v. White*, 7 Wall. 700 (1869), at 725.

2000 presidential election

None are more conscious of the vital limits on judicial authority than are the members of this Court, and none stand more in admiration of the Constitution's design to leave the selection of the President to the people, through their legislatures, and to the political sphere. When contending parties invoke the process of the courts, however, it becomes our unsought responsibility to resolve the federal and constitutional issues the judicial system has been forced to confront.

> Per curiam, *Bush v. Gore*, 531 U.S. 98 (2000), at 111.

What must underlie petitioners' entire federal assault on the Florida election procedures is an unstated lack of confidence in the impartiality and capacity of the state judges who would make the critical decisions if the vote count were to proceed. . . . The endorsement of that position by the majority of this Court can only lend credence to the most cynical appraisal of the work of judges throughout the land. It is confidence in the men and women who administer the judicial system that is the true backbone of the rule of law. Time will one day heal the wound to that confidence that will be inflicted by today's decision. One thing, however, is certain. Although we may never know with complete certainty the identity of the winner of this year's Presidential election, the identity of the loser is perfectly clear. It is the Nation's confidence in the judge as an impartial guardian of the rule of law.

> John Paul Stevens, dissenting, *Bush v. Gore*, 531 U.S. 98 (2000), at 128–129.

Note: This table reflects the judgment of the authors.

Table 5-14 Published Biographies of the Justices

Justice (appointment number)	Biographies[a]
Baldwin, Henry (23)	Taylor, Flavia M. "The Political and Civil Career of Henry Baldwin." *Western Pennsylvania Historical Magazine* 24 (March 1941): 37–50.
Barbour, Philip P. (26)	Cynn, Paul P. "Philip Pendleton Barbour." *John P. Branch Historical Papers of Randolph-Macon College* 4 (1913): 67–77.
Black, Hugo L. (79)	Ball, Howard. *The Vision and the Dream of Justice Hugo L. Black*. University: University of Alabama Press, 1975.
	Black, Hugo L., Jr. *My Father: A Remembrance*. New York: Random House, 1975.
	Dunne, Gerald T. *Hugo Black and the Judicial Revolution*. New York: Simon and Schuster, 1977.
	Frank, John P. *Mr. Justice Black*. New York: Alfred A. Knopf, 1949.
	Hamilton, Virginia V. *Hugo Black: The Alabama Years*. Baton Rouge: Louisiana State University Press, 1972.
	Newman, Roger K. *Hugo Black: A Biography*, 2d. ed. New York: Fordham University Press, 1997.
	Yarbrough, Tinsley E. *Mr. Justice Black and His Critics*. Durham, N.C.: Duke University Press, 1988.
Blackmun, Harry A. (102)	Foote, Joseph. "Mr. Justice Blackmun." *Harvard Law School Bulletin* 21 (June 1970): 18–21.
Blair, John, Jr. (5)	Drinard, J. Elliott. "John Blair." *Proceedings of the Virginia State Bar Association* 39 (1927): 436–449.
Blatchford, Samuel (49)	Hall, A. Oakey. "Justice Samuel Blatchford." *Green Bag* 5 (November 1893): 489–492.
Bradley, Joseph P. (42)	Parker, Cortlandt. *Mr. Justice Bradley of the United States Supreme Court*. Newark, N.J.: Advertiser Printing House, 1893.
Brandeis, Louis D. (69)	Freund, Paul A. *A Portrait of a Liberal Judge: Mr. Justice Brandeis, on Understanding the Supreme Court*. Boston: Little, Brown, 1957.

Table 5-14   *(Continued)*

Justice (appointment number)	*Biographies*[a]
	Gal, Allon. *Brandeis of Boston.* Cambridge, Mass.: Harvard University Press, 1980.
	Mason, Alpheus T. *Brandeis: A Free Man's Life.* New York: Viking Press, 1946.
	Murphy, Bruce. *The Brandeis-Frankfurter Connection.* Oxford, England: Oxford University Press, 1982.
	Strum, Philippa. *Louis D. Brandeis: Justice for the People.* Cambridge, Mass.: Harvard University Press, 1984.
	Urofsky, Melvin I. *Louis D. Brandeis and the Progressive Tradition.* Boston: Little, Brown, 1981.
Brennan, William J., Jr. (94)	Clark, Hunter R. *Justice Brennan: The Great Conciliator.* Secaucus, N.J.: Carol Publishing, 1995.
	Goldman, Roger L., with David Gallen. *Justice William J. Brennan, Jr.: Freedom First.* New York: Carroll and Graf, 1994.
	Hopkins, W. Wat. *Mr. Justice Brennan and Freedom of Expression.* New York: Praeger, 1991.
	Michelman, Frank L. *Brennan and Democracy.* Princeton, N.J.: Princeton University Press, 1999.
Brewer, David J. (52)	Brodhead, Michael J. *David J. Brewer: The Life of a Supreme Court Justice 1837–1910.* Carbondale.: Southern Illinois University Press, 1994.
	Eitzen, D. Stanley. *David J. Brewer, 1837–1910: A Kansan on the United States Supreme Court.* Emporia: Kansas State Teacher's College, 1964.
Brown, Henry B. (53)	Kent, Charles A. *A Memoir of Henry Billings Brown.* New York: Duffield and Company, 1915.
Burger, Warren E. (101)	Blasi, Vincent (ed.). *The Burger Court: The Counter-Revolution That Wasn't.* New Haven, Conn.: Yale University Press, 1983.
	Lamb, Charles M., and Stephen C. Halpern (eds.). *The Burger Court: Political and Judicial Profiles.* Urbana: University of Illinois Press, 1991.

(Table continues)

Table 5-14 *(Continued)*

Justice (appointment number)	Biographies[a]
	Maltz, Earl M. *The Chief Justiceship of Warren Burger, 1969–1986.* Columbia: University of South Carolina Press, 2000.
	Schwartz, Bernard. *The Assent of Pragmatism: The Burger Court in Action.* Reading, Mass.: Addison-Wesley, 1990.
Burton, Harold H. (88)	Berry, Mary F. *Stability, Security and Continuity: Mr. Justice Burton and Decision-Making in the Supreme Court, 1945–1958.* Westport, Conn.: Greenwood Press, 1978.
Butler, Pierce (73)	Brown, Francis J. *The Social and Economic Philosophy of Pierce Butler.* Washington, D.C.: Catholic University of America Press, 1945.
	Danelski, David J. *A Supreme Court Justice Is Appointed.* New York: Random House, 1964.
Byrnes, James F. (85)	Burns, Ronald. *James F. Byrnes.* New York: McGraw-Hill, 1961.
	Byrnes, James F. *All in One Lifetime.* New York: Harper, 1958 (autobiography).
	Robertson, David. *Sly and Able: A Political Biography of James F. Byrnes.* New York: Norton, 1994.
Campbell, John A. (34)	Connor, Henry G. *John Archibald Campbell, Associate Justice of the United States Supreme Court, 1853–1861.* Boston: Houghton Mifflin, 1920.
	Duncan, George W. *John Archibald Campbell.* Montgomery: Alabama Historical Society, 1905.
	Saunders, Robert, Jr. *John Archabald Campbell: Southern Moderate.* Tuscaloosa: University of Alabama Press, 1997.
Cardozo, Benjamin (78)	Hellman, George S. *Benjamin N. Cardozo, American Judge.* New York: McGraw-Hill, 1940.
	Kaufman, Andrew L. *Cardozo.* Cambridge, Mass.: Harvard University Press, 1998.
	Levy, Berl H. *Cardozo and Frontiers of Legal Thinking.* Cleveland, Ohio: Case Western Reserve University, 1969.

Table 5-14 *(Continued)*

Justice (appointment number)	Biographies[a]
	Polenberg, Richard. *The World of Benjamin Cardozo.* Cambridge, Mass.: Harvard University Press, 1997.
	Pollard, Joseph P. *Mr. Justice Cardozo: A Liberal Mind in Action.* New York: Yorktown Press, 1935.
	Posner, Richard A. *Cardozo: A Study in Reputation.* Chicago: University of Chicago Press, 1990.
Catron, John (27)	Chandler, Walter. *Address on the Centenary of Associate Justice John Catron of the United States Supreme Court.* Washington, D.C.: Government Printing Office, 1937.
Chase, Salmon P. (40)	Blue, Frederick J. *Salmon P. Chase: A Life in Politics.* Kent, Ohio: Kent State University Press, 1987.
	Hart, Albert B. *Salmon Portland Chase.* Boston: Houghton Mifflin, 1899.
	Niven, John. *Salmon P. Chase.* New York: Oxford University Press, 1995.
Chase, Samuel (10)	Elsmere, Jane S. *Justice Samuel Chase.* Muncie, Ind.: Janevar, 1980.
	Haw, James A., Francis F. Beirne, Rosamond R. Beirne, and R. Samuel Jett. *Stormy Patriot: The Life of Samuel Chase.* Baltimore: Maryland Historical Society, 1980.
Clark, Tom C. (90)	Dutton, C.B. "Mr. Justice Tom C. Clark." *Indiana Law Journal* 26 (Winter 1951): 169–184.
Clarke, John H. (70)	Warner, Hoyt L. *The Life of Mr. Justice Clarke, A Testament to the Power of Liberal Dissent in America.* Cleveland, Ohio: Case Western Reserve University, 1959.
Clifford, Nathan (35)	Clifford, Philip G. *Nathan Clifford, Democrat, 1803–1881.* New York: Putnam's, 1922.
Curtis, Benjamin R. (33)	Leach, Richard H. "Benjamin Robbins Curtis: Judicial Misfit." *New England Quarterly* 25 (December 1952): 448–462.
Cushing, William (3)	Rugg, Arthur P. "William Cushing." *Yale Law Journal* 30 (December 1920): 128–144.

(Table continues)

Table 5-14   *(Continued)*

Justice (appointment number)	Biographies[a]
Daniel, Peter V. (29)	Frank, John P. *Justice Daniel Dissenting: A Biography of Peter V. Daniel, 1784–1860.* Cambridge, Mass.: Harvard University Press, 1964.
Davis, David (38)	King, Willard L. *Lincoln's Manager, David Davis.* Cambridge, Mass.: Harvard University Press, 1960.
Day, William R. (60)	McLean, Joseph E. *William Rufus Day: Supreme Court Justice From Ohio.* Baltimore: Johns Hopkins Press, 1946.
Douglas, William O. (82)	Douglas, William O. *Go East, Young Man.* New York: Random House, 1974 (autobiography).
	Douglas, William O. *The Court Years, 1939–1975: The Autobiography of William O. Douglas.* New York: Random House, 1980 (autobiography).
	Durham, James C. *Justice William O. Douglas.* Boston: Twayne, 1981.
	Simon, James F. *Independent Journey: The Life of William O. Douglas.* New York: Harper and Row, 1980.
Duvall, Gabriel (18)	Currie, David P. "The Most Insignificant Justice: A Preliminary Inquiry." *University of Chicago Law Review* 50 (Spring 1983): 466–480.
Ellsworth, Oliver (11)	Brown, William G. *The Life of Oliver Ellsworth.* New York: Macmillan, 1905.
	Lettieri, Ronald J. *Connecticut's Young Man of the Revolution, Oliver Ellsworth.* Hartford: American Revolution Bicentennial Commission of Connecticut, 1978.
Field, Stephen J. (39)	Kens, Paul. *Justice Stephen Field: Shaping Liberty from the Gold Rush to the Guilded Age.* Lawrence: University Press of Kansas, 1997.
	Swisher, Carl B. *Stephen J. Field: Craftsman of the Law.* Washington, D.C.: Brookings, 1930.
Fortas, Abe (99)	Kalman, Laura. *Abe Fortas: A Biography.* New Haven, Conn.: Yale University Press, 1990.
	Murphy, Bruce A. *Fortas: The Rise and Ruin of a Supreme Court Justice.* New York: Morrow, 1987.

Table 5-14   *(Continued)*

Justice (appointment number)	Biographies[a]
	Shogan, Robert. *A Question of Judgment: The Fortas Case and the Struggle for the Supreme Court.* Indianapolis: Bobbs-Merrill, 1972.
Frankfurter, Felix (81)	Baker, Liva. *Felix Frankfurter.* New York: Coward-McCann, 1969.
	Hirsch, Harry N. *The Enigma of Felix Frankfurter.* New York: Basic Books, 1981.
	Kurland, Philip B. *Mr. Justice Frankfurter and the Constitution.* Chicago: University of Chicago Press, 1971.
	Parrish, Michael E. *Felix Frankfurter and His Times.* New York: Free Press, 1982.
Fuller, Melville W. (51)	Ely, James W. *The Chief Justiceship of Melville W. Fuller, 1888–1910.* Columbia: University of South Carolina Press 1995.
	King, Willard L. *Melville Weston Fuller: Chief Justice of the United States, 1888–1910.* New York: Macmillan, 1950.
Ginsburg, Ruth Bader (112)	Halberstam, Malvina. "Ruth Bader Ginsburg: The First Jewish Woman on the United States Supreme Court." *Cardozo Law Review* 19 (1998): 1441–1454.
Goldberg, Arthur J. (98)	Goldberg, Dorothy. *A Private View of a Public Life.* New York: Charthouse, 1975.
	Stebenne, David. *Arthur J. Goldberg: New Deal Liberal.* New York: Oxford University Press, 1996.
Gray, Horace (48)	Hoar, George F. "Memoir of Horace Gray." *Massachusetts Historical Society Proceedings* 18 (January 1904): 155–187.
Grier, Robert C. (32)	Jones, Francis R. "Robert Cooper Grier." *Green Bag* 16 (April 1904): 221–224.
Harlan, John Marshall I (45)	Beth, Loren P. *John Marshall Harlan: The Last Great Whig Justice.* Lexington: University Press of Kentucky, 1992.
	Clark, Floyd B. *Constitutional Doctrines of Justice Harlan.* Baltimore: Johns Hopkins Press, 1915.

(Table continues)

Table 5-14   *(Continued)*

Justice (appointment number)	*Biographies*[a]
	Latham, Frank B. *The Great Dissenter: Supreme Court Justice John Marshall Harlan, 1833–1911.* New York: Cowles, 1970.
	Przybszewski, Linda. *The Republic According to John Marshall Harlan.* Chapel Hill: University of North Carolina Press, 1999.
	Yarbrough, Tinsley E. *Judicial Enigma: The First Justice Harlan.* New York: Oxford University Press, 1995.
Harlan, John Marshall II (93)	Yarbrough, Tinsley E. *John Marshall Harlan: Great Dissenter of the Warren Court.* New York: Oxford University Press, 1992.
Holmes, Oliver W., Jr. (59)	Alschuler, Albert W. *Law Without Values: The Life, Work, and Legacy of Justice Holmes.* Chicago: University of Chicago Press, 2000.
	Baker, Liva. *The Justice from Beacon Hill: The Life and Times of Oliver Wendell Holmes.* New York: HarperCollins, 1991.
	Bent, Silas. *Justice Oliver Wendell Holmes, A Biography.* New York: Vanguard Press, 1932.
	Biddle, Francis. *Mr. Justice Holmes.* New York: Charles Scribner's Sons, 1942.
	Bowen, Catherine D. *Yankee from Olympus: Justice Holmes and His Family.* Boston: Little, Brown, 1944.
	Howe, Mark D. *Justice Oliver Wendell Holmes*, 2 vols. Cambridge, Mass.: Harvard University Press, 1957–1963.
	Pohlman, H. L. *Justice Oliver Wendell Holmes and Utilitarian Jurisprudence.* Cambridge, Mass.: Harvard University Press, 1984.
	White, G. Edward. *Oliver Wendell Holmes: Sage of the Supreme Court.* New York: Oxford University Press, 2000.
Hughes, Charles E. (63, 76)	Hendel, Samuel. *Charles Evans Hughes and the Supreme Court.* New York: King's Crown Press, 1951.

Table 5-14   *(Continued)*

Justice (appointment number)	*Biographies*[a]
	Pusey, Merlo J. *Charles Evans Hughes*, 2 vols. New York: Macmillan, 1951.
	———. *Mr. Chief Justice Hughes.* Chicago: University of Chicago Press, 1956.
	Vinson, John C. *Charles Evans Hughes.* New York: McGraw-Hill, 1961.
Hunt, Ward (43)	"Old Judge and New." *Albany Law Journal* 6 (December 14, 1872): 400–401.
Iredell, James (6)	McRee, Griffith J. *Life and Correspondence of James Iredell.* New York: D. Appleton, 1857.
	Whichard, Willis P. *Justice James Iredell.* Durham, N.C.: Carolina Academic Press, 2000.
Jackson, Howell E. (55)	Calvani, Terry. "The Early Legal Career of Howell Jackson." *Vanderbilt Law Review* 30 (January 1977): 39–72.
Jackson, Robert H. (86)	Gerhart, Eugene C. *America's Advocate: Robert H. Jackson.* Indianapolis: Bobbs-Merrill, 1958.
	———. *Supreme Court Justice Jackson: Lawyer's Judge.* New York: Q Corporation, 1961.
	Schubert, Glendon. *Dispassionate Justice.* New York: Bobbs-Merrill, 1969.
Jay, John (1)	Hubbard, Elbert. *John Jay, the First Chief Justice of the United States.* New York: Hartford Lunch Company, 1918.
	Morris, Richard B. *John Jay, the Nation, and the Court.* Boston: Boston University Press, 1967.
	Pellew, George. *John Jay.* Boston: Houghton Mifflin, 1890.
Johnson, Thomas (7)	Delaplaine, Edward S. *The Life of Thomas Johnson.* New York: F. H. Hitchock, 1927.
Johnson, William (15)	Morgan, Donald G. *Justice William Johnson, the First Dissenter.* Columbia: University of South Carolina Press, 1971.

(Table continues)

Table 5-14   *(Continued)*

Justice (appointment number)	*Biographies*[a]
Kennedy, Anthony (109)	Williams, Charles F. "The Opinions of Anthony Kennedy: No Time for Ideology." *American Bar Association Journal* 74 (March 1988): 56–61.
Lamar, Joseph R. (66)	Lamar, Clarinda. *The Life of Joseph Rucker Lamar, 1857–1916.* New York: Putnam's, 1926.
	Sibley, Samuel H. *Georgia's Contribution to Law: The Lamars.* New York: Newcomen Society of England, American Branch, 1948.
Lamar, Lucius Q. C. (50)	Murphy, James B. *L. Q. C. Lamar: Pragmatic Patriot.* Baton Rouge: Louisiana State University Press, 1973.
	Sibley, Samuel H. *Georgia's Contribution to Law: The Lamars.* New York: Newcomen Society of England, American Branch, 1948.
Livingston, H. Brockholst (16)	Livingston, Edwin B. *The Livingstons of Livingston Manor.* New York: Knickerbocker Press, 1910.
Lurton, Horace (62)	Tucker, David M. "Justice Horace Harmon Lurton: The Shaping of a Natural Progressive." *American Journal of Legal History* 13 (July 1969): 223–232.
Marshall, John (14)	Baker, Leonard. *John Marshall: A Life in Law.* New York: Macmillan, 1974.
	Beveridge, Albert J. *The Life of John Marshall*, 4 vols. Boston: Houghton Mifflin, 1916–1919.
	Corwin, Edward S. *John Marshall and the Constitution.* New Haven, Conn.: Yale University Press, 1919.
	Crosskey, William W. *Mr. Chief Justice Marshall.* Chicago: University of Chicago Press, 1956.
	Hobson, Charles F. *The Great Chief Justice: John Marshall and the Rule of Law.* Lawrence: University Press of Kansas, 1996.
	Johnson, Herbert Alan. *The Chief Justiceship of John Marshall.* Columbia: University of South Carolina Press, 1997.

Table 5-14   *(Continued)*

Justice (appointment number)	*Biographies*[a]
	Smith, Jean Edward. *John Marshall: Definer of a Nation.* New York: Holt, 1996.
	Swindler, William F. *The Constitution and Chief Justice Marshall.* New York: Dodd, Mead, 1979.
Marshall, Thurgood (100)	Ball, Howard. *A Defiant Life: Thurgood Marshall and the Persistence of Racism in America.* New York: Crown Publishers, 1998.
	Bland, Randall W. *Private Pressure on Public Law: The Legal Career of Justice Thurgood Marshall.* Port Washington, N.Y.: Kennikat Press, 1973.
	Davis, Michael D., and Hunter R. Clark. *Thurgood Marshall: Warrior at the Bar, Rebel on the Bench.* Secaucus, N.J.: Carol Publishing, 1992.
	Haskins, James. *Thurgood Marshall: A Life for Justice.* New York: H. Holt, 1992.
	Rowan, Carl T. *Dream Makers, Dream Breakers: World of Justice Thurgood Marshall.* Boston: Little, Brown, 1993.
	Tushnet, Mark V. *Making Constitutional Law: Thurgood Marshall and the Supreme Court.* New York: Oxford University Press, 1997.
	Williams, Juan. *Thurgood Marshall: American Revolutionary.* New York: Times Books, 1998.
Matthews, Stanley (47)	Jager, Ronald B. "Stanley Matthews for the Supreme Court: 'Lord Roscoe's' Downfall." *Cincinnati Historical Society Bulletin* 38 (Fall 1980): 191–208.
McKenna, Joseph (58)	McDevitt, Matthew. *Joseph McKenna, Associate Justice of the United States.* Washington, D.C.: Catholic University of America Press, 1946.
McKinley, John (28)	Hicks, Jimmie. "Associate Justice John McKinley: A Sketch." *Alabama Review* 18 (July 1965): 227–233.
McLean, John (22)	Weinsenberger, Francis P. *The Life of John McLean: A Politician on the United States Supreme Court.* Columbus: Ohio State University Press, 1937.

(Table continues)

Table 5-14   *(Continued)*

Justice (appointment number)	*Biographies*[a]
McReynolds, James C. (68)	Fletcher, R. V. "Mr. Justice McReynolds: An Appreciation." *Vanderbilt Law Review* 2 (December 1948): 35–46.
Miller, Samuel (37)	Fairman, Charles. *Mr. Justice Miller and the Supreme Court, 1862–1890*. Cambridge, Mass.: Harvard University Press, 1939.
	Gregory, Charles N. *Samuel Freeman Miller*. Iowa City: State Historical Society of Iowa, 1907.
Minton, Sherman (91)	Gugin, Linda C., and James E. St. Clair. *Sherman Minton: New Deal Senator, Cold War Justice*. Indianapolis: Indiana Historical Society, 1997.
Moody, William H. (61)	Heffron, Paul T. "Profile of a Public Man." *Supreme Court Historical Society Yearbook*, 1980 (1980): 30–31, 48.
Moore, Alfred (13)	Davis, Junius. *Alfred Moore and James Iredell: Revolutionary Patriots and Associate Justices of the Supreme Court of the United States*. Raleigh: North Carolina Society of the Sons of the Revolution, 1899.
Murphy, Frank (83)	Fine, Sidney. *Frank Murphy: The Detroit Years*. Ann Arbor: University of Michigan Press, 1975.
	———. *Frank Murphy: The New Deal Years*. Chicago: University of Chicago Press, 1979.
	———. *Frank Murphy: The Washington Years*. Ann Arbor: University of Michigan Press, 1984.
	Howard, J. Woodford, Jr. *Mr. Justice Murphy: A Political Biography*. Princeton, N.J.: Princeton University Press, 1968.
Nelson, Samuel (30)	Leach, Richard H. "Rediscovery of Samuel Nelson." *New York History* 34 (January 1953): 64–71.
O'Connor, Sandra Day (106)	Bentley, Judith. *Justice Sandra Day O'Connor*. Englewood Cliffs, N.J.: Messner, 1983.
	Maveety, Nancy. *Justice Sandra Day O'Connor: Strategist on the Supreme Court*. Lanham, Md.: Rowman and Littlefield, 1996.

Table 5-14   *(Continued)*

Justice (appointment number)	*Biographies*[a]
	Spaeth, Harold J. "Justice Sandra Day O'Connor: An Assessment." In *An Essential Safeguard,* ed. D.G. Stephenson, Jr. New York: Greenwood Press, 1991.
	Woods, Harold, and Geraldine Woods. *Equal Justice: A Biography of Sandra Day O'Connor.* Minneapolis: Dillon Press, 1985.
Paterson, William (8)	O'Connor, John E. *William Paterson: Lawyer and Statesman, 1745–1806.* New Brunswick, N.J.: Rutgers University Press, 1979.
Peckham, Rufus W. (57)	Proctor, L. B. "Rufus W. Peckham." *Albany Law Journal* 55 (May 1, 1897): 286–288.
Pitney, Mahlon (67)	Belknap, Michael R. "Mr. Justice Pitney and Progressivism." *Seton Hall Law Review* 16 (1986): 381–428.
Powell, Lewis F., Jr. (103)	Jeffries, John C., Jr. *Justice Lewis F. Powell, Jr.* New York: Charles Scribner's Sons, 1994.
	Kahn, Paul W. "The Court, the Community, and the Judicial Balance: The Jurisprudence of Justice Powell." *Yale Law Journal* 97 (November 1987): 1–60.
	Wilkinson, J. Harvie. *Serving Justice: A Supreme Court Clerk's View.* New York: Charterhouse, 1974.
Reed, Stanley F. (80)	Fassett, John D. *New Deal Justice: The Life of Stanley Reed of Kentucky.* New York: Vantage Press, 1994.
	O'Brien, F. William. *Justice Reed and the First Amendment: The Religion Clauses.* Washington, D.C.: Georgetown University Press, 1958.
	Prickett, Morgan D. "Stanley Forman Reed: Perspectives on a Judicial Epitaph." *Hastings Constitutional Law Quarterly* 8 (Winter 1981): 343–369.
Rehnquist, William (104, 107)	Boles, Donald E. *Mr. Justice Rehnquist, Judicial Activist: The Early Years.* Ames: Iowa State University Press, 1987.

(Table continues)

Table 5-14   *(Continued)*

Justice (appointment number)	Biographies[a]
	Davis, Derek. *Original Intent: Chief Justice Rehnquist and the Course of American Church-State Relations*. Buffalo, N.Y.: Prometheus Books, 1991.
	Davis, Sue. *Justice Rehnquist and the Constitution*. Princeton, N.J.: Princeton University Press, 1989.
	Gottlieb, Stephen E. *Morality Imposed: The Rehnquist Court and Liberty in America*. New York: New York University Press, 2000.
	Yarbrough, Tinsley E. *The Rehnquist Court and the Constitution*. New York: Oxford University Press, 2000.
Roberts, Owen J. (77)	Leonard, Charles. *A Search for a Judicial Philosophy: Mr. Justice Roberts and the Constitutional Revolution of 1937*. Port Washington, N.Y.: Kennikat Press, 1971.
Rutledge, John (2, 9)	Barry, Richard. *Mr. Rutledge of South Carolina*. New York: Duell Sloan, and Pearce, 1942.
	Haw, James. *John and Edward Rutledge of South Carolina*. Athens: University of Georgia, 1997.
Rutledge, Wiley B. (87)	Harper, Fowler V. *Justice Rutledge and the Bright Constellation*. Indianapolis: Bobbs-Merrill, 1965.
	Stevens, John P. *Mr. Justice Rutledge*. Chicago: University of Chicago Press, 1956.
Sanford, Edward T. (74)	Fowler, James A. "Mr. Justice Edward Terry Sanford." *American Bar Association Journal* 17 (April 1931): 229–233.
Scalia, Antonin (108)	Brisbin, Richard A. *Justice Antonin Scalia and the Conservative Revival*. Baltimore: Johns Hopkins University Press, 1997.
	Schultz, David Andrew, and Christopher E. Smith. *The Jurisprudential Vision of Justice Antonin Scalia*. Lanham, Md.: Rowman and Littlefield, 1996.
	Smith, Christopher E. *Justice Antonin Scalia and the Supreme Court's Conservative Movement*. Westport, Conn.: Praeger, 1993.

Table 5-14   *(Continued)*

Justice (appointment number)	Biographies[a]
Shiras, George, Jr. (54)	Shiras, George III. *Justice George Shiras, Jr., of Pittsburgh: A Chronicle of His Family, Life, and Times.* Edited by Winfield Shiras. Pittsburgh: University of Pittsburgh Press, 1953.
Souter, David H. (110)	Smith, Christopher E., and Scott P. Johnson. "Newcomer on the High Court." *South Dakota Law Review* 37 (1991): 21–43.
Stevens, John Paul (105)	Sickels, Robert J. *John Paul Stevens and the Constitution: The Search for Balance.* University Park: Pennsylvania State University Press, 1988.
Stewart, Potter (96)	Barnett, Helaine M., and Kenneth Levine. "Mr. Justice Potter Stewart." *New York University Law Review* 40 (May 1965): 526–562.
Stone, Harlan Fiske (75, 84)	Konefsky, Samuel J. *Chief Justice Stone and the Supreme Court.* New York: Macmillan, 1945.
	Mason, Alpheus T. *Harlan Fiske Stone: Pillar of the Law.* New York: Viking, 1956.
Story, Joseph (19)	Dunne, Gerald T. *Justice Joseph Story and the Rise of the Supreme Court.* New York: Simon and Schuster, 1970.
	McClellan, James. *Joseph Story and the American Constitution: Study in Political and Legal Thought.* Norman: University of Oklahoma Press, 1971.
	Newmyer, R. Kent. *Supreme Court Justice Joseph Story: Statesman of the Old Republic.* Chapel Hill: University of North Carolina Press, 1985.
Strong, William (41)	"Political Portrait of William Strong." *United States Democratic Review* 27 (September 1850): 269–275.
Sutherland, George (72)	Arkes, Hadley. *The Return of George Sutherland: Restoring a Jurisprudence of Natural Rights.* Princeton, N.J.: Princeton University Press, 1994.
	Pascal, Joel F. *Mr. Justice Sutherland, a Man Against the State.* Princeton, N.J.: Princeton University Press, 1951.
	———. *Mr. Justice Sutherland.* Chicago: University of Chicago Press, 1956.

(Table continues)

Table 5-14 *(Continued)*

Justice (appointment number)	*Biographies*[a]
Swayne, Noah H. (36)	Swayne, Norman W. *The Descendants of Francis Swayne*. Philadelphia: Lippincott, 1921.
Taft, William H. (71)	Anderson, Judith I. *William Howard Taft: An Intimate History*. New York: W. W. Norton, 1981.
	Mason, Alpheus T. *William Howard Taft, Chief Justice*. New York: Simon and Schuster, 1965.
	Pringle, Henry F. *Life and Times of William Howard Taft, Chief Justice*. New York: Farrar and Rhinehart, 1939.
Taney, Roger B. (25)	Lewis, Walker. *Without Fear or Favor: A Biography of Chief Justice Roger Brooke Taney*. Boston: Houghton Mifflin, 1965.
	Schumacher, Alvin J. *Thunder on Capitol Hill: The Life of Chief Justice Roger B. Taney*. Milwaukee: Bruce Publishing Company, 1964.
	Swisher, Carl B. *Roger B. Taney*. Macmillan, 1935.
	————. *Mr. Chief Justice Taney*. Chicago: University of Chicago Press, 1956.
Thomas, Clarence (111)	Gerber, Scott Douglas. *First Principles: The Jurisprudence of Clarence Thomas*. New York: New York University Press, 1999.
	Halliburton, Warren J. *Clarence Thomas: Supreme Court Justice*. Hillside, N.J.: Enslow Publishers, 1993.
	McCarghey, Elizabeth P. "Clarence Thomas's Record as a Judge." *Presidential Studies Quarterly* 21 (Fall 1991): 833–835.
Thompson, Smith (20)	Roper, Donald Malcolm. *Mr. Justice Thompson and the Constitution*. New York: Garland, 1987.
Todd, Thomas (17)	O'Rear, Edward C. "Justice Thomas Todd." *Kentucky State Historical Society Record* 38 (February 1940): 112–119.
Trimble, Robert (21)	Goff, John S. "Mr. Justice Trimble of the United States Supreme Court." *Kentucky Historical Society Register* 58 (January 1960): 6–28.

Table 5-14   *(Continued)*

Justice (appointment number)	Biographies[a]
Van Devanter, Willis (65)	Holsinger, M. Paul. "The Appointment of Supreme Court Justice Van Devanter." *American Journal of Legal History* 12 (October 1968): 324–335.
Vinson, Fred M. (89)	Frank, John P. "Fred Vinson and the Chief Justiceship." *University of Chicago Law Review* 21 (Winter 1954): 212–246.
Waite, Morrison (44)	Magrath, C. Peter. *Morrison R. Waite: The Triumph of Character*. New York: Macmillan, 1963.
	Trimble, Bruce R. *Chief Justice Waite: Defender of the Public Interest*. Princeton, N.J.: Princeton University Press, 1938.
Warren, Earl (92)	Cray, Ed. *Chief Justice: A Biography of Earl Warren*. New York: Simon and Schuster, 1997.
	Katcher, Leo. *Earl Warren: A Political Biography*. New York: McGraw-Hill, 1967.
	Pollack, Jack H. *Earl Warren, the Judge Who Changed America*. Englewood Cliffs, N.J.: Prentice Hall, 1979.
	Schwartz, Bernard. *Super Chief*. New York: New York University Press, 1983.
	White, G. Edward. *Earl Warren: A Public Life*. New York: Oxford University Press, 1982.
Washington, Bushrod (12)	Binney, Horace. *Bushrod Washington*. Philadelphia: C. Sherman and Son, 1858.
Wayne, James M. (24)	Lawrence, Alexander A. *James Moore Wayne, Southern Unionist*. Chapel Hill: University of North Carolina Press, 1943.
White, Byron R. (97)	Hutchinson, Dennis. *The Man Who Once Was Whizzer White: A Portrait of Justice Byron R. White*. New York: Free Press, 1998.
	Liebman, Lance. "Swing Man on the Supreme Court." *New York Times Magazine*, October 8, 1972, 16–17, 94–95, 98, 100.
White, Edward D. (56, 64)	Hagemann, Gerard. *The Man on the Bench: A Story of Chief Justice Edward Douglass White*. Notre Dame, Ind.: Dujarie Press, 1962.

(Table continues)

Table 5-14 *(Continued)*

Justice (appointment number)	Biographies[a]
	Highsaw, Robert B. *Edward Douglass White: Defender of the Conservative Faith.* Baton Rouge: Louisiana State University Press, 1981.
Whittaker, Charles E. (95)	Christensen, Barbara B. "Mister Justice Whittaker: The Man on the Right." *Santa Clara Law Review* 19 (1979): 1039–1062.
Wilson, James (4)	Hall, Mark David. *The Political and Legal Philosophy of James Wilson.* Columbia: University of Missouri Press, 1997.
	O'Donnell, May G. *James Wilson and the Natural Law Basis of Positive Law.* New York: Fordham University Press, 1937.
	Smith, Page. *James Wilson: Founding Father, 1742–1798.* Chapel Hill: University of North Carolina Press, 1956.
Woodbury, Levi (31)	Cole, Donald B. *Jacksonian Democracy in New Hampshire, 1800–1851.* Cambridge: Harvard University Press, 1970.
	Rantoul, Robert. "Mr. Justice Woodbury." *Law Reporter* 14 (November 1851): 349–361.
Woods, William B. (46)	Baynes, Thomas E. "Yankee from Georgia: A Search for Justice Woods." *Supreme Court Historical Society Yearbook,* 1978 (1978): 31–42.

[a] Wherever possible book length biographies are listed. Where full volumes are not available, articles describing the life and career of the justice are provided. The listings included here are not exhaustive.

Sources: Fenton S. Martin and Robert U. Goehlert, *The United States Supreme Court: A Bibliography* (Washington, D.C.: Congressional Quarterly, 1990); and Leon Friedman and Fred L. Israel, eds, *The Justices of the United States Supreme Court: Their Lives and Major Opinions* (New York: R. R. Bowker, 1969–1978). Updated by the authors.

6

The Justices: Voting
Behavior and Opinions

In Chapter 6 we examine the official voting behavior and opinion-writing records of the justices of the Supreme Court. This includes liberal versus conservative voting tendencies; voting interagreement among the justices; voting to overturn legislation or precedent; assignment of the majority opinion; writing the majority, concurring, and dissenting opinions; and joining one or more of the same. The justices must also decide whether or not to hear cases appealed to them, but the vast majority of their individual votes in such cases are not officially reported and are typically available only from the docket books of the justices. (An exception is the expanded version of the U.S. Supreme Court Judicial Database, which includes pre-merits votes of justices who served during the Vinson and Warren Court eras.) The crucial question here is why do the justices behave as they do?

Legal professionals maintain that a justice's vote is based on some combination of the plain meaning of statutes, the intent of the framers, and precedent (also called *stare decisis*). Political scientists are more likely to look at the attitudes and values of each justice as an answer to this question. Still others argue that judicial tradition bounded by judicial restraint leads justices to defer to the wishes of Congress, the president, or the public. The data on the voting behavior of the justices in Tables 6-1 through 6-9 (most of which we derived from the Supreme Court Database) will help students of the Court assess these and other competing explanations. The voting data consist of all formally decided cases on the Court's appellate docket from the 1946 through 2001 terms.

Table 6-1 presents variously derived ideological scores for the justices. In Tables 6-2 and 6-3, we look at each justice's tendency to vote in a liberal versus conservative direction, though in some issue areas (for example, criminal justice) this label fits better than in others (for example, federalism). (See the notes following the tables for further explanation.) Table 6-2 presents the aggregate voting behavior for each justice who served between the 1946 and 1994 terms of the Court. Pre–1946 votes by those who served during the 1946 term are not included in the database or in this table. Votes are broken down by the eleven aggregate issue areas defined by the database, plus a separate civil liberties column that combines the votes from criminal procedure, civil rights, First Amendment, due process, privacy, and attorneys' cases. In the combined civil liberties cases, Justice Goldberg is the most liberal of the justices, supporting that position nearly 90 percent of the time. Not far behind is Justice Douglas, who supported the liberal position 88 percent of the time. A second rung of liberals consists of Justices Marshall, Fortas, Brennan, and Warren, all of whom supported the liberal position approximately 80 percent of the time. Justice Black is the remaining liberal of the group, with almost three-quarters of his votes in the liberal direction. A plurality of the justices are moderate on civil liberties issues. This group includes Frankfurter, Jackson, Burton, Clark, Minton, Harlan, Whittaker, Stewart, White, Blackmun, Powell, Stevens, Souter, Ginsburg, and Breyer. Reed, Burger, Rehnquist, O'Connor, Scalia, and Kennedy rank as conservative in civil liberties cases. In economics cases, the same tendencies hold, with some exceptions. Clark, for instance, is decidedly more liberal in economic matters than in civil liberties concerns, while Marshall approaches the moderate camp.

Because aggregate voting patterns can mask change through the judicial life cycle, we provide the annual voting behavior of each justice in Table 6-3. Data here are limited to those issues where enough cases have been decided to make annual comparisons meaningful. In addition, we have combined economics and union cases into a single economics category, as relatively few union cases are heard in any given year. While most justices demonstrate a fair amount of consistency from term to term, there are exceptions: Justice Black became markedly more moderate following the 1963 term. Justice Blackmun, who originally voted as a moderate conservative, in later terms voted as a moderate liberal.

Tables 6-4 through 6-7 present voting interagreement among the justices by issue area on the Vinson, Warren, Burger, and Rehnquist Courts, respectively. There is little surprise here: like-minded justices tend to vote alike. Thus, Douglas voted with Goldberg over 90 percent of the time in civil rights and First Amendment cases during the Warren Court, and Brennan and Marshall were nearly inseparable on the three Courts on which they served together. Thomas began his career as a virtual clone of Scalia.

Data on voting behavior conclude with Tables 6-8 and 6-9, which look at cases where the Court declared legislation unconstitutional (Table 6-8) or explicitly overturned previous decisions (Table 6-9). The data are limited here because they do not tell us how justices voted in every case that the Court was asked to strike a law or overturn precedent, but only in those cases that a majority of justices in fact did so. Nevertheless, interesting results are evident. For example, Justice Frankfurter, who was reputedly opposed to the Warren Court's activism, was three times more likely to join the Court than not when it voided legislation. Rehnquist is the only justice who has consistently refused to join the Court when it strikes legislation.

After the Court reaches a decision on the merits of the case, the chief justice, or the senior associate justice in the majority if the chief justice dissents or does not participate, assigns the majority opinion to one of the members of the majority. The justices not assigned the majority opinion can either write a concurring opinion (agreeing with the decision of the majority, but not necessarily with the reasoning in its opinion), a dissenting opinion (disagreeing with both the results and the reasoning of the majority opinion), or not write at all, silently joining one or more of the opinions written by others. We detail the extent of opinion writing from the 1790 through 2001 terms of the Court in Table 6-10. Some points are worth noting. Extensive dissent and concurrence writing is a fairly recent phenomenon. John Marshall Harlan (I) is the only justice who did not sit on the Warren, Burger, or Rehnquist Courts who wrote more than 100 dissents. Oliver Wendell Holmes, who wrote only 72 dissenting opinions in more than 5,700 cases, was known as the "Great Dissenter" not because of the quantity of his dissents, but because of their quality. No justice predating the Warren Court wrote more than 100 concurrences.

The Supreme Court Database provides additional data on the opinion writing of the justices, including the number of judgments of the Court written by each justice (these are plurality rulings that occur when no majority agrees on the justification for a decision) and a division of concurring opinions into regular concurrences (joining the majority opinion, but writing separately as well) and special concurrences (explicitly disagreeing with the rationale in the majority opinion). This information appears in Table 6-11.

Table 6-12 presents the number of solo dissents authored since the 1946 term. We would expect that such dissents would come from justices at the liberal or conservative extremes of the Court's ideological spectrum. Not surprisingly, Douglas and Rehnquist have authored solo dissents on a regular basis. What cannot be explained is the solo dissent record of Justice Stevens, who is by no means an extremist. Presumably, his decision-making behavior cannot be explained by the simple liberal-conservative scale.

Yet another aspect of opinion writing concerns the importance of the justices' decisions. Table 6-13 lists the most significant opinions of each justice. Of course, such lists are subjective. Nonetheless, we are confident that ours, at the very least, hits the highlights of the justices' careers.

Finally, in Tables 6-14 through 6-19, we examine the opinion assignment patterns of each justice who assigned an opinion between the 1946 and 2001 terms. In most of these tables, we assume that the senior justice in the majority decision coalition assigned the opinion. (An exception is Table 6-14 for which we used the chief justice's assignment sheet to ascertain the opinion assigner.) This assumption does not always hold, however, as sometimes justices switch votes and are not in the majority when the assignment is made. Thus, in cases where the chief justice dissents at the original conference vote but subsequently switches to the majority, we may have incorrectly listed the chief justice as having assigned the majority opinion. The same may happen when senior associate justices switch their votes.

The chief justice assigns the overwhelming number of opinions in any term. During the Warren Court, non–Warren assignments fell largely to Frankfurter, for when Warren dissented, Douglas and Black usually did too. On the Burger Court, Douglas, and then Brennan, assigned the overwhelming majority of cases when Burger dissented. On the Rehnquist Court, Brennan, until his retirement, made every assignment when the chief justice dissented. Most assigners give preference to justices who are ideologically close to them, especially in the most important cases. As an extreme example, the liberal Warren assigned but one opinion to the moderate Frankfurter in the 1959 term, while assigning ten or more opinions to five other justices. Frankfurter, however, was able to overcome this imbalance by assigning to himself the seven cases where Warren dissented and he was the senior associate in the majority.

Table 6-1 Ideological Values of Supreme Court Justices, Vinson, Warren, Burger, and Rehnquist Courts

Justice	Segal/Cover[a]	Schubert[b] C	Schubert[b] E	Spaeth[c] Freedom	Spaeth[c] Equality	Spaeth[c] New Deal
Black	.75	9	2	.53	−.55	.43
Reed	.45	20	8	—	—	—
Frankfurter	.33	12.5	19	−.12	−.81	−.36
Douglas	.46	3	4	.73	.76	.73
Murphy	1.00	1	3	—	—	—
Jackson	1.00	14.5	20	—	—	—
Rutledge	1.00	2	1	—	—	—
Burton	−.44	16	15.5	—	—	—
Vinson	.50	17	9	—	—	—
Clark	.00	18	10	−.51	−.20	.25
Minton	.44	19	6.5	—	—	—
Warren	.50	6	5	.65	.61	.43
Harlan	.75	14.5	17.5	−.30	−.36	−.64
Brennan	1.00	7	6.5	.38	.58	.37
Whittaker	.00	12.5	17.5	−.38	−.67	−.06
Stewart	.50	11	15.5	.09	−.08	−.32
White	.00	10	11	−.40	−.07	−.02
Goldberg	.50	8	12.5	.63	.64	.18
Fortas	1.00	4	12.5	.63	.63	.24
Marshall	1.00	5	14	.45	.57	.23
Burger	−.77	—	—	−.49	−.42	−.38
Blackmun	−.77	—	—	−.34	−.27	−.22
Powell	−.67	—	—	−.26	−.26	−.49
Rehnquist	−.91	—	—	−.58	−.58	−.55
Stevens	−.50	—	—	.05	.31	−.15
O'Connor	−.17	—	—	—	—	—
Rehnquist	−.91	—	—	—	—	—
Scalia	−1.00	—	—	—	—	—
Kennedy	−.27	—	—	—	—	—
Souter	−.34	—	—	—	—	—
Thomas	−.68	—	—	—	—	—
Ginsburg	.36	—	—	—	—	—
Breyer	−.05	—	—	—	—	—

Note: "—" indicates justice not covered in study.

[a] Values are from 1.00 (most liberal) to −1.00 (most conservative); values derived from content analyses of newspaper editorials prior to confirmation.

[b] Values range from 1 (justice most supportive of civil liberties (C) or economic liberties (E)) through 20 (justice least supportive); scores derived from factor analyses and multidimensional scaling of the votes of justices in nonunanimous cases.

[c] Values represent justices' support of or opposition to the three values of freedom, equality, and New Deal economics. Values range from 1.00 (highest level of support) to −1.00 (lowest level of support). Scores derived from factor analyses and multidimensional scaling of the votes of justices in nonunanimous cases.

Sources: Segal/Cover: Jeffrey A. Segal and Albert D. Cover, "Ideological Values and the Votes of U.S. Supreme Court Justices," *American Political Science Review* 83 (1989): 560; and Jeffrey A. Segal, Lee Epstein, Charles M. Cameron, and Harold J. Spaeth, "Ideological Values and the Votes of U.S. Supreme Court Justices Revisited," *Journal of Politics* 57 (1995): 816. Schubert: Glendon Schubert, *The Judicial Mind Revisited* (New York: Oxford University Press, 1974), 60; Spaeth: Harold J. Spaeth, *Supreme Court Policy Making* (San Francisco: Freeman, 1979), 135.

Table 6-2 Aggregate Liberal Voting of Justices, 1946–2001 Terms

Justice	CivL	Crim	CivR	1st	DP	Priv	Atty	Un'n	Econ	FTax	Fed	JudP
Black	74.0 (1,202)	69.8 (514)	73.5 (347)	84.6 (234)	73.6 (87)	42.9 (7)	76.9 (13)	74.3 (179)	83.2 (691)	84.5 (174)	64.0 (139)	53.2 (479)
Blackmun	52.8 (1,893)	42.3 (724)	62.1 (607)	56.9 (281)	52.0 (173)	50.9 (55)	73.6 (53)	61.9 (134)	54.3 (587)	74.4 (90)	65.9 (138)	35.7 (384)
Brennan	79.5 (2,416)	76.2 (944)	83.6 (768)	83.3 (408)	74.5 (192)	59.2 (49)	85.5 (55)	66.2 (234)	71.6 (867)	70.6 (180)	67.0 (191)	42.7 (527)
Breyer	61.2 (358)	52.9 (155)	73.8 (107)	60.4 (48)	67.7 (31)	46.2 (13)	50.0 (4)	84.2 (19)	52.4 (105)	75.0 (20)	69.0 (42)	40.2 (97)
Burger	29.6 (1,429)	19.8 (515)	37.3 (499)	31.9 (213)	38.0 (129)	12.5 (40)	39.4 (33)	43.9 (107)	42.5 (424)	72.1 (68)	67.8 (87)	22.2 (266)
Burton	38.9 (494)	31.1 (212)	48.1 (129)	32.5 (80)	54.8 (62)	0.0 (5)	66.7 (6)	50.9 (79)	49.9 (371)	73.2 (86)	43.3 (60)	35.1 (205)
Clark	43.7 (764)	35.6 (326)	56.2 (217)	34.0 (159)	70.6 (51)	33.3 (3)	62.5 (8)	64.6 (130)	71.0 (482)	75.6 (131)	53.3 (104)	43.8 (340)
Douglas	88.8 (1,496)	73.9 (631)	90.7 (463)	94.4 (285)	75.5 (110)	73.3 (15)	84.5 (13)	64.1 (209)	83.5 (770)	39.5 (190)	69.1 (152)	67.3 (553)
Fortas	81.0 (205)	80.2 (91)	83.6 (61)	77.3 (44)	100.0 (5)	— (0)	75.0 (4)	60.0 (20)	69.3 (75)	50.0 (16)	64.3 (14)	39.6 (48)
Frankfurter	53.5 (664)	54.2 (288)	61.8 (157)	47.1 (121)	55.9 (68)	50.0 (4)	83.3 (6)	44.4 (108)	38.5 (460)	69.0 (116)	52.5 (80)	29.2 (267)

Ginsburg	64.6 (407)	58.7 (179)	68.3 (120)	75.0 (52)	61.8 (34)	62.5 (16)	100.0 (6)	80.0 (20)	53.8 (130)	72.7 (22)	63.8 (47)	40.2 (107)
Goldberg	88.9 (153)	80.0 (60)	98.3 (58)	89.3 (28)	80.0 (5)	100.0 (1)	100.0 (1)	65.0 (20)	65.5 (84)	78.3 (23)	61.1 (18)	40.0 (45)
Harlan	43.6 (869)	39.4 (371)	45.0 (258)	44.1 (186)	66.7 (39)	33.3 (3)	66.7 (12)	55.4 (130)	37.8 (402)	71.2 (111)	55.7 (79)	32.5 (231)
Jackson	40.8 (294)	38.3 (128)	52.1 (73)	30.2 (43)	40.0 (45)	25.0 (4)	100.0 (1)	40.8 (49)	39.8 (236)	56.0 (50)	53.1 (32)	30.8 (120)
Kennedy	36.6 (767)	28.7 (341)	41.4 (210)	52.8 (108)	36.2 (58)	21.4 (28)	54.5 (22)	35.7 (42)	47.2 (254)	77.3 (44)	50.6 (87)	40.5 (205)
Marshall	81.4 (1,888)	80.2 (722)	85.1 (619)	82.9 (287)	75.8 (165)	60.4 (48)	83.0 (47)	68.1 (138)	65.2 (557)	74.2 (93)	67.5 (123)	44.4 (369)
Minton	36.4 (231)	28.4 (88)	41.2 (68)	27.5 (40)	63.3 (30)	0.0 (3)	50.0 (2)	56.8 (37)	60.2 (186)	75.6 (45)	48.5 (33)	28.2 (99)
Murphy	79.1 (134)	81.8 (66)	87.5 (32)	64.3 (14)	71.4 (21)	0.0 (1)	0.0 (0)	74.1 (27)	77.9 (113)	87.5 (24)	46.2 (13)	51.1 (47)
O'Connor	35.7 (1,348)	25.6 (559)	45.7 (392)	42.9 (189)	39.7 (121)	40.5 (42)	28.9 (45)	40.2 (82)	42.9 (413)	57.1 (70)	48.1 (133)	37.7 (310)
Powell	37.4 (1,285)	28.8 (482)	41.0 (432)	47.8 (182)	44.3 (122)	32.4 (37)	36.7 (30)	51.1 (94)	44.5 (357)	56.1 (57)	62.7 (83)	25.9 (239)
Reed	34.9 (387)	27.2 (169)	41.0 (100)	27.6 (58)	57.4 (54)	0.0 (4)	50.0 (2)	62.1 (66)	52.0 (323)	72.6 (73)	43.5 (46)	37.9 (161)

(Table continues)

Table 6-2 (*Continued*)

Justice	CivL	Crim	CivR	1st	DP	Priv	Atty	Un'n	Econ	FTax	Fed	JudP
Rehnquist	21.8 (2,127)	16.7 (840)	26.8 (671)	21.3 (301)	27.7 (191)	16.4 (67)	26.3 (57)	41.8 (141)	43.1 (666)	69.4 (108)	40.3 (181)	28.4 (468)
Rutledge	76.3 (135)	77.3 (66)	76.7 (30)	75.0 (16)	77.3 (22)	0.0 (1)	0.0 (0)	65.4 (26)	82.5 (120)	83.3 (24)	69.2 (13)	56.3 (48)
Scalia	28.4 (902)	25.3 (395)	30.9 (249)	33.1 (127)	28.9 (76)	25.0 (28)	29.6 (27)	35.3 (51)	43.1 (288)	67.3 (52)	54.5 (99)	32.2 (230)
Souter	60.8 (571)	51.2 (256)	68.5 (168)	76.7 (73)	61.9 (42)	60.0 (20)	58.3 (12)	61.3 (31)	52.1 (194)	64.7 (34)	62.3 (61)	44.4 (160)
Stevens	64.5 (1,783)	64.8 (714)	63.2 (552)	68.0 (241)	63.2 (163)	51.7 (60)	75.5 (53)	64.1 (117)	58.0 (562)	56.2 (89)	55.8 (165)	45.3 (393)
Stewart	51.4 (1,550)	46.1 (607)	50.0 (518)	63.9 (274)	54.8 (104)	41.4 (29)	72.2 (18)	56.9 (167)	45.0 (564)	65.9 (123)	59.8 (102)	34.7 (346)
Thomas	25.1 (506)	20.4 (226)	25.7 (148)	34.8 (66)	28.2 (39)	27.8 (18)	44.4 (9)	26.1 (23)	37.8 (172)	50.0 (32)	43.1 (58)	37.5 (144)
Vinson	36.5 (277)	29.6 (115)	47.2 (72)	25.6 (43)	52.4 (42)	0.0 (4)	0.0 (1)	34.1 (44)	52.9 (225)	75.5 (49)	48.3 (29)	32.7 (113)
Warren	78.6 (771)	75.1 (346)	82.8 (221)	79.9 (159)	81.8 (33)	50.0 (2)	80.0 (10)	72.0 (125)	81.9 (442)	79.1 (115)	73.3 (75)	46.4 (222)
White	42.4 (2,308)	33.3 (894)	55.8 (756)	38.3 (363)	48.4 (182)	14.8 (54)	39.0 (59)	62.6 (195)	58.4 (753)	85.5 (138)	67.0 (179)	36.8 (500)

| Whittaker | 43.3 (240) | 43.5 (115) | 46.3 (54) | 37.0 (54) | 60.0 (15) | 00.0 (1) | 100.0 (1) | 42.5 (40) | 32.0 (150) | 57.1 (42) | 60.0 (25) | 37.5 (64) |

Note: Figures listed are the percentage of cases in which the justice took the liberal position. Figures in parentheses are the total number of cases in issue area in which the justice participated.

The issue areas are defined as follows: Civil liberties (CivL): combines criminal procedure, civil rights, First Amendment, due process, privacy, and attorneys; Criminal procedure (Crim): the rights of persons accused of crime except for the due process rights of prisoners; Civil rights (CivR): non-First Amendment freedom cases that pertain to classifications based on race (including Native Americans), age, indigence, voting, residence, military or handicapped status, sex, or alienage; First Amendment (1st): guarantees contained therein; Due process (DP): noncriminal procedural guarantees, plus court jurisdiction over nonresident litigants and the takings clause of the Fifth Amendment; Privacy (Priv): abortion, contraception, the Freedom of Information Act and related federal statutes; Attorneys (Atty): attorneys' fees, commercial speech, admission to and removal from the bar, and disciplinary matters; Unions (Un'n): labor union activity; Economics (Econ): commercial business activity, plus litigation involving injured persons or things, employee actions vis-à-vis employers, zoning regulations, and governmental regulation of corruption other than that involving campaign spending; Federal taxation (FTax): the Internal Revenue Code and related statutes; Federalism (Fed): conflicts between the federal and state governments, excluding those between state and federal courts, and those involving the priority of federal fiscal claims; Judicial power (JudP): the exercise of the judiciary's own power and authority. Federalism and judicial power are undercounted somewhat because they frequently occur in cases containing a substantive issue area. In such situations, typically only the substantive issue is counted.

The term *liberal* represents the voting direction of the justices across the various issue areas. It is most appropriate in the areas of civil liberties, criminal procedure, civil rights, First Amendment, due process, privacy, and attorneys, where it signifies pro-defendant votes in criminal procedure cases, pro-women or -minorities in civil rights cases, pro-individual against the government in First Amendment, due process, and privacy cases, and pro-attorney in attorneys' fees and bar membership cases. In takings clause cases, however, a pro-government/anti-owner vote is considered liberal. The use of the term is perhaps less appropriate in union cases, where it represents pro-union votes against both individuals and the government, and in economic cases, where it represents pro-government votes against challenges to federal regulatory authority and pro-competition, anti-business, pro-liability, pro-injured person, and pro-bankruptcy votes. In federalism and federal taxation, liberal indicates pro-national government positions; in judicial power cases, the term represents pro-judiciary positions.

Source: U.S. Supreme Court Judicial Database, with analu = 0 or 4 and dec_type = 1, 6, or 7.

Table 6-3 Liberal Voting of the Justices, by Term, 1946–2001

Term	Civil liberties	Criminal procedure	Civil rights	First Amendment	Economics
			Black		
1946	48.7 (39)	50.0 (20)	50.0 (6)	50.0 (8)	80.6 (62)
1947	77.6 (58)	70.8 (24)	83.3 (18)	80.0 (5)	87.9 (33)
1948	66.7 (39)	63.6 (22)	75.0 (8)	66.7 (3)	78.4 (51)
1949	71.4 (35)	88.9 (9)	80.0 (10)	57.1 (7)	80.8 (26)
1950	74.2 (31)	88.9 (9)	75.0 (12)	71.4 (7)	62.9 (35)
1951	86.1 (36)	88.2 (17)	100.0 (6)	100.0 (6)	73.3 (30)
1952	87.2 (39)	85.7 (14)	80.0 (10)	100.0 (6)	90.3 (31)
1953	82.1 (28)	66.7 (15)	100.0 (8)	100.0 (4)	81.1 (37)
1954	78.4 (37)	66.7 (18)	80.0 (10)	100.0 (5)	84.6 (26)
1955	83.3 (30)	66.7 (12)	100.0 (11)	100.0 (5)	87.2 (39)
1956	94.2 (52)	100.0 (18)	75.0 (12)	100.0 (15)	86.8 (38)
1957	87.3 (63)	81.3 (32)	100.0 (14)	100.0 (9)	85.3 (34)
1958	88.1 (42)	84.0 (25)	83.3 (6)	100.0 (11)	85.7 (49)
1959	91.7 (36)	87.5 (16)	100.0 (10)	100.0 (7)	89.7 (39)
1960	83.6 (67)	90.0 (30)	78.6 (14)	81.8 (22)	78.9 (38)

Table 6-3 *(Continued)*

Term	Civil liberties	Criminal procedure	Civil rights	First Amendment	Economics
1961	92.1 (38)	87.5 (16)	88.9 (9)	100.0 (8)	76.3 (38)
1962	88.2 (51)	81.8 (22)	94.1 (17)	87.5 (8)	88.9 (45)
1963	87.9 (58)	90.9 (22)	85.2 (27)	88.9 (9)	82.5 (40)
1964	73.8 (42)	68.8 (16)	69.2 (13)	90.0 (10)	79.3 (29)
1965	71.7 (46)	75.0 (16)	50.0 (14)	92.3 (13)	76.9 (26)
1966	56.9 (58)	53.6 (28)	57.9 (19)	70.0 (10)	86.7 (30)
1967	60.0 (70)	47.2 (36)	62.5 (16)	78.6 (14)	73.5 (34)
1968	50.0 (62)	33.3 (27)	54.5 (22)	80.0 (10)	85.7 (21)
1969	51.6 (64)	50.0 (26)	46.2 (26)	70.0 (10)	66.7 (15)
1970	55.6 (81)	41.7 (24)	55.2 (29)	72.7 (22)	70.8 (24)
Blackmun					
1970	34.6 (81)	12.5 (24)	51.7 (29)	31.8 (22)	47.8 (23)
1971	37.4 (91)	20.6 (34)	46.4 (28)	35.3 (17)	47.4 (38)
1972	38.9 (95)	25.7 (35)	54.5 (33)	27.8 (18)	63.6 (33)
1973	37.1 (89)	26.7 (30)	41.7 (36)	50.0 (14)	46.4 (28)
1974	46.6 (73)	45.8 (24)	48.3 (29)	55.6 (9)	64.7 (34)

(Table continues)

Table 6-3   *(Continued)*

Term	Civil liberties	Criminal procedure	Civil rights	First Amendment	Economics
1975	32.2 (90)	9.1 (33)	50.0 (28)	64.3 (14)	43.8 (32)
1976	33.3 (93)	23.3 (30)	34.3 (35)	33.3 (15)	50.0 (26)
1977	51.6 (64)	48.0 (25)	45.8 (24)	66.7 (6)	63.3 (30)
1978	45.8 (83)	37.9 (29)	52.9 (34)	37.5 (8)	46.9 (32)
1979	51.2 (84)	34.4 (32)	63.6 (22)	60.0 (10)	56.8 (37)
1980	44.8 (67)	44.0 (25)	50.0 (26)	44.4 (9)	66.7 (30)
1981	59.3 (81)	36.8 (19)	73.5 (34)	75.0 (12)	63.6 (33)
1982	61.0 (82)	40.0 (30)	78.6 (28)	63.6 (11)	55.0 (40)
1983	43.6 (94)	20.5 (39)	65.5 (29)	75.0 (12)	48.5 (33)
1984	51.1 (88)	39.4 (33)	68.0 (25)	63.6 (11)	52.8 (36)
1985	64.9 (97)	55.8 (43)	72.4 (29)	61.5 (13)	47.4 (19)
1986	74.5 (94)	68.3 (41)	82.6 (23)	83.3 (12)	51.9 (27)
1987	65.4 (78)	53.1 (32)	76.2 (21)	76.9 (13)	54.3 (35)
1988	68.7 (83)	58.6 (29)	96.2 (26)	53.3 (15)	63.6 (22)
1989	58.6 (70)	54.3 (35)	70.0 (10)	57.1 (14)	46.2 (26)
1990	77.6 (58)	66.7 (30)	93.8 (16)	100.0 (6)	59.4 (32)

Table 6-3   *(Continued)*

Term	Civil liberties	Criminal procedure	Civil rights	First Amendment	Economics
1991	73.2 (56)	57.1 (21)	83.3 (18)	87.5 (8)	67.9 (28)
1992	78.2 (55)	72.4 (29)	78.6 (14)	87.5 (8)	52.4 (21)
1993	72.3 (47)	65.2 (23)	75.0 (12)	75.0 (4)	75.0 (24)
			Brennan		
1956	72.7 (44)	83.3 (18)	50.0 (12)	62.5 (8)	74.4 (39)
1957	78.7 (61)	70.0 (30)	85.7 (14)	100.0 (9)	79.4 (34)
1958	79.1 (43)	73.1 (26)	66.7 (6)	100.0 (11)	75.5 (49)
1959	77.8 (36)	68.8 (16)	100.0 (10)	85.7 (7)	81.0 (42)
1960	79.1 (67)	80.0 (30)	64.3 (14)	86.4 (22)	63.2 (38)
1961	84.6 (39)	76.5 (17)	88.9 (9)	100.0 (8)	68.4 (38)
1962	84.3 (51)	77.3 (22)	94.1 (17)	87.5 (8)	82.2 (45)
1963	86.0 (57)	77.3 (22)	92.3 (26)	88.9 (9)	67.5 (40)
1964	70.5 (44)	50.0 (16)	85.7 (14)	72.7 (11)	65.5 (29)
1965	73.9 (46)	56.3 (16)	85.7 (14)	76.9 (13)	82.1 (28)
1966	78.0 (59)	75.0 (28)	84.2 (19)	81.8 (11)	73.3 (30)
1967	77.1 (70)	80.6 (36)	81.3 (16)	64.3 (14)	66.7 (33)

(Table continues)

Table 6-3 *(Continued)*

Term	Civil liberties	Criminal procedure	Civil rights	First Amendment	Economics
1968	79.4 (63)	66.7 (27)	82.6 (23)	100.0 (10)	76.2 (21)
1969	69.2 (65)	55.6 (27)	84.6 (26)	70.0 (10)	62.5 (16)
1970	75.9 (79)	70.8 (24)	82.1 (28)	68.2 (22)	68.0 (25)
1971	81.8 (88)	71.0 (31)	92.9 (28)	82.4 (17)	66.7 (39)
1972	86.3 (95)	74.3 (35)	93.9 (33)	94.4 (18)	70.0 (30)
1973	80.9 (89)	76.7 (30)	86.1 (36)	85.7 (14)	82.8 (29)
1974	80.8 (73)	83.3 (24)	86.2 (9)	66.7 (9)	73.5 (34)
1975	84.4 (90)	78.8 (33)	85.7 (28)	100.0 (14)	63.6 (33)
1976	75.5 (94)	71.0 (31)	74.3 (35)	93.3 (15)	73.1 (26)
1977	79.3 (58)	95.0 (20)	69.6 (23)	85.7 (7)	80.6 (31)
1978	79.3 (82)	78.6 (28)	82.4 (34)	62.5 (8)	51.6 (31)
1979	82.4 (85)	78.1 (32)	86.4 (22)	100.0 (10)	80.6 (36)
1980	72.1 (68)	72.0 (25)	85.2 (27)	77.8 (9)	71.9 (32)
1981	76.5 (81)	78.9 (19)	85.3 (34)	75.0 (12)	67.6 (34)
1982	74.1 (81)	66.7 (30)	78.6 (28)	80.0 (10)	60.0 (40)
1983	74.0 (96)	75.0 (40)	82.8 (29)	84.6 (13)	57.6 (33)

Table 6-3 *(Continued)*

Term	Civil liberties	Criminal procedure	Civil rights	First Amendment	Economics
1984	76.4 (89)	78.8 (33)	72.0 (25)	90.9 (11)	63.9 (36)
1985	76.5 (98)	76.7 (43)	72.4 (29)	71.4 (14)	66.7 (18)
1986	92.7 (96)	95.1 (41)	92.0 (25)	91.7 (12)	64.3 (28)
1987	82.9 (76)	83.3 (30)	81.0 (21)	100.0 (13)	69.4 (36)
1988	85.7 (84)	79.3 (29)	96.2 (26)	80.0 (15)	68.2 (22)
1989	84.3 (71)	88.6 (35)	100.0 (10)	71.4 (14)	69.2 (26)
Breyer					
1994	63.4 (41)	42.1 (19)	81.8 (11)	87.5 (8)	42.9 (14)
1995	65.0 (40)	44.4 (18)	75.0 (8)	88.9 (9)	50.0 (20)
1996	57.4 (47)	52.9 (17)	62.5 (16)	60.0 (5)	64.7 (17)
1997	56.3 (48)	52.0 (25)	70.6 (17)	0.0 (2)	68.4 (19)
1998	57.1 (42)	37.5 (16)	78.9 (19)	50.0 (2)	47.1 (17)
1999	66.0 (50)	63.0 (27)	90.0 (10)	37.5 (8)	54.5 (11)
2000	72.1 (43)	82.3 (17)	76.9 (13)	50.0 (6)	72.7 (11)
2001	53.3 (43)	46.7 (15)	58.3 (12)	55.6 (9)	53.9 (13)
Burger					
1969	30.8 (65)	22.2 (27)	34.6 (26)	40.0 (10)	23.1 (13)

(Table continues)

Table 6-3   *(Continued)*

Term	Civil liberties	Criminal procedure	Civil rights	First Amendment	Economics
1970	36.3 (80)	17.4 (23)	48.3 (29)	31.8 (22)	44.0 (2425)
1971	34.1 (91)	17.6 (34)	42.9 (28)	35.3 (17)	36.8 (38)
1972	29.5 (95)	17.1 (35)	45.5 (33)	16.7 (18)	57.1 (35)
1973	30.3 (89)	20.0 (30)	38.9 (36)	28.6 (14)	37.9 (29)
1974	38.4 (73)	41.7 (24)	41.4 (29)	22.2 (9)	41.2 (34)
1975	26.7 (90)	9.1 (33)	46.4 (28)	42.9 (14)	42.4 (33)
1976	17.0 (94)	19.4 (31)	17.1 (35)	20.0 (15)	36.0 (25)
1977	36.0 (75)	48.3 (29)	25.0 (28)	50.0 (8)	51.4 (35)
1978	27.7 (83)	31.0 (29)	17.6 (34)	37.5 (8)	40.6 (32)
1979	35.3 (85)	15.6 (32)	50.0 (22)	50.0 (10)	47.2 (36)
1980	31.3 (67)	32.0 (25)	33.3 (27)	25.0 (8)	43.8 (32)
1981	23.8 (80)	0.0 (18)	26.5 (34)	50.0 (12)	35.3 (34)
1982	28.0 (82)	10.0 (30)	39.3 (28)	45.5 (11)	50.0 (40)
1983	30.9 (94)	12.8 (39)	55.2 (29)	25.0 (12)	39.4 (33)
1984	28.1 (89)	9.1 (33)	56.0 (25)	18.2 (11)	41.7 (36)
1985	23.5 (98)	18.6 (43)	27.6 (29)	21.4 (14)	42.1 (19)

Table 6-3   *(Continued)*

Term	Civil liberties	Criminal procedure	Civil rights	First Amendment	Economics
			Burton		
1946	25.6 (39)	20.0 (20)	16.7 (6)	37.5 (8)	51.6 (64)
1947	50.8 (59)	37.5 (24)	66.7 (18)	40.0 (5)	36.4 (33)
1948	23.1 (39)	18.2 (22)	37.5 (8)	0.0 (3)	49.0 (51)
1949	31.1 (35)	22.2 (9)	60.0 (10)	0.0 (7)	60.0 (25)
1950	53.1 (32)	55.6 (9)	66.7 (12)	37.5 (8)	47.1 (34)
1951	39.5 (38)	47.1 (17)	37.5 (8)	33.3 (6)	45.2 31
1952	42.5 (40)	13.3 (15)	50.0 (10)	66.7 (6)	41.9 (31)
1953	35.7 (28)	33.3 (15)	37.5 (8)	25.0 (4)	51.3 (39)
1954	52.8 (36)	47.1 (17)	60.0 (10)	40.0 (5)	61.5 (26)
1955	43.3 (30)	33.3 (12)	45.5 (11)	40.0 (5)	56.4 (39)
1956	30.2 (53)	35.0 (20)	8.3 (12)	21.4 (14)	53.5 (43)
1957	36.5 (63)	25.0 (32)	50.0 (14)	44.4 (9)	47.1 (34)
1958	100.0 (2)	—	100.0 (2)	—	—
			Clark		
1949	36.0 (25)	20.0 (5)	57.1 (7)	0.0 (5)	59.1 (22)

(Table continues)

Table 6-3   *(Continued)*

Term	Civil liberties	Criminal procedure	Civil rights	First Amendment	Economics
1950	50.0 (24)	60.0 (5)	60.0 (10)	28.6 (7)	57.6 (33)
1951	37.9 (29)	53.3 (15)	40.0 (5)	20.0 (5)	46.2 (26)
1952	37.8 (37)	7.1 (14)	40.0 (10)	66.7 (6)	46.4 (28)
1953	44.4 (27)	26.7 (15)	62.5 (8)	66.7 (3)	60.0 (35)
1954	62.2 (37)	50.0 (18)	60.0 (10)	80.0 (5)	81.5 (27)
1955	48.3 (29)	45.5 (11)	54.4 (11)	40.0 (5)	81.1 (37)
1956	32.1 (53)	45.0 (20)	16.7 (12)	7.1 (14)	80.0 (40)
1957	30.6 (62)	25.0 (32)	21.4 (14)	11.1 (9)	66.7 (33)
1958	41.9 (43)	34.6 (26)	50.0 (6)	54.5 (11)	67.4 (46)
1959	36.1 (36)	18.8 (16)	60.0 (10)	28.6 (7)	69.0 (42)
1960	31.3 (67)	30.0 (30)	42.9 (14)	22.7 (22)	54.1 (37)
1961	43.6 (39)	35.3 (17)	66.7 (9)	25.0 (8)	71.1 (38)
1962	47.1 (51)	31.8 (22)	64.7 (17)	50.0 (8)	90.9 (44)
1963	55.2 (58)	45.5 (22)	70.4 (27)	33.3 (9)	80.0 (40)
1964	59.1 (44)	37.5 (16)	85.7 (14)	45.5 (11)	69.0 (29)
1965	58.7 (46)	37.5 (16)	78.6 (14)	53.8 (13)	75.0 (28)

Table 6-3 *(Continued)*

Term	Civil liberties	Criminal procedure	Civil rights	First Amendment	Economics
1966	43.9 (57)	46.2 (26)	52.6 (19)	27.3 (11)	81.5 (27)
			Douglas		
1946	52.6 (38)	55.0 (20)	83.3 (6)	37.5 (8)	69.5 (59)
1947	79.3 (58)	75.0 (24)	88.9 (18)	100.0 (5)	78.1 (32)
1948	79.5 (39)	81.8 (22)	87.5 (8)	66.7 (3)	82.0 (50)
1949	77.8 (9)	100.0 (2)	75.0 (4)	—	100.0 (5)
1950	71.9 (32)	66.7 (9)	75.0 (12)	87.5 (8)	77.1 (35)
1951	71.1 (38)	76.5 (17)	75.0 (8)	83.3 (6)	61.3 (31)
1952	72.5 (40)	73.3 (15)	60.0 (10)	100.0 (6)	64.5 (31)
1953	85.7 (28)	73.3 (15)	100.0 (8)	100.0 (4)	77.8 (36)
1954	78.4 (37)	72.2 (18)	80.0 (10)	100.0 (5)	88.9 (27)
1955	86.7 (30)	75.0 (12)	100.0 (11)	100.0 (5)	87.2 (39)
1956	94.3 (53)	95.0 (20)	90.9 (11)	100.0 (15)	90.7 (43)
1957	92.1 (63)	93.8 (32)	100.0 (14)	100.0 (9)	91.2 (34)
1958	93.0 (43)	92.3 (26)	83.3 (6)	100.0 (11)	93.8 (48)
1959	91.7 (36)	87.5 (16)	100.0 (10)	100.0 (7)	90.5 (42)

(Table continues)

Table 6-3 *(Continued)*

Term	Civil liberties	Criminal procedure	Civil rights	First Amendment	Economics
1960	95.5 (67)	93.3 (30)	92.9 (14)	100.0 (22)	81.6 (38)
1961	92.3 (39)	94.1 (17)	88.9 (9)	100.0 (8)	84.2 (38)
1962	94.1 (51)	90.9 (22)	94.1 (17)	100.0 (8)	77.8 (45)
1963	98.3 (58)	100.0 (22)	100.0 (27)	88.9 (9)	68.4 (38)
1964	97.7 (44)	93.8 (16)	100.0 (14)	100.0 (11)	72.4 (29)
1965	93.5 (46)	87.5 (16)	92.9 (14)	100.0 (13)	85.7 (28)
1966	91.2 (57)	96.3 (27)	89.5 (19)	90.0 (10)	93.3 (30)
1967	91.4 (70)	91.7 (36)	81.3 (16)	100.0 (14)	66.7 (30)
1968	87.1 (62)	81.5 (27)	91.3 (23)	100.0 (9)	81.0 (21)
1969	83.1 (65)	77.8 (27)	88.5 (26)	80.0 (10)	73.3 (15)
1970	90.9 (77)	86.4 (22)	85.7 (28)	100.0 (21)	75.0 (24)
1971	94.5 (91)	88.2 (34)	96.4 (28)	100.0 (17)	68.4 (38)
1972	91.6 (95)	88.6 (35)	93.9 (33)	94.4 (18)	71.4 (35)
1973	93.3 (89)	93.3 (30)	94.4 (36)	85.7 (14)	77.8 (27)
1974	89.1 (64)	95.5 (22)	91.3 (23)	88.9 (9)	80.0 (30)
1975	—	—	—	—	100.0 (1)

Table 6-3   *(Continued)*

Term	Civil liberties	Criminal procedure	Civil rights	First Amendment	Economics
			Fortas		
1965	83.7 (43)	73.3 (15)	100.0 (13)	75.0 (12)	68.2 (22)
1966	82.5 (57)	92.6 (27)	78.9 (19)	70.0 (10)	76.9 (26)
1967	80.0 (70)	80.6 (36)	75.0 (16)	78.6 (14)	57.6 (33)
1968	77.1 (35)	61.5 (13)	84.6 (13)	87.5 (8)	71.4 (14)
			Frankfurter		
1946	33.3 (39)	20.0 (20)	66.7 (6)	37.5 (8)	48.4 (64)
1947	55.9 (59)	58.3 (24)	66.7 (18)	20.0 (5)	24.2 (33)
1948	48.7 (39)	63.6 (22)	50.0 (8)	0.0 (3)	37.3 (51)
1949	61.8 (34)	66.7 (9)	88.9 (9)	28.6 (7)	18.2 (22)
1950	56.3 (32)	77.8 (9)	58.3 (12)	50.0 (8)	39.4 (33)
1951	75.8 (33)	87.5 (16)	83.3 (6)	60.0 (5)	39.3 (28)
1952	79.5 (39)	64.3 (14)	80.0 (10)	83.3 (6)	37.5 (32)
1953	57.1 (28)	46.7 (15)	62.5 (8)	75.0 (4)	46.2 (39)
1954	70.3 (37)	55.6 (18)	90.9 (10)	80.0 (5)	61.5 (26)
1955	67.9 (28)	50.0 (12)	88.9 (9)	80.0 (5)	52.6 (38)

(Table continues)

Table 6-3 *(Continued)*

Term	Civil liberties	Criminal procedure	Civil rights	First Amendment	Economics
1956	51.9 (54)	65.0 (20)	25.0 (12)	53.3 (15)	33.3 (36)
1957	54.1 (61)	50.0 (32)	53.8 (13)	66.7 (9)	33.3 (33)
1958	42.5 (40)	37.5 (24)	40.0 (5)	54.5 (11)	42.2 (45)
1959	36.1 (36)	25.0 (16)	50.0 (10)	28.6 (7)	30.8 (39)
1960	34.8 (66)	36.7 (30)	42.9 (14)	23.8 (21)	41.9 (31)
1961	57.9 (19)	57.1 (7)	57.1 (7)	50.0 (2)	33.3 (18)
			Ginsburg		
1993	55.3 (47)	47.8 (23)	41.7 (12)	75.0 (4)	66.7 (24)
1994	68.3 (41)	52.6 (19)	63.6 (11)	100.0 (8)	50.0 (16)
1995	60.0 (40)	44.4 (18)	75.0 (8)	88.9 (9)	35.0 (20)
1996	55.3 (47)	47.1 (17)	68.8 (16)	60.0 (5)	64.7 (17)
1997	66.7 (48)	64.0 (25)	76.5 (17)	50.0 (2)	63.2 (19)
1998	64.3 (42)	62.5 (16)	63.2 (19)	100.0 (2)	50.0 (18)
1999	78.0 (50)	70.4 (27)	90.0 (10)	75.0 (8)	54.5 (11)
2000	68.9 (45)	73.7 (19)	76.9 (13)	66.7 (6)	90.9 (11)
2001	63.6 (44)	60.0 (15)	61.5 (13)	55.6 (9)	46.2 (13)

Table 6-3   *(Continued)*

Term	Civil liberties	Criminal procedure	Civil rights	First Amendment	Economics
			Goldberg		
1962	88.2 (51)	77.3 (22)	100.0 (17)	100.0 (8)	75.6 (40)
1963	96.6 (58)	95.5 (22)	100.0 (27)	88.9 (9)	64.9 (37)
1964	79.5 (44)	62.5 (16)	92.9 (14)	81.8 (11)	50.0 (26)
			Harlan		
1954	81.8 (11)	50.0 (4)	100.0 (4)	100.0 (1)	33.3 (3)
1955	50.0 (24)	37.5 (8)	44.4 (9)	60.0 (5)	65.6 (32)
1956	50.0 (54)	50.0 (20)	25.0 (12)	60.0 (15)	39.0 (41)
1957	42.9 (63)	43.8 (32)	35.7 (14)	44.4 (9)	32.4 (34)
1958	44.2 (43)	38.5 (26)	33.3 (6)	63.6 (11)	45.7 (46)
1959	36.1 (36)	25.0 (16)	40.0 (10)	42.9 (7)	38.1 (42)
1960	35.4 (65)	33.3 (30)	58.3 (12)	22.7 (22)	43.2 (37)
1961	51.3 (39)	52.9 (17)	55.6 (9)	37.5 (8)	36.8 (38)
1962	35.3 (41)	36.4 (22)	29.4 (17)	37.5 (8)	47.7 (44)
1963	38.6 (57)	40.9 (22)	42.3 (26)	22.2 (9)	33.3 (39)
1964	54.5 (44)	43.8 (16)	57.1 (14)	63.6 (11)	39.3 (28)
1965	37.0 (46)	18.8 (16)	35.7 (14)	53.8 (13)	37.0 (27)

(Table continues)

Table 6-3 *(Continued)*

Term	Civil liberties	Criminal procedure	Civil rights	First Amendment	Economics
1966	30.5 (59)	28.6 (28)	36.8 (19)	27.3 (11)	33.3 (30)
1967	45.7 (70)	44.4 (36)	50.0 (16)	28.6 (14)	45.5 (33)
1968	55.6 (63)	44.4 (27)	52.2 (23)	90.0 (10)	52.6 (19)
1969	46.9 (64)	37.0 (27)	52.0 (25)	60.0 (10)	37.5 (16)
1970	42.0 (81)	45.8 (24)	44.8 (29)	27.3 (22)	50.0 (24)
			Jackson		
1946	30.6 (36)	20.0 (20)	60.0 (5)	33.3 (6)	45.9 (61)
1947	48.2 (56)	58.3 (24)	43.8 (16)	20.0 (5)	25.0 (28)
1948	30.8 (39)	40.9 (22)	37.5 (8)	0.0 (3)	30.4 (46)
1949	40.0 (35)	33.3 (9)	60.0 (10)	28.6 (7)	21.7 (23)
1950	35.5 (31)	44.4 (9)	54.5 (11)	12.5 (8)	53.1 (32)
1951	47.4 (38)	41.2 (17)	75.0 (8)	50.0 (6)	46.7 (30)
1952	43.8 (32)	23.1 (13)	28.6 (7)	50.0 (4)	41.9 (31)
1953	48.1 (27)	35.7 (14)	62.5 (8)	50.0 (4)	47.1 (34)
			Kennedy		
1987	45.7 (35)	29.4 (17)	57.1 (7)	60.0 (5)	47.4 (19)
1988	28.2 (85)	16.7 (30)	34.6 (26)	33.3 (15)	42.9 (21)

Table 6-3   *(Continued)*

Term	Civil liberties	Criminal procedure	Civil rights	First Amendment	Economics
1989	24.6 (69)	14.3 (35)	25.0 (8)	35.7 (14)	46.2 (26)
1990	36.2 (58)	30.0 (30)	50.0 (16)	50.0 (6)	46.9 (32)
1991	48.2 (56)	38.1 (21)	61.1 (18)	75.0 (8)	42.9 (28)
1992	38.2 (55)	34.5 (29)	28.6 (14)	62.5 (8)	47.6 (21)
1993	44.7 (47)	43.5 (23)	33.3 (12)	50.0 (4)	45.8 (24)
1994	41.5 (41)	31.6 (19)	27.3 (11)	75.0 (8)	43.8 (16)
1995	55.0 (40)	38.9 (18)	37.5 (8)	100.0 (9)	35.0 (20)
1996	27.7 (47)	29.4 (17)	31.3 (16)	20.0 (5)	58.8 (17)
1997	33.3 (48)	20.0 (25)	64.7 (17)	0.0 (2)	47.4 (19)
1998	35.7 (42)	25.0 (16)	36.8 (19)	100.0 (2)	44.4 (18)
1999	38.0 (50)	33.3 (27)	60.0 (10)	37.5 (8)	36.4 (11)
2000	33.3 (45)	36.8 (19)	38.5 (13)	50.0 (6)	63.6 (11)
2001	29.5 (44)	13.3 (15)	30.8 (13)	44.4 (9)	32.5 (13)
Marshall					
1967	77.6 (49)	80.8 (26)	81.8 (11)	63.6 (11)	44.4 (9)
1968	84.5 (58)	69.6 (23)	91.3 (23)	100.0 (9)	68.4 (18)

(Table continues)

Table 6-3   *(Continued)*

Term	Civil liberties	Criminal procedure	Civil rights	First Amendment	Economics
1969	69.5 (59)	58.3 (24)	87.0 (23)	60.0 (10)	70.0 (10)
1970	78.2 (78)	79.2 (24)	82.8 (29)	65.0 (20)	50.0 (24)
1971	85.7 (91)	85.3 (34)	78.6 (28)	94.1 (17)	53.8 (39)
1972	85.7 (91)	79.4 (34)	84.4 (32)	94.1 (17)	76.5 (34)
1973	83.9 (87)	80.0 (30)	85.7 (35)	92.9 (14)	75.9 (29)
1974	79.5 (73)	79.2 (24)	89.7 (29)	66.7 (9)	55.9 (34)
1975	83.9 (87)	75.0 (32)	88.5 (26)	100.0 (14)	54.5 (33)
1976	76.1 (92)	74.2 (31)	75.8 (33)	86.7 (15)	61.5 (26)
1977	79.7 (74)	86.2 (29)	75.0 (28)	85.7 (7)	77.1 (35)
1978	78.3 (83)	75.9 (29)	85.3 (34)	50.0 (8)	59.4 (32)
1979	86.1 (79)	86.7 (30)	86.4 (22)	100.0 (8)	70.6 (34)
1980	76.5 (68)	76.0 (25)	85.2 (27)	88.9 (9)	72.7 (30)
1981	75.9 (79)	77.8 (18)	88.2 (34)	72.7 (11)	70.6 (34)
1982	82.5 (80)	72.4 (29)	92.6 (27)	81.8 (11)	67.5 (40)
1983	75.0 (92)	76.3 (38)	82.8 (29)	76.9 (13)	56.3 (32)
1984	74.7 (87)	75.8 (33)	72.0 (25)	80.0 (10)	67.6 (34)

Table 6-3   *(Continued)*

Term	Civil liberties	Criminal procedure	Civil rights	First Amendment	Economics
1985	81.4 (97)	81.4 (43)	75.0 (28)	85.7 (14)	57.9 (19)
1986	90.5 (95)	95.0 (40)	96.0 (25)	91.7 (12)	67.9 (28)
1987	83.3 (78)	87.1 (31)	81.0 (21)	100.0 (13)	75.0 (36)
1988	86.9 (84)	80.0 (30)	100.0 (26)	80.0 (15)	68.2 (22)
1989	88.6 (70)	94.3 (35)	100.0 (10)	71.4 (14)	69.2 (26)
1990	86.2 (58)	83.3 (30)	93.8 (16)	100.0 (6)	71.9 (32)
			Minton		
1949	41.2 (34)	22.2 (9)	60.0 (10)	16.7 (6)	58.3 (24)
1950	40.6 (32)	44.4 (9)	41.7 (12)	37.5 (8)	52.9 (34)
1951	26.7 (30)	20.0 (10)	28.6 (7)	16.7 (6)	57.1 (28)
1952	35.0 (40)	6.7 (15)	40.0 (10)	66.7 (6)	51.6 (31)
1953	39.3 (28)	40.0 (15)	37.5 (8)	25.0 (4)	53.8 (39)
1954	36.1 (36)	29.4 (17)	40.0 (10)	20.0 (5)	74.1 (27)
1955	33.3 (30)	33.3 (12)	36.4 (11)	0.0 (5)	71.8 (39)
1956	100.0 (1)	100.0 (1)	—	—	0.0 (1)
			Murphy		
1946	64.9 (37)	65.0 (20)	83.3 (6)	50.0 (6)	77.8 (63)

(Table continues)

Table 6-3   *(Continued)*

Term	Civil liberties	Criminal procedure	Civil rights	First Amendment	Economics
1947	81.4 (59)	83.3 (24)	88.9 (18)	80.0 (5)	83.3 (30)
1948	89.5 (38)	95.5 (22)	87.5 (8)	66.7 (3)	72.3 (47)
O'Connor					
1981	34.6 (81)	10.5 (19)	41.2 (34)	58.3 (12)	53.1 (32)
1982	26.8 (82)	13.3 (30)	42.9 (28)	36.4 (11)	46.2 (39)
1983	31.3 (96)	17.5 (40)	55.2 (29)	23.1 (13)	41.9 (31)
1984	32.6 (89)	21.2 (33)	52.0 (25)	27.3 (11)	45.7 (35)
1985	34.7 (98)	20.9 (43)	44.8 (29)	50.0 (14)	52.6 (19)
1986	30.5 (95)	22.0 (41)	33.3 (24)	50.0 (12)	46.4 (28)
1987	33.8 (77)	33.3 (30)	38.1 (21)	23.1 (13)	33.3 (36)
1988	33.3 (84)	20.0 (30)	44.0 (25)	33.3 (15)	28.6 (21)
1989	21.4 (71)	14.3 (35)	11.1 (20)	28.6 (14)	40.0 (25)
1990	39.7 (58)	26.7 (30)	62.5 (16)	50.0 (6)	43.8 (30)
1991	57.1 (56)	52.4 (21)	61.1 (18)	87.5 (8)	42.9 (28)
1992	43.6 (55)	41.4 (29)	35.7 (14)	50.0 (8)	42.9 (21)
1993	36.2 (47)	26.1 (23)	33.3 (12)	75.0 (4)	34.8 (23)

Table 6-3 *(Continued)*

Term	Civil liberties	Criminal procedure	Civil rights	First Amendment	Economics
1994	48.8 (41)	42.1 (19)	54.5 (11)	62.5 (8)	37.5 (16)
1995	52.5 (40)	44.4 (18)	50.0 (8)	66.7 (9)	30.0 (20)
1996	36.2 (47)	29.4 (17)	37.5 (16)	(60.0) (5)	47.1 (17)
1997	29.2 (48)	20.0 (25)	52.9 (17)	0.0 (2)	47.4 (19)
1998	38.1 (42)	12.5 (16)	57.9 (19)	50.0 (2)	29.4 (17)
1999	40.0 (50)	33.3 (27)	50.0 (10)	25.0 (8)	(36.4) (11)
2000	38.6 (44)	42.1 (19)	50.0 (12)	33.3 (6)	63.6 (11)
2001	36.4 (44)	26.7 (15)	38.5 (13)	33.3 (9)	50.0 (12)
			Powell		
1971	34.7 (49)	17.4 (23)	60.0 (10)	33.3 (12)	33.3 (15)
1972	36.2 (94)	22.9 (35)	50.0 (32)	22.2 (18)	56.7 (30)
1973	42.0 (88)	23.3 (30)	44.4 (36)	78.6 (14)	44.0 (25)
1974	52.9 (68)	54.2 (24)	51.9 (27)	55.6 (9)	45.2 (31)
1975	35.6 (90)	18.2 (33)	50.0 (28)	50.0 (14)	48.4 (31)
1976	35.1 (94)	35.5 (31)	34.3 (35)	40.0 (15)	45.8 (24)
1977	47.3 (74)	55.2 (29)	42.9 (28)	57.1 (7)	53.1 (32)

(Table continues)

Table 6-3   *(Continued)*

Term	Civil liberties	Criminal procedure	Civil rights	First Amendment	Economics
1978	30.4 (69)	36.4 (22)	16.1 (31)	33.3 (6)	36.0 (25)
1979	42.7 (82)	37.5 (32)	40.0 (20)	44.4 (9)	51.4 (37)
1980	34.8 (66)	36.0 (25)	34.6 (26)	37.5 (8)	48.3 (29)
1981	38.3 (81)	21.1 (19)	38.2 (34)	66.7 (12)	45.5 (33)
1982	26.8 (82)	20.0 (30)	25.0 (28)	54.5 (11)	50.0 (36)
1983	34.7 (95)	17.5 (28)	50.0 (13)	53.8 (10)	28.1 (32)
1984	40.7 (59)	24.0 (25)	66.7 (15)	62.5 (8)	41.7 (24)
1985	31.6 (98)	25.6 (43)	31.0 (29)	35.7 (14)	47.4 (19)
1986	37.5 (96)	26.8 (41)	48.0 (25)	50.0 (12)	51.9 (27)

		Reed			
1946	25.6 (39)	15.0 (20)	50.0 (6)	25.0 (8)	59.7 (62)
1947	45.6 (57)	37.5 (24)	50.0 (16)	20.0 (5)	51.5 (33)
1948	30.8 (39)	27.3 (22)	25.0 (8)	33.3 (3)	51.0 (49)
1949	34.3 (35)	11.1 (9)	50.0 (10)	14.3 (7)	34.6 (26)
1950	40.6 (32)	44.4 (9)	58.3 (12)	25.0 (8)	68.6 (35)
1951	31.6 (38)	35.3 (17)	25.0 (8)	33.3 (6)	35.5 (31)

Table 6-3   *(Continued)*

Term	Civil liberties	Criminal procedure	Civil rights	First Amendment	Economics
1952	35.9 (39)	13.3 (15)	33.3 (9)	66.7 (6)	50.0 (32)
1953	40.0 (25)	33.3 (12)	37.5 (8)	50.0 (4)	45.9 (37)
1954	27.0 (37)	22.2 (18)	30.0 (10)	0.0 (5)	63.0 (27)
1955	26.7 (30)	33.3 (12)	27.3 (11)	0.0 (5)	66.7 (39)
1956	50.0 (16)	27.3 (11)	100.0 (2)	100.0 (1)	55.6 (18)
Rehnquist					
1971	25.5 (47)	10.5 (19)	40.0 (10)	33.3 (12)	33.3 (21)
1972	17.2 (93)	14.3 (35)	28.1 (32)	11.1 (18)	45.7 (35)
1973	25.0 (88)	17.2 (29)	27.8 (36)	35.7 (14)	34.5 (29)
1974	31.9 (72)	41.7 (24)	31.0 (29)	0.0 (8)	50.0 (34)
1975	18.9 (90)	9.1 (33)	35.7 (28)	28.6 (14)	36.4 (33)
1976	9.9 (81)	4.0 (25)	18.6 (32)	7.1 (14)	38.1 (21)
1977	18.7 (75)	20.7 (29)	14.3 (28)	37.5 (8)	40.0 (35)
1978	21.7 (83)	27.6 (29)	8.8 (34)	25.0 (8)	41.9 (31)
1979	10.7 (84)	0.0 (32)	13.6 (22)	0.0 (10)	38.9 (36)
1980	19.7 (66)	20.0 (25)	23.1 (26)	0.0 (8)	41.9 (31)

(Table continues)

Table 6-3   *(Continued)*

Term	Civil liberties	Criminal procedure	Civil rights	First Amendment	Economics
1981	21.0 (81)	5.3 (19)	17.6 (34)	50.0 (12)	50.0 (34)
1982	17.1 (82)	16.7 (30)	21.4 (28)	18.2 (11)	50.0 (40)
1983	24.0 (96)	7.5 (40)	44.8 (29)	15.4 (13)	41.9 (31)
1984	22.5 (89)	15.2 (33)	36.0 (25)	9.1 (11)	41.2 (34)
1985	16.5 (97)	14.0 (43)	17.9 (28)	7.1 (14)	36.8 (19)
1986	15.6 (96)	12.2 (41)	20.0 (25)	8.3 (12)	46.4 (28)
1987	29.9 (77)	25.8 (31)	33.3 (21)	25.0 (12)	37.1 (35)
1988	22.6 (84)	20.0 (30)	26.9 (26)	14.3 (14)	36.4 (22)
1989	14.3 (71)	11.4 (35)	0.0 (10)	14.3 (14)	46.2 (26)
1990	20.7 (58)	13.3 (30)	37.5 (16)	16.7 (6)	46.9 (32)
1991	32.1 (56)	23.8 (21)	50.0 (18)	37.5 (8)	50.0 (28)
1992	27.3 (55)	24.1 (29)	21.4 (14)	37.5 (8)	52.4 (21)
1993	26.1 (46)	17.4 (23)	25.0 (12)	25.0 (4)	62.5 (24)
1994	29.3 (41)	15.8 (19)	36.4 (11)	50.0 (8)	37.5 (16)
1995	32.5 (40)	27.8 (18)	25.0 (8)	44.4 (9)	30.0 (20)
1996	25.5 (47)	11.8 (17)	31.3 (16)	40.0 (5)	47.1 (17)

Table 6-3   *(Continued)*

Term	Civil liberties	Criminal procedure	Civil rights	First Amendment	Economics
1997	31.3 (48)	28.0 (25)	47.1 (17)	0.0 (2)	47.4 (19)
1998	23.8 (42)	18.8 (16)	26.3 (19)	50.0 (2)	27.8 (18)
1999	32.0 (50)	25.9 (27)	50.0 (10)	12.5 (8)	36.4 (11)
2000	17.8 (45)	21.1 (19)	23.1 (13)	16.7 (6)	63.6 (11)
2001	15.9 (44)	0.0 (15)	23.1 (13)	22.2 (9)	30.8 (13)
			Rutledge		
1946	61.5 (39)	60.0 (20)	50.0 (6)	75.0 (8)	76.6 (64)
1947	84.2 (57)	83.3 (24)	87.5 (16)	80.0 (5)	81.3 (32)
1948	79.5 (39)	86.4 (22)	75.0 (8)	66.7 (3)	82.0 (50)
			Scalia		
1986	27.7 (94)	25.0 (40)	32.0 (25)	36.4 (11)	63.0 (27)
1987	36.8 (76)	32.3 (31)	35.0 (20)	46.2 (13)	40.0 (35)
1988	33.3 (84)	30.0 (30)	38.5 (26)	33.3 (15)	40.9 (22)
1989	24.3 (70)	17.1 (35)	22.2 (9)	28.6 (14)	38.5 (26)
1990	29.3 (58)	30.0 (30)	43.8 (16)	0.0 (6)	43.8 (32)
1991	25.0 (56)	14.3 (21)	38.9 (18)	37.5 (8)	39.3 (28)
1992	34.5 (55)	31.0 (29)	28.6 (14)	50.0 (8)	47.6 (21)

(Table continues)

Table 6-3 *(Continued)*

Term	Civil liberties	Criminal procedure	Civil rights	First Amendment	Economics
1993	29.8 (47)	26.1 (23)	16.7 (12)	50.0 (4)	37.5 (24)
1994	29.3 (41)	26.3 (19)	27.3 (11)	37.5 (8)	43.8 (16)
1995	25.0 (40)	27.8 (18)	12.5 (8)	22.2 (9)	35.0 (20)
1996	25.5 (47)	17.6 (17)	25.0 (16)	60.0 (5)	35.3 (17)
1997	25.0 (48)	28.0 (25)	29.4 (17)	0.0 (2)	52.6 (19)
1998	38.1 (42)	37.5 (16)	36.8 (19)	100.0 (2)	27.8 (18)
1999	28.0 (50)	25.9 (27)	50.0 (10)	0.0 (8)	36.4 (11)
2000	17.8 (45)	21.1 (19)	15.4 (13)	16.7 (6)	63.6 (11)
2001	13.6 (44)	6.7 (15)	15.4 (13)	33.9 (9)	16.7 (12)
Souter					
1990	32.1 (53)	14.8 (27)	73.3 (15)	33.3 (6)	41.4 (29)
1991	50.9 (55)	42.9 (21)	50.0 (18)	100.0 (8)	53.6 (28)
1992	58.2 (55)	55.2 (29)	42.9 (14)	75.0 (8)	57.1 (21)
1993	59.6 (47)	56.5 (23)	50.0 (12)	50.0 (4)	75.0 (24)
1994	73.2 (41)	57.9 (19)	81.8 (11)	87.5 (8)	43.8 (16)
1995	62.5 (40)	38.9 (18)	75.0 (8)	88.9 (9)	35.0 (20)

Table 6-3   *(Continued)*

Term	Civil liberties	Criminal procedure	Civil rights	First Amendment	Economics
1996	54.3 (46)	35.3 (17)	75.0 (16)	75.0 (4)	58.8 (17)
1997	64.6 (48)	56.0 (25)	76.5 (17)	100.0 (2)	63.2 (19)
1998	64.3 (42)	62.5 (16)	68.4 (19)	100.0 (2)	44.4 (18)
1999	82.0 (50)	77.8 (27)	90.0 (10)	75.0 (8)	50.0 (10)
2000	66.7 (45)	63.2 (19)	76.9 (13)	83.3 (6)	81.8 (11)
2001	65.9 (44)	60.0 (15)	69.2 (13)	66.7 (9)	46.2 (13)
			Stevens		
1975	54.8 (42)	33.3 (15)	87.5 (16)	50.0 (4)	66.7 (18)
1976	58.1 (93)	54.8 (31)	58.8 (34)	66.7 (15)	53.8 (26)
1977	52.7 (74)	60.7 (28)	42.9 (28)	87.5 (8)	76.5 (34)
1978	60.5 (81)	65.5 (29)	53.1 (32)	25.0 (8)	56.7 (30)
1979	60.7 (84)	56.3 (32)	52.4 (21)	100.0 (10)	61.1 (36)
1980	53.7 (67)	58.3 (24)	51.9 (27)	66.7 (9)	51.5 (33)
1981	51.3 (78)	36.8 (19)	57.6 (33)	80.0 (10)	54.5 (33)
1982	57.9 (81)	62.1 (29)	64.3 (28)	72.7 (11)	43.6 (39)
1983	57.3 (96)	55.0 (40)	72.4 (29)	38.5 (13)	57.6 (33)

(Table continues)

Table 6-3 *(Continued)*

Term	Civil liberties	Criminal procedure	Civil rights	First Amendment	Economics
1984	56.3 (87)	61.3 (31)	56.0 (25)	72.7 (11)	47.2 (36)
1985	55.7 (97)	60.5 (43)	51.7 (29)	42.9 (14)	47.4 (19)
1986	66.7 (93)	69.2 (39)	54.2 (24)	66.7 (12)	71.4 (28)
1987	62.8 (78)	71.0 (31)	57.1 (21)	53.8 (13)	62.9 (35)
1988	61.9 (84)	50.0 (30)	73.1 (26)	66.7 (15)	54.5 (22)
1989	71.4 (70)	77.1 (35)	77.8 (9)	50.0 (14)	46.2 (26)
1990	81.0 (58)	83.3 (30)	87.5 (16)	66.7 (6)	71.9 (32)
1991	80.4 (56)	76.2 (21)	77.8 (18)	100.0 (8)	53.6 (28)
1992	76.4 (55)	75.9 (29)	64.3 (14)	87.5 (8)	71.4 (21)
1993	66.0 (47)	65.2 (23)	50.0 (12)	75.0 (4)	66.7 (24)
1994	85.4 (41)	84.2 (19)	72.7 (11)	100.0 (8)	62.5 (16)
1995	75.0 (40)	66.7 (18)	75.0 (8)	77.8 (9)	52.6 (19)
1996	66.0 (47)	70.6 (17)	75.0 (16)	40.0 (5)	70.6 (17)
1997	62.5 (48)	64.0 (25)	64.7 (17)	50.0 (2)	68.4 (19)
1998	78.6 (42)	75.0 (16)	78.9 (19)	100.0 (2)	55.6 (18)
1999	82.0 (50)	77.8 (27)	90.0 (10)	87.5 (8)	63.6 (11)

Table 6-3   *(Continued)*

Term	Civil liberties	Criminal procedure	Civil rights	First Amendment	Economics
2000	71.1 (45)	68.4 (19)	69.2 (13)	83.3 (6)	72.7 (11)
2001	68.2 (44)	73.3 (15)	53.8 (13)	66.7 (9)	61.5 (13)
			Stewart		
1958	41.0 (39)	34.6 (26)	33.3 (3)	60.0 (10)	48.8 (43)
1959	41.7 (36)	37.5 (16)	50.0 (10)	42.9 (7)	50.0 (40)
1960	53.0 (66)	58.6 (29)	50.0 (14)	45.5 (22)	48.6 (35)
1961	66.7 (39)	52.9 (17)	88.9 (9)	75.0 (8)	54.1 (37)
1962	54.9 (51)	40.9 (22)	70.6 (17)	50.0 (8)	51.1 (44)
1963	68.4 (57)	50.0 (22)	77.8 (27)	87.5 (8)	50.0 (36)
1964	55.8 (43)	43.8 (16)	64.3 (14)	60.0 (10)	53.8 (26)
1965	54.3 (46)	37.5 (16)	50.0 (14)	69.2 (13)	50.0 (28)
1966	41.4 (58)	40.7 (27)	36.8 (19)	45.5 (11)	48.3 (29)
1967	63.8 (69)	63.9 (36)	62.5 (16)	57.1 (14)	47.1 (34)
1968	54.0 (63)	37.0 (27)	47.8 (23)	100.0 (10)	42.9 (21)
1969	41.5 (65)	29.6 (27)	50.0 (26)	50.0 (10)	40.0 (15)
1970	47.5 (80)	29.2 (24)	51.7 (29)	50.0 (22)	48.0 (25)

(Table continues)

Table 6-3   *(Continued)*

Term	Civil liberties	Criminal procedure	Civil rights	First Amendment	Economics
1971	64.8 (91)	52.9 (34)	71.4 (28)	70.6 (17)	45.9 (37)
1972	57.4 (94)	48.6 (35)	56.3 (32)	77.8 (18)	41.4 (29)
1973	52.3 (88)	40.0 (30)	54.3 (35)	78.6 (14)	36.0 (25)
1974	57.5 (73)	75.0 (24)	51.7 (29)	55.6 (9)	38.2 (34)
1975	47.8 (90)	36.4 (33)	53.6 (28)	71.4 (14)	40.6 (32)
1976	40.4 (94)	41.9 (31)	34.3 (35)	66.7 (15)	36.0 (25)
1977	54.7 (75)	62.1 (29)	39.3 (28)	75.0 (8)	61.8 (34)
1978	42.2 (83)	48.3 (29)	23.5 (34)	50.0 (8)	48.4 (31)
1979	45.9 (85)	40.6 (32)	36.4 (22)	80.0 (10)	50.0 (34)
1980	36.4 (66)	48.0 (25)	25.9 (27)	62.5 (8)	53.1 (32)
Thomas					
1991	25.6 (43)	16.7 (18)	42.9 (14)	16.7 (6)	40.0 (25)
1992	30.9 (55)	24.1 (29)	35.7 (14)	37.5 (8)	42.9 (21)
1993	23.4 (47)	13.0 (23)	16.7 (12)	50.0 (4)	25.0 (24)
1994	26.8 (41)	15.8 (19)	27.3 (11)	50.0 (8)	37.5 (16)
1995	25.6 (39)	27.8 (18)	14.3 (7)	22.2 (9)	30.0 (20)

Table 6-3   *(Continued)*

Term	Civil liberties	Criminal procedure	Civil rights	First Amendment	Economics
1996	25.5 (47)	17.6 (17)	25.0 (16)	60.0 (5)	35.3 (17)
1997	16.7 (48)	16.0 (25)	23.5 (17)	0.0 (2)	42.1 (19)
1998	26.2 (42)	31.3 (16)	15.8 (19)	100.0 (2)	27.8 (18)
1999	30.0 (50)	25.9 (27)	40.0 (10)	12.5 (8)	36.4 (11)
2000	17.8 (45)	21.1 (19)	15.4 (13)	16.7 (6)	63.6 (11)
2001	22.7 (44)	13.3 (15)	23.1 (13)	44.4 (9)	30.8 (13)

<table>
<tr><td colspan="6" align="center">Vinson</td></tr>
</table>

Term	Civil liberties	Criminal procedure	Civil rights	First Amendment	Economics
1946	23.1 (39)	20.0 (20)	33.3 (6)	12.5 (8)	57.1 (63)
1947	52.6 (57)	33.3 (24)	66.7 (18)	60.0 (5)	51.5 (33)
1948	23.7 (38)	27.3 (22)	25.0 (8)	0.0 (3)	43.1 (51)
1949	32.4 (34)	22.2 (9)	60.0 (10)	0.0 (7)	56.0 (25)
1950	43.8 (32)	55.6 (9)	50.0 (12)	25.0 (8)	55.9 (34)
1951	36.8 (38)	41.2 (17)	37.5 (8)	16.7 (6)	48.4 (31)
1952	35.9 (39)	14.3 (14)	30.0 (10)	66.7 (6)	34.4 (32)

<table>
<tr><td colspan="6" align="center">Warren</td></tr>
</table>

Term	Civil liberties	Criminal procedure	Civil rights	First Amendment	Economics
1953	38.5 (26)	21.4 (14)	62.5 (8)	50.0 (4)	66.7 (39)
1954	61.1 (36)	47.1 (17)	70.0 (10)	80.0 (5)	81.5 (27)

(Table continues)

Table 6-3 *(Continued)*

Term	Civil liberties	Criminal procedure	Civil rights	First Amendment	Economics
1955	75.9 (29)	45.5 (11)	100.0 (11)	100.0 (5)	87.2 (39)
1956	75.0 (52)	85.0 (20)	50.0 (12)	73.3 (15)	90.5 (42)
1957	83.3 (60)	75.0 (32)	92.9 (14)	100.0 (7)	82.4 (34)
1958	85.7 (42)	80.0 (25)	83.3 (6)	100.0 (11)	87.5 (48)
1959	80.0 (35)	75.0 (16)	100.0 (10)	83.3 (6)	85.7 (42)
1960	82.1 (67)	96.7 (30)	64.3 (14)	77.3 (22)	65.8 (38)
1961	92.1 (38)	94.1 (17)	87.5 (8)	100.0 (8)	78.9 (38)
1962	84.3 (51)	77.3 (22)	94.1 (17)	87.5 (8)	85.7 (42)
1963	87.9 (58)	86.4 (22)	92.6 (27)	77.8 (9)	80.0 (40)
1964	78.6 (42)	66.7 (15)	92.3 (13)	72.7 (11)	64.3 (28)
1965	77.3 (44)	66.7 (15)	84.6 (13)	76.9 (13)	78.6 (28)
1966	78.0 (59)	85.7 (28)	78.9 (19)	63.6 (11)	75.9 (29)
1967	73.9 (69)	74.3 (35)	81.3 (16)	64.3 (14)	72.7 (33)
1968	79.4 (63)	74.1 (27)	78.3 (23)	90.0 (10)	85.7 (21)
			White		
1961	50.0 (2)	0.0 (1)	100.0 (1)	—	80.0 (8)

Table 6-3   *(Continued)*

Term	Civil liberties	Criminal procedure	Civil rights	First Amendment	Economics
1962	60.8 (51)	50.0 (22)	70.6 (17)	62.5 (8)	76.2 (42)
1963	63.2 (57)	50.0 (22)	73.1 (26)	66.7 (9)	61.5 (39)
1964	60.0 (40)	43.8 (16)	69.2 (13)	62.5 (8)	67.9 (28)
1965	58.1 (43)	42.9 (14)	78.6 (14)	41.7 (12)	85.2 (27)
1966	52.6 (57)	50.0 (26)	57.9 (19)	54.5 (11)	66.7 (27)
1967	50.0 (70)	44.4 (36)	75.0 (16)	28.6 (14)	67.6 (34)
1968	61.3 (62)	50.0 (26)	56.5 (23)	90.0 (10)	66.7 (21)
1969	49.2 (65)	44.4 (27)	57.7 (26)	40.0 (10)	60.0 (15)
1970	40.0 (80)	13.0 (23)	58.6 (29)	36.4 (22)	54.2 (24)
1971	49.5 (91)	41.2 (34)	57.1 (28)	41.2 (17)	48.7 (39)
1972	31.2 (93)	26.5 (34)	56.3 (32)	5.6 (18)	57.1 (35)
1973	44.9 (89)	23.3 (30)	61.1 (36)	50.0 (14)	72.4 (29)
1974	49.3 (73)	50.0 (24)	62.1 (29)	11.1 (9)	64.7 (34)
1975	37.8 (90)	18.2 (33)	53.6 (28)	50.0 (14)	38.5 (31)
1976	35.1 (94)	32.3 (31)	45.7 (35)	20.0 (15)	46.2 (26)
1977	53.3 (75)	65.5 (29)	46.4 (28)	62.5 (8)	71.4 (35)

(Table continues)

Table 6-3 *(Continued)*

Term	Civil liberties	Criminal procedure	Civil rights	First Amendment	Economics
1978	49.4 (83)	44.8 (29)	61.8 (34)	37.5 (8)	58.1 (31)
1979	41.7 (84)	19.4 (31)	63.6 (22)	60.0 (10)	70.3 (37)
1980	44.1 (68)	40.0 (25)	55.6 (27)	44.4 (9)	56.7 (30)
1981	45.7 (81)	31.6 (19)	52.9 (34)	50.0 (12)	60.6 (33)
1982	36.6 (82)	23.3 (30)	57.1 (28)	45.5 (11)	55.0 (40)
1983	33.7 (95)	20.0 (40)	58.6 (29)	23.1 (13)	45.2 (31)
1984	30.7 (88)	18.2 (33)	52.0 (25)	9.1 (11)	51.4 (35)
1985	32.7 (98)	27.9 (43)	41.4 (29)	28.6 (14)	44.4 (18)
1986	26.3 (95)	15.0 (40)	36.0 (25)	33.3 (12)	42.9 (28)
1987	39.7 (78)	35.5 (31)	38.1 (21)	46.2 (13)	48.6 (35)
1988	31.8 (85)	20.0 (30)	38.5 (26)	26.7 (15)	45.5 (22)
1989	27.1 (70)	22.9 (35)	44.4 (9)	21.4 (14)	57.7 (26)
1990	43.1 (58)	36.7 (30)	68.8 (16)	16.7 (6)	50.0 (32)
1991	41.1 (56)	38.1 (21)	61.1 (18)	37.5 (8)	57.1 (28)
1992	40.0 (55)	37.9 (29)	35.7 (14)	37.5 (8)	61.9 (21)
Whittaker					
1956	47.1 (17)	83.3 (6)	0.0 (6)	33.3 (3)	57.1 (14)

Table 6-3 *(Continued)*

Term	Civil liberties	Criminal procedure	Civil rights	First Amendment	Economics
1957	47.6 (63)	40.6 (32)	57.1 (14)	44.4 (9)	32.4 (34)
1958	46.5 (43)	38.5 (26)	66.7 (6)	54.5 (11)	38.8 (49)
1959	33.3 (36)	31.3 (16)	40.0 (10)	28.6 (7)	28.6 (42)
1960	38.8 (67)	46.7 (30)	42.9 (14)	27.3 (22)	31.6 (38)
1961	57.1 (14)	60.0 (5)	75.0 (4)	50.0 (2)	28.6 (14)

Note: "—" indicates that no issue area was decided during tenure overlap. Figures listed are the percentage of cases in which the justice took the liberal position. Figures in parentheses are the total number of cases in issue area in which the justice participated. Readers should take care in interpreting the percentages since some of the figures on which they are based are quite small.

The issue areas are defined as follows: Civil liberties: combines criminal procedure, civil rights, First Amendment, due process, privacy, and attorneys; Criminal procedure: the rights of persons accused of crime except for the due process rights of prisoners; Civil rights: non-First Amendment freedom cases that pertain to classifications based on race (including Native Americans), age, indigence, voting, residence, military or handicapped status, sex, or alienage; First Amendment: guarantees contained therein; Economics: labor union activity, commercial business activity, litigation involving injured persons or things, employee actions vis-à-vis employers, zoning regulations, and governmental regulation of corruption other than that involving campaign spending.

The term *liberal* represents the voting direction of justices across the various issue areas. It is most appropriate in the areas of civil liberties, criminal procedure, civil rights, First Amendment, due process, privacy, and attorneys, where it signifies pro-defendant votes in criminal procedure cases, pro-women or -minorities in civil rights cases, pro-individual against the government in First Amendment, due process, and privacy cases, and pro-attorney in attorneys' fees and bar membership cases. In takings clause cases, however, a pro-government/anti-owner vote is considered liberal. The use of the term is perhaps less appropriate in union cases, where it represents pro-union votes against both individuals and the government, and in economic cases, where it represents pro-government votes against challenges to its regulatory authority and pro-competition, anti-business, pro-liability, pro-injured person, and pro-bankruptcy votes. In federalism and federal taxation, liberal indicates pro-national government positions; in judicial power cases, the term represents pro-judiciary positions.

Source: U.S. Supreme Court Judicial Database, with analu = 0 or 4 and dec_type = 1, 6, or 7.

Table 6-4 Voting Interagreements Among the Justices, by Issue Area: The Vinson Court, 1946–1952 Terms

Justice	Crim	CivR	1st	DP	Priv	Atty	Un'n	Econ	JudP	Fed	IR	FTax	Misc
						Black							
Burton	48.7 (113)	68.2 (63)	52.6 (38)	69.7 (43)	50.0 (4)	0.0 (1)	53.5 (43)	45.1 (208)	62.8 (113)	74.1 (27)	50.0 (12)	70.9 (48)	100.0 (1)
Clark	50.0 (38)	63.3 (30)	54.5 (22)	72.2 (18)	0.0 (2)	100.0 (1)	68.8 (16)	58.2 (91)	68.1 (66)	73.3 (15)	75.0 (4)	72.7 (22)	100.0 (1)
Douglas	81.5 (108)	81.3 (64)	88.6 (35)	81.6 (38)	75.0 (4)	—	70.7 (41)	78.8 (198)	74.3 (101)	69.6 (23)	75.0 (12)	50.0 (40)	100.0 (1)
Frankfurter	68.4 (114)	82.9 (70)	59.6 (42)	77.7 (45)	66.7 (3)	0.0 (1)	59.1 (44)	47.5 (221)	60.3 (116)	57.7 (26)	41.7 (12)	63.8 (47)	100.0 (1)
Jackson	48.7 (113)	68.2 (63)	52.6 (38)	69.7 (43)	50.0 (4)	0 (1)	53.5 (43)	45.1 (208)	62.8 (113)	74.1 (27)	50.0 (12)	70.9 (48)	100.0 (1)
Minton	33.3 (42)	64.9 (37)	56.0 (25)	62.5 (24)	0.0 (3)	100.0 (1)	88.3 (17)	58.1 (98)	56.4 (62)	60.0 (15)	66.7 (3)	75.0 (24)	0.0 (1)
Murphy	74.3 (66)	87.5 (32)	92.9 (14)	75.0 (120)	100.0 (1)	—	96.3 (27)	94.6 (111)	76.0 (46)	92.3 (13)	62.5 (8)	95.8 (24)	—
Reed	52.2 (115)	58.2 (67)	57.2 (42)	75.5 (45)	25.0 (4)	100.0 (1)	70.5 (44)	57.7 (220)	66.9 (115)	69.2 (26)	58.3 (12)	67.3 (49)	0.0 (1)
Rutledge	75.8 (66)	83.3 (30)	87.5 (16)	85.8 (21)	100.0 (1)	—	96.3 (27)	94.6 (111)	76.0 (46)	92.3 (13)	62.5 (8)	95.8 (24)	—

	59.4 (114)	67.1 (70)	52.4 (42)	68.3 (41)	25.0 (4)	100.0 (1)	61.4 (44)	62.0 (221)	65.2 (112)	82.1 (28)	58.3 (12)	81.6 (49)	0.0 (1)
Vinson	59.4 (114)	67.1 (70)	52.4 (42)	68.3 (41)	25.0 (4)	100.0 (1)	61.4 (44)	62.0 (221)	65.2 (112)	82.1 (28)	58.3 (12)	81.6 (49)	0.0 (1)
Burton													
Black	53.0 (115)	70.0 (70)	50.0 (42)	75.6 (45)	25.0 (4)	100.0 (1)	65.9 (44)	56.6 (221)	66.3 (116)	67.9 (28)	58.3 (12)	68.8 (48)	100.0 (1)
Clark	87.2 (39)	93.7 (32)	91.3 (23)	88.9 (18)	100.0 (2)	100.0 (1)	81.3 (16)	80.0 (90)	83.3 (66)	93.8 (16)	100.0 (4)	91.3 (23)	100.0 (1)
Douglas	56.9 (109)	71.2 (66)	55.5 (36)	66.7 (39)	50.0 (4)	—	58.5 (41)	59.3 (199)	53.5 (101)	56.5 (23)	83.3 (12)	55.0 (40)	100.0 (1)
Frankfurter	56.5 (115)	72.8 (70)	79.1 (43)	76.1 (46)	66.7 (3)	0.0 (1)	88.7 (44)	69.2 (221)	78.4 (116)	81.5 (27)	50.0 (12)	68.1 (47)	100.0 (1)
Jackson	72.8 (114)	72.3 (65)	74.4 (39)	75.0 (44)	75.0 (4)	0.0 (1)	76.8 (43)	70.1 (207)	77.9 (113)	85.7 (28)	75.0 (12)	66.0 (47)	100.0 (1)
Minton	81.4 (43)	87.2 (39)	84.6 (26)	66.7 (24)	100.0 (3)	100.0 (1)	76.5 (17)	80.4 (97)	85.3 (61)	93.8 (16)	100.0 (3)	84.0 (25)	0.0 (1)
Murphy	43.9 (66)	62.5 (32)	42.9 (14)	61.9 (21)	100.0 (1)	—	55.6 (27)	62.8 (113)	70.2 (47)	76.9 (13)	87.5 (8)	60.9 (23)	—
Reed	87.1 (116)	86.9 (69)	79.0 (43)	69.6 (46)	100.0 (4)	100.0 (1)	81.8 (44)	78.1 (220)	82.6 (115)	85.2 (27)	100.0 (12)	75.5 (49)	0.0 (1)
Rutledge	48.0 (66)	70.0 (30)	43.8 (16)	72.7 (22)	100.0 (1)	—	65.4 (26)	63.3 (120)	70.8 (48)	53.9 (13)	50.0 (8)	73.9 (23)	—
Vinson	86.1 (115)	86.1 (72)	83.7 (43)	76.2 (42)	100.0 (4)	100.0 (1)	86.4 (44)	78.8 (221)	84.0 (112)	86.2 (29)	100.0 (12)	83.6 (49)	100.0 (1)

(Table continues)

Table 6-4 (*Continued*)

Justice	Crim	CivR	1st	DP	Priv	Atty	Un'n	Econ	JudP	Fed	IR	FTax	Misc
						Clark							
Black	50.0 (38)	63.3 (30)	54.5 (22)	72.2 (18)	0.0 (2)	100.0 (1)	68.8 (16)	58.2 (91)	68.1 (66)	73.3 (15)	75.0 (4)	72.7 (22)	100.0 (1)
Burton	87.2 (39)	93.7 (32)	91.3 (23)	88.9 (18)	100.0 (2)	100.0 (1)	81.3 (16)	80.0 (90)	83.3 (66)	93.8 (16)	100.0 (4)	91.3 (23)	100.0 (1)
Douglas	54.3 (32)	82.1 (28)	50.0 (18)	71.4 (14)	50.0 (2)	—	26.7 (15)	54.7 (75)	52.9 (51)	60.0 (10)	100.0 (4)	60.0 (15)	100.0 (1)
Frankfurter	61.5 (39)	70.0 (30)	69.6 (23)	72.2 (18)	0.0 (1)	0.0 (1)	75.0 (16)	64.4 (90)	76.9 (65)	78.6 (14)	50.0 (4)	66.7 (21)	100 (1)
Jackson	84.2 (38)	71.4 (28)	76.2 (21)	76.5 (17)	50.0 (2)	0.0 (1)	75.1 (16)	74.1 (89)	79.7 (64)	86.7 (15)	100.0 (4)	91.3 (23)	100.0 (1)
Minton	93.7 (32)	84.4 (32)	91.3 (23)	83.4 (18)	100.0 (2)	100.0 (1)	68.8 (16)	84.9 (86)	88.1 (59)	87.5 (16)	100.0 (3)	86.4 (22)	100.0 (1)
Reed	82.1 (39)	96.8 (31)	91.3 (23)	83.3 (18)	100.0 (2)	100.0 (1)	62.5 (16)	75.0 (92)	89.2 (65)	86.7 (15)	100.0 (4)	87.0 (23)	0.0 (2)
Vinson	92.1 (38)	90.6 (32)	100.0 (23)	88.3 (17)	100.0 (2)	100.0 (1)	93.8 (16)	85.5 (90)	90.7 (64)	93.8 (16)	100.0 (4)	100.0 (23)	0.0 (1)
						Douglas							
Black	81.5 (108)	81.3 (64)	87.6 (35)	81.6 (38)	75.0 (4)	—	70.7 (41)	78.8 (198)	74.3 (101)	69.6 (23)	75.0 (12)	50.0 (40)	100.0 (1)

Burton	56.9 (109)	71.2 (66)	55.5 (36)	66.7 (39)	50.0 (2)	—	58.5 (41)	59.3 (199)	53.5 (101)	83.3 (23)	83.3 (12)	55.0 (40)	100.0 (1)
Clark	54.3 (35)	82.1 (28)	50.0 (18)	71.4 (14)	50.0 (2)	—	26.7 (15)	54.7 (75)	52.9 (51)	60.0 (10)	100.0 (4)	60.0 (15)	100.0 (1)
Frankfurter	67.6 (108)	71.9 (64)	52.8 (36)	61.6 (39)	33.3 (3)	—	61.0 (41)	51.7 (199)	53.9 (102)	61.9 (21)	33.3 (12)	52.5 (40)	100.0 (1)
Jackson	50.4 (107)	59.3 (59)	37.5 (32)	68.4 (38)	25.0 (4)	—	55.0 (40)	48.7 (187)	57.1 (98)	59.1 (22)	75.0 (12)	52.5 (40)	100.0 (1)
Minton	44.4 (36)	66.7 (33)	50.0 (20)	52.7 (19)	33.3 (3)	—	33.3 (15)	60.0 (80)	48.0 (50)	50.0 (10)	100.0 (3)	66.7 (18)	0.0 (1)
Murphy	83.3 (66)	93.8 (32)	85.7 (14)	52.7 (19)	100.0 (1)	—	80.7 (26)	80.4 (107)	80.4 (46)	69.2 (13)	87.5 (8)	56.5 (23)	—
Reed	54.1 (109)	66.7 (63)	55.6 (36)	69.2 (39)	50.0 (4)	—	70.7 (41)	63.6 (198)	64.0 (100)	71.4 (21)	83.3 (12)	51.2 (41)	0.0 (1)
Rutledge	81.8 (66)	83.4 (30)	75.1 (16)	65.0 (20)	100.0 (1)	—	88.0 (25)	85.1 (114)	72.3 (47)	61.6 (13)	75.0 (8)	47.8 (23)	—
Vinson	54.7 (108)	68.2 (66)	52.8 (36)	57.1 (35)	50.0 (4)	—	53.7 (41)	62.0 (200)	59.6 (99)	56.5 (23)	83.3 (12)	56.1 (41)	0.0 (1)
Frankfurter													
Black	68.4 (114)	82.9 (70)	59.6 (42)	77.7 (45)	66.7 (3)	0.0 (1)	59.1 (44)	47.5 (221)	60.3 (116)	57.7 (26)	41.7 (12)	63.8 (47)	100.0 (1)
Burton	56.5 (115)	72.8 (70)	79.1 (43)	76.1 (46)	66.7 (3)	0.0 (1)	88.7 (44)	69.2 (221)	78.4 (116)	81.5 (27)	50.0 (12)	68.1 (47)	100.0 (1)

(Table continues)

Table 6-4 (Continued)

Justice	Crim	CivR	1st	DP	Priv	Atty	Un'n	Econ	JudP	Fed	IR	FTax	Misc
Clark	61.5 (39)	70.0 (30)	69.6 (23)	72.2 (18)	0.0 (1)	0.0 (1)	75.0 (16)	64.4 (90)	76.9 (65)	78.6 (14)	50.0 (4)	66.7 (21)	100.0 (1)
Douglas	67.6 (108)	71.9 (64)	52.8 (36)	61.6 (39)	33.3 (3)	—	61.0 (41)	51.7 (199)	53.9 (102)	61.9 (21)	33.3 (12)	52.5 (40)	100.0 (1)
Jackson	76.1 (113)	77.8 (63)	79.5 (39)	79.6 (44)	100.0 (3)	100.0 (1)	79.0 (43)	81.6 (207)	80.6 (113)	76.9 (26)	58.4 (12)	68.1 (47)	100.0 (1)
Minton	47.6 (42)	70.3 (37)	61.5 (26)	54.2 (24)	50.0 (2)	0.0 (1)	64.7 (17)	56.7 (97)	78.7 (61)	92.9 (14)	66.7 (3)	69.5 (23)	0.0 (1)
Murphy	63.6 (66)	68.7 (32)	50.0 (14)	71.4 (21)	100.0 (1)	—	51.9 (27)	56.6 (113)	76.6 (47)	69.2 (13)	37.5 (8)	62.5 (24)	—
Reed	58.2 (115)	64.2 (67)	62.8 (43)	63.0 (46)	66.7 (3)	0.0 (1)	70.5 (44)	71.4 (220)	73.9 (115)	72.0 (25)	50.0 (12)	68.8 (48)	0.0 (1)
Rutledge	62.1 (66)	63.3 (30)	50.0 (16)	63.6 (22)	100.0 (1)	—	61.5 (26)	51.6 (120)	60.4 (48)	61.6 (13)	50.0 (8)	66.7 (24)	—
Vinson	57.0 (114)	72.8 (70)	72.1 (43)	69.1 (42)	66.7 (3)	0.0 (1)	84.1 (44)	67.4 (221)	77.7 (112)	77.8 (27)	50.0 (12)	68.8 (48)	0.0 (1)
						Jackson							
Burton	72.8 (114)	72.3 (65)	74.4 (39)	75.0 (44)	75.0 (4)	0.0 (1)	76.8 (43)	70.1 (207)	77.9 (113)	85.7 (28)	75.0 (12)	66.0 (47)	100.0 (1)

Clark	84.2 (38)	71.4 (28)	76.2 (21)	76.5 (17)	50.0 (2)	0.0 (1)	75.1 (16)	74.1 (89)	79.7 (64)	86.7 (15)	100.0 (4)	76.2 (21)	100.0 (1)
Douglas	50.4 (107)	59.3 (59)	37.5 (32)	68.4 (38)	25.0 (4)	—	55.0 (40)	48.7 (187)	57.1 (98)	59.1 (22)	75.0 (12)	52.5 (40)	100.0 (1)
Frankfurter	76.1 (113)	77.8 (63)	79.5 (39)	79.6 (44)	100.0 (3)	100.0 (1)	76.0 (43)	81.6 (207)	80.6 (113)	76.9 (26)	58.4 (12)	80.4 (46)	100.0 (1)
Minton	92.7 (41)	74.3 (35)	66.7 (24)	60.8 (23)	66.7 (3)	0.0 (1)	52.9 (17)	67.1 (94)	72.1 (61)	86.7 (15)	100.0 (3)	69.6 (23)	0.0 (1)
Murphy	59.1 (66)	51.7 (29)	42.9 (14)	45.0 (20)	100 (1)	—	50.0 (26)	52.9 (106)	79.8 (47)	84.6 (13)	50.0 (8)	62.5 (24)	—
Reed	78.1 (114)	73.9 (65)	71.8 (39)	70.4 (44)	75.0 (4)	0.0 (1)	79.1 (43)	69.7 (208)	79.6 (113)	80.8 (26)	75.0 (12)	64.6 (48)	0.0 (1)
Rutledge	51.6 (66)	58.6 (29)	50.0 (14)	57.1 (21)	100.0 (1)	—	60.0 (25)	52.3 (109)	68.1 (47)	61.5 (13)	37.5 (8)	66.7 (24)	—
Vinson	76.1 (113)	75.4 (65)	76.9 (39)	72.5 (40)	75.0 (4)	0.0 (1)	76.7 (43)	70.5 (207)	78.0 (109)	85.7 (28)	75.0 (12)	75.0 (48)	0.0 (1)
Minton													
Black	33.3 (42)	64.9 (37)	56.0 (25)	62.5 (24)	0.0 (3)	100.0 (1)	88.3 (17)	57.1 (98)	56.4 (62)	60.0 (15)	66.7 (3)	75.0 (24)	0.0 (1)
Burton	81.4 (43)	87.2 (39)	84.6 (26)	66.7 (24)	100.0 (3)	100.0 (1)	76.5 (17)	80.4 (97)	85.3 (61)	93.8 (16)	100.0 (3)	84.0 (25)	100 (1)

(Table continues)

Table 6-4 *(Continued)*

Justice	Crim	CivR	1st	DP	Priv	Atty	Un'n	Econ	JudP	Fed	IR	FTax	Misc
Clark	93.7 (32)	84.4 (32)	91.3 (23)	(83.4) (18)	100.0 (2)	100.0 (1)	68.8 (16)	84.9 (86)	88.1 (59)	87.5 (16)	100.0 (3)	86.4 (22)	100.0 (1)
Douglas	44.4 (36)	66.7 (33)	50.0 (20)	52.7 (19)	33.1 (3)	—	33.3 (15)	60.0 (80)	48.0 (50)	50.0 (10)	100.0 (3)	66.7 (18)	0.0 (1)
Frankfurter	47.6 (42)	70.3 (37)	61.5 (26)	54.2 (24)	50.0 (2)	0.0 (1)	64.7 (17)	56.7 (97)	78.7 (61)	92.9 (14)	66.7 (3)	69.5 (23)	0.0 (1)
Jackson	92.7 (41)	74.3 (35)	66.7 (24)	60.8 (23)	66.7 (3)	0.0 (1)	52.9 (17)	67.1 (94)	72.1 (61)	86.7 (15)	100.0 (3)	69.6 (23)	0.0 (1)
Reed	88.4 (43)	86.8 (38)	92.3 (26)	83.4 (24)	100.0 (3)	100.0 (1)	58.8 (17)	73.7 (99)	88.5 (61)	73.3 (15)	100.0 (3)	88.0 (25)	100.0 (1)
Vinson	90.5 (42)	89.8 (39)	92.3 (26)	78.3 (23)	100.0 (3)	100.0 (1)	76.5 (17)	85.6 (97)	85.0 (60)	81.3 (16)	100.0 (3)	88.0 (25)	100.0 (1)
Murphy													
Burton	42.4 (66)	62.5 (32)	42.9 (14)	61.9 (21)	100.0 (1)	—	55.6 (27)	62.8 (113)	70.2 (47)	76.9 (13)	87.5 (8)	60.9 (25)	—
Jackson	59.1 (66)	51.7 (29)	42.9 (14)	45.0 (20)	100.0 (1)	—	50.0 (26)	52.9 (106)	80.8 (147)	84.6 (13)	50.0 (8)	62.5 (24)	—
Douglas	83.3 (66)	93.8 (32)	85.7 (14)	52.7 (19)	100.0 (1)	—	80.7 (26)	80.4 (46)	80.4 (46)	69.2 (13)	87.5 (8)	56.5 (23)	—

Frankfurter	63.6 (66)	68.7 (32)	50.0 (14)	71.4 (21)	100.0 (1)	—	51.9 (27)	56.5 (113)	76.6 (47)	69.2 (13)	37.5 (8)	62.5 (24)	—
Reed	45.5 (66)	56.6 (30)	64.3 (14)	61.9 (21)	100.0 (1)	—	74.1 (27)	67.0 (109)	69.6 (46)	91.7 (12)	87.5 (8)	66.7 (24)	—
Black	74.3 (66)	87.5 (32)	92.9 (14)	75.0 (20)	100.0 (1)	—	96.3 (27)	94.6 (111)	76.0 (46)	92.3 (13)	62.5 (18)	95.8 (24)	—
Rutledge	89.4 (66)	90.0 (30)	92.8 (14)	90.4 (21)	100.0 (1)	—	92.3 (26)	90.3 (113)	78.7 (47)	61.5 (13)	62.5 (18)	87.5 (24)	—
Vinson	42.4 (66)	62.5 (32)	64.3 (114)	50.0 (18)	100.0 (1)	—	55.6 (27)	71.5 (112)	81.8 (144)	92.3 (13)	87.5 (8)	83.3 (24)	—
Reed													
Black	52.2 (115)	58.2 (67)	57.2 (42)	75.5 (45)	25.0 (4)	100.0 (1)	70.5 (44)	57.7 (220)	66.9 (115)	69.2 (26)	58.3 (12)	67.3 (49)	0.0 (1)
Burton	87.1 (116)	86.9 (69)	79.0 (43)	69.6 (46)	100.0 (4)	100.0 (1)	81.8 (44)	78.1 (220)	82.6 (115)	85.2 (27)	100.0 (12)	75.5 (49)	0.0 (1)
Clark	82.1 (39)	96.8 (31)	91.3 (23)	83.3 (18)	100.0 (2)	100.0 (1)	62.5 (16)	75.0 (92)	89.2 (65)	86.7 (15)	100.0 (4)	87.0 (23)	0.0 (1)
Douglas	54.1 (109)	66.7 (63)	55.6 (36)	69.2 (39)	50.0 (4)	—	70.7 (41)	63.6 (198)	64.0 (100)	71.4 (21)	83.3 (12)	51.2 (41)	0.0 (1)
Frankfurter	58.2 (115)	64.2 (67)	62.8 (43)	63.0 (46)	66.7 (3)	0.0 (1)	70.5 (44)	71.4 (220)	73.9 (115)	72.0 (25)	50.0 (12)	68.8 (48)	0.0 (1)

(Table continues)

Table 6-4 (Continued)

Justice	Crim	CivR	1st	DP	Priv	Atty	Un'n	Econ	JudP	Fed	IR	FTax	Misc
Jackson	78.1 (114)	73.9 (65)	71.8 (39)	70.4 (44)	75.0 (4)	0.0 (1)	79.1 (43)	69.7 (208)	79.6 (113)	80.8 (26)	75.0 (12)	64.6 (48)	0.0 (1)
Minton	88.4 (43)	86.8 (38)	92.3 (26)	83.4 (24)	100.0 (3)	100.0 (1)	58.8 (17)	73.7 (99)	88.5 (61)	73.3 (15)	100.0 (3)	88.0 (25)	100.0 (1)
Murphy	45.5 (66)	56.6 (30)	64.3 (14)	61.9 (21)	100.0 (1)	—	74.1 (27)	67.0 (109)	69.6 (46)	91.7 (12)	87.5 (8)	66.7 (24)	—
Rutledge	47.0 (66)	66.7 (30)	50.0 (16)	72.7 (22)	100.0 (1)	—	84.6 (26)	69.0 (116)	76.6 (47)	50.0 (12)	50.0 (8)	79.2 (24)	—
Vinson	93.0 (115)	85.5 (69)	86.0 (43)	80.9 (42)	100.0 (4)	100.0 (1)	72.7 (44)	79.1 (220)	84.0 (112)	85.2 (27)	100.0 (12)	84.0 (50)	100.0 (1)
						Rutledge							
Black	75.8 (66)	83.3 (30)	87.5 (16)	85.8 (21)	100.0 (1)	—	96.2 (26)	91.5 (118)	80.9 (47)	53.9 (13)	100.0 (8)	91.7 (24)	—
Burton	48.5 (66)	70.0 (30)	43.8 (16)	72.7 (22)	100.0 (1)	—	65.4 (26)	63.3 (120)	70.8 (48)	53.9 (13)	50.0 (8)	73.9 (23)	—
Douglas	81.8 (66)	83.4 (30)	75.1 (16)	65.0 (20)	100.0 (1)	—	88.0 (25)	85.1 (114)	72.3 (47)	61.5 (13)	37.5 (8)	66.7 (24)	—
Frankfurter	62.1 (66)	63.3 (30)	50.0 (16)	63.6 (22)	100.0 (1)	—	61.5 (26)	51.6 (120)	60.4 (48)	61.6 (113)	50.0 (8)	66.7 (24)	—

Jackson	51.6 (66)	58.6 (29)	50.0 (14)	57.1 (21)	100.0 (1)	—	60.0 (25)	52.3 (109)	68.1 (47)	61.5 (13)	37.5 (8)	66.7 (24)	—
Murphy	89.4 (66)	90.0 (30)	92.8 (14)	90.4 (21)	100.0 (1)	—	92.3 (26)	90.3 (113)	78.7 (47)	61.5 (13)	62.5 (8)	87.5 (24)	—
Reed	47.0 (66)	66.7 (30)	50.0 (16)	72.7 (22)	100.0 (1)	—	84.6 (26)	69.0 (116)	76.6 (47)	50.0 (12)	50.0 (8)	79.2 (254)	—
Vinson	43.9 (66)	63.3 (30)	50.0 (16)	63.2 (19)	100.0 (1)	—	65.4 (26)	68 (119)	66.6 (45)	53.9 (13)	50.0 (18)	95.8 (24)	—

Vinson

Black	54.4 (114)	67.1 (70)	52.4 (42)	68.3 (41)	25 (4)	100.0 (1)	61.4 (44)	62.0 (221)	65.2 (112)	82.1 (28)	58.3 (12)	81.6 (49)	0.0 (1)
Burton	86.1 (115)	86.1 (72)	83.7 (43)	76.2 (42)	100.0 (4)	100.0 (1)	86.4 (44)	78.8 (221)	84.0 (112)	86.2 (29)	100.0 (12)	83.6 (49)	0.0 (1)
Clark	92.1 (38)	90.6 (32)	100.0 (23)	88.3 (17)	100.0 (2)	100.0 (1)	93.8 (16)	85.5 (90)	90.7 (64)	93.8 (16)	100.0 (4)	100.0 (23)	0.0 (1)
Douglas	54.7 (108)	68.2 (66)	52.8 (36)	57.1 (35)	50.0 (4)	—	53.7 (41)	62.0 (200)	59.6 (99)	56.5 (23)	83.3 (12)	56.1 (41)	0.0 (1)
Frankfurter	57.0 (114)	72.8 (70)	72.1 (43)	69.1 (42)	66.7 (3)	0.0 (1)	84.1 (44)	67.4 (221)	77.7 (112)	77.8 (27)	50.0 (12)	68.8 (48)	0.0 (1)
Jackson	76.1 (113)	75.4 (65)	76.9 (39)	72.5 (40)	75.0 (4)	0.0 (1)	76.7 (43)	70.5 (207)	78.0 (109)	85.7 (28)	75.0 (12)	75.0 (48)	0.0 (1)

(Table continues)

Table 6-4 *(Continued)*

Justice	Crim	CivR	1st	DP	Priv	Atty	Un'n	Econ	JudP	Fed	IR	FTax	Misc
Minton	90.5 (42)	89.8 (39)	92.3 (26)	78.3 (23)	100.0 (3)	100.0 (1)	76.5 (17)	85.6 (97)	85.0 (60)	81.3 (16)	100.0 (3)	88.0 (25)	100.0 (1)
Reed	93.0 (115)	85.5 (69)	86.0 (43)	80.9 (42)	100.0 (4)	100.0 (1)	72.7 (44)	79.1 (220)	84.0 (112)	85.2 (27)	100.0 (12)	84.0 (50)	100.0 (1)
Rutledge	43.9 (66)	63.3 (30)	50.0 (16)	63.2 (19)	100.0 (1)	—	65.4 (26)	68.0 (119)	66.6 (45)	53.9 (13)	50.0 (8)	95.8 (24)	—
Murphy	42.4 (66)	62.6 (32)	64.3 (14)	50.0 (18)	100.0 (1)	—	55.6 (27)	71.5 (112)	81.8 (44)	92.3 (13)	87.5 (18)	83.3 (24)	—

Note: "—" indicates that no case in issue areas was decided during tenure overlap. Figures listed are the percentage of cases in which the justices voted together. Figures in parentheses are the total number of cases decided in the issue area in which both justices participated during their tenures on the Vinson Court. The data include all orally argued citations. Percentages should be interpreted with care since some of the figures on which they are based are quite small.

Definitions of issue areas: Criminal procedure (Crim): the rights of persons accused of a crime except for the due process rights of prisoners; Civil rights (CivR): non–First Amendment freedom cases that pertain to classifications based on race (including Native Americans), age, indigence, voting residence, military or handicapped status, sex, or alienage; First Amendment (1st): guarantees contained therein; Due process (DP): noncriminal procedural guarantees, plus court jurisdiction over nonresident litigants and the takings clause of the Fifth Amendment; Privacy (Priv): abortion, contraception, the Freedom of Information Act and related federal statutes; Attorneys (Atty): attorneys' fees, commercial speech, admission to and removal from the bar, and disciplinary matters; Unions (Un'n): labor union activity; Economics (Econ): commercial business activity, plus litigation involving injured persons or things, employee actions vis-à-vis employers, zoning regulations, governmental regulation of corruption other than that involving campaign spending; Judicial power (JudP): the exercise of the judiciary's own power and authority; Federalism (Fed): conflicts between the federal and state governments, excluding those between state and federal courts, and those involving the priority of federal fiscal claims; Interstate relations (IR): conflicts between states, such as boundary disputes, and nonproperty disputes commonly arising under the full faith and credit clause of the Constitution; Federal taxation (FTax): the Internal Revenue Code and related statutes; Miscellaneous (Misc.): legislative veto, separation of powers, and matters not included in any other issue area.

Source: U.S. Supreme Court Judicial Database, with analu = 0 or 4 and dec_type = 1, 6, or 7.

Table 6-5 Voting Interagreements Among the Justices, by Issue Area: The Warren Court, 1953–1968 Terms

Justice	Crim	CivR	1st	DP	Priv	Atty	Un'n	Econ	JudP	Fed	IR	FTax	Misc
						Black							
Brennan	71.0 (300)	79.7 (192)	83.5 (139)	80.0 (30)	50.0 (2)	88.9 (9)	76.5 (98)	82.7 (358)	83.8 (185)	81.5 (65)	100 (6)	76.6 (94)	100 (1)
Burton	52.2 (94)	47.4 (57)	32.4 (37)	62.5 (16)	100 (1)	80.0 (5)	77.4 (31)	57.7 (142)	75.8 (66)	42.9 (21)	66.7 (3)	76.3 (38)	50.0 (4)
Clark	51.4 (284)	63.6 (184)	41.7 (134)	69.7 (33)	0.0 (1)	85.7 (7)	82.3 (107)	83.1 (384)	81.7 (192)	65.2 (66)	100 (9)	83.3 (108)	60.0 (5)
Douglas	79.1 (349)	82.8 (221)	90.6 (159)	86.5 (37)	50.0 (2)	90.0 (10)	79.0 (119)	86.9 (435)	78.9 (219)	77.5 (80)	100 (9)	54.0 (113)	80.0 (5)
Fortas	60.4 (91)	66.7 (60)	66.7 (45)	80.0 (5)	—	100 (4)	70.0 (20)	80.8 (73)	80.5 (46)	64.2 (14)	—	62.5 (16)	—
Frankfurter	54.3 (171)	65.6 (95)	51.9 (79)	45.4 (22)	100 (1)	80.0 (5)	63.1 (57)	47.7 (254)	70.0 (110)	71.1 (38)	80.0 (5)	82.9 (70)	80.0 (5)
Goldberg	75.0 (60)	86.0 (57)	85.2 (27)	80.0 (5)	0.0 (1)	100 (1)	85.0 (20)	73.8 (84)	75.5 (45)	83.3 (18)	75.0 (4)	78.3 (23)	—
Harlan	50.7 (316)	59.6 (203)	53.9 (152)	55.8 (34)	50.0 (4)	80.0 (13)	68.5 (108)	46.3 (374)	71.8 (202)	68.5 (70)	87.5 (9)	66.6 (99)	66.7 (4)
Jackson	71.4 (14)	62.5 (8)	50.0 (4)	100 (1)	—	—	66.7 (6)	57.7 (26)	57.1 (7)	50.0 (4)	—	33.3 (3)	—

(Table continues)

Table 6-5 (Continued)

Justice	Crim	CivR	1st	DP	Priv	Atty	Un'n	Econ	JudP	Fed	IR	FTax	Misc
Marshall	51.0 (49)	66.6 (33)	70.0 (20)	66.7 (3)	—	100 (1)	100 (4)	66.7 (24)	95.2 (21)	75.0 (4)	—	100 (3)	—
Minton	67.3 (46)	44.8 (29)	14.3 (14)	66.7 (6)	—	100 (1)	70.0 (20)	79.5 (83)	58.8 (34)	61.5 (13)	100 (3)	100 (21)	50.0 (4)
Reed	51.9 (52)	41.9 (31)	20.0 (15)	87.5 (8)	—	100 (1)	90.5 (21)	60.0 (95)	61.0 (41)	53.3 (15)	100 (3)	87.5 (27)	75.0 (4)
Stewart	58.8 (252)	70.7 (164)	63.4 (120)	66.7 (21)	100 (2)	75.0 (4)	74.5 (86)	56.4 (287)	76.4 (157)	71.9 (57)	66.7 (6)	61.8 (76)	100 (1)
Warren	74.3 (343)	80.8 (219)	82.8 (157)	78.8 (33)	50.0 (2)	90.0 (10)	84.8 (118)	89.2 (437)	86.7 (219)	84.5 (71)	100 (8)	86.0 (114)	60.0 (5)
White	65.7 (163)	73.5 (128)	67.1 (70)	75.0 (12)	0.0 (1)	80.0 (5)	76.8 (56)	75.7 (169)	86.2 (108)	76.3 (38)	100 (4)	72.5 (40)	—
Whittaker	53.5 (114)	55.6 (54)	44.4 (54)	66.7 (15)	100 (1)	0.0 (1)	41.2 (34)	47.0 (151)	82.3 (62)	66.7 (21)	100 (2)	65.9 (41)	100 (1)
Brennan													
Black	71.0 (300)	79.7 (192)	83.5 (139)	80.0 (30)	50.0 (2)	88.9 (9)	76.5 (98)	82.7 (358)	83.8 (185)	81.5 (65)	100 (6)	76.6 (94)	100 (1)
Burton	52.1 (48)	64.3 (28)	56.3 (16)	66.7 (9)	100 (1)	75.0 (4)	85.7 (14)	61.0 (59)	87.1 (31)	60.0 (10)	—	70.6 (17)	—

Clark	60.0 (240)	74.2 (155)	46.6 (116)	80.8 (26)	100 (1)	83.3 (6)	82.8 (93)	91.2 (307)	87.8 (156)	84.9 (53)	100 (6)	93.1 (88)	100 (1)
Douglas	78.2 (304)	90.2 (193)	85.7 (140)	86.7 (30)	100 (2)	77.8 (9)	77.8 (104)	81.4 (353)	75.2 (198)	73.1 (67)	100 (6)	59.2 (93)	100 (1)
Fortas	86.8 (91)	93.5 (61)	80.4 (46)	100 (5)	—	75.0 (4)	94.7 (19)	84.0 (75)	93.3 (45)	85.7 (14)	—	75.0 (16)	—
Frankfurter	64.8 (125)	70.5 (61)	53.4 (58)	53.3 (15)	100 (1)	75.0 (4)	69.7 (43)	53.6 (170)	77.7 (76)	92.6 (27)	100 (2)	88.0 (50)	100 (1)
Goldberg	90.0 (60)	93.0 (57)	92.9 (28)	100 (5)	100 (1)	100 (1)	95.0 (20)	88.1 (84)	84.4 (45)	93.8 (16)	75.0 (4)	82.6 (23)	—
Harlan	62.5 (304)	58.1 (191)	52.5 (141)	66.7 (30)	100 (2)	66.7 (9)	87.7 (105)	58.1 (348)	76.3 (186)	86.4 (66)	100 (6)	78.9 (95)	100 (1)
Marshall	93.9 (49)	94.1 (34)	100 (20)	100 (3)	—	100 (1)	100 (4)	87.5 (24)	100 (22)	75.0 (4)	—	80.0 (5)	—
Reed	33.3 (9)	100 (2)	100 (1)	100 (1)	—	—	100 (1)	61.5 (13)	85.7 (7)	100 (2)	—	100 (3)	—
Stewart	72.5 (254)	71.5 (165)	71.9 (121)	95.2 (21)	0.0 (1)	50.0 (4)	81.8 (88)	69.6 (289)	81.6 (157)	92.7 (55)	66.7 (6)	79.2 (77)	100 (1)
Warren	86.0 (301)	96.3 (191)	94.2 (138)	92.6 (27)	100 (2)	88.9 (9)	94.2 (103)	92.1 (355)	91.9 (186)	89.8 (59)	100 (6)	93.7 (95)	100 (1)
White	74.2 (163)	80.5 (128)	70.8 (72)	100 (12)	100 (1)	80.0 (5)	90.9 (55)	89.4 (170)	92.5 (107)	94.4 (36)	100 (4)	90.0 (40)	—

(Table continues)

537

Table 6-5 (Continued)

Justice	Crim	CivR	1st	DP	Priv	Atty	Un'n	Econ	JudP	Fed	IR	FTax	Misc
Whittaker	66.4 (113)	64.8 (54)	46.3 (54)	73.3 (15)	100 (1)	0.0 (1)	52.5 (40)	55.0 (151)	81.3 (64)	87.0 (23)	100 (2)	73.8 (42)	100 (1)
Burton													
Black	52.2 (94)	47.4 (57)	32.4 (37)	62.5 (16)	100 (1)	80.0 (5)	77.4 (31)	57.7 (142)	75.8 (66)	42.9 (21)	66.7 (3)	76.3 (38)	50.0 (4)
Brennan	52.1 (48)	64.3 (28)	56.3 (16)	66.7 (9)	100 (1)	75.0 (4)	85.7 (14)	61.0 (59)	87.1 (31)	60.0 (10)	—	70.6 (17)	—
Clark	88.4 (95)	79.0 (57)	68.6 (35)	68.8 (16)	—	60.0 (5)	85.7 (35)	71.4 (136)	86.1 (65)	91.3 (23)	66.7 (3)	84.2 (38)	75.0 (4)
Douglas	43.7 (96)	48.2 (56)	32.4 (37)	68.8 (16)	100 (1)	80.0 (5)	68.6 (35)	57.3 (143)	58.5 (65)	47.8 (23)	66.7 (3)	57.9 (38)	75.0 (4)
Frankfurter	79.2 (96)	73.2 (56)	62.2 (37)	53.3 (15)	100 (1)	60.0 (5)	71.4 (35)	72.6 (146)	85.1 (67)	73.9 (23)	66.7 (3)	76.3 (38)	75.0 (4)
Harlan	82.3 (63)	75.6 (41)	75.9 (29)	53.9 (13)	100 (1)	80.0 (5)	82.6 (23)	72.1 (86)	89.4 (47)	78.6 (14)	50.0 (4)	81.8 (22)	100 (2)
Jackson	71.4 (14)	75.0 (8)	50.0 (4)	100 (1)	—	—	100 (6)	85.7 (28)	57.1 (7)	100 (4)	—	33.3 (3)	—
Minton	80.0 (45)	89.6 (29)	64.3 (14)	66.7 (6)	—	100 (1)	75.0 (20)	74.1 (85)	85.3 (34)	92.3 (13)	66.7 (3)	85.7 (21)	100 (4)

Reed	84.6 (52)	80.6 (31)	66.7 (9)	75.0 (8)	—	100 (1)	95.5 (22)	80.6 (98)	87.8 (41)	86.7 (15)	66.7 (3)	83.4 (24)	75.0 (4)
Warren	62.8 (94)	64.9 (57)	48.6 (35)	50.0 (12)	100 (1)	80.0 (5)	88.6 (35)	62.8 (145)	81.3 (64)	63.6 (22)	100 (2)	73.0 (37)	100 (4)
Whittaker	86.8 (38)	86.4 (22)	100 (12)	75.0 (8)	100 (1)	100 (1)	75.0 (8)	77.5 (40)	95.4 (22)	80.0 (5)	—	55.6 (9)	—

Clark

Black	51.4 (284)	63.6 (184)	41.7 (134)	69.7 (33)	0.0 (1)	85.7 (7)	82.3 (107)	83.1 (384)	81.7 (192)	65.2 (66)	100 (9)	83.3 (108)	60.0 (5)
Brennan	60.0 (240)	74.2 (155)	46.6 (116)	80.8 (26)	100 (1)	83.3 (6)	82.8 (93)	91.2 (307)	87.8 (156)	84.9 (53)	100 (6)	93.1 (88)	100 (1)
Burton	88.4 (95)	79.0 (57)	68.6 (35)	68.8 (16)	—	60.0 (5)	85.7 (35)	71.4 (136)	86.1 (65)	91.3 (23)	66.7 (3)	84.2 (38)	75.0 (4)
Douglas	44.1 (288)	63.6 (181)	36.0 (136)	78.8 (33)	100 (1)	71.4 (7)	72.6 (113)	79.7 (384)	70.6 (191)	72.0 (68)	100 (9)	57.0 (107)	60.0 (5)
Fortas	58.5 (41)	78.1 (32)	62.5 (24)	100 (3)	—	100 (1)	77.8 (9)	86.1 (36)	86.7 (30)	71.4 (7)	—	70.0 (10)	—
Frankfurter	80.3 (173)	73.3 (90)	77.9 (77)	59.0 (22)	—	80.0 (5)	75.0 (64)	61.5 (244)	79.8 (109)	75.7 (37)	80.0 (5)	88.7 (71)	60.0 (5)
Goldberg	58.3 (60)	74.1 (58)	53.6 (28)	80.0 (5)	100 (1)	100 (1)	85.0 (20)	80.7 (83)	84.1 (44)	70.6 (17)	75.0 (4)	82.6 (23)	—

(Table continues)

Table 6-5 (Continued)

Justice	Crim	CivR	1st	DP	Priv	Atty	Un'n	Econ	JudP	Fed	IR	FTax	Misc
Harlan	80.8 (256)	74.1 (166)	79.8 (129)	76.7 (30)	100 (1)	85.7 (7)	76.5 (102)	57.9 (330)	79.9 (174)	81.0 (58)	87.5 (8)	78.5 (93)	100 (3)
Jackson	85.7 (14)	75.0 (8)	66.7 (3)	100 (1)	—	—	100 (6)	80.8 (26)	71.4 (7)	100 (4)	—	33.3 (3)	—
Minton	80.0 (45)	79.3 (29)	53.9 (13)	66.7 (6)	—	100 (1)	75.0 (20)	85.1 (80)	73.5 (34)	100 (13)	100 (3)	100 (21)	75.0 (4)
Reed	82.6 (52)	74.2 (31)	57.2 (14)	97.5 (7)	—	100 (1)	95.5 (22)	76.1 (92)	75.0 (40)	93.3 (15)	100 (3)	87.5 (24)	75.0 (4)
Stewart	80.0 (190)	81.1 (127)	71.1 (97)	88.2 (17)	0.0 (1)	50.0 (2)	82.8 (76)	69.5 (239)	83.0 (129)	90.7 (43)	66.7 (6)	76.1 (71)	100 (1)
Warren	58.8 (282)	73.1 (182)	52.6 (133)	82.8 (29)	100 (1)	85.7 (7)	88.5 (113)	90.6 (383)	87.4 (191)	77.3 (66)	100 (8)	92.6 (108)	80.0 (5)
White	81.0 (100)	83.4 (90)	73.0 (48)	87.5 (8)	100 (1)	100 (2)	83.7 (43)	86.5 (126)	90.1 (81)	81.5 (27)	100 (4)	93.9 (33)	—
Whittaker	84.4 (115)	77.8 (54)	88.7 (53)	73.3 (15)	—	0.0 (1)	70.0 (40)	62.8 (145)	90.3 (62)	90.0 (20)	100 (2)	64.3 (42)	100 (1)
Douglas													
Black	79.1 (349)	82.8 (221)	90.6 (159)	86.5 (37)	50.0 (2)	90.0 (10)	79.0 (119)	86.9 (435)	78.9 (219)	77.5 (80)	100 (9)	54.0 (113)	80.0 (5)

540

Justice												
Brennan	100 (1)	59.2 (93)	100 (6)	73.1 (67)	75.2 (198)	81.4 (355)	77.8 (104)	77.8 (9)	100 (2)	86.7 (30)	85.7 (140)	90.2 (193)	78.2 (304)
Burton	75.0 (4)	57.9 (38)	66.7 (3)	47.8 (23)	58.5 (65)	57.3 (143)	68.6 (35)	80.0 (5)	100 (1)	68.8 (16)	32.4 (37)	48.2 (56)	43.7 (96)
Clark	60.0 (5)	57.0 (107)	100 (9)	72.0 (68)	70.6 (191)	79.7 (384)	72.6 (113)	71.4 (7)	100 (1)	78.8 (33)	36.0 (136)	63.6 (181)	44.1 (288)
Fortas	—	68.8 (16)	—	85.7 (14)	74.5 (47)	73.2 (71)	65.0 (20)	100 (4)	—	100 (5)	78.2 (46)	95.1 (61)	84.6 (91)
Frankfurter	80.0 (5)	55.7 (70)	80.0 (5)	65.0 (40)	54.5 (110)	43.6 (255)	59.4 (64)	60.0 (5)	100 (1)	45.4 (22)	49.3 (79)	61.8 (89)	54.6 (174)
Goldberg	—	50.0 (22)	75.0 (4)	72.2 (18)	72.7 (44)	74.7 (83)	73.7 (19)	100 (1)	100 (1)	80.0 (5)	92.9 (28)	96.6 (58)	85.0 (60)
Harlan	66.7 (4)	51.0 (98)	87.5 (8)	63.9 (72)	61.8 (204)	46.1 (373)	69.3 (114)	90.0 (10)	100 (2)	55.9 (34)	46.4 (153)	50.0 (204)	43.8 (320)
Jackson	—	33.3 (3)	—	75.0 (4)	42.9 (7)	60.0 (25)	16.7 (6)	—	—	100 (1)	50.0 (4)	62.5 (8)	64.2 (14)
Marshall	—	20.0 (5)	—	50.0 (4)	77.3 (22)	73.9 (23)	50.0 (4)	100 (1)	—	66.7 (3)	78.9 (19)	97.1 (34)	79.6 (49)
Minton	75.0 (4)	61.9 (21)	100 (3)	76.9 (13)	50.0 (32)	73.5 (83)	75.0 (20)	100 (1)	—	50.0 (6)	14.3 (14)	44.8 (29)	60.8 (46)
Reed	50.0 (4)	70.8 (24)	100 (3)	66.7 (15)	64.1 (39)	59.4 (96)	77.3 (22)	100 (1)	—	75.0 (8)	20.0 (15)	41.9 (31)	49.1 (53)

(Table continues)

541

Table 6-5 *(Continued)*

Justice	Crim	CivR	1st	DP	Priv	Atty	Un'n	Econ	JudP	Fed	IR	FTax	Misc
Stewart	53.2 (254)	63.9 (166)	62.5 (120)	81.0 (21)	0.0 (1)	75.0 (4)	73.9 (88)	54.4 (283)	68.1 (157)	70.2 (57)	66.7 (6)	58.7 (75)	100 (1)
Warren	81.3 (347)	90.0 (220)	81.1 (158)	84.9 (33)	100 (2)	80.0 (10)	77.4 (124)	86.7 (434)	78.0 (218)	83.5 (73)	100 (8)	54.9 (113)	80.0 (5)
White	55.2 (163)	73.6 (129)	57.7 (71)	83.3 (12)	100 (1)	80.0 (5)	67.3 (55)	76.3 (165)	76.6 (107)	73.7 (38)	100 (4)	48.8 (39)	—
Whittaker	46.1 (115)	52.9 (53)	37.0 (54)	60.0 (15)	100 (1)	100 (1)	40.0 (40)	41.3 (150)	71.9 (64)	65.2 (23)	100 (2)	68.3 (41)	100 (1)
Fortas													
Black	60.4 (91)	66.7 (60)	66.7 (45)	80.0 (5)	—	100 (4)	70.0 (20)	80.8 (73)	80.5 (46)	64.2 (14)	—	62.5 (16)	—
Brennan	86.8 (91)	93.5 (61)	80.4 (46)	100 (5)	—	75.0 (4)	94.7 (19)	84.0 (75)	93.3 (45)	85.7 (14)	—	75.0 (16)	—
Clark	58.5 (41)	78.1 (32)	62.5 (24)	100 (3)	—	100 (1)	77.8 (9)	86.1 (36)	86.7 (30)	71.4 (7)	—	70.0 (10)	—
Douglas	84.6 (91)	95.1 (61)	78.2 (46)	100 (5)	—	100 (4)	65.0 (20)	73.2 (71)	74.5 (47)	85.7 (14)	—	68.8 (16)	—
Harlan	53.8 (91)	57.3 (61)	52.2 (46)	80.0 (5)	—	100 (4)	90.0 (20)	69.8 (73)	72.9 (48)	85.7 (14)	—	50.0 (16)	—

Marshall	88.6 (35)	100 (24)	72.2 (18)	100 (1)	—	100 (1)	100 (3)	84.2 (19)	91.7 (12)	100 (1)	—	75.0 (4)	—
Stewart	66.6 (90)	59.0 (27)	63.0 (46)	100 (5)	—	66.7 (3)	70.0 (20)	70.7 (75)	83.0 (47)	85.7 (14)	—	50.0 (16)	—
Warren	84.6 (91)	90.0 (60)	87.0 (46)	100 (5)	—	75.0 (4)	100 (19)	83.8 (74)	93.6 (47)	90.9 (11)	—	81.3 (16)	—
White	59.8 (87)	73.8 (61)	55.5 (45)	100 (5)	—	75.0 (4)	90.0 (20)	86.1 (72)	85.4 (48)	71.4 (14)	—	73.4 (15)	—

Frankfurter

Black	54.3 (171)	65.6 (90)	51.9 (79)	45.4 (22)	100 (1)	80.0 (5)	63.1 (57)	47.7 (234)	70.0 (110)	71.1 (38)	90.0 (4)	82.9 (70)	80.0 (5)
Brennan	64.8 (125)	70.5 (61)	53.4 (58)	53.3 (15)	100 (1)	75.0 (4)	69.7 (43)	53.6 (170)	77.7 (76)	92.6 (27)	100 (2)	88.0 (50)	100 (1)
Burton	79.2 (96)	73.2 (56)	62.2 (37)	53.3 (15)	100 (1)	60.0 (5)	71.4 (35)	72.6 (146)	85.1 (67)	73.9 (23)	66.7 (3)	76.3 (38)	75.0 (4)
Clark	80.3 (173)	73.3 (90)	77.9 (77)	59.0 (22)	—	80.0 (5)	75.0 (64)	61.5 (244)	70.8 (123)	75.7 (37)	80.0 (5)	88.7 (71)	60.0 (5)
Douglas	54.6 (174)	61.8 (89)	49.3 (79)	45.4 (22)	100 (1)	60.0 (5)	59.4 (64)	43.6 (255)	54.5 (110)	65.0 (40)	80.0 (5)	55.7 (70)	80.0 (5)
Harlan	91.5 (141)	88.9 (72)	87.3 (71)	84.2 (19)	100 (1)	80.0 (5)	80.8 (52)	87.2 (195)	89.2 (92)	86.7 (30)	75.0 (4)	76.4 (55)	66.7 (4)

(Table continues)

544

Table 6-5 (Continued)

Justice	Crim	CivR	1st	DP	Priv	Atty	Un'n	Econ	JudP	Fed	IR	FTax	Misc
Jackson	78.6 (14)	75.0 (8)	25.0 (4)	100 (1)	—	—	83.3 (6)	92.8 (28)	57.1 (7)	75.0 (4)	—	66.6 (3)	—
Minton	71.7 (46)	55.2 (29)	35.7 (14)	50.0 (6)	—	100 (1)	75.0 (20)	76.7 (86)	85.3 (34)	76.9 (13)	66.7 (3)	85.7 (21)	75.0 (4)
Reed	67.9 (53)	48.4 (31)	40.0 (15)	37.5 (8)	—	100 (1)	72.7 (22)	70.7 (99)	70.7 (41)	73.3 (15)	66.7 (3)	83.4 (24)	50.0 (4)
Stewart	82.9 (76)	78.8 (33)	85.0 (40)	71.4 (7)	—	—	74.1 (26)	76.2 (102)	75.5 (42)	81.3 (16)	100 (2)	69.7 (33)	100 (1)
Warren	56.7 (171)	74.4 (90)	60.5 (76)	50.0 (18)	100 (1)	80.0 (5)	68.8 (64)	51.0 (257)	68.8 (109)	69.4 (36)	100 (4)	90.0 (70)	80.0 (5)
Whittaker	83.2 (113)	75.0 (52)	88.7 (53)	64.2 (14)	100 (1)	100 (1)	63.9 (36)	80.5 (148)	82.8 (64)	81.8 (22)	100 (2)	69.1 (42)	100 (1)
Goldberg													
Black	75.0 (60)	86.0 (57)	85.2 (27)	80.0 (5)	0.0 (1)	100 (1)	85.0 (20)	73.8 (84)	75.5 (45)	83.3 (18)	75.0 (4)	78.3 (23)	—
Brennan	90.0 (60)	93.0 (57)	92.9 (28)	100 (5)	100 (1)	100 (1)	95.0 (20)	88.1 (84)	84.4 (45)	93.8 (16)	75.0 (4)	82.6 (23)	—
Clark	58.3 (60)	74.1 (58)	53.6 (28)	80.0 (5)	100 (1)	100 (1)	85.0 (20)	80.7 (83)	84.1 (44)	70.6 (17)	75.0 (4)	82.6 (23)	—

Douglas	85.0 (60)	96.6 (58)	92.9 (28)	80.0 (5)	100 (1)	100 (1)	73.7 (19)	74.7 (83)	72.7 (44)	72.2 (18)	75.0 (4)	50.0 (22)	—
Harlan	56.7 (60)	43.9 (57)	39.3 (28)	60.0 (5)	100 (1)	100 (1)	85.0 (20)	63.0 (81)	86.4 (44)	83.4 (18)	75.0 (4)	82.6 (23)	—
Stewart	65.0 (60)	74.1 (58)	76.9 (26)	100 (5)	0.0 (1)	100 (1)	85.0 (20)	81.7 (82)	80.0 (45)	83.4 (18)	50.0 (4)	87.0 (23)	—
Warren	91.6 (59)	94.8 (57)	89.3 (28)	100 (5)	100 (1)	100 (1)	90.0 (20)	80.2 (81)	84.4 (45)	82.4 (17)	75.0 (4)	86.9 (23)	—
White	68.3 (60)	73.2 (56)	68.0 (25)	100 (5)	100 (1)	100 (1)	85.0 (20)	82.2 (79)	82.2 (45)	87.5 (16)	75.0 (4)	78.3 (23)	—

Harlan

Black	50.7 (316)	59.6 (203)	53.9 (152)	55.8 (34)	50.0 (4)	80.0 (13)	68.5 (108)	46.3 (374)	71.8 (202)	68.5 (70)	87.5 (9)	66.6 (99)	66.7 (4)
Brennan	62.5 (304)	58.1 (191)	52.5 (141)	66.7 (30)	100 (2)	66.7 (9)	87.7 (105)	58.1 (348)	76.3 (186)	83.8 (68)	100 (6)	78.9 (95)	100 (1)
Burton	82.3 (63)	75.6 (41)	75.9 (29)	53.9 (13)	100 (1)	80.0 (5)	82.6 (23)	72.1 (86)	89.4 (47)	78.6 (14)	50.0 (4)	81.8 (22)	100 (2)
Clark	80.8 (256)	74.1 (166)	79.8 (129)	76.7 (30)	100 (1)	85.7 (7)	76.5 (102)	57.9 (330)	79.9 (174)	81.0 (58)	87.5 (8)	78.5 (93)	100 (3)
Douglas	43.8 (320)	50.0 (204)	46.4 (153)	55.9 (34)	100 (2)	90.0 (10)	69.3 (114)	46.1 (373)	61.8 (204)	63.9 (72)	87.5 (8)	51.0 (98)	66.7 (4)

(Table continues)

Table 6-5 (Continued)

Justice	Crim	CivR	1st	DP	Priv	Atty	Un'n	Econ	JudP	Fed	IR	FTax	Misc
Fortas	53.8 (91)	57.3 (61)	52.2 (46)	80.0 (5)	—	100 (4)	90.0 (20)	69.8 (73)	72.9 (48)	85.7 (14)	—	50.0 (16)	—
Frankfurter	91.5 (141)	88.9 (72)	87.3 (71)	84.2 (19)	100 (1)	80.0 (5)	80.8 (52)	87.2 (195)	89.2 (92)	86.7 (30)	75.0 (4)	76.4 (55)	66.7 (4)
Goldberg	56.7 (60)	43.9 (57)	39.3 (28)	60.0 (5)	100 (1)	100 (1)	85.0 (20)	63.0 (81)	86.4 (44)	83.4 (18)	75.0 (4)	82.6 (23)	—
Marshall	57.1 (49)	64.7 (34)	75.0 (20)	66.7 (3)	—	100 (1)	100 (4)	72.7 (22)	81.8 (22)	75.0 (4)	—	60.0 (5)	—
Minton	76.9 (13)	76.9 (13)	33.3 (18)	33.3 (3)	—	100 (1)	75.0 (8)	60.7 (28)	80.0 (15)	75.0 (4)	50.0 (2)	80.0 (5)	100 (2)
Reed	73.9 (23)	73.4 (15)	42.9 (7)	60.0 (5)	—	100 (1)	60.0 (7)	59.5 (42)	76.2 (21)	83.3 (6)	50.0 (2)	75.0 (8)	100 (2)
Stewart	79.9 (254)	77.3 (163)	73.6 (121)	76.2 (21)	0.0 (1)	75.0 (4)	83.2 (89)	80.7 (279)	82.9 (158)	92.8 (56)	66.7 (6)	89.6 (77)	100 (1)
Warren	50.8 (317)	57.4 (202)	56.3 (151)	67.7 (31)	100 (1)	70.0 (10)	83.2 (113)	53.0 (372)	69.8 (202)	81.3 (64)	100 (7)	75.0 (100)	100 (3)
White	74.8 (163)	66.4 (128)	76.3 (72)	66.7 (12)	100 (1)	80.0 (5)	80.4 (56)	65.6 (163)	80.7 (109)	84.2 (38)	100 (4)	82.5 (40)	—
Whittaker	83.5 (115)	73.1 (52)	92.6 (54)	73.4 (15)	100 (1)	0.0 (1)	55.0 (40)	83.7 (147)	84.4 (64)	77.2 (22)	100 (2)	73.8 (42)	100 (1)

	Jackson												
Black	71.4 (14)	62.5 (8)	50.0 (4)	100 (1)	—	—	66.7 (6)	57.7 (26)	57.1 (7)	50.0 (4)	—	33.3 (3)	—
Burton	71.4 (14)	75.0 (8)	50.0 (4)	100 (1)	—	—	100 (6)	85.7 (28)	57.1 (7)	100 (4)	—	33.3 (3)	—
Clark	85.7 (14)	75.0 (8)	66.7 (3)	100 (1)	—	—	100 (6)	80.8 (26)	71.4 (7)	100 (4)	—	33.3 (3)	—
Douglas	64.2 (14)	62.5 (8)	50.0 (4)	100 (1)	—	—	16.7 (6)	60.0 (25)	42.9 (7)	75.0 (4)	—	33.3 (3)	—
Frankfurter	78.6 (14)	75.0 (8)	25.0 (4)	100 (1)	—	—	83.3 (6)	92.8 (28)	57.1 (7)	75.0 (4)	—	66.6 (3)	—
Minton	92.9 (14)	75.0 (8)	50.0 (4)	100 (1)	—	—	66.7 (6)	75.0 (28)	71.5 (7)	100 (4)	—	33.3 (3)	—
Reed	72.7 (11)	75.0 (8)	50.0 (4)	100 (1)	—	—	100 (6)	81.5 (27)	28.6 (7)	75.0 (4)	—	33.3 (3)	—
Warren	84.6 (13)	75.0 (8)	50.0 (4)	—	—	—	100 (6)	75.0 (28)	50.0 (6)	100 (3)	—	50.0 (4)	—
	Marshall												
Black	51.0 (49)	66.6 (33)	70.0 (20)	66.7 (3)	100 (1)	100 (4)	100 (4)	66.7 (24)	95.2 (21)	75.0 (4)	—	100 (5)	—

(Table continues)

Table 6-5 (Continued)

Justice	Crim	CivR	1st	DP	Priv	Atty	Un'n	Econ	JudP	Fed	IR	FTax	Misc
Brennan	93.9 (49)	94.1 (34)	100 (20)	100 (3)	—	100 (1)	100 (4)	87.5 (24)	100 (22)	75.0 (4)	—	80.0 (5)	—
Douglas	79.6 (49)	100 (34)	78.9 (19)	66.7 (3)	—	100 (1)	50.0 (4)	73.9 (23)	77.3 (22)	50.0 (4)	—	20.0 (10)	—
Fortas	88.6 (35)	100 (24)	72.2 (18)	100 (1)	—	100 (1)	100 (3)	84.2 (19)	91.7 (12)	100 (1)	—	75.0 (4)	—
Stewart	71.4 (49)	64.7 (34)	95.0 (20)	100 (3)	—	—	75.0 (4)	66.6 (24)	90.9 (22)	75.0 (4)	—	50.0 (4)	—
Warren	93.9 (49)	91.2 (34)	95.0 (20)	100 (3)	—	100 (1)	100 (4)	79.2 (24)	95.5 (22)	75.0 (4)	—	80.0 (5)	—
White	68.8 (48)	67.6 (34)	75.0 (20)	100 (1)	—	100 (1)	100 (4)	83.3 (24)	90.9 (22)	75.0 (4)	—	100 (5)	—
Minton													
Black	67.3 (46)	44.8 (29)	14.3 (14)	66.7 (6)	—	100 (1)	70.0 (20)	79.5 (83)	58.8 (34)	61.5 (13)	100 (3)	100 (21)	50.0 (4)
Burton	80.0 (45)	89.6 (29)	64.3 (14)	66.7 (6)	—	100 (1)	75.0 (20)	74.1 (85)	85.3 (34)	92.3 (13)	66.7 (3)	85.7 (21)	100 (4)
Clark	80.0 (45)	79.3 (29)	53.9 (13)	66.7 (6)	—	100 (1)	75.0 (20)	85.1 (80)	73.5 (34)	100 (13)	100 (3)	100 (21)	75.0 (4)

549

Douglas	60.8 (46)	44.8 (29)	14.3 (14)	50.0 (6)	—	100 (1)	75.0 (20)	73.5 (83)	50.0 (32)	76.9 (13)	100 (3)	61.9 (21)	75.0 (4)
Frankfurter	71.7 (46)	55.2 (29)	35.7 (14)	50.0 (6)	—	100 (1)	75.0 (20)	76.7 (86)	85.3 (34)	76.9 (13)	66.7 (3)	85.7 (21)	75.0 (4)
Harlan	76.9 (13)	76.9 (13)	33.3 (18)	33.3 (3)	—	100 (1)	75.0 (8)	60.7 (28)	80.0 (15)	75.0 (4)	50.0 (2)	80.0 (5)	100 (2)
Jackson	92.9 (14)	75.0 (8)	50.0 (4)	100 (1)	—	—	66.7 (6)	75.0 (28)	71.5 (7)	100 (4)	—	33.3 (3)	—
Reed	90.7 (43)	93.1 (29)	85.7 (14)	83.4 (6)	—	100 (1)	80.0 (20)	75.0 (84)	85.3 (34)	92.3 (13)	100 (3)	85.7 (21)	75.0 (4)
Warren	72.0 (50)	54.8 (31)	40.0 (15)	71.4 (7)	—	100 (1)	100 (22)	66.7 (99)	71.8 (39)	85.7 (14)	100 (2)	87.0 (23)	75.0 (4)
Reed													
Black	51.9 (52)	41.9 (31)	20.0 (15)	87.5 (8)	—	100 (1)	90.5 (21)	60.0 (95)	61.0 (41)	53.3 (15)	100 (3)	87.5 (27)	75.0 (4)
Brennan	33.3 (9)	100 (2)	100 (1)	100 (1)	—	—	100 (1)	61.5 (13)	85.7 (7)	100 (2)	—	100 (3)	—
Burton	84.6 (52)	80.6 (31)	66.7 (9)	75.0 (8)	—	100 (1)	95.5 (22)	80.6 (98)	87.8 (41)	86.7 (15)	66.7 (3)	83.4 (24)	75.0 (4)
Clark	82.6 (52)	74.2 (31)	57.2 (14)	97.5 (7)	—	100 (1)	95.5 (22)	76.1 (92)	75.0 (40)	93.3 (15)	100 (3)	87.5 (24)	75.0 (4)

(Table continues)

Table 6-5 (Continued)

Justice	Crim	CivR	1st	DP	Priv	Atty	Un'n	Econ	JudP	Fed	IR	FTax	Misc
Douglas	49.1 (53)	41.9 (31)	20.0 (15)	75.0 (8)	—	100 (1)	77.3 (22)	59.4 (96)	64.1 (39)	66.7 (15)	100 (3)	70.8 (24)	50.0 (4)
Frankfurter	67.9 (53)	48.4 (31)	40.0 (15)	37.5 (8)	—	100 (1)	72.7 (22)	70.7 (99)	70.7 (41)	73.3 (15)	66.7 (3)	83.4 (24)	50.0 (4)
Harlan	73.9 (23)	73.4 (15)	42.9 (7)	60.0 (5)	—	100 (1)	60.0 (7)	59.5 (42)	76.2 (21)	83.3 (6)	50.0 (2)	75.0 (8)	100 (2)
Jackson	72.7 (11)	75.0 (8)	50.0 (4)	100 (1)	—	—	100 (6)	81.5 (27)	28.6 (7)	75.0 (4)	—	33.3 (3)	—
Minton	90.7 (43)	93.1 (29)	85.7 (14)	83.4 (6)	—	100 (1)	80.0 (20)	75.0 (84)	85.3 (34)	92.3 (13)	100 (3)	85.7 (21)	75.0 (4)
Warren	72.0 (50)	54.8 (31)	40.0 (15)	71.4 (7)	—	100 (1)	100 (22)	66.7 (99)	71.8 (39)	85.7 (14)	100 (2)	87.0 (23)	75.0 (4)
Stewart													
Black	58.8 (252)	70.7 (164)	63.4 (120)	66.7 (21)	100 (2)	75.0 (4)	74.5 (86)	56.4 (287)	76.4 (157)	71.9 (57)	66.7 (6)	61.8 (76)	100 (1)
Brennan	72.5 (254)	71.5 (165)	71.9 (121)	95.2 (21)	0.0 (1)	50.0 (4)	81.8 (88)	69.6 (289)	81.6 (157)	92.7 (55)	66.7 (6)	79.2 (77)	100 (1)
Clark	80.0 (190)	81.1 (127)	71.1 (97)	88.2 (17)	0.0 (1)	50.0 (2)	82.8 (76)	69.5 (239)	83.0 (129)	90.7 (43)	66.7 (6)	76.1 (71)	100 (1)

Douglas	53.2 (254)	63.9 (166)	62.5 (120)	81.0 (21)	0.0 (1)	75.0 (4)	73.9 (88)	54.4 (283)	68.1 (157)	70.2 (57)	66.7 (6)	58.7 (75)	100 (1)
Fortas	66.6 (90)	59.0 (27)	63.0 (46)	100 (5)	—	66.7 (3)	70.0 (20)	70.7 (75)	83.0 (47)	85.7 (14)	—	50.0 (16)	—
Frankfurter	82.9 (76)	78.8 (33)	85.0 (40)	71.4 (7)	—	—	74.1 (27)	76.2 (101)	75.5 (45)	81.3 (16)	100 (2)	69.7 (33)	100 (1)
Goldberg	65.0 (60)	74.1 (58)	76.9 (26)	100 (5)	0.0 (1)	100 (1)	85.0 (20)	81.7 (82)	80.0 (45)	83.4 (18)	50.0 (4)	87.0 (23)	—
Harlan	79.9 (254)	77.3 (163)	73.6 (121)	76.2 (21)	0.0 (1)	75.0 (4)	83.2 (89)	80.7 (279)	82.9 (158)	92.8 (56)	66.7 (6)	89.6 (77)	100 (1)
Marshall	71.4 (49)	64.7 (34)	95.0 (20)	100 (3)	—	—	75.0 (4)	66.6 (24)	90.9 (22)	75.0 (4)	—	50.0 (4)	—
Warren	61.8 (251)	69.9 (163)	69.2 (120)	90.5 (21)	0.0 (1)	50.0 (4)	83.9 (87)	62.4 (284)	75.9 (158)	88.0 (50)	66.7 (6)	76.6 (77)	100 (1)
White	82.1 (162)	75.2 (129)	78.6 (70)	100 (12)	0.0 (1)	50.0 (4)	78.2 (55)	71.9 (167)	83.5 (109)	89.5 (38)	50.0 (4)	79.5 (39)	—
Whittaker	76.3 (76)	87.1 (31)	85.4 (41)	85.7 (7)	—	—	56.6 (23)	76.2 (101)	83.3 (42)	100 (16)	100 (2)	90.9 (33)	100 (1)
							Warren						
Black	74.3 (343)	80.8 (219)	82.8 (157)	78.8 (33)	50.0 (2)	90.0 (10)	84.8 (118)	89.2 (437)	86.7 (219)	84.5 (71)	100 (8)	86.0 (114)	60.0 (5)

(Table continues)

Table 6-5 *(Continued)*

Justice	Crim	CivR	1st	DP	Priv	Atty	Un'n	Econ	JudP	Fed	IR	FTax	Misc
Brennan	86.0 (301)	96.3 (191)	94.2 (138)	92.6 (27)	100 (2)	88.9 (9)	94.2 (103)	92.1 (355)	91.9 (186)	89.8 (59)	100 (6)	93.7 (95)	100 (1)
Burton	62.8 (94)	64.9 (57)	48.6 (35)	50.0 (12)	100 (1)	80.0 (5)	88.6 (35)	62.8 (145)	81.3 (64)	63.6 (22)	100 (2)	73.0 (37)	100 (4)
Clark	58.8 (282)	73.1 (182)	52.6 (133)	82.8 (29)	100 (1)	85.7 (7)	88.5 (113)	90.6 (383)	87.4 (191)	77.3 (66)	100 (8)	92.6 (108)	80.0 (5)
Douglas	81.3 (347)	90.0 (220)	81.1 (158)	84.9 (33)	100 (2)	80.0 (10)	77.4 (124)	86.7 (434)	78.0 (218)	83.5 (73)	100 (8)	54.9 (113)	80.0 (5)
Fortas	84.6 (91)	90.0 (60)	87.0 (46)	100 (5)	—	75.0 (4)	100 (19)	83.8 (74)	93.6 (47)	90.9 (11)	—	81.3 (16)	—
Frankfurter	56.7 (171)	74.4 (90)	60.5 (76)	50.0 (18)	100 (1)	80.0 (5)	68.8 (64)	51.0 (257)	68.8 (109)	69.4 (36)	100 (4)	90.0 (70)	80.0 (5)
Goldberg	91.6 (59)	94.8 (57)	89.3 (28)	100 (5)	100 (1)	100 (1)	90.0 (20)	80.2 (81)	84.4 (45)	82.4 (17)	75.0 (4)	86.9 (23)	—
Harlan	50.8 (317)	57.4 (202)	56.3 (151)	67.7 (31)	100 (1)	70.0 (10)	83.2 (113)	53.0 (372)	69.8 (202)	81.3 (64)	100 (7)	75.0 (100)	100 (3)
Jackson	84.6 (13)	75.0 (8)	50.0 (4)	—	—	—	100 (6)	75.0 (28)	50.0 (6)	100 (3)	—	50.0 (4)	—
Marshall	93.9 (49)	91.2 (34)	95.0 (20)	100 (3)	—	100 (1)	100 (4)	79.2 (24)	95.5 (22)	75.0 (4)	—	80.0 (5)	—

Minton	79.1 (43)	58.6 (29)	35.7 (14)	40.0 (5)	—	100 (1)	80.0 (20)	81.4 (86)	62.5 (32)	91.7 (12)	100 (2)	100 (20)	100 (4)
Reed	72.0 (50)	54.8 (31)	40.0 (15)	71.4 (7)	—	100 (1)	100 (22)	66.7 (99)	71.8 (39)	85.7 (14)	100 (2)	87.0 (23)	75.0 (4)
Stewart	61.8 (251)	69.9 (163)	69.2 (120)	90.5 (21)	0.0 (1)	50.0 (4)	83.9 (87)	62.4 (284)	75.9 (158)	88.0 (50)	66.7 (6)	76.6 (77)	100 (1)
White	65.8 (161)	78.6 (126)	68.1 (72)	100 (12)	100 (1)	80.0 (5)	94.4 (54)	84.3 (166)	87.0 (108)	91.2 (34)	100 (4)	87.5 (40)	—
Whittaker	57.0 (114)	64.9 (54)	49.0 (51)	75.0 (16)	100 (1)	0.0 (1)	50.0 (40)	49.0 (149)	84.1 (63)	63.2 (19)	100 (2)	71.4 (42)	100 (1)

White

Black	65.7 (163)	73.5 (128)	67.1 (70)	75.0 (12)	0.0 (1)	80.0 (5)	76.8 (56)	75.7 (169)	86.2 (108)	76.3 (38)	100 (4)	72.5 (40)	—
Brennan	74.2 (163)	80.5 (128)	70.8 (72)	100 (12)	100 (1)	80.0 (5)	90.9 (55)	89.4 (170)	92.5 (107)	94.4 (36)	100 (4)	90.0 (40)	—
Clark	81.0 (100)	83.4 (90)	73.0 (48)	87.5 (8)	100 (1)	100 (2)	83.7 (43)	86.5 (126)	90.1 (81)	81.5 (27)	100 (4)	93.9 (33)	—
Douglas	55.2 (163)	73.6 (129)	57.7 (71)	83.3 (12)	100 (1)	80.0 (5)	67.3 (55)	76.3 (165)	76.6 (107)	73.7 (38)	100 (4)	48.8 (39)	—
Fortas	59.8 (87)	73.8 (61)	55.5 (45)	100 (5)	—	75.0 (4)	90.0 (20)	86.1 (72)	85.4 (48)	71.4 (14)	—	73.4 (15)	—

(Table continues)

Table 6-5 (Continued)

Justice	Crim	CivR	1st	DP	Priv	Atty	Un'n	Econ	JudP	Fed	IR	FTax	Misc
Goldberg	68.3 (60)	73.2 (56)	68.0 (25)	100 (5)	100 (1)	100 (1)	85.0 (20)	82.2 (79)	82.2 (45)	87.5 (16)	75.0 (4)	78.3 (23)	—
Harlan	74.8 (163)	66.4 (128)	76.3 (72)	66.7 (12)	100 (1)	80.0 (5)	80.4 (56)	65.6 (163)	80.7 (109)	84.2 (38)	100 (4)	82.5 (40)	—
Marshall	68.8 (48)	67.6 (34)	75.0 (20)	100 (3)	—	100 (1)	100 (4)	83.3 (24)	90.9 (22)	75.0 (4)	—	100 (5)	—
Stewart	82.1 (162)	75.2 (129)	78.6 (70)	100 (12)	0.0 (1)	50.0 (4)	78.2 (55)	71.9 (167)	83.5 (109)	89.5 (38)	50.0 (4)	79.5 (39)	—
Warren	65.8 (161)	78.6 (126)	68.1 (72)	100 (12)	100 (1)	80.0 (5)	94.4 (54)	84.3 (166)	87.0 (108)	91.2 (34)	100 (4)	87.5 (40)	—
Whittaker													
Black	53.5 (114)	55.6 (54)	44.4 (54)	66.7 (15)	100 (1)	0.0 (1)	41.2 (34)	47.0 (151)	82.3 (62)	66.7 (21)	100 (2)	65.9 (41)	100 (1)
Brennan	66.4 (113)	64.8 (54)	46.3 (54)	73.3 (15)	100 (1)	0.0 (1)	52.5 (40)	55.0 (151)	81.3 (64)	87.0 (23)	100 (2)	73.8 (42)	100 (1)
Burton	86.8 (38)	86.4 (22)	100 (12)	75.0 (8)	100 (1)	100 (1)	75.0 (8)	77.5 (40)	95.4 (22)	80.0 (5)	—	55.6 (9)	—
Clark	84.4 (115)	77.8 (54)	88.7 (53)	73.3 (15)	—	0.0 (1)	70.0 (40)	62.8 (145)	90.3 (62)	90.0 (20)	100 (2)	64.3 (42)	100 (1)

	Crim	CivR	1st	DP	Priv	Atty	Un'n	Econ	JudP	Fed	IR	FTax	Misc
Douglas	46.1 (115)	52.9 (53)	37.0 (54)	60.0 (15)	100 (1)	100 (1)	40.0 (40)	41.3 (150)	71.9 (64)	65.2 (23)	100 (2)	68.3 (41)	100 (1)
Frankfurter	83.2 (113)	75.0 (52)	88.7 (53)	64.2 (14)	100 (1)	100 (1)	63.9 (36)	80.5 (148)	82.8 (64)	81.8 (22)	100 (2)	69.1 (42)	100 (1)
Harlan	83.5 (115)	73.1 (52)	92.6 (54)	73.4 (15)	0.0 (1)	100 (1)	55.0 (40)	83.7 (147)	84.4 (64)	77.2 (22)	100 (2)	73.8 (42)	100 (1)
Stewart	76.3 (76)	87.1 (31)	85.4 (41)	85.7 (7)	—	—	56.6 (23)	76.2 (101)	83.3 (42)	100 (16)	100 (2)	90.9 (33)	100 (1)
Warren	57.0 (114)	64.9 (54)	49.0 (51)	75.0 (16)	100 (1)	0.0 (1)	50.0 (40)	49.0 (149)	84.1 (63)	63.2 (19)	100 (2)	71.4 (42)	100 (1)

Note: "—" indicates that no case in issue area was decided during tenure overlap. Figures listed are the percentage of cases in which the justices voted together. Figures in parentheses are the total number of cases decided in the issue area in which both justices participated during their tenures on the Warren Court. The data include all orally argued citations. Percentages should be interpreted with care since some of the figures on which they are based are quite small.

Definitions of issue areas: Criminal procedure (Crim): the rights of persons accused of a crime except for the due process rights of prisoners; Civil rights (CivR): non–First Amendment freedom cases that pertain to classifications based on race (including Native Americans), age, indigence, voting, residence, military or handicapped status, sex, or alienage; First Amendment (1st): guarantees contained therein; Due process (DP): noncriminal procedural guarantees, plus court jurisdiction over nonresident litigants and the takings clause of the Fifth Amendment; Privacy (Priv): abortion, contraception, the Freedom of Information Act and related federal statutes; Attorneys (Atty): attorneys' fees, commercial speech, admission to and removal from the bar, and disciplinary matters; Unions (Un'n): labor union activity; Economics (Econ): commercial business activity, plus litigation involving injured persons or things, employee actions vis-à-vis employers, zoning regulations, and governmental regulation of corruption other than that involving campaign spending; Judicial power (JudP): the exercise of the judiciary's own power and authority; Federalism (Fed): conflicts between the federal and state governments, excluding those between state and federal courts, and those involving the priority of federal fiscal claims; Interstate relations (IR): conflicts between states, such as boundary disputes, and nonproperty disputes commonly arising under the full faith and credit clause of the Constitution; Federal taxation (FTax): the Internal Revenue Code and related statutes; Miscellaneous (Misc.): legislative veto, separation of powers, and matters not included in any other issue area.

Source: U.S. Supreme Court Judicial Database, with analu = 0 or 4 and dec_type = 1, 6, or 7.

Table 6-6 Voting Interagreements Among the Justices, by Issue Area: The Burger Court, 1969–1985 Terms

Justice	Crim	CivR	1st	DP	Priv	Atty	Un'n	Econ	JudP	Fed	IR	FTax	Misc
Black													
Blackmun	70.8 (24)	75.9 (29)	59.1 (22)	75.0 (4)	100 (1)	0.0 (1)	66.7 (9)	71.4 (14)	86.7 (15)	100 (1)	—	75.0 (4)	—
Brennan	58.0 (50)	59.3 (54)	71.9 (32)	40.0 (5)	0.0 (1)	50.0 (2)	66.7 (15)	83.4 (24)	75.8 (29)	80.0 (5)	100 (1)	63.6 (11)	—
Burger	65.3 (49)	80.0 (55)	62.6 (32)	60.0 (5)	100 (1)	50.0 (2)	60.0 (15)	59.0 (22)	78.6 (28)	80.0 (5)	100 (1)	81.8 (11)	—
Douglas	64.6 (48)	61.2 (54)	71.0 (31)	60.0 (5)	0.0 (1)	50.0 (2)	66.6 (15)	81.8 (22)	70.4 (27)	60.0 (5)	100 (1)	54.5 (11)	—
Harlan	52.0 (50)	66.7 (54)	53.1 (32)	40.0 (5)	100 (1)	0.0 (2)	80.0 (15)	60.8 (23)	79.3 (29)	100 (5)	100 (1)	81.8 (11)	—
Marshall	54.1 (48)	65.4 (52)	73.3 (30)	40.0 (5)	0.0 (1)	50.0 (2)	83.3 (12)	76.2 (21)	81.5 (27)	75.0 (4)	100 (1)	81.8 (11)	—
Stewart	56.0 (50)	74.6 (55)	65.6 (32)	40.0 (5)	0.0 (1)	0.0 (1)	53.3 (15)	43.5 (23)	82.8 (29)	60.0 (5)	100 (1)	90.9 (11)	—
White	65.3 (49)	70.9 (55)	65.7 (32)	40.0 (5)	100 (1)	0.0 (2)	64.3 (14)	73.9 (23)	75.9 (29)	80.0 (5)	100 (1)	81.8 (11)	—
Blackmun													
Black	70.8 (24)	75.9 (29)	59.1 (22)	75.0 (4)	100 (1)	0.0 (1)	66.7 (9)	71.4 (14)	86.7 (15)	100 (1)	—	75.0 (4)	—

Brennan	54.9 (472)	70.4 (463)	61.8 (199)	66.4 (128)	87.2 (39)	78.5 (28)	78.9 (100)	73.8 (393)	81.0 (248)	86.3 (80)	81.3 (16)	79.7 (59)	66.7 (6)
Burger	82.6 (483)	78.6 (469)	76.1 (201)	86.7 (128)	66.7 (39)	63.3 (30)	73.3 (101)	80.4 (403)	85.1 (248)	91.4 (82)	87.5 (16)	81.4 (59)	50.0 (6)
Douglas	35.0 (143)	55.5 (148)	39.3 (79)	51.5 (33)	44.4 (9)	50.0 (4)	58.4 (36)	61.1 (113)	54.2 (72)	64.3 (14)	20.0 (5)	38.9 (18)	—
Harlan	66.7 (24)	93.1 (29)	77.2 (22)	75.0 (4)	100 (1)	100 (1)	77.8 (9)	76.9 (13)	93.3 (15)	100 (1)	—	75.0 (4)	—
Marshall	52.7 (478)	71.0 (461)	62.4 (194)	67.2 (125)	87.2 (39)	77.8 (27)	79.2 (101)	78.2 (399)	81.7 (246)	85.2 (74)	81.3 (16)	78.0 (59)	50.0 (6)
O'Connor	71.3 (164)	66.9 (145)	71.2 (59)	84.4 (45)	75.0 (12)	52.9 (17)	60.0 (30)	77.8 (126)	79.2 (77)	73.7 (38)	75.0 (4)	78.9 (19)	60.0 (5)
Powell	81.7 (435)	75.4 (402)	79.0 (167)	75.9 (108)	71.4 (35)	68.0 (25)	70.5 (88)	77.9 (327)	84.2 (221)	80.3 (71)	87.6 (16)	70.6 (51)	50.0 (6)
Rehnquist	77.6 (439)	65.3 (417)	65.3 (173)	80.1 (116)	58.4 (36)	51.7 (29)	69.3 (88)	75.2 (367)	82.4 (227)	60.8 (79)	87.6 (16)	72.2 (54)	33.3 (6)
Stevens	65.9 (317)	72.4 (297)	68.2 (110)	68.9 (87)	72.4 (29)	72.0 (25)	75.0 (64)	72.4 (268)	78.4 (157)	75.0 (64)	72.7 (11)	57.9 (38)	66.7 (6)
Stewart	74.4 (321)	79.2 (323)	68.3 (142)	74.4 (82)	63.0 (27)	91.7 (12)	64.8 (71)	73.1 (257)	81.7 (169)	61.5 (39)	75.0 (12)	59.5 (37)	0.0 (1)
White	79.4 (482)	79.5 (468)	73.6 (201)	83.5 (127)	59.0 (39)	66.6 (30)	84.1 (101)	78.5 (399)	83.9 (249)	90.2 (182)	87.6 (16)	79.7 (59)	66.7 (6)

(Table continues)

Table 6-6 (Continued)

Justice	Crim	CivR	1st	DP	Priv	Atty	Un'n	Econ	JudP	Fed	IR	FTax	Misc
						Brennan							
Black	58.0 (50)	59.3 (54)	71.9 (32)	40.0 (5)	0.0 (1)	50.0 (2)	66.7 (15)	83.4 (24)	75.8 (29)	80.0 (5)	100 (1)	63.6 (11)	—
Blackmun	54.9 (472)	70.4 (463)	61.8 (199)	66.4 (128)	87.2 (39)	78.5 (28)	78.9 (100)	73.8 (393)	81.0 (248)	86.3 (80)	81.3 (16)	79.7 (59)	66.7 (6)
Burger	43.9 (503)	53.0 (494)	45.2 (212)	55.0 (129)	52.5 (40)	51.6 (31)	58.3 (108)	66.8 (410)	73.6 (265)	80.0 (85)	94.1 (17)	79.4 (68)	85.7 (7)
Douglas	80.2 (167)	89.6 (173)	78.7 (89)	79.4 (34)	77.7 (9)	80.0 (5)	59.5 (42)	80.5 (123)	66.3 (86)	72.2 (18)	50.0 (6)	69.2 (26)	—
Harlan	66.6 (51)	64.2 (53)	68.8 (32)	100 (5)	0.0 (1)	50.0 (2)	60.0 (15)	68.0 (25)	75.9 (29)	80.0 (5)	100 (1)	81.8 (11	—
Marshall	92.9 (496)	94.9 (483)	92.7 (205)	89.7 (126)	94.9 (39)	100 (28)	93.3 (105)	84.4 (405)	93.5 (261)	93.6 (78)	88.2 (17)	86.8 (68)	85.7 (7)
O'Connor	41.2 (165)	64.2 (145)	55.0 (60)	62.2 (45)	75.0 (12)	33.3 (18)	63.3 (30)	72.0 (125)	81.8 (77)	75.0 (36)	75.0 (4)	68.4 (19)	80.0 (5)
Powell	51.1 (429)	56.9 (402)	56.5 (170)	62.9 (108)	63.9 (36)	56.0 (25)	64.0 (89)	69.9 (322)	72.5 (222)	77.1 (70)	81.3 (16)	83.1 (53)	85.7 (7)
Rehnquist	36.3 (435)	41.2 (417)	31.4 (175)	45.7 (116)	48.6 (37)	37.9 (29)	55.1 (89)	64.4 (363)	71.7 (230)	60.3 (78)	81.3 (16)	75.0 (56)	71.4 (7)

Stevens	71.6 (310)	75.4 (297)	71.4 (112)	67.8 (87)	70.0 (30)	80.0 (25)	73.9 (65)	72.1 (265)	74.2 (159)	74.6 (63)	72.7 (11)	69.2 (39)	85.7 (7)
Stewart	64.1 (340)	60.1 (348)	75.2 (153)	61.4 (83)	57.2 (28)	83.3 (12)	60.2 (78)	65.3 (268)	73.6 (186)	63.6 (44)	92.3 (13)	67.3 (46)	100 (2)
White	55.4 (502)	71.2 (493)	49.3 (213)	64.1 (128)	50.0 (40)	48.4 (31)	83.2 (107)	80.6 (408)	81.2 (266)	88.3 (85)	82.4 (17)	82.4 (68)	42.9 (7)
Burger													
Black	65.3 (49)	80.0 (55)	62.6 (32)	60.0 (5)	100 (1)	50.0 (2)	60.0 (15)	59.0 (22)	78.6 (28)	80.0 (5)	100 (1)	81.8 (11)	—
Blackmun	82.6 (483)	78.6 (469)	76.1 (201)	86.7 (128)	66.7 (39)	63.3 (30)	73.3 (101)	80.4 (403)	85.1 (248)	91.4 (82)	87.5 (16)	81.4 (59)	50.0 (6)
Brennan	43.9 (503)	53.0 (494)	45.2 (212)	55.0 (129)	52.5 (40)	51.6 (31)	58.3 (108)	66.8 (410)	73.6 (265)	80.0 (85)	94.1 (17)	79.4 (68)	85.7 (7)
Douglas	34.3 (169)	49.4 (174)	34.9 (89)	52.9 (34)	33.3 (9)	80.0 (5)	54.8 (42)	52.4 (126)	56.0 (84)	66.7 (18)	50.0 (6)	57.6 (26)	—
Harlan	78.0 (50)	87.1 (54)	78.2 (32)	80.0 (5)	100 (1)	50.0 (2)	80.0 (15)	82.6 (23)	96.5 (28)	80.0 (5)	100 (1)	81.8 (11)	—
Marshall	41.3 (508)	53.0 (489)	43.7 (206)	57.1 (126)	53.8 (39)	53.3 (30)	59.1 (105)	73.4 (414)	72.8 (261)	80.1 (80)	94.1 (17)	80.9 (68)	100 (7)
O'Connor	90.2 (164)	86.2 (145)	85.0 (60)	93.3 (45)	83.3 (12)	100 (18)	86.7 (30)	85.8 (126)	88.4 (78)	78.9 (38)	75.0 (4)	84.2 (19)	100 (5)

(Table continues)

Table 6-6 (Continued)

Justice	Crim	CivR	1st	DP	Priv	Atty	Un'n	Econ	JudP	Fed	IR	FTax	Misc
Powell	87.3 (440)	87.0 (407)	78.2 (170)	82.4 (108)	83.3 (36)	96.3 (27)	83.1 (89)	86.1 (331)	91.5 (223)	80.8 (73)	87.5 (16)	81.1 (53)	100 (7)
Rehnquist	90.1 (440)	86.0 (422)	85.8 (176)	93.1 (116)	91.9 (37)	87.1 (31)	86.5 (89)	85.8 (374)	92.6 (231)	61.7 (81)	87.5 (16)	78.6 (56)	85.7 (7)
Stevens	57.1 (322)	67.2 (302)	58.4 (113)	70.1 (87)	70.0 (30)	66.7 (27)	67.7 (65)	72.6 (270)	73.8 (160)	68.2 (66)	63.6 (11)	66.7 (39)	85.7 (7)
Stewart	76.7 (352)	82.2 (354)	63.6 (154)	79.5 (83)	71.4 (28)	92.8 (14)	67.9 (78)	82.3 (271)	84.3 (185)	64.5 (45)	92.3 (13)	69.5 (46)	100 (2)
White	85.0 (513)	76.1 (499)	86.0 (214)	84.4 (128)	82.5 (40)	84.9 (33)	63.6 (107)	79.8 (416)	86.8 (266)	87.5 (88)	88.2 (17)	76.5 (68)	57.1 (7)
							Douglas						
Black	64.6 (48)	61.2 (54)	71.0 (31)	60.0 (5)	0.0 (1)	50.0 (2)	66.6 (15)	81.8 (22)	70.4 (27)	60.0 (5)	100 (1)	54.5 (11)	—
Blackmun	35.0 (143)	55.5 (148)	39.3 (79)	51.5 (33)	44.4 (9)	50.0 (4)	58.4 (36)	61.1 (113)	54.2 (72)	64.3 (14)	20.0 (5)	38.9 (18)	—
Brennan	80.2 (167)	89.6 (173)	78.7 (89)	79.4 (34)	77.7 (9)	80.0 (5)	59.5 (42)	80.5 (123)	66.3 (86)	72.2 (18)	50.0 (6)	69.2 (26)	—
Burger	34.3 (169)	49.4 (174)	34.9 (89)	52.9 (34)	33.3 (9)	80.0 (5)	54.8 (42)	52.4 (126)	56.0 (84)	66.7 (18)	50.0 (6)	57.6 (26)	—

Harlan	57.1 (49)	82.3 (40)	38.7 (31)	80.0 (5)	0.0 (1)	50.0 (2)	60.0 (15)	56.5 (23)	63.0 (27)	60.0 (5)	100 (1)	72.7 (11)	—
Marshall	86.8 (167)	85.8 (169)	79.1 (86)	85.3 (34)	77.7 (9)	66.7 (3)	66.7 (39)	69.9 (123)	68.2 (85)	70.6 (17)	50.0 (6)	57.7 (26)	—
Powell	37.3 (110)	55.5 (99)	45.3 (53)	50.0 (22)	60.0 (5)	50.0 (2)	50.0 (24)	57.7 (71)	56.0 (50)	50.0 (12)	20.0 (5)	76.9 (13)	—
Rehnquist	28.6 (105)	35.3 (102)	24.5 (53)	33.4 (24)	16.7 (6)	33.3 (3)	62.5 (24)	53.9 (89)	54.7 (53)	63.7 (11)	20.0 (5)	50.0 (14)	—
Stewart	55.3 (170)	64.7 (173)	65.2 (89)	61.8 (34)	66.6 (9)	75.0 (4)	54.7 (42)	53.1 (115)	62.8 (86)	66.7 (18)	50.0 (6)	64.0 (25)	—
White	44.1 (168)	65.3 (173)	37.0 (89)	55.8 (34)	22.2 (9)	40.0 (5)	51.2 (41)	69.2 (127)	58.1 (86)	55.6 (18)	50.0 (6)	57.6 (26)	—
						Harlan							
Black	52.0 (50)	66.7 (54)	53.1 (32)	40.0 (5)	100 (1)	0.0 (2)	80.0 (15)	60.8 (23)	79.3 (29)	100 (5)	100 (1)	81.8 (11)	—
Blackmun	66.7 (24)	93.1 (29)	77.2 (22)	75.0 (4)	100 (1)	100 (1)	77.8 (9)	76.9 (13)	93.3 (15)	100 (1)	—	75.0 (4)	—
Brennan	66.6 (51)	64.2 (53)	68.8 (32)	100 (5)	0.0 (1)	50.0 (2)	60.0 (15)	68.0 (25)	75.9 (29)	80.0 (5)	100 (1)	81.8 (11)	—
Burger	78.0 (50)	87.1 (54)	78.2 (32)	80.0 (5)	100 (1)	50.0 (2)	80.0 (15)	82.6 (23)	96.5 (28)	80.0 (5)	100 (1)	81.8 (11)	—

(Table continues)

Table 6-6 (Continued)

Justice	Crim	CivR	1st	DP	Priv	Atty	Un'n	Econ	JudP	Fed	IR	FTax	Misc
Douglas	57.1 (49)	82.3 (40)	38.7 (31)	80.0 (5)	0.0 (1)	50.0 (2)	60.0 (15)	56.5 (23)	63.0 (27)	60.0 (5)	100 (1)	72.7 (11)	—
Marshall	71.5 (49)	64.7 (51)	70.0 (30)	100 (5)	0.0 (1)	50.0 (2)	83.3 (12)	77.3 (22)	77.8 (27)	75.0 (4)	100 (1)	100 (11)	—
Stewart	80.4 (51)	87.1 (54)	81.2 (32)	100 (5)	0.0 (1)	100 (1)	60.0 (15)	83.3 (24)	89.7 (29)	60.0 (5)	100 (1)	72.7 (11)	—
White	78.0 (50)	88.9 (54)	75.1 (32)	100 (5)	100 (1)	50.0 (2)	42.9 (14)	68.0 (25)	82.8 (29)	80.0 (5)	100 (1)	100 (11)	—
						Marshall							
Black	54.1 (48)	65.4 (52)	73.3 (30)	40.0 (5)	0.0 (1)	50.0 (2)	83.3 (12)	76.2 (21)	81.5 (27)	75.0 (4)	100 (1)	81.8 (11)	—
Blackmun	52.7 (478)	71.0 (461)	62.4 (194)	67.2 (125)	87.2 (39)	77.8 (27)	79.2 (101)	78.2 (399)	81.7 (246)	85.2 (74)	81.3 (16)	78.0 (59)	50.0 (6)
Brennan	92.9 (496)	94.9 (483)	92.7 (205)	89.7 (126)	94.9 (39)	100 (28)	93.3 (105)	84.4 (405)	93.5 (261)	93.6 (78)	88.2 (17)	86.8 (68)	85.7 (7)
Burger	41.3 (508)	53.0 (489)	43.7 (206)	57.1 (126)	53.8 (39)	53.3 (30)	59.1 (105)	73.4 (414)	72.8 (261)	80.1 (80)	94.1 (17)	80.9 (68)	100 (7)
Douglas	86.8 (167)	85.8 (169)	79.1 (86)	85.3 (34)	77.7 (9)	66.7 (3)	66.7 (39)	69.9 (123)	68.2 (85)	70.6 (17)	50.0 (6)	57.7 (26)	—

Harlan	71.5 (49)	64.7 (51)	70.0 (30)	100 (5)	0.0 (1)	50.0 (2)	83.3 (12)	77.3 (22)	77.8 (27)	75.0 (4)	100 (1)	100 (11)	—
O'Connor	36.4 (162)	60.8 (143)	55.9 (59)	65.1 (43)	75.0 (12)	35.3 (17)	60.0 (30)	70.9 (124)	77.6 (76)	70.6 (34)	75.0 (4)	73.7 (19)	100 (5)
Powell	49.8 (434)	55.7 (399)	56.6 (166)	63.8 (105)	71.5 (35)	60.0 (25)	66.3 (89)	74.4 (329)	74.1 (220)	74.2 (66)	81.3 (16)	81.1 (53)	100 (7)
Rehnquist	33.6 (438)	39.1 (414)	32.2 (171)	46.9 (113)	50.0 (36)	39.3 (28)	57.3 (89)	67.9 (371)	72.3 (228)	56.8 (74)	81.3 (16)	76.8 (56)	85.7 (7)
Stevens	69.9 (318)	71.3 (296)	73.3 (109)	69.1 (84)	68.9 (29)	84.6 (26)	72.3 (65)	68.7 (268)	73.1 (156)	72.9 (59)	54.5 (11)	69.3 (39)	85.7 (7)
Stewart	63.4 (347)	59.7 (345)	77.0 (148)	68.3 (82)	66.7 (27)	83.3 (12)	66.7 (75)	72.9 (270)	78.2 (183)	65.9 (41)	92.3 (13)	67.4 (46)	100 (2)
White	53.2 (506)	71.5 (488)	49.7 (207)	61.6 (125)	51.3 (39)	53.3 (30)	82.8 (105)	80.9 (412)	77.9 (263)	87.5 (80)	82.4 (17)	89.7 (68)	57.1 (7)
							O'Connor						
Blackmun	71.3 (164)	66.9 (145)	71.2 (59)	84.4 (45)	75.0 (12)	52.9 (17)	60.0 (30)	77.8 (126)	79.2 (77)	73.7 (38)	75.0 (4)	78.9 (19)	60.0 (5)
Brennan	41.2 (165)	64.2 (145)	55.0 (60)	62.2 (45)	75.0 (12)	33.3 (18)	63.3 (30)	72.0 (125)	81.8 (77)	75.0 (36)	75.0 (4)	68.4 (19)	80.0 (5)
Burger	90.2 (164)	86.2 (145)	85.0 (60)	93.3 (45)	83.3 (12)	100 (18)	86.7 (30)	85.8 (126)	88.4 (78)	78.9 (38)	75.0 (4)	84.2 (19)	100 (5)

(Table continues)

Table 6-6 (Continued)

Justice	Crim	CivR	1st	DP	Priv	Atty	Un'n	Econ	JudP	Fed	IR	FTax	Misc
Marshall	36.4 (162)	60.8 (143)	55.9 (59)	65.1 (43)	75.0 (12)	35.3 (17)	60.0 (30)	70.9 (124)	77.6 (76)	70.6 (34)	75.0 (4)	73.7 (19)	100 (5)
Powell	86.7 (157)	84.4 (134)	81.0 (58)	86.8 (38)	75.0 (12)	93.8 (16)	80.0 (30)	83.5 (109)	88.1 (76)	77.4 (31)	75.0 (4)	77.8 (18)	100 (5)
Rehnquist	93.3 (165)	79.2 (144)	80.4 (61)	91.1 (45)	91.7 (12)	100 (18)	90.0 (30)	86.3 (124)	97.5 (77)	89.5 (38)	75.0 (4)	84.2 (19)	80.0 (5)
Stevens	60.3 (164)	70.9 (144)	58.4 (60)	68.2 (44)	58.3 (12)	61.1 (18)	70.0 (30)	75.0 (124)	72.4 (76)	70.3 (37)	75.0 (4)	68.5 (19)	80.0 (5)
White	81.8 (165)	80.6 (145)	78.7 (61)	81.8 (44)	91.7 (12)	94.5 (18)	66.7 (30)	73.5 (121)	85.9 (78)	73.7 (38)	75.0 (4)	73.7 (19)	60.0 (5)
Powell													
Blackmun	81.7 (435)	75.4 (402)	79.0 (167)	75.9 (108)	71.4 (35)	68.0 (25)	70.5 (88)	77.9 (327)	84.2 (221)	80.3 (71)	87.6 (16)	70.6 (51)	50.0 (6)
Brennan	51.1 (429)	56.9 (402)	56.5 (170)	62.9 (108)	63.9 (36)	56.0 (25)	64.0 (89)	69.9 (322)	72.5 (222)	77.1 (70)	81.3 (16)	83.1 (53)	85.7 (7)
Burger	87.3 (440)	87.0 (407)	78.2 (170)	82.4 (108)	83.3 (36)	96.3 (27)	83.1 (89)	86.1 (331)	91.5 (223)	80.8 (73)	87.5 (16)	81.1 (53)	100 (7)
Douglas	37.3 (110)	55.5 (99)	45.3 (53)	50.0 (22)	60.0 (5)	50.0 (2)	50.0 (24)	57.7 (71)	56.0 (50)	50.0 (12)	20.0 (5)	76.9 (13)	—

Marshall	49.8 (434)	55.7 (399)	56.6 (166)	63.8 (105)	71.5 (35)	60.0 (25)	66.3 (89)	74.4 (329)	74.1 (220)	74.2 (66)	81.3 (16)	81.1 (53)	100 (7)
O'Connor	86.7 (157)	84.4 (134)	81.0 (58)	86.8 (38)	75.0 (12)	93.8 (16)	80.0 (30)	83.5 (109)	88.1 (76)	77.4 (31)	75.0 (4)	77.8 (18)	100 (5)
Rehnquist	83.2 (430)	83.4 (398)	70.0 (170)	77.1 (105)	74.3 (35)	81.5 (27)	78.5 (88)	81.9 (326)	89.2 (221)	62.5 (72)	100 (16)	75.5 (53)	85.7 (7)
Stevens	63.6 (308)	68.3 (287)	61.6 (107)	62.9 (78)	76.7 (30)	72.0 (25)	71.9 (64)	72.5 (240)	74.0 (154)	82.7 (58)	54.5 (11)	67.6 (37)	85.7 (7)
Stewart	79.9 (284)	85.3 (272)	68.1 (113)	78.3 (69)	95.9 (23)	90.9 (11)	82.4 (58)	82.8 (210)	82.1 (145)	64.1 (39)	75.0 (12)	72.8 (33)	100 (2)
White	82.2 (439)	74.6 (406)	73.6 (171)	83.2 (107)	77.8 (36)	85.2 (27)	68.5 (89)	78.9 (328)	85.2 (223)	79.5 (73)	87.6 (16)	71.7 (53)	57.1 (7)

Rehnquist

Blackmun	77.6 (439)	65.3 (417)	65.3 (173)	80.1 (116)	58.4 (36)	51.7 (29)	69.3 (88)	75.2 (367)	82.4 (227)	60.8 (79)	87.6 (16)	72.2 (54)	33.3 (6)
Brennan	36.3 (435)	41.2 (417)	31.4 (175)	45.7 (116)	48.6 (37)	37.9 (29)	55.1 (89)	64.4 (363)	71.7 (230)	60.3 (78)	81.3 (16)	75.0 (56)	71.4 (7)
Burger	90.1 (444)	86.0 (422)	85.8 (176)	93.1 (116)	91.9 (37)	87.1 (31)	86.5 (89)	85.8 (374)	92.6 (231)	61.7 (81)	87.5 (16)	78.6 (56)	85.7 (7)
Douglas	28.6 (105)	35.3 (102)	24.5 (53)	33.4 (24)	16.7 (6)	33.3 (3)	62.5 (24)	53.9 (89)	54.7 (53)	63.7 (11)	20.0 (5)	50.0 (14)	—

(Table continues)

Table 6-6 *(Continued)*

Justice	Crim	CivR	1st	DP	Priv	Atty	Un'n	Econ	JudP	Fed	IR	FTax	Misc
Marshall	33.6 (438)	39.1 (414)	32.2 (171)	46.9 (113)	50.0 (36)	39.3 (28)	57.3 (89)	67.9 (371)	72.3 (228)	56.8 (74)	81.3 (16)	76.8 (56)	85.7 (7)
O'Connor	93.3 (165)	79.2 (144)	80.4 (61)	91.1 (45)	91.7 (12)	100 (18)	90.0 (30)	86.3 (124)	97.5 (77)	89.5 (38)	75.0 (4)	84.2 (19)	80.0 (5)
Powell	83.2 (430)	83.4 (398)	70.0 (170)	77.1 (105)	74.3 (35)	81.5 (27)	78.5 (88)	81.9 (326)	89.2 (221)	62.5 (72)	100 (16)	75.5 (53)	85.7 (7)
Stevens	54.2 (317)	63.3 (297)	51.3 (113)	64.3 (84)	66.6 (30)	55.6 (27)	62.5 (64)	69.4 (262)	74.1 (158)	69.7 (66)	54.5 (11)	77.0 (39)	71.4 (7)
Stewart	67.5 (280)	79.4 (277)	49.1 (116)	72.9 (70)	68.0 (25)	61.5 (13)	78.0 (59)	85.3 (231)	84.1 (151)	68.4 (38)	75.0 (12)	85.3 (34)	100 (2)
White	79.7 (443)	67.0 (421)	77.9 (177)	80.0 (115)	91.9 (37)	87.1 (31)	66.2 (89)	76.5 (370)	85.3 (231)	61.7 (81)	87.6 (16)	67.9 (56)	71.4 (7)
Stevens													
Blackmun	65.9 (317)	72.4 (297)	68.2 (110)	68.9 (87)	72.4 (29)	72.0 (25)	75.0 (64)	72.4 (268)	78.4 (157)	75.0 (64)	72.7 (11)	57.9 (38)	66.7 (6)
Brennan	71.6 (310)	75.4 (297)	71.4 (112)	67.8 (87)	70.0 (30)	80.0 (25)	73.9 (65)	72.1 (265)	74.2 (159)	74.6 (63)	72.7 (11)	69.2 (39)	85.7 (7)
Burger	57.1 (322)	67.2 (302)	58.4 (113)	70.1 (87)	70.0 (30)	66.7 (27)	67.7 (65)	72.6 (270)	73.8 (160)	68.2 (66)	63.6 (11)	66.7 (39)	85.7 (7)

Marshall	69.9 (318)	71.3 (296)	73.3 (109)	69.1 (84)	68.9 (29)	84.6 (26)	72.3 (65)	68.7 (268)	73.1 (156)	72.9 (59)	54.5 (11)	69.3 (39)	85.7 (7)
O'Connor	60.3 (164)	70.9 (144)	58.4 (60)	68.2 (44)	58.3 (12)	61.1 (18)	70.0 (30)	75.0 (124)	72.4 (76)	70.3 (37)	75.0 (4)	68.5 (19)	80.0 (5)
Powell	63.6 (308)	68.3 (287)	61.6 (107)	62.9 (78)	76.7 (30)	72.0 (25)	71.9 (64)	72.5 (240)	74.0 (154)	82.7 (58)	54.5 (11)	67.6 (37)	85.7 (7)
Rehnquist	54.2 (317)	63.3 (297)	51.3 (113)	64.3 (84)	66.6 (30)	55.6 (27)	62.5 (64)	69.4 (262)	74.1 (158)	69.7 (66)	54.5 (11)	77.0 (39)	71.4 (7)
Stewart	74.9 (159)	70.9 (158)	72.3 (54)	59.6 (42)	77.8 (18)	88.9 (9)	71.5 (35)	73.7 (137)	77.5 (80)	50.0 (24)	57.1 (7)	83.4 (18)	100 (2)
White	63.0 (322)	71.5 (302)	57.9 (114)	66.3 (86)	66.6 (30)	70.4 (27)	73.9 (65)	74.1 (267)	72.3 (159)	78.8 (66)	63.6 (11)	61.6 (39)	42.9 (7)

Stewart

Black	56.0 (50)	74.6 (55)	65.6 (32)	40.0 (5)	0.0 (1)	0.0 (1)	53.3 (15)	43.5 (23)	82.8 (29)	60.0 (5)	100 (1)	90.9 (11)	—
Blackmun	74.4 (321)	79.2 (323)	68.3 (142)	74.4 (82)	63.0 (27)	91.7 (12)	64.8 (71)	73.1 (257)	81.7 (169)	61.5 (39)	75.0 (12)	59.5 (37)	0.0 (1)
Brennan	64.1 (340)	60.1 (348)	75.2 (153)	61.4 (83)	57.2 (28)	83.3 (12)	60.2 (78)	65.3 (268)	73.6 (186)	63.6 (44)	92.3 (13)	67.3 (46)	100 (2)
Burger	76.7 (352)	82.2 (354)	63.6 (154)	79.5 (83)	71.4 (28)	92.8 (14)	67.9 (78)	82.3 (271)	84.3 (185)	64.5 (45)	92.3 (13)	69.5 (46)	100 (2)

(Table continues)

Table 6-6 (*Continued*)

Justice	Crim	CivR	1st	DP	Priv	Atty	Un'n	Econ	JudP	Fed	IR	FTax	Misc
Douglas	55.3 (170)	64.7 (173)	65.2 (89)	61.8 (34)	66.6 (9)	75.0 (4)	54.7 (42)	53.1 (115)	62.8 (86)	66.7 (18)	50.0 (6)	64.0 (25)	—
Harlan	80.4 (51)	87.1 (54)	81.2 (32)	100 (5)	0.0 (1)	100 (1)	60.0 (15)	83.3 (24)	89.7 (29)	60.0 (5)	100 (1)	72.7 (11)	—
Marshall	63.4 (347)	59.7 (345)	77.0 (148)	68.3 (82)	66.7 (27)	83.3 (12)	66.7 (75)	72.9 (270)	78.2 (183)	65.9 (41)	92.3 (13)	67.4 (46)	100 (2)
Powell	79.9 (284)	85.3 (272)	68.1 (113)	78.3 (69)	95.9 (23)	90.9 (11)	82.4 (58)	82.8 (210)	82.1 (145)	64.1 (39)	75.0 (12)	72.8 (33)	100 (2)
Rehnquist	67.5 (280)	79.4 (277)	49.1 (116)	72.9 (70)	68.0 (25)	61.5 (13)	78.0 (59)	85.3 (231)	84.1 (151)	68.4 (38)	75.0 (12)	85.3 (34)	100 (2)
Stevens	74.9 (159)	70.9 (158)	72.3 (54)	59.6 (42)	77.8 (18)	88.9 (9)	71.5 (35)	73.7 (137)	77.5 (80)	50.0 (24)	57.1 (7)	83.4 (18)	100 (2)
White	77.2 (350)	73.7 (353)	66.2 (154)	78.3 (83)	71.4 (28)	71.4 (14)	59.7 (77)	75.9 (274)	78.0 (186)	60.0 (45)	76.9 (13)	60.9 (46)	50.0 (2)
							White						
Black	65.3 (49)	70.9 (55)	65.7 (32)	40.0 (5)	100 (1)	0.0 (2)	64.3 (14)	73.9 (23)	75.9 (29)	80.0 (5)	100 (1)	81.8 (11)	—
Blackmun	79.4 (482)	79.5 (468)	73.6 (201)	83.5 (127)	59.0 (39)	66.6 (30)	84.1 (101)	78.5 (399)	83.9 (249)	90.2 (82)	87.6 (16)	79.7 (59)	66.7 (6)

Justice												
Brennan	55.4 (502)	71.2 (493)	49.3 (213)	64.1 (128)	50.0 (40)	48.4 (31)	83.2 (107)	80.6 (408)	81.2 (266)	88.3 (85)	82.4 (17)	82.4 (68)	42.9 (7)
Burger	85.0 (513)	76.1 (499)	86.0 (214)	84.4 (128)	82.5 (40)	84.9 (33)	63.6 (107)	79.8 (416)	86.8 (266)	87.5 (88)	88.2 (17)	76.5 (68)	57.1 (7)
Douglas	44.1 (168)	65.3 (173)	37.0 (89)	55.8 (34)	22.2 (9)	40.0 (5)	51.2 (41)	69.2 (127)	58.1 (86)	55.6 (18)	50.0 (6)	57.6 (26)	—
Harlan	78.0 (50)	88.9 (54)	75.1 (32)	100 (5)	100 (1)	50.0 (2)	42.9 (14)	68.0 (25)	82.8 (29)	80.0 (5)	100 (1)	100 (11)	—
Marshall	53.2 (506)	71.5 (488)	49.7 (207)	61.6 (125)	51.3 (39)	53.3 (30)	82.8 (105)	80.9 (412)	77.9 (263)	87.5 (80)	82.4 (17)	89.7 (68)	57.1 (7)
O'Connor	81.8 (165)	80.6 (145)	78.7 (61)	81.8 (44)	91.7 (12)	94.5 (18)	66.7 (30)	73.5 (121)	85.9 (78)	73.7 (38)	75.0 (4)	73.7 (19)	60.0 (5)
Powell	82.2 (439)	74.6 (406)	73.6 (171)	83.2 (107)	77.8 (36)	85.2 (27)	68.5 (89)	78.9 (328)	85.2 (223)	79.5 (73)	87.6 (16)	71.7 (53)	57.1 (7)
Rehnquist	79.7 (443)	67.0 (421)	77.9 (177)	80.0 (115)	91.9 (37)	87.1 (31)	66.2 (89)	76.5 (370)	85.3 (231)	61.7 (81)	87.6 (16)	67.9 (56)	71.4 (7)
Stevens	63.0 (322)	71.5 (302)	57.9 (114)	66.3 (86)	66.6 (30)	70.4 (27)	73.9 (65)	74.1 (267)	72.3 (159)	78.8 (66)	63.6 (11)	61.6 (39)	42.9 (7)
Stewart	77.2 (350)	73.7 (353)	66.2 (154)	78.3 (83)	71.4 (28)	71.4 (14)	59.7 (77)	75.9 (274)	78.0 (186)	60.0 (45)	76.9 (13)	60.9 (46)	50.0 (2)

Note: "—" indicates that no case in issue area was decided during tenure overlap. Figures listed are the percentage of cases in which the justices voted together. Figures in parentheses are the total number of cases decided in the issue area in which both justices participated during their tenures on the Burger

(Notes continue)

Court. The data include all orally argued citations. Readers should take care in interpreting the percentages since some of the figures on which they are based are quite small.

The issue areas are defined as follows: Criminal procedure (Crim): the rights of persons accused of crime except for the due process rights of prisoners; Civil rights (CivR): non–First Amendment freedom cases that pertain to classifications based on race (including Native Americans), age, indigence, voting, residence, military or handicapped status, sex, or alienage; First Amendment (1st): guarantees contained therein; Due process (DP): noncriminal procedural guarantees, plus court jurisdiction over nonresident litigants and the takings clause of the Fifth Amendment; Privacy (Priv): abortion, contraception, the Freedom of Information Act and related federal statutes; Attorneys (Atty): attorneys' fees, commercial speech, admission to and removal from the bar, and disciplinary matters; Unions (Un'n): labor union activity; Economics (Econ): commercial business activity, plus litigation involving injured persons or things, employee actions vis-à-vis employers, zoning regulations, and governmental regulation of corruption other than that involving campaign spending; Judicial power (JudP): the exercise of the judiciary's own power and authority; Federalism (Fed): conflicts between the federal and state governments, excluding those between state and federal courts, and those involving the priority of federal fiscal claims; Interstate relations (IR): conflicts between states, such as boundary disputes, and nonproperty disputes commonly arising under the full faith and credit clause of the Constitution; Federal taxation (FTax): the Internal Revenue Code and related statutes; Miscellaneous (Misc): legislative veto, separation of powers, and matters not included in any other issue area.

Source: U.S. Supreme Court Judicial Database, with analu = 0 or 4 and dec_type = 1, 6, or 7.

Table 6-7 Voting Interagreements Among the Justices, by Issue Area: The Rehnquist Court, 1986–2001 Terms

Justice	Crim	CivR	1st	DP	Priv	Atty	Un'n	Econ	JudP	Fed	IR	FTax	Misc
						Blackmun							
Brennan	71.3 (136)	88.8 (80)	81.5 (54)	72.8 (33)	87.5 (8)	93.3 (15)	81.0 (21)	82.0 (89)	97.1 (69)	86.8 (38)	100.0 (6)	76.5 (17)	100.0 (5)
Ginsburg	65.2 (23)	66.7 (12)	50.0 (4)	100.0 (3)	100.0 (3)	100.0 (2)	100.0 (1)	61.9 (21)	77.8 (9)	100.0 (4)	—	100.0 (1)	—
Kennedy	57.3 (185)	52.5 (101)	73.3 (60)	60.7 (28)	57.1 (14)	72.2 (18)	69.5 (23)	71.8 (145)	81.3 (107)	79.5 (44)	55.6 (9)	86.9 (23)	100.0 (1)
Marshall	71.4 (168)	90.7 (96)	83.3 (60)	83.4 (36)	80.0 (10)	93.8 (16)	79.3 (29)	81.4 (113)	94.2 (85)	90.2 (41)	87.5 (8)	70.0 (20)	85.7 (7)
O'Connor	55.7 (239)	55.8 (138)	57.6 (80)	60.8 (46)	81.3 (16)	52.1 (23)	72.8 (33)	65.5 (177)	88.0 (134)	76.3 (55)	80.0 (10)	77.5 (31)	85.7 (7)
Powell	58.5 (41)	56.5 (23)	50.0 (12)	78.5 (14)	100.0 (1)	0.0 (3)	80.0 (5)	76.2 (21)	93.3 (15)	90.9 (11)	100.0 (1)	75.0 (4)	100.0 (1)
Rehnquist	52.1 (240)	44.6 (139)	47.5 (78)	52.2 (46)	62.5 (16)	47.8 (23)	69.7 (33)	72.1 (179)	78.5 (135)	79.3 (58)	70.0 (10)	77.4 (31)	85.7 (7)
Scalia	49.6 (24)	50.0 (138)	51.9 (79)	56.5 (46)	42.9 (14)	52.2 (23)	78.8 (33)	66.8 (178)	79.6 (132)	81.0 (58)	60.0 (10)	74.2 (31)	57.1 (7)
Souter	65.0 (100)	71.2 (59)	73.1 (26)	75.0 (12)	85.7 (7)	62.5 (8)	75.0 (12)	70.1 (87)	83.9 (62)	88.9 (18)	75.0 (4)	69.2 (13)	100.0 (2)

(Table continues)

Table 6-7 (Continued)

Justice	Crim	CivR	1st	DP	Priv	Atty	Un'n	Econ	JudP	Fed	IR	FTax	Misc
Stevens	76.3 (24)	79.9 (139)	71.3 (80)	80.5 (46)	81.3 (16)	95.5 (22)	75.7 (33)	72.6 (179)	84.4 (135)	82.5 (57)	88.9 (9)	74.2 (31)	85.7 (7)
Thomas	48.6 (70)	52.5 (40)	33.3 (18)	25.0 (8)	60.0 (5)	60.0 (5)	50.0 (4)	57.9 (64)	82.6 (46)	68.8 (16)	50.0 (2)	72.7 (11)	—
White	60.7 (216)	60.7 (127)	55.2 (76)	69.8 (43)	53.8 (13)	57.2 (21)	71.9 (32)	71.5 (158)	87.3 (126)	83.4 (54)	90 (10)	83.3 (30)	85.7 (7)
						Brennan							
Blackmun	71.3 (136)	88.8 (80)	81.5 (54)	72.8 (33)	87.5 (8)	93.3 (15)	81.0 (21)	82.0 (89)	97.1 (69)	86.8 (38)	100 (6)	76.5 (17)	100 (5)
Kennedy	35.3 (82)	38.1 (42)	52.9 (34)	60.0 (15)	57.1 (7)	80.0 (10)	45.5 (11)	74.5 (55)	81.4 (43)	79.2 (24)	60.0 (5)	80.0 (10)	100 (2)
Marshall	94.9 (136)	97.6 (82)	100 (54)	90.9 (33)	87.5 (8)	100 (14)	95.2 (21)	97.8 (91)	97.1 (69)	97.3 (37)	83.3 (6)	100 (17)	100 (5)
O'Connor	34.1 (135)	41.3 (80)	44.5 (54)	48.5 (33)	75.0 (8)	46.7 (15)	57.1 (21)	64.0 (89)	88.3 (68)	68.6 (35)	100 (6)	82.4 (17)	80.0 (5)
Powell	31.7 (41)	56.0 (25)	58.3 (12)	57.1 (14)	100 (1)	0.0 (3)	80.0 (5)	68.2 (22)	86.7 (15)	72.7 (11)	100 (1)	100 (4)	100 (1)
Rehnquist	29.4 (136)	31.7 (82)	30.8 (52)	42.4 (33)	62.5 (8)	46.7 (15)	66.7 (21)	66.7 (90)	76.8 (69)	73.7 (38)	83.3 (6)	82.4 (17)	100 (5)

Scalia	39.0 (136)	42.0 (81)	47.2 (53)	48.5 (33)	42.9 (7)	46.7 (15)	61.9 (21)	68.5 (89)	80.6 (67)	73.7 (38)	66.7 (6)	82.4 (17)	40.0 (5)
Stevens	77.2 (136)	78.3 (72)	70.4 (54)	81.8 (33)	75.0 (8)	92.9 (14)	66.7 (21)	77.8 (90)	84.1 (69)	83.8 (37)	80.0 (5)	82.4 (17)	80.0 (5)
White	35.6 (135)	47.6 (82)	46.3 (54)	63.7 (33)	62.5 (8)	53.3 (15)	61.9 (21)	72.3 (77)	84.1 (69)	81.5 (38)	83.3 (6)	76.5 (17)	100.0 (5)

Breyer

Ginsburg	83.8 (155)	84.3 (107)	77.1 (48)	87.1 (31)	76.9 (13)	50.0 (4)	94.8 (19)	85.7 (105)	89.6 (96)	90.5 (42)	100.0 (6)	85.0 (20)	60.0 (5)
Kennedy	67.7 (155)	65.4 (107)	68.8 (48)	71.0 (31)	61.5 (13)	50.0 (4)	63.2 (19)	85.8 (105)	85.5 (97)	61.9 (42)	100.0 (6)	80.0 (20)	100.0 (5)
O'Connor	75.5 (155)	71.7 (106)	72.9 (48)	74.2 (31)	76.9 (13)	100.0 (4)	47.4 (19)	86.4 (103)	88.5 (95)	60.0 (40)	83.5 (6)	78.9 (19)	80.0 (5)
Rehnquist	61.9 (155)	57.0 (107)	58.4 (48)	61.3 (31)	76.9 (13)	100.0 (4)	42.1 (19)	79.0 (105)	84.5 (97)	61.9 (42)	100.0 (6)	85.0 (20)	100.0 (5)
Scalia	57.4 (155)	51.4 (107)	43.8 (48)	58.0 (31)	61.5 (13)	50.0 (4)	50.0 (18)	81.0 (105)	77.3 (97)	48.8 (41)	66.7 (6)	75.0 (20)	80.0 (5)
Souter	79.3 (155)	90.7 (107)	79.2 (48)	93.5 (31)	76.9 (13)	75.0 (4)	89.5 (19)	88.4 (104)	89.7 (97)	90.5 (42)	100.0 (5)	80.0 (20)	80.0 (5)
Stevens	74.2 (155)	92.5 (107)	75.0 (48)	83.8 (31)	61.5 (13)	50.0 (4)	100.0 (19)	86.5 (104)	88.6 (97)	83.3 (42)	83.3 (6)	72.2 (18)	40.0 (5)

(Table continues)

Table 6-7 (*Continued*)

Justice	Crim	CivR	1st	DP	Priv	Atty	Un'n	Econ	JudP	Fed	IR	FTax	Misc
Thomas	60.6 (155)	50.0 (106)	45.8 (48)	58.0 (31)	69.2 (13)	100.0 (4)	42.1 (19)	78.1 (105)	77.3 (97)	42.9 (42)	50.0 (6)	55.0 (20)	100.0 (5)
Ginsburg													
Blackmun	65.2 (23)	66.6 (12)	50.0 (4)	100.0 (3)	100.0 (3)	100.0 (2)	100.0 (1)	63.6 (22)	77.8 (9)	100.0 (4)	—	100.0 (1)	—
Breyer	83.8 (155)	84.3 (107)	77.1 (48)	87.1 (31)	76.9 (13)	50.0 (4)	94.8 (19)	85.7 (105)	89.6 (96)	90.5 (42)	100.0 (6)	85.0 (20)	60.0 (5)
Kennedy	65.9 (179)	70.0 (120)	63.4 (52)	70.6 (34)	56.3 (16)	66.7 (18)	65.0 (20)	86.9 (130)	86.9 (107)	63.8 (47)	100.0 (6)	95.5 (22)	100.0 (5)
O'Connor	69.2 (179)	72.2 (119)	57.7 (52)	70.6 (34)	87.6 (16)	33.3 (6)	50.0 (20)	77.2 (127)	89.5 (105)	60.0 (45)	83.3 (6)	85.7 (21)	40.0 (5)
Rehnquist	58.1 (179)	61.7 (120)	40.4 (52)	64.7 (34)	75.0 (16)	33.3 (6)	45.0 (20)	85.5 (130)	85.9 (107)	65.9 (47)	100.0 (6)	90.9 (22)	100.0 (5)
Scalia	59.2 (179)	55.8 (120)	36.5 (52)	61.8 (34)	56.3 (16)	33.3 (6)	52.6 (19)	80.8 (130)	78.5 (107)	54.3 (46)	66.7 (6)	77.2 (22)	40.0 (5)
Souter	87.1 (179)	93.3 (120)	80.8 (52)	94.1 (34)	87.6 (16)	83.3 (6)	95.0 (20)	86.1 (129)	90.6 (107)	95.7 (47)	100.0 (5)	86.4 (22)	80.0 (5)
Stevens	78.2 (179)	91.7 (120)	86.6 (52)	79.4 (34)	87.5 (16)	100.0 (6)	95.0 (20)	78.3 (129)	87.8 (126)	89.3 (47)	83.3 (6)	85.0 (20)	80.0 (5)

	55.6 (179)	52.1 (119)	42.3 (52)	61.8 (34)	62.5 (16)	100.0 (6)	45.0 (20)	80.8 (130)	81.3 (107)	48.9 (47)	50.0 (6)	63.6 (22)	100.0 (5)
Thomas							Kennedy						
Blackmun	57.3 (185)	53.0 (102)	73.3 (60)	63.0 (27)	53.3 (15)	72.2 (18)	69.5 (23)	71.8 (145)	81.1 (106)	79.5 (44)	55.6 (9)	87.0 (23)	100.0 (2)
Brennan	35.8 (81)	39.0 (41)	52.9 (34)	64.3 (14)	50.0 (8)	80.0 (10)	45.5 (11)	74.5 (55)	78.3 (46)	79.2 (24)	100.0 (5)	80.0 (10)	100.0 (2)
Breyer	67.7 (155)	65.4 (107)	68.8 (48)	71.0 (31)	61.5 (13)	50.0 (4)	63.2 (19)	85.8 (105)	85.5 (97)	61.9 (42)	100.0 (6)	80.0 (20)	100.0 (5)
Ginsburg	65.9 (179)	70.0 (120)	63.4 (52)	70.6 (34)	56.3 (16)	66.7 (18)	65.0 (20)	86.9 (130)	86.9 (107)	63.8 (47)	100.0 (6)	95.5 (22)	100.0 (5)
Marshall	32.2 (112)	42.2 (57)	52.5 (40)	64.7 (17)	33.3 (9)	72.7 (11)	52.6 (19)	72.2 (79)	76.7 (60)	78.6 (28)	42.9 (7)	83.3 (12)	75.0 (4)
O'Connor	85.3 (340)	82.2 (208)	74.1 (108)	86.2 (58)	67.9 (28)	68.2 (22)	92.8 (42)	86.7 (249)	89.6 (202)	79.3 (82)	80.0 (15)	79.1 (43)	88.9 (9)
Rehnquist	86.2 (341)	86.6 (210)	68.2 (107)	88.0 (58)	78.5 (28)	77.2 (22)	85.8 (42)	95.8 (254)	90.7 (205)	85.1 (87)	93.3 (15)	93.2 (44)	88.9 (9)
Scalia	80.7 (341)	84.7 (210)	74.1 (108)	86.2 (58)	92.6 (27)	75.2 (22)	80.5 (41)	88.2 (254)	90.2 (204)	84.9 (86)	73.3 (15)	79.9 (44)	77.8 (9)
Souter	72.3 (256)	70.8 (168)	69.0 (74)	69.7 (43)	65.0 (20)	83.3 (12)	80.6 (31)	88.6 (194)	88.6 (158)	73.7 (61)	88.9 (9)	82.4 (34)	100.0 (7)

(Table continues)

Table 6-7 (*Continued*)

Justice	Crim	CivR	1st	DP	Priv	Atty	Un'n	Econ	JudP	Fed	IR	FTax	Misc
Stevens	53.7 (341)	65.2 (210)	63.9 (108)	60.3 (58)	57.2 (28)	66.7 (21)	64.3 (42)	73.1 (253)	78.9 (204)	62.8 (86)	60.0 (15)	76.2 (42)	88.9 (9)
Thomas	76.6 (226)	82.4 (148)	65.1 (66)	82.0 (39)	88.8 (18)	88.9 (9)	82.6 (23)	85.5 (172)	88.2 (144)	83.1 (59)	100.0 (8)	68.7 (32)	100.0 (5)
White	83.4 (162)	78.9 (90)	71.4 (56)	79.2 (24)	91.6 (12)	87.6 (16)	81.8 (22)	82.9 (123)	85.6 (97)	82.5 (40)	44.4 (9)	81.8 (22)	75.0 (4)
							Marshall						
Blackmun	71.4 (168)	90.7 (96)	83.3 (60)	83.4 (36)	80.0 (10)	93.8 (16)	79.3 (29)	81.4 (113)	94.2 (85)	90.2 (41)	87.5 (8)	70.0 (20)	85.7 (7)
Brennan	94.9 (136)	97.6 (82)	100 (54)	90.9 (33)	87.5 (8)	100 (14)	95.2 (21)	97.8 (91)	97.1 (69)	97.3 (37)	83.3 (6)	100 (17)	100 (5)
Kennedy	32.8 (113)	41.4 (58)	52.5 (40)	61.1 (18)	37.5 (8)	72.7 (11)	52.6 (19)	72.2 (79)	79.0 (57)	78.6 (28)	42.9 (7)	83.3 (12)	75.0 (4)
O'Connor	32.3 (167)	45.8 (96)	45.0 (60)	58.4 (36)	70.0 (10)	50.0 (16)	55.2 (29)	61.1 (113)	85.7 (84)	65.8 (38)	75.0 (8)	80.0 (20)	71.4 (7)
Powell	31.7 (41)	52.0 (25)	58.3 (12)	78.5 (14)	100 (1)	0.0 (3)	80.0 (5)	63.6 (22)	86.7 (15)	81.8 (11)	100 (1)	100 (4)	100 (1)
Rehnquist	26.8 (168)	31.6 (98)	29.3 (58)	52.8 (36)	50.0 (10)	50.0 (16)	65.5 (29)	66.7 (114)	72.9 (85)	75.6 (41)	62.5 (8)	85.0 (20)	100 (7)

Scalia	36.3 (168)	41.2 (97)	42.4 (59)	58.3 (36)	50.0 (8)	50.0 (16)	62.0 (29)	67.3 (113)	76.8 (82)	78.0 (41)	50.0 (8)	80.0 (20)	42.9 (7)
Souter	25.9 (27)	80.0 (15)	33.3 (6)	50.0 (2)	0.0 (1)	50.0 (2)	62.5 (8)	61.9 (21)	80.0 (15)	100 (3)	100 (2)	100 (2)	50.0 (2)
Stevens	78.6 (168)	72.4 (98)	70.0 (60)	80.6 (36)	90.0 (10)	93.3 (15)	79.3 (29)	77.2 (114)	81.1 (85)	85.0 (40)	71.4 (7)	85.0 (20)	71.4 (7)
White	35.9 (168)	50.0 (98)	43.3 (60)	75.0 (36)	50.0 (10)	50.0 (16)	62.1 (29)	72.0 (114)	82.4 (85)	85.3 (41)	100 (8)	70.0 (20)	100 (7)
O'Connor													
Blackmun	55.7 (239)	56.1 (139)	57.6 (80)	62.2 (45)	76.5 (17)	52.1 (23)	72.8 (33)	65.5 (177)	88.0 (133)	76.3 (55)	80.0 (10)	77.5 (31)	85.7 (7)
Brennan	43.3 (134)	41.5 (79)	44.5 (54)	50.0 (32)	66.7 (9)	46.7 (15)	57.1 (21)	64.0 (89)	85.9 (71)	68.6 (35)	100.0 (6)	82.4 (17)	100.0 (5)
Breyer	75.5 (155)	71.7 (106)	72.9 (48)	74.2 (31)	76.9 (13)	100.0 (4)	47.4 (19)	86.4 (103)	88.5 (95)	60.0 (40)	83.5 (6)	78.9 (19)	80.0 (5)
Ginsburg	69.2 (179)	72.2 (119)	57.7 (52)	70.6 (34)	87.6 (16)	33.3 (6)	50.0 (20)	77.2 (127)	89.5 (105)	60.0 (45)	83.3 (6)	85.7 (21)	40.0 (5)
Kennedy	85.3 (340)	82.2 (208)	74.1 (108)	86.2 (58)	67.9 (28)	68.2 (22)	92.8 (42)	86.7 (249)	89.6 (202)	79.3 (82)	80.0 (15)	79.1 (43)	88.9 (9)
Marshall	31.4 (166)	46.4 (95)	45.0 (60)	60.0 (35)	63.6 (11)	50.0 (16)	55.2 (29)	61.1 (113)	83.9 (87)	65.8 (38)	75.0 (8)	80.0 (20)	71.4 (7)

(Table continues)

Table 6-7 (Continued)

Justice	Crim	CivR	1st	DP	Priv	Atty	Un'n	Econ	JudP	Fed	IR	FTax	Misc
Powell	80.5 (41)	70.8 (24)	100.0 (12)	78.5 (14)	100.0 (1)	100.0 (3)	80.0 (5)	81.5 (22)	100.0 (15)	100.0 (11)	100.0 (1)	100.0 (4)	100.0 (1)
Rehnquist	86.1 (395)	80.2 (247)	70.6 (126)	84.2 (76)	76.7 (30)	84.9 (27)	93.2 (52)	84.5 (284)	89.1 (230)	86.4 (96)	87.6 (16)	78.4 (51)	75.0 (12)
Scalia	79.0 (395)	78.8 (246)	70.8 (127)	82.9 (76)	60.7 (28)	81.5 (27)	86.3 (51)	85.9 (283)	85.9 (227)	83.2 (95)	81.3 (16)	78.4 (51)	83.4 (12)
Souter	72.2 (262)	75.5 (167)	64.9 (74)	74.5 (43)	95.0 (20)	58.3 (12)	70.9 (31)	84.8 (191)	89.9 (158)	64.4 (59)	77.8 (9)	84.8 (33)	71.4 (778)
Stevens	53.9 (395)	66.4 (247)	57.8 (128)	59.2 (76)	83.3 (30)	50.0 (26)	55.8 (52)	67.2 (283)	80.4 (229)	63.5 (96)	66.7 (15)	76.0 (50)	83.3 (12)
Thomas	77.5 (226)	74.2 (147)	62.1 (66)	77.0 (39)	61.1 (18)	77.8 (9)	95.6 (23)	88.7 (169)	89.4 (142)	70.2 (57)	75.0 (8)	87.1 (31)	80.0 (5)
White	80.0 (215)	78.9 (128)	71.1 (76)	78.6 (42)	78.6 (14)	76.2 (21)	78.1 (32)	76.4 (157)	86.3 (124)	76.5 (51)	70.0 (10)	60.0 (30)	71.4 (7)
Powell													
Blackmun	58.5 (41)	56.5 (23)	50.0 (12)	78.5 (14)	100 (1)	0.0 (3)	80.0 (5)	76.2 (21)	93.3 (15)	90.9 (11)	100 (1)	75.0 (4)	100 (1)

Brennan	31.7 (41)	56.0 (25)	58.3 (12)	57.1 (14)	100 (1)	0.0 (3)	80.0 (5)	68.2 (22)	86.7 (15)	72.7 (11)	100 (1)	100 (4)	100 (1)
Marshall	31.7 (41)	52.0 (25)	58.3 (12)	78.5 (14)	100 (1)	0.0 (3)	80.0 (5)	63.6 (22)	86.7 (15)	81.8 (11)	100 (1)	100 (4)	100 (1)
O'Connor	80.5 (41)	70.8 (24)	83.3 (12)	78.5 (14)	100 (1)	100 (3)	80.0 (5)	81.8 (22)	100 (15)	72.7 (11)	100 (1)	75.0 (4)	100 (1)
Rehnquist	85.4 (41)	72.0 (25)	58.3 (12)	78.5 (14)	100 (1)	100 (3)	80.0 (5)	86.3 (22)	100 (15)	90.9 (11)	100 (1)	75.0 (4)	100 (1)
Scalia	75.6 (41)	52.0 (25)	81.8 (11)	78.5 (14)	100 (1)	100 (3)	80.0 (5)	90.5 (21)	100 (13)	90.9 (11)	100 (1)	75.0 (4)	100 (1)
Stevens	51.2 (41)	60.0 (25)	66.7 (12)	50.0 (14)	100 (1)	33.3 (9)	60.0 (5)	54.5 (22)	80.0 (15)	72.7 (11)	—	50.0 (4)	100 (1)
White	82.5 (40)	80.0 (25)	83.3 (12)	78.6 (14)	100 (1)	100 (3)	40.0 (5)	86.3 (22)	86.7 (15)	72.7 (11)	100 (1)	75.0 (4)	100 (1)
Rehnquist													
Blackmun	52.1 (240)	45.0 (140)	47.5 (78)	53.3 (45)	58.8 (17)	47.8 (23)	69.7 (33)	72.1 (179)	78.4 (134)	79.3 (58)	70.0 (10)	77.4 (31)	85.6 (7)
Brennan	29.6 (135)	32.1 (81)	30.8 (52)	43.8 (32)	55.6 (9)	46.7 (15)	66.7 (21)	66.7 (90)	75.0 (72)	73.7 (38)	83.3 (6)	82.4 (17)	100.0 (5)

(Table continues)

Table 6-7 *(Continued)*

Justice	Crim	CivR	1st	DP	Priv	Atty	Un'n	Econ	JudP	Fed	IR	FTax	Misc
Breyer	61.9 (155)	57.0 (107)	58.4 (48)	61.3 (31)	76.9 (13)	100.0 (4)	42.1 (19)	79.0 (105)	84.5 (97)	61.9 (42)	100.0 (6)	85.0 (20)	100.0 (5)
Ginsburg	58.1 (179)	61.7 (120)	40.4 (52)	64.7 (34)	75.0 (16)	33.3 (6)	45.0 (20)	85.5 (130)	85.9 (107)	65.9 (47)	100.0 (6)	90.9 (22)	100.0 (5)
Kennedy	86.2 (341)	86.6 (210)	68.2 (107)	88.0 (58)	78.5 (28)	77.2 (22)	85.8 (42)	95.8 (254)	90.7 (205)	85.1 (87)	93.3 (15)	93.2 (44)	88.9 (9)
Marshall	26.3 (167)	32.0 (97)	29.3 (58)	54.3 (35)	45.5 (11)	50.0 (16)	65.5 (29)	66.7 (114)	71.6 (88)	75.6 (41)	62.5 (8)	85.0 (20)	85.7 (7)
O'Connor	86.1 (395)	80.2 (247)	70.6 (126)	84.2 (76)	76.7 (30)	84.9 (27)	93.2 (52)	84.5 (284)	89.1 (230)	86.4 (96)	87.6 (16)	78.4 (51)	75.0 (12)
Powell	85.4 (41)	72.0 (25)	58.3 (12)	78.5 (14)	100.0 (1)	100.0 (3)	80.0 (5)	86.3 (22)	100.0 (15)	90.9 (11)	100.0 (1)	75.0 (4)	100.0 (1)
Scalia	84.6 (396)	86.8 (249)	81.6 (125)	90.7 (76)	78.6 (28)	92.6 (27)	82.3 (51)	89.6 (288)	89.1 (230)	88.0 (100)	69.8 (16)	86.5 (52)	58.3 (12)
Souter	66.1 (256)	110.0 (168)	51.3 (74)	60.5 (43)	75.0 (20)	66.7 (12)	64.5 (31)	81.9 (194)	88.2 (160)	68.9 (61)	88.9 (9)	91.1 (34)	71.4 (7)
Stevens	45.4 (396)	57.6 (250)	48.4 (126)	48.7 (76)	60.0 (30)	46.2 (26)	59.6 (52)	64.1 (287)	76.7 (232)	65.0 (100)	66.7 (15)	70.0 (50)	75.0 (12)

Thomas	87.6 (226)	79.9 (148)	78.9 (66)	92.3 (39)	77.8 (18)	88.9 (9)	100.0 (23)	85.5 (172)	88.2 (144)	76.3 (59)	62.5 (8)	71.9 (32)	100.0 (5)
White	86.1 (216)	82.3 (130)	86.5 (74)	78.6 (42)	100.0 (14)	80.9 (21)	87.5 (32)	77.2 (158)	84.8 (125)	83.4 (54)	60.0 (10)	86.7 (30)	100.0 (7)

Scalia

Blackmun	49.6 (240)	50.4 (139)	51.9 (79)	57.8 (45)	40.0 (15)	52.2 (23)	78.8 (33)	67.4 (178)	79.4 (131)	81.0 (58)	60.0 (10)	74.2 (31)	100.0 (7)
Brennan	35.2 (135)	42.5 (80)	47.2 (53)	50.0 (32)	37.5 (8)	46.7 (15)	61.9 (21)	68.5 (89)	78.5 (70)	73.7 (38)	100.0 (6)	82.4 (17)	100.0 (5)
Breyer	57.4 (155)	51.4 (107)	43.8 (48)	58.0 (31)	61.5 (13)	50.0 (4)	50.0 (18)	81.0 (105)	77.3 (97)	48.8 (41)	66.7 (6)	75.0 (20)	80.0 (5)
Ginsburg	59.2 (179)	55.8 (120)	36.5 (52)	61.8 (34)	56.3 (16)	33.3 (6)	52.6 (19)	80.8 (130)	78.5 (107)	54.3 (46)	66.7 (6)	77.2 (22)	40.0 (5)
Kennedy	80.7 (341)	84.7 (210)	74.1 (108)	86.2 (58)	92.6 (27)	75.2 (22)	80.5 (41)	88.2 (254)	90.2 (204)	84.9 (86)	73.3 (15)	79.9 (44)	77.8 (9)
Marshall	35.9 (167)	41.7 (96)	42.4 (59)	60.0 (35)	44.4 (9)	50.0 (16)	62.0 (29)	67.3 (113)	75.3 (85)	78.0 (41)	50.0 (8)	80.0 (20)	42.9 (7)
O'Connor	79.0 (395)	78.8 (246)	70.8 (127)	82.9 (76)	60.7 (28)	81.5 (27)	86.3 (51)	85.9 (283)	85.9 (227)	83.2 (95)	81.3 (16)	78.4 (51)	83.4 (12)
Powell	75.6 (41)	52.0 (25)	100.0 (11)	78.5 (14)	100.0 (1)	100.0 (3)	80.0 (5)	90.5 (21)	100.0 (13)	100.0 (11)	100.0 (1)	100.0 (4)	100.0 (1)

(Table continues)

Table 6-7 (*Continued*)

Justice	Crim	CivR	1st	DP	Priv	Atty	Un'n	Econ	JudP	Fed	IR	FTax	Misc
Rehnquist	84.6 (396)	86.8 (249)	81.6 (125)	90.7 (76)	78.6 (28)	92.6 (27)	82.3 (51)	89.6 (288)	89.1 (230)	88.0 (100)	69.8 (16)	86.5 (52)	58.3 (12)
Souter	66.4 (256)	58.9 (168)	45.9 (74)	58.1 (43)	60.0 (20)	66.7 (12)	70.0 (30)	84.0 (194)	84.3 (159)	66.7 (60)	66.7 (9)	85.3 (34)	71.4 (7)
Stevens	46.7 (396)	57.0 (249)	42.5 (127)	52.6 (76)	57.1 (28)	46.2 (26)	64.7 (51)	63.9 (286)	74.6 (229)	63.6 (99)	73.3 (15)	66.0 (50)	66.6 (12)
Thomas	90.3 (226)	92.5 (128)	92.4 (66)	100.0 (39)	94.4 (18)	88.9 (9)	90.9 (22)	94.1 (172)	93.0 (144)	86.2 (58)	87.5 (8)	78.1 (32)	80.0 (5)
White	78.7 (216)	76.0 (129)	81.4 (75)	83.4 (42)	91.7 (12)	80.9 (21)	71.9 (32)	78.4 (157)	81.1 (122)	85.2 (54)	50.0 (10)	83.4 (30)	42.9 (7)
						Souter							
Blackmun	65.0 (100)	71.6 (60)	73.1 (26)	75.0 (12)	85.7 (7)	62.5 (8)	75.0 (12)	70.1 (87)	83.6 (61)	88.9 (18)	75.0 (4)	69.2 (13)	100.0 (2)
Breyer	79.3 (155)	90.7 (107)	79.2 (48)	93.5 (31)	76.9 (13)	75.0 (4)	89.5 (19)	88.4 (104)	89.7 (97)	90.5 (42)	100.0 (5)	80.0 (20)	80.0 (5)
Ginsburg	87.1 (179)	93.3 (120)	80.8 (52)	94.1 (34)	87.6 (16)	83.3 (6)	95.0 (20)	86.1 (129)	90.6 (107)	95.7 (47)	100.0 (5)	86.4 (22)	80.0 (5)
Kennedy	72.3 (256)	70.8 (168)	69.0 (74)	69.7 (43)	65.0 (20)	83.3 (12)	80.6 (31)	88.6 (194)	88.6 (158)	73.7 (61)	88.9 (9)	82.4 (34)	100.0 (7)

Marshall	25.9 (27)	80.0 (15)	33.4 (6)	50.0 (2)	100.0 (1)	50.0 (2)	62.5 (8)	60.0 (20)	80.0 (15)	100.0 (3)	100.0 (2)	100.0 (2)	50.0 (2)
O'Connor	72.2 (262)	75.5 (167)	64.9 (74)	74.5 (43)	95.0 (20)	58.3 (12)	70.9 (31)	84.8 (191)	89.9 (158)	64.4 (59)	77.8 (9)	84.8 (33)	71.4 (7)
Rehnquist	66.1 (256)	110.0 (168)	51.3 (74)	60.5 (43)	75.0 (20)	66.7 (12)	64.5 (31)	81.9 (194)	88.2 (160)	68.9 (61)	88.9 (9)	91.1 (34)	71.4 (7)
Scalia	66.4 (256)	58.9 (168)	45.9 (74)	58.1 (43)	60.0 (20)	66.7 (12)	70.0 (30)	84.0 (194)	84.3 (159)	66.7 (60)	66.7 (9)	85.3 (34)	71.4 (7)
Stevens	70.3 (256)	84.5 (168)	81.1 (74)	81.4 (43)	85.0 (20)	66.7 (12)	80.6 (31)	76.2 (193)	83.0 (159)	85.2 (61)	77.8 (9)	68.8 (32)	71.4 (7)
Thomas	61.5 (226)	55.4 (148)	45.4 (66)	53.8 (39)	61.1 (18)	66.7 (9)	56.5 (23)	80.7 (171)	86.1 (144)	60.3 (58)	100.0 (7)	75.1 (32)	80.0 (5)
White	75.3 (77)	93.8 (48)	50.0 (22)	66.7 (9)	75.0 (4)	100.0 (6)	81.8 (11)	84.6 (65)	86.5 (52)	85.7 (14)	75.0 (4)	75.0 (12)	50.0 (2)
Stevens													
Blackmun	76.3 (240)	80.0 (140)	71.3 (80)	80.0 (45)	82.3 (17)	95.5 (22)	75.7 (33)	72.6 (179)	84.4 (134)	82.5 (57)	88.9 (9)	74.2 (31)	100.0 (7)
Brennan	77.8 (135)	67.9 (81)	70.4 (54)	80.3 (32)	77.8 (9)	92.9 (14)	66.7 (21)	77.8 (90)	82.0 (72)	83.8 (37)	100.0 (5)	82.4 (17)	100.0 (5)
Breyer	74.2 (155)	92.5 (107)	75.0 (48)	83.8 (31)	61.5 (13)	50.0 (4)	100.0 (19)	86.5 (104)	88.6 (97)	83.3 (42)	83.3 (6)	72.2 (18)	40.0 (5)

(Table continues)

Table 6-7 (*Continued*)

Justice	Crim	CivR	1st	DP	Priv	Atty	Un'n	Econ	JudP	Fed	IR	FTax	Misc
Ginsburg	78.2 (179)	91.7 (120)	86.6 (52)	79.4 (34)	87.5 (16)	100.0 (6)	95.0 (20)	78.3 (129)	87.8 (126)	89.3 (47)	83.3 (6)	85.0 (20)	80.0 (5)
Kennedy	53.7 (341)	65.2 (210)	63.9 (108)	60.3 (58)	57.2 (28)	66.7 (21)	64.3 (42)	73.1 (253)	78.9 (204)	62.8 (86)	60.0 (15)	76.2 (42)	88.9 (9)
Marshall	78.4 (167)	72.1 (97)	70.0 (60)	80.0 (35)	90.9 (11)	93.3 (15)	73.3 (29)	77.2 (114)	81.8 (88)	85.0 (40)	71.4 (7)	85.0 (20)	71.4 (7)
O'Connor	53.9 (395)	66.4 (247)	57.8 (128)	59.2 (76)	83.3 (30)	50.0 (26)	55.8 (52)	67.2 (283)	80.4 (229)	63.5 (96)	66.7 (15)	76.0 (50)	83.3 (12)
Powell	85.4 (41)	72.0 (25)	58.3 (12)	78.5 (14)	100.0 (1)	100.0 (3)	80.0 (5)	86.3 (22)	100.0 (15)	90.9 (11)	100.0 (1)	75.0 (4)	100.0 (1)
Rehnquist	45.4 (396)	57.6 (250)	48.4 (126)	48.7 (76)	60.0 (30)	46.2 (26)	59.6 (52)	64.1 (287)	76.7 (232)	65.0 (100)	66.7 (15)	70.0 (50)	75.0 (12)
Scalia	46.7 (396)	57.0 (249)	42.5 (127)	52.6 (76)	57.1 (28)	46.2 (26)	64.7 (51)	63.9 (286)	74.6 (229)	63.6 (99)	73.3 (15)	66.0 (50)	66.6 (12)
Souter	70.3 (256)	84.5 (168)	81.1 (74)	81.4 (43)	85.0 (20)	66.7 (12)	80.6 (31)	76.2 (193)	83.0 (159)	85.2 (61)	77.8 (9)	68.8 (32)	71.4 (7)
Thomas	43.8 (226)	54.1 (148)	36.4 (66)	43.6 (39)	50.0 (18)	44.4 (9)	43.5 (23)	64.9 (171)	74.8 (143)	47.5 (59)	62.5 (8)	70.0 (30)	80.0 (5)
White	54.2 (216)	68.5 (130)	59.2 (76)	64.3 (42)	57.1 (14)	60.0 (20)	78.2 (32)	69.0 (158)	84.0 (125)	83.0 (53)	77.8 (9)	56.6 (30)	71.4 (7)

	Thomas												
Blackmun	48.6 (70)	53.6 (41)	33.3 (18)	25.0 (8)	100.0 (5)	60.0 (5)	50.0 (4)	56.9 (64)	82.2 (45)	68.8 (16)	50.0 (2)	72.7 (11)	—
Breyer	60.6 (155)	50.0 (106)	45.8 (48)	58.0 (31)	69.2 (13)	100.0 (4)	42.1 (19)	78.1 (105)	77.3 (97)	42.9 (42)	50.0 (6)	55.0 (20)	100.0 (5)
Ginsburg	55.6 (179)	52.1 (119)	42.3 (52)	61.8 (34)	62.5 (16)	100.0 (6)	45.0 (20)	80.8 (130)	81.3 (107)	48.9 (47)	50.0 (6)	63.6 (22)	100.0 (5)
Kennedy	76.6 (226)	82.4 (148)	65.1 (66)	82 (39)	88.8 (18)	88.9 (9)	82.6 (23)	85.5 (172)	88.2 (144)	83.1 (59)	100 (8)	68.7 (32)	100 (5)
O'Connor	77.5 (226)	74.2 (147)	62.1 (66)	77.0 (39)	61.1 (18)	77.8 (9)	95.6 (23)	88.7 (169)	89.4 (142)	70.2 (57)	75.0 (8)	87.1 (31)	80.0 (5)
Rehnquist	87.6 (226)	79.9 (148)	78.9 (66)	92.3 (39)	77.8 (18)	88.9 (9)	100.0 (23)	85.5 (172)	88.2 (144)	76.3 (59)	62.5 (8)	71.9 (32)	100.0 (5)
Scalia	90.3 (226)	92.5 (128)	92.4 (66)	100 (39)	94.4 (18)	88.9 (9)	90.9 (22)	94.1 (172)	93 (144)	86.2 (58)	87.5 (8)	78.1 (32)	80.0 (5)
Souter	61.5 (226)	55.4 (148)	45.4 (66)	53.8 (39)	61.1 (18)	66.7 (9)	56.5 (23)	80.7 (171)	86.1 (144)	60.3 (58)	100.0 (7)	75.1 (32)	80.0 (5)
Stevens	43.8 (226)	54.1 (148)	36.4 (66)	43.6 (39)	50.0 (18)	44.4 (9)	43.5 (23)	64.9 (171)	74.8 (143)	47.5 (59)	62.5 (8)	70.0 (30)	80.0 (5)
White	70.3 (47)	79.3 (29)	92.9 (14)	100.0 (5)	100.0 (2)	66.7 (3)	66.7 (3)	66.7 (42)	91.7 (36)	75.0 (12)	50.0 (2)	60.0 (10)	—

(Table continues)

Table 6-7 (Continued)

Justice	Crim	CivR	1st	DP	Priv	Atty	Un'n	Econ	JudP	Fed	IR	FTax	Misc
White
Blackmun	60.7 (216)	60.7 (127)	55.2 (76)	69.8 (43)	53.8 (13)	57.2 (21)	71.9 (32)	71.5 (158)	87.3 (126)	83.4 (54)	90.0 (10)	83.3 (30)	85.7 (7)
Brennan	35.6 (135)	47.6 (82)	46.3 (54)	63.7 (33)	62.5 (8)	53.3 (15)	61.9 (21)	72.3 (77)	84.1 (69)	81.5 (69)	83.3 (6)	76.5 (17)	100.0 (5)
Kennedy	83.4 (162)	78.6 (89)	71.4 (56)	80.0 (25)	90.9 (11)	87.6 (16)	81.8 (22)	82.3 (124)	85.7 (98)	82.5 (40)	44.4 (9)	81.8 (22)	75.0 (4)
Marshall	35.9 (168)	50.0 (98)	43.3 (60)	75.0 (36)	50.0 (10)	50.0 (16)	62.1 (29)	72.0 (114)	82.4 (85)	85.3 (41)	100.0 (8)	70.0 (20)	100.0 (7)
O'Connor	80.0 (215)	78.7 (127)	71.6 (76)	79.1 (43)	76.9 (13)	76.2 (21)	78.1 (32)	76.0 (158)	86.4 (125)	83.0 (53)	77.8 (9)	56.6 (30)	71.4 (7)
Powell	82.5 (40)	80.0 (25)	83.3 (12)	78.6 (14)	100.0 (1)	100.0 (3)	40.0 (5)	86.3 (22)	86.7 (15)	72.7 (11)	100.0 (1)	75.0 (4)	100.0 (1)
Rehnquist	86.1 (216)	82.2 (129)	86.5 (74)	79.1 (43)	100.0 (13)	80.9 (21)	87.5 (32)	77.4 (159)	84.9 (126)	83.4 (54)	60.0 (10)	86.7 (30)	100.0 (7)
Scalia	78.7 (216)	75.8 (128)	81.4 (75)	83.8 (43)	90.9 (11)	80.9 (21)	71.9 (32)	77.9 (158)	81.3 (123)	85.2 (54)	50.0 (10)	83.4 (30)	42.9 (7)
Souter	75.3 (77)	93.6 (47)	50.0 (22)	66.7 (9)	75.0 (4)	83.3 (6)	81.8 (11)	84.8 (66)	86.6 (53)	85.7 (14)	75.0 (4)	75.0 (12)	50.0 (2)

Stevens	54.2	68.2	59.2	62.8	61.5	60.0	78.2	69.2	84.2	83.0	77.8	56.6	71.4
	(216)	(129)	(76)	(43)	(13)	(20)	(32)	(159)	(126)	(53)	(9)	(30)	(7)
Thomas	70.3	78.6	92.9	80.0	100.0	66.7	66.7	65.1	91.9	75.0	50.0	60.0	—
	(47)	(28)	(14)	(5)	(2)	(3)	(3)	(43)	(37)	(12)	(2)	(10)	

Note: "—" indicates no case in issue area was decided during tenure overlap. Figures listed are the percentage of cases in which the justices voted together. Figures in parentheses are the total number of cases decided in the issue area in which both justices participated during their tenures on the Rehnquist Court, through the end of the 1994 term. The data include all orally argued citations. Readers should take care in interpreting the percentages since some of the figures on which they are based are quite small.

The issue areas are defined as follows: Criminal procedure (Crim): the rights of persons accused of crime except for the due process rights of prisoners; Civil rights (CivR): non–First Amendment freedom cases that pertain to classifications based on race (including Native Americans), age, indigence, voting, residence, military or handicapped status, sex, or alienage; First Amendment (1st): guarantees contained therein; Due process (DP): noncriminal procedural guarantees, plus court jurisdiction over nonresident litigants and the takings clause of the Fifth Amendment; Privacy (Priv): abortion, contraception, the Freedom of Information Act and related federal statutes; Attorneys (Atty): attorneys' fees, commercial speech, admission to and removal from the bar, and disciplinary matters; Unions (Un'n): labor union activity; Economics (Econ): commercial business activity, plus litigation involving injured persons or things, employee actions vis-à-vis employers, zoning regulations, and governmental regulation of corruption other than that involving campaign spending; Judicial power (JudP): the exercise of the judiciary's own power and authority; Federalism (Fed): conflicts between the federal and state governments, excluding those between state and federal courts, and those involving the priority of federal fiscal claims; Interstate relations (IR): conflicts between states, such as boundary disputes, and nonproperty disputes commonly arising under the full faith and credit clause of the Constitution; Federal taxation (FTax): the Internal Revenue Code and related statutes; Miscellaneous (Misc): legislative veto, separation of powers, and matters not included in any other issue area.

Source: U.S. Supreme Court Judicial Database, with analu = 0 or 4 and dec_type = 1, 6, or 7.

Table 6-8 Votes in Support of and Opposition to Decisions Declaring Legislation Unconstitutional, 1946–2001 Terms

| | Court | | | | | | | | | | Congressional laws[a] | |
Justice	Vinson	%	Warren	%	Burger	%	Rehnquist	%	Total	%		%
Black	11-7	61.1	131-30	81.4	21-9	70.0	—	—	163-46	78.0	25-6	80.6
Blackmun	—	—	—	—	196-42	82.4	59-39	60.2	255-81	75.9	22-9	71.0
Brennan	—	—	145-0	100.0	235-14	94.4	41-1	97.6	421-15	96.6	51-3	94.4
Breyer	—	—	—	—	—	—	35-24	59.3	35-24	59.3	13-31	41.9
Burger	—	—	—	—	174-80	69.0	—	—	174-80	69.0	20-8	71.4
Burton	14-4	77.8	16-10	61.5	—	—	—	—	30-14	68.2	0-4	0.0
Clark	9-1	90.0	94-31	75.2	—	—	—	—	103-32	76.3	7-8	46.7
Douglas	13-4	76.5	158-4	97.5	97-9	91.5	—	—	268-17	94.0	31-3	91.2
Fortas	—	—	46-3	93.9	—	—	—	—	46-3	93.9	11-0	100.0
Frankfurter	14-4	77.8	35-11	76.1	—	—	—	—	49-15	76.6	4-3	57.1
Ginsburg	—	—	—	—	—	—	42-24	63.6	42-24	63.6	15-16	48.4
Goldberg	—	—	55-3	94.8	—	—	—	—	55-3	94.8	6-0	100.0
Harlan	—	—	88-66	57.1	26-4	86.7	—	—	114-70	62.0	16-14	53.3

Jackson	13-5	72.2	8-0	100.0	—	—	—	—	21-5	80.8	1-0	100.0
Kennedy	—	—	—	—	—	—	106-7	93.8	106-7	93.8	25-2	92.6
Marshall	—	—	28-0	100.0	237-15	94.9	41-4	91.1	306-19	94.4	35-5	87.5
Minton	6-4	60.0	11-2	84.6	—	—	—	—	17-6	73.9	1-0	100.0
Murphy	5-2	71.4	—	—	—	—	—	—	5-2	71.4	0-0	—
O'Connor	—	—	—	—	42-22	65.6	101-24	80.8	143-46	75.7	38-8	82.6
Powell	—	—	—	—	181-22	89.2	10-1	90.9	191-23	89.3	20-3	87.0
Reed	14-4	77.8	13-2	86.7	—	—	—	—	27-6	81.8	1-0	100.0
Rehnquist	—	—	—	—	78-129	37.7	68-57	54.4	146-186	44.0	38-21	64.4
Rutledge	7-1	87.5	—	—	—	—	—	—	7-1	87.5	0-0	—
Scalia	—	—	—	—	—	—	87-39	69.0	87-39	69.0	29-9	76.3
Souter	—	—	—	—	—	—	66-18	78.6	66-18	78.6	21-12	63.6
Stevens	—	—	—	—	115-20	85.2	93-32	74.4	244-49	83.3	29-22	56.9
Stewart	—	—	98-35	73.7	166-20	89.2	—	—	264-55	82.8	29-10	74.4
Thomas	—	—	—	—	—	—	59-21	73.8	59-21	73.8	26-6	81.3
Vinson	17-1	94.4	—	—	—	—	—	—	17-1	94.4	1-0	100.0

(Table continues)

Table 6-8 (*Continued*)

| | | | | | Court | | | | | | Congressional | |
Justice	Vinson	%	Warren	%	Burger	%	Rehnquist	%	Total	%	laws[a]	%
Warren	—	—	147-12	92.5	—	—	—	—	147-12	92.5	18-6	75.0
White	—	—	91-21	81.3	196-58	77.2	44-17	72.1	331-96	77.5	30-22	57.7
Whittaker	—	—	22-5	81.5	—	—	—	—	22-5	81.5	2-2	50.0
Totals	123-37	76.9	1,186-235	83.5	1,764-444	79.9	1,082-410	72.5	5,180-1,290	80.1	649-264	71.1

Note: Includes only those cases in which a majority voted to declare legislation unconstitutional. Figures to the left of the dash indicate the number of votes in favor of striking down legislation; figures to the right indicate the number of votes in favor of upholding the legislation. Percentages indicate the percent of cases in which the justice voted with the majority to declare legislation unconstitutional.

Determination of which decisions have voided acts of Congress and declared state and local legislation unconstitutional is not a clear-cut matter. The database lists only decisions in which the Court clearly indicates that it has voided a legislative enactment of some level of government. More specifically, declarations of unconstitutionality extend only to acts of Congress; state and territorial statutes, regulations, and constitutional provisions; and municipal or other local ordinances. Federal pre-emption of state or local legislation or regulations are excluded from consideration unless the opinion of the Court expressly states that the state or local enactment is unconstitutional.

[a] Excludes legislation passed by state and local power.

Source: U.S. Supreme Court Judicial Database, with analu = 0 and dec_type = 1, 6, or 7.

Table 6-9 Votes in Support of and Opposition to Decisions Formally Altering Precedent, 1946–2001 Terms

Justice	Court												
	Vinson	%	Warren	%	Burger	%	Rehnquist	%	Total	%
Black	2-4	33.3	33-7	82.5	3-1	75.0	—	—	38-12	76.0
Blackmun	—	—	—	—	42-4	91.3	15-9	62.5	57-13	81.4
Brennan	—	—	38-0	100.0	31-16	66.0	9-6	60.0	78-22	78.0
Breyer	—	—	—	—	—	—	13-3	81.3	13-3	81.3
Burger	—	—	—	—	41-8	83.7	—	—	41-8	83.7
Burton	5-1	83.3	2-1	66.7	—	—	—	—	7-2	77.8
Clark	3-0	100.0	13-15	46.4	—	—	—	—	16-15	51.6
Douglas	2-2	50.0	37-3	92.5	9-3	75.0	—	—	48-8	85.7
Fortas	—	—	15-1	93.8	—	—	—	—	15-1	93.8
Frankfurter	2-4	33.3	3-5	37.5	—	—	—	—	5-9	35.7
Ginsburg	—	—	—	—	—	—	13-5	72.2	13-5	72.2
Goldberg	—	—	12-0	100.0	—	—	—	—	12-0	100.0
Harlan	—	—	16-23	41.0	3-1	75.0	—	—	19-24	44.2

(Table continues)

Table 6-9 (Continued)

				Court						
Justice	Vinson	%	Warren	%	Burger	%	Rehnquist	%	Total	%
Jackson	4-2	66.7	1-0	100.0	—	—	—	—	5-2	71.4
Kennedy	—	—	—	—	—	—	36-1	97.3	36-1	97.3
Marshall	—	—	9-0	100.0	33-15	68.8	9-9	50.0	51-24	68.0
Minton	3-0	100.0	1-0	100.0	—	—	—	—	4-0	100.0
Murphy	2-1	66.7	—	—	—	—	—	—	2-1	66.7
O'Connor	—	—	—	—	11-2	84.6	31-8	79.5	36-1	97.3
Powell	—	—	—	—	39-4	90.7	4-1	80.0	43-5	89.6
Reed	4-2	66.7	1-0	100.0	—	—	—	—	5-2	71.4
Rehnquist	—	—	—	—	32-11	74.4	31-9	77.5	63-20	75.9
Rutledge	2-1	66.7	—	—	—	—	—	—	2-1	66.7
Scalia	—	—	—	—	—	—	35-5	83.5	35-5	87.5
Souter	—	`'`	—	—	—	—	19-6	76.0	19-6	76.0
Stevens	—	—	—	—	24-9	72.7	23-16	59.0	47-25	65.3
Stewart	—	—	24-13	64.9	33-3	91.7	—	—	57-16	78.1

Thomas	—	—	—	—	—	—	—	—	18-4	81.8
Vinson	6-0	100.0	—	—	—	—	—	—	6-0	100.0
Warren	—	—	37-2	94.9	—	—	37-2	94.9	37-2	94.9
White	—	—	21-11	65.6	39-8	83.0	18-4	81.8	78-23	77.2
Whittaker	—	—	3-2	60.0	—	—	—	—	3-2	60.0
Total	35-17	67.3	266-83	76.2	340-85	80.0	269-86	75-8	553-149	78.8

Note: Includes only those cases in which a majority voted to formally alter precedent. Figures to the left of the dash indicate the number of votes in favor of striking down legislation; figures to the right indicate the number of votes in favor of upholding legislation. Percentages indicate the percent of cases in which the justice voted with the majority to formally alter precedent.

Determination of whether or not the Court has formally altered precedent is not a clear-cut judgment. Only those decisions in which the Court says that the decision has formally altered or "overruled" a previous decision of the Court are included. "Distinguished" precedents are not considered to have been formally altered. But those that "are disapproved," "are no longer good law," "can no longer be considered controlling," or "modify and narrow" are. Note further that the Court will occasionally assert that an earlier decision overruled a precedent even though that earlier decision contains no language to that effect. See, for example, the statement in *International Paper Co. v. Ouellette*, 479 U.S. 481 (1987), at 488, that *Illinois v. Milwaukee*, 406 U.S. 91 (1972), overruled *Ohio v. Wyandotte Chemicals Corp.*, 401 U.S. 493 (1971). Consequently, the list of overrulings for a given period of time need not remain constant because language in cases decided subsequent to that period may indicate that an earlier case overruled decisions even where not explicitly stated.

Source: U.S. Supreme Court Judicial Database, with analu = 0 and dec_type = 1, 6, or 7.

Table 6-10 Opinions of the Court, Dissenting Opinions, and
Concurring Opinions, 1790–2001 Terms

Justice	Participations[a] (N)	Opinions of the Court (N)	Dissenting opinions (N)	Concurring opinions (N)
Baldwin	609	39	11	7
Barbour	210	17	2	1
Black	3,754	481	310	88
Blackmun	3,239	304	256	256
Blair	29	0	0	0
Blatchford	3,496	427	2	0
Bradley	5,343	389	60	17
Brandeis	3,874	455	65	10
Brennan	4,427	428	456	258
Brewer	4,405	533	57	8
Breyer	709	71	81	54
Brown	3,408	453	44	10
Burger	2,394	247	118	119
Burton	1,259	96	50	15
Butler	2,811	325	35	6
Byrnes	147	16	0	0
Campbell	696	92	18	5
Cardozo	2,134	129	23	2
Catron	1,730	157	26	12
Salmon Chase	1,226	134	8	2
Samuel Chase	188	1	1	1
Clark	1,717	214	98	24
Clarke	1,200	128	22	2
Clifford	3,428	395	60	8
Curtis	427	48	8	3
Cushing	217	4	0	3
Daniel	1,253	87	47	9
Davis	2,250	192	10	2
Day	4,160	430	22	2
Douglas	4,157	524	486	154
Duvall	958	16	1	1
Ellsworth	35	9	0	0
Field	7,455	544	84	19
Fortas	379	38	33	24
Frankfurter	2,681	247	251	132
Fuller	4,687	750	32	1
Ginsburg	816	85	53	47
Goldberg	345	36	23	28
Gray	5,366	450	11	4
Grier	1,903	194	12	2
Harlan I	7,927	737	119	17
Harlan II	1,826	165	311	204
Holmes	5,767	873	72	14
Hughes	3,155	395	17	2

Table 6-10   *(Continued)*

Justice	Participations[a] (N)	Opinions of the Court (N)	Dissenting opinions (N)	Concurring opinions (N)
Hunt	1,902	141	5	4
Iredell	55	0	1	1
H. Jackson	762	46	4	0
R. Jackson	1,441	150	107	47
Jay	25	1	0	0
T. Johnson	10	0	0	0
W. Johnson	1,057	109	30	11
Kennedy	1,635	163	63	122
J. Lamar	1,485	112	2	0
L. Q. C. Lamar	1,304	101	2	1
Livingston	513	38	7	3
Lurton	1,211	96	2	0
J. Marshall	1,111	508	6	0
T. Marshall	3,187	317	328	105
Matthews	2,668	233	5	2
McKenna	5,580	646	30	4
McKinley	793	19	3	1
McLean	1,855	245	33	5
McReynolds	4,789	488	65	7
Miller	5,839	608	67	6
Minton	603	66	35	7
Moody	700	62	4	0
Moore	25	0	0	0
Murphy	1,336	132	66	18
Nelson	2,408	290	22	6
O'Connor	2,664	302	168	210
Paterson	112	1	1	0
Peckham	2,695	312	8	2
Pitney	2,455	249	19	5
Powell	2,126	242	152	186
Reed	2,215	228	79	21
Rehnquist	4,246	483	342	120
Roberts	2,237	296	67	2
J. Rutledge	5	0	0	0
W. Rutledge	873	65	59	34
Sanford	1,457	129	3	1
Scalia	1,819	195	171	234
Shiras	2,381	251	15	0
Souter	1,168	120	81	67
Stevens	3,582	363	619	368
Stewart	2,863	304	225	173
Stone	3,392	456	93	37
Story	1,340	270	13	1
Strong	2,126	238	19	2

(Table continues)

Table 6-10   *(Continued)*

Justice	Participations[a] (N)	Opinions of the Court (N)	Dissenting opinions (N)	Concurring opinions (N)
Sutherland	2,535	288	23	2
Swayne	2,874	335	9	3
Taft	1,680	255	2	1
Taney	1,708	260	14	7
Thomas	1,034	92	87	84
Thompson	834	87	10	2
Todd	608	12	0	1
Trimble	127	16	0	0
Van Devanter	5,220	360	4	1
Hughes	3,155	395	17	2
Vinson	654	76	12	0
Waite	3,863	872	23	2
Warren	1,754	165	56	21
Washington	851	69	1	0
Wayne	2,040	144	5	6
B. White	4,089	456	302	236
E. White	5,807	680	49	11
Whittaker	561	42	52	18
Wilson	48	2	1	0
Woodbury	406	42	9	2
Woods	2,144	164	1	0

Note: Given that we used two data sources to assemble this table, readers should be aware that differences probably exist in the way those collecting the data defined opinions of the Court, dissenting opinions, and concurring opinions. We only report their results and make no attempt to impose consistency on the data.

[a] Figures for justices seated prior to 1953 are approximations based on the number of majority opinions decided during their tenures.

Sources: For justices seated before the 1953 term: Albert P. Blaustein and Roy M. Mersky, *The First One Hundred Justices* (Hamden, Conn.: Shoe String Press, 1978), 142–146; for justices seated during and after the 1953 term: U.S. Supreme Court Judicial Database, with analu = 0 and dec_type = 1, 6, or 7.

Table 6-11 Opinion Writing, 1946–2001 Terms

Justice[a]	Participation	Opinions of the Court	Judgments of the Court[b]	Dissents	Concurrences		Dissents (jurisdictional)[e]	Wrote no opinion
					Regular[c]	Special[d]		
Black	2,743	300 (10.9)	10 (0.4)	339 (12.4)	59 (2.2)	92 (3.4)	1 (0.0)	1,942 (70.8)
Blackmun	3,239	304 (9.4)	10 (0.3)	256 (7.9)	111 (3.4)	145 (4.5)	3 (0.1)	2,510 (77.5)
Brennan	4,427	428 (9.7)	24 (0.5)	456 (10.3)	113 (2.6)	145 (3.3)	0 (—)	3,261 (73.7)
Breyer	709	71 (10.0)	7 (0.9)	81 (11.4)	32 (4.5)	22 (3.1)	0 (—)	496 (70.0)
Burger	2,394	247 (10.3)	11 (0.5)	118 (4.9)	76 (3.1)	43 (1.8)	1 (0.0)	1,898 (79.3)
Burton	1,277	89 (7.0)	1 (0.1)	77 (6.0)	8 (0.6)	10 (0.8)	0 (—)	1,092 (85.5)
Clark	1,914	215 (11.2)	1 (0.1)	112 (5.9)	15 (0.8)	24 (1.3)	1 (0.1)	1,546 (80.8)
Douglas	3,261	364 (11.2)	3 (0.1)	595 (18.2)	106 (3.3)	108 (3.3)	7 (0.2)	2,078 (63.7)
Fortas	379	38 (10.0)	2 (0.5)	33 (8.7)	11 (2.9)	13 (3.4)	1 (0.3)	281 (74.1)
Frankfurter	1,668	140 (8.4)	14 (0.8)	236 (14.1)	59 (3.5)	86 (5.2)	31 (1.9)	1,102 (66.1)
Ginsburg	816	85 (10.4)	0 (—)	33 (6.5)	30 (3.7)	17 (2.1)	0 (—)	631 (77.3)

Table 6-11 (*Continued*)

Justice[a]	Participation	Opinions of the Court	Judgments of the Court[b]	Dissents	Concurrences Regular[c]	Concurrences Special[d]	Dissents (jurisdictional)[e]	Wrote no opinion
Goldberg	345	36 (10.4)	0 —	23 (6.7)	14 (4.6)	14 (4.6)	1 (0.3)	257 (74.5)
Harlan	1,826	165 (9.0)	6 (0.3)	311 (17.0)	81 (4.4)	123 (6.7)	2 (0.1)	1,138 (62.3)
Jackson	795	87 (10.9)	3 (0.4)	103 (13.0)	13 (1.6)	26 (3.3)	3 (0.4)	560 (70.4)
Kennedy	1,635	163 (10.0)	25 (0.3)	63 (3.9)	72 (4.4)	50 (3.1)	0 —	1,282 (78.4)
Marshall	3,187	317 (9.9)	5 (0.2)	328 (10.3)	2 (1.3)	63 (2.0)	2 (0.1)	2,430 (76.3)
Minton	636	64 (10.0)	0 —	40 (6.3)	0 —	4 (0.6)	1 (0.2)	527 (82.9)
Murphy	363	35 (9.6)	0 —	36 (9.9)	4 (1.1)	2 (0.6)	0 —	286 (78.9)
O'Connor	2,664	302 (11.3)	12 (0.5)	168 (6.3)	124 (4.7)	86 (3.2)	1 —	1,971 (74.1)
Powell	2,126	242 (11.4)	12 (0.6)	152 (7.1)	109 (5.1)	77 (3.6)	0 —	1,534 (72.2)
Reed	1,065	98 (9.2)	6 (0.6)	79 (7.4)	4 (0.4)	19 (1.8)	0 —	859 (80.7)
Rehnquist	4,246	483 (11.4)	15 (0.4)	342 (9.1)	52 (1.2)	68 (1.6)	2 (0.0)	3,284 (77.3)
Rutledge	371	27 (7.3)	1 (0.3)	40 (10.8)	12 (3.2)	22 (5.9)	0 —	26.9 (72.5)

Scalia	1,819	185 (10.2)	4 (0.2)	171 (7.9)	92 (4.8)	142 (9.1)	1,225 (68.3)	1 (—)
Souter	1,168	120 (10.3)	3 (0.2)	81 (6.9)	42 (3.6)	25 (2.1)	895 (76.6)	2 (0.2)
Stevens	3,582	323 (10.1)	21 (0.6)	619 (17.3)	160 (4.5)	208 (5.8)	2,204 (61.5)	7 (0.2)
Stewart	2,863	304 (10.6)	10 (0.3)	225 (7.9)	72 (2.5)	101 (3.5)	2,147 (75.0)	4 (0.1)
Thomas	1,034	92 (8.9)	2 (0.2)	87 (8.4)	48 (4.6)	36 (3.5)	768 (74.4)	0 (—)
Vinson	747	74 (9.9)	3 (0.4)	21 (2.8)	0 (—)	0 (—)	649 (86.9)	0 (—)
Warren	1,754	165 (9.4)	5 (0.3)	56 (3.2)	10 (0.6)	11 (0.6)	1,506 (85.9)	1 (0.1)
White	4,089	456 (11.2)	19 (0.5)	302 (7.4)	98 (2.4)	138 (3.4)	3,073 (75.2)	3 (0.1)
Whittaker	561	42 (7.5)	0 (—)	52 (9.3)	6 (1.1)	12 (2.1)	449 (80.0)	0 (—)

Note: Figures in parentheses are percentage of listed activity relative to overall participation. Data include all orally argued case citations.

[a] For those justices seated prior to 1946, data are not completely descriptive of their careers.
[b] Plurality rulings that occur when no majority agrees on the justification for a decision.
[c] Joined majority opinion but wrote separately as well.
[d] Explicitly disagreed with rationale in majority opinion.
[e] Includes dissent (in the form of an opinion) from a dismissal or denial of certiorari, dissent from summary affirmation of an appeal, or dissent from the Court's assertion of jurisdiction.

Source: U.S. Supreme Court Judicial Database, analu = 0 and dec_type = 1, 6, or 7.

Table 6-12   Number of Solo Dissents, 1946–2001 Terms

Justice[a]	Solo dissents	Solo dissents as % of participations in solo dissent cases[b]
Black	86	17.0
Blackmun	27	6.9
Brennan	22	3.3
Breyer	4	8.0
Burger	14	4.3
Burton	21	9.9
Clark	21	6.4
Douglas	240	42.6
Fortas	2	1.8
Frankfurter	35	13.4
Ginsburg	2	3.9
Goldberg	0	0.0
Harlan	79	22.5
Jackson	20	16.4
Kennedy	2	1.6
Marshall	33	8.1
Minton	2	1.9
Murphy	2	3.4
O'Connor	9	4.1
Powell	11	4.2
Reed	16	9.3
Rehnquist	71	17.6
Rutledge	4	6.7
Scalia	18	4.3
Souter	4	7.8
Stevens	126	38.9
Stewart	28	5.6
Thomas	6	6.7
Vinson	1	0.7
Warren	4	1.2
White	36	6.1
Whittaker	13	17.1

Note: Jurisdictional dissents and dissents from denials of certiorari are excluded. Unit of analysis is docket number of orally argued cases.

[a] For those justices seated prior to 1946, data are not completely descriptive of their careers.

[b] Indicates percentage of cases in which justice was the solo dissenter in cases containing solo dissents.

Source: U.S. Supreme Court Judicial Database.

Table 6-13 Significant Opinions Based on Congressional Quarterly's List of Major Decisions

Justice (appointment number)	Case	Opinion[a]	Subject matter
Baldwin, Henry (23)	Groves v. Slaughter (1841)	C	Slavery
Barbour, Philip P. (26)	City of New York v. Miln (1837)	M	Commerce
Black, Hugo L. (79)	Johnson v. Zerbst (1938)	M	Right to counsel
	Korematsu v. United States (1944)	M	War powers
	United States v. Lovett (1944)	M	Bills of attainder
	United States v. South-Eastern Underwriters Assn. (1944)	M	Commerce
	Everson v. Board of Education (1947)	M	Freedom of religion
	United States v. California (1947)	M	Offshore lands
	Illinois ex rel. McCollum v. Board of Education (1948)	M	Freedom of religion
	Youngstown Sheet and Tube v. Sawyer (1952)	M	Powers of the president
	Terry v. Adams (1953)	J	Voting rights
	Engle v. Vitale (1962)	M	Freedom of religion
	Gideon v. Wainwright (1963)	M	Right to counsel
	Griffin v. County School Board of Prince Edward County (1964)	M	Civil rights
	Wesberry v. Sanders (1964)	M	Voting rights
	Pointer v. Texas (1965)	M	Due process
	Oregon v. Mitchell; Texas v. Mitchell; United States v. Idaho; United States v. Arizona (1970)	J	Voting rights
	Younger v. Harris (1971)	M	Federal courts
Blackmun, Harry A. (102)	Graham v. Richardson (1971)	M	Equal protection
	McKeiver v. Pennsylvania, In re Burris (1971)	J	Due process
	Roe v. Wade (1973)	M	Abortion
	Bigelow v. Virginia (1975)	M	Freedom of speech
	Complete Auto Transit Inc. v. Brady (1977)	M	Taxes

(Table continues)

Table 6-13 *(Continued)*

Justice (appointment number)	Case	Opinion[a]	Subject matter
	Ballew v. Georgia (1978)	J	Jury trials
	Garcia v. San Antonio Metropolitan Transit Authority (1985)	M	Powers of Congress
	Thornburgh v. American College of Obstetricians and Gynecologists (1986)	M	Abortion
	Allegheny County v. American Civil Liberties Union, Greater Pittsburgh Chapter (1989)	J	Freedom of religion
	Mistretta v. United States (1989)	M	Powers of Congress
	International Union, United Automobile, Aerospace & Agricultural Implement Workers of America, UAW v. Johnson Controls, Inc. (1991)	M	Civil rights
	Austin v. United States (1993)	M	Excessive fines
	J.E.B. v. Alabama ex rel. T.B. (1994)	M	Equal protection
Blair, John, Jr. (5)	*Chisholm v. Georgia* (1793)	S	Federal courts
Blatchford, Samuel (49)	*Chicago, Milwaukee & St. Paul Railroad Co. v. Minnesota* (1890)	M	Due process
	Counselman v. Hitchcock (1892)	M	Self-incrimination
Bradley, Joseph P. (42)	*Ex parte Siebold* (1880)	M	Voting rights
	The Civil Rights Cases (1883)	M	Civil rights
	Boyd v. United States (1886)	M	Search and seizure
Brandeis, Louis D. (69)	*Truax v. Corrigan* (1921)	D	Labor, due process, equal protection
	Olmstead v. United States (1928)	D	Wiretapping, privacy
Brennan, William J., Jr. (94)	*Roth v. United States* (1957)	M	Obscenity
	Baker v. Carr (1962)	M	Voting rights

Case		Category
NAACP v. Button (1963)	M	Freedom of association
Fay v. Noia (1963)	M	Federal courts
Malloy v. Hogan (1964)	M	Self-incrimination
New York Times Co. v. Sullivan (1964)	M	Freedom of press
Dombrowski v. Pfister (1965)	M	Freedom of association
Albertson v. Subversive Activities Control Board (1965)	M	Self-incrimination
Keyishian v. Board of Regents (1967)	M	Freedom of association
Warden v. Hayden (1967)	M	Search and seizure
United States v. Wade (1967)	M	Right to counsel
Green v. County School Board of New Kent County, Va. (1968)	M	Civil rights
Kirkpatrick v. Preisler (1969)	M	Voting rights
Shapiro v. Thompson, Washington v. Legrant; Reynolds v. Smith (1969)	M	Personal liberty
In re Winship (1970)	M	Due process
Keyes v. Denver School District No. 1 (1973)	M	Civil rights
Weinberger v. Wiesenfeld (1975)	M	Equal protection
Craig v. Boren (1976)	M	Equal protection
Michelin Tire Corp. v. Wages (1976)	M	Taxes
Elrod v. Burns (1976)	M	Freedom of association
Monell v. Department of Social Services, City of New York (1978)	M	Federal courts
Orr v. Orr (1979)	M	Equal protection
Davis v. Passman (1979)	M	Due process
United Steelworkers of America v. Weber; Kaiser Aluminum v. Weber; United States v. Weber (1979)	M	Civil rights
County of Washington v. Gunther (1981)	M	Equal protection
Plyler v. Doe, Texas v. Certain Named and Unnamed Undocumented Alien Children (1982)	M	Equal protection
Board of Education, Island Trees Union Free School District #26 v. Pico (1982)	J	Freedom of expression
Karcher v. Daggett (1983)	M	Voting rights
Roberts v. U.S. Jaycees (1984)	M	Freedom of association
Aguilar v. Felton (1985)	M	Freedom of religion

(Table continues)

Table 6-13 (*Continued*)

Justice (appointment number)	Case	Opinion[a]	Subject matter
	Local #28 of the Sheet Metal Workers' International v. Equal Employment Opportunity Commission (1986)	J	Civil rights
	Local #93, International Association of Firefighters v. City of Cleveland and Cleveland Vanguards (1986)	M	Civil rights
	United States v. Paradise (1987)	J	Civil rights
	Johnson v. Transportation Agency of Santa Clara County (1987)	M	Civil rights
	Edwards v. Aguillard (1987)	M	Freedom of religion
	South Carolina v. Baker (1988)	M	Powers of Congress
	Texas v. Johnson (1989)	M	Freedom of expression
	Metro Broadcasting Inc. v. Federal Communications Commission; Astroline Communications Co. v. Shurberg Broadcasting of Hartford Inc. (1990)	M	Civil rights
	Rutan v. Republican Party of Illinois; Frech v. Rutan (1990)	M	Freedom of association
	United States v. Eichman; United States v. Haggerty (1990)	M	Freedom of expression
Brewer, David J. (52)	Louisville, New Orleans and Texas Railway Co. v. Mississippi (1890)	M	Civil rights
	In re Debs (1895)	M	Commerce
	Muller v. Oregon (1908)	M	State powers
Breyer, Stephen G. (113)	United States v. Lopez (1995)	D	Commerce
Brown, Henry B. (53)	Pollock v. Farmers' Loan and Trust Co. (1895)	D	Taxes
	Plessy v. Ferguson (1896)	M	Civil rights
	Holden v. Hardy (1898)	M	Due process
	The Insular Cases: DeLima v. Bidwell (1901)	M	Territories
Burger, Warren E. (101)	Griggs v. Duke Power Co. (1971)	M	Civil rights
	Harris v. New York (1971)	M	Self-incrimination

Lemon v. Kurtzman (1971)	M	Freedom of religion
Reed v. Reed (1971)	M	Equal protection
Swann v. Charlotte-Mecklenburg Board of Education (1971)	M	Civil rights
United States v. Brewster (1972)	M	Official immunity
Miller v. California (1973)	M	Obscenity
Strunk v. United States (1973)	M	Due process
Milliken v. Bradley (1974)	M	Civil rights
United States v. Nixon (1974)	M	Powers of the president
Goldfarb v. Virginia State Bar (1975)	M	Commerce
Nebraska Press Association v. Stuart (1976)	M	Freedom of press
United States v. Helstoski (1979)	M	Official immunity
Hutchinson v. Proxmire (1979)	M	Official immunity
Fullilove v. Klutznick (1980)	J	Civil rights
Richmond Newspapers Inc. v. Commonwealth of Virginia (1980)	J	Right of access
Chandler v. Florida (1981)	M	Due process
H.L. v. Matheson (1981)	M	Abortion
Bob Jones University v. United States; Goldsboro Christian Schools v. United States (1983)	M	Civil rights
INS v. Chadha (1983)	M	Powers of Congress
Lynch v. Donnelly (1984)	M	Freedom of religion
Nix v. Williams (1984)	M	Due process
Bowsher v. Synar; Senate v. Synar; O'Neill v. Synar (1986)	M	Powers of Congress
Burton, Harold H. (88)		
Joint Anti-Fascist Refugee Committee v. McGrath (1951)	M	Freedom of association
Butler, Pierce (73)		
Powell v. Alabama (1932)	D	Right to counsel
Morehead v. New York ex rel. Tipaldo (1936)	M	Due process
Breedlove v. Suttles (1937)	M	Voting rights
Byrnes, James F. (85)		
Edwards v. California (1941)	M	Commerce
Campbell, John A. (34)		
Dodge v. Woolsey (1856)	D	Contracts, state taxation
Scott v. Sandford (1857)	C	Slavery

(Table continues)

Table 6-13 (*Continued*)

Justice (appointment number)	Case	Opinion[a]	Subject matter
Cardozo, Benjamin (78)	Nixon v. Condon (1932)	M	Voting rights
	Helvering v. Davis (1937)	M	Spending power
	Palko v. Connecticut (1937)	M	Due process
	Steward Machine Co. v. Davis (1937)	M	Spending power
Catron, John (27)	The License Cases (1847)	C	Commerce
	Scott v. Sandford (1857)	C	Slavery
Chase, Salmon P. (40)	Mississippi v. Johnson (1867)	M	Federal courts
	Ex parte McCardle (1869)	M	Federal courts
	Texas v. White (1869)	M	State powers
	Veazie Bank v. Fenno (1869)	M	State powers
	Hepburn v. Griswold (1870)	M	Currency
Chase, Samuel (10)	Hylton v. United States (1796)	S	Taxes
	Ware v. Hylton (1796)	S	Treaties
	Calder v. Bull (1798)	S	Ex post facto laws
Clark, Tom C. (90)	Garner v. Board of Public Works (1951)	M	Freedom of association
	Slochower v. Board of Higher Education of New York City (1956)	M	Self-Incrimination
	Watkins v. United States (1957)	D	Powers of Congress
	Mapp v. Ohio (1961)	M	Search and seizure
	Ker v. California (1963)	J	Search and seizure
	Heart of Atlanta Motel v. United States (1964)	M	Civil rights
Clarke, John H. (70)	Abrams v. United States (1919)	M	Freedom of expression
Clifford, Nathan (35)	Knox v. Lee, Parker v. Davis (1871)	D	Legal tender

Curtis, Benjamin R. (33)	*Cooley v. Board of Wardens of Port of Philadelphia* (1852)	M	Commerce
	Murray's Lessee v. Hoboken Land and Improvement Co. (1856)	M	Due process
	Scott v. Sandford (1857)	D	Slavery
Cushing, William (3)	*Chisholm v. Georgia* (1793)	S	Federal courts
	Ware v. Hylton (1796)	S	Treaties
Daniel, Peter V. (29)	*Scott v. Sandford* (1857)	C	Slavery
Davis, David (38)	*Ex parte Milligan* (1866)	M	Powers of the president
Day, William R. (60)	*Muskrat v. United States* (1911)	M	Federal courts
	Weeks v. United States (1914)	M	Search and seizure
	Buchanan v. Warley (1917)	M	Due process
	Hammer v. Dagenhart (1918)	M	Commerce
Douglas, William O. (82)	*Sunshine Anthracite Coal Co. v. Adkins* (1940)	M	Taxes
	Skinner v. Oklahoma (1942)	M	Equal protection
	Murdock v. Pennsylvania (1943)	M	Freedom of religion
	Girourard v. United States (1946)	M	Freedom of religion
	Terminiello v. Chicago (1949)	M	Freedom of speech
	Kent v. Dulles (1958)	M	Personal liberty
	Lassiter v. Northhampton County Board of Education (1959)	M	Voting rights
	Gray v. Sanders (1963)	M	Voting rights
	Griffin v. California (1965)	M	Self-incrimination
	Griswold v. Connecticut (1965)	M	Personal privacy
	Adderley v. Florida (1966)	D	Freedom of expression
	Elfbrandt v. Russell (1966)	M	Freedom of association
	Harper v. Virginia State Board of Elections (1966)	M	Voting rights
	Argersinger v. Hamlin (1972)	M	Right to counsel
Duvall, Gabriel (18)	*Mima Queen and Child v. Hepburn* (1813)	D	Slavery

(Table continues)

Table 6-13 *(Continued)*

Justice (appointment number)	Case	Opinion[a]	Subject matter
Ellsworth, Oliver (11)	None		
Field, Stephen J. (39)	Cummings v. Missouri, Ex parte Garland (1867)	M	Ex post facto laws
	Paul v. Virginia (1869)	M	Commerce
	Bradley v. Fisher (1872)	M	Federal courts
	Low v. Austin (1872)	M	Taxes
	Munn v. Illinois (1877)	D	State powers
	Chae Chan Ping v. United States (Chinese Exclusion Cases) (1889)	M	Immigration
	Geofroy v. Riggs (1890)	M	Treaties
	Virginia v. Tennessee (1893)	M	Compacts
Fortas, Abe (99)	In re Gault (1967)	M	Due process
	Tinker v. Des Moines Independent School District (1969)	M	Freedom of expression
Frankfurter, Felix (81)	Lane v. Wilson (1939)	M	Voting rights
	Minersville School District v. Gobitis (1940)	M	Freedom of religion
	McNabb v. United States (1943)	M	Due process
	Colegrove v. Green (1946)	J	Voting rights
	Wolf v. Colorado (1949)	M	Search and seizure
	Rochin v. California (1952)	M	Search and seizure
	Ullman v. United States (1956)	M	Self-incrimination
	Mallory v. United States (1957)	M	Due process
	Wiener v. United States (1958)	M	Powers of the president
	Gomillion v. Lightfoot (1960)	M	Voting rights
	Communist Party v. Subversive Activities Control Board (1961)	M	Freedom of association
Fuller, Melville W. (51)	California v. Southern Pacific Co. (1895)	M	Federal courts
	Pollock v. Farmers' Loan and Trust Co. (1895)	M	Taxes

Justice	Case		Topic
	United States v. E.C. Knight (1895)	M	Commerce
	Champion v. Ames (1903)	D	Commerce
	Loewe v. Lawler (1908)	M	Commerce
Ginsburg, Ruth Bader (112)	Miller v. Johnson (1995)	D	Voting rights
	United States v. Virginia (1996)	M	Equal protection
Goldberg, Arthur J. (98)	Aptheker v. Secretary of State (1964)	M	Freedom of association
	Escobedo v. Illinois (1964)	M	Self-incrimination, counsel
	Murphy v. The Waterfront Commission of New York Harbor (1964)	M	Self-incrimination
	Griswold v. Connecticut (1965)	C	Personal privacy
Gray, Horace (48)	Wisconsin v. Pelican Insurance Company (1888)	M	Federal courts
	United States v. Wong Kim Ark (1898)	M	Citizenship
Grier, Robert C. (32)	The Prize Cases (1863)	M	Powers of the president
Harlan, John Marshall I (45)	Santa Clara County v. Southern Pacific Railroad Co. (1886)	M	Equal protection
	Mugler v. Kansas (1887)	M	State powers
	United States v. Texas (1892)	M	Federal courts
	Pollock v. Farmers' Loan and Trust Co. (1895)	D	Taxes
	Plessy v. Ferguson (1896)	D	Civil rights
	Chicago, Burlington & Quincy Railroad Company v. Chicago (1897)	M	Due process
	Smyth v. Ames (1898)	M	Due process
	Champion v. Ames (1903)	M	Commerce
	Northern Securities Co. v. United States (1904)	M	Commerce
	Adair v. United States (1908)	M	Commerce
Harlan, John Marshall II (93)	Yates v. United States (1957)	M	Freedom of speech
	NAACP v. Alabama ex rel. Patterson (1958)	M	Freedom of association
	Barenblatt v. United States (1959)	M	Powers of Congress

(Table continues)

Table 6-13 (Continued)

Justice (appointment number)	Case	Opinion[a]	Subject matter
	Hoyt v. Florida (1961)	M	Equal protection
	Scales v. United States, Noto v. United States (1961)	M	Freedom of association
	Reynolds v. Sims (1964)	D	Voting rights
	Miranda v. Arizona (1966)	D	Self-incrimination
	Gaston County v. United States (1969)	M	Voting rights
Holmes, Oliver W., Jr. (59)	Swift and Co. v. United States (1905)	M	Commerce
	Georgia v. Tennessee Copper Company (1907)	M	State powers
	United States v. Mosley (1915)	M	Voting rights
	Abrams v. United States (1919)	D	Freedom of expression
	Schenck v. United States (1919)	M	Freedom of expression
	Missouri v. Holland (1920)	M	Treaties
	Moore v. Dempsey (1923)	M	Due process
	Buck v. Bell (1927)	M	Due process
	Nixon v. Herndon (1927)	M	Voting rights
Hughes, Charles E. (63, 76)	Shreveport Rate Case (1914)	M	Commerce
	Virginia v. West Virginia (1915)	M	Interstate relations
	Near v. Minnesota (1931)	M	Freedom of the press
	Stromberg v. California (1931)	M	Freedom of speech
	Wood v. Broom (1932)	M	Voting rights
	Home Building and Loan Association v. Blaisdell (1934)	M	Contracts
	Gold Clause Cases: Norman v. Baltimore and Ohio Railroad Co.; Nortz v. United States; Perry v. United States (1935)	M	Currency
	Norris v. Alabama (1935)	M	Jury trials
	Panama Refining Co. v. Ryan (1935)	M	Powers of Congress
	Schechter Poultry Corp. v. United States (1935)	M	Commerce
	Ashwander v. Tennessee Valley Authority (1936)	M	Powers of Congress

Justice	Case		Topic
	Brown v. Mississippi (1936)	M	Due process
	DeJonge v. Oregon (1937)	M	Freedom of assembly
	N.L.R.B. v. Jones & Laughlin Steel Corp. (1937)	M	Commerce
	West Coast Hotel v. Parrish (1937)	M	Due process
	Lovell v. Griffin (1938)	M	Freedom of the press
	Missouri ex rel. Gaines v. Canada (1938)	M	Civil rights
	Coleman v. Miller (1939)	M	Federal courts
	Cox v. New Hampshire (1941)	M	Freedom of assembly
Hunt, Ward (43)	*United States v. Reese* (1876)	D	Voting rights
Iredell, James (6)	*Chisholm v. Georgia* (1793)	D	Federal court jurisdiction
	Hylton v. United States (1796)	S	Taxes
	Calder v. Bull (1798)	S	Ex post facto laws
Jackson, Howell E. (55)	*Pollock v. Farmers' Loan and Trust* (1895)	D	Taxes
Jackson, Robert H. (86)	*Wickard v. Filburn* (1942)	M	Commerce
	West Virginia State Board of Education v. Barnette (1943)	M	Freedom of religion
	Korematsu v. United States (1944)	D	War powers
	Fay v. New York (1947)	M	Jury trials
	Youngstown Sheet and Tube Co. v. Sawyer (1952)	C	Powers of the president
Jay, John (1)	*Chisholm v. Georgia* (1793)	S	Federal courts
Johnson, Thomas (7)	None		
Johnson, William (15)	*Martin v. Hunter's Lessee* (1816)	C	Judicial review
	Gibbons v. Ogden (1824)	C	Commerce
Kennedy, Anthony (109)	*National Treasury Employees Union v. Raab* (1989)	M	Search and seizure
	Skinner v. Railway Labor Executives Association (1989)	M	Search and seizure

(Table continues)

Table 6-13 (*Continued*)

Justice (appointment number)	Case	Opinion[a]	Subject matter
	Ohio v. Akron Center for Reproductive Health (1990)	J	Abortion
	Masson v. New Yorker Magazine (1991)	M	Freedom of the press
	Planned Parenthood of Southeastern Pennsylvania v. Casey (1992)	J	Abortion
	Lee v. Weisman (1992)	M	Freedom of religion
	Holder v. Hall (1994)	J	Voting rights
	Turner Broadcasting System, Inc. v. Federal Communications Commission (1994)	J	Freedom of expression
	Miller v. Johnson (1995)	M	Voting rights
	Rosenberger v. Rector and Visitors of University of Virginia (1995)	M	Freedom of religion
	O'Hara Truck Service v. Northlake (1996)	M	Freedom of expression
	Romer v. Evans (1996)	M	Civil rights
Lamar, Joseph R. (66)	*Gompers v. Buck's Stove and Range Co.* (1911)	M	Contempt
Lamar, Lucius Q. C. (50)	*Kidd v. Pearson* (1888)	M	Commerce
	In re Neagle (1890)	D	Powers of the president
Livingston, H. Brockholst (16)	None		
Lurton, Horace (62)	*Coyle v. Smith* (1911)	M	State powers
Marshall, John (14)	*Marbury v. Madison* (1803)	M	Judicial review
	Bank of United States v. Deveaux (1809)	M	Federal courts
	Fletcher v. Peck (1810)	M	Contracts
	Dartmouth College v. Woodward (1819)	M	Contracts
	McCulloch v. Maryland (1819)	M	Powers of Congress
	Sturges v. Crowninshield (1819)	M	Contracts
	Cohens v. Virginia (1821)	M	Judicial review

	Gibbons v. Ogden (1824)	M	Commerce
	Osborn v. Bank of the United States (1824)	M	Federal courts
	Wayman v. Southard (1825)	M	Powers of Congress
	Brown v. Maryland (1827)	M	Taxes
	Foster v. Neilson (1829)	M	Federal courts
	Weston v. City Council of Charleston (1829)	M	Taxes
	Willson v. Blackbird Creek Marsh Co. (1829)	M	Commerce
	Craig v. Missouri (1830)	M	Bills of credit
	Worcester v. Georgia (1832)	M	State powers
	Barron v. Baltimore (1838)	M	Individual rights
Marshall, Thurgood (100)	Benton v. Maryland (1969)	M	Due process
	Furman v. Georgia (1972)	C	Cruel and unusual punishment
	San Antonio Independent School District v. Rodriguez (1973)	D	Equal protection
	Ake v. Oklahoma (1985)	M	Right to counsel
	Ford v. Wainwright (1986)	J	Cruel and unusual punishment
	Vasquez v. Hillery (1986)	M	Equal protection
	Tashjian v. Republican Party of Connecticut (1987)	M	Freedom of association
Matthews, Stanley (47)	Hurtado v. California (1884)	M	Due process
	Yick Wo v. Hopkins (1886)	M	Civil rights
McKenna, Joseph (58)	Weems v. United States (1910)	M	Cruel and unusual punishment
	Hadacheck v. Los Angeles (1915)	M	State powers
	Bunting v. Oregon (1917)	M	Due process
McKinley, John (28)	Bank of Augusta v. Earle (1839)	D	Corporations

(Table continues)

Table 6-13 (*Continued*)

Justice (appointment number)	Case	Opinion[a]	Subject matter
McLean, John (22)	Briscoe v. Bank of the Commonwealth of Kentucky (1837)	M	Bills of credit
	Rhode Island v. Massachusetts (1846)	M	Interstate boundaries
	Smith v. Turner; Norris v. Boston (The Passenger Cases) (1849)	M	Commerce
	Cooley v. Board of Wardens of Port of Philadelphia (1852)	D	Commerce
	Pennsylvania v. Wheeling and Belmont Bridge (1852)	M	Commerce
	Scott v. Sandford (1857)	D	Slavery
McReynolds, James C. (68)	Newberry v. United States (1921)	M	Powers of Congress
	Pierce v. Society of Sisters (1925)	M	Freedom of religion
	The Gold Clause Cases (1935)	D	Currency
	N.L.R.B. v. Jones & Laughlin Steel Corp. (1937)	D	Commerce
Miller, Samuel (37)	Woodruff v. Parham (1869)	M	Taxes
	Bradwell v. State of Illinois (1873)	M	Privileges and immunities
	Slaughterhouse Cases (1873)	M	Privileges and immunities
	Henderson v. Wickham; Commissioners of Immigration v. The North German Lloyd; Chy Lung v. Freeman (1876)	M	Commerce
	Kilbourn v. Thompson (1881)	M	Powers of Congress
	Ex parte Yarbrough (1884)	M	Voting rights
	Head Money Cases (1884)	M	Taxes
	Wabash, St. Louis and Pacific Railway Co. v. Illinois (1886)	M	Commerce
Minton, Sherman (91)	United States v. Rabinowitz (1950)	M	Search and seizure
Moody, William H. (61)	First Employers' Liability Case (1908)	D	Commerce
	Twining v. New Jersey (1908)	M	Due process
Moore, Alfred (13)	None		

Justice / Case	Code	Topic
Murphy, Frank (83)		
Chaplinsky v. New Hampshire (1942)	M	Freedom of speech
Wolf v. Colorado (1949)	D	Search and seizure
Nelson, Samuel (30)		
Scott v. Sandford (1857)	C	Slavery
O'Connor, Sandra Day (106)		
Garcia v. San Antonio Metropolitan Transit Authority (1985)	D	Powers of Congress
Tison v. Arizona (1987)	M	Cruel and unusual punishment
City of Richmond v. J.A. Croson Co. (1989)	J	Civil rights
Penry v. Lynaugh (1989)	J	Cruel and unusual punishment
Board of Education of the Westside Community Schools v. Mergens (1990)	J	Freedom of religion
Simon & Schuster v. Members of New York State Crime Victims Board (1991)	M	Freedom of press
Planned Parenthood of Southeastern Pennsylvania v. Casey (1992)	J	Abortion
Harris v. Forklift Systems (1993)	M	Civil rights
Shaw v. Reno (1993)	M	Voting rights
Adarand Constructors Inc. v. Peña (1995)	J	Civil rights
Board of County Commissioners v. Umbehr (1996)	M	Freedom of speech
Bush v. Vera (1996)	J	Voting rights
Paterson, William (8)		
Hylton v. United States (1796)	S	Taxes
Peckham, Rufus W. (57)		
Allgeyer v. Louisiana (1897)	M	Due process
Maxwell v. Dow (1900)	M	Due process
Lochner v. New York (1905)	M	Due process
Ex parte Young (1908)	M	Federal courts
Pitney, Mahlon (67)		
Frank v. Mangum (1915)	M	Due process
Duplex Printing Press Co. v. Deering (1921)	M	Commerce

(Table continues)

Table 6-13 (*Continued*)

Justice (appointment number)	Case	Opinion[a]	Subject matter
Powell, Lewis F., Jr. (103)	*Kastigar v. United States* (1972)	M	Self-incrimination
	San Antonio Independent School District v. Rodriguez (1973)	M	Equal protection
	Stone v. Powell; Wolff v. Rice (1976)	M	Federal courts
	Gregg v. Georgia, Proffitt v. Florida (1976)	J	Cruel and unusual punishment
	Village of Arlington Heights v. Metropolitan Housing Development Corp. (1977)	M	Civil rights
	First National Bank of Boston v. Bellotti (1978)	M	Freedom of speech
	Regents of the University of California v. Bakke (1978)	M	Civil rights
	Youngberg v. Romeo (1982)	M	Equal protection
	Nixon v. Fitzgerald (1982)	M	Official immunity
	Harlow v. Fitzgerald (1982)	M	Official immunity
	City of Akron v. Akron Center for Reproductive Health Inc.; Akron Center for Reproductive Health Inc. v. City of Akron (1983) *Planned Parenthood Association of Kansas City, Missouri v. Ashcroft; Ashcroft v. Planned Parenthood Association of Kansas City, Missouri* (1983)	M	Abortion
	Brown v. Thomson (1983)	M	Voting rights
	Solem v. Helm (1983)	M	Cruel and unusual punishment
	Wygant v. Jackson Board of Education (1986)	J	Civil rights
	Batson v. Kentucky (1986)	M	Equal protection
	McCleskey v. Kemp (1987)	M	Cruel and unusual punishment
Reed, Stanley F. (80)	*McNabb v. United States* (1943)	D	Self-incrimination
	Smith v. Allwright (1944)	M	Voting rights

Case		Topic
Morgan v. Virginia (1946)	M	Civil rights
Louisiana ex rel. Francis v. Resweber (1947)	J	Cruel and unusual punishment
United Public Workers v. Mitchell (1947)	M	Powers of Congress
Carlson v. Landon (1952)	M	Excessive bail
Rehnquist, William (104, 107)		
Mahan v. Howell; City of Virginia Beach v. Howell; Weinberg v. Prichard (1973)	M	Voting rights
Edelman v. Jordan (1974)	M	Federal courts
National League of Cities v. Usery (1976)	M	Commerce
Pasadena City Board of Education v. Spangler (1976)	M	Civil rights
Scott v. Illinois (1979)	M	Right to counsel
Burch v. Louisiana (1979)	M	Jury trials
Rostker v. Goldberg (1981)	M	Equal protection
Dames & Moore v. Regan (1981)	M	Powers of the president
Mueller v. Allen (1983)	M	Freedom of religion
New York v. Quarles (1984)	M	Self-incrimination
Schall v. Martin; Abrams v. Martin (1984)	M	Due process
Federal Election Commission v. National Conservative Political Action Committee; Democratic Party of United States v. National Conservative Political Action Committee (1985)	M	Freedom of expression
Lockhart v. McCree (1986)	M	Cruel and unusual punishment
United States v. Salerno (1987)	M	Due process
Morrison v. Olson (1988)	M	Powers of Congress
Webster v. Reproductive Health Services (1989)	J	Abortion
Cruzan v. Director, Missouri Department of Health (1990)	M	Personal liberty
Michigan, Department of State Police v. Sitz (1990)	M	Search and seizure
Arizona v. Fulminante (1991)	M	Due process
Barnes v. Glen Theatre (1991)	J	Freedom of expression
Payne v. Tennessee (1991)	M	Cruel and unusual punishment

(Table continues)

Table 6-13 (*Continued*)

Justice (appointment number)	Case	Opinion[a]	Subject matter
	Rust v. Sullivan (1991)	M	Freedom of speech
	Herrera v. Collins (1993)	M	Cruel and unusual punishment
	Zobrest v. Catalina Foothills School District (1993)	M	Freedom of religion
	Dolan v. City of Tigard (1994)	M	Due process
	Madsen v. Women's Health Center, Inc. (1994)	M	Freedom of speech
	Missouri v. Jenkins (1995)	M	Civil rights
	United States v. Lopez (1995)	M	Commerce
	Bennis v. Michigan (1996)	M	Due process
	Felkin v. Turpin (1996)	M	Habeas corpus
	Seminole Tribe of Florida v. Florida (1996)	M	State sovereignty
	Shaw v. Hunt (1996)	M	Voting rights
Roberts, Owen J. (77)	*Nebbia v. New York* (1934)	M	Due process
	Grovey v. Townsend (1935)	M	Voting rights
	Railroad Retirement Board v. Alton Railroad Co. (1935)	M	Commerce
	United States v. Butler (1936)	M	Spending power
	Mulford v. Smith (1938)	M	Commerce
	Cantwell v. Connecticut (1940)	M	Freedom of religion
	Betts v. Brady (1942)	M	Right to counsel
Rutledge, John (2, 9)	None		
Rutledge, Wiley B. (87)	*In re Yamashita* (1946)	D	War tribunals
Sanford, Edward T. (74)	*Gitlow v. New York* (1925)	M	Freedom of speech
	Corrigan v. Buckley (1926)	M	Civil rights
	Whitney v. California (1927)	M	Freedom of association

Scalia, Antonin (108)	Johnson v. Transportation Agency of Santa Clara County (1987)	D	Civil rights
	Stanford v. Kentucky (1989)	J	Cruel and unusual punishment
	Employment Division, Department of Human Resources of Oregon v. Smith (1990)	M	Freedom of religion
	R.A.V. v. City of St. Paul (1992)	M	Freedom of expression
	Capital Square Review and Advisory Board v. Pinette (1995)	J	Freedom of religion
	Veronica School District 47J v. Acton (1995)	M	Search and seizure
Shiras, George, Jr. (54)	DeLima v. Bidwell (1901)	D	Territories
Souter, David H. (110)	Planned Parenthood of Southeastern Pennsylvania v. Casey (1992)	J	Abortion
	Board of Education of Kiryas Joel Village School District v. Grumet (1994)	J	Freedom of religion
	Hurley v. Irish-American Gay, Lesbian and Bisexual Group of Boston (1995)	M	Freedom of expression
Stevens, John Paul (105)	Jurek v. Texas (1976)	J	Cruel and unusual punishment
	Roberts v. Louisiana (1976)	J	Cruel and unusual punishment
	Payton v. New York, Riddick v. New York (1980)	M	Search and seizure
	NAACP v. Claiborne Hardware Co. (1982)	M	Freedom of expression
	Wallace v. Jaffree (1985)	M	Freedom of religion
	Thompson v. Oklahoma (1988)	J	Cruel and unusual punishment
	Chisom v. Roemer; United States v. Roemer (1991)	M	Voting rights
	Sale v. Haitian Centers Council (1993)	M	Powers of the president
	McIntyre v. Ohio Elections Commission (1995)	M	Freedom of expression
	U.S. Term Limits v. Thornton (1995)	M	State powers
	44 Liquormart v. Rhode Island (1996)	J	Freedom of speech

(Table continues)

Table 6-13 *(Continued)*

Justice (appointment number)	Case	Opinion[a]	Subject matter
Stewart, Potter (96)	Elkins v. United States (1960)	M	Search and seizure
	Robinson v. California (1962)	M	Cruel and unusual punishment
	Edwards v. South Carolina (1963)	M	Freedom of speech
	Katz v. United States (1967)	M	Search and seizure
	Jones v. Alfred H. Mayer (1968)	M	Civil rights
	Chimel v. California (1969)	M	Search and seizure
	Geduldig v. Aiello (1974)	M	Equal protection
	Albemarle Paper Co. v. Moody (1975)	M	Civil rights
	Gregg v. Georgia (1976)	J	Cruel and unusual punishment
	Hills v. Gautreaux (1976)	M	Civil rights
	Runyon v. McCrary; Fairfax-Brewster School, Inc. v. Gonzales; Southern Independent School Assoc. v. McCrary (1976)	M	Civil rights
	Woodson v. North Carolina, Roberts v. Louisiana (1976)	J	Cruel and unusual punishment
	Gannett Co. Inc. v. DePasquale (1979)	M	Freedom of the press
	City of Mobile, Ala. v. Bolden (1980)	J	Voting rights
	Harris v. McRae (1980)	M	Powers of Congress
	Rhode Island v. Innis (1980)	M	Right to counsel
Stone, Harlan Fiske (75, 84)	United States v. Butler (1936)	D	Spending power
	Graves v. New York ex rel. O'Keefe (1939)	M	Taxes
	Minersville School District v. Gobitis (1940)	D	Freedom of religion
	United States v. Classic (1941)	M	Voting rights
	United States v. Darby Lumber Company (1941)	M	Commerce
	Ex parte Quirin (1942)	M	War powers

	Hirabayashi v. United States (1943)	M	War powers
	Yakus v. United States (1944)	M	Powers of Congress
Story, Joseph (19)	*Martin v. Hunter's Lessee* (1816)	M	Judicial review
	Martin v. Mott (1827)	M	Powers of the president
	Charles River Bridge v. Warren Bridge (1837)	D	Contracts
	Prigg v. Pennsylvania (1842)	M	Slavery
Strong, William (41)	*Knox v. Lee, Parker v. Davis* (1871)	M	Currency
Sutherland, George (72)	*Adkins v. Children's Hospital* (1923)	M	Due process
	Massachusetts v. Mellon; Frothingham v. Mellon (1923)	M	Federal courts
	Euclid v. Ambler Realty Co. (1926)	M	State powers
	Patton v. United States (1930)	M	Jury trials
	Powell v. Alabama (1932)	M	Right to counsel
	Humphrey's Executor v. United States (1935)	M	Powers of the president
	Carter v. Carter Coal Co. (1936)	M	Commerce
	Grosjean v. American Press Co. (1936)	M	Freedom of the press
	United States v. Curtiss-Wright Export Corp. (1936)	M	Powers of the president
Swayne, Noah H. (36)	*Slaughterhouse Cases* (1873)	D	Privileges and immunities
Taft, William H. (71)	*Bailey v. Drexel Furniture Co.* (1922)	M	Taxes
	Ponzi v. Fessenden (1922)	M	State powers
	United States v. Lanza (1922)	M	Double jeopardy
	Adkins v. Children's Hospital (1923)	D	Due process
	Carroll v. United States (1925)	M	Search and seizure
	Myers v. United States (1926)	M	Powers of the president
	Tumey v. Ohio (1927)	M	Due process
	J.W. Hampton Jr. & Co. v. United States (1928)	M	Taxes
	Olmstead v. United States (1928)	M	Search and seizure

(Table continues)

Table 6-13 *(Continued)*

Justice *(appointment number)*	Case	Opinion[a]	Subject matter
Taney, Roger B. (25)	*Charles River Bridge v. Warren Bridge* (1837)	M	Contracts
	Holmes v. Jennison (1840)	M	Foreign affairs
	Luther v. Borden (1849)	M	Federal courts
	Scott v. Sandford (1857)	M	Slavery
	Ableman v. Booth; United States v. Booth (1859)	M	Federal courts
	Kentucky v. Dennison (1861)	M	Extradition
Thomas, Clarence (111)	*Hudson v. McMillan* (1992)	D	Cruel and unusual punishment
	U.S. Term Limits, Inc. v. Thornton (1995)	D	State powers
Thompson, Smith (20)	*Mason v. Haile* (1827)	M	Contracts
	Cherokee Nation v. Georgia (1831)	D	Native Americans
	Kendall v. United States ex rel. Stokes (1838)	M	Federal courts
Todd, Thomas (17)	None		
Trimble, Robert (21)	*Ogden v. Saunders* (1827)	C	Contracts
Van Devanter, Willis (65)	*Dillon v. Gloss* (1921)	M	Constitutional amendment ratification
Vinson, Fred M. (89)	*United States v. United Mine Workers* (1947)	M	Contempt
	Shelley v. Kraemer (1948)	M	Civil rights
	American Communications Assn. v. Douds (1950)	M	Freedom of association
	McLaurin v. Oklahoma State Regents for Higher Education (1950)	M	Civil rights
	Sweatt v. Painter (1950)	M	Civil rights
	Feiner v. New York (1951)	M	Freedom of speech
	Kunz v. New York (1951)	M	Freedom of speech

	Dennis v. United States (1951)	J	Freedom of speech
	Stack v. Boyle (1951)	M	Excessive bail
	Rosenberg v. United States (1953)	M	War powers
Waite, Morrison (44)	*Minor v. Happersett* (1875)	M	Privileges and immunities
	United States v. Cruikshank (1876)	M	Voting rights
	United States v. Reese (1876)	M	Voting rights
	Walker v. Sauvinet (1876)	M	Jury trials
	Munn v. Illinois (1877)	M	State powers
	Hall v. DeCuir (1878)	M	Civil rights
	Stone v. Mississippi (1880)	M	Contracts
Warren, Earl (92)	*Brown v. Board of Education* (1954)	M	Civil rights
	Pennsylvania v. Nelson (1956)	M	State powers
	Watkins v. United States (1957)	M	Powers of Congress
	Cooper v. Aaron (1958)	M	Civil rights
	Trop v. Dulles (1958)	J	Cruel and unusual punishment
	Reynolds v. Sims (1964)	M	Voting rights
	Harman v. Forssenius (1965)	M	Voting rights
	Miranda v. Arizona (1966)	M	Self-incrimination
	South Carolina v. Katzenbach (1966)	M	Voting rights
	Klopfer v. North Carolina (1967)	M	Due process
	Loving v. Virginia (1967)	M	Civil rights
	United States v. Robel (1967)	M	Freedom of association
	Washington v. Texas (1967)	M	Due process
	Flast v. Cohen (1968)	M	Federal courts
	Terry v. Ohio (1968)	M	Search and seizure
	Powell v. McCormack (1969)	M	Powers of Congress
Washington, Bushrod (12)	*Dartmouth College v. Woodward* (1819)	C	Contracts
	Ogden v. Saunders (1827)	M	Contracts

(Table continues)

Table 6-13 *(Continued)*

Justice (appointment number)	Case	Opinion[a]	Subject matter
Wayne, James M. (24)	*Dobbins v. Erie County* (1842)	M	Taxes
	Louisville Railroad Co. v. Letson (1844)	M	Federal courts
	Cooley v. Board of Wardens of Port of Philadelphia (1852)	D	Commerce
	Dodge v. Woolsey (1856)	M	Contracts
White, Byron R. (97)	*Duncan v. Louisiana* (1968)	M	Due process
	Williams v. Florida (1970)	M	Due process
	Branzburg v. Hayes (1972)	M	Freedom of the press
	Johnson v. Louisiana; Apodaca v. Oregon (1972)	M	Due process
	Taylor v. Louisiana (1975)	M	Jury trials
	Washington v. Davis (1976)	M	Civil rights
	Coker v. Georgia (1977)	J	Cruel and unusual punishment
	United Jewish Organizations of Williamsburgh v. Carey (1977)	J	Voting rights
	Butz v. Economou (1978)	M	Official immunity
	Marshall v. Barlows, Inc. (1978)	M	Search and seizure
	Zurcher v. The Stanford Daily (1978)	M	Search and seizure
	Columbus Board of Education v. Penick; Dayton Board of Education v. Brinkman (1979)	M	Civil rights
	Enmund v. Florida (1982)	M	Cruel and unusual punishment
	Firefighters Local Union #1794 v. Stotts (1984)	M	Civil rights
	Grove City College v. Bell (1984)	M	Equal protection
	United States v. Leon (1984)	M	Search and seizure
	City of Cleburne, Texas v. Cleburne Living Center (1985)	M	Equal protection
	Tennessee v. Garner (1985)	M	Search and seizure
	Bowers v. Hardwick (1986)	M	Personal privacy

Justice	Case	Opinion	Subject
	Davis v. Bandemer (1986)	J	Voting rights
	Shaare Tefila Congregation v. Cobb; Saint Francis College v. Al-Khazraji (1987)	M	Civil rights
	New York State Club Association Inc. v. New York City (1988)	M	Freedom of association
	Wards Cove Packing Co. v. Atonio (1989)	M	Civil rights
	Cohen v. Cowles Media Co. (1991)	M	Freedom of press
	United States v. Fordice; Ayers v. Fordice (1992)	M	Civil rights
	Lamb's Chapel v. Center Moriches Union Free School District (1993)	M	Freedom of religion
White, Edward D. (56, 64)	Knowlton v. Moore (1900)	M	Taxes
	McCray v. United States (1904)	M	Taxes
	Standard Oil Co. v. United States (1911)	M	Commerce
	Guinn v. United States (1915)	M	Voting rights
	Brushaber v. Union Pacific Railroad Co. (1916)	M	Taxes
	Clark Distilling Co. v. Western Maryland Railway (1917)	M	Powers of Congress
	Selective Draft Law Cases (1918)	M	Powers of Congress
Whittaker, Charles E. (95)	None		
Wilson, James (4)	Chisholm v. Georgia (1793)	S	Federal courts
	Hylton v. United States (1796)	S	Taxes
Woodbury, Levi (31)	None		
Woods, William B. (46)	None		

Note: Data cover 1790–1996.

[a] M = majority opinion; C = concurring opinion; D = dissenting opinion; J = judgment of the Court; S = seriatim opinion.

Sources: Majority opinions/judgments: Joan Biskupic and Elder Witt, *Guide to the U.S. Supreme Court*, 3d ed. (Washington, D.C.: Congressional Quarterly, 1996); other opinions: the judgment of the authors.

Table 6-14 Assignment and Authorship of Majority Opinion, 1946–1952 Terms

Term/Assigner[a]	Author											Total
	Vinson	Black	Reed	Frankfurter	Douglas	Murphy	Jackson	Rutledge	Burton	Clark	Minton	
1946												
Vinson	12	22	11	8	19	12	12	7	4	—	—	107
Black	0	5	2	1	7	5	3	3	1	—	—	27
Reed	0	0	1	1	1	0	0	0	0	—	—	3
Frankfurter	0	0	0	1	0	0	0	0	0	—	—	1
Douglas	0	0	0	0	0	0	0	0	1	—	—	1
Total	12	27	14	11	27	17	15	10	6	—	—	139
1947												
Vinson	12	15	9	6	15	4	13	7	4	—	—	85
Black	0	3	1	2	5	4	2	2	0	—	—	19
Reed	0	0	1	0	1	0	1	1	0	—	—	4
Frankfurter	0	0	0	0	0	1	1	0	0	—	—	2
Total	12	18	11	8	21	9	17	10	4	—	—	110
1948												
Vinson	10	14	13	11	17	8	8	9	4	—	—	94
Black	0	5	4	4	2	2	1	1	2	—	—	21
Reed	0	0	0	0	0	0	1	0	1	—	—	2
Frankfurter	0	0	0	0	1	0	0	0	0	—	—	1
Total	10	19	17	15	20	10	10	10	7	—	—	118
1949												
Vinson	11	13	4	6	2	—	11	—	6	12	10	75
Black	0	2	0	0	0	—	2	—	3	0	2	9
Reed	0	0	3	1	0	—	0	—	0	0	0	4
Total	11	15	7	7	2	—	13	—	9	12	12	88

1950											
Vinson	12	8	8	7	7	—	8	—	7	8	6	71
Black	0	4	0	0	3	—	1	—	1	1	3	13
Reed	0	0	2	1	2	—	1	—	0	1	0	7
Frankfurter	0	0	0	0	0	—	0	—	1	0	0	1
Total	12	12	10	8	12	—	10	—	9	10	9	92
1951											
Vinson	9	6	6	3	10	—	9	—	7	8	9	67
Black	0	5	0	3	0	—	0	—	1	0	0	9
Reed	0	0	1	0	1	—	0	—	0	0	0	2
Frankfurter	0	0	0	4	0	—	0	—	0	1	1	6
Total	9	11	7	10	11	—	9	—	8	9	10	84
1952											
Vinson	12	6	10	6	11	—	8	—	6	9	7	75
Black	0	4	1	2	1	—	2	—	4	4	2	20
Reed	0	0	3	2	1	—	0	—	1	0	2	9
Total	12	10	14	10	13	—	10	—	11	13	11	104

[a] Assignment determined by reference to the chief justice's assignment sheets.

Source: Expanded U.S. Supreme Court Judicial Database, with analu = 0, dec_type = 1 or 7, and jur ≠ 9.

Table 6-15 Assignment and Authorship of Majority Opinion, 1953–1960 Terms

Term/assigner[a]	Author													
	Black	Reed	Frankfurter	Douglas	Jackson	Burton	Clark	Minton	Warren	Harlan	Whittaker	Brennan	Stewart	Total
1953														
Warren	5	3	4	5	2	4	4	3	7	—	—	—	—	37
Black	4	1	1	0	1	1	3	3	2	—	—	—	—	16
Reed	0	3	3	0	4	1	0	0	0	—	—	—	—	11
Total	9	7	8	5	7	6	7	6	9	—	—	—	—	64
1954														
Warren	8	3	7	11	—	6	14	6	12	1	—	—	—	68
Black	1	2	1	0	—	0	0	1	0	0	—	—	—	5
Reed	0	1	3	0	—	0	0	0	0	1	—	—	—	5
Total	9	6	11	11	—	6	14	7	12	2	—	—	—	78
1955														
Warren	9	3	9	9	—	5	7	9	8	8	—	—	—	67
Black	0	0	0	1	—	1	0	0	0	0	—	—	—	2
Reed	0	6	0	0	—	2	4	0	0	1	—	—	—	13
Total	9	9	9	10	—	8	11	9	8	9	—	—	—	82
1956														
Warren	9	1	6	12	—	7	10	—	12	10	3	7	—	77
Black	2	0	0	1	—	1	0	—	0	0	0	1	—	5
Reed	0	4	2	0	—	1	1	—	0	1	0	2	—	11
Frankfurter	0	0	3	0	—	0	3	—	0	0	0	—	—	6
Total	11	5	11	13	—	9	14	—	12	11	3	10	—	99

1957															
Warren	9	—	3	12	—	3	—	9	—	11	7	8	10	—	72
Black	3	—	0	1	—	0	—	1	—	0	2	0	2	—	9
Frankfurter	0	—	7	0	—	4	—	5	—	0	6	0	2	—	24
Total	12	—	10	13	—	7	—	15	—	11	15	8	14	—	105
1958															
Warren	10	—	4	11	—	8	—	10	—	4	9	11	5	—	72
Black	0	—	1	0	—	0	—	0	—	2	1	0	0	—	4
Frankfurter	0	—	6	1	—	3	—	0	—	6	0	2	5	—	23
Total	10	—	11	12	—	11	—	10	—	12	10	13	10	—	99
1959															
Warren	10	—	2	10	—	11	—	11	—	6	5	11	9	—	75
Black	0	—	1	0	—	0	—	0	—	0	0	0	0	—	1
Frankfurter	0	—	6	1	—	5	—	0	—	2	2	1	2	—	19
Douglas	0	—	0	0	—	0	—	0	—	1	0	0	0	—	1
Total	10	—	9	11	—	16	—	11	—	9	7	12	11	—	96
1960															
Warren	12	—	6	13	—	9	—	11	—	4	8	10	7	—	80
Black	2	—	0	0	—	1	—	0	—	1	2	0	0	—	6
Frankfurter	0	—	6	0	—	3	—	0	—	6	2	2	5	—	24
Total	14	—	12	13	—	13	—	11	—	11	12	12	12	—	110

[a] Assignment determined by reference to the chief justice's assignment sheets.

Source: Expanded U.S. Supreme Court Judicial Database, with analu = 0, dec_type = 1 or 7, and jur ≠ 9.

Table 6-16 Assignment and Authorship of Majority Opinion, 1961–1968 Terms

Term/assigner[a]		Author												
	Black	Frankfurter	Douglas	Clark	Warren	Harlan	Whittaker	Brennan	Stewart	White	Goldberg	Fortas	Marshall	Total
1961														
Warren	12	3	11	7	10	5	1	9	8	3	—	—	—	69
Black	0	0	0	1	0	2	0	0	2	0	—	—	—	5
Frankfurter	0	1	0	3	0	3	1	1	1	0	—	—	—	10
Clark	0	0	0	0	0	0	0	0	1	0	—	—	—	1
Total	12	4	11	11	10	10	2	10	12	3	—	—	—	85
1962														
Warren	9	—	11	8	12	8	—	11	12	11	10	—	—	92
Black	1	—	0	3	0	2	—	0	0	1	0	—	—	7
Douglas	0	—	2	1	0	1	—	2	0	0	1	—	—	7
Clark	0	—	0	0	0	1	—	0	0	0	1	—	—	2
Brennan	0	—	0	0	0	0	—	0	0	1	0	—	—	1
Total	10	—	13	12	12	12	—	13	12	13	12	—	—	109
1963														
Warren	10	—	12	10	11	10	—	13	13	10	13	—	—	102
Black	0	—	0	2	0	2	—	0	0	1	0	—	—	5
Douglas	0	—	0	0	0	0	—	0	1	0	0	—	—	1
Clark	0	—	0	1	0	0	—	0	0	0	1	—	—	2
Harlan	0	—	0	0	0	0	—	0	0	1	0	—	—	1
Total	10	—	12	13	11	12	—	13	14	12	14	—	—	111
1964														
Warren	9	—	8	9	10	8	—	10	6	4	8	—	—	72
Black	0	—	2	0	0	1	—	0	2	4	2	—	—	11
Douglas	0	—	0	0	0	0	—	0	1	1	0	—	—	2
Clark	0	—	0	2	0	0	—	1	0	1	0	—	—	4
Total	9	—	10	11	10	9	—	11	9	10	10	—	—	89

														Total
1965														
Warren	9	—	11	8	8	6	—	11	7	10	—	10	—	80
Black	2	—	1	0	0	1	—	1	4	1	—	0	—	10
Clark	0	—	0	2	0	1	—	1	1	0	—	0	—	5
Douglas	0	—	0	1	0	0	—	0	0	0	—	0	—	1
Total	11	—	12	11	8	8	—	13	12	11	—	10	—	96
1966														
Warren	7	—	11	11	11	6	—	7	7	11	—	10	—	81
Black	4	—	1	1	0	3	—	1	4	1	—	0	—	15
Clark	0	—	0	0	0	0	—	3	0	0	—	0	—	3
Douglas	0	—	0	0	0	0	—	0	0	0	—	1	—	1
Total	11	—	12	12	11	9	—	11	11	12	—	11	—	100
1967														
Warren	12	—	11	—	11	8	—	12	14	11	—	10	9	98
Black	0	—	2	—	0	4	—	0	0	1	—	0	0	7
Douglas	0	—	0	—	0	0	—	1	0	0	—	1	0	2
Harlan	0	—	0	—	0	1	—	0	0	0	—	0	0	1
Total	12	—	13	—	11	13	—	13	14	12	—	11	9	108
1968														
Warren	10	—	11	—	11	8	—	9	10	9	—	8	12	88
Black	2	—	1	—	0	1	—	0	0	1	—	0	1	6
Douglas	0	—	0	—	0	0	—	1	0	0	—	0	0	1
Harlan	0	—	0	—	0	1	—	1	0	0	—	0	0	2
Total	12	—	12	—	11	10	—	11	10	10	—	8	13	97

[a] Assignment determined by reference to the chief justice's assignment sheets.

Source: Expanded U.S. Supreme Court Judicial Database, with analu = 0, dec_type = 1 or 7, and jur ≠ 9.

Table 6-17 Assignment and Authorship of Majority Opinion, 1969–1977 Terms

Term/assigner[a]	Author												
	Black	Douglas	Harlan	Brennan	Stewart	White	Marshall	Burger	Blackmun	Powell	Rehnquist	Stevens	Total
1969													
Burger	6	8	6	4	10	9	7	11	—	—	—	—	61
Black	4	3	1	3	1	4	2	0	—	—	—	—	18
Douglas	0	2	2	3	1	0	1	0	—	—	—	—	9
Total	10	13	9	10	12	13	10	11	—	—	—	—	88
1970													
Burger	11	11	6	10	13	12	9	13	10	—	—	—	95
Black	3	1	2	0	1	1	0	0	0	—	—	—	8
Douglas	0	2	2	1	2	0	0	0	0	—	—	—	7
Total	14	14	10	11	16	13	9	13	10	—	—	—	110
1971													
Burger	—	10	—	11	12	15	11	12	12	12	11	—	106
Douglas	—	3	—	7	6	2	4	0	0	0	0	—	22
Brennan	—	0	—	0	0	1	0	0	0	0	0	—	1
Total	—	13	—	18	18	18	15	12	12	12	11	—	129
1972													
Burger	—	13	—	9	12	15	12	19	14	13	15	—	122
Douglas	—	3	—	4	2	2	0	0	0	3	0	—	14
Brennan	—	0	—	0	2	0	0	0	0	1	1	—	4
Total	—	16	—	13	16	17	12	19	14	17	16	—	140
1973													
Burger	—	13	—	12	14	16	11	14	14	14	16	—	124
Douglas	—	1	—	3	2	3	2	0	1	1	1	—	14

											Total
Brennan	0	0	2	0	0	0	0	1	1	—	4
Stewart	0	0	0	0	0	0	0	1	0	—	1
Total	14	15	18	19	13	14	15	17	18	—	143
1974											
Burger	6	12	10	13	10	14	11	16	15	—	107
Douglas	0	3	5	3	0	0	2	1	0	—	14
Brennan	0	0	1	0	1	0	0	0	0	—	2
Total	6	15	16	16	11	14	13	17	15	—	123
1975											
Burger	—	13	14	13	16	17	14	16	16	6	125
Brennan	—	3	2	2	1	0	2	0	0	3	13
Total	—	16	16	15	17	17	16	16	16	9	138
1976											
Burger	—	6	10	13	11	15	11	12	15	12	105
Brennan	—	7	3	2	1	0	3	3	0	1	20
Stewart	—	0	1	0	0	0	0	0	0	0	1
Total	—	13	14	15	12	15	14	15	15	13	126
1977											
Burger	—	7	9	10	15	16	10	13	12	11	103
Brennan	—	7	6	3	0	0	2	2	0	2	22
Stewart	—	0	0	0	0	0	0	0	2	1	3
White	—	0	0	1	0	0	0	0	0	0	1
Total	—	14	15	14	15	16	12	15	14	14	129

a Assumes senior justice in the majority opinion coalition assigned the opinion. The reader should be aware, however, that sometimes justices switch votes after the original conference. Therefore, where the chief justice dissents initially, but switches to the majority after the original conference, he is possibly listed incorrectly as having assigned the majority opinion. The same holds when senior associate justices switch their votes.

Source: U.S. Supreme Court Judicial Database, with analu = 0.

Table 6-18 Assignment and Authorship of Majority Opinion, 1978–1985 Terms

Term/ assigner[a]	Author										
	Brennan	Stewart	White	Marshall	Burger	Blackmun	Powell	Rehnquist	Stevens	O'Connor	Total
1978											
Burger	6	13	15	12	17	9	10	16	13	—	111
Brennan	7	1	1	1	0	4	2	0	2	—	18
Stewart	0	1	0	0	0	0	0	0	0	—	1
Total	13	15	16	13	17	13	12	16	15	—	130
1979											
Burger	9	12	13	12	15	13	15	15	11	—	115
Brennan	5	3	2	1	0	1	1	0	3	—	16
Stewart	0	0	0	1	0	0	0	0	0	—	1
Total	14	15	15	14	15	14	16	15	14	—	132
1980											
Burger	5	14	11	12	13	11	13	15	10	—	104
Brennan	8	0	3	1	0	1	2	0	1	—	16
Stewart	0	2	0	0	0	0	0	0	0	—	2
White	0	0	1	0	0	0	0	0	0	—	1
Total	13	16	15	13	13	12	15	15	11	—	123
1981											
Burger	3	—	16	9	16	9	14	16	12	11	106
Brennan	12	—	3	5	0	5	2	1	3	1	32
White	0	—	0	0	0	0	0	0	0	1	1
Blackmun	0	—	0	0	0	1	0	0	0	0	1
Marshall	0	—	0	1	0	0	0	0	0	0	1
Total	15	—	19	15	16	15	16	17	15	13	141

1982											
Burger	7	—	18	16	17	14	16	20	15	16	139
Brennan	8	—	1	0	0	1	2	0	0	0	12
Total	15	—	19	16	17	15	18	20	15	16	151
1983											
Burger	9	—	17	15	18	14	17	19	16	17	142
Brennan	5	—	1	0	0	2	1	0	0	0	9
Total	14	—	18	15	18	16	18	19	16	17	151
1984											
Burger	6	—	15	12	17	13	12	16	15	16	122
Brennan	7	—	3	1	0	3	1	1	1	0	17
Total	13	—	18	13	17	16	13	17	16	16	139
1985											
Burger	6	—	17	12	14	10	16	18	15	16	124
Brennan	7	—	1	3	0	4	2	0	2	1	20
White	0	—	1	0	0	0	0	1	0	0	2
Total	13	—	19	15	14	14	18	19	17	17	146

[a] Assumes senior justice in the majority decision coalition assigned the opinion. The reader should be aware, however, that sometimes justices switch votes after the original conference. Therefore, where the chief justice dissents initially, but switches to the majority after the original conference, he is possibly listed incorrectly as having assigned the opinion. The same holds when senior associate justices switch their votes.

Source: U.S. Supreme Court Judicial Database, with analu = 0.

Table 6-19 Assignment and Authorship of Majority Opinion, 1986–2001 Terms

Term/ assigner[a]	Author														Total
	Brennan	White	Marshall	Blackmun	Powell	Rehnquist	Stevens	O'Connor	Scalia	Kennedy	Souter	Thomas	Ginsburg	Breyer	
1986															
Rehnquist	4	15	10	7	18	17	12	18	10	—	—	—	—	—	111
Brennan	12	2	6	6	2	0	4	0	2	—	—	—	—	—	34
Total	16	17	16	13	20	17	16	18	12	—	—	—	—	—	145
1987															
Rehnquist	10	19	13	11	—	15	14	14	14	4	—	—	—	—	114
Brennan	6	1	2	4	—	0	5	2	2	3	—	—	—	—	25
Total	16	20	15	15	—	15	19	16	16	7	—	—	—	—	139
1988															
Rehnquist	8	17	12	12	—	15	14	12	11	13	—	—	—	—	114
Brennan	8	0	2	2	—	0	2	1	1	2	—	—	—	—	18
Total	16	17	14	14	—	15	16	13	12	15	—	—	—	—	132
1989															
Rehnquist	5	14	12	11	—	15	10	14	14	12	—	—	—	—	107
Brennan	8	3	2	2	—	0	3	3	0	1	—	—	—	—	22
Total	13	17	14	13	—	15	13	17	14	13	—	—	—	—	129
1990															
Rehnquist	—	10	11	10	—	14	9	15	11	9	7	—	—	—	96
White	—	4	0	0	—	0	3	0	0	3	1	—	—	—	11
Marshall	—	0	1	1	—	0	1	1	0	1	0	—	—	—	5
Blackmun	—	0	0	0	—	0	1	0	0	0	0	—	—	—	1
Total	—	14	12	11	—	14	14	16	11	13	8	—	—	—	113

															Total
1991															
Rehnquist	—	11	—	9	—	11	9	13	10	7	10	8	—	—	88
White	—	4	—	0	—	0	3	1	2	2	2	0	—	—	14
Blackmun	—	0	—	1	—	0	0	0	0	2	1	0	—	—	4
Total	—	15	—	10	—	11	12	14	12	11	13	8	—	—	106
1992															
Rehnquist	—	13	—	9	—	14	9	13	12	10	9	10	—	—	99
White	—	0	—	0	—	0	0	0	1	0	1	1	—	—	3
Blackmun	—	0	—	1	—	0	4	0	1	0	0	0	—	—	6
Total	—	13	—	10	—	14	13	13	14	10	10	11	—	—	108
1993															
Rehnquist	—	—	—	6	—	10	8	12	8	8	7	7	5	—	71
Blackmun	—	—	—	2	—	0	2	0	0	1	1	0	3	—	9
Stevens	—	—	—	0	—	0	1	0	0	1	0	1	2	—	5
Total	—	—	—	8	—	10	11	12	8	10	8	8	10	—	85
1994															
Rehnquist	—	—	—	—	—	11	3	10	7	9	8	8	5	8	69
Stevens	—	—	—	—	—	0	6	0	0	1	1	0	3	1	12
Total	—	—	—	—	—	11	9	10	7	10	9	8	8	9	81
1995															
Rehnquist	—	—	—	—	—	10	4	9	7	7	9	8	4	6	64
Stevens	—	—	—	—	—	0	4	0	1	1	0	0	4	1	11
Total	—	—	—	—	—	10	8	9	8	8	9	8	8	7	75
1996															
Rehnquist	—	—	—	—	—	11	8	8	7	10	6	7	6	7	70
Stevens	—	—	—	—	—	0	2	1	1	0	2	0	3	1	10
Total	—	—	—	—	—	11	10	9	8	10	8	7	9	8	80

(Table continues)

Table 6-19 (*Continued*)

Term/assigner[a]	Brennan	White	Marshall	Blackmun	Powell	Rehnquist	Stevens	O'Connor	Scalia	Kennedy	Souter	Thomas	Ginsburg	Breyer	Total
1997															
Rehnquist	—	—	—	—	—	12	5	9	10	7	10	9	10	8	80
Stevens	—	—	—	—	—	0	3	1	0	3	0	1	0	2	10
Total	—	—	—	—	—	12	8	10	10	10	10	10	10	10	90
1998															
Rehnquist	—	—	—	—	—	10	6	9	8	7	6	7	6	5	64
Stevens	—	—	—	—	—	0	3	2	0	1	1	0	3	3	13
Total	—	—	—	—	—	10	9	11	8	8	7	7	9	8	77
1999															
Rehnquist	—	—	—	—	—	10	3	8	8	9	8	7	6	7	66
Stevens	—	—	—	—	—	0	4	0	0	1	1	1	1	1	9
Total	—	—	—	—	—	10	7	8	8	10	9	8	7	8	76
2000															
Rehnquist	—	—	—	—	—	8	4	6	7	7	5	8	8	7	60
Stevens	—	—	—	—	—	0	5	2	0	1	3	0	0	2	13
O'Connor	—	—	—	—	—	0	0	0	0	0	0	0	1	0	1
Scalia	—	—	—	—	—	0	0	0	1	0	0	0	0	0	1
Total	—	—	—	—	—	8	9	8	8	8	8	8	9	9	75
2001															
Rehnquist	—	—	—	—	—	10	3	7	8	7	6	6	7	8	62
Stevens	—	—	—	—	—	0	5	0	0	1	2	1	2	1	12
O'Connor	—	—	—	—	—	0	0	1	0	0	0	0	0	0	1
Total	—	—	—	—	—	10	8	8	8	8	8	7	9	9	75

[a] Assumes senior justice in the majority decision coalition assigned the opinion. The reader should be aware, however, that sometimes justices switch votes. Therefore, where the chief justice dissents initially, but switches to the majority after the original conference, he is possibly listed incorrectly as having assigned the majority opinion. The same holds when senior associate justices switch their votes.

Source: U.S. Supreme Court Judicial Database, with analu = 0.

7

The Supreme Court:
Its Political and Legal Environments

In the preceding chapters we present data on the internal processes and behavior of the Supreme Court and its members. Here, we consider the relationship between the Court and its political and legal environments. In the first part of the chapter we look at the actors that make up the Court's political environment—Congress, the executive branch, state governments, and interest groups. Each of these actors interacts with the judiciary in a distinctive fashion that is oftentimes bounded by tradition or even constitutional mandate. Consider Congress, which is the focus of Tables 7-1 through 7-9. At least five points of interaction exist between Congress and the Court. First, Congress can propose amendments that are designed to overturn Court decisions[1] or change the Court's jurisdiction, composition, benefits, and so forth. Table 7-1 lists amendments proposed by Congress and ratified by the states in response to Supreme Court decisions. Note that this has occurred only five times in the more than two hundred years of government operation, and despite the fact that "the number of [proposed] constitutional amendments designed to overcome a ruling of the Supreme Court would fill a congressman's wastebasket."[2] Tables 7-2 and 7-3 detail state action and public opinion on some constitutional amendments that have been proposed but not ratified. (For more data on public opinion and the Court, see Chapter 8.)

Another aspect of the Court-congressional dynamic is more direct and increasingly employed. As shown in Table 7-4, members of Congress are filing amicus curiae ("friend of the Court") briefs in Court cases with growing regularity. The overwhelming majority of all such filings have occurred since 1980. In addition, participation in amicus curiae activity has taken on a pluralistic gloss. In more cases than ever members of Congress are filing on both sides of the issue under consideration. The briefs submitted in *Webster v. Reproductive Health Services* (1989),[3] which involved state-imposed restrictions on abortion, provide a good example: 9 senators and 44 representatives filed on behalf of the pro-life side, while

25 senators and 115 representatives filed in support of the pro-choice position.

A third point of interaction between Congress and the Court is congressionally enacted legislation, which itself often becomes the subject of litigation. In Chapter 2, we provide information on congressional acts overturned by the Court (see Table 2-13). Table 7-5 lists those laws most litigated during the Vinson, Warren, Burger, and Rehnquist Court eras. Table 7-6 provides parallel data on highly litigated constitutional provisions. Some issues remain perennial subjects of Court litigation. For example, the Internal Revenue Code and the National Labor Relations Act appear in high numbers in all four eras. Others, though, change with the times. Title VII of the Civil Rights Act of 1964, enacted five years prior to the end of the Warren Court era, does not appear until the Burger years, where it trailed the Social Security Act, the National Labor Relations Act, and the Internal Revenue Code. By the Rehnquist Court years, however, few other laws surpassed it in frequency.

A fourth point of interaction occurs between the Court and the judiciary committees of Congress. Among other things, these committees make budgetary recommendations for the federal judiciary and consider bills of interest to the Court. The Senate Judiciary Committee has the additional function of holding confirmation hearings on nominees to the federal bench, including the Supreme Court. In Chapter 4, we provide information on the outcomes of the confirmation process as it pertains to Supreme Court justices (Table 4-13). Tables 7-7 and 7-8 list the names of those who have served as chairs of the judiciary committees of the Senate and House, respectively.

Finally, Congress can impeach federal judges, including Supreme Court justices. Article I of the Constitution specifies that the House "shall have the sole Power of Impeachment" and that the Senate "shall have the sole Power to try all Impeachments." Members of Congress have threatened to initiate proceedings against at least three justices (see Table 5-6), but, as is evident in Table 7-9, the House has voted articles of impeachment against only one, Samuel Chase; the Senate has never convicted a member of the Supreme Court. This has not been true of lower court judges, seven of whom have been convicted of impeachable charges. Interestingly, three of those seven convictions were handed down in the 1980s.

The executive branch is another participant in judicial affairs. Most notably, presidents are responsible for nominating Supreme Court justices. This is a subject we consider in some detail in Chapter 4 (see Tables 4-11 and 4-12). Another less obvious though no less important activity is the role of the executive branch as a participant in Court cases. The office of the U.S. solicitor general, located within the Department of Justice (see Figures 7-1 and 7-2), is responsible for representing the U.S. government, including many (but not all) of its agencies, before the Court. In

Tables 7-10 and 7-11 we provide the names of those who have served as attorney general and solicitor general, respectively. More interesting still may be Tables 7-12 through 7-20, where we present varied data on the relative success of the U.S. government and its agencies from 1946–1994. Readers can draw their own conclusions about the government's record, but one thing is certain: regardless of the particular ideology or partisanship of the administration in office, or even the legal issue under review, solicitors general carry great weight with the justices. Why is the U.S. government, as represented by the solicitor general, typically such a successful courtroom player? Those who have studied the issue offer a variety of reasons. Most significantly, the solicitor general brings before the Court only those cases he or she deems important. This helps explain the solicitor general's high rate of success in getting the Court to hear his or her cases. The solicitor general's legal expertise and the embodiment of the interests of the nation are additional explanations.[4]

The United States is not the only government entity to litigate before the Supreme Court. The states and the officials and offices under their authority often appear as parties and amici curiae. Taken collectively, the data in Tables 7-21 through 7-23 suggest that the states are significantly less successful than the U.S. government. Yet definitive conclusions cannot be drawn simply by comparing percentages. While it is true that the federal government has a better aggregated rate of success than the states, these statistics can be deceiving. For one thing, we must take into account the states' comparative success within the distinct Court eras. As political scientists Sheehan, Mishler, and Songer note, "state governments fared better against the federal government during the early Burger years but much worse during the Rehnquist years."[5] However, it may not be simply a matter of parties determining their own fates. Research by Sheehan and his colleagues indicates that the ideology of the Court affects its disposition of all kinds of cases, including those brought by states. Those readers who are interested in comparing the relative success of the various governmental entities before the Court should use the tables contained in this chapter in conjunction with data presented in Chapters 3 and 6 to obtain a fair assessment.

That government units such as legislatures, executives, states, and so forth play some role in Court litigation is not surprising. After all, the doctrines of checks and balances and federalism suggest that "dialogues" will inevitably occur between and among the branches and components of our government.[6] What may be surprising is that points of interaction also exist between the Court and extra-institutional entities, in particular, interest groups. Attorneys representing a range of organized interests commonly lobby the Court. On average, in recent terms, nearly two thousand organized interests participated in about 90 percent of the cases decided with an opinion.

While it is certainly true that interest groups wish to influence the Court as ardently as they do Congress and the executive, judicial lobbying is nevertheless a significantly different enterprise from that which occurs in congressional or executive corridors. The "rules of the legal game" simply prohibit groups from directly approaching judges and justices in the same manner as they would members of Congress or the executive. Instead, interest group organizations have had to develop a uniquely "judicial" approach to lobbying the Court: they sponsor cases (that is, interest groups provide legal representation to parties to suits),[7] they intervene in litigation (that is, interest groups "voluntarily interpose" in suits),[8] and they file or cosign amicus curiae briefs.[9]

Tables 7-24 through 7-27 provide information on interest group involvement as amici curiae. We limit our look into the world of organizational litigation to the amicus curiae strategy for many reasons, not the least of which is that attorneys filing as amici curiae generally list their organizational affiliation on the cover of their briefs, while those sponsoring cases often do not. Accordingly, it is relatively easy to discern whether a group participated as an amicus and far more difficult to determine if it sponsored a case.[10] Table 7-24 provides the Court's rules governing amicus curiae participation. As Table 7-25 shows, such participation has increased considerably over the past four decades. In 1953 only 13.3 percent of Court cases contained one or more amicus curiae briefs; that figure was 92.5 just forty years later, in 1993. Table 7-26 shows the wide array of groups that participate as amicus curiae. Table 7-27 indicates that the justices occasionally cite amicus curiae briefs in their opinions. While these data do not prove that justices are swayed by amici arguments, they do show that some members of the Court consider them in developing their opinions.

In the second part of this chapter we look at the role of the Supreme Court in the American legal system (Figure 7-3). Tables 7-28 through 7-33 focus on the federal judiciary. Today's lower federal courts fall into three categories. The courts of appeals occupy the rung of the judicial ladder immediately below the Supreme Court. The business of the courts of appeals is to review the decisions of the federal trial courts and various federal administrative agencies when disappointed litigants appeal. Each of the twelve regular courts of appeals has jurisdiction over a particular geographical area, known as a circuit (Figure 7-4). Appeals are normally heard by panels of three appellate judges. The decisions of the courts of appeals are reviewable only by the Supreme Court. The legal interpretations of the courts of appeals, if not reversed by the Supreme Court, are binding on all lower federal and state courts within that particular circuit. Table 7-28 shows the development of the circuit court system, and Table 7-29 provides information on how the Supreme Court has treated appeals from the various circuit courts.

The district courts constitute the second level of federal tribunals. The United States today is divided into ninety-four judicial districts (see Figure 7-4). Eighty-nine of these operate within the various states, with each state having between one and four districts, depending upon caseload demands. Additional districts exist for the District of Columbia, Puerto Rico, and three federal territories (Guam, Northern Mariana Islands, and the Virgin Islands). Each of these judicial districts has a district court.

The federal district courts function as the primary trial court of general jurisdiction for the federal system. Most federal court cases begin at this level and move up to the courts of appeals, but others go directly to the Supreme Court. Table 7-30 examines how the decisions of the district courts have been reviewed when appealed directly to the Supreme Court without intervention by the courts of appeals.

The final group of federal courts are those of limited jurisdiction. Such courts normally hear cases on specific subject matter and fall into one of two categories. The first we call Article I, or legislative, courts (Table 7-31). These tribunals have been created by Congress to help the legislature carry out its responsibilities as outlined in Article I of the Constitution. Examples are the United States Tax Court, the United States Court of Appeals for the Armed Services, and the United States Court of Federal Claims. Because these courts have been created under Article I, the judges sitting on them do not enjoy the same constitutional benefits as judges serving on courts that are part of the regular judiciary. For example, Article I judges do not enjoy life tenure, instead serving designated terms.

The second category of special courts contains those tribunals we call Article III, or constitutional, courts (Table 7-32). These courts have been created by Congress under Article III of the Constitution to create courts inferior to the Supreme Court. Judges on these bodies have life tenure and the other Article III provisions designed to ensure judicial independence. Examples are the United States Court of International Trade and the Court of Appeals for the Federal Circuit. Table 7-33 reveals how decisions appealed from these specialized courts have fared when reviewed by the Supreme Court.

The Supreme Court interacts with state judiciaries as well as with the lower federal courts. The final table in this chapter examines the state judiciaries. Over the past two centuries, state judiciaries have flourished. This growth has run contrary to the fears of many state advocates at the time of the Constitutional Convention who predicted that if the federal judiciary grew in size and power, the state courts would decline or even disappear. Table 7-34 reviews the U.S. Supreme Court's record on decisions appealed to the justices from the various state courts.

Notes

1. There are four routes by which to amend the Constitution: (1) Proposal passed by two-thirds vote of both houses of Congress and ratified by approval of three-fourths of the state legislatures, (2) proposal passed by two-thirds vote of both houses of Congress and ratified by approval of three-fourths of the state conventions, (3) proposal passed by national convention established by Congress upon request of two-thirds of the states and ratified by approval of three-fourths of the state legislatures, and (4) proposal passed by national convention established by Congress upon request of two-thirds of the states and ratified by approval of three-fourths of the state conventions.

2. Joseph T. Keenan, *The Constitution of the United States* (Chicago: Dorsey, 1988), 43.

3. 492 U.S. 490.

4. For a review of this literature, see Jeffrey A. Segal, "Courts, Executives, and Legislatures," in John B. Gates and Charles A. Johnson, eds., *The American Courts* (Washington, D.C.: CQ Press, 1991).

5. Reginald S. Sheehan, William Mishler, and Donald R. Songer, "Ideology, Status, and Differential Success of Direct Parties before the Supreme Court," *American Political Science Review* 86 (1992): 466.

6. For more on this point, see Louis Fisher, *Constitutional Dialogues* (Princeton, N.J.: Princeton University Press, 1988).

7. *Brown v. Board of Education,* 347 U.S. 483 (1954), sponsored by the NAACP Legal Defense and Educational Fund, provides a classic example. For other examples, see Jack Greenberg, *Judicial Process and Social Change* (St. Paul, Minn.: West Publishing, 1977); Clement E. Vose, *Caucasians Only* (Berkeley: University of California Press, 1959); and Karen O'Connor, *Women's Organizations' Use of the Court* (Lexington, Mass.: Lexington Books, 1980).

8. *Harris v. McRae,* 448 U.S. 297 (1980), which involved the constitutionality of a federal act (the Hyde Amendment) limiting the use of Medicaid funds for abortions, provides an example. In that case, a pro-life organization (Americans United for Life Legal Defense Fund) represented intervenor Henry Hyde (R-Ill.), who did not believe that the Carter administration would ably defend the amendment. For more on intervention, see Emma Coleman Jones's articles, "Litigation Without Representation: The Need for Intervention in Affirmative Action Litigation," *Harvard Civil Rights-Civil Liberties* 14 (1979): 31, and "Problems and Prospects of Participation in Affirmative Action Litigation: A Role for Intervenors," *University of California, Davis, Law Review* 13 (1980): 221.

9. For more information on the role of amici curiae and their history in the Supreme Court, see Samuel Krislov, "The *Amicus Curiae* Brief: From Friendship to Advocacy," *Yale Law Journal* 72 (1963): 694, and Gregory A. Caldeira and John R. Wright, "The Discuss List: Agenda Building in the Supreme Court," *Law and Society Review* 24 (1990): 807.

10. We want to stress that researchers interested in amicus curiae participation should not rely on the *U.S. Reports* as they do not provide complete information. Rather, researchers should consult the briefs filed in cases. Consider *Coker v. Georgia,* 433 U.S. 583 (1977), in which the American Civil Liberties Union (ACLU) filed an amicus curiae brief. It appears in the *U.S. Reports* in the following form: "*Ruth Bader Ginsburg, Melvin L. Wulf, Marjorie Mazen Smith,* and *Nancy Stearns* filed a brief for the American Civil Liberties Union et al. as *amici curiae* urging reversal." The *U.S. Reports* identifies this as an "et

al." brief. This means that "others" signed on to it. The brief within the micro-
fiche record of *Coker* names these "others" specifically: "Brief *amici curiae* of
the American Civil Liberties Union, the Center for Constitutional Rights, the
National Organization for Women Legal Defense and Education Fund, the
Women's Law Project, the Center for Women Policy Studies, the Women's
Legal Defense Fund, and Equal Rights Advocates, Inc." The ACLU may have
been the lead interest, but six other groups (the "et al." in the *U.S. Reports)*
signed the brief.

Table 7-1   Amendments to the U.S. Constitution Overturning Supreme Court Decisions

Amendment	Date ratified	Supreme Court decision overturned
Eleventh	February 7, 1795	*Chisholm v. Georgia* (1793)
Thirteenth	December 6, 1865	*Scott v. Sandford* (1857)
Fourteenth	July 9, 1868	*Scott v. Sandford* (1857)
Sixteenth	February 3, 1913	*Pollock v. Farmer's Loan and Trust Co.* (1895)
Twenty-sixth	July 1, 1971	*Oregon v. Mitchell* (1970)

Table 7-2   State Action on Proposed Constitutional Amendments

	Proposed amendment				
State	Reapportionment[a]	Equal rights[b]	Balanced budget[c]	Ban on Abortion[d]	Line-item veto[e]
Alabama	yes	na	r	yes	na
Alaska	na	yes	yes	na	na
Arizona	yes	na	yes	na	yes
Arkansas	yes	na	yes	yes	na
California	na	yes	na[f]	na	na
Colorado	yes	yes	yes	na	na
Connecticut	na	yes	na	na	na
Delaware	na	yes	yes	yes	na
Florida	yes	na	r	na	na
Georgia	yes	na	yes	na	na
Hawaii	na	yes	na	na	na
Idaho	yes	r	yes	yes	yes
Illinois	r[g]	na	na[f]	na	yes
Indiana	yes	yes	yes	yes	na
Iowa	yes	yes	yes	na	na
Kansas	r[g]	yes	yes	na	yes
Kentucky	yes	r	na[f]	yes	na
Louisiana	yes	na	r	yes	yes
Maine	na	yes	na	na	na
Maryland	r[g]	yes	yes	na	na
Massachusetts	na	yes	na	yes	na
Michigan	na	yes	na	na	yes
Minnesota	yes	yes	na	na	na
Mississippi	yes	na	yes	yes	na
Missouri	yes	na	yes	yes	na
Montana	yes	yes	na[f]	na	na
Nebraska	yes	r	yes	yes	na
Nevada	yes	na	r[g]	yes	yes
New Hampshire	yes	yes	yes	na	na
New Jersey	na	yes	na	yes	na
New Mexico	yes	yes	yes	na	na
New York	na	yes	na	na	na

Table 7-2 *(Continued)*

State	Reapportionment[a]	Proposed amendment Equal rights[b]	Proposed amendment Balanced budget[c]	Proposed amendment Ban on Abortion[d]	Proposed amendment Line-item veto[e]
North Carolina	r[g]	na	yes	na	na
North Dakota	yes	yes	yes	na	na
Ohio	na	yes	na	na	na
Oklahoma	yes	na	yes	yes	na
Oregon	na	yes	yes	na	na
Pennsylvania	na	yes	yes	yes	na
Rhode Island	na	yes	na	yes	na
South Carolina	yes	na	yes	na	na
South Dakota	yes	r	yes	yes	yes
Tennessee	yes	r	yes	yes	yes
Texas	r[g]	yes	yes	na	na
Utah	yes	na	yes	yes	na
Vermont	na	yes	na	na	na
Virginia	yes	na	yes	na	yes
Washington	yes	yes	na	na	na
West Virginia	yes	yes	na	na	na
Wisconsin	yes	yes	na	na	na
Wyoming	yes	yes	yes	na	na

Note: "Yes" indicates state legislature approved of the amendment or sent a petition to Congress for a constitutional convention; "na" indicates no action was taken or the state legislature rejected the amendment or proposal to petition for a convention; "r" indicates previous appeal was rescinded. The Equal Rights Amendment was initiated by Congress and submitted to the states for ratification. The other proposed amendments were initiated by petition from state legislatures.

[a] Following two Supreme Court "one-person, one vote" decisions concerning how states were apportioned for their legislatures, some states acted to petition Congress for a constitutional convention to consider an amendment that would allow one house of a state legislature to be apportioned on a basis other than population.

[b] The time limit for approval of this amendment has expired. As proposed by Congress and voted on by the states, it read: "Section 1. Equality of rights under law shall not be denied or abridged by the United States or any State on account of sex. Section 2. The Congress shall have the power to enforce, by appropriate legislation, the provisions of this article. Section 3. This amendment shall take effect two years after the date of ratification."

[c] This proposed amendment has various forms. In its simplest form, Congress would be required to approve a balanced federal budget each year. In other forms there is a provision that a three-fifths majority of Congress could vote not to balance the budget in any given year.

[d] Some states have called for a constitutional convention to consider an amendment that would ban abortions. The most common approach among the various proposed amendments is to apply the constitutional protection of due process against the denial of life and property to unborn children.

[e] Some states have called for a constitutional convention to consider an amendment that would give the president a line-item veto.

[f] The state did not endorse the call for a constitutional convention but petitioned Congress to propose a balanced budget amendment to the states.

[g] Passed by only one house of the state legislature.

Source: Harold W. Stanley and Richard G. Niemi, *Vital Statistics on American Politics, 1999–2000* (Washington, D.C.: CQ Press, 2001), 304–305.

Table 7-3   Public Opinion on Issues Related to Proposed Constitutional
Amendments (Percentage)

Proposed amendment/year	Favor	Oppose	Don't know or no opinion
Abortion			
1985 (January)	38	58	4
1985 (September)	37	55	8
1987	25	69	6
1988	34	60	6
1989 (January)	29	68	3
1989 (March)	28	63	9
1989 (April)	27	65	8
1989 (June)	31	60	9
1989 (July)	27	62	11
1989 (October)	29	62	2
1990	21	73	6
1992	25	67	8
1996 (June)	24	75	1
1996 (August)	26	72	2
Balanced Budget[a]			
1976	78	13	9
1981 (April)	70	22	8
1981 (September)	73	19	8
1982	74	17	9
1983	71	21	8
1985	49	27	24
1987	53	23	24
1989	59	24	17
1994	80	12	8
1995	76	18	6
Equal Rights[a]			
1975	58	24	18
1976	57	24	19
1978	58	31	11
1980	58	31	11
1981	63	32	5
1982	56	34	10
1984	63	31	6
Flag Burning			
1989 (June)	71	24	5
1989 (June)	67	29	4
1989 (July)	67	28	5
1990 (June)	68	25	5
1990 (June)	57	42	1
School Prayer			
1963	24	70	6
1971	28	67	6

Table 7-3 *(Continued)*

Proposed amendment/year	Favor	Oppose	Don't know or no opinion
1974	31	66	3
1975	35	62	3
1977	33	64	2
1981	31	66	3
1982	37	60	3
1983	40	57	4
1985 (March)	43	54	3
1985 (September)	37	62	1
1986	37	61	2
1988	37	59	4
1989	41	56	3
1990	40	56	5
1991	38	58	4
1993	39	58	4
1994	37	58	4
1996	40	56	4
1998	43	53	5
2000	37	58	5

Note: All results are based on national, adult samples. The questions were as follows: Abortion: "Do you favor or oppose a constitutional amendment to ban abortions?" (or similar wording). Balanced Budget: "Have you heard (or read) about the proposal for a constitutional amendment which would require the federal government to balance the national budget each year? A proposed amendment to the Constitution would require Congress to approve a balanced federal budget each year. Government spending would have to be limited to no more than expected revenues, unless a three-fifths majority of Congress voted to spend more than expected revenues. Would you favor or oppose this amendment to the Constitution?" (Slightly different wording in 1976 and 1989.) Equal Rights: "Have you heard or read about the Equal Rights Amendment to the U.S. Constitution which would prohibit discrimination on the basis of sex? Do you favor or oppose this amendment?" Flag Burning: "Do you favor or oppose a constitutional amendment which would make it illegal to burn the American flag?" (or similar wording). School Prayer: "The U.S. Supreme Court has ruled that no state or local government may require the reading of the Lord's Prayer or Bible verses in public schools. What are your views on this—do you approve or disapprove of the court ruling?"

[a] Of those who were aware of the proposed amendment, except 1984 for equal rights and 1976 and 1987–1989 for balanced budget. Between 88 percent and 91 percent of those asked were aware of the Equal Rights Amendment. Between 48 percent and 66 percent of those asked were aware of the proposed Balanced Budget Amendment.

Source: Harold W. Stanley and Richard G. Niemi, *Vital Statistics on American Politics, 1999–2000* (Washington, D.C.: CQ Press, 2001), 151–153.

Table 7-4   Cases in Which Members of Congress Filed Amicus
Curiae Briefs, 1912–1997

Pacific States Telegraph and Telephone Co. v. Oregon, 223 U.S. 118 (1912)
Myers v. United States, 272 U.S. 52 (1926)
National Life Insurance Co. v. United States, 277 U.S. 508 (1928)
The Pocket Veto Case, 279 U.S. 655 (1929)
Edwards v. United States, 286 U.S. 482 (1932)
Jurney v. MacCracken, 294 U.S. 125 (1935)
Wright v. United States, 302 U.S. 583 (1938)
United States v. Bekins, 304 U.S. 27 (1938)
Edwards v. California, 314 U.S. 160 (1941)
Shapiro v. United States, 335 U.S. 1 (1948)
Henderson v. United States, 339 U.S. 816 (1950)
United States v. Louisiana, 363 U.S. 1 (1960)
United States v. Florida, 363 U.S. 121 (1960)
New York Times v. United States, 403 U.S. 713 (1971)
Williamson v. United States, 405 U.S. 1026 (1972)
United States v. United States District Court, 407 U.S. 297 (1972)
Laird v. Tatum, 408 U.S. 1 (1972)
Regional Rail Reorganization Act Cases, 419 U.S. 102 (1974)
Ripon Society v. National Republican Party, 424 U.S. 933 (1976)
Hutchinson v. Proxmire, 443 U.S. 111 (1979)
Harris v. McRae, 448 U.S. 297 (1980)
Rostker v. Goldberg, 453 U.S. 57 (1981)
Lehman v. Nakshian, 453 U.S. 156 (1981)
McCarty v. McCarty, 453 U.S. 210 (1981)
Federal Election Commission v. Democratic Senatorial Campaign Committee,
   454 U.S. 27 (1981)
Weinberger v. Rossi, 456 U.S. 25 (1982)
North Haven Board of Education v. Bell, 456 U.S. 512 (1982)
Nixon v. Fitzgerald, 457 U.S. 731 (1982)
Harlow v. Fitzgerald, 457 U.S. 800 (1982)
Crawford v. Board of Education of City of Los Angeles, 458 U.S. 527 (1982)
Bob Jones University v. United States, 461 U.S. 574 (1983)
United States v. Ptasynski, 462 U.S. 74 (1983)
Bush v. Lucas, 462 U.S. 367 (1983)
Immigration and Naturalization Service v. Chadha, 462 U.S. 919 (1983)
Grove City College v. Bell, 465 U.S. 555 (1984)
Consolidated Rail Corp. v. Darrone, 465 U.S. 624 (1984)
Heckler v. Mathews, 465 U.S. 728 (1984)
Monsanto v. Spray-Rite Service Corp., 465 U.S. 752 (1984)
Federal Communications Commission v. League of Women Voters, 468 U.S. 364 (1984)
Wallace v. Jaffree, 472 U.S. 38 (1985)
Jean v. Nelson, 472 U.S. 846 (1985)
Atascadero State Hospital v. Scanlon, 473 U.S. 234 (1985)
Bender v. Williamsport Area School District, 475 U.S. 534 (1986)
Diamond v. Charles, 476 U.S. 54 (1986)
Wygant v. Jackson Board of Education, 476 U.S. 267 (1986)
Bowen v. American Hospital Association, 476 U.S. 610 (1986)
Thornburgh v. American College of Obstetricians and Gynecologists, 476 U.S. 747 (1986)
Meritor Savings Bank v. Vinson, 477 U.S. 57 (1986)

Table 7-4   *(Continued)*

Riverside v. Rivera, 477 U.S. 561 (1986)
Japan Whaling Association v. American Cetacean Society, 478 U.S. 221 (1986)
Tashjian v. Republican Party of Connecticut, 479 U.S. 208 (1986)
California Federal Savings and Loan v. Guerra, 479 U.S. 272 (1987)
School Board of Nassau County v. Arline, 480 U.S. 273 (1987)
Meese v. Keene, 481 U.S. 465 (1987)
Edwards v. Aguillard, 482 U.S. 578 (1987)
South Dakota v. Dole, 483 U.S. 203 (1987)
Honig v. Doe, 484 U.S. 305 (1988)
United States v. Providence Journal Co., 485 U.S. 305 (1988)
Huffman v. Western Nuclear, 486 U.S. 663 (1988)
Pierce v. Underwood, 487 U.S. 552 (1988)
Bowen v. Kendrick, 487 U.S. 589 (1988)
Morrison v. Olson, 487 U.S. 654 (1988)
Communications Workers v. Beck, 487 U.S. 735 (1988)
United States v. Mistretta, 488 U.S. 361 (1989)
Board of Estimate of the City of New York v. Morris, 489 U.S. 688 (1989)
U.S. Department of Justice v. Reporters Committee for Freedom of Press, 489 U.S.
  749 (1989)
American Foreign Service Association v. Garfinkel, 490 U.S. 153 (1989)
Patterson v. McLean Credit Union, 491 U.S. 164 (1989)
Sable Communications v. Federal Communications Commission, 492 U.S. 115 (1989)
Webster v. Reproductive Health Services, 492 U.S. 490 (1989)
Dole v. United Steelworkers, 494 U.S. 26 (1990)
Adams Fruit Co. v. Ramsford Barrett, 494 U.S. 638 (1990)
United States v. Eichman, 496 U.S. 310 (1990)
Eli Lilly v. Medtronic, 496 U.S. 661 (1990)
Minnesota v. Hodgson, 497 U.S. 490 (1989)
Metro Broadcasting v. Federal Communications Commission, 497 U.S. 547 (1990)
Lujan v. National Wildlife Federation, 497 U.S. 871 (1990)
Rust v. Sullivan, Secretary of Health and Human Services, 500 U.S. 173 (1991)
Payne v. Tennessee, 501 U.S. 808 (1991)
Arkansas et al. v. Oklahoma et al., 503 U.S. 91 (1992)
Jacobson v. United States, 503 U.S. 540 (1992)
United States v. Thompson/Center Arms Company, 504 U.S. 505 (1992)
Lujan, Secretary of the Interior v. Defenders of Wildlife et al., 504 U.S. 555 (1992)
Wright v. West, 505 U.S. 277 (1992)
Planned Parenthood of Southeastern Pennsylvania v. Casey, 505 U.S. 833 (1992)
Lucas v. South Carolina Coastal Council, 505 U.S. 1003 (1992)
Farrar v. Hobby, 506 U.S. 103 (1992)
Nixon v. United States, 506 U.S. 224 (1993)
Voinovich v. Quilter, 507 U.S. 146 (1993)
Building and Trades Council v. Associated Builders, 507 U.S. 218 (1993)
Sale v. Haitian Centers Council, 509 U.S. 155 (1993)
Wisconsin v. Mitchell, 509 U.S. 476 (1993)
Shaw v. Reno, 509 U.S. 630 (1993)
John Hancock Mutual Life Insurance Co. v. Harris Trust and Savings Bank, 510 U.S.
  86 (1993)
Barclays Bank, P.L.C. v. Franchise Tax Board of California, 512 U.S. 298 (1994)

(Table continues)

Table 7-4 *(Continued)*

Johnson v. De Grandy, 512 U.S. 997 (1994)
Anderson v. Green, 513 U.S. 557 (1995)
United States v. Lopez, 514 U.S. 549 (1995)
U.S. Term Limits, Inc. v. Thornton, 514 U.S. 779 (1995)
Babbitt v. Sweet Home Chapter of Communities for a Great Oregon, 515 U.S. 687 (1995)
United States v. Hays, 515 U.S. 737 (1995)
Miller v. Johnson, 515 U.S. 900 (1995)
Wisconsin v. New York, 517 U.S. 1 (1996)
Shaw v. Hunt, 517 U.S. 899 (1966)
Colorado Republican Fed. Campaign Comm. v. FEC, 518 U.S. 604 (1996)
Felker v. Turpin, 518 U.S. 1051 (1996)
Arizonans for Official English v. Arizona, 520 U.S. 43 (1997)
Bennet v. Spear, 520 U.S. 154 (1997)
Agostini v. Felton, 521 U.S. 203 (1997)
Printz v. United States, 521 U.S. 898 (1997)
Kansas v. Hendricks, 521 U.S. 346 (1997)
Vacco v. Quill, 521 U.S. 793 (1997)
City of Boerne v. Flores, 521 U.S. 507 (1997)
Reno v. American Civil Liberties Union, 521 U.S. 844 (1997)

Note: Amicus curiae (or "friend of the court") is a person (or group), not a party to a case, who submits views in the form of written briefs and/or oral arguments on how the case should be decided.

Source: Cases obtained by authors through LEXIS and from a list maintained by Rorie Spill. We are greatful to Professor Spill for providing us with her data. Data for more recent terms, because of LEXIS's reporting system are not yet available.

Table 7-5 Most Litigated Laws, Vinson Through Rehnquist Courts

Court (terms)	Law	Number of cases
Vinson (1946–1952)	Internal Revenue Code	53
	Sherman Anti-Trust Act	51
	Federal Rules of Civil Procedure, including Appellate Procedure	35
	Interstate Commerce Act, as amended	29
	Labor-Management Relations Act	27
	Bankruptcy Code, Bankruptcy Act	25
	Selective Service, Military Selective Service, and Universal Military Service and Training Act	23
	Federal Employees' Liability Act	22
	Fair Labor Standards Act	21
	National Labor Relations Act, as amended	21
	Trading with the Enemy Act, as amended	18
	Robinson-Patman Act	17
	Criminal Procedure, Federal Rules of	16
	Federal Trade Commission Act	15
Warren (1953–1968)	Internal Revenue Code	122
	National Labor Relations Act, as amended	116
	Interstate Commerce Act, as amended	103
	Natural Gas and Natural Gas Policy Acts	62
	Immigration and Naturalization, Immigration, and Nationality Acts, as amended	53
	Sherman Anti-Trust Act	49
	Criminal Procedure, Federal Rules of	46
	Clayton Act	40
	Federal Rules of Civil Procedure, including Appellate Procedure	40
	Labor-Management Relations Act	32
	Federal Employers' Liability Act	25
	Railway Labor Act	25
	Bankruptcy Code, Bankruptcy Act, and Bankruptcy Reform Act of 1978	23
	Supreme Court Jurisdiction: State Courts, Appeal, Certiorari (28 USC 1257)	21
	Selective Service, Military Selective Service, and Universal Military Service and Training Acts	19
Burger (1969–1985)	Social Security Act (Aid to Families with Dependent Children, Medicaid, Medicare, Social Security Disability Benefits Reform Act, and Supplemental Security Income)	92
	National Labor Relations Act, as amended	91
	Internal Revenue Code	77
	Civil Rights Act of 1964, Title VII	67
	Civil Rights Act, section 1983	48

(Table continues)

Table 7-5   *(Continued)*

Court (terms)	Law	Number of cases
	Federal Rules of Civil Procedure, including Appellate Procedure	46
	Securities Act of 1933, Securities and Exchange Act, and Williams Act	38
	Sherman Anti-Trust Act	35
	Habeas Corpus (28 USC 2241–2255)	30
	Clayton Act	26
	Natural Gas and Natural Gas Policy Acts	25
	Interstate Commerce Act, as amended	24
	Omnibus Crime Control and Safe Streets, National Firearms, Organized Crime Control, and Gun Control Acts (excluding RICO)	24
	Communications Act of 1934	21
	Freedom of Information, Sunshine, and Privacy Acts	21
	Longshoremen and Harbor Workers' Compensation Act	21
	Voting Rights Act of 1965, plus amendments	21
Rehnquist (1986–2001)	Internal Revenue Code	50
	Federal Rules of Civil Procedure	46
	Bankruptcy Code and Acts	37
	Employee Retirement Income Security	34
	Civil Rights Act, section 1983	28
	Social Security Act (Aid to Families with Dependent Children, Medicaid, Medicare, Supplemental Security Income)	28
	Civil Rights Act of 1964, Title 7	26
	Habeas Corpus (28 USC 2241–2255)	26
	Federal Rules of Criminal Procedure	23
	Immigration and Naturalization	19
	National Labor Relations	19
	Administrative Procedure	17
	Securities Act of 1933, Securities and Exchange, and Williams Act	17
	Racketeer Influenced and Corrupt Organizations	16
	Voting Rights Act of 1965	16
	Americans with Disabilities	15
	Federal Rules of Evidence	15
	Age Discrimination in Employment	12
	Civil Rights Attorneys' Fees Awards	11

Source: U.S. Supreme Court Judicial Database, with analu = 0, 3, or 5 and dec_type = 1, 6, or 7.

Table 7-6 Most Litigated Constitutional Provisions, Vinson Through Rehnquist Courts

Court (terms)	Constitutional provision	Number of cases
Vinson (1946–1952)	Fourteenth Amendment, due process clause	56
	Fourteenth Amendment, equal protection clause	43
	Article I, section 8, interstate commerce clause	40
	First Amendment, freedom of speech, press, and assembly clauses	37
	Fifth Amendment, due process clause	28
	Fifth Amendment, takings clause	25
	Article IV, section 1, full faith and credit	19
	Fifth Amendment, self-incrimination clause	18
	Fourth Amendment	11
	Sixth Amendment, right to counsel	11
	Article I, section 10, contract clause	10
Warren (1953–1968)	Fourteenth Amendment, equal protection clause	127
	Fourteenth Amendment, due process clause	125
	First Amendment, freedom of speech, press, and assembly clauses	74
	Fourth Amendment[a]	62
	Fifth Amendment, self-incrimination clause[a]	54
	Article I, section 8, interstate commerce clause	37
	Article VI, supremacy clause	36
	Sixth Amendment, right to counsel[a]	36
	Fifth Amendment, due process clause	31
	First Amendment, freedom of association[a]	24
	Sixth Amendment, confrontation, cross examination, and compulsory process clauses[a]	21
	Fifth Amendment, double jeopardy clause[a]	20
	Fifth Amendment, takings clause[a]	20
	Article IV, section 1, full faith and credit	12
	Sixth Amendment, trial by jury clause[a]	12
Burger (1969–1985)	Fourteenth Amendment, due process clause	214
	Fourteenth Amendment, equal protection clause	185
	First Amendment, freedom of speech, press, and assembly clauses[a]	168
	Fourth Amendment[a]	112
	Article III, section 2, case or controversy requirement	88
	Article I, section 8, interstate commerce clause	71
	Fifth Amendment, due process clause	62
	Fifth Amendment, double jeopardy clause[a]	50
	Fifth Amendment, equal protection component	50
	Fifth Amendment, self-incrimination clause[a]	47
	Fifth Amendment, takings clause[a]	42
	First Amendment, establishment of religion clause[a]	41

(Table continues)

Table 7-6   *(Continued)*

Court (terms)	Constitutional provision	Number of cases
	Sixth Amendment, right to counsel[a]	40
	Eighth Amendment, cruel and unusual punishment clause[a]	35
	First Amendment, freedom of association[a]	24
	Article VI, supremacy clause	23
Rehnquist (1986–2001)	First Amendment, freedom of speech, press, and assembly clauses[a]	109
	Fourteenth Amendment, due process clause	99
	Article III, section 2, case or controversy requirement	58
	Fourth Amendment[a]	58
	Eighth Amendment, cruel and unusual punishment clause[a]	42
	Fourteenth Amendment, equal protection clause	42
	Article I, section 8, interstate commerce clause	37
	Fifth Amendment, due process clause[a]	32
	First Amendment, establishment of religion clause[a]	24
	Fifth Amendment, takings clause[a]	24
	Eleventh Amendment	23
	Sixth Amendment, right to counsel[a]	20
	First Amendment, freedom of association clause[a]	19
	Fifth Amendment, double jeopardy clause[a]	19
	Fifth Amendment, equal protection clause	15
	Article VI, supremacy clause	15
	Sixth Amendment, confrontation clause[a]	15
	Fifth Amendment, self-incrimination clause[a]	14
	Sixth Amendment, jury trial[a]	13
	First Amendment, free exercise of religion clause[a]	10

[a] Where a state or local government allegedly abridged a provision of the Bill of Rights that has been made binding on the states because it has been incorporated into the due process clause of the Fourteenth Amendment, identification is to the specific provision rather than the due process clause.

Source: U.S. Supreme Court Judicial Database, with analu = 0, 3, or 5 and dec_type = 1, 6, or 7.

Table 7-7   Chairs of the Senate Committee on the Judiciary

Name	Years of service	State	Party[a]
Dudley Chase	1815–1817	Vermont	Jacksonian Democrat
John J. Crittenden	1817–1818	Kentucky	Unionist
James Burrill, Jr.	1818–1819	Rhode Island	[b]
William Smith	1819–1823	South Carolina	Democrat
Martin Van Buren	1823–1828	New York	Democrat
John M. Berrien	1828–1829	Georgia	Democrat
John Rowan	1829–1831	New York	Democrat
William L. Marcy	1831–1832	New York	Jacksonian Democrat
William Wilkins	1832–1833	Pennsylvania	Democrat
John M. Clayton	1833–1836	Delaware	National Republican
Felix Grundy	1836–1838	Tennessee	War Democrat
Garret D. Wall	1838–1841	New Jersey	Democrat
John M. Berrien	1841–1844	Georgia	Whig
Chester Ashley	1844–1847	Arkansas	Democrat
Andrew P. Butler	1847–1857	South Carolina	States Rights Democrat
James A. Bayard	1857–1860	Delaware	Democrat
Lyman Trumbull	1860–1872	Illinois	Republican
George F. Edmunds	1872–1879	Vermont	Republican
Allen G. Thurman	1879–1881	Ohio	Democrat
George F. Edmunds	1881–1891	Vermont	Republican
George F. Hoar	1891–1893	Massachusetts	Republican
James L. Pugh	1893–1895	Alabama	Democrat
George F. Hoar	1895–1904	Massachusetts	Republican
Orville H. Platt	1904–1905	Connecticut	Republican
Clarence D. Clark	1905–1913	Wyoming	Republican
Charles A. Culberson	1913–1919	Texas	Democrat
Knute Nelson	1919–1923	Minnesota	Republican
Frank B. Brandegee	1923–1925	Connecticut	Republican
Albert B. Cummins	1925–1926	Iowa	Republican
William E. Borah	1926–1927	Idaho	Republican
George W. Norris	1927–1933	Nebraska	Republican
Henry F. Ashurst	1933–1941	Arizona	Democrat
Frederick Van Nuys	1941–1945	Indiana	Democrat
Pat McCarran	1945–1947	Nevada	Democrat
Alexander Wiley	1947–1949	Wisconsin	Republican
Pat McCarran	1949–1953	Nevada	Democrat
William Langer	1953–1955	North Dakota	Republican
Harley M. Kilgore	1955–1957	West Virginia	Democrat
James O. Eastland	1957–1979	Mississippi	Democrat
Edward M. Kennedy	1979–1981	Massachusetts	Democrat
Strom Thurmond	1981–1987	South Carolina	Republican
Joseph Biden	1987–1994	Delaware	Democrat
Orrin G. Hatch	1995–2001	Utah	Republican
Patrick J. Leahy	Jan. 2–Jan. 20, 2001	Vermont	Democrat

(Table continues)

Table 7-7   *(Continued)*

Name	Years of service	State	Party[a]
Orrin G. Hatch	Jan. 20– June 5, 2001	Utah	Republican
Patrick J. Leahy	June 6, 2001–	Vermont	Democrat

[a] During the nineteenth century, members of Congress commonly changed political parties. Listed here is party with which member was affiliated at time of service as chair.
[b] No party affiliation.

Source: U.S. Senate, *History of the Committee on the Judiciary United States Senate 1816–1967,* Sen. Doc. No. 78, 90th Cong., 2d sess. (Washington, D.C.: Government Printing Office, 1968), 131–133; *CQ's Guide to Congress* (Washington, D.C.: Congressional Quarterly, 1982); www.senate.gov/~judiciary/chair.htm.

Table 7-8   Chairs of the House Committee on the Judiciary

Name	Years of service	State	Party[a]
Charles Jared Ingersoll	1813–1815	Pennsylvania	Democrat
Hugh Nelson	1815–1819	Virginia	Democrat
John Sergeant	1819–1822	Pennsylvania	Federalist
Hugh Nelson	1822–1823	Virginia	Democrat
Daniel Webster	1823–1827	Massachusetts	Federalist
Philip Pendelton Barbour	1827–1829	Virginia	Democrat
James Buchanan	1829–1831	Pennsylvania	Democrat
Warren Ransom Davis	1831–1832	South Carolina	States' Rights Democrat
John Bell	1832–1834	Tennessee	Whig
Thomas Flournoy Foster	1834–1835	Georgia	Democrat
Samuel Beardsley	1835–1836	New York	Democrat
Francis Thomas	1836–1839	Maryland	Democrat
John Sergeant	1839–1841	Pennsylvania	Federalist
Daniel Dewey Barnard	1841–1843	New York	Whig
William Wilkins	1843–1844	Pennsylvania	Democrat
Romulus Mitchell Saunders	1844–1845	North Carolina	Democrat
George Oscar Rathbun	1845–1847	New York	Democrat
Joseph Reed Ingersoll	1847–1849	Pennsylvania	Whig
James Thompson	1849–1851	Pennsylvania	Democrat
James Xavier McLanahan	1851–1853	Pennsylvania	Democrat
Frederick Perry Stanton	1853–1855	Tennessee	Democrat
George Abel Simmons	1855–1857	New York	Whig
George Smith Houston	1857–1859	Alabama	Democrat
John Hickman	1859–1861	Pennsylvania	Douglas Democrat
John Hickman	1861–1863	Pennsylvania	Republican
James Falcolner Wilson	1863–1869	Iowa	Republican
John Armour Bingham	1869–1873	Ohio	Republican
Ben Franklin Butler	1873–1875	Massachusetts	Republican
James Proctor Knott	1875–1881	Kentucky	Democrat
Thomas Bracket Reed	1881–1883	Maine	Republican
John Randolph Tucker	1883–1887	Virginia	Democrat
David Browning Culberson	1887–1889	Texas	Democrat
Ezra Booth Taylor	1889–1891	Ohio	Republican
David Browning Culberson	1891–1895	Texas	Democrat
David Bremner Henderson	1895–1899	Iowa	Republican
George Washington Ray	1899–1903	New York	Republican
John James Jenkins	1903–1909	Wisconsin	Republican
Richard Wayne Parker	1909–1911	New Jersey	Republican
Henry De Lamar Clayton	1911–1915	Alabama	Democrat
Edwin Yates Webb	1915–1919	North Carolina	Democrat
Andrew John Volstead	1919–1923	Minnesota	Republican
George Scott Graham	1923–1931	Pennsylvania	Republican
Hatton William Sumners	1931–1946	Texas	Democrat
Earl Cory Michener	1947–1948	Michigan	Republican
Emanuel Celler	1949–1952	New York	Democrat
Chauncey W. Reed	1953–1954	Illinois	Republican

(Table continues)

Table 7-8 *(Continued)*

Name	Years of service	State	Party[a]
Emanuel Celler	1955–1972	New York	Democrat
Peter W. Rodino, Jr.	1973–1988	New Jersey	Democrat
Jack Brooks	1989–1994	Texas	Democrat
Henry J. Hyde	1995–2001	Illinois	Republican
F. James Sensenbrenner, Jr.	2001–	Wisconsin	Republican

[a] During the nineteenth century, members of Congress commonly changed political parties. Listed here is party with which member was affiliated at time of service as chair.

Source: U.S. House, *History of the Committee on the Judiciary of the House of Representatives,* Committee Print, Serial no. 15, 97th Cong., 2d sess. (Washington, D.C.: Government Printing Office, 1982), 144–145; *CQ's Guide to Congress* (Washington, D.C.: Congressional Quarterly, 1982). Updated by authors.

Table 7-9 Impeachment of Federal Judges and Justices

Name (Court)	House	Senate
John Pickering (District Court, N.H.)	Voted (45–8) four articles of impeachment, most of which involved his judicial conduct (e.g., his handling of a lawsuit; being drunk and committing blasphemy on the bench), in December 1803.	Convicted (19–7) on all charges in March 1804.
Samuel Chase (Supreme Court)	Voted (72–32) eight articles of impeachment, six of which involved his actions "while presiding on circuit at treason and sedition trials," in March 1804. The other two centered on "addresses delivered to grand juries."	Acquitted (varying votes) on all charges in March 1805.
James H. Peck (District Court, Fla.)	Voted (123–49) one article charging him with "wrongfully convicting an attorney of contempt" in April 1830.	Acquitted (22–21) in January 1831.
Wes H. Humphreys (District Court, Tenn.)	Voted (voice vote) seven articles, all centering on the fact that he "ceased holding court and acted as a judge for the Confederacy," in May 1862.	Convicted (38–0) on six of seven charges in June 1862.
Charles Swayne; (District Court, Fla.)	Voted (voice vote) twelve articles, charged with "padding expense accounts, using railroad property in receivership, and misusing contempt of power," in December 1904.	Acquitted (varying votes) on all charges in February 1905.
Robert W. Archibald (Commerce Court)	Voted (223–1) thirteen articles, many of which involved allegations of influence peddling, in July 1912.	Convicted (voice vote) on five charges in January 1913.
George W. English (District Court, Ill.)	Voted (306–2) five articles, charged with "partiality, tyranny, and oppression" (e.g., accepting gifts) in November 1926.	Resigned in December 1926; proceedings dismissed (70–9) in December.

(Table continues)

Table 7-9 *(Continued)*

Name *(Court)*	House	Senate
Harold Louderback (District Court, Calif.)	Voted (183–142) five articles, including "registering to vote at a fictitious residence" and "appointing incompetent receivers and allowing them excessive fees," in February 1933.	Acquitted (varying votes) on all charges in May 1933.
Halstead L. Ritter (District Court, Fla.)	Voted (181–146) seven articles, including income tax evasion and continuing to practice law while a judge, in March 1936. The last article charged that he brought "his court into scandal and disrepute."	Convicted (56–28) on the last count only in April 1936.
Harry E. Claibourne (District Court, Nev.)	Voted (406–0) four articles, stemming from his conviction of income tax evasion, in July 1986.	Convicted (varying votes) on three of the four counts in October 1986.
Alcee L. Hastings (District Court, Fla.)	Voted (413–3) seventeen articles, centering on a bribery charge for which he was acquitted in February 1983, in August 1988.	Convicted on eight of the seventeen counts in October 1989.
Walter L. Nixon (District Court, Miss.)	Voted (417–0) three articles, stemming from his 1986 conviction for perjury, in May 1989.	Convicted on two of the three counts in November 1989.

Note: In 1873, the House impeached Mark H. Delahay, with the "most grievous charge" being that "he was intoxicated off the bench as well as on the bench." After he was impeached, but before articles were drawn up, Delahay resigned. This is "the only impeachment in American history in which articles were never drafted." See Emily Field Von Tassel and Paul Finkelman, *Impeachable Offenses* (Washington, D.C.: CQ Press, 1998), 119.

Sources: U.S. Department of Justice, *The Law of Impeachment* (Washington, D.C.: Government Printing Office, February 22, 1974), Appendix 1; Henry J. Abraham, *The Judicial Process*, 5th ed. (New York: Oxford University Press, 1986), 46–48; Congressional Quarterly, *1989 Almanac* (Washington, D.C.: Congressional Quarterly, 1990), 231, 234. For further information on the articles of impeachment voted by the House of Representatives (prior to 1973), see U.S. House, Committee on the Judiciary, *Impeachment—Selected Materials*, 93d Cong., 1st sess. (Washington, D.C.: Government Printing Office, 1973), 125–203.

Figure 7-1 Organizational Chart of the Department of Justice

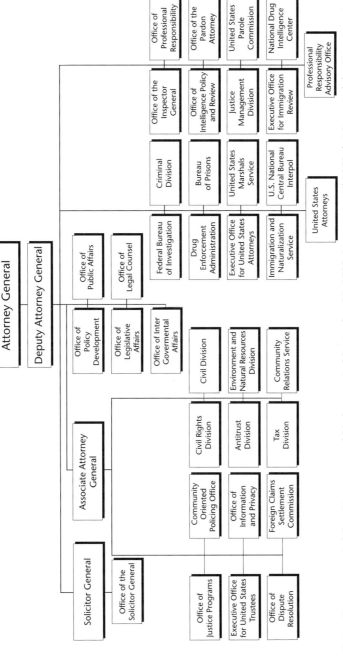

Note: Congress created the attorney generalship by an act of September 24, 1789. It was not until 1870 that it created the Department of Justice.

Source: www.usdoj.gov/dojorg.htm.

Table 7-10 Attorneys General of the United States

Name	Term	Appointing president
Edmund Jennings Randolph	September 26, 1789–January 2, 1794	Washington
William Bradford	January 27, 1794–August 23, 1795	Washington
Charles Lee	December 10, 1795–February 18, 1801	Washington/J. Adams
Levi Lincoln	March 5, 1801– March 3, 1805	Jefferson
John Breckenridge	August 7, 1805–December 14, 1806	Jefferson
Caesar Augustus Rodney	January 20, 1807–December 11, 1811	Jefferson/Madison
William Pinkney	December 11, 1811–February 10, 1814	Madison
Richard Rush	February 10, 1814–November 13, 1817	Madison
William Wirt	November 13, 1817–March 3, 1829	Monroe/J.Q. Adams
John MacPherson Berrien	March 9, 1829–July 20, 1831	Jackson
Roger Brooke Taney	July 20, 1831–September 24, 1833	Jackson
Benjamin Franklin Butler	July 5, 1833–September 1, 1838	Jackson/Van Buren
Felix Grundy	July 5, 1838–December 1, 1839ª	Van Buren
Henry Dilworth Gilpin	January 11, 1840–March 4, 1841	Van Buren
John Jordan Crittenden	March 3, 1841–September 13, 1841	W. Harrison//Tyler
Hugh Swinton Legare	September 13, 1841–June 20, 1843	Tyler
John Nelson	July 1, 1843–March 3, 1845	Tyler
John Young Mason	March 6, 1845–September 9, 1846	Polk
Nathan Clifford	September 17, 1846–March 17, 1848	Polk
Isaac Toucey	June 21, 1848–March 3, 1849	Polk
Reverdy Johnson	March 8, 1849–July 20, 1850	Taylor
John Jordan Crittenden	July 22, 1850–March 3, 1853	Fillmore
Caleb Cushing	March 7, 1853–March 3, 1857	Pierce
Jeremiah Sullivan Black	March 6, 1857–December 17, 1860	Buchanan
Edwin McMasters Stanton	December 20, 1860–March 3, 1861	Buchanan
Edward Bates	March 5, 1861–September 1864	Lincoln
James Speed	December 2, 1864–July 17, 1866	Lincoln/A. Johnson
Henry Stanbery	July 23, 1866–March 12, 1868	A. Johnson

William Maxwell Evarts	July 15, 1868–March 3, 1869	A. Johnson
Ebenezer Rockwood Hoar	March 5, 1869–June 23, 1870	Grant
Amos Tappan Akerman	June 23, 1870–January 10, 1872	Grant
George Henry Williams	December 14, 1871–May 15, 1875[b]	Grant
Edwards Pierrepont	April 26, 1875–May 22, 1876[c]	Grant
Alphonso Taft	May 22, 1876–March 11, 1877	Grant
Charles Devens	March 12, 1877–March 6, 1881	Hayes
(Isaac) Wayne MacVeagh	March 5, 1881–September 24, 1881[d]	Garfield
Benjamin Harris Brewster	December 19, 1881– March 5, 1885[e]	Arthur
Augustus Hill Garland	March 6, 1885–March 5, 1889	Cleveland
William Henry Harrison Miller	March 5, 1889–March 6, 1893	B. Harrison
Richard Oliney	March 6, 1893–June 7, 1895	Cleveland
Judson Harmon	June 8, 1895–March 5, 1897	Cleveland
Joseph McKenna	March 5, 1897–January 25, 1898	McKinley
John William Griggs	June 25, 1898–March 29, 1901	McKinley
Philander Chase Knox	April 5, 1901–June 30, 1904	McKinley
William Henry Moody	July 1, 1904–December 17, 1906	T. Roosevelt
Charles Joseph Bonaparte	December 17, 1906–March 4, 1909	T. Roosevelt
George Woodward Wickersham	March 5, 1909–March 5, 1913	Taft
James Clark McReynolds	March 5, 1913–August 29, 1914	Wilson
Thomas Watt Gregory	August 20, 1914–March 4, 1919	Wilson
Alexander Mitchell Palmer	March 5, 1919–March 5, 1921	Wilson
Harry Micajah Daugherty	March 4, 1921–March 28, 1924	Harding
Harlan Fiske Stone	April 7, 1924–February 3, 1925	Coolidge
John T. Sargent	March 17, 1925–March 5, 1929	Coolidge
William DeWitt Mitchell	March 5, 1929–March 3, 1933	Hoover
Homer Stille Cummings	March 4, 1933–January 2, 1939	F. Roosevelt
Frank Murphy	January 2, 1939–January 18, 1940	F. Roosevelt
Robert Houghwout Jackson	January 18, 1940–July 10, 1941	F. Roosevelt
Francis Biddle	September 15, 1941–June 30, 1945	F. Roosevelt
Tom Campbell Clark	June 15, 1945–August 24, 1949[f]	Truman
James Howard McGrath	August 24, 1949–April 7, 1952	Truman
James Patrick McGranery	May 27, 1952–January 20, 1953	Truman

(Table continues)

Table 7-10 *(Continued)*

Name	Term	Appointing president
Herbert Brownell, Jr.	January 21, 1953–November 8, 1957	Eisenhower
William Pierce Rogers	November 8, 1957–January 20, 1961	Eisenhower
Robert Francis Kennedy	January 21, 1961–September 3, 1964	Kennedy
Nicholas deBelleville Katzenbach	February 11, 1965–October 2, 1966[g]	L. Johnson
Ramsey Clark	February 3, 1967–January 20, 1969	L. Johnson
John Newton Mitchell	January 21, 1969–March 1, 1972	Nixon
Richard Gordon Kleindienst	June 12, 1972–May 24, 1973[h]	Nixon
Elliot Lee Richardson	May 25, 1973–October 20, 1973	Nixon
William Bart Saxbe	January 4, 1974–February 3, 1975	Nixon
Edward Hirsch Levi	February 6, 1975–January 20, 1977	Ford
Griffin Boyette Bell	January 26, 1977–August 16, 1979	Carter
Benjamin R. Civiletti	August 16, 1979–January 19, 1981	Carter
William French Smith	January 23, 1981–February 24, 1985	Reagan
Edwin Meese III	February 25, 1985–August 12, 1988	Reagan
Richard L. Thornburgh	August 12, 1988–August 9, 1991	Reagan/G. Bush
William P. Barr	November 25, 1991–January 20, 1993	G. Bush
Janet Reno	March 12, 1993–January 20, 2001	Clinton
John Ashcroft	January 21, 2001–	G. W. Bush

[a] Appointed July 5, 1838, to take effect September 1, 1838.
[b] Appointed December 14, 1871, to take effect January 10, 1872.
[c] Appointed April 26, 1875, to take effect May 15, 1875.
[d] Resigned September 22, 1881, but served to October 23, 1881.
[e] Did not take the oath of office until January 2, 1882.
[f] Entered on duty July 1, 1945.
[g] Served as acting attorney general from September 4, 1964, until appointed.
[h] Served as acting attorney general from March 2, 1972, until appointed.

Sources: U.S. Department of Justice, *Register of the U.S. Department of Justice and the Federal Courts*, 56th ed. (Washington, D.C.: Government Printing Office, 1992), 151; www.usdoj.gov/jmd/ls/agbib2000.htm#agchart.

Figure 7-2 Organizational Chart of the Office of the Solicitor General

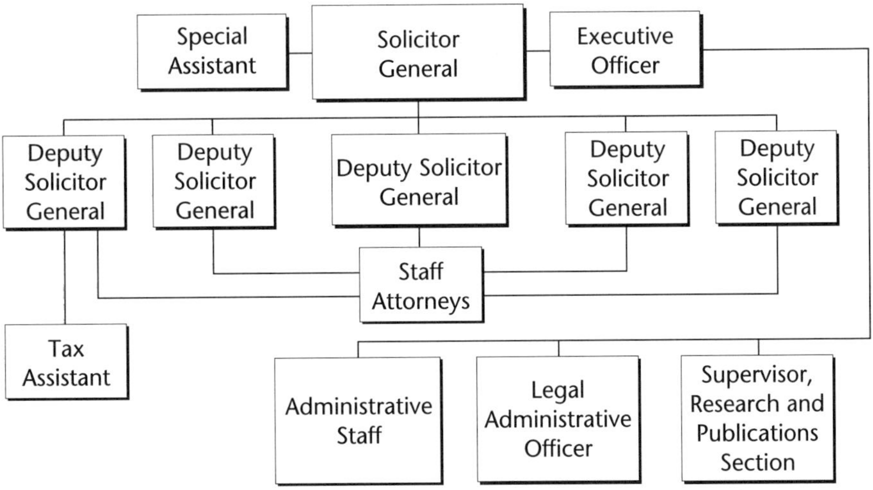

Source: www.usdoj.gov/jmd/msp/OMFM-3.gif.

Table 7-11 Solicitors General of the United States

Name	Term	Appointing president
Benjamin H. Bristow	October 11, 1870–November 15, 1872	Grant
Samuel F. Phillips	November 15, 1872–May 3, 1885	Grant
John Goode	May 1, 1885–August 5, 1886	Cleveland
George A. Jenks	July 30, 1886–May 29, 1889	Cleveland
Orlow W. Chapman	May 29, 1889–January 19, 1890	B. Harrison
William Howard Taft	February 4, 1890–March 20, 1892	B. Harrison
Charles H. Aldrich	March 21, 1892–May 28, 1893	B. Harrison
Lawrence Maxwell, Jr.	April 6, 1893–January 30, 1895	Cleveland
Holmes Conrad	February 6, 1895–July 8, 1897	Cleveland
John K. Richards	July 1, 1897–March 6, 1903	McKinley
Henry M. Hoyt	February 25, 1903–March 31, 1909[a]	T. Roosevelt
Lloyd Wheaton Bowers	April 1, 1909–September 9, 1910	Taft
Frederick W. Lehman	December 12, 1910–July 15, 1912	Taft William
Marshall Bullitt	July 16, 1912–March 11, 1913	Taft
John William Davis	August 30, 1913–November 26, 1918	Wilson
Alexander C. King	November 27, 1918–May 23, 1920	Wilson
William L. Frierson	June 11, 1920–June 30, 1921	Wilson
James M. Beck	June 30, 1921–June 7, 1925	Harding
William D. Mitchell	June 4, 1925–April 5, 1929[b]	Coolidge
Charles Evans Hughes, Jr.	May 27, 1929–March 16, 1930	Hoover
Thomas D. Thacher	March 22, 1930–May 4, 1933[c]	Hoover
James Crawford Biggs	May 4, 1933–March 24, 1935	F. Roosevelt
Stanley Reed	March 23, 1935–January 30, 1938[d]	F. Roosevelt
Robert H. Jackson	March 5, 1938–January 17, 1940	F. Roosevelt
Francis Biddle	January 22, 1940–September 4, 1941	F. Roosevelt
Charles Fahy	November 15, 1941–September 27, 1945	F. Roosevelt
J. Howard McGrath	October 4, 1945–October 7, 1946[e]	Truman

Philip B. Perlman	July 30, 1947–August 15, 1952[f]	Truman
Walter J. Cummings, Jr.	December 2, 1952–March 1, 1953	Truman
Simon E. Sobeloff	February 10, 1954–July 19, 1956[g]	Eisenhower
J. Lee Rankin	August 4, 1956–January 23, 1961	Eisenhower
Archibald Cox	January 24, 1961–July 31, 1965	Kennedy
Thurgood Marshall	August 11, 1965–August 30, 1967	L. Johnson
Erwin N. Griswold	October 12, 1967–June 25, 1973	L. Johnson
Robert H. Bork	June 19, 1973–January 20, 1977	Nixon
Wade Hampton McCree, Jr.	March 28, 1977–August 5, 1981	Carter
Rex E. Lee	August 6, 1981–May 31, 1985	Reagan
Charles Fried	October 25, 1985–January 20, 1989	Reagan
Kenneth Starr	May 27, 1989–January 20, 1993	G. Bush
Drew S. Days III	June 7, 1993–June 28, 1996	Clinton
Walter Dellinger (acting)	August 1996–August 1997	Clinton
Seth P. Waxman	August 1997–January 20, 2001	Clinton
Theodore B. Olson	June 2001–	G.W. Bush

[a] Took the oath of office and entered on duty March 16, 1909.
[b] Took the oath of office and entered on duty June 8, 1925.
[c] Took the oath of office and entered on duty April 17, 1930.
[d] Took the oath of office and entered on duty March 25, 1935.
[e] Took the oath of office and entered on duty October 8, 1945.
[f] Took the oath of office and entered on duty July 31, 1947.
[g] Took the oath of office and entered on duty February 25, 1954.

Sources: U.S. Department of Justice, *Register of the U.S. Department of Justice and the Federal Courts,* 56th ed. (Washington, D.C.: Government Printing Office, 1992), 143; www.usdoj.gov/osg/aboutosg/sglist.html.

Table 7-12   Success Rate of the United States as a Party to a
Case Before the Supreme Court, 1946–2001 Terms

Term	Total number of cases[a]	Percentage won
1946	68	69.1
1947	51	66.7
1948	39	56.4
1949	38	57.9
1950	51	64.7
1951	37	62.2
1952	43	58.1
1953	26	61.5
1954	34	61.8
1955	41	46.3
1956	59	44.1
1957	48	58.3
1958	35	62.9
1959	56	62.5
1960	51	68.6
1961	36	44.4
1962	36	61.1
1963	37	56.8
1964	24	79.2
1965	39	56.4
1966	30	60.0
1967	40	65.0
1968	31	61.3
1969	26	65.4
1970	40	70.0
1971	23	43.5
1972	40	72.5
1973	31	71.0
1974	38	68.4
1975	33	84.8
1976	30	50.0
1977	33	57.6
1978	20	65.0
1979	38	65.8
1980	16	66.8
1981	18	72.2
1982	25	52.0
1983	30	83.3
1984	25	76.0
1985	25	88.0
1986	26	61.5
1987	24	66.7
1988	15	80.0
1989	23	56.5
1990	14	64.3
1991	21	57.1

Table 7-12   *(Continued)*

Term	Total number of cases[a]	Percentage won
1992	30	60.0
1993	21	61.9
1994	14	46.7
1995	27	55.6
1996	17	70.6
1997	26	65.4
1998	11	45.5
1999	21	52.4
2000	12	50.0
2001	14	87.5

[a] Includes those cases where the *U.S. Reports* names the United States a party to the case, and criminal and habeas corpus cases where the *U.S. Reports* lists as the party the name of the official or office of the person who prosecutes or has custody of the accused or convicted person. If the United States is not the first named party in multiple party litigation, the case is not included.

Source: U.S. Supreme Court Judicial Database, with analu = 0 or 1 and dec_type = 1, 6, or 7.

Table 7-13 Success Rate of the United States as a Party
to a Case Before the Supreme Court, by
Issue Area, 1946–2001 Terms

Issue area	Total number of cases[a]	Percentage won
Criminal procedure	689	63.3
Civil rights	136	61.0
First Amendment	110	45.5
Due process	75	73.3
Privacy	3	100.0
Attorneys	5	60.0
Unions	15	53.3
Economic activity	381	63.0
Judicial power	142	65.5
Federalism	56	57.1
Federal taxation	177	70.6
Miscellaneous	9	77.8
Total	1,818	63.0

Note: The issue areas are defined as follows: Criminal procedure: the rights of persons accused of crime except for the due process rights of prisoners; Civil rights: non–First Amendment freedom cases that pertain to classifications based on race (including Native Americans), age, indigence, voting, residence, military or handicapped status, sex, or alienage; First Amendment: guarantees contained therein; Due process: noncriminal procedural guarantees, plus court jurisdiction over non-resident litigants and the takings clause of the Fifth Amendment; Privacy: abortion, contraception, the Freedom of Information Act and related federal statutes; Attorneys: attorneys' fees, commercial speech, admission to and removal from the bar, and disciplinary matters; Unions: labor union activity; Economic activity: commercial business activity, plus litigation involving injured persons or things, employee actions vis-à-vis employers, zoning regulations, and governmental regulation of corruption other than that involving campaign spending; Judicial power: the exercise of the judiciary's own power and authority; Federalism: conflicts between the federal and state governments, excluding those between state and federal courts, and those involving the priority of federal fiscal claims; Federal taxation: the Internal Revenue Code and related statutes; Miscellaneous: Legislative veto, separation of powers, and matters not included in any other issue area.

[a] Includes those cases where the *U.S. Reports* names the United States a party to the case, and criminal and habeas corpus cases where the *U.S. Reports* lists as the party the name of the official or office of the person who prosecutes or has custody of the accused or convicted person. If the United States is not the first named party in multiple party litigation, the case is not included.

Source: U.S. Supreme Court Judicial Database, with analu = 0 or 1 and dec_type = 1, 6, or 7.

Table 7-14   Position Taken by the Solicitor General as an
Amicus Curiae in Cases Before the Supreme
Court, 1953–1989 Terms

Term	Liberal	Conservative	Mixed
1953	2	2	0
1954	4	1	0
1955	2	3	0
1956	4	3	0
1957	3	0	0
1958	4	3	1
1959	5	1	0
1960	6	2	0
1961	9	0	0
1962	10	5	0
1963	20	4	0
1964	7	2	0
1965	3	5	2
1966	7	2	0
1967	8	2	5
1968	3	2	2
1969	12	6	1
1970	11	5	3
1971	5	6	3
1972	10	8	4
1973	6	12	0
1974	7	4	4
1975	14	6	11
1976	12	4	4
1977	10	4	3
1978	11	11	3
1979	14	8	3
1980	18	12	4
1981	16	10	5
1982	14	15	3
1983	16	15	2
1984	11	24	1
1985	10	27	2
1986	11	26	3
1987	12	17	3
1988	14	21	2
1989	8	26	2

Note: Figures represent number of cases in which position was taken.

Source: James A. Stimson, Michael B. MacKuen, and Robert S. Erikson, "Dynamic Representation," *American Political Science Review* 89 (1995): 543–565.

Table 7-15 Success Rate of the Solicitor General as an Amicus Curiae in Cases Before the Supreme Court, 1954–1996 Terms

Term	Total number of cases	Percentage won
1954	5	80.0
1955	5	60.0
1956	7	57.1
1957	3	100.0
1958	7	85.7
1959	5	100.0
1960	9	100.0
1961	8	75.0
1962	15	73.3
1963	25	100.0
1964	9	88.9
1965	8	87.5
1966	9	66.7
1967	10	90.0
1968	5	80.0
1969	18	66.7
1970	16	62.5
1971	11	63.6
1972	17	70.6
1973	17	88.2
1974	9	55.6
1975	19	84.2
1976	16	56.3
1977	12	50.0
1978	23	65.2
1979	20	70.0
1980	25	72.0
1981	29	75.9
1982	30	80.0
1983	29	79.3
1984	28	67.9
1985	36	58.3
1986	37	73.0
1987	27	40.7
1988	19	52.6
1989	31	74.2
1990	29	86.2
1991	21	90.5
1992	24	75.0
1993	18	44.4
1994	18	61.1
1995	15	66.7
1996	14	64.3

Note: Includes cases decided by the Court with an opinion on the merits and those in which the solicitor general's brief took a clear position on the merits of the case.

Sources: 1954–1982: Jeffrey A. Segal, "Courts, Executives, and Legislatures," in John B. Gates and Charles A. Johnson, eds., *The American Courts: A Critical Assessment* (Washington, D.C.: CQ Press, 1991); 1983–1988: Valerie Hoekstra, Washington University, personal communication; 1989–1993: Christina Wolbrecht, Washington University, personal communication; 1994–1996: Calculated by the authors from data available at www.usdoj.gov/osg/briefs/search.html#type.

Table 7-16 Success Rate of the Solicitor General as an
Amicus Curiae in Cases Before the Supreme
Court, by President, 1952–1999 Terms

President	Total number of cases[a]	Percentage won
Eisenhower	42	83.3
Kennedy	48	87.5
Johnson	41	82.9
Nixon	79	70.9
Ford	38	71.1
Carter	86	65.1
Reagan[b]	239	72.8
G. Bush[c]	110	78.2
Clinton[d]	148	68.2

[a] Includes all cases where solicitor general filed an amicus curiae brief that took a clear position and the Court decided the case with an opinion on the merits.

[b] Includes 1980–1987 terms.

[c] Includes 1988–1991 terms.

[d] Includes 1992–1999 terms.

Sources: 1952–1982: Jeffrey A. Segal. "Courts, Executives, and Legislatures," in John B. Gates and Charles A. Johnson, eds., *The American Courts: A Critical Assessment* (Washington, D.C.: CQ Press, 1991), 379; 1983–1999: calculated by the authors.

Table 7-17   Success Rate of Federal Agencies as a Party to a
Case Before the Supreme Court, 1946–2001 Terms

Term	Total number of cases[a]	Percentage won
1946	57	84.2
1947	44	88.6
1948	33	78.8
1949	34	79.4
1950	36	63.9
1951	26	65.4
1952	34	73.5
1953	28	50.0
1954	18	77.8
1955	29	55.2
1956	28	78.6
1957	39	41.0
1958	25	80.0
1959	29	69.0
1960	21	52.4
1961	18	61.1
1962	22	68.2
1963	16	68.8
1964	29	72.4
1965	19	68.4
1966	30	63.3
1967	34	82.4
1968	14	78.6
1969	24	45.8
1970	18	44.4
1971	26	73.1
1972	25	80.0
1973	32	65.6
1974	24	75.0
1975	38	57.9
1976	25	84.0
1977	27	77.8
1978	25	64.0
1979	24	70.8
1980	33	78.8
1981	24	83.3
1982	44	72.7
1983	41	80.5
1984	34	82.4
1985	28	57.1
1986	21	71.4
1987	37	59.5
1988	24	62.5
1989	24	70.8
1990	16	37.5

Table 7-17   *(Continued)*

Term	Total number of cases[a]	Percentage won
1991	16	93.8
1992	14	78.6
1993	9	66.7
1994	10	60.0
1995	8	87.5
1996	11	72.7
1997	8	62.5
1998	11	63.6
1999	6	50.0
2000	13	31.8
2001	20	70.0
Total	1,403	69.6

Note: See Table 7-19 for list of federal agencies included.

[a] Includes cases where the *U.S. Reports* lists name of federal agency or the head of the agency as a party to a case.

Source: U.S. Supreme Court Judicial Database, with analu = 0 or 1 and dec_type = 1, 6, or 7.

Table 7-18 Success Rate of Federal Agencies as a Party to a Case Before the Supreme Court, by Issue Area, 1946–2001 Terms

Issue	Total number of cases[a]	Percentage won
Criminal procedure	32	75.0
Civil rights	215	61.4
First Amendment	104	61.5
Due process	57	84.2
Privacy	33	81.8
Attorneys	13	53.8
Unions	210	68.1
Economic activity	332	76.3
Judicial power	204	65.2
Federalism	28	53.6
Federal taxation	166	74.7
Miscellaneous	9	66.7
Total	1,403	69.4

Note: Issue areas are defined as follows: Criminal procedure: the rights of persons accused of crime except for the due process rights of prisoners; Civil rights: non–First Amendment freedom cases that pertain to classifications based on race (including Native Americans), age, indigence, voting, residence, military or handicapped status, sex, or alienage; First Amendment: guarantees contained therein; Due process: noncriminal procedural guarantees, plus court jurisdiction over nonresident litigants and the takings clause of the Fifth Amendment; Privacy: abortion, contraception, the Freedom of Information Act and related federal statutes; Attorneys: attorneys' fees, commercial speech, admission to and removal from the bar, and disciplinary matters; Unions: labor union activity; Economic activity: commercial business activity, plus litigation involving injured persons or things, employee actions vis-à-vis employers, zoning regulations, and governmental regulation of corruption other than that involving campaign spending; Judicial power: the exercise of the judiciary's own power and authority; Federalism: conflicts between the federal and state governments, excluding those between state and federal courts, and those involving the priority of federal fiscal claims; Federal taxation: the Internal Revenue Code and related statutes; Miscellaneous: legislative veto, separation of powers, and matters not included in any other issue area.

[a] Includes cases where the *U.S. Reports* lists name of federal agency or the head of the agency as a party to a case.

Source: U.S. Supreme Court Judicial Database, with analu = 0 or 1 and dec_type = 1, 6, or 7.

Table 7-19   Success Rate of Federal Agencies as a Party to a Case Before the Supreme Court, by Agency, 1946–2001 Terms

Agency[a]	Total number of cases[b]	Percentage won
Air Force	4	50.0
Alien Property Custodian	6	50.0
Amtrak	1	0.0
Army	8	50.0
Atomic Energy Commission	1	0.0
Benefits Review Board	2	50.0
Board of Immigration Appeals	3	100.0
Bureau of Prisons	1	100.0
Central Intelligence Agency	3	66.7
Civil Aeronautics Board	9	66.7
Commodity Futures Trading Commission	3	66.7
Comptroller of Currency	8	50.0
Comptroller General	7	42.9
Consumer Product Safety Commission	2	50.0
Civil Rights Commission	2	100.0
Civil Service Commission	11	54.5
Customs Service	1	100.0
Defense Base Closure and Realignment Commission	1	100.0
Department of Agriculture	31	64.5
Department of Commerce	4	100.0
Department of Defense	44	86.4
Department of Education	6	83.3
Department of Energy	2	50.0
Department of Health and Human Services	46	69.6
Department of Health, Education and Welfare	30	86.7
Department of Housing and Urban Development	7	57.1
Department of Interior	46	71.7
Department of Justice	52	50.0
Department of Labor	62	69.4
Department of State	21	33.3
Department of Transportation	7	85.7
Department of Treasury	18	66.7
Employees' Compensation Commission	7	71.4
Environmental Protection Agency	32	78.1
Equal Employment Opportunity Commission	16	75.0
Farm Credit Administration	1	100.0
Federal Aviation Administration	1	100.0
Federal Bureau of Investigation	1	100.0
Federal Communications Commission	28	75.0
Federal Deposit Insurance Corporation	3	100.0
Federal Elections Commission	12	54.0
Federal Energy Administration	1	100.0
Federal Energy Regulatory Commission	20	85.0
Federal Home Loan Bank Board	1	100.0
Federal Housing Administration	1	100.0
Federal Labor Relations Authority	7	42.9

(Table continues)

Table 7-19   *(Continued)*

Agency[a]	Total number of cases[b]	Percentage won
Federal Maritime Board	7	42.9
Federal Maritime Commission	6	33.3
Federal Power Commission	59	76.3
Federal Reserve Board	11	81.8
Federal Savings and Loan Insurance Corporation	2	50.0
Federal Trade Commission	59	84.7
Federal Works Administration	2	100.0
Food and Drug Administration	3	100.0
General Services Administration	2	100.0
Immigration and Naturalization Service	81	61.7
Information Security Oversight Office	1	0.0
Internal Revenue Service	164	75.4
Interstate Commerce Commission	84	70.2
Legal Services Corporation	1	0.0
National Endowment for the Arts	1	0.0
National Labor Relations Board	194	70.1
National Mediation Board	2	100.0
National Railway Adjustment Board	3	100.0
Navy	2	100.0
Nuclear Regulatory Commission	4	100.0
Occupational Safety and Health Administration	1	0.0
Occupational Safety and Health Review Commission	3	66.7
Office of Management and Budget	1	0.0
Office of Personnel Management	5	60.0
Office of Price Administration	11	90.9
Office of Workers' Compensation Programs	7	14.3
Patent Office	3	100.0
Pension Benefit Guaranty Corporation	1	100.0
Public Health Service	2	50.0
Railroad Retirement Board	1	100.0
Renegotiation Board	2	100.0
Securities and Exchange Commission	24	70.8
Selective Service System	5	60.0
Small Business Administration	1	100.0
Social Security Administration	3	33.3
Subversive Activities Control Board	5	20.0
Tennessee Valley Authority	2	50.0
United States Forest Service	1	100.0
United States Parole Commission	12	41.7
United States Postal Service	10	60.0
Veterans' Administration	9	66.7
Wage Stabilization Board	1	0.0

[a] Note that agencies occasionally change names or otherwise alter their structure. They may also cease to exist.

[b] Includes cases where the *U.S. Reports* lists federal agency or the head of the agency as a party to a case.

Source: U.S. Supreme Court Judicial Database, with analu = 0 or 1 and dec_type = 1, 6, or 7.

Table 7-20   Supreme Court Rulings Against Presidents, Washington
to Clinton

President	Number of decisions	President	Number of decisions
Washington	0	Arthur	2
Adams	0	Cleveland	1
Jefferson	2	Harrison	0
Madison	3	McKinley	0
Monroe	1	T. Roosevelt	0
J.Q. Adams	0	Taft	0
Jackson	0	Wilson	2
Van Buren	0	Harding	2
Harrison	0	Coolidge	3
Tyler	1	Hoover	1
Polk	0	F. Roosevelt	8
Taylor	0	Truman	3
Fillmore	1	Eisenhower	3
Pierce	0	L. Johnson	2
Buchanan	0	Nixon	25
Lincoln	5	Ford	3
A. Johnson	2	Carter	2
Grant	0	Reagan	0
Hayes	1	G. Bush	0
Garfield	0	Clinton[a]	3

[a] Data for Clinton are through 1997.

Source: Lyn Ragsdale, *Vital Statistics on the Presidency,* rev. ed. (Washington, D.C.: Congressional Quarterly, 1998), 444.

Table 7-21 Success Rate of States as a Party to a Case Before the Supreme Court, 1946–2001 Terms

Term	Total number of cases[a]	Percentage won
1946	13	46.2
1947	21	57.1
1948	20	30.0
1949	8	62.5
1950	9	55.6
1951	11	54.5
1952	12	75.0
1953	17	35.3
1954	7	14.3
1955	10	60.0
1956	13	23.1
1957	21	66.7
1958	18	55.6
1959	15	33.3
1960	33	51.5
1961	20	35.0
1962	29	27.6
1963	23	21.7
1964	27	14.8
1965	19	26.3
1966	34	38.2
1967	30	26.7
1968	31	35.5
1969	41	43.9
1970	57	54.4
1971	64	42.2
1972	62	59.7
1973	37	48.6
1974	43	46.5
1975	44	59.1
1976	62	45.2
1977	48	52.1
1978	46	60.9
1979	35	37.1
1980	36	61.1
1981	46	34.8
1982	55	58.2
1983	45	48.9
1984	37	56.8
1985	52	65.4
1986	48	54.2
1987	31	45.2
1988	33	63.6
1989	38	68.4
1990	31	58.1
1991	28	28.6

Table 7-21 *(Continued)*

Term	Total number of cases[a]	Percentage won
1992	22	72.7
1993	14	71.4
1994	10	50.0
1995	14	50.0
1996	17	70.6
1997	15	60.0
1998	11	63.6
1999	20	55.0
2000	21	52.4
2001	13	38.3
Total	1,617	49.2

[a] Includes those cases where the *U.S. Reports* names a state a party to a case, and criminal and habeas corpus cases where the *U.S. Reports* list as the party the name of the official or office of the person who prosecutes or has custody of the accused or convicted person. If a state is not the first named party in multiple party litigation, the case is not included. Excludes original jurisdiction cases in which one state sues another.

Source: U.S. Supreme Court Judicial Database, with analu = 0 or 1 and dec_type = 1, 6, or 7.

Table 7-22   Success Rate of States as a Party to a Case Before the
Supreme Court, by Issue Area, 1946–2001 Terms

Issue	Total number of cases[a]	Percentage won
Criminal procedure	682	54.0
Civil rights	287	38.7
First Amendment	136	37.5
Due process	74	60.8
Privacy	27	51.9
Attorneys	10	50.0
Unions	4	50.0
Economic activity	143	46.9
Judicial power	162	61.7
Federalism	87	35.6
Federal taxation	4	25.0
Miscellaneous	1	100.0
Total	1,617	49.2

Note: The issue areas are defined as follows: Criminal procedure: the rights of persons accused of crime except for the due process rights of prisoners; Civil rights: non–First Amendment freedom cases that pertain to classifications based on race (including Native Americans), age, indigence, voting, residence, military or handicapped status, sex, or alienage; First Amendment: guarantees contained therein; Due process: noncriminal procedural guarantees, plus court jurisdiction over nonresident litigants and the takings clause of the Fifth Amendment; Privacy: abortion, contraception, the Freedom of Information Act and related federal statutes; Attorneys: attorneys' fees, commercial speech, admission to and removal from the bar, and disciplinary matters; Unions: labor union activity; Economic activity: commercial business activity, plus litigation involving injured persons or things, employee actions vis-à-vis employers, zoning regulations, and governmental regulation of corruption other than that involving campaign spending; Judicial power: the exercise of the judiciary's own power and authority; Federalism: conflicts between the federal and state governments, excluding those between state and federal courts, and those involving the priority of federal fiscal claims; Federal taxation: the Internal Revenue Code and related statutes; Miscellaneous: legislative veto, separation of powers, and matters not included in any other issue area.

[a] Includes those cases where the *U.S. Reports* name a state a party to a case, and criminal and habeas corpus cases where the *U.S. Reports* list as the party the name of the official or office of the person who prosecutes or has custody of the accused or convicted person. If a state is not the first named party in multiple party litigation, the case is not included. Excludes original jurisdiction cases in which one state sues another.

Source: U.S. Supreme Court Judicial Database, with analu = 0 or 1 and dec_type = 1, 6, or 7.

Table 7-23   Success Rates of States as a Party to a Case Before
the Supreme Court, by State, 1946–2001 Terms

State	Total number of cases[a]	Percentage won
Alabama	44	29.5
Alaska	15	46.7
Arizona	50	48.0
Arkansas	20	35.0
California	159	60.4
Colorado	11	63.6
Connecticut	23	34.8
Delaware	6	50.0
Florida	78	53.8
Georgia	54	40.7
Hawaii	8	25.0
Idaho	11	27.3
Illinois	98	50.0
Indiana	22	54.5
Iowa	21	42.9
Kansas	8	50.0
Kentucky	26	50.0
Louisiana	63	33.3
Maine	10	40.0
Maryland	49	61.2
Massachusetts	39	66.7
Michigan	32	62.5
Minnesota	17	52.9
Mississippi	35	28.6
Missouri	26	38.5
Montana	14	57.1
Nebraska	11	63.6
Nevada	11	45.5
New Hampshire	9	11.1
New Jersey	30	50.0
New Mexico	15	33.3
New York	131	58.8
Noth Carolina	34	41.2
North Dakota	5	40.0
Ohio	60	41.7
Oklahoma	26	42.3
Oregon	20	70.0
Pennsylvania	66	42.4
Rhode Island	10	30.0
South Carolina	20	35.0
South Dakota	11	54.5
Tennessee	25	60.0
Texas	82	41.4
Utah	6	66.7
Vermont	5	20.0

(Table continues)

Table 7-23   *(Continued)*

State	Total number of cases[a]	Percentage won
Virginia	47	44.7
Washington	30	56.7
West Virginia	8	75.0
Wisconsin	22	50.0
Wyoming	4	50.0

[a] Includes those cases where the *U.S. Reports* name a state a party to a case, and criminal and habeas corpus cases where the *U.S. Reports* list as the party the name of the official or office of the person who prosecutes or has custody of the accused or convicted person. If a state is not the first named party in multiple party litigation, the case is not included. Excludes original jurisdiction cases in which one state sues another.

Source: U.S. Supreme Court Judicial Database, with analu = 0 or 1 and dec_type = 1, 6, or 7.

1. An amicus curiae brief that brings to the attention of the Court relevant matter not already brought to its attention by the parties may be of considerable help to the Court. An amicus curiae brief that does not serve this purpose burdens the Court, and its filing is not favored.

2. (a) An amicus curiae brief submitted before the Court's consideration of a petition for a writ of certiorari, motion for leave to file a bill of complaint, jurisdictional statement, or petition for an extraordinary writ, may be filed if accompanied by the written consent of all parties, or if the Court grants leave to file under subparagraph 2(b) of this Rule. The brief shall be submitted within the time allowed for filing a brief in opposition or for filing a motion to dismiss or affirm. The amicus curiae brief shall specify whether consent was granted, and its cover shall identify the party supported.

(b) When a party to the case has withheld consent, a motion for leave to file an amicus curiae brief before the Court's consideration of a petition for a writ of certiorari, motion for leave to file a bill of complaint, jurisdictional statement, or petition for an extraordinary writ may be presented to the Court. The motion, prepared as required by Rule 33.1 and as one document with the brief sought to be filed, shall be submitted within the time allowed for filing an amicus curiae brief, and shall indicate the party or parties who have withheld consent and state the nature of the movant's interest. Such a motion is not favored.

3. (a) An amicus curiae brief in a case before the Court for oral argument may be filed if accompanied by the written consent of all parties, or if the Court grants leave to file under subparagraph 3(b) of this Rule. The brief shall be submitted within the time allowed for filing the brief for the party supported, or if in support of neither party, within the time allowed for filing the petitioner's or appellant's brief. The amicus curiae brief shall specify whether consent was granted, and its cover shall identify the party supported or indicate whether it suggests affirmance or reversal. The Clerk will not file a reply brief for an amicus curiae, or a brief for an amicus curiae in support of, or in opposition to, a petition for rehearing.

(b) When a party to a case before the Court for oral argument has withheld consent, a motion for leave to file an amicus curiae brief may be presented to the Court. The motion, prepared as required by Rule 33.1 and as one document with the brief sought to be filed, shall be submitted within the time allowed for filing an amicus curiae brief, and shall indicate the party or parties who have withheld consent and state the nature of the movant's interest.

4. No motion for leave to file an amicus curiae brief is necessary if the brief is presented on behalf of the United States by the Solicitor General; on behalf of any agency of the United States allowed by law to appear before this Court when submitted by the agency's authorized legal representative; on behalf of a State, Commonwealth, Territory, or Possession when submitted by its Attorney General; or on behalf of a city, county, town, or similar entity when submitted by its authorized law officer.

5. A brief or motion filed under this Rule shall be accompanied by proof of service as required by Rule 29, and shall comply with the applicable provisions of Rules 21, 24, and 33.1 (except that it suffices to set out in the brief the interest of the amicus curiae, the summary of the argument, the argument, and the conclusion). A motion for leave to file may not exceed five pages. A party served with the motion may file an objection thereto, stating concisely the reasons for withholding consent; the objection shall be prepared as required by Rule 33.2.

6. Except for briefs presented on behalf of amicus curiae listed in Rule 37.4, a brief filed under this Rule shall indicate whether counsel for a party authored the brief in whole or in part and shall identify every person or entity, other than the amicus curiae, its members, or its counsel, who made a monetary contribution to the preparation or submission of the brief. The disclosure shall be made in the first footnote on the first page of text.

Source: Rules of the Supreme Court of the United States, Part VII. Practice and Procedure, Rule 37. Brief for an Amicus Curiae (available at www.law.cornell.edu/rules/supct/37.html).

Table 7-25   Supreme Court Cases Containing at Least One Amicus
Curiae Brief, 1953–1994 Terms

Term	Percentage	Number of cases
1953	13.3	126
1954	23.3	109
1955	20.2	128
1956	17.0	162
1957	20.8	194
1958	26.7	167
1959	15.3	157
1960	23.8	160
1961	25.5	148
1962	38.5	188
1963	46.3	224
1964	45.7	156
1965	33.6	187
1966	33.3	201
1967	37.1	285
1968	37.1	207
1969	39.0	188
1970	48.4	224
1971	55.9	259
1972	50.0	272
1973	52.2	267
1974	51.4	223
1975	60.0	253
1976	46.1	254
1977	58.4	244
1978	66.7	244
1979	53.8	221
1980	70.3	255
1981	75.3	269
1982	67.4	277
1983	72.3	298
1984	64.8	301
1985	70.0	308
1986	86.5	163
1987	82.8	157
1988	83.2	161
1989	86.1	144
1990	79.0	119
1991	84.8	118
1992	81.7	109
1993	92.5	93
1994	93.9	82

Sources: 1953–1985: National Science Foundation, Preliminary Version of the Codebook for
Phase II of the Supreme Court Database; 1986–1990: Lee Epstein, "Interest Group Litigation
during the Rehnquist Court Era," *Journal of Law and Politics* 9 (1993): 680; 1991–1993:
Andrew Koshner, *Interest Group Participation and the U.S. Supreme Court: A Longitudinal
Analysis of the Rise of Interest Group Litigation,* Ph.D. diss., Washington University; 1994: updated by authors via LEXIS. Due to reporting limitations, data cannot presently be further
updated with LEXIS.

Table 7-26   Participation as an Amicus Curiae on the Merits of Supreme Court Cases, by Group Type, 1958–1990 Terms

Group type	Briefs submitted[a]				
	1958–1961	*1978–1981*	*1982*	*1984*	*1986–1990*
Corporations	18.3%	9.2%	9.2%	17.7%	11.1%
Business, trade, and professional associations	46.8	36.2	37.5	30.2	32.7
Labor unions	17.4	11.6	5.0	5.3	5.1
Citizen, advocacy, public interest, and charitable groups and public interest law firms	17.4	43.0	48.3	46.8	51.1
Total number of briefs submitted by groups falling under these categories	(N=109)	(N=423)	(N=666)	(N=1,298)	(N=1,008)

Note: Only groups falling under these four categories were coded (for example, Indian tribes, individuals, and state governments were excluded), and only the group listed first on the brief on the merits was counted.

[a] Figures are percentage of all briefs submitted by group types.

Sources: 1958–1961 and 1978–1981: Kay Lehman Schlozman and John Tierney, *Organized Interests and American Democracy* (New York: Harper and Row, 1986), 383; 1982: Gregory A. Caldeira and John R. Wright, "Amici Before the Supreme Court," 52 *Journal of Politics* (1990): 793; 1984: Patrick Bruer, "Amicus Curiae and Supreme Court Litigation," (Paper presented at the 1988 annual meeting of the Law & Society Meeting) (on file with the author); 1988–1990: Lee Epstein, "Interest Group Litigation during the Rehnquist Court Era," 9 *Journal of Law and Politics* (1993): 639–717.

Table 7-27   Justices' Citations to Amicus Curiae Briefs, 1953–2000 Terms

Justice[a]	Number of citations to amici curiae	Number of citations to amici curiae divided by total opinions written[b]
Black	297	.53
Blackmun	559	.68
Brennan	755	.65
Breyer	47	.31
Burger	337	.68
Burton	17	.21
Clark	109	.36
Douglas	416	.45
Fortas	43	.44
Frankfurter	74	.29
Ginsburg	48	.31
Goldberg	87	.39
Harlan	252	.37
Jackson	10	.63
Kennedy	129	.45
Marshall	505	.71
Minton	8	.20
O'Connor	338	.60
Powell	458	.77
Reed	20	.33
Rehnquist	494	.61
Scalia	219	.44
Souter	57	.26
Stevens	688	.60
Stewart	363	.51
Thomas	60	.29
Warren	99	.40
White	670	.66
Whittaker	28	.25

[a] For justices joining the Court prior to 1953, data are not completely descriptive of careers.
[b] Includes opinions of the Court, judgments, and dissenting and concurring (regular and special) opinions.

Sources: LEXIS; U.S. Supreme Court Judicial Database.

Figure 7-3 The American Court System

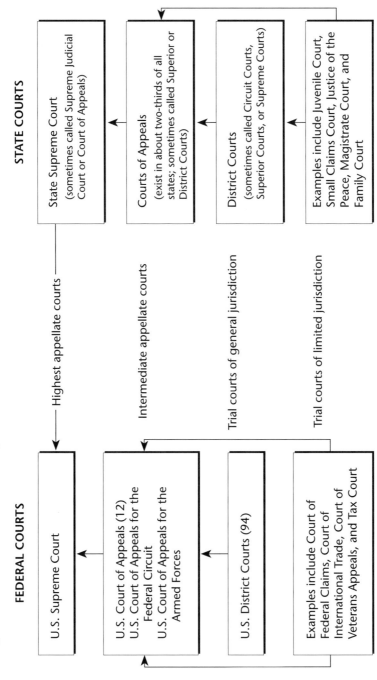

Source: Lee Epstein and Thomas G. Walker, *Constitutional Law for a Changing America: Rights, Liberties, and Justice,* 4th ed. (Washington, D.C.: CQ Press, 2001), 13.

Figure 7-4 The Federal Court System

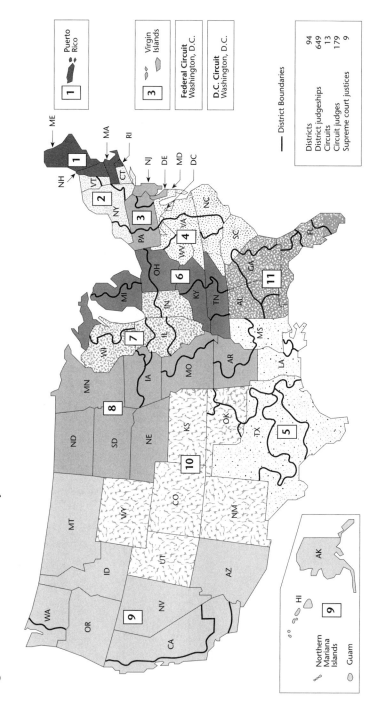

Note: Number and composition of circuits set forth by 28 U.S.C. § 4. The large numerals indicate the Courts of Appeals.

Source: Administrative Office of the United States Courts.

Table 7-28 The Development of the Federal Courts of Appeals

	Circuit/states in circuit													
Year of congressional action	First	Second	Third	Fourth	Fifth	Sixth	Seventh	Eighth	Ninth	California	District of Columbia	Tenth	Eleventh	Federal
1802	NH, MA, RI	CT, NY, VT	NJ, PA	MD, DE	VA, NC	SC, GA					[a]			
1807							TN, KY, OH							
1837	NH, MA, RI, ME						IL, IN, OH	MO, KY, TN	AL, LA[b], MS, AR					
1842				MD, DE, VA	AL, LA	SC, NC, GA	MI, IN, IL, OH		MS, AR					
1855										CA				
1862				MD, DE, VA, NC, SC, WV	FL, GA, AL, MS	TX, LA, AR, TN, KY	IN, OH	WI, IL, MI	MN, IA, MO, KS					

(Table continues)

Table 7-28 (Continued)

| | Circuit/states in circuit | | | | | | | | | | District of Columbia | | | |
Year of congressional action	First	Second	Third	Fourth	Fifth	Sixth	Seventh	Eighth	Ninth	California		Tenth	Eleventh	Federal
1863										Abolished	a	CA, OR		
1866			PA, NJ, DE	MD, VA, NC, SC, WV	FL, GA, AL, MS, LA, TX	TN, KY, OH, MI	WI, IN, IL	KS, MO, IA, MN, AR[c]	CA, NV, OR			Abolished		
1891				MD, VA, NC, SC, WV				KS, MO, IA, MN, AR, ND, SD, NE, CO, WY	CA, NV, OR, WA, ID, MT					
1893											a			
1929	PR, ME, NH,							ND, SD, NE,	CA, NV, OR,			NM, CO, OK,		

Year						
1948	MA, RI	PA, NJ, DE, VI	FL, GA, AL, MS, LA, TX, CZ	MN, IA, MO, AR	WA, ID, MT, HI, AZ	KS, WY, UT
					CA, NV, OR, WA, ID, MT, HI, AZ, AK	Formally specified circuit
1980			TX, MS, LA			
1982			FL, GA, AL			Created[d]
Present					CA, NV, OR, WA, ID, MT, HI, AZ, AK, GU, MP	

(Table continues)

Table 7-28 *(Continued)*

Note: The Judiciary Act of 1789 created three circuits, the Eastern, Middle, and Southern. By an act of February 13, 1801, Congress provided for the establishment of six circuit courts, "comprising the Thirteen original states, the States of Kentucky, Tennessee, and Vermont, and the districts of Maine and Ohio." Congress repealed the 1801 Act, but an act passed in 1802 retained some elements of its predecessor, including the enlarged number of circuits.

Three other important laws relating to the development of the courts of appeals were passed in 1802, 1869, and 1891. In 1802 Congress provided "that circuits shall consist of a Supreme Court Justice residing within the district and the district judge of the district. This act thereby dispenses with specifically designated circuit judges." In 1869 a circuit court judge was appointed for each of the "then existing nine judicial circuits." Not until 1891, however, did Congress create separate federal intermediate appellate courts.

[a] The Judiciary Act of 1801 created separate circuit court judgeships and a federal intermediate court for the District of Columbia. In 1802 Congress repealed that part of the law establishing circuit judgeships, but not that which created the D.C. Court. In 1863 it replaced the D.C. intermediate court with the Supreme Court for the District of Columbia and, finally, in 1893 it replaced the D.C. Supreme Court with the Court of Appeals for the District of Columbia.
[b] Except for the Western District of Louisiana.
[c] Except for the Western District of Arkansas.
[d] Created out of the Court of Claims and Court of Customs and Patent Appeals.

Sources: Russell R. Wheeler and Cynthia Harrison, *Creating the Federal Judicial System* (Washington, D.C.: Federal Judicial Center, 1989). For more information on the development of the circuit courts of appeals, see U.S. Senate, Committee on the Judiciary, *Legislative History of the United States Circuit Courts of Appeals and the Judges Who Served during the Period 1801 through March 1958*, 85th Cong., 2d sess. (Washington, D.C.: Government Printing Office, 1958); 3. For more information on the evolution of the District of Columbia District Court, see John R. Schmidhauser, *Judges and Justices* (Boston: Little, Brown, 1979), 45–47.

Table 7-29   U.S. Court of Appeals Decisions Affirmed by the Supreme Court, 1946–2001 Terms

	Circuit					
Term	First	Second	Third	Fourth	Fifth	Sixth
1946	4 (50.0)	12 (58.3)	17 (23.5)	7 (71.4)	3 (66.7)	27 (66.7)
1947	2 (100.0)	9 (77.8)	3 (33.3)	1 (100.0)	8 (12.5)	7 (14.3)
1948	—	19 (57.9)	16 (37.5)	7 (28.6)	12 (16.7)	2 (0.0)
1949	2 (50.0)	12 (66.7)	4 (75.0)	—	8 (12.5)	4 (25.0)
1950	—	16 (43.8)	2 (50.0)	3 (100.0)	11 (45.5)	4 (50.0)
1951	1 (100.0)	8 (100.0)	10 (80.0)	2 (50.0)	5 (80.0)	3 (0.0)
1952	3 (66.7)	16 (31.3)	8 (62.5)	7 (71.4)	6 (33.3)	5 (20)
1953	2 (100.0)	8 (50.0)	2 (100.0)	2 (100.0)	16 (31.3)	3 (66.7)
1954	3 (66.7)	15 (46.7)	7 (57.1)	2 (50.0)	13 (38.5)	7 (42.9)
1955	—	14 (57.1)	8 (75.0)	4 (0.0)	11 (36.4)	3 (33.3)
1956	3 (66.7)	14 (42.9)	7 (28.6)	3 (66.7)	10 (20.0)	6 (33.3)
1957	3 (33.3)	12 (41.7)	6 (66.7)	3 (0.0)	12 (25.0)	11 (45.5)
1958	2 (0.0)	12 (66.7)	13 (61.5)	7 (85.7)	12 (25.0)	2 (50.0)
1959	1 (0.0)	11 (72.2)	8 (50.0)	4 (25.0)	18 (38.9)	8 (37.5)
1960	8 (50.0)	7 (76.5)	5 (0.0)	4 (25.0)	6 (50.0)	7 (57.1)
1961	4 (0.0)	11 (36.4)	4 (0.0)	3 (33.3)	10 (30.0)	3 (33.3)
1962	5 (40.0)	15 (46.7)	3 (0.0)	2 (0.0)	9 (11.1)	6 (16.7)
1963	3 (33.3)	14 (28.6)	3 (33.3)	1 (0.0)	11 (0.0)	2 (0.0)
1964	4 (0.0)	12 (58.3)	5 (60.0)	4 (0.0)	11 (18.2)	6 (50.0)
1965	1 (0.0)	12 (33.3)	1 (100.0)	3 (66.7)	17 (35.3)	7 (14.3)
1966	3 (100.0)	12 (50.0)	4 (0.0)	3 (0.0)	12 (50.0)	7 (71.4)
1967	4 (50.0)	16 (50.0)	11 (18.2)	3 (66.7)	5 (20.0)	9 (22.2)
1968	3 (33.3)	4 (25.0)	4 (0.0)	3 (33.3)	9 (33.3)	6 (16.7)
1969	—	10 (30.0)	2 (100.0)	3 (0.0)	12 (25.0)	8 (37.5)
1970	2 (50.0)	5 (60.0)	3 (33.3)	4 (50.0)	16 (31.3)	7 (42.9)
1971	4 (25.0)	14 (57.1)	1 (100.0)	6 (16.7)	17 (29.4)	7 (85.7)
1972	2 (50.0)	10 (60.0)	4 (25.0)	9 (77.8)	7 (42.9)	8 (25.0)
1973	3 (33.3)	14 (28.6)	8 (12.5)	8 (50.0)	9 (66.7)	18 (27.8)
1974	1 (100.0)	14 (50.0)	11 (54.5)	7 (0.0)	10 (30.0)	6 (16.7)
1975	3 (0.0)	11 (54.5)	7 (28.6)	9 (66.7)	18 (22.2)	10 (30.0)
1976	2 (100.0)	10 (30.0)	6 (50.0)	12 (41.7)	19 (36.8)	11 (27.3)
1977	5 (80.0)	16 (25.0)	4 (50.0)	6 (50.0)	16 (43.8)	10 (20.0)
1978	—	12 (25.0)	8 (50.0)	5 (40.0)	14 (28.6)	7 (28.6)
1979	3 (0.0)	14 (64.3)	10 (20.0)	4 (75.0)	20 (65.0)	6 (33.3)
1980	2 (0.0)	9 (44.4)	17 (17.6)	4 (0.0)	16 (56.3)	7 (57.1)
1981	6 (50.0)	10 (65.0)	16 (18.8)	9 (33.3)	20 (35.0)	6 (50.0)
1982	6 (33.3)	14 (35.7)	5 (40.0)	10 (60.0)	20 (30.0)	6 (50.0)
1983	7 (28.6)	11 (36.4)	15 (53.3)	9 (55.6)	8 (37.5)	9 (44.4)
1984	6 (66.7)	15 (53.3)	10 (30.0)	8 (37.5)	4 (25.0)	18 (50.0)
1985	4 (25.0)	7 (86.7)	13 (69.2)	14 (35.7)	7 (42.9)	16 (43.8)
1986	4 (75.0)	11 (11.1)	14 (64.3)	6 (16.7)	13 (53.8)	8 (25.0)
1987	6 (83.3)	4 (75.0)	7 (42.9)	11 (45.5)	13 (69.2)	10 (70.0)
1988	1 (100.0)	18 (55.6)	11 (54.5)	10 (60.0)	10 (60.0)	6 (16.7)
1989	2 (100.0)	11 (27.3)	12 (75.0)	10 (40.0)	10 (20.0)	4 (0.0)
1990	1 (0.0)	8 (87.5)	6 (83.3)	10 (30.0)	19 (42.1)	5 (40.0)
1991	6 (33.3)	11 (27.3)	7 (57.1)	5 (40.0)	14 (50.0)	7 (14.3)
1992	5 (20.0)	4 (25.0)	3 (66.7)	8 (12.5)	8 (75.0)	6 (33.3)
1993	—	1 (100.0)	9 (44.4)	4 (100.0)	5 (40.0)	6 (66.7)
1994	1 (100.0)	5 (20.0)	5 (60.0)	3 (33.3)	9 (33.3)	7 (42.9)
1995	3 (33.3)	7 (28.6)	2 (100.0)	10 (20.0)	1 (0.0)	4 (50.0)

(Table continues)

Table 7-29 *(Continued)*

				Circuit		
Term	*First*	*Second*	*Third*	*Fourth*	*Fifth*	*Sixth*
1996	1 (00.0)	7 (14.3)	3 (66.7)	2 (50.0)	5 (20.0)	3 (33.3)
1997	5 (60.0)	3 (66.7)	4 (75.0)	1 (100.0)	12 (50.0)	3 (33.3)
1998	—	4 (25.0)	7 (42.9)	6 (33.3)	5 (20.0)	4 (50.0)
1999	1 (100.0)	3 (0.0)	2 (50.0)	9 (55.6)	8 (37.5)	5 (20.0)
2000	2 (0.0)	8 (75.0)	5 (60.0)	5 (60.0)	7 (42.9)	7 (28.6)
2001	1 (100)	4 (0.0)	1 (0.0)	14 (33.3)	1 (0.0)	9 (11.1)
Total	155 (46.5)	592 (47.8)	386 (44.8)	315 (42.5)	601 (36.1)	383 (36.6)

				Circuit		
Term	*Seventh*	*Eighth*	*Ninth*	*Tenth*	*Eleventh*	*District of Columbia*
1946	13 (69.2)	12 (41.7)	14 (28.6)	12 (91.7)		15 (33.3)
1947	16 (0.0)	6 (66.7)	16 (50.0)	5 (60.0)		25 (40.0)
1948	8 (37.5)	1 (0.0)	7 (28.6)	7 (57.1)		9 (33.3)
1949	7 (57.1)	4 (0.0)	4 (50.0)	3 (66.7)		18 (22.2)
1950	9 (22.2)	5 (80.0)	3 (0.0)	5 (20.0)		10 (30.0)
1951	3 (33.3)	1 (100.0)	10 (80.0)	1 (100.0)		13 (53.8)
1952	5 (60.0)	3 (0.0)	7 (42.9)	1 (0.0)		8 (25.0)
1953	—	3 (66.7)	8 (80.0)	1 (0.0)		13 (69.2)
1954	5 (0.0)	1 (0.0)	5 (20.0)	4 (75.0)		9 (11.1)
1955	4 (50.0)	3 (100.0)	10 (50.0)	4 (25.0)		8 (0.0)
1956	11 (45.5)	5 (80.0)	16 (25.0)	1 (0.0)		9 (33.3)
1957	9 (55.6)	3 (66.7)	9 (66.7)	7 (71.4)		17 (23.5)
1958	5 (40.0)	8 (62.5)	9 (11.1)	3 (33.3)		18 (22.2)
1959	11 (36.4)	1 (0.0)	11 (36.4)	4 (75.0)		9 (44.4)
1960	15 (40.0)	2 (100.0)	8 (37.5)	2 (0.0)		12 (33.3)
1961	6 (33.3)	—	6 (16.7)	2 (50.0)		19 (15.8)
1962	5 (40.0)	1 (100.0)	9 (22.2)	1 (0.0)		8 (75.0)
1963	8 (50.0)	3 (0.0)	8 (25.0)	3 (0.0)		4 (50.0)
1964	6 (50.0)	3 (66.7)	5 (60.0)	3 (33.3)		12 (16.7)
1965	8 (25.0)	4 (25.0)	6 (16.7)	2 (50.0)		6 (33.3)
1966	8 (12.5)	2 (0.0)	8 (25.0)	6 (50.0)		7 (28.6)
1967	8 (0.0)	4 (0.0)	13 (15.4)	18 (50.0)		11 (9.1)
1968	6 (16.7)	6 (16.7)	7 (14.3)	6 (33.3)		4 (25.0)
1969	4 (0.0)	5 (20.0)	8 (37.5)	5 (20.0)		3 (33.3)
1970	9 (44.4)	—	14 (42.9)	3 (33.3)		4 (50.0)
1971	8 (37.5)	7 (14.3)	11 (54.5)	5 (20.0)		6 (16.7)
1972	8 (25.0)	5 (20.0)	17 (23.5)	1 (0.0)		15 (26.7)
1973	11 (18.2)	2 (50.0)	16 (56.3)	3 (33.3)		17 (35.3)
1974	5 (60.0)	3 (0.0)	11 (36.4)	4 (0.0)		18 (22.2)
1975	6 (50.0)	4 (50.0)	27 (33.3)	5 (0.0)		17 (41.2)
1976	10 (40.0)	11 (33.3)	9 (55.6)	3 (33.3)		6 (16.7)
1977	12 (8.3)	7 (28.6)	16 (6.3)	2 (50.0)		16 (18.8)
1978	14 (57.1)	13 (23.1)	8 (27.3)	7 (0.0)		4 (0.0)
1979	6 (66.7)	3 (33.3)	12 (8.3)	6 (66.7)		12 (25.0)
1980	5 (20.0)	6 (16.7)	19 (36.8)	1 (0.0)		16 (31.3)
1981	11 (38.4)	8 (62.5)	10 (70.0)	5 (80.0)		15 (0.0)
1982	9 (44.4)	11 (36.4)	29 (34.5)	3 (66.7)		27 (18.5)

Table 7-29   *(Continued)*

	Circuit					
Term	*Seventh*	*Eighth*	*Ninth*	*Tenth*	*Eleventh*	*District of Columbia*
1983	7 (85.7)	12 (33.3)	33 (6.1)	6 (16.7)	6 (33.3)	11 (0.0)
1984	11 (45.5)	6 (33.3)	28 (25.0)	6 (50.0)	10 (70.0)	7 (14.3)
1985	6 (66.7)	6 (16.7)	18 (44.4)	2 (50.0)	6 (33.3)	13 (23.1)
1986	6 (33.3)	7 (42.9)	29 (57.1)	5 (0.0)	12 (33.3)	7 (14.3)
1987	5 (20.0)	10 (40.0)	18 (55.6)	9 (55.6)	5 (60.0)	14 (64.3)
1988	9 (44.4)	10 (40.0)	21 (42.9)	2 (0.0)	10 (50.0)	8 (50.0)
1989	6 (50.0)	9 (66.7)	16 (50.0)	4 (25.0)	6 (83.3)	8 (50.0)
1990	8 (25.0)	3 (33.3)	13 (23.1)	7 (0.0)	5 (40.0)	7 (28.6)
1991	5 (40.0)	3 (33.3)	14 (35.7)	7 (28.6)	10 (30.0)	2 (0.00)
1992	6 (50.0)	9 (44.4)	24 (37.5)	4 (50.0)	12 (16.7)	6 (50.0)
1993	8 (62.5)	4 (50.0)	16 (37.5)	4 (50.0)	5 (40.0)	2 (100.0)
1994	8 (75.0)	3 (0.0)	17 (29.4)	4 (25.0)	3 (33.3)	4 (50.0)
1995	7 (42.9)	3 (33.3)	13 (15.4)	4 (50.0)	6 (50.0)	7 (71.4)
1996	4 (00.0)	8 (50.0)	24 (16.7)	4 (75.0)	6 (66.7)	1 (100.0)
1997	8 (50.0)	13 (38.5)	17 (23.5)	1 (100.0)	3 (33.3)	10 (60.0)
1998	4 (0.0)	5 (50.0)	16 (31.3)	4 (75.0)	8 (25.0)	1 (100.0)
1999	9 (22.2)	5 (80.0)	12 (16.7)	1 (100.0)	6 (66.7)	2 (100.0)
2000	4 (50.0)	2 (100.0)	14 (35.7)	4 (24.0)	2 (0.0)	2 (50.0)
2001	2 (100.0)	9 (22.2)	14 (35.7)	6 (50.0)	6 (16.7)	4 (50.0)
Total	414 (37.9)	290 (38.6)	759 (33.3)	236 (41.5)	12.7 (41.7)	537 (30.9)

Note: "—" indicates no cases decided. Figures are total number of cases. Figures in parentheses are percentage of cases affirmed. All orally argued docket numbers, excluding cases arising under the Court's original jurisdiction, are included. Because the formal dispositions the Court makes do not necessarily correspond to who wins the case, the focus here is on the prevailing party. If the petitioning party prevails in whole or in part, the case is counted as a reversal; otherwise as an affirmation.

Source: U.S. Supreme Court Judicial Database, with analu = 0 or 1, dec_type = 1, 6, or 7, and jur ≠ 9.

Table 7-30 U.S. District Court Decisions Affirmed by the Vinson, Warren, Burger, and Rehnquist Courts

District court	Vinson (1946–1952) N	Percentage	Warren (1953–1968) N	Percentage	Burger (1969–1985) N	Percentage	Rehnquist (1986–2001) N	Percentage	Total N	Percentage
Alabama, MD	2	0.0	7	42.9	3	0.0	2	100.0	14	35.7
Alabama, ND	1	100.0	2	0.0	5	40.0	—	—	8	37.5
Alaska, D	—	—	2	0.0	1	0.0	—	—	3	0.0
Arizona, D	—	—	1	100.0	5	80.0	—	—	6	83.3
Arkansas, ED	—	—	1	0.0	—	—	—	—	1	0.0
Arkansas, WD	—	—	8	37.5	5	0.0	—	—	13	23.1
California, CD	—	—	—	—	21	33.3	3	66.7	24	37.5
California, ED	—	—	—	—	2	50.0	1	0.0	3	33.3
California, ND	4	25.0	10	40.0	20	30.0	2	50.0	36	35.3
California, SD	10	50.0	10	30.0	3	0.0	—	—	23	34.8
Colorado, D	1	100.0	8	62.5	2	50.0	—	—	11	63.6
Connecticut, D	—	—	9	33.3	9	11.9	—	—	18	22.2
Delaware, D	2	100.0	3	66.7	—	—	—	—	5	80.0
District of Columbia, D	14	35.7	25	48.0	36	44.4	15	42.0	90	45.6
Florida, MD	—	—	5	40.0	5	0.0	1	100.0	11	27.3
Florida, ND	1	100.0	1	0.0	1	0.0	3	66.7	6	50.0
Florida, SD	1	0.0	5	0.0	3	0.0	—	—	9	0.0
Georgia, MD	—	—	2	0.0	2	50.0	—	—	4	25.0
Georgia, ND	1	0.0	11	9.1	6	83.3	1	100.0	19	36.8
Georgia, SD	—	—	3	100.0	1	0.0	5	100.0	9	88.9
Hawaii, D	1	100.0	3	0.0	—	—	—	—	4	25.0
Idaho, D	—	—	—	—	1	100.0	—	—	1	100.0
Illinois, ED	1	100.0	—	—	—	—	—	—	1	100.0
Illinois, ND	14	64.3	22	36.4	24	12.5	—	—	60	33.3
Illinois, SD	—	—	4	25.0	1	0.0	—	—	5	20.0

Indiana, ND	2	0.0	1	100.0	2	0.0	—	—	5	20.0
Indiana, SD	4	75.0	2	0.0	7	0.0	—	—	13	23.1
Iowa, ND	—	—	1	0.0	1	100.0	1	0.0	3	33.3
Iowa, SD	—	—	1	100.0	2	0.0	—	—	3	33.3
Kansas, D	—	—	3	0.0	3	33.3	—	—	6	16.7
Kentucky, ED	—	—	1	0.0	2	50.0	—	—	3	33.3
Kentucky, WD	2	50.0	4	0.0	—	—	—	—	4	0.0
Louisiana, ED	—	—	9	44.4	3	33.3	—	—	14	42.9
Louisiana, MD	1	0.0	—	—	—	—	1	0.0	1	0.0
Louisiana, WD	2	0.0	2	0.0	—	—	2	0.0	4	0.0
Maryland, D	3	100.0	3	33.3	8	37.5	—	—	11	36.4
Massachusetts, D	—	—	8	12.5	14	35.7	1	0.0	25	24.0
Michigan, ED	1	0.0	3	33.3	2	50.0	—	—	8	62.5
Michigan, WD	—	—	1	100.0	—	—	—	—	1	100.0
Minnesota, D	1	0.0	3	100.0	8	37.5	2	0.0	14	42.9
Mississippi, ND	—	—	—	—	1	0.0	—	—	1	0.0
Mississippi, SD	1	0.0	7	14.3	9	0.0	1	0.0	17	5.9
Missouri, ED	3	33.3	5	20.0	3	0.0	—	—	11	18.2
Missouri, WD	2	100.0	6	66.7	1	0.0	2	50.0	11	63.6
Montana, D	—	—	—	—	4	75.0	1	0.0	5	60.0
Nebraska, D	—	—	3	33.3	2	50.0	—	—	5	40.0
Nevada, D	—	—	—	—	1	0.0	—	—	1	0.0
New Hampshire, D	—	—	—	—	1	100.0	—	—	1	100.0
New Jersey, D	1	0.0	4	0.0	4	50.0	—	—	9	22.2
New Mexico, D	—	—	—	—	3	0.0	—	—	3	0.0
New York, ED	—	—	6	16.7	6	33.3	—	—	12	25.0
New York, ND	4	100.0	1	0.0	2	100.0	—	—	7	85.7
New York, SD	18	88.9	44	43.2	45	33.3	1	100.0	108	47.2
New York, WD	2	100.0	2	0.0	5	20.0	—	—	9	44.4
North Carolina, ED	—	—	—	—	3	66.7	6	50.0	9	55.6
North Carolina, MD	—	—	3	0.0	—	—	—	—	3	0.0

(Table continues)

Table 7-30 (Continued)

District court	Vinson (1946–1952) N	Percentage	Warren (1953–1968) N	Percentage	Burger (1969–1985) N	Percentage	Rehnquist (1986–2001) N	Percentage	Total N	Percentage
North Carolina, WD	—	—	—	—	4	50.0	2	0.0	6	33.3
North Dakota, D	—	—	—	—	2	0.0	1	—	2	0.0
Ohio, ND	3	66.7	4	0.0	2	0.0	1	0.0	10	20.0
Ohio, SD	1	0.0	5	40.0	4	75.0	—	—	10	50.0
Oklahoma, ND	—	—	—	—	—	—	1	0.0	1	0.0
Oklahoma, WD	4	50.0	4	25.0	6	33.3	—	—	14	35.7
Oregon, D	1	100.0	—	—	3	0.0	—	—	4	25.0
Pennsylvania, ED	1	0.0	8	50.0	18	38.9	1	100.0	28	42.9
Pennsylvania, MD	—	—	4	50.0	2	0.0	—	—	6	33.3
Pennsylvania, WD	—	—	1	0.0	2	0.0	—	—	3	0.0
Puerto Rico, D	—	—	—	—	2	50.0	—	—	2	50.0
Rhode Island, D	1	0.0	5	80.0	4	50.0	—	—	10	60.0
South Carolina, D	—	—	—	—	3	33.3	—	—	3	33.3
South Carolina, ED	2	0.0	3	0.0	—	—	—	—	5	0.0
South Dakota, D	—	—	1	0.0	—	—	—	—	6	16.7
Tennessee, ED	2	100.0	—	—	—	—	—	—	2	100.0
Tennessee, MD	—	—	4	25.0	1	0.0	—	—	5	20.0
Tennessee, WD	—	—	1	0.0	—	—	—	—	1	0.0
Texas, ED	—	—	—	—	3	33.3	—	—	3	33.3
Texas, ND	3	0.0	2	0.0	7	57.1	—	—	12	33.3
Texas, SD	—	—	9	44.4	5	0.0	3	100.0	17	41.2
Texas, WD	1	100.0	3	66.7	11	18.2	—	—	15	33.3
Utah, D	1	0.0	11	9.1	1	100.0	3	33.3	16	18.8
Vermont, D	—	—	3	0.0	3	100.0	—	—	6	50.0
Virginia, ED	1	0.0	8	12.5	8	25.0	1	100.0	18	22.2

	N	%	N	%	N	%	N	%	N	%
Virginia, WD	—	—	—	—	2	50.0	—	—	2	50.0
Washington, ED	—	—	—	—	2	0.0	—	—	2	0.0
Washington, WD	—	—	5	60.0	4	25.0	1	100.0	10	50.0
West Virginia, SD	—	—	2	100.0	2	0.0	1	0.0	4	50.0
West Virginia, WD	—	—	—	—	—	—	—	—	1	0.0
Wisconsin, ED	3	66.7	4	50.0	6	33.3	—	—	13	46.2
Wisconsin, WD	—	—	—	—	1	0.0	—	—	1	0.0
Wyoming, D	—	—	—	—	3	33.3	—	—	3	33.3
Total	123	56.1	352	34.1	409	31.5	65	52.3	949	37.0

Note: "—" indicates no cases decided. *N*s are the total number of cases. Percentages are the number of cases affirmed expressed as a percentage of the total number of cases. District courts having no decisions directly reviewed by the Supreme Court do not appear. Only district court decisions directly reviewed by the Supreme Court are included. Because the disposition made of district court decisions after intervention by the courts of appeals is problematic at best, they are excluded from consideration. D = single-district state; ED = eastern district; MD = middle district; ND = northern district; SD = southern district; WD = western district. All orally argued docket numbers, excluding cases arising under the Court's original jurisdiction, are included. Because the formal dispositions the Court makes do not necessarily correspond to who wins the case, the focus here is on the prevailing party. If the petitioning party prevails in whole or in part, the case is counted as a reversal; otherwise as an affirmation.

Source: U.S. Supreme Court Judicial Database, with analu = 0 and dec_type = 1, 6, or 7.

Table 7-31 Article I Special Jurisdiction Courts

Court	Characteristics
Bankruptcy Courts	*Status:* After years of controversy over the question of Article I versus Article III status for bankruptcy judges, Congress reorganized the federal bankruptcy courts in 1984. The result is a hybrid creation. Bankruptcy courts are established as a unit within the federal district court, yet the bankruptcy judges are Article I officers.
	Jurisdiction: The bankruptcy courts, operating within the federal district court system, have jurisdiction over personal and corporate bankruptcy filings.
	Judges: Congress has authorized a number of bankruptcy judge positions for each judicial district based on the district's caseload demands. The judges are chosen by the judges of the court of appeals for the respective circuit. In those districts with more than one bankruptcy judge, the district court designates a chief judge of the bankruptcy court. Bankruptcy judges serve for terms of 14 years. They may be removed from office by the Judicial Council of the circuit, but only for reasons of incompetence, misconduct, neglect of duty, or physical or mental disability.
	Location: One in each federal judicial district.
	Appeals: Go to the federal district court. Legislation also authorizes the establishment of an appeals panel of bankruptcy judges within the districts. After a bankruptcy judge's decisions are reviewed by the district court or the appeals panel, further appeal may be made to the appropriate court of appeals.
Territorial Courts	*Status:* From time to time Congress has created courts to deal with legal disputes arising in territories administered by the United States. Three such courts currently exist: Guam, Virgin Islands, and the Northern Mariana Islands. While the courts in these territories function in much the same manner as the United States district courts, their judges do not have Article III status.
	Jurisdiction: Jurisdiction over disputes involving federal and local law arising within their geographical jurisdiction.
	Judges: Guam and the Northern Mariana Islands courts have one judge each; the court for the Virgin Islands has two judges. Judges are appointed by the president and confirmed by the Senate, and serve for 10-year terms.
	Location: Located in their respective territories.
	Appeals: Appeals from the decisions of the territorial courts of Guam and the Northern Mariana Islands go to the Court of Appeals for the Ninth Circuit. Appeals from the decisions of the territorial court for the Virgin Islands go to the Court of Appeals for the Third Circuit.

Table 7-31 *(Continued)*

Court	Characteristics
United States Court of Federal Claims	*Status:* Created by Congress in 1982 as a successor to the Court of Claims, which operated from 1855–1982.
	Jurisdiction: Trial court having authority to hear suits involving monetary claims against the United States government.
	Judges: Staffed by 16 judges who are nominated by the president and confirmed by the Senate. Members of the court serve for terms of 15 years. The chief judge must be under 70 years of age when chosen and may serve until reaching the age of 70 or until the president designates another judge to be chief. Judges may be removed from office by the United States Court of Appeals for the Federal Circuit, but only for reasons of incompetency, misconduct, neglect of duty, engaging in the practice of law, or physical or mental disability.
	Location: Washington, D.C., but cases may be heard nationwide.
	Appeals: Decisions may be appealed to the United States Court of Appeals for the Federal Circuit.
United States Court of Appeals for the Armed Forces	*Status:* Created by Congress in 1950.
	Jurisdiction: An appellate tribunal to review the decisions of military courts martial.
	Judges: Staffed by five judges, who are nominated by the president and confirmed by the Senate. Judges must be civilians at the time of their appointment and persons who have served 20 or more years in the military are not eligible. No more than three judges may be of the same political party. They serve terms of 15 years. The chief judge is designated by the president. Judges may be removed by the president only for neglect of duty, malfeasance in office, or mental or physical disability.
	Location: Washington, D.C.
	Appeals: Decisions are reviewable only on certiorari to the United States Supreme Court.
United States Court of Appeals for Veterans Claims	*Status:* Created by Congress in 1988.
	Jurisdiction: Exclusive appellate jurisdiction over decisions of the Board of Veterans Appeals, a unit of the Veterans Administration.
	Judges: Staffed by one chief judge and two to six associate judges. The judges are appointed by the president, confirmed by the Senate, and serve 15-year terms. No more than the smallest possible majority of the judges may be of the same political party. Judges may be removed by the president only on

(Table continues)

Table 7-31 *(Continued)*

Court	Characteristics
	grounds of misconduct, neglect of duty, or engaging in the practice of law.
	Location: Washington, D.C., but cases may be heard nationwide.
	Appeals: Decisions may be appealed to the Court of Appeals for the Federal Circuit.
United States Tax Court	*Status:* Originally created by Congress in 1924 as an administrative agency in the executive branch. It was known as the United States Board of Tax Appeals until 1942, when it received its current name. In 1969, Congress moved it out of the executive branch and made it an Article I tribunal.
	Jurisdiction: A trial court that handles suits filed by taxpayers who are dissatisfied with the decisions of the appeals division of the Internal Revenue Service.
	Judges: Staffed by 19 judges, who are appointed by the president, confirmed by the Senate, and serve a term of 15 years. The chief judge is elected by the members of the court for a two-year term. The court is empowered to appoint special trial judges who assist the court with its work and serve at the pleasure of the court. Judges must be under the age of 65 when appointed and can be removed by the president only for inefficiency, neglect of duty, or malfeasance.
	Location: Headquartered in Washington, D.C., but judges hear cases throughout the United States at locations convenient to taxpayers.
	Appeals: Taken to the United States court of appeals for the appropriate circuit.

Note: Article I courts, also known as legislative courts, are those created by Congress to assist the legislature in carrying out congressional functions described in Article I of the Constitution. Because they are created under Article I of the Constitution, these courts do not enjoy the same status ascribed to federal courts. Article I judges, for example, do not serve during good behavior and are not protected against salary reduction.

Sources: United States Code; *The United States Government Manual 1999/2000* (Washington, D.C.: Office of the Federal Register of the National Archives and Records Administration, 1995); Kenneth R. Redden, *Federal Special Court Litigation* (Charlottesville, Va.: The Michie Company, 1982).

Table 7-32 Article III Special Jurisdiction Courts

Court	Characteristics
Court of Appeals for the Federal Circuit	*Status:* Created by Congress in 1982. It is the result of a merger of the appellate jurisdictions of the United States Court of Claims and the United States Court of Customs and Patent Appeals. It enjoys the same status as the regional courts of appeals.
	Jurisdiction: Jurisdiction over patent, trademark, and copyright disputes, and certain administrative law issues. It hears cases appealed from district courts, the United States Court of Federal Claims, the United States Court of International Trade, the United States Court of Veterans Appeals, and designated administrative agencies.
	Judges: Staffed by twelve judges appointed by the president and confirmed by the Senate. The chief judge is the member of the court with the greatest seniority who is under the age of 65. The chief judge serves for a term of seven years.
	Location: Washington, D.C.
	Appeals: Reviewable under writ of certiorari to the United States Supreme Court.
Foreign Intelligence Surveillance Court	*Status:* Established by Congress in 1978.
	Jurisdiction: Jurisdiction over executive branch requests for warrants to engage in domestic electronic surveillance for the purposes of gathering foreign intelligence.
	Judges: Staffed by seven district court judges from seven different circuits designated by the chief justice of the United States. Judges may serve no more than seven years. All hearings, procedures, and decisions are classified. Staffed on a monthly rotational basis with the judge on duty authorized to act individually. Service is part time and is in addition to judges' regular judicial duties.
	Location: Washington, D.C.
	Appeals: The chief justice is authorized to appoint three federal judges to serve as a review panel for cases in which the government wishes to appeal a warrant denial. Decisions of this appeal panel may be reviewed upon government petition for a writ of certiorari to the Supreme Court.
Judicial Panel on Multidistrict Litigation	*Status:* Created by Congress in 1968 in an effort to streamline the judicial process with respect to law-suits filed in separate districts that involve common factual questions.
	Jurisdiction: Empowered to transfer temporarily to a single district civil cases pending in different districts that involve

(Table continues)

Court	Characteristics
	common questions of fact. This action allows pretrial and discovery procedures to be conducted at a single location to improve the efficiency of the system.

Judges: Staffed by seven judges, who are designated by the chief justice of the United States from among district and court of appeals judges. The chief justice from time to time changes the members of the panel. Two or more of the judges may not be from the same circuit. The chief judge of the panel is also appointed by the chief justice. Duty on the panel is part time and is in addition to the other responsibilities the members of the panel may have.

Location: Headquartered in Washington, D.C., but the panel holds hearings in each of the circuits on a rotating basis.

Appeals: No review of panel decisions is permitted except by extraordinary writ to the relevant court of appeals.

United States Court of International Trade

Status: Created by Congress in 1980. It traces its roots to 1890 as the Board of United States General Appraisers, which became the United States Customs Court in 1926. In 1956, the Customs Court became an Article III tribunal. The 1980 legislation reorganized the Customs Court into its present form as the Court of International Trade.

Jurisdiction: Jurisdiction over civil cases arising from federal trade and import laws. This includes such matters as customs, duties, and trade regulations.

Judges: Nine judges serve on the Court of International Trade. They are appointed by the president and confirmed by the Senate. Not more than five of the judges may be of the same political party. The chief judge is designated by the president. The chief judge is the member of the court under the age of sixty-five with the most seniority who has not previously served as chief judge. The chief judge serves a term of seven years or until reaching the age of seventy, whichever comes first.

Location: Headquartered in New York City, but may hear cases in other cities as well.

Appeals: Taken to the Court of Appeals for the Federal Circuit.

Note: Article III courts, also known as constitutional courts, are those created by Congress under its authority in Article III of the Constitution to establish lower federal courts. These courts are part of the judicial branch and judges serving on them enjoy all of the protections specified in Article III (terms of good behavior, no reduction in salary, removeable only by impeachment, etc.).

Sources: United States Code; *The United States Government Manual 1999/2000* (Washington, D.C.: Office of the Federal Register of the National Archives and Records Administration, 1995); Kenneth R. Redden, *Federal Special Court Litigation* (Charlottesville, Va.: The Michie Company, 1982).

Table 7-33 Specialized Court Decisions Affirmed by the Vinson, Warren, Burger, and Rehnquist Courts

Specialized court	Vinson (1946–1952)		Warren (1953–1969)		Burger (1969–1986)		Rehnquist (1986–2001)		Total	
	N	Percentage	N	Percentage	N	Percentage	N	Percentage	N	Percentage
Customs and Patent Appeals	—	—	1	0.0	6	50.0	—	—	7	42.9
Court of Claims[a]	37	48.6	37	29.7	19	36.8	7	71.4	63	36.5
Federal Circuit	—	—	—	—	7	14.3	38	44.7	45	40.0
International trade	—	—	—	—	—	—	3	33.3	3	33.3
Temporary Emergency Court of Appeals	1	0.0	—	—	1	100.0	—	—	1	100.0
Military Appeals	—	—	—	—	—	—	8	62.5	8	62.5
Military review	—	—	—	—	—	—	4	75.0	4	75.0

Note: "—" indicates no cases decided. *N*s are the total number of cases. Percentages are the number of cases affirmed expressed as a percentage of the total number of cases. All orally argued docket numbers, excluding cases arising under the Court's original jurisdiction, are included. Because the formal dispositions the Court makes do not necessarily correspond to who wins the case, the focus here is on the prevailing party. If the petitioning party prevails in whole or in part, the case is counted as a reversal; otherwise, as an affirmation.

[a] This court is now called the Court of Federal Claims.

Source: U.S. Supreme Court Judicial Database, with analu = 0 and dec_type = 1, 6, or 7.

Table 7-34 State and Territorial Court Decisions Affirmed by the Vinson, Warren, Burger, and Rehnquist Courts

State/territory	Vinson (1946–1952) N	Percentage	Warren (1953–1969) N	Percentage	Burger (1969–1986) N	Percentage	Rehnquist (1986–2001) N	Percentage	Total N	Percentage
Alabama	5	60.0	29	17.2	14	35.7	14	42.9	62	30.6
Alaska	—	—	3	33.3	3	0.0	—	—	6	16.7
Arizona	1	100.0	8	12.5	14	35.7	12	50.0	35	37.1
Arkansas	3	66.7	10	0.0	3	66.7	10	50.0	26	34.6
California	31	58.1	57	52.6	58	39.7	35	58.3	182	52.7
Colorado	3	66.7	3	0.0	6	83.3	5	40.0	17	52.9
Connecticut	2	100.0	8	37.5	6	66.7	1	0.0	17	52.9
Delaware	—	—	7	85.7	5	40.0	1	0.0	13	61.5
District of Columbia	1	0.0	—	—	8	50.0	1	100.0	9	55.6
Florida	3	33.3	31	45.2	32	46.9	20	35.0	86	47.7
Georgia	7	42.9	17	17.6	28	35.7	5	40.0	57	31.6
Hawaii	—	—	—	—	3	0.0	2	100.0	5	40.0
Idaho	1	42.9	1	0.0	3	0.0	4	25.0	9	11.1
Illinois	25	36.0	19	31.6	32	31.3	23	43.5	99	35.4
Indiana	3	33.3	4	75.0	6	33.3	2	50.0	14	50.0
Iowa	—	—	9	33.3	3	66.7	4	25.0	16	37.5
Kansas	—	—	8	12.5	2	50.0	6	33.3	16	25.0
Kentucky	1	100.0	7	14.3	14	35.7	5	40.0	27	33.3
Louisiana	3	100.0	28	32.1	18	22.2	6	33.3	55	34.6
Maine	—	—	—	—	4	50.0	4	50.0	8	50.0
Maryland	6	66.7	16	25.0	13	69.2	10	0.0	45	33.3
Massachusetts	2	0.0	5	40.0	16	43.8	4	0.0	27	33.0
Michigan	9	44.4	11	54.5	14	35.7	11	54.5	45	46.7
Minnesota	—	—	2	50.0	9	33.3	6	33.3	17	35.3
Mississippi	5	40.0	4	25.0	10	20.0	9	33.3	28	28.6
Missouri	8	25.0	10	30.0	7	0.0	6	50.0	31	25.8

State	N	%	N	%	N	%	N	%	N	%
Montana	1	100.0	—	—	2	50.0	4	50.0	7	57.1
Nebraska	3	66.7	4	50.0	4	25.0	3	33.3	14	42.9
Nevada	—	—	1	0.0	—	—	5	20.0	6	16.7
New Hampshire	2	50.0	11	25.0	7	14.3	—	—	13	23.1
New Jersey	6	83.3	8	50.0	14	35.7	5	40.0	33	48.5
New Mexico	—	—	3	66.7	8	12.5	1	100.0	12	33.3
New York	39	66.7	54	50.0	39	33.3	14	42.9	146	49.3
North Carolina	3	100.0	12	16.7	10	50.0	4	50.0	29	42.4
North Dakota	—	—	1	100.0	3	0.0	2	50.0	6	33.3
Ohio	8	12.5	29	31.0	24	25.0	12	41.7	73	28.8
Oklahoma	12	58.3	6	33.3	6	0.0	8	37.5	32	37.5
Oregon	2	100.0	5	0.0	11	36.4	7	0.0	25	24.0
Pennsylvania	8	12.5	10	30.0	12	41.7	12	33.3	42	31.0
Puerto Rico	—	—	—	—	3	66.7	1	—	3	66.7
Rhode Island	3	33.3	1	0.0	2	50.0	1	0.0	7	28.6
South Carolina	3	0.0	10	10.0	5	40.0	8	12.5	26	15.4
South Dakota	2	0.0	—	—	5	20.0	1	100.0	8	25.0
Tennessee	4	100.0	6	16.7	7	28.6	5	80.0	22	50.0
Texas	6	50.0	41	19.5	21	14.3	9	22.2	77	20.8
Utah	3	0.0	4	25.0	2	50.0	1	100.0	10	30.0
Vermont	1	0.0	—	—	3	66.7	1	100.0	5	60.0
Virginia	2	100.0	16	25.0	7	14.3	7	14.3	32	25.0
Washington	3	100.0	20	30.0	15	20.0	6	16.7	44	29.5
West Virginia	1	0.0	5	60.0	4	50.0	5	20.0	15	40.0
Wisconsin	12	33.3	7	57.1	9	22.2	10	50.0	38	42.1
Wyoming	—	—	—	—	1	100.0	1	0.0	2	50.0
Total	245	51.0	544	34.4	555	34.6	338	38.5	1,437	35.4

Note: "—" indicates no cases decided. *N*s are the total number of cases. Percentages are the number of cases affirmed expressed as a percentage of the total number of cases. All orally argued docket numbers, excluding cases arising under the Court's original jurisdiction, are included. Because the formal dispositions the Court makes do not necessarily correspond to who wins the case, the focus here is on the prevailing party. If the petitioning party prevails in whole or in part, the case is counted as a reversal; otherwise, as an affirmation.

Source: U.S. Supreme Court Judicial Database, analu = 0 or dec_type = 1, 6, or 7.

8

The Supreme Court and Public Opinion

The relationship between the Supreme Court and public opinion brings together questions of vital interest to Court-watchers. First, is the Supreme Court influenced by public opinion? Second, does the Supreme Court have the capability to influence public opinion through its rulings? The latter question can be expanded to include issues of public support for the Court and the extent to which the Court is able to influence the public's opinion about itself.

High-profile decisions by and large reflect public opinion.[1] Whether the Court is actually *influenced* by public opinion is harder to gauge. There is little reason to think so. The justices, unlike state court judges, are immune from majoritarian pressures. The public neither elects nor removes them from office. Moreover, the justices are not supposed to represent majoritarian concerns. Justice Robert H. Jackson stated this convincingly in *West Virginia Board of Education v. Barnette* (1943):

> The very purpose of a Bill of Rights was to withdraw certain subjects from the vicissitudes of political controversy, to place them beyond the reach of majorities and officials and to establish them as legal principles to be applied by the courts. One's right to life, liberty, and property, to free speech, a free press, freedom of worship and assembly, and other fundamental rights may not be submitted to vote; they depend on the outcome of no elections.[2]

With the exceptions of the Court's interpretation of the cruel and unusual punishments clause, the due process clause, and its definition of obscenity, the Court has stood by Jackson's exhortation. In the three excepted areas, however, justification for the Court's results, as laid out in the majority opinion, if not the result itself, often rests on public opinion.

The question as to whether the Court influences public opinion and legitimates public policy was first asked by Robert Dahl in 1957.[3] Dahl, in the course of arguing that the Court had not historically filled its normative role as the protector of minority rights, claimed that its power could nevertheless be justified by its ability to legitimate the decisions of other branches of government. The overwhelming majority of research on this subject, however, has found the Court to be without power to influence public opinion.[4]

In this chapter we present a series of polls on public opinion concerning matters with which the Court has dealt. (See also Table 7-3, detailing public opinion on various proposed Constitutional amendments.) The four basic sources used to compile this data are The General Social Survey, The Harris Survey, The Gallup Poll, and the *New York Times* surveys. Some care must be taken in interpreting survey results, as small differences in question wording can lead to substantial differences in aggregate responses. For instance, a majority of Americans support a woman's right to terminate her pregnancy, while at the same time a majority of Americans also believe that the killing of the unborn should be prohibited. Moreover, special care should be taken in interpreting Harris surveys, whose questions tend to lean in the Democratic/liberal direction. For example, The Harris Survey's questions on affirmative action contain the tag "provided there are no strict quotas." Jane Mansbridge's award-winning *Why We Lost the ERA*[5] documents Harris's change to a more favorable question wording about the proposed amendment in the days before the Illinois legislature was scheduled to vote, in an effort to claim increased support for women's rights.

We begin with political tolerance (Tables 8-1 through 8-5). Americans are notably inconsistent in response to questions about political tolerance. On the one hand, there is almost universal support of statements such as "The right of everyone to freedom of speech, no matter what his or her views, must be upheld." On the other hand, when questions are phrased in the context of particular groups, for example, communists, homosexuals, or atheists, libertarianism drops markedly. Thus, only a bare majority of Americans believe that atheists, communists, or militarists should be allowed to teach at colleges or universities. With the exception of racists' rights, however, a trend toward respect for the rights of all groups is evident.

We next turn from the rights of association to the rights of the accused. Table 8-6 demonstrates strong support for capital punishment, dating as far back as 1936. And despite twelve years of Reagan-Bush appointments to the federal bench, about 80 percent of the survey respondents believe that courts are too lenient with criminals (see Table 8-7). Presumably, such responses are based on the actions of state courts, where the overwhelming majority of criminal cases are tried. Nevertheless, the public's support for the "peace forces" in society does not extend to the use of wiretapping (see Table 8-8).

We next consider the "American dilemma": the question of race (Tables 8-9 through 8-13). *Brown v. Board of Education*,[6] the school desegregation case, mustered support by a majority of Americans (54 percent) in 1954, and that support grew throughout the decade. Laws against intermarriage are supported today by only the most insistent racists (13.4 percent), as is the "right" of whites to live in segregated housing (15.0 percent). On the other hand, racial busing remains anathema to most Americans. Support for racial preference in hiring garners a less than majority approval rate, while support for affirmative action appears high, though, as noted in Table 8-13, it drops markedly when the question wording is changed.

Women's rights and abortion are the subjects of Tables 8-14 through 8-19. The percentage of Americans who believe that a woman's job is to take care of the home (13.6 percent) is at about the same level as the percentage of people who are opposed to racial intermarriage. On abortion, the results are far more complex. The most interesting results are in Table 8-18, which shows that something short of a majority of Americans support abortion on demand (44.8 percent) or advocate a total ban on abortion (see, for example, the "chance of defect" column). Thus, the middle ground taken by the Court in *Planned Parenthood of Southeastern Pennsylvania v. Casey*[7] may be closest to the public's opinion on this issue. Support for *Roe v. Wade*[8] appears high, though only 20 percent of Americans support abortions in the second trimester of pregnancy (see the note to Table 8-19). More so than many other issues, the answers received on matters of abortion depend on the exact manner in which the question is asked.

Other social and political issues are presented in Tables 8-20 through 8-25. We note briefly the American public's opposition to homosexuality and pornography, and support for school prayer and the right to die. Only the general public's response to the school prayer issue differs from the most relevant Court decisions (see also Table 7-3). But a more specialized group—attorneys—take issue with Court decisions that have a direct bearing on them: those that permit some form of advertising. Contrary to the Court's ruling, most attorneys believe such advertising should be banned (see Table 8-25).

We present the public's perception of the Court itself in Tables 8-26 through 8-35. Some pertain to views of the Court in the wake of *Bush v. Gore*;[9] others provide a broader scale. Note that overall, while only a minority of Americans have a great deal of confidence in the Court, confidence in Congress is certainly no higher. As is evident in Tables 8-33 and 8-35, one plausible explanation as to why the Supreme Court is unable to influence public opinion is that Americans are largely unaware of its activities. Less than 10 percent of Americans can name the chief justice of the United States (William Rehnquist) or the most well known associate justice (Sandra Day O'Connor). Only 6 out of 1,005 persons were able to name John Paul Stevens as an associate justice. Yet 54 percent of survey respondents were able to name correctly the judge on the television program "The People's Court" (Table 8-34). Such data provide a stunning picture of the American public's general ignorance of the Court and its day-to-day activity.

Notes

1. Thomas Marshall, *Public Opinion and the Supreme Court* (New York: Unwin/ Hyman, 1989).
2. 319 U.S. 624, at 638.
3. Robert Dahl, "Decision-Making in a Democracy: The Supreme Court as National Policy-Maker," *Journal of Public Law* 6 (1957): 279–296.
4. See Gregory A. Caldeira, "Courts and Public Opinion," in *The American Courts: A Critical Assessment,* ed. John B. Gates and Charles A. Johnson (Washington, D.C.: CQ Press, 1991), and Charles H. Franklin and Liane C. Kosaki, "The Republican Schoolmaster: The Supreme Court, Public Opinion, and Abortion," *American Political Science Review* 83 (1989): 751–772.
5. Jane Mansbridge, *Why We Lost the ERA* (Chicago: University of Chicago Press, 1986).
6. 347 U.S. 483 (1954).
7. 505 U.S. 833 (1992).
8. 410 U.S. 113 (1973).
9. 531 U.S. 98 (2000).

Table 8-1   Respondents Allowing Atheists to Perform Specified Activity (Percentage)

Year	Community	Library	College
1972	66.6	62.8	41.9
1973	65.8	62.2	42.0
1974	62.6	61.4	43.3
1976	64.7	61.1	42.2
1977	62.7	59.7	39.5
1980	66.7	63.6	46.9
1982	62.5	59.8	45.1
1984	68.6	65.3	47.4
1985	65.6	62.1	46.8
1987	68.7	66.0	47.6
1988	70.9	65.3	46.8
1989	72.5	69.4	53.5
1990	73.7	69.1	53.3
1991	72.8	71.1	53.9
1993	72.5	70.1	54.2
1994	73.6	71.3	54.3
1996	74.5	70.5	58.0
1998	75.3	71.7	60.2
2000	75.4	70.6	58.9

Note: Questions: (Community) "Suppose someone who is against all churches and religion wanted to make a speech in your community. Should he be allowed to speak or not?" (Library) "If some people in your community suggested that a book he wrote against churches and religion should be taken out of the library, would you favor removing this book or not?" (College) "Should such a person be allowed to teach in a college or university, or not?"

Source: General Social Survey, National Opinion Research Center, University of Chicago, various years.

Table 8-2   Respondents Allowing Racists to Perform Specified Activity (Percentage)

Year	Community	Library	College
1976	60.6	62.1	42.0
1977	58.4	62.7	41.9
1980	61.4	66.3	45.0
1982	56.2	59.2	41.8
1984	57.3	65.1	42.2
1985	55.3	61.8	43.5
1987	59.0	63.2	43.1
1988	61.0	63.8	43.0
1989	61.7	67.2	47.6
1990	62.5	67.0	47.4
1991	62.1	67.5	43.7
1993	60.4	67.1	45.2
1994	61.3	67.9	44.1
1996	60.5	66.3	47.7
1998	62.3	65.7	48.7
2000	—	65.4	48.1

Note: Questions: (Community) "Suppose someone who believes blacks are genetically inferior wanted to make a speech in your community. Should he be allowed to speak or not?" (Library) "If someone in your community suggested that a book he wrote that said blacks are inferior should be taken out of the library, would you favor removing it?" (College) "Should such a person be allowed to teach in a college or university, or not?" Due to differences in computation we advise against comparing "community" with "library" and "college."

Source: General Social Survey, National Opinion Research Center, University of Chicago, various years.

Table 8-3   Respondents Allowing Homosexuals to Perform Specified Activity (Percentage)

Year	Community	Library	College
1973	63.2	55.0	49.4
1974	65.3	57.2	53.0
1976	64.0	57.5	53.9
1977	64.1	57.2	51.4
1980	68.0	59.5	56.8
1982	66.9	56.7	57.0
1984	70.6	61.3	61.3
1985	69.1	57.1	59.7
1987	69.2	58.2	58.4
1988	72.6	62.7	59.5
1989	78.4	66.2	66.6
1990	76.6	65.9	65.9
1991	77.8	70.6	65.8
1993	80.8	69.5	71.7
1994	81.3	70.9	73.0
1996	82.7	71.2	77.3
1998	83.2	73.3	77.0
2000	83.0	73.5	79.3

Note: Questions: (Community) "Suppose someone who admits he is a homosexual wanted to make a speech in your community, should he be allowed to speak or not?" (Library) "If some people in your community suggested that a book he wrote in favor of homosexuality should be taken out of the library, would you favor removing this book, or not?" (College) "Should such a person be allowed to teach in a college or university, or not?"

Source: General Social Survey, National Opinion Research Center, University of Chicago, various years.

Table 8-4 Respondents Allowing Communists to Perform Specified Activity (Percentage)

Year	Community	Library	College
1972	53.7	55.5	34.6
1973	61.2	59.9	41.5
1974	59.6	60.7	44.4
1976	55.8	58.2	43.6
1977	56.6	56.7	40.5
1980	56.6	59.5	43.2
1982	56.6	57.6	46.5
1984	60.8	61.6	48.3
1985	58.6	59.4	46.4
1987	60.2	61.6	49.3
1988	61.7	61.3	50.4
1989	65.9	64.4	53.8
1990	66.4	66.1	55.2
1991	68.7	69.5	57.0
1993	70.5	69.7	60.6
1994	68.3	68.2	58.3
1996	65.8	67.5	60.4
1998	68.4	69.9	60.7
2000	67.5	68.2	60.7

Note: Questions: (Community) "Suppose someone who admits he is a communist wanted to make a speech in your community. Should he be allowed to speak, or not?" (Library) "Suppose he wrote a book that is in your public library. Somebody in the community suggests that the book should be removed from the public library. Would you favor removing it, or not?" (College) "Suppose he is teaching in a college. Should he be fired or not?"

Source: General Social Survey, National Opinion Research Center, University of Chicago, various years.

Table 8-5 Respondents Allowing Militarists to Perform Specified Activity (Percentage)

Year	Community	Library	College
1976	55.3	58.2	38.4
1977	51.4	56.1	34.9
1980	58.1	60.1	41.1
1982	53.6	55.3	39.0
1984	57.9	60.4	42.4
1985	55.8	57.6	41.1
1987	56.6	58.4	40.0
1988	57.6	59.0	38.6
1989	60.3	61.8	42.5
1990	58.9	63.0	45.0
1991	63.6	68.4	45.3
1993	66.1	69.7	49.8
1994	65.2	65.8	47.4
1996	64.2	66.7	50.7
1998	67.9	70.0	54.1
2000	64.6	66.3	50.3

Note: Questions: (Community) "Suppose someone who advocates doing away with elections and letting the military run the country wanted to make a speech in your community. Should he be allowed to speak or not?" (Library) "Suppose he wrote a book advocating doing away with elections and letting the military run the country. Somebody in your community suggests the book be removed from the public library. Would you favor removing it, or not?" (College) "Should such a person be allowed to teach in a college or university, or not?"

Source: General Social Survey, National Opinion Research Center, University of Chicago, various years.

Table 8-6 Respondents Favoring Capital Punishment, Various Polls (Percentage)

Year	General Social Survey	Harris	Gallup	New York Times
1936	—	—	61	—
1937	—	—	65	—
1953	—	—	68	—
1960	—	—	51	—
1965	—	38	45	—
1966	—	—	42	—
1969	—	48	51	—
1970	—	47	—	—
1971	—	—	49	—
1972	—	—	57	—
1973	—	59	—	—
1974	66.5	—	64	—
1975	64.4	—	—	—
1976	68.7	67	65	—
1977	71.8	—	—	—
1978	70.4	—	62	—
1980	71.6	—	—	—
1981	—	—	66	—
1982	72.7	—	—	—
1983	76.8	68	—	—
1984	74.8	—	—	—
1985	79.5	—	—	—
1986	75.3	—	—	—
1987	69.2	—	—	—
1988	76.1	—	—	77
1989	78.3	—	—	71
1990	79.4	—	—	72
1991	76.2	—	76	—
1993	77.4	—	59	—
1994	79.2	—	—	—
1995	—	—	77	65
1996	76.8	—	—	—
1997	—	75	—	—
1998	73.3	—	—	—
1999	—	71	71	—
2000	68.8	64	67	—
2001	—	67	68	67
2002	—	—	72	—

Note: "—" indicates survey not conducted in that year. Question for General Social Survey, Gallup, and *New York Times* (through 1994): Do you believe in capital punishment for persons convicted of murder or are you opposed to it? Question for General Social Survey (1996–2000) and *New York Times*/CBS (2001): Do you favor or oppose death penalty for a person convicted of murder? Question for *New York Times* (1995) and Gallup (1995–2002): Are you in favor of death penalty for a person convicted of murder? The Harris Survey asked: Do you believe in capital punishment or are you opposed to it?

Sources: General Social Survey, National Opinion Research Center, University of Chicago, various years; The Harris Survey, February 10, 1983, 2; *The Gallup Poll* (1985), 36, (1991), 43, and (1993), 35; *New York Times* press release; LEXIS-NEXIS Academic Universe.

Table 8-7 Respondents Believing Courts Not Harsh Enough with Criminals

Year	Percentage	Year	Percentage
1972	74.2	1986	88.5
1973	80.5	1987	87.8
1974	83.6	1988	88.6
1975	85.1	1989	88.0
1976	86.1	1990	86.9
1977	87.9	1991	83.9
1978	89.6	1993	86.1
1980	88.4	1994	89.3
1982	86.3	1996	83.5
1983	89.4	1998	79.3
1984	85.3	2000	74.8
1985	87.1		

Note: Question: "In general, do you think the courts in this area deal too harshly or not harshly enough with criminals?"

Source: General Social Survey, National Opinion Research Center, University of Chicago, various years.

Table 8-8 Respondents Approving of Wiretapping

Year	General Social Survey	Gallup
1949	—	22
1969	—	46
1974	17.2	—
1975	16.9	—
1977	19.1	—
1978	19.6	—
1982	17.5	—
1983	19.3	—
1985	23.6	—
1986	23.1	—
1988	21.6	—
1989	27.6	—
1990	23.3	—
1991	25.6	—
1993	24.2	—
1994	19.5	—

Note: "—" indicates survey not conducted in that year. Question: (General Social Survey) "Everything considered, would you say that, in general, you approve or disapprove of wiretapping?" (The Gallup Poll) "Do you think it is right, or not, to get evidence for use in a court trial by means of wiretapping?"

Sources: General Social Survey, National Opinion Research Center, University of Chicago, various years; *The Gallup Poll* 2 (1935–1971), 844.

Table 8-9 Respondents Approving of *Brown v. Board of Education*

Date	Percentage
May 1954	54
April 1955	56
November 1955	59
December 1956	63
April 1957	62
July 1957	58
September 1957	59
May 1959	57
May 1961	62

Source: The Gallup Poll (1981), 26.

Table 8-10   Respondents Disapproving of Racial Intermarriage and Approving of Segregated Housing (Percentage)

Year	Favor laws against racial intermarriage	Believe whites have right to segregated housing
1970	35.0	—
1971	—	—
1972	39.3	22.3
1973	37.9	—
1974	34.5	—
1975	38.6	—
1976	32.6	21.5
1977	28.3	22.1
1978	—	—
1979	—	—
1980	29.9	15.6
1981	—	—
1982	25.7	12.1
1983	—	—
1984	25.0	10.5
1985	26.0	10.2
1986	—	—
1987	21.0	8.4
1988	22.5	7.6
1989	21.3	7.8
1990	19.2	8.3
1991	17.6	6.8
1992	—	—
1993	17.2	4.0
1994	13.8	5.2
1996	11.1	5.4
1998	11.2	—
2000	10.1	—

Note: "—" indicates survey not conducted in that year. Questions asked of non-blacks only through 1977. Questions: (General Social Survey) "Do you think there should be laws against marriage between (Negroes/blacks) and whites?" (The Gallup Poll) "Some states have laws making it a crime for a white person and a Negro to marry. Do you approve or disapprove of such laws?" (General Social Survey and The Gallup Poll). "White people have a right to keep (Negroes/blacks) out of their neighborhoods if they want to and (Negroes/blacks) should respect that right. Do you agree?"

Source: 1970: *The Gallup Poll* 3 (1935–1971), 2263; 1971–1998: General Social Survey, National Opinion Research Center, University of Chicago, various years.

Table 8-11   Respondents Approving of Busing, Various Polls (Percentage)

Year	General Social Survey	Harris	Gallup
1970	—	—	11
1971	—	17	18
1972	19.4	17	—
1973	—	—	—
1974	20.1	—	35[a]
1975	17.2	20	—
1976	15.7	14	—
1977	16.2	—	—
1978	20.0	—	—
1979	—	—	—
1980	—	—	22
1981	—	—	—
1982	25.8	—	—
1983	22.8	—	—
1984	—	—	—
1985	21.9	—	—
1986	29.3	41	—
1987	—	—	—
1988	32.4	—	—
1989	27.6	—	—
1990	32.9	—	—
1991	34.2	—	—
1992	—	—	—
1993	28.7	—	—
1994	31.5	—	—
1996	35.3	—	—

Note: "—" indicates survey not conducted in that year. Questions: (General Social Survey, The Harris Survey) "In general, do you favor or oppose the busing of black and white school children from one school district to another?" (The Gallup Poll) "Do you favor or oppose busing children to achieve a better racial balance?"

[a] Percentage of respondents giving a positive response out of those giving a positive or negative response.

Sources: General Social Survey, National Opinion Research Center, University of Chicago, various years; The Harris Survey, January 5, 1987, 3; *The Gallup Poll* 3 (1935–1971), 2243, 2323, and (1981), 21.

Table 8-12   Respondents Favoring Racial Preferences in Hiring or Promotion Where There Has Been Past Discrimination

Date	Percentage
May 1985	42
April 1987	50
July 1987	40
September 1987	37
May 1990	33
December 1990	32
January 1992	49
February 1992	39
March 1993	33
February 1995	33
April 1995	29
August 1995	32
October 1995	36
April 1996	29
December 1997	35

Note: Question: "Do you believe that where there has been job discrimination against blacks in the past, preference in hiring or promotion should be given to blacks today?"

Source: New York Times press release; CBS/*New York Times.*

Table 8-13   Respondents Favoring Affirmative Action

Date	Percentage
January 1982	72
July 1982	69
September 1983	61
July 1984	65
September 1985	75
July 1987	69
June 1991	75
September 1991[a]	70

Note: Question: "Do you favor or oppose federal laws requiring affirmative action programs for women and minorities provided there are no rigid quotas?"

[a] When "affirmative action" is replaced by "racial preferences," support drops to 46 percent.

Source: The Harris Poll, July 14, 1991, 3, and September 15, 1991, 2.

Table 8-14   Respondents Believing a Woman's Job Is to Take Care of the Home

Date	Percentage
1974	35.6
1975	35.6
1977	38.2
1978	31.9
1982	28.2
1983	23.2
1985	26.4
1986	24.2
1988	21.2
1989	20.0
1990	17.9
1991	19.3
1993	14.8
1994	14.1
1996	16.3
1998	15.4

Note: Question: "Women should take care of running their homes and leave running the country to men (agree/disagree)?"

Source: General Social Survey, National Opinion Research Center, University of Chicago, various years. Data not available for 2000.

Table 8-15   Respondents Believing Past Job Discrimination Against Women Should Result in Hiring Preferences Today

Date	Percentage
May 1985	48
April 1987	50
September 1991	28
February 1995	43
April 1995	44
August 1995	40
October 1995	44
April 1996	32
December 1997	37

Note: Question: "Do you believe that where there has been job discrimination against women in the past, preferences in hiring should be given to women today?"

Sources: New York Times press release; CBS/*New York Times.*

Table 8-16 Respondents Believing Abortion Should Be
Legal, Select Polls (Percentage)

Date	New York Times	Gallup
April 1975	—	21
December 1977	—	22
February 1979	—	22
July 1980	—	25
May 1981	—	23
May 1983	—	23
September 1988	—	24
September 1989	40	—
November 1989	41	—
January 1990	39	—
April 1990	—	31
August 1990	41	—
June 1991	37	—
August 1991	41	—
September 1991	42	33
January 1992	40	—
March 1992	44	—
June 1992	42	—
July 1992	41	—
August 1992	41	—
October 1992	41	—
March 1993	42	33
July 1994	40	—
February 1995	43	—
April 1995	38	—
August 1995	40	—
September 1995	—	31
October 1995	37	—
February 1996	40	—
April 1996	37	—
June 1996	35	—
July 1996	37	—
September 1996	—	24
August 1997	—	22
November 1997	—	26
January 1998	32	23
May 1999	—	27
November 1999	34	—
September 2000	32	—
March 2001	33	—
August 2001	—	26
May 2002	—	25

Note: "—" indicates survey not conducted in that year. Questions: *(New York Times)*
"Which of these comes closest to your views? 1) Abortion should be generally available to all who want it, or 2) Abortion should be available but under stricter limits
than it is now, or 3) Abortion should not be permitted." (The Gallup Poll) "Do you
think abortion should be legal under any circumstances, legal only under some circumstances, or illegal under all circumstances?" The percentages represent those
who selected "1" in the *New York Times* poll and "under any circumstances" in the
Gallup; LEXIS-NEXIS Academic Universe.

Sources: New York Times press release; *The Gallup Poll* (1978), 29, 509, (1988), 206,
(April 1990), 3, (September 1991), 52, and (1993), 38.

Table 8-17   Respondents Believing Information on Birth Control Should Be Legally Available, Select Polls (Percentage)

Year	General Social Survey	Gallup
1936	—	70
1959	—	72
1964	—	81
1974	91.2	—
1975	89.3	—
1977	90.8	—
1982	89.5	—
1983	90.1	—

Note: "—" indicates survey not conducted in that year. Questions: (General Social Survey) "Do you think birth control information should be available to anyone who wants it, or not?" (The Gallup Poll) 1936, "Should the distribution of information on birth control be made legal?" After 1936, "Do you think birth control information should be available to anyone who wants it, or not?"

Sources: General Social Survey, National Opinion Research Center, University of Chicago, various years; *The Gallup Poll* 1 (1936), 41; 3 (1959), 1654; 3 (1964), 1915.

Table 8-18   Respondents Supporting Legal Abortion Under Special Circumstances (Percentage)

Year	Chance of defect	Wants no more children	Health endangered	Can't afford	Rape	Not married	Any reason
1965	54.0	—	77.0	18.0	—	—	—
1972	78.6	39.7	86.9	48.8	79.1	43.5	—
1973	84.5	47.7	92.3	53.4	83.5	49.1	—
1974	85.1	46.9	92.4	54.8	86.5	50.1	—
1975	83.2	45.7	90.7	53.2	83.7	48.2	—
1976	83.9	46.2	90.8	53.1	83.7	50.3	—
1977	85.5	46.5	90.5	53.4	83.8	49.8	37.7
1978	82.0	40.3	90.6	47.4	83.2	41.1	33.3
1979	—	—	—	—	—	—	—
1980	83.1	47.1	90.1	51.7	83.4	48.4	41.1
1981	—	—	—	—	—	—	—
1982	82.1	45.8	90.4	49.0	83.9	45.5	38.5
1983	78.9	38.9	89.7	43.7	82.8	39.4	34.3
1984	80.2	42.7	89.5	46.3	80.4	44.2	38.6
1985	78.5	40.3	89.3	43.7	81.2	41.2	36.9
1986	—	—	—	—	—	—	—
1987	78.0	41.0	87.9	44.7	79.6	40.1	39.2
1988	78.8	39.9	88.7	42.0	81.1	39.4	36.1
1989	81.3	44.5	90.1	47.7	83.2	45.4	40.3
1990	81.2	45.1	91.8	48.1	84.8	45.3	43.4
1991	83.5	44.6	91.5	48.5	86.5	44.8	42.6
1992	—	—	—	—	—	—	—
1993	81.3	47.1	89.8	49.9	82.9	48.1	45.3
1994	82.3	48.3	90.6	50.4	83.6	47.6	46.3
1996	81.8	46.7	91.6	46.6	84.3	44.9	45.0
1998	78.6	42.3	87.9	44.3	80.1	42.3	40.9
2000	78.7	40.7	88.5	42.2	80.6	39.1	39.9

Note: "—" indicates survey not conducted in that year. Questions: "Please tell me whether or not you think it should be possible for a pregnant woman to obtain a *legal* abortion if A) there is a strong chance of serious defect in the baby, B) She is married and does not want any more children, C) the woman's own health is seriously endangered by the pregnancy, D) the family has a very low income and can't afford any more children, E) She became pregnant as the result of rape, F) She is not married and does not want to marry the man, or G) the woman wants it for any reason?"

Sources: The Gallup Poll 3 (1935–1971), 1985; General Social Survey, National Opinion Research Center, University of Chicago, various years.

Table 8-19   Respondents Supporting *Roe v. Wade,* Select Polls (Percentage)

Date	Harris	Gallup
February 1974	52	—
November 1974	—	47
April 1975	54	—
March 1976	54	—
August 1976	59	—
October 1976	60	—
July 1977	53	—
July 1978	—	—
February 1979	60	—
February 1980	—	—
May 1981	56	45
May 1982	—	—
June 1983	—	50
June 1984	—	—
September 1985	50	—
January 1986	—	49
January 1987	—	—
December 1988	—	57
January 1989	56	—
July 1989	61	58
August 1989	59	—
October 1989	58	—
October 1990	—	—
June 1991	—	52
July 1991	—	56
September 1991	—	57
January 1992	—	65
August 1992	65	—
October 1993	56	—
September 1996	52	—
January 1998	57	—
March 2002	—	60

Note: "—" indicates survey not conducted in that year. Questions: (The Harris Survey) "In 1973, the U.S. Supreme Court decided that state laws which made it a crime to have an abortion up to three months of pregnancy were unconstitutional, and that the decision of whether or not to have an abortion should be left to the woman and her doctor to decide. In general, do you favor or oppose the U.S. Supreme Court decision making abortion up to three months of pregnancy legal?" (The Gallup Poll) "In 1973, the Supreme Court ruled that states cannot place restrictions on a woman's right to an abortion during the first three months of pregnancy. Would you like to see this ruling overturned or not?" The wording of these questions is inaccurate. The decision in fact legalized abortion in the first six months of pregnancy. In 1975, Harris found only 20 percent approval for legalized abortions between the third and sixth months of pregnancy. The 2002 Gallup survey qualified "during the first three months" with "at least in the first three . . . ."

Sources: The Harris Survey, August 18, 1977, 2, March 7, 1979, 2, January 29, 1989, 2, and November 26, 1989, 2; *The Gallup Poll* (1981), 113, (1983), 139, (1986), 49, (1989), 20, (July 1991), 21, (September 1992), 52; and (1992), 5; LEXIS-NEXIS Academic Universe.

Table 8-20   Respondents Believing Homosexual
Behavior Is Wrong

Year	Percentage[a]
1973	79.3
1974	75.5
1976	76.3
1977	77.7
1980	79.3
1982	80.1
1984	78.3
1985	79.3
1987	82.3
1988	81.5
1989	78.3
1990	81.2
1991	79.6
1993	70.6
1994	70.5
1996	65.6
1998	63.7
2000	63.3

Note: Question: "Do you believe that sexual relations between two adults of the same sex is always wrong, almost always wrong, wrong only sometimes, or not wrong at all?"

[a] Includes "always" and "almost always" responses.

Source: General Social Survey, National Opinion Research Center, University of Chicago, various years.

Table 8-21   Respondents Believing Homosexuals
Should Have Equal Rights in Job
Opportunities

Date	Percentage
1977	56
1982	59
1989	71
June 1992	74
August 1992	79
February 1993	78
February 1996	83

Note: Question: "Do you think homosexuals should or should not have equal rights in terms of job opportunities?"

Source: New York Times press release; CBS News/*New York Times.*

Table 8-22   Respondents Believing Pornography Leads to a Breakdown in Morals

Year	Percentage
1973	52.8
1975	51.3
1976	54.6
1978	56.8
1980	60.0
1983	58.3
1984	61.3
1986	61.9
1987	59.0
1988	61.8
1989	62.1
1990	60.8
1991	59.6
1993	63.5
1994	56.7

Note: Question: "Sexual materials lead to a breakdown in morals (yes/no)?"

Source: General Social Survey, National Opinion Research Center, University of Chicago, various years.

Table 8-23   Respondents Approving of Supreme Court Decisions Preventing Organized Prayer or Bible Readings in Schools, Select Polls (Percentage)

Year	General Social Survey	Gallup
1963	—	24
1974	31.8	—
1975	36.4	—
1977	34.2	—
1982	35.4	—
1983	41.1	—
1985	44.4	—
1986	37.9	—
1988	38.8	—
1989	42.2	—
1990	41.5	—
1991	39.8	—
1993	40.9	—
1994	39.1	—
1996	41.5	—
1998	44.6	—
2000	38.8	—

Note: "—" indicates survey not conducted in that year. Question: "The U.S. Supreme Court has ruled that no state or local government may require the reading of the Lord's Prayer or Bible verses in public schools. What are your views on this?"

Sources: General Social Survey, National Opinion Research Center, University of Chicago, various years; *The Gallup Poll* 3 (1935–1971), 1837.

Table 8-24   Respondents Supporting an Individual's Right to Die, Various Polls (Percentage)

Year	General Social Survey	Gallup	Harris
1936	—	—	—
1947	—	37	—
1973	—	53	—
1977	62.4	—	66
1978	60.1	—	—
1981	—	—	73
1982	58.2	—	—
1983	65.9	—	—
1985	65.5	—	80
1986	68.3	—	—
1988	69.3	—	—
1989	68.7	—	—
1990	72.3	—	—
1991	73.8	65	—
1993	68.3	—	63
1994	71.3	40	—
1996	70.8	69	—
1998	71.6	—	—
2000	68.1	—	—

Note: "—" indicates survey not conducted in that year. Questions: (General Social Survey, The Gallup Poll) "Do you believe that doctors should be allowed by law to end an incurable patient's life if the patient and his family request it?" (The Harris Survey) "Do you believe families should be allowed to tell doctors to end life support for comatose terminally ill patients?"

Sources: General Social Survey, National Opinion Research Center, University of Chicago, various years; *The Gallup Poll* 1 (1935–1971), 656, (January 1991), 51, 2d (1994), 194; The Harris Survey, March 4, 1985, 3 and (1993), 2.

Table 8-25 Attorneys' Attitudes About the Propriety of Advertising in the Legal Profession

Survey statement	Agree		Disagree	
	N	%	N	%
The law is a profession, not a trade, and advertising should be banned.	454	57	328	41
The public is ill-equipped to evaluate lawyer advertising.	530	67	252	32
Lawyer advertising provides useful information to the public.	162	21	620	78
Advertising by lawyers is inherently misleading.	266	34	515	65
Advertising by lawyers must be allowed because of the First Amendment.	27	34	515	65
Advertising is necessary for new lawyers entering the profession.	61	8	721	91
Only factual advertising (change of address, etc.) is appropriate.	318	40	464	59

Note: Data are from surveys mailed to the senior partner of small law firms located in Illinois, Kentucky, Louisiana, and Massachusetts between November 1988 and March 1989.

Source: Lauren Bowen, "Do Court Decisions Matter?" In *Contemplating Courts,* ed. Lee Epstein (Washington, D.C.: CQ Press, 1995), 380.

Table 8-26 Respondents Believing the Supreme Court Is Too Liberal or Too Conservative (Percentage)

Year	Too liberal	Too conservative	About right	Unsure
1973	35	26	17	22
1986	34	38	10	17
1987	38	38	8	18
1991	30	42	9	19

Note: Question: "In general, do you think the U.S. Supreme Court is too liberal or too conservative?"

Source: New York Times press release.

Table 8-27 Respondents Having a Great Deal of Confidence in the Supreme Court, Various Polls (Percentage)

Year	General Social Survey	Harris	Gallup 1	Gallup 2
1963	—	—	43	—
1966	—	50	—	—
1967	—	—	45	—
1968	—	—	36	—
1969	—	—	33	—
1971	—	23	—	—
1972	—	28	—	17
1973	32.6	33	37	—
1974	34.8	40	—	17
1975	32.2	28	49	—
1976	37.5	22	—	16
1977	37.2	29	—	—
1978	29.4	29	—	—
1979	—	28	45	—
1980	26.1	28	47	—
1981	—	29	—	—
1982	30.5	25	—	—
1983	28.3	33	42	—
1984	34.5	35	—	—
1985	—	28	55	—
1986	30.9	32	53	—
1987	35.8	30	52	—
1988	36.3	32	56	—
1989	36.2	15	—	—
1990	36.6	32	—	—
1991	38.6	23	—	—
1991	—	30	—	—
1992	—	30	—	—
1993	31.9	26	18	—
1994	31.2	31	18	—
1995	—	32	20	—
1996	29.8	31	17	—
1997	—	28	25	19
1998	32.7	37	24	27
1999	—	42	20	29
2000	33.9	—	—	—
2000, January	—	34	—	—
2000, July	—	—	—	23
2000, December 15	—	—	49	—
2001, January	—	35	—	—
2001, June	—	—	50	—
2002, January	—	41	—	—

Note: "—" indicates survey not conducted that year. Questions: (General Social Survey, The Harris Poll) "As far as people running the U.S. Supreme Court are concerned, would you say you have a great deal of confidence, only some confidence, or hardly any confidence?" (The Gallup Poll 1) 1963–1973, "In general, what kind of rating would you give the Supreme Court?" After 1975, "Would you tell me how much confidence you have in the Supreme Court: a great deal, quite a lot, some, or very little?" (The Gallup Poll 2) "Let me ask you how much trust and confidence you have at this time in the judicial branch, headed by the U.S. Supreme Court: a great deal, a fair amount, not very much, or none at all?"

Sources: General Social Survey, National Opinion Research Center, University of Chicago, various years; The Harris Poll, March 22, 1992, 2, (1992), 2, (1993), and (1994); *The Gallup Poll* 3 (1935–1971), 1836, 2147, 2200, 1 (1972–1977), 140, 528, (1980), 245, (1983), 174, (1986), 275, (1987), 141, (1993), 23, and (1994), 5.

Table 8-28   Public Reaction to Franklin D. Roosevelt's Plan to Enlarge the Supreme Court

Interview dates (1937)	Favor plan	Oppose plan	Don't know
February 10–15	38.4%	44.8%	17%
February 17–22	44.1	45.9	10
February 24–March 1	42.3	45.1	12
March 3–March 8	41.9	49.1	9
March 12–March 17	45.9	44.1	10
March 17–March 22	45.4	43.6	11
March 24–March 29	44.2	40.8	15
April 1–April 6	43.7	42.1	14
April 7–April 12	44.1	45.9	10
April 14–April 19	40.9	46.1	13
April 21–April 26	39.9	45.1	15
April 28–May 1	38.7	47.3	14
May 5–May 10	36.5	46.5	17
May 12–May 17	37.4	45.7	17
May 19–May 24	30.7	44.3	25
May 26–May 31	30.8	46.2	23
June 3–June 8	34.9	48.2	17
June 9–June 14	37.4	49.6	13

Note: On February 5, 1937, President Franklin D. Roosevelt announced a plan to reorganize the federal court system. Among his proposals was the creation of one new seat on the Supreme Court for every justice who had attained the age of 70 but remained in active service. At the time of his proposal, six sitting justices were over 70.

Questions: February 10–April 12, "Are you in favor of President Roosevelt's proposal regarding the Supreme Court?" April 14–June 14, "Should Congress pass the President's Supreme Court plan?"

Source: American Institute of Public Opinion (Gallup), 1937 Studies: #68–86.

Table 8-29   Members of State, District, and Territorial Bars Favoring
Franklin D. Roosevelt's Plan to Enlarge the Supreme Court
(1937)

State	Percentage	Total number of respondents
Alabama	27.0	596
Arizona	23.4	274
Arkansas	35.1	501
California	21.1	4,585
Colorado	15.2	794
Connecticut	16.6	757
Delaware	18.3	115
District of Columbia	19.2	1,298
Florida	31.1	1,007
Georgia	31.1	809
Idaho	20.3	256
Illinois	18.3	6,457
Indiana	17.2	1,861
Iowa	11.5	1,430
Kansas	13.7	931
Kentucky	22.9	955
Louisiana	22.6	702
Maine	10.9	384
Maryland	18.1	1,084
Massachusetts	12.0	2,515
Michigan	18.1	2,281
Minnesota	16.5	1,606
Mississippi	41.2	461
Missouri	19.3	2,529
Montana	21.1	322
Nebraska	15.0	1,130
Nevada	23.1	134
New Hampshire	10.5	191
New Jersey	26.3	2,149
New Mexico	15.5	148
New York	22.9	10,788
North Carolina	32.1	842
North Dakota	17.3	294
Ohio	16.9	4,375
Oklahoma	27.2	1,465
Oregon	14.4	785
Pennsylvania	19.1	3,932
Rhode Island	10.6	322
South Carolina	31.2	343
South Dakota	14.5	413
Tennessee	26.5	861
Texas	25.7	2,736
Utah	14.1	327
Vermont	7.6	184
Virginia	23.4	1,085
Washington	16.3	1,261

(Table continues)

Table 8-29   *(Continued)*

State	Percentage	Total number of respondents
West Virginia	16.5	672
Wisconsin	21.6	1,391
Wyoming	15.4	130
Territorial	26.3	19
Total	20.3	70,487

Note: On February 5, 1937, President Franklin D. Roosevelt announced a plan to reorganize the federal court system. Among his proposals was the creation of one new seat on the Supreme Court for every justice who had attained the age of 70 but remained in active service. At the time of his proposal, six sitting justices were over 70.

Source: U.S. Senate, Committee on the Judiciary, *Hearings on a Bill to Reorganize the Judicial Branch of Government, April 5 to 15, 1937,* 76th Cong., 1st sess., 1937 (Supplement to hearing of April 15, 1937).

Table 8-30   Respondents Believing That the Supreme Court's Decision in *Bush v. Gore* Mainly Reflected the Political Views or Partisan Politics of the Justices (Percentage)

	Harris	CBS News	News-week	Reuters/ NBC News/ Zogby	ABC News/ Washington Post	CNN/ USA Today/ Gallup
All voters	41	37	33	43	35	35
Bush voters		10	13	—	—	6
Gore voters		65	54	—	—	65

Note: "—" indicates survey not conducted that year. Questions: (Harris) December 14–21, 2000, "Do you believe that the decisions made by individual judges in the Supreme Court mainly reflect the political views of the judges or mainly reflect their impartial legal judgments?" (CBS News) December 14–16, 2000, "Do you think the Supreme Court's decision was based more on partisan politics, or more on an objective interpretation of the law?" (*Newsweek*) December 14–15, 2000, "What role, if any, do you think politics or partisanship played in the Supreme Court justices' decision? Do you think politics or partisanship played a major role in their decision, somewhat of a role, or no role at all?" (Reuters/NBC/Zogby) December 13, 2000, "Do you believe the U.S. Supreme Court has ruled in the best interests of the nation, or do you believe the ruling reveals the personal political interests of the justices?" (ABC/*Washington Post*) December 14, 2000, "Do you think the majority in the U.S. Supreme Court that ruled in Bush's favor did so mainly on the law and evidence in the case, or mainly because it wanted to help Bush become president?" (CNN/*USA Today*/Gallup) December 13, 2000, "Do you think the Justices of the U.S. Supreme Court who voted to end the recount in Florida did so mostly based on the legal merits of the case OR mostly based on their own desire to have Bush as the next president?"

Source: All data available at www.pollingreport.com/wh2post.htm.

Table 8-31   Respondents Approving of or Agreeing with the Supreme Court's Decision in *Bush v. Gore* (Percentage)

	CBS News	ABC News/ Washington Post	CNN/ USA Today/ Gallup
All	54	50	52
Bush voters	95		93
Gore voters	16		13

Note: Question: (CBS News) December 14–16, 2000, "As you may know, on Tuesday the United States Supreme Court ruled in George W. Bush's favor, and stopped the manual recounting of votes in Florida that had been ordered by the Florida Supreme Court. Do you approve or disapprove of the U.S. Supreme Court's ruling that stopped the manual recount?" (ABC/*Washington Post*) December 14, 2000, "From what you've heard or read about it, do you approve or disapprove of the U.S. Supreme Court's decision rejecting the recount in Florida?" (CNN/*USA Today*/Gallup) December 13, 2000, "As you may know, the U.S. Supreme Court reached a decision last night which effectively ended the vote recount in Florida, meaning that George W. Bush will be the next president. Do you agree or disagree with the U.S. Supreme Court's decision?"

Source: All data available at: www.pollingreport.com/wh2post.htm.

Table 8-32   Respondents Supporting or Opposing Nominees for the
Supreme Court

Nominee	Date of survey	Favor	Oppose	Not sure
Black	September 1937[a]	56	44	0
Carswell	April 1970[b]	32	34	34
O'Connor	July 1981[a]	86	8	6
O'Connor	July 1981[b]	79	14	7
Rehnquist	August 1986[b, c]	30	58	12
Bork	August 1987[a]	31	25	44
Bork	September 1987[d]	14	13	73
Bork	September 1987[d]	21	27	52
Bork	October 1987[b, c]	29	57	14
Thomas	July 1991[a]	52	17	31
Thomas	July 1991[b]	59	27	14
Thomas	August 1991[a]	56	23	21
Thomas	August 1991[b]	59	32	9
Thomas	September 1991[a]	54	25	21
Thomas	September 1991[b]	53	39	8
Thomas	October 9, 1991[d]	24	11	65
Thomas	October 9–13, 1991[b, c]	58	38	4
Thomas	October 10–13, 1991[a, c]	53	30	17
Thomas	October 13, 1991[d]	45	20	35
Thomas	October 14, 1991[d]	57	19	24
Thomas	October 14, 1991[a, c]	58	30	12
Ginsburg	June 1993[a]	54	12	34
Ginsburg	January 1994[a]	58	22	20
Breyer	May 1994	53	11	36

[a] The Gallup Poll
[b] The Harris Survey
[c] Respondents were informed of charges against nominee prior to being asked question.
[d] *New York Times* Poll

Sources: The Harris Survey Yearbook of Public Opinion (1971), 21; The Harris Survey, July 20, 1981, 3, August 3, 1986, 3, September 28, 1987, 2, and October 15, 1991, 4; *The Gallup Poll* 1 (1935–1971), 71, (1987), 221, (July 1991), 18, (August 1991), 53, (September 1991), 45, (October 1991), 26, (1993), 19, and (1994), 10; *New York Times* press release.

Table 8-33   Respondents Able to Name 1989
Supreme Court Justices

Justice	Percentage
O'Connor	23
Rehnquist	9
Kennedy	7
Scalia	6
Marshall	5
Blackmun	4
Brennan	3
White	3
Stevens	1

Note: 71 percent of respondents could not name any justice;
only two of the 1,005 respondents correctly named all nine.

Source: Washington Post National Weekly Edition, June 26–July 2,
1989, 37.

Table 8-34   Respondents Able to Name the Judge
of the Television Show "The People's
Court"

Justice	Percentage
Wapner	54
Other	1
Don't Know	42

Source: Washington Post National Weekly Edition, June 26–July 2,
1989, 37.

Table 8-35 Respondents' Impressions of Chief Justice Rehnquist (Percentage)

	Favorable or positive			Not familiar, not sure, no opinion		
	CNN/ Time	Gallup/ CNN/ USA Today	NBC News/ Wall Street Journal	NBC News/ CNN/ Time	Gallup/ CNN/ USA Today	Wall Street Journal
January 1999	48	51	28	42	41	37
January 2001	—	—	24	—	—	39

Note: Questions: (CNN/*Times*) "I'd like to get your overall opinion of some people in the news. As I read each name, please say if you have a favorable or unfavorable opinion of this person—or if you have never heard of him or her. . . . Supreme Court Chief Justice William Rehnquist." (Gallup/CNN/*USA Today*) "I'd like to get your overall opinion of some people in the news. As I read each name, please say if you have a favorable or unfavorable opinion of this person—or if you have never heard of him or her. . . . Supreme Court Chief Justice William Rehnquist." (NBC News/*Wall Street Journal*) "I'm going to read you the names of several public figures and institutions. I'd like you to rate your feelings toward each one as either very positive, somewhat positive, neutral, somewhat negative, or very negative. If you don't know the name, please just say so. William Rehnquist." Percentage favorable or positive for NBC News/*Wall Street Journal* combines the "very positive" and "somewhat positive" responses.

Source: www.pollingreport.com/Q-Z.htm#Rehnquist.

9

The Impact of the Supreme Court

Once the U.S. Supreme Court hands down a decision, does that ruling have any legal, political, or social impact? Answers provided by scholars range from the definite "no" to the absolute "yes." Most analysts, however, are circumspect, suggesting that the impact of a Court decision depends on the way various "populations" (for example, judges, lawyers, politicians, citizens) respond to it.[1]

Addressing the question of the Court's impact is beyond the scope of this book.[2] What we do provide, however, are data pertaining to specific Supreme Court rulings in the areas of abortion, capital punishment, school desegregation, voting rights, campaign contributions, and reapportionment. This information can help analysts and students better understand the Court and provide a base from which to conduct further scholarly endeavors. We wish to make clear from the outset that we do not assume causal links between specific Court cases and the data presented. Simply because we present data on voter registration rates, for example, does not necessarily mean that the Court's rulings have had any impact on those figures. This said, we may now consider the tables appearing in this chapter and the Court cases associated with them.

Table 9-1 presents data on legal abortions carried out in the United States, providing information on the number of abortions and on the characteristics of women who have had the procedure. The Supreme Court's involvement in the issue of abortion began in earnest with *Roe v. Wade* (1973).[3] In this landmark decision, the Court found that the right to privacy encompasses the decision whether or not to bear a child, and it set out a "trimester" scheme, which legalized the abortion procedure prior to viability. As evident in Table 9-1, in absolute terms the number of legal abortions skyrocketed from 18,000 in 1968 to 1,528,900 in 1992 (although it has fallen in the last decade). Percentagewise, though, the biggest growth period occurred just prior to the *Roe* decision. This has led some scholars to conclude that the Court's 1973 decision did not have much impact on exercise of the abortion right. Others argue that these numbers would have remained flat had the Court not acted.

Tables 9-2 and 9-3 present data on another highly charged issue: capital punishment. Prior to the 1970s, the Supreme Court had never issued an explicit ruling on the constitutionality of capital punishment.[5] Accordingly, states were free to impose sentences of death. The data displayed in Table 9-2 indicate that, at least through the 1950s, many states did in fact use execution as a form of criminal punishment. By the 1960s and 1970s, however, the pace of executions had slowed considerably. Although a number of reasons exist for this slowdown, two in particular are important. The first is that in the mid-1960s a civil rights litigating group, the NAACP Legal Defense and Educational Fund, developed a legal strategy to stop all executions in the United States. Now referred to as "moratorium," this strategy proved quite effective. In 1968, for the first time in U.S. history, no legalized executions occurred.[6] The second explanation derives from a Supreme Court case, *Furman v. Georgia* (1972),[7] in which five of the justices held that the procedures used by the states to impose capital punishment violated the Constitution.[8]

Largely as a result of the moratorium strategy and *Furman*, no executions took place in the United States between 1968 and 1976. This is not to say that states had eradicated capital punishment or that judges and juries were not imposing sentences of death. In fact, immediately after the *Furman* decision, many states rewrote their laws to conform to the Court's ruling. In *Gregg v. Georgia* (1976),[9] the Court held that these new laws were constitutional so long as they met certain procedural standards and did not impose mandatory death sentences. Accordingly, states are once again free to invoke the death penalty and, in fact, if they continue at their current pace, over nine hundred individuals will be executed during the 1990s.

Tables 9-4, 9-5, and 9-6 present data pertaining to yet another controversial issue: school desegregation. Beginning in the late 1930s, the Supreme Court chipped away at the "separate but equal" doctrine it had articulated in *Plessy v. Ferguson* (1896).[10] But it was not until 1954, in the landmark case of *Brown v. Board of Education*,[11] that it fully overturned *Plessy*. A year later, the Court ordered that school desegregation take place "with all deliberate speed" and gave federal district courts the requisite oversight responsibilities. In *Swann v. Charlotte-Mecklenburg County Board of Education* (1971),[12] the justices reaffirmed the broad powers of district courts in enforcing *Brown*, allowing them to use "a wide arsenal of student placement strategies, including rearrangement of attendance zones and the politically unpopular imposition of forced busing."[13]

Three trends visible in the tables are particularly worth noting. The first is simply that change has occurred. In the 1950s schools in the South were almost completely segregated (see Table 9-4); thirty years later, 56.5

percent of black students attended schools with more than half minority students (see Table 9-5). The second trend is that, while change has occurred, it has been slow to arrive. As important as *Brown v. Board of Education* was, it (and its progeny of the 1960s) did not lead to overnight desegregation of public schools. As the data reveal, it was not until the late 1960s and into the 1970s that the promise of *Brown* seemed at least somewhat fulfilled. Finally, and relatedly, many school systems today remain segregated, though not unconstitutionally so. To be sure, the data support a trend toward desegregation, yet they also reveal that in the South 24 percent of black students are in schools that are 90 percent to 100 percent minority; moreover, they show that less than 35 percent of black students are enrolled in majority white schools.

The remaining tables present data on voting and the electoral process. Table 9-7 contains information on white versus minority voter registration rates in eleven southern states. The Court's long involvement in the area of race discrimination in the electoral process stems from the attempts of southern states to circumvent the Fifteenth Amendment by keeping blacks out of the voting booth. As Chief Justice Earl Warren wrote in *South Carolina v. Katzenbach* (1966),

> beginning in 1890, the States of Alabama, Georgia, Louisiana, Mississippi, North Carolina, South Carolina, and Virginia enacted tests still in use which were specifically designed to prevent Negroes from voting. Typically they made the ability to read and write a registration qualification and also required completion of a registration form. These laws were based on the fact that as of 1890 in each of the named States, more than two-thirds of the adult Negroes were illiterate while less than one-quarter of the adult whites were unable to read or write. At the same time, alternate tests were prescribed in all of the named States to assure that white illiterates would not be deprived of the franchise. These included grandfather clauses, property qualifications, "good character" tests, and the requirement that registrants "understand" or "interpret" certain matter.[14]

Despite the efforts of the Supreme Court, Congress, and the Justice Department to remove these and other barriers, the South continued to stymie black voting. Table 9-7 shows that as late as 1960 registration rates for nonwhites hovered around 29 percent compared with 61 percent for whites. "Figures such as these convinced Congress . . . that a more aggressive policy was required. . . The result was the Voting Rights Act of 1965, the most comprehensive statute ever enacted by Congress to enforce the guarantees of the Fifteenth Amendment."[15] Led by South Carolina, five southern states immediately challenged the act as exceeding the constitutional power of the federal government. In *South Carolina v. Katzenbach* (1965),[16] however, the Supreme Court upheld the Act, writing that "[h]opefully, millions of non-white Americans will now be able to participate for the first time on an equal basis in the government under which they live." Based on the data presented in Table 9-7, at the very least, minority and white registration in the South are now roughly comparable.

Tables 9-8 and 9-9 contain information on another dimension of electoral activity, that involving political action committees (PACs). PACs are nonpolitical party committees set up in accordance with federal law to collect money and disburse it to preferred candidates. As the tables reveal, there were only about 700 PACs prior to 1976, and they spent relatively little: about $53 million compared with $358 million in 1990. What happened? What explains the astounding growth of PACs? Part of the answer lies with a 1976 Supreme Court decision, *Buckley v. Valeo*.[17] There the Court reviewed several 1974 amendments to the Federal Election Campaign Act of 1971 designed to reform political campaigns. The resulting decision was mixed: the justices struck down provisions mandating ceilings on independent political expenditures but upheld limits on direct campaign contributions. PACs were a natural, albeit perhaps unintended, outgrowth of this ruling.[18] To circumvent the individual spending limits, individuals and organizations created these PACs. Some were established by existing interest groups (connected PACs); others (nonconnected PACs) were formed solely to acquire and then give money to candidates and campaigns. In any case, they are now a major, institutionalized force operating in the electoral process.

Finally, Table 9-10 provides data on a third dimension of voting: reapportionment. Prior to 1963, states were free to devise (or "apportion") legislative districts as they saw fit. Some states, however, never bothered to reapportion, even after massive population shifts that saw large numbers emigrate from rural areas into the cities. In *Colegrove v. Green* (1946),[19] the Supreme Court dismissed a challenge to Illinois' congressional districts (which the legislature had failed to reapportion since 1901), ruling that the case presented a political rather than legal question. In the early 1960s, the justices had a change of heart. In a series of cases beginning with *Baker v. Carr* (1962),[20] the Court mandated that states reapportion their districts on the basis of the one person, one vote principle. The results of those rulings are depicted in Table 9-10.

Notes

1. See, for example, Charles A. Johnson and Bradley C. Canon, *Judicial Policies: Implementation and Impact* (Washington, D.C.: CQ Press, 1984).
2. See Selected Readings list at the end of the book for some leading works on the Court's impact. Also, given the limited focus of this book, we do not provide data on lower federal and state court responses to Supreme Court rulings (that is, the "legal" impact of decisions). For readers interested in this literature, we highly recommend the following articles: Charles A. Johnson, "Lower Court Reactions to Supreme Court Decisions: A Quantitative Examination," *American Journal of Political Science* 23 (1979): 792–804; Charles A.

Johnson, "Law, Politics, and Judicial Decision Making: Lower Federal Court Uses of Supreme Court Decisions," *Law and Society Review* 21 (1987): 325–340; Bradley C. Canon, "Organizational Contumacy in the Transmission of Legal Policies: The *Mapp, Escobedo, Miranda*, and *Gault* Cases," *Villanova Law Review* 20 (1974): 50–79; Donald Songer, "Alternative Approaches to the Study of Judicial Impact: *Miranda* in Five State Courts," *American Politics Quarterly* 16 (1988): 425–444.

3. 410 U.S. 113. Prior to 1973, the Court decided several cases involving reproductive issues, with *Griswold v. Connecticut*, 381 U.S. 479 (1965) among the most significant. It also decided at least one abortion-related case prior to *Roe, United States v. Vuitch*, 402 U.S. 62 (1971).
4. 505 U.S. 833.
5. Of course, it had decided cases in which defendants had been sentenced to death, but the primary issue in those cases was not the constitutionality of capital punishment. In addition, prior to 1972 the Court decided cases examining procedures surrounding the imposition of death sentences.
6. For more information on moratorium, see Lee Epstein and Joseph Kobylka, *The Supreme Court and Legal Change* (Chapel Hill: University of North Carolina Press, 1992), and Michael Meltsner, *Cruel and Unusual* (New York: Random House, 1973).
7. 408 U.S. 238.
8. The Court issued a per curiam opinion. Each justice wrote separately.
9. 428 U.S. 153.
10. 163 U.S. 537.
11. 347 U.S. 483.
12. 402 U.S. 1.
13. Lee Epstein and Thomas G. Walker, *Constitutional Law for a Changing America—Rights, Liberties, and Justice*, 2d ed. (Washington, D.C.: CQ Press, 1995), 734.
14. 383 U.S. 301, at 310–311.
15. Epstein and Walker, *Constitutional Law for a Changing America*, 786.
16. 383 U.S. 301.
17. 424 U.S. 1.
18. A 1975 Federal Election Commission (FEC) ruling also paved the way for the creation of corporate PACs. More specifically, in 1975 the Sun Oil Company sought the FEC's permission to use its funds to create a PAC, which would solicit contributions from employees and stockholders. The FEC granted the company's request, with the proviso that contributions be truly voluntary.
19. 328 U.S. 459.
20. 369 U.S. 186.

Table 9-1   Legal Abortions, 1966–1997

Year	Number	Change from previous year	Percentage change from previous year
1966	8,000		
1967	9,000	+1,000	+13
1968	18,000	+9,000	+100
1969	22,700	+4,700	+26
1970	193,500	+170,800	+752
1971	485,800	+292,300	+151
1972	586,800	+101,000	+21
1973	744,600	+157,800	+27
1974	898,600	+154,000	+21
1975	1,034,200	+135,600	+15
1976	1,179,300	+145,100	+14
1977	1,316,700	+137,400	+12
1978	1,409,600	+92,900	+7
1979	1,497,700	+88,100	+6
1980	1,553,900	+56,200	+4
1981	1,577,300	+23,400	+2
1982	1,573,900	−3,400	−0.2
1983	1,575,000	+1,100	−0.07
1984	1,577,200	+2,200	+0.1
1985	1,588,600	+11,400	+0.7
1986	1,574,000	−14,600	−0.92
1987	1,559,100	−14,900	−0.95
1988	1,590,800	+31,700	+2
1989	1,566,900	−23,900	−1.5
1990	1,608,600	+41,700	+2.7
1991	1,556,500	−52,100	−3.3
1992	1,528,900	−27,600	−1.8
1993	1,500,000	−28,900	−0.02
1994	1,431,000	−69,000	−0.05
1995	1,363,700	−67,300	−0.05
1996	1,365,700	−2,000	−0.001
1997	1,186,039	−179,661	−0.97

Sources: 1966–1973: Gerald N. Rosenberg, *The Hollow Hope* (Chicago: University of Chicago Press, 1991), 180; 1973–1988: Harold W. Stanley and Richard G. Niemi, *Vital Statistics on American Politics,* 3d ed. (Washington, D.C.: CQ Press, 1992), 34; 1989–1992: Stanley K. Henshaw and Jennifer Van Vort, "Abortion Services in the United States, 1991–1992," *Family Planning Perspectives* 26 (1994): 101; 1993–1996: Stanley K. Henshaw, "Abortion Incidence and Services in the United States," *Family Planning Perspectives* 30: 263–270; 1997 (most recent available data): Center for Disease Control and Prevention, *CDC Surveillance Summaries,* December 8, 2000.

Table 9-2 The Death Penalty: Numbers Executed (1930–2002)

				Number executed				
State or authority	*1930s*	*1940s*	*1950s*	*1960s*	*1970s*	*1980s*	*1990s*	*2000–2002[a]*
Alabama	60	50	20	5	0	7	12	5
Alaska	0	0	0[b]	—	—	—	—	—
Arizona	17	9	8	4	0	0	19	3
Arkansas	53	8	18	9	0	0	21	3
California	108	80	74	30	0	0	8	3
Colorado	25	13	3	6	0	0	1	0
Connecticut	5	10	5	1	0	0	0	0
Delaware	8	4	0[d]	0[c]	0	0	10	3
District of Columbia	20	NA	4	0	0[d]	—	—	—
Florida	44	65	49	12	1	20	23	7
Georgia	137	130	85	14	0	14	9	5
Hawaii	0	NA	0[e]	—	—	—	—	—
Idaho	0	NA	3	0	0	0	1	0
Illinois	61	18	9	2	0	0	12	0
Indiana	31	7	2	1	0	2	5	2
Iowa	8	7	1	2[f]	—	—	—	—
Kansas	7[g]	5	5	5	0[h]	—	—	—
Kentucky	52	34	16	1	0	0	2	0
Louisiana	58	47	27	1	0	18	7	2
Maine	—	—	—	—	—	—	—	—
Maryland	16	45	6	1	0	0	3	0
Massachusetts	18	9	0	0	0	0[i]	—	—
Michigan	0	0	0	0[j]	—	—	—	—
Minnesota	—	—	—	—	—	—	—	—
Mississippi	48	60	36	10	0	4	0	0

(Table continues)

Table 9-2 (*Continued*)

State or authority				Number executed				
	1930s	1940s	1950s	1960s	1970s	1980s	1990s	2000–2002[a]
Missouri	36	15	7	4	0	1	40	13
Montana	5	1	0	0	0	0	2	0
Nebraska	0	2	2	0	0	0	3	0
Nevada	8	0	9	2	1	3	4	1
New Hampshire	1	0	0	0	0	0	0	0
New Jersey	40	NA	17	3	0	0	0	0
New Mexico	2	NA	3	1	0	0	0	0
New York	153	114	52	10[k]	0[l]	—	—	—
North Carolina	131	12	19	1	0	3	12	6
North Dakota	—	—	—	—	—	—	—	—
Ohio	82	1	32	7	0	0	1	3
Oklahoma	34	NA	7	6	0	0	19	31
Oregon	2	12	4	1[m]	0[n]	0	2	0
Pennsylvania	82	6	31	3	0	0	3	0
Rhode Island	—	—	—	—	—	—	—	—
South Carolina	67	61	26	8	0	2	22	2
South Dakota	0[o]	1	0	0	0	0	0	0
Tennessee	47	37	8	1	0	0	0	1
Texas	120	NA	74	29	0	33	166	75
Utah	2	NA	6	1	1	2	3	0
Vermont	1	1	2	0[p]	—	—	—	—
Virginia	28	35	23	6	0	8	65	13
Washington	23	NA	6	2	0	0	3	1
West Virginia	20	11	9	q	—	—	—	—
Wisconsin	—	—	—	—	—	—	—	—
Wyoming	4	2	0	1	0	0	1	0

U.S. government	10	13	9	1	0	0	0	0
U.S. military[r]	NA	NA	NA	NA	NA	NA	0	0
Total[s]	1,667	925	717	191	3	117	478	186

Note: "—" indicates death penalty abolished prior to 1930. "NA" indicates data not available.

[a] Through June 2002.

[b] Death penalty abolished in 1957.

[c] Death penalty abolished in 1958 but restored in 1961.

[d] Death penalty abolished in 1972.

[e] Death penalty abolished in 1957.

[f] Death penalty abolished in 1872, restored in 1876, and abolished again in 1965.

[g] Death penalty restored in 1935 after having been abolished in 1907.

[h] Death penalty abolished in 1972.

[i] Death penalty declared unconstitutional in 1980.

[j] Death penalty abolished in 1846 but retained for treason until 1963.

[k] Death penalty abolished in 1966 but retained for some civil offenses.

[l] Death penalty restored in 1974, then declared unconstitutional in 1977.

[m] Death penalty abolished in 1964.

[n] Death penalty restored in 1970s.

[o] Death penalty restored in 1939 after having been abolished in 1915.

[p] Death penalty abolished in 1965.

[q] Death penalty abolished in 1965 but retained for some civil offenses.

[r] Since 1930, 160 executions have been carried out under military authority. Breakdown by decade is not available.

[s] The national total counts multiple death-sentence inmates once. However, they are included in the state total for each state where they are sentenced to death.

Sources: 1930–1989: Harold W. Stanley and Richard G. Niemi, *Vital Statistics on American Politics*, 5th ed. (Washington, D.C.: CQ Press, 1995), 30–32, and Franklin E. Zimring and Gordon Hawkins, *Capital Punishment and the American Agenda* (New York: Cambridge University Press, 1986), 31, 43; 1990–2002: web.cis.smu.edu/~deathpen/.

Table 9-3   U.S. Death Row Inmate Statistics, 2002

Defendant	Number of death row inmates	Percentage
Race		
White	1,691	45.59
Black	1,598	43.08
Latino/Latina	337	9.09
Native American	42	1.13
Asian	40	1.08
Unknown	1	.03
Total	3,709	100.00
Gender		
Male	3,655	98.54
Female	54	1.46
Total	3,709	100.00
Juveniles[a]		
Male	82	2.21 (of total)

Note: Data as of October 1, 2002.

[a] There were no female juveniles on death row.

Source: www.naacpldf.org.

Table 9-4   Black Children in Elementary and Secondary Schools with White Children: Southern and Border States, 1954–1973

| Year | Southern states[a] | | Border states[b] | |
	Percentage[c]	Number	Percentage[c]	Number
1954–1955	0.001	23	NA	NA
1955–1956	0.12	2,782	NA	NA
1956–1957	0.14	3,514	39.6	106,878
1957–1958	0.15	3,829	41.4	127,677
1958–1959	0.13	3,456	44.4	142,352
1959–1960	0.16	4,216	45.4	191,114
1960–1961	0.16	4,308	49.0	212,895
1961–1962	0.24	6,725	52.5	240,226
1962–1963	0.45	12,868	51.8	251,797
1963–1964	1.20	34,105	54.8	281,731
1964–1965	2.30	66,135	58.3	313,919
1965–1966	6.10	184,308	68.9	384,992
1966–1967	16.90	489,900	71.4	456,258
1968–1969	32.00	942,600	74.7	475,000
1970–1971	85.90	2,707,000	76.8	512,000
1972–1973	91.30	2,886,300	77.3	524,800

Note: "NA" indicates not available.

[a] Includes Alabama, Arkansas, Florida, Georgia, Louisiana, Mississippi, North Carolina, South Carolina, Tennessee, Texas, and Virginia.

[b] Includes Delaware, the District of Columbia, Kentucky, Maryland, Missouri, Oklahoma, and West Virginia.

[c] Percentage of black students out of all black schoolchildren attending school with white students.

Source: Gerald N. Rosenberg, *The Hollow Hope* (Chicago: University of Chicago Press, 1991), 50.

Table 9-5 School Desegregation by Region, 1968–1998

Region/year	Percentage of black students in schools with more than half minority students	Percentage of Hispanic students in schools with more than half minority students	Percentage of black students in schools 90–100 percent minority	Percentage of Hispanic students in schools 90–100 percent minority
South[a]				
1968	80.9	69.6	77.8	33.7
1972	55.3	69.9	24.7	31.4
1976	54.9	70.9	22.4	32.2
1980	57.1	76.0	23.0	37.3
1984	56.9	75.4	24.2	37.3
1986	58.0	75.2	25.1	38.6
1988	56.5	80.2	24.0	37.9
1991	60.8	76.8	26.6	38.6
1994	—	75.6	—	38.0
1996	65.3	75.9	27.9	38.3
1998	67.2	76.1	29.7	39.1
Change from 1968 to 1998	−13.7	+6.5	−48.1	+5.4
Border[b]				
1968	71.6	—	60.2	—
1972	67.2	—	54.7	—
1976	60.1	—	42.5	—
1980	59.2	—	37.0	—
1984	62.5	—	37.4	—
1986	59.3	29.9	35.6	—
1988	59.6	—	34.5	—
1991	59.3	37.4	33.2	10.8

1994	—	40.8	—	12.3
1996	63.2	43.5	37.3	12.6
1998	64.7	46.1	39.2	13.1
Change from 1968 to 1998	−6.9	—	−21.0	—
Northeast[c]				
1968	66.8	74.8	42.7	44.0
1972	69.9	74.4	46.9	44.1
1976	72.5	74.9	51.4	45.8
1980	79.9	76.3	48.7	45.8
1984	73.1	77.5	47.4	47.1
1986	72.8	78.2	49.8	46.4
1988	77.3	79.7	48.0	44.2
1991	76.2	78.1	50.1	46.2
1994	—	77.6	—	45.1
1996	77.3	78.2	50.5	46.0
1998	77.5	78.5	50.9	45.7
Change from 1968 to 1998	+10.7	+3.7	+8.2	+1.7
Midwest[d]				
1968	77.3	31.8	58.0	6.8
1972	75.3	34.4	57.4	9.5
1976	70.3	39.3	51.1	14.1
1980	69.5	46.6	43.6	19.6
1984	70.7	53.9	43.6	24.2
1986	69.8	54.3	38.5	23.5
1988	70.1	52.3	41.8	24.9
1991	69.9	53.5	39.4	21.1
1994	—	53.1	—	21.8
1996	72.0	54.0	43.4	22.3
1998	72.8	55.6	45.5	24.1
Change from 1968 to 1998	−4.5	+23.8	−12.5	+17.3

(Table continues)

Table 9-5 (*Continued*)

Region/year	Percentage of black students in schools with more than half minority students	Percentage of Hispanic students in schools with more than half minority students	Percentage of black students in schools 90–100 percent minority	Percentage of Hispanic students in schools 90–100 percent minority
West[e]				
1968	72.2	42.4	50.8	11.7
1972	68.1	44.7	42.7	11.5
1976	67.4	52.7	36.3	13.3
1980	66.8	63.5	33.7	18.5
1984	66.9	68.4	29.4	22.9
1986	68.2	69.9	28.3	24.7
1988	67.1	71.3	28.6	27.5
1991	69.7	73.5	26.4	29.7
1994	—	75.9	—	32.1
1996	73.5	77.1	27.5	33.0
1998	74.0	78.3	28.8	35.2
Change from 1968 to 1998	+1.8	+35.9	+22.0	+23.5
Total[f]				
1968	76.6	54.8	64.3	23.1
1972	63.6	56.6	38.7	23.3
1976	62.4	60.8	35.9	24.8
1980	62.9	68.1	33.2	28.8
1984	63.5	70.6	33.2	31.0
1986	63.3	71.5	32.5	32.2
1988	63.2	—	32.1	—
1991	66.0	73.4	33.9	34.0

1994	67.1	74.0	33.6	34.8
1996	68.8	74.8	35.0	35.4
1998	70.1	75.6	36.5	36.7
Change from 1968 to 1998	-6.5	+20.8	-27.8	+13.6

Note: "—" indicates data not available.

[a] Includes Alabama, Arkansas, Florida, Georgia, Louisiana, Mississippi, North Carolina, South Carolina, Tennessee, Texas, and Virginia.
[b] Includes Delaware, District of Columbia, Kentucky, Maryland, Missouri, Oklahoma, and West Virginia.
[c] Includes Connecticut, Maine, Massachusetts, New Hampshire, New Jersey, New York, Pennsylvania, Rhode Island, and Vermont.
[d] Includes Illinois, Indiana, Iowa, Kansas, Michigan, Minnesota, Nebraska, North Dakota, Ohio, South Dakota, and Wisconsin.
[e] Includes Arizona, California, Colorado, Idaho, Montana, Nevada, New Mexico, Oregon, Utah, Washington, and Wyoming.
[f] Excludes Alaska and Hawaii.

Source: Harold W. Stanley and Richard G. Niemi, *Vital Statistics on American Politics, 2001–2002* (Washington, D.C.: CQ Press, 2001), 376–377.

Table 9-6   Percentage of Black Students in Majority White Schools

Year	Percentage
1954	.001
1960	.1
1964	2.3
1967	13.9
1968	23.4
1970	33.1
1972	36.4
1976	37.6
1980	37.1
1986	42.9
1988	43.5
1991	39.2
1994	36.6
1996	34.7

Source: Gary Orfield and John T. Yun, *Resegregation in American Schools.* Cambridge, Mass.: Harvard University, The Civil Rights Project, 1999. Data available at www.law.harvard.edu/groups/civilrights/publications/resegregation99/resegregation99.html.

Table 9-7 Voter Registration Rates in Eleven Southern States, by Race, 1960–2000

Year/state	Whites		Nonwhites	
	Number registered	*Percentage of white voting age population*	*Number registered*	*Percentage of nonwhite voting age population*
1960				
Alabama	860,000	63.6	66,000	13.7
Arkansas	518,000	60.9	73,000	38.0
Florida	1,819,000	69.3	183,000	39.4
Georgia	1,020,000	56.8	180,000	29.3
Louisiana	993,000	76.9	159,000	31.1
Mississippi	478,000	63.9	22,000	5.2
North Carolina	1,861,000	92.1	210,000	39.1
South Carolina	481,000	57.1	58,000	13.7
Tennessee	1,300,000	73.0	185,000	59.1
Texas	2,079,000	42.5	227,000	35.5
Virginia	867,000	46.1	100,000	23.1
Total	12,276,000	61.1	1,463,000	29.1
1970				
Alabama	1,311,000	85.0	315,000	66.0
Arkansas	728,000	74.1	153,000	82.3
Florida	2,495,000	65.5	302,000	55.3
Georgia	1,615,000	71.7	395,000	57.2
Louisiana	1,143,000	77.0	319,000	57.4
Mississippi	690,000	82.1	286,000	71.0
North Carolina	1,640,000	68.1	305,000	51.3
South Carolina	668,000	62.3	221,000	56.1
Tennessee	1,600,000	78.5	242,000	71.6
Texas	3,599,000	62.0	550,000	72.6
Virginia	1,496,000	64.5	269,000	57.0
Total	16,985,000	69.2	3,357,000	62.0
1980				
Alabama	1,700,000	81.4	350,000	55.8
Arkansas	1,056,000	76.9	130,000	57.2
Florida	4,331,000	67.7	489,000	58.3
Georgia	1,800,000	63.0	450,000	48.6
Louisiana	1,550,000	74.8	465,000	60.7
Mississippi	1,152,000	98.9	330,000	62.3
North Carolina	2,314,000	70.1	440,000	51.3
South Carolina	916,000	58.5	320,000	53.7
Tennessee	2,200,000	78.5	300,000	64.0
Texas	6,020,000	75.1	620,000	56.0
Virginia	1,942,000	62.2	360,000	53.2
Total	24,981,000	71.9	4,254,000	55.8

(Table continues)

Table 9-7   *(Continued)*

Year/state	Whites		Nonwhites	
	Number registered	*Percentage of white voting age population*	*Number registered*	*Percentage of nonwhite voting age population*
1996				
Alabama	1,783,000	75.8	532,000	69.2
Arkansas	972,000	64.5	203,000	65.8
Florida	5.927,000	63.7	754,000	53.1
Georgia	2,460,000	67.8	1,015,000	64.6
Louisiana	1,613,000	74.5	653,000	71.9
Mississippi	942,000	75.0	445,000	67.4
North Carolina	2,930,000	70.4	660,000	65.5
South Carolina	1,399,000	69.7	436,000	64.3
Tennessee	2,170,000	66.3	471,000	65.7
Texas	7,234,000	62.7	914,000	63.2
Virginia	2,576,000	68.4	659,000	64.0
Total	30,006,000		6,742,000	
2000				
Alabama	1,783,000	74.5	619,000	72.0
Arkansas	916,000	59.5	199,000	60.0
Florida	6,176,000	62.5	773,000	52.7
Georgia	2,221,000	59.3	1,296,000	66.3
Louisiana	1,700,000	77.5	656,000	73.5
Mississippi	1,006,000	72.2	450,000	73.7
North Carolina	2,812,000	67.9	827,000	62.9
South Carolina	1,524,000	68.2	454,000	68.6
Tennessee	2,160,000	61.9	427,000	64.9
Texas	7,771,000	61.8	971,000	69.5
Virginia	2,658,000	67.6	586,000	58.0
Total	30,727,000		7,258,000	

[a] As of August 1986.

Source: U.S. Bureau of the Census, *Statistical Abstract of the United States* (Washington, D.C.: Government Printing Office, 1980, 1989, 1990). Original data source is Voter Educational Project, Atlanta, Georgia. Data for 2000 are available at www.ceasus.gov/.

Table 9-8 Political Action Committees (PACs), 1974–2000

Date	Connected PACs[a] Corporate	Labor	Trade/ health/ membership	Cooperative	Corporation without stock	Nonconnected PACs[b]	Total
December 1974	89	201	318[c]	[c]	[c]	[c]	608
November 1975	139	226	357[c]	[c]	[c]	[c]	722
December 1976	433	224	489[c]	[c]	[c]	[c]	1,146
December 1977	550	234	438	8	20	110	1,360
December 1978	785	217	453	12	24	162	1,653
December 1979	950	240	514	12	32	247	1,995
December 1980	1,206	297	576	42	56	374	2,551
December 1981	1,329	318	614	41	68	531	2,901
December 1982	1,469	380	649	47	103	723	3,371
December 1983	1,538	378	643	51	122	793	3,525
December 1984	1,682	394	698	52	130	1,053	4,009
December 1985	1,710	388	695	54	142	1,003	3,992
December 1986	1,744	384	745	56	151	1,077	4,157
December 1987	1,775	364	865	59	145	957	4,165
December 1988	1,816	354	786	59	138	1,115	4,268
December 1989	1,796	349	777	59	137	1,060	4,178
December 1990	1,795	346	774	59	136	1,062	4,172
December 1991	1,738	338	742	57	136	1,083	4,094
December 1992	1,735	347	770	56	142	1,145	4,195
December 1993	1,789	337	761	56	146	1,121	4,210
December 1994	1,660	333	792	53	136	980	3,954
December 1995	1,674	334	815	44	129	1,020	3,982
December 1996	1,642	332	838	41	123	1,103	4,079
December 1997	1,597	332	825	42	117	931	3,844
December 1998	1,567	321	821	39	115	935	3,798

(Table continues)

Table 9-8 (Continued)

Date	Connected PACs[a]					Nonconnected PACs[b]	Total
	Corporate	Labor	Trade/ health/ membership	Cooperative	Corporation without stock		
December 1999	1,548	318	844	38	115	972	3835
December 2000	1,523	316	812	39	114	902	3706

[a] Operate in association with sponsoring organization that often covers operating and fund-raising costs.
[b] Operate independently.
[c] Trade/membership/health category includes all PACs except corporate and labor.

Sources: 1974–1992: Harold W. Stanley and Richard G. Niemi, *Vital Statistics on American Politics*, 5th ed. (Washington, D.C.: CQ Press, 1995), 161; 1993–2000: *Statistical Abstract of the United State, 2001.*

Table 9-9   Receipts, Expenditures, and Contributions of PACs, 1975–2000

Election cycle	Receipts (millions)	Expenditures (millions)	Contributions to congressional candidates (millions)	Percentage contributed to congressional candidates
1975–1976	$54.0	$52.9	$22.6	42
1977–1978	80.0	77.4	34.1	43
1979–1980	137.7	131.2	60.2	44
1981–1982	199.5	190.2	87.6	44
1983–1984	288.7	266.8	113.0	39
1985–1986	353.4	340.0	139.8	40
1987–1988	384.6	364.2	159.2	41
1989–1990	372.1	357.6	159.1	43
1991–1992	385.5	394.9	188.9	49
1993–1994	391.8	388.1	189.6	48
1995–1996	437.4	429.9	217.8	50
1997–1998	502.6	470.8	219.9	44
1999–2000	604.9	579.4	259.8	43

Note: Figures are in current dollars.

Source: Harold W. Stanley and Richard G. Niemi, *Vital Statistics on American Politics, 2001–2000* (Washington, D.C.: CQ Press, 2001), 101.

Table 9-10   Legislative Districting: Deviations from Equality in Congressional Districts

State	1960s[a]	1980s[b]	1990s[c]
Alabama	38.6	2.45	[d]
Alaska	AL	AL	AL
Arizona	107.2	.08	[d]
Arkansas	54.2	.73	.73
California	451.4	.08	.49
Colorado	104.5	[d]	[d]
Connecticut	87.7	.46	.05
Delaware	AL	AL	AL
Florida	102.5	.13	[d]
Georgia	139.9	NA	.93
Hawaii	AL	[d]	[d]
Idaho	45.8	.04	[d]
Illinois	65.2	.03	NA
Indiana	96.0	2.96	[d]
Iowa	22.7	.05	.05
Kansas	38.2	.34	.01
Kentucky	60.0	1.39	[d]
Louisiana	66.8	.42	.04
Maine	8.6	[d]	NA
Maryland	123.6	.35	[d]
Massachusetts	23.9	1.09	[d]
Michigan	156.7	[d]	NA
Minnesota	25.2	.01	[d]
Mississsippi	72.2	NA	.02
Missouri	29.7	.18	.20
Montana	37.4	NA	AL
Nebraska	26.8	.23	.20
Nevada	AL	.60	[d]
New Hampshire	18.6	.24	.07
New Jersey	81.7	.69	[d]
New Mexico	AL	.87	.16
New York	29.5	1.64	[d]
North Carolina	55.6	1.76	[d]
North Dakota	10.8	AL	AL
Ohio	121.1	.68	[d]
Oklahoma	83.8	.58	[d]
Oregon	58.2	.15	[d]
Pennsylvania	59.6	.24	.01
Rhode Island	14.0	.02	.02
South Carolina	65.3	.28	[a]
South Dakota	92.6	AL	AL
Tennessee	101.8	2.40	NA
Texas	167.0	.28	[d]
Utah	57.2	.43	.02
Vermont	AL	AL	AL
Virginia	57.1	1.81	[d]
Washington	41.2	.06	[d]

Table 9-10   *(Continued)*

State	1960s[a]	1980s[b]	1990s[c]
West Virginia	32.0	.50	.09
Wisconsin	74.3	.14	[d]
Wyoming	AL	AL	AL

Note: Figures represent the absolute sum of the maximum percentage deviations (positive and negative) from the average district populations. "AL" indicates at-large district (only one congressional representative); "NA" indicates not available.

[a] From 1962.
[b] As of April 1983.
[c] As of August 1994.
[d] Less than .01 percent.

Source: Harold W. Stanley and Richard G. Niemi, *Vital Statistics on American Politics, 2001–2002* (Washington, D.C.: CQ Press, 2001), 74–75.

Selected Readings

The books listed here may be useful to readers who would like to explore further subjects covered in our tables.

Introduction, Chapter One, and General

Abraham, Henry J. *The Judiciary: The Supreme Court in the Governmental Process.* 10th ed. New York: NYU Press, 1996.

Baum, Lawrence. *The Supreme Court.* 7th ed. Washington, D.C.: CQ Press, 2000.

Biskupic, Joan, and Elder Witt. *Guide to the U.S. Supreme Court.* 3d ed. Washington, D.C.: Congressional Quarterly, 1997.

Brigham, John. *The Cult of the Court.* Philadelphia: Temple University Press, 1987.

Cooper, Phillip J., and Howard Ball. *The United States Supreme Court: From the Inside Out.* Upper Saddle River, N.J.: Prentice Hall, 1996.

Currie, David P. *The Constitution in the Supreme Court, 1789–1986.* Chicago: University of Chicago Press, 1985.

Epstein, Lee, and Thomas G. Walker. *Constitutional Law for a Changing America: Institutional Powers and Constraints.* 4th ed. Washington, D.C.: CQ Press, 2001.

Frank, John P. *Marble Palace: The Supreme Court in American Life.* New York: Knopf, 1958.

Gillman, Howard, and Cornell Clayton, eds. *The Supreme Court in American Politics: New Institutionalist Interpretations.* Lawrence: University Press of Kansas, 1999.

Goebel, Julius, Jr. *Antecedents and Beginnings to 1801: The History of the Supreme Court of the United States.* New York: Macmillan, 1971.

Hall, Kermit L., ed. *The Oxford Companion to the Supreme Court of the United States.* New York: Oxford University Press, 1992.

_____. *The Magic Mirror: Law in American History.* New York: Oxford University Press, 1989.

Jost, Kenneth, ed. *The Supreme Court A to Z.* 2d ed. Washington, D.C.: Congressional Quarterly, 1998.

Kelly, Alfred H., Winfred A. Harbison, and Herman Belz. *The American Constitution: Its Origins and Development.* New York: W. W. Norton, 1991.

Krislov, Samuel. *The Supreme Court in the Political Process.* New York: Macmillan, 1965.

Martin, Fenton, and Robert U. Goehlert. *The U.S. Supreme Court: A Bibliography.* Washington, D.C.: CQ Press, 1990.

McCloskey, Robert G. *The American Supreme Court.* 3d ed. Revised by Sanford Levinson. Chicago: University of Chicago Press, 2000.

_____. *The Modern Supreme Court.* Cambridge: Harvard University Press, 1972.

_____. *The American Supreme Court.* Chicago: University of Chicago Press, 1960.

McGuire, Kevin T. *Understanding the U.S. Supreme Court: Cases and Controversies.* New York: McGraw-Hill, 2002.

O'Brien, David M. *Storm Center.* 6th ed. New York: W. W. Norton, 2002.

Pacelle, Richard L., Jr. *The Role of the Supreme Court in American Politics.* Boulder: Westview Press, 2002.

Rehnquist, William H. *The Supreme Court.* New York: Knopf, 2001.

Rohde, David W., and Harold J. Spaeth. *Supreme Court Decision Making.* San Francisco: Freeman, 1976.

Schmidhauser, John R. *The Supreme Court: Its Politics, Personality, and Procedures.* New York: Holt, Rinehart, and Winston, 1960.

Schwartz, Bernard. *A History of the Supreme Court.* 1994. Reprint, New York: Oxford University Press, 1995.

Segal, Jeffrey A., and Harold J. Spaeth. *The Supreme Court and the Attitudinal Model Revisited.* New York: Cambridge University Press, 2002.

Spaeth, Harold J. *Supreme Court Policy Making.* San Francisco: Freeman, 1979.

Urofsky, Melvin I., and Paul Finkelman. *A March of Liberty: A Constitutional History of the United States.* 2d ed. New York: Oxford University Press, 2001.

Warren, Charles. *The Supreme Court in United States History.* Boston: Little, Brown, 1926.

Wasby, Stephen L. *The Supreme Court in the Federal Judicial System.* 4th ed. Chicago: Nelson-Hall, 1993.

Chapter Two

Bickel, Alexander M. *The Caseload of the Supreme Court, and What, If Anything, to Do About It.* Washington, D.C.: American Enterprise Institute for Public Policy Research, 1973.

———. *The Least Dangerous Branch of Government.* New Haven: Yale University Press, 1986.

Casper, Gerhard, and Richard Posner. *The Workload of the Supreme Court.* Chicago: American Bar Foundation, 1974.

Choper, Jesse H. *Judicial Review and the National Political Process.* Chicago: University of Chicago Press, 1980.

Dahl, Robert A. *Pluralist Democracy in the United States.* Chicago: Rand McNally, 1967.

Ely, John Hart. *Democracy and Distrust.* Cambridge: Harvard University Press, 1980.

Epp, Charles. *The Rights Revolution: Lawyers, Activists, and Supreme Courts in Comparative Perspective.* Chicago: University of Chicago Press, 1998.

Epstein, Lee, and Joseph F. Kobylka. *The Supreme Court and Legal Change: Abortion and the Death Penalty.* Chapel Hill: University of North Carolina Press, 1992.

Estreicher, Samuel, and John Sexton. *Redefining the Supreme Court's Role.* New Haven: Yale University Press, 1986.

Federal Judicial Center. *Case Load of the Supreme Court: A Report of the Study Group.* Washington, D.C.: Administrative Office of the U.S. Courts, 1972.

Frankfurter, Felix, and James M. Landis. *The Business of the Supreme Court: A Study in the Federal Judicial System.* New York: Macmillan, 1928.

Gates, John B. *The Supreme Court and Partisan Realignment.* Boulder: Westview Press, 1991.

Halpern, Stephen, and Charles Lamb, eds. *Supreme Court Activism and Restraint.* Lexington, Mass.: Lexington Books, 1982.

Kloppenberg, Lisa A. *Playing it Safe: How the Supreme Court Sidesteps Hard Cases and Stunts the Development of Law.* New York: NYU Press, 2001.

Lasser, William. *The Limits of Judicial Power.* Chapel Hill: University of North Carolina Press, 1988.

McLauchlan, William P. *Federal Court Caseloads.* New York: Praeger, 1984.

Pacelle, Richard L., Jr. *The Transformation of the Supreme Court's Agenda.* Boulder: Westview Press, 1991.

Perry, H. W. *Deciding to Decide: Agenda Setting in the United States Supreme Court.* Cambridge: Harvard University Press, 1991.

Provine, Doris Marie. *Case Selection in the United States Supreme Court*. Chicago: University of Chicago Press, 1980.

Sunstein, Cass R. *One Case at a Time: Judicial Minimalism on the Supreme Court*. Cambridge: Harvard University Press, 1999.

Chapters Three and Six

Baum, Lawrence. *The Puzzle of Judicial Behavior*. Ann Arbor: University of Michigan Press, 1997.

Brenner, Saul, and Harold J. Spaeth. *Stare Indecisis: The Alteration of Precedent on the Supreme Court*. New York: Cambridge University Press, 1996.

Clayton, Cornell W., and Howard Gillman, eds. *Supreme Court Decision Making: New Institutionalist Approaches*. Chicago: University of Chicago Press, 1999.

Cooper, Phillip J. *Battles on the Bench*. Lawrence: University Press of Kansas, 1995.

Dickson, Del, ed. *The Supreme Court in Conference (1940–1985): The Private Discussions Behind Nearly 300 Supreme Court Decisions*. New York: Oxford University Press, 2001.

Epstein, Lee, and Jack Knight. *The Choices Justices Make*. Washington, D.C.: CQ Press, 1998.

Maltzman, Forrest, James R. Spriggs II, and Paul J. Wahlbeck. *Crafting Law on the Supreme Court*. Cambridge: Cambridge University Press, 2000.

Murphy, Walter F. *Elements of Judicial Strategy*. Chicago: University of Chicago Press, 1964.

Pritchett, C. Herman. *The Roosevelt Court*. New York: Macmillan, 1948.

Rohde, David W., and Harold J. Spaeth. *Supreme Court Decision Making*. San Francisco: Freeman, 1976.

Savage, David G. *Turning Right: The Making of the Rehnquist Court*. New York: Wiley, 1992.

Schubert, Glendon A. *The Judicial Mind Revisited*. New York: Oxford University Press, 1985.

_____. *Quantitative Analysis of Judicial Behavior*. Glencoe, Ill.: Free Press, 1959.

Schwartz, Bernard, ed. *The Burger Court: Counter-Revolution or Confirmation?* New York: Oxford University Press, 1998.

_____. *Decision: How the Supreme Court Decides Cases*. New York: Oxford University Press, 1996.

Segal, Jeffrey A., and Harold J. Spaeth. *The Supreme Court and the Attitudinal Model Revisited*. New York: Cambridge University Press, 2002.

Smolla, Rodney A., ed. *A Year in the Life of the Supreme Court*. Durham: Duke University Press, 1995.

Spaeth, Harold J., and Jeffrey A. Segal. *Majority Rule or Minority Will: Adherence to Precedent on the U.S. Supreme Court*. New York: Cambridge University Press, 1999.

Stearns, Maxwell L. *Constitutional Process: A Social Choice Analysis of Supreme Court Decision Making*. Ann Arbor: University of Michigan Press, 2000.

Van Geel, Tyll. *Understanding Supreme Court Opinions*. 3d ed. New York: Longman, 2001.

Chapters Four and Five

Abraham, Henry J. *Justices, Presidents, and Senators: A History of the U.S. Supreme Court Appointments from Washington to Clinton*. Rev. ed. Lanham, Md.: Rowman and Littlefield, 1999.

Atkinson, David N. *Leaving the Bench: Supreme Court Justices at the End*. Lawrence: University Press of Kansas, 1999.

Berger, Raoul. *Impeachment: The Constitutional Problems*. Cambridge: Harvard University Press, 1973.

Bork, Robert H. *The Tempting of America*. New York: Simon and Schuster, 1990.

Bronner, Ethan. *Battle for Justice: How the Bork Nomination Shook America*. New York: W. W. Norton, 1989.

Cushman, Clare. *The Supreme Court Justices: Illustrated Biographies, 1789–1995*. 2d ed. Washington, D.C.: Congressional Quarterly, 1995.

Danelski, David J. *A Supreme Court Justice Is Appointed*. New York: Random House, 1964.

Goldman, Sheldon. *Picking Federal Judges*. New Haven: Yale University Press, 1997.

Harris, Richard. *Decision*. New York: Dutton, 1970.

Maltese, John Anthony. *The Selling of Supreme Court Nominees*. 1995. Reprint, Baltimore: Johns Hopkins University Press, 1998.

Perry, Barbara A. *A "Representative" Supreme Court? The Impact of Race, Religion, and Gender on Appointments*. New York: Greenwood, 1991.

Schmidhauser, John R. *Judges and Justices*. Boston: Little, Brown, 1979.

Silverstein, Mark. *Judicious Choices: The New Politics of Supreme Court Confirmations*. New York: W. W. Norton, 1994.

Simon, James F. *In His Own Image*. New York: McKay, 1973.

Tribe, Laurence H. *God Save This Honorable Court: How the Choice of Justice Shapes Our History*. New York: Random House, 1985.

Van Tassel, Emily Field, and Paul Finkelman. *Impeachable Offenses: A Documentary History from 1787 to the Present*. Washington, D.C.: Congressional Quarterly, 1999.

Vieira, Norman, and Leonard Gross, eds. *Supreme Court Appointments: Judge Bork and the Politicization of Senate Confirmations*. Carbondale: Southern Illinois University Press, 1999.

Ward, Artemus. *Deciding to Leave: The Politics of Retirement from the United States Supreme Court*. Albany: SUNY Press, 2003.

Watson, George L., and John A. Stookey. *Shaping America: The Politics of Supreme Court Appointments*. New York: HarperCollins, 1995.

Yalof, David Alistair. *Pursuit of Justices: Presidential Politics and the Selection of Supreme Court Nominees*. Chicago: University of Chicago Press, 1999.

Chapter Seven

Abraham, Henry J. *Justices, Presidents, and Senators: A History of the U.S. Supreme Court Appointments from Washington to Clinton*. Rev. ed. Lanham, Md: Rowman and Littlefield, 1999.

Berger, Raoul. *Congress v. The Supreme Court*. Cambridge: Harvard University Press, 1969.

Campbell, Colton C., and John F. Stack Jr., eds. *Congress Confronts the Court: The Struggle for Legitimacy and Authority in Lawmaking*. Lanham, Md: Rowman and Littlefield, 2001.

Caplan, Lincoln. *The Tenth Justice*. New York: Knopf, 1987.

Carp, Robert A., and C. K. Rowland. *Policymaking and Politics in the Federal District Courts*. Knoxville: University of Tennessee Press, 1983.

Epstein, Lee. *Conservatives in Court*. Knoxville: University of Tennessee Press, 1985.

Eskridge, William N., Jr. *Dynamic Statutory Interpretation*. Cambridge: Harvard University Press, 1994.

Fisher, Louis. *Constitutional Conflicts between Congress and the President*. Lawrence: University Press of Kansas, 1997.

_____. *Constitutional Dialogues*. Princeton: Princeton University Press, 1988.

Harriger, Katy J. *The Special Prosecutor in American Politics*. 2d rev. ed. Lawrence: University Press of Kansas, 2000.

Howard, J. Woodford, Jr. *Courts of Appeals in the Federal Judicial System*. Princeton: Princeton University Press, 1981.

Katzmann, Robert A. *Courts and Congress*. Washington, D.C.: Brookings Institution, 1997.

Kluger, Richard. *Simple Justice*. New York: Knopf, 1976.

Kobylka, Joseph F. *The Politics of Obscenity*. Westport, Conn.: Greenwood Press, 1990.

Koshner, Andrew Jay. *Solving the Puzzle of Interest Group Litigation*. Westport, Conn.: Greenwood Press, 1998.

Lawrence, Susan E. *The Poor in Court*. Princeton: Princeton University Press, 1990.

Lyles, Kevin. *The Gatekeepers: Federal District Courts in the Political Process*. Westport, Conn: Greenwood Press, 1997.

Murphy, Walter F. *Congress and the Court*. Chicago: University of Chicago Press, 1962.

O'Connor, Karen. *Women's Organizations' Use of the Court*. Lexington, Mass.: Lexington Books, 1980.

Posner, Richard A. *Federal Courts: Crisis and Reform*. Cambridge: Harvard University Press, 1985.

Pritchett, C. Herman. *Congress versus the Supreme Court*. Minneapolis: University of Minnesota Press, 1961.

Richardson, Richard J., and Kenneth N. Vines. *The Politics of Federal Courts*. Boston: Little, Brown, 1970.

Rowland, C. K. and Robert Carp. *Politics and Judgment in the Federal District Courts*. Lawrence: University Press of Kansas, 1996.

Salokar, Rebecca Mae. *The Solicitor General: The Politics of Law*. Philadelphia: Temple University Press, 1992.

Schmidhauser, John R., and Larry L. Berg. *The Supreme Court and Congress*. New York: Free Press, 1972.

Scigliano, Robert. *The Supreme Court and the Presidency*. New York: Free Press, 1971.

Shapiro, Martin. *The Supreme Court and Administrative Agencies*. New York: Free Press, 1968.

Sorauf, Frank J. *The Wall of Separation: Constitutional Politics of Church and State*. Princeton: Princeton University Press, 1976.

Stanley, Harold W., and Richard G. Niemi. *Vital Statistics on American Politics, 2001–2002*. Washington, D.C.: CQ Press, 2001.

Stumpf, Harry P., and John H. Culver. *The Politics of State Courts*. New York: Longman, 1992.

Tarr, G. Alan, and Mary C. A. Porter. *State Supreme Courts in State and Nation*. New Haven: Yale University Press, 1988.

Vose, Clement E. *Caucasians Only*. Berkeley and Los Angeles: University of California Press, 1959.

Waltenburg, Eric N., and Bill Swinford. *Litigating Federalism: The States Before the U.S. Supreme Court*. Westport, Conn.: Greenwood Press, 1999.

Warren, Charles. *Congress, the Constitution, and the Supreme Court*. Boston: Little, Brown, 1925.

Wasby, Stephen L. *Race Relations Litigation in an Age of Complexity*. Charlottesville: University of Virginia Press, 1995.

Yates, Jeff. *Popular Justice: Presidential Prestige and Executive Success in the Supreme Court*. Albany: SUNY Press, 2002.

Chapter Eight

Gillman, Howard. *The Votes That Counted*. Chicago: University of Chicago Press, 2001.

Haltom, William. *Reporting on the Courts*. Chicago: Nelson-Hall, 1998.

Hoekstra, Valerie J. *From the Marble Temple to Main Street: The Effect of Court Decisions on Local Public Opinion*. New York: Cambridge University Press, forthcoming.

Marshall, Thomas. *Public Opinion and the Supreme Court.* New York: Longman, 1989.

Perry, Barbara A. *The Priestly Tribe: The Supreme Court's Image in the American Mind.* Westport, Conn: Praeger, 1999.

Semonche, John E. *Keeping the Faith: A Cultural History of the U.S. Supreme Court.* Lanham, Md.: Rowman and Littlefield, 1998.

Slotnick, Elliot E., and Jennifer A. Segal. *Television News and the Supreme Court: All the News That's Fit to Air?* New York: Cambridge University Press, 1998.

Chapter Nine

Bass, Jack. *Unlikely Heroes.* New York: Simon and Schuster, 1981. Reprint, Tuscaloosa: University of Alabama Press, 1990.

Becker, Theodore L., ed. *The Impact of Supreme Court Decisions.* New York: Oxford University Press, 1969.

Becker, Theodore L., and Malcolm Feeley, eds. *The Impact of Supreme Court Decisions.* 2d ed. New York: Oxford University Press, 1985.

Bullock, Charles S., III, and Charles M. Lamb, eds. *Implementation of Civil Rights Policy.* Monterey, Calif.: Brooks-Cole, 1984.

Craig, Barbara Hinkson, and David M. O'Brien. *Abortion and American Politics.* Chatham, N.J.: Chatham House, 1993.

Dolbeare, Kenneth M., and Phillip E. Hammond. *The School Prayer Decisions.* Chicago: University of Chicago Press, 1971.

Johnson, Charles A., and Bradley C. Canon. *Judicial Policies: Implementation and Impact.* 2d ed. Washington, D.C.: CQ Press, 1998.

McCann, Michael. *Rights at Work.* Chicago: University of Chicago Press, 1994.

Peltason, Jack W. *Fifty-eight Lonely Men: Southern Federal Judges and School Desegregation.* New York: Harcourt, Brace, and World, 1961.

Rosenberg, Gerald N. *The Hollow Hope.* Chicago: University of Chicago Press, 1991.

Wasby, Stephen L. *The Impact of the United States Supreme Court.* Homewood, Ill.: Dorsey Press, 1970.

Index

APR 2004

100.00